# FAULT LINES OF DEMOCRACY
# IN POST-TRANSITION LATIN AMERICA

# Fault Lines of Democracy in Post-Transition Latin America

EDITED BY
FELIPE AGÜERO AND JEFFREY STARK

North·South Center Press
UNIVERSITY OF MIAMI

The publisher of this book is the North-South Center Press at the University of Miami.

The mission of the North-South Center is to promote better relations and serve as a catalyst for change among the United States, Canada, and the nations of Latin America and the Caribbean by advancing knowledge and understanding of the major political, social, economic, and cultural issues affecting the nations and peoples of the Western Hemisphere.

© 1998 North-South Center Press at the University of Miami.

 Published by the North-South Center Press at the University of Miami and distributed by Lynne Rienner Publishers, Inc., 1800 30th Street, Suite 314, Boulder, CO 80301-1026. All rights reserved under International and Pan-American Conventions. No portion of the contents may be reproduced or transmitted in any form, or by any means, including photocopying, recording, or any information storage retrieval system, without prior permission in writing from the North-South Center Press.

All copyright inquiries should be addressed to the publisher: North-South Center Press, 1500 Monza Avenue, Coral Gables, Florida 33146-3027, U.S.A., phone 305-284-8912, fax 305-284-5089, or e-mail mmapes@nsc.msmail.miami.edu.

To order or to return books, contact Lynne Rienner Publishers, Inc., 1800 30th Street, Suite 314, Boulder, CO 80301-1026, 303-444-6684, fax 303-444-0824.

Cover photo of Floridian coral rock "fault lines" by Mary M. Mapes.

**Library of Congress Cataloging-in-Publication Data**

Fault lines of democracy in post-transition Latin America / edited by
Felipe Agüero and Jeffrey Stark
p. cm.
Includes bibliographical references and index.
ISBN 1-57454-046-7 (alk. paper: pbk.)
1. Democracy—Latin America. 2. Civil-military relations—Latin America.
I. Agüero, Felipe. II. Stark, Jeffrey.
JL966.F38 1998                                                    98-42225
320.98'09'048—dc21                                                  CIP

Printed in the United States of America/EBNC

02 01 00 99      6 5 4 3 2

# Contents

# Preface and Acknowledgments

## FELIPE AGÜERO AND JEFFREY STARK

This volume is the result of a multi-year project, supported by the North-South Center at the University of Miami, that has sought to lay the groundwork for a new research agenda on the problems (or "fault lines" in our chosen metaphor) of democracy in post-transition Latin America. Its point of departure has been the recognition that, with Latin America's transition from authoritarian to democratic regimes essentially accomplished and with quite dramatic social and economic restructuring well underway, there is a clear need for revisiting our understanding of the region's democratic experiences. The guiding thread to this inquiry has been a concern with the scope, depth, and quality of Latin America's democratic regimes. We believe that the "fault lines" metaphor[1] has engendered within the book a distinctive approach not found in other volumes. Adopting an analytic posture different from those used by studies operating within the democratic consolidation framework, the "fault lines" approach to democracy probes at the tensions and weaknesses in Latin America's democracies in their own right, without seeking to link them to explicit assessments of the durability of those regimes. Our approach opens the possibility of new vistas on democracy in the hemisphere and facilitates an understanding of the often disjunctive and diverse expressions of political life to be found there.

The project leading to the book progressed in several stages. First, a small preparatory workshop involving about a dozen scholars was held in Miami in November 1994 to develop a set of themes and issues to be explored in much greater detail at a major conference on "Fault Lines of Democratic Governance in the Americas" the following year. Based on this planning session, papers were commissioned from an international, interdisciplinary group of social scientists, including participants from across the hemisphere with backgrounds in political science, economics, sociology, law, anthropology, political theory, history, and international relations. Panel discussants and other attendees from diverse fields were also selected, and the conference, which brought together some 40 participants, was held at the North-South Center in May 1995. Both of these events were coordinated and directed by Felipe Agüero, who was then spending a year in residence as a senior research associate at the Center. Subsequent to the conference, a comprehensive rapporteur's report was prepared by Carlos Monge of the Centro Peruano de Estudios Sociales.[2] The report was published in early 1996 and

---

[1.] We owe the "fault lines" metaphor to our former North-South Center colleague Gustavo Gorriti (now associate director of *La Prensa* in Panama), who offered it during informal discussions that preceded the project.

[2.] The conference report, entitled "Fault Lines of Democratic Governance in the Americas," was a superlative document that elicited much favorable comment, and it has proved to be a useful reference throughout the preparation of this volume, including the preface. We are extremely grateful to Carlos Monge for the diligence and intelligence that he brought to his task.

i

circulated widely. In preparation for this book, the authors updated and revised their papers for publication, based on the commentaries of discussants at the conference, the general discussion that took place there, other commentaries sought individually by authors, and written comments by the editors. At a later stage, in a number of instances, authors also responded to comments by the book's reviewer. Two papers were translated from Spanish into English.

## THE STRUCTURE AND CONTENT OF THE BOOK

Discussions leading to the book focused on the quality of democratic processes in the Americas and the need for new analytic tools commensurate with the complexity of the processes underway. Many of the participants in the project's workshop and conference stressed repeatedly that the terrain upon which democracy is unfolding in Latin America is shifting rapidly, due to fundamental economic reforms, large-scale social restructuring, changes in political practices, and the influences of globalization. The coeditors and other contributors, therefore, sought to address these contextual concerns, and they are examined in the four chapters that compose Part I of the volume.

Similarly, it was recognized that the components of democratization in many cases involve contradictory or arrhythmic patterns, especially with regard to institutions, practices, and procedures of representation and participation that manifest great variability in the provision of citizens' civil, social, and economic rights. Particularly crucial is the question of representation and whether it is in decline, due to the increasing irrelevance of previously existing political and institutional mechanisms, or simply awaiting a new institutionalization, as reflected in the spread of new social movements, non-governmental organizations, and other alternative arrangements. At the same time, matters related to gender and ethnicity were deemed to be of the utmost importance for the Latin American democracies. Such clearly fundamental but heretofore largely neglected issues open a window onto new relationships among associational life, identity formation, public spaces, and institutional change. These themes — citizenship, representation, gender, and ethnicity — are the focus of Part II.

Another principal topic running through all our discussions was the need for advances in the adequacy and performance of democratic institutions dealing with justice, the rule of law, and the judiciary. It is perhaps in this context that Latin American citizens most frequently encounter the scope and limits of democratic rule. For a project such as ours, it was essential to incorporate studies on law-related issues directly within the broader social science debates on democratic governance. Two such efforts are offered in Part III.

Finally, it was recognized that, while civil-military relations have clearly improved in recent years, difficult questions remain concerning the proper role and function of the military in the context of what are obviously major changes in the international system and the political scenarios of Latin America. These new circumstances pose the double-sided question of how the military institution will accommodate itself to these new realities and how civilian authorities will conceive of and execute their oversight responsibilities. Three chapters provide a variety of cases and concepts dealing with this unfinished story in Part IV.

In the opening chapter, "Conflicting Assessments of Democratization: Exploring the Fault Lines," Felipe Agüero reviews the recent literature on Latin America's new democracies, locating key debates and critiquing the analytic shortcomings in the uses of the concept of democracy. With democracy now in a post-transition phase in most of Latin America, assessments of the status attained by the new regimes depend in large measure on the combination of variables selected for analysis, which may vary widely (for example, representation, participation, institutionalization, legitimacy, rule of law, and accountability), the comparative strategies adopted, and the notions of democracy employed. Agüero, criticizing the uses of the concept of democratic consolidation, views the geological metaphor of "fault lines of democratic governance" as providing a more sophisticated view of democratization in the hemisphere by allowing us to acknowledge that the area's democracies rest upon variegated and shifting terrains encompassing both democratization's accomplishments and faults.

Chapter two, Norbert Lechner's essay on "The Transformations of Politics," stresses the importance of a phenomenon that has received rather slight attention — the sustained focus on democratic transition has obscured the fact that politics itself is undergoing transition. Lechner discusses three aspects of such change: the loss of the centrality *(descentramiento)* of politics; the informalization of politics; and the redefinition and rearticulation of private and public domains. The loss of the centrality of politics is related to the explosive burst of a "market society" that challenges the traditional roles of politics and the state as the primary sites where the social order is built and acquires legitimacy. He finds that today the political domain overflows the institutional framework and operates through informal networks and technical institutions, leading to an emptying *(vaciamiento)* of the political system. The redefinition and rearticulation of private and public domains and issues imply a new notion of citizenship. While the public sphere is increasingly shaped by the market (including consumers' rights), individuals discover in their private experiences issues concerning gender, sexuality, and ethnicity that broaden the public agenda.

Atilio A. Borón's contribution in chapter three, "Faulty Democracies? A Reflection on the Capitalist 'Fault Lines' in Latin America," mounts a provocative critique of the effects of neoliberal economic reforms and globalization on Latin American democratization. This critique is rooted in a definition of democracy that extends beyond procedural routines to view the inclusion of social, economic, and ethical considerations as indispensable. According to Borón, representative, electoral democracy has become dominant in the hemisphere at the very time that neoliberal reforms are taking away from large segments of the population the basic social and economic rights that — in tandem with political rights — give meaning and substance to democracy. This is taking place at a time when the state is losing autonomy and sovereignty in relation to its capacity to define the economic and social policies needed to allow citizens to gain access to such basic rights. Borón anticipates a democratic resurgence in response to this conundrum that will call into question the viability of the current economic model.

In chapter four's examination of "Globalization and Democracy in Latin America," Jeffrey Stark traces globalization's impact on democratization through four conceptual categories: the world economy, communications, consumerism, and new political cultures. Stark finds that, although globalization produces or reinforces conditions of social and economic insecurity and inequality through the frequently anti-democratic influences of "market civilization," it also contributes to the circulation of ideas, norms, and practices that bolster democracy. He points out that even embedded within the challenges and disequilibration resulting from economic globalization are important opportunities for the strengthening of transparency, accountability, and the rule of law. At the same time, he argues that considerably more attention needs to be paid to significant changes that are occurring through the influences of "international political culture" on the cognitive universes of citizens, altering in important ways the intersubjective basis of democratic governance.

The discussion shifts in chapter five to Frances Hagopian's inquiry on "Democracy and Political Representation in Latin America in the 1990s: Pause, Reorganization, or Decline?" Hagopian examines in detail the issue of political representation in Latin America, with attention to indicators of volatility, abstention, and party identification. She argues that a decline in political representation has taken place for a variety of reasons, including: 1) parties were weakened by authoritarian regimes prior to the democratic transitions; 2) representative institutions, such as labor unions, that were adapted to the corporative realities of the authoritarian period have not adjusted to the transformations associated with the market-based democracies of contemporary Latin America; and 3) changes in the economy — especially the decline of the importance of the state and of populist policies — challenge traditional party programs, policies, and social constituencies. As a result of these changes, Hagopian finds not party realignment but party dealignment, with no clear evidence that new social movements or NGOs can fill the gap. While finding it too early to determine how interests might reorganize in the near future, she identifies decentralized and transnationalized networks of representation as potentially important alternatives.

In chapter six, "Democratization in Latin America: A Citizen Responsibility," Augusto Varas argues for strengthening democratic accountability through the empowerment of the citizenry. His central argument is that even with basic institutional mechanisms in place, democracy remains limited when civil society does not find ways to further its direct participation in the democratic process. This is especially so in a context in which globalization and rapid changes in technology and communications contribute to new forms and intensities of concentrated economic and political power. At the same time, Varas notes that Latin America faces the persistence of pre-modern cultural and political traditions during a phase when it needs to entrench democratic minimums and reach broad consensus on the economic and political reforms to be implemented. Responses to these challenges, says Varas, must include citizen efforts to construct new networks of social organization and collective action to assure democratic accountability and develop the necessary accompanying institutions.

One of the principal fault lines of democracy in the hemisphere is to be found in the exclusion of women from participation in the political systems of many countries, and this is the focus of Marysa Navarro and Susan C. Bourque's reflections in chapter seven on "Fault Lines of Democratic Governance: A Gender Perspective." Navarro and Bourque place their discussion in context by providing a review of the historical process by which women have fought for and sought to acquire basic political and social rights in modern Latin America. As they point out, in many countries, while women gained basic political rights (the vote), a set of civil and economic regulations still subjugated them to their fathers and husbands and limited their citizenship. In the 1970s and 1980s, in response to exclusionary military regimes, second-wave feminist movements, and national liberation movements in Central America, there was a marked upswing in women's involvement in social movements and political activism. Yet, they conclude, women still tend to be excluded from institutional politics, and it remains to be seen whether international influences and changes in Latin American political culture will be sufficient to lead to the long-term expansion of women's political participation.

In chapter eight's discussion of "Ethnicity and Democratic Governability in Latin America: Reflections from Two Central Andean Countries," Carlos Iván Degregori seeks to place the political experiences of indigenous peoples in Peru and Bolivia in comparative context through an examination of their respective histories. He notes that while ethnic movements exist in Bolivia, they do not in Peru. In Peru, the demand for citizenship from indigenous groups combined somewhat with the state's discourse on national integration, and the state's increasing adoption of *indigenista* policies became part of a more general modernization of society. Degregori notes that, as Peruvian Andean peoples became internally more complex and differentiated, union leaders and well-educated young people imagined political communities along class lines. Combined with large-scale, rural-urban migration, this led over time to a mix of gender, regional, class, and ethnic identities. In Bolivia, with the final crisis of populism in the early 1970s and the distancing of the state from the indigenous peoples, Aymara intellectuals placed ethnic-cultural grievances at the center of their political concerns. Degregori asserts that, although prone to ideological excesses and not successful in electoral politics, their movement, *katarismo*, brought attention to the politics of cultural diversity and the need for the inclusion of original peoples in the democratic life of the country. Today, says Degregori, the challenge for democratic consolidation in both Peru and Bolivia is to provide full citizenship in ways that encompass but go beyond ethnic-cultural demands.

In chapter nine, "Judicial Reform and Democratization in Latin America," Hugo Frühling presents an overview of the failure of past attempts at socio-legal and judicial reforms in Latin America and an examination of how and why such attempts are beginning to bear fruit today. According to Frühling, earlier reform efforts were cut off by the repressive regimes of the 1970s and the resistance within the bar and traditional law schools to an instrumental conception of the law as a means to shape new social relations. In recent years, Latin American justice systems and judiciaries have suffered from a lack of real independence from partisan politics, widespread citizen mistrust, serious delays in adjudication, and an inability to process heavy caseloads due to significant increases in common crime. For citizens of many Latin

American democracies, Frühling says, there is a fundamental lack of access to justice, among other reasons, as a result of a lack of knowledge about legal rights and prohibitive costs attached to litigation. In the 1990s, however, the panorama is slowly beginning to change due to the efforts of human rights advocates, various forms of assistance from foreign governments and international institutions, and the influence of local businesspeople concerned about the challenges of global integration.

In their treatment in chapter ten of "Democracy, Law, and Violence: Disjunctions of Brazilian Citizenship," James Holston and Teresa P.R. Caldeira put forward the notion of "disjunctive democracy" to characterize the coexistence of noteworthy progress in the development of democratic political institutions, including fair and legitimate electoral processes, with massive violations of civil rights, exemplified by the killings of prisoners by the military police in São Paulo and Rio de Janeiro, lethal assaults by military police on residents of *favelas,* and — such atrocities notwithstanding — a sense of impunity on the part of the police. The authors argue that, in Brazil and other "uncivil democracies" in Latin America, the civil component of citizenship is significantly impaired; yet, without the creation of the conditions of fairness, access, universality, and legality associated with the rule of law, democratic politics loses its legitimacy. Holston and Caldeira remark upon the dismaying lack of attention paid to law and the judiciary in the democratization literature, and they argue for a conception of democracy that encompasses political, civil, social, and cultural components of citizenship, while recognizing that disjunctions among these mutually constituitive elements are to be anticipated.

In chapter eleven, "Civil-Military Relations in Argentina, Brazil, and Chile: Present Trends, Future Prospects," Wendy Hunter maintains that the initial phases of democratic transitions are normally plagued by uncertainty and that public officials and the military tend to test each other, raising the levels of conflict — but never to the point of challenging the transition. Later, based upon such mutual testing, a certain degree of accommodation is usually reached. Hunter points out that Argentina, Brazil, and Chile exemplify different results of such accommodations. In Argentina, the disastrous Malvinas experience weakened the military to the point that civilian governments eventually reduced the political power of the armed forces and subordinated them (albeit at the cost of concessions concerning crimes committed during the "dirty war") to the elected civilian leaderships. In Brazil, the civil-military equilibrium rests at a higher level of military influence than in Argentina, in part as a result of the significant control the military governments exercised over the transition from authoritarianism. In Chile, the very nature of the transition, based on a political accommodation between the civilian leadership and the military, left the military with extended political prerogatives. In Hunter's view, in none of the three countries is the stability of democracy in question in the foreseeable future; however, economic crisis, crime, and concern over public security have the potential to create situations just as problematic as those intrinsic to the process of military reform.

In evaluating "The Changing International Environment and Civil-Military Relations in Post-Cold War Southern Latin America" in chapter twelve, Michael Desch asks whether the end of the Cold War will coincide with improved civil-military relations in South America. As a conceptual point of departure, he posits at the outset that a challenging external threat environment tends to lead to relatively good civil-military relations, while a challenging internal threat environment undermines civil-military relations. Accordingly, he argues that in recent years difficult civil-military relations in Latin America have resulted as much from perceived internal threats as external threats and, therefore, the end of the Cold War may not produce all of the dividends anticipated by some observers. In fact, the persistence of internal problems such as crime and corruption have the potential to sour civil-military relations at crucial moments. However, the technological competition that characterizes the new "revolution in military affairs" and trends toward greater military professionalism may, in some circumstances, have the effect of actually improving civil-military relations. Desch concludes that civilian government institutions need continued strengthening and civilian officials need to develop higher levels of competence and expertise to oversee continued professionalization in the armed forces.

Fernando Bustamante's analysis of "Democracy, Civilizational Change, and the Latin American Military" in chapter thirteen links the debates over civil-military relations to a larger and long-standing preoccupation in Latin America with the "civilizing mission" of the military, the construction of threats from the "other," and the search for order within society. Bustamante notes that the transformations associated with the end of the Cold War recast these concerns but do not make them go away. Operational questions about the role of the military remain embedded within the dilemma of identifying a historical mission for the military and the ways in which the military can serve as a stabilizing force for the nation and its citizens. Globalization and lingering concerns about state sovereignty increase the difficulty of addressing these issues. At the same time, he suggests, it has become important to think through the steps that can contribute to the institutionalization of an ethos of citizenship within and toward military life. Ultimately, Bustamante argues, the military's role as the provider of order must be inscribed within a new paradigm that is shared by civilian and military authorities alike.

## ACKNOWLEDGMENTS

A great many people contributed in various ways to the project upon which this book is based as well as to the completion of the book itself. Those who participated in the stimulating discussions of the project's initial workshop included Robert Kaufman, Arturo Valenzuela, Lourdes Sola, Bill Smith, Mark Warren, Eduardo Gamarra, Katherine Hite, Norbert Lechner, Kimberley Stanton, and Mark Everingham. Julie Diehl and Rebecca Wisot provided important assistance as rapporteurs for the workshop. We are deeply saddened by the passing of one of our workshop participants — Enrique Baloyra — who was not only a distinguished political scientist but a person who exemplified the democratic spirit throughout his life.

The success of the much larger conference that followed seven months later was due to the participation and contributions of numerous scholars and analysts to whom we are most grateful. Conference papers were presented by Atilio A. Borón, Norbert Lechner, Jeffrey Stark, Rob Walker, Alvaro Díaz, Frances Hagopian,

Augusto Varas, Hugo Frühling, Marysa Navarro, Carlos Iván Degregori, Wendy Hunter, Michael Desch, and James Holston and Teresa Caldeira. Those who contributed greatly by taking on the role of discussant were Terry Karl, Robert Kaufman, Alberto Van Klaveren, Robert Pastor, Carlos Portales, Mark Everingham, Juan Manuel Villasuso, Scott Mainwaring, Jonathan Hartlyn, Bill Smith, Philippe Schmitter, Paulo Sergio Pinheiro, Rogelio Pérez Perdomo, Donna Lee Van Cott, Edward LiPuma, Kathryn Hochstetler, and Fernando Bustamante. Panels were chaired by North-South Center colleagues Luigi Manzetti, Tommie Sue Montgomery, Anthony Bryan, Mary Uebersax, and Elena Alvarez. Other invited participants who enriched our discussions were Tim Power, Phil Oxhorn, Gustavo Gorriti, Lynn Kuzma, and Tamara Sorger. The Center's Director, Ambler Moss, and Deputy Director, Robin Rosenberg, welcomed the conference participants and were supportive of the project from start to finish. Valuable assistance with conference planning, logistics, and materials was provided by Mark Everingham, Julie Diehl, Ben Recarey, Mary Mapes, Sherry Tross, and Nancy Colón.

Assembling the present volume was a lengthy and labor-intensive process. Philip Oxhorn provided the North-South Center Press with a thorough review of the entire manuscript, including many helpful comments and observations on individual chapters that we shared with the authors. We are indebted to Robert Barros for excellent translations of two of the chapters. Early in the process, Patricia Rosas and Martha Reiner made contributions to the copy editing efforts. Our thanks go to Mary D'León for assisting with copy editing and patiently entering edits on numerous chapter drafts. Christina Jaramillo typed in preliminary edits on all the chapter drafts. At the end of the project, Susan Holler good naturedly dealt with the jumble of terms that the editors sought to include in the index.

Our greatest debt, however, goes to Kathleen Hamman, editorial director, and Mary Mapes, publications director, of the North-South Center Press. It was only through their tireless efforts and unflagging professionalism that this book was brought to a successful conclusion.

*Felipe Agüero and Jeffrey Stark*

# Part I

## Thinking About Problems of Democratic Governance in Post-Transition Latin America

# CHAPTER ONE

# Conflicting Assessments of Democratization: Exploring the Fault Lines

## FELIPE AGÜERO

It has been about two decades since Latin America started joining democratization's third wave (Huntington 1991). Ecuador, Bolivia, and Peru began moving away from authoritarianism in the late 1970s. The Central American countries, Argentina, Uruguay, Brazil, Paraguay, and Chile followed, establishing democratic regimes in the 1980s and 1990s, and Mexico joined by holding unprecedented competitive elections in 1997. In all these countries, incumbent presidents and most members of congress have been elected in competitive elections under at least minimal standards of freedom and fairness.

Democratization imported noteworthy changes. The military, for the most part, gradually receded backstage, and outright fear ceased to be employed as political currency. Competition substituted for monopolized political decisionmaking, and alternation in office took place peacefully between historical adversaries, such as Peronists and Radicals in Argentina, and former combatants, such as Sandinistas and their opposition in Nicaragua. Accountability of government officials acquired greater weight, to the point that presidents were forced out of office when caught in corrupt or illegal activity, as occurred in Brazil and Venezuela, giving credence to the strength of constitutional norms and procedures.

These changes have been accompanied by equally momentous transformations in the economies and the international relations of Latin America (Smith and Korzeniewicz 1997). Economic reforms have enhanced the role of the market via deregulation, privatization, and trade liberalization. Case by case, at varying rhythms, these reforms have been sealing the fate of the developmentalist state that prevailed in the past. In the end, reforms aided the region's vigorous economic recovery, which took off from the low points of the debt crisis and the "lost decade" of the 1980s.

The nature of the connections between these reforms and democratization has been a matter of contention. Economic reforms, with the exception of Chile's, were seriously promoted only after the demise of authoritarian regimes, and, when pursued effectively, they assisted the legitimation of successor democratic governments. The ensuing strengthening of private sectors was viewed by some as adding a fundamental component of democratization by limiting the discretionary arbitrary power of the state and creating possibilities for the expansion of civil society. For many others, however, market reforms resulting in a speedy weakening of the state have troubled the advancement of democracy by exacerbating the problems of poverty and inequality, by limiting public action and regulation in several other important areas, and by denying civil society dialogue with necessary counterparts in the state (Smith, Acuña, and Gamarra 1994; Chalmers et al. 1997).

A vastly changed international context also accompanied democratization and economic reforms. Although the end of the Cold War was not as directly related to democratization in Latin America as it was in other regions, its cessation did eliminate the strategic entrenchment of the region within the confines of bipolarity. This alleviated domestic conflicts that had been distorted by outside pressures and helped to make possible agreements necessary for democratization.

Expansive military roles and the inward orientation of national security doctrines could no longer be sustained on the bipolar logic. At the same time, increased regional and subregional cooperation on political issues as well as on issues of trade and economic integration provided hope that military roles and expenses would be diminished or reshaped in favor of shared development goals.

## ASSESSMENTS OF DEMOCRATIZATION

Despite progress, democratization, embedded in economic and international change, has remained the subject of controversial and inconclusive evaluation (Shin 1994). A quick glance at the literature reveals the frequent use of conditional terms to address the new democracies: fragile, hybrid regimes, unsettling, delegative, debilitating, illiberal, in crisis, in need of deepening and consolidation, inchoate, and many more (Schmitter 1994; Collier and Levitsky 1995; Diamond 1996; Lowenthal and Domínguez 1997). Scholarly writing on the subject often reveals caution and hesitation in the approaches to assessment, signaling the inadequacy of concepts utilized in handling the question.[1] Analyses often appear to be rooted in a sort of preconceived view about the chances that true democratization has of surviving in Latin American polities.

Conflicting assessments of democratization should be no reason to worry in a field that has been marked by disagreement and whose health, in fact, relies on the contrast of diverse points of view. It is troubling, however, that conflicting assessments are made of the same cases with the same information and from roughly similar schema. Argentina, for instance, has been praised for the alternation of Radicals and Peronists, the shift to a new development course, and the reemergence of a sense of optimism that puts behind the years of military contestation and hyperinflation. However, at the same time, Argentina's democracy is deemed to have suffered under Carlos Menem's administrations, viewed as reenactments of personalistic, authoritarian features typical of old-style Peronism, visible in the maneuvers around constitutional reform and the proliferation of corrupt practices. Thus, while Argentina's democracy is evaluated positively as having attained substantial progress, it is assessed negatively for receding back to authoritarian features.[2]

Similarly, Brazil has been praised for the ability of its institutions under democracy to cope with the crisis of presidential corruption (Weyland 1993), to maintain the military on the fringes (Hunter 1997), and to facilitate economic reform and the advancement of a new growth model (Kingstone 1997). Scholars, in this regard, have been sensitive to the vigorous reformist leadership of President Fernando Henrique Cardoso, thought to be relevant in many areas to the promotion of democracy.[3] In contrast, it is noted that individual leaders prevail over political parties that remain weak (Mainwaring 1992-1993); that state and institutional bottlenecks prevent the revamping of the economy and its ability to deal with the pressing issues of poverty and inequality (Power 1997; Weyland 1996); and that the military retains powers that are incompatible with fully democratic arrangements (Zaverucha 1997). Weaknesses in several arenas have led to assessments of unconsolidated democracy in Brazil (Linz and Stepan 1996).

Chile's democratization is another example of differences in evaluation. Since the transition from Gen. Augusto Pinochet's military government to democratically elected civilian officials in 1990, Chilean politics has resumed many of its historical traits, such as a vigorous party system and stable electoral alignments. The old traits also acquired patterns that were new: reduced polarization and consensus across much of the political spectrum on substantive areas, such as the overall orientation of development and economic policies. As democratic institutions seemed to take firm hold anew, the new democracy was described as "possibly consolidating" or moving in the direction of democratic consolidation (Burton, Gunther, and Higley 1992, 325). Other scholars, however, while acknowledging the presence of those favorable traits, gave greater weight to constitutional restrictions on the new democracy inherited from the authoritarian period (Linz and Stepan 1996) and to the difficulties of promoting democratic reforms from within the new institutions, given the nature of cleavages still prevailing among elites (Agüero 1993, 1998).[4] And one could go down the list of countries, finding similar differences in assessment.

What results, then, is a difference between positions of systematic optimism and systematic pessimism. For optimists, democracy has been quickly consolidated, inaugurating a new era with no chances of reversal. For pessimists, many of the changes experienced are close to being just façades, behind which authoritarian structures remain well entrenched, albeit in disguise, or ready to resurface at any sign of crisis. Pessimists wonder whether Latin American democracies are riding through yet another wave in the cyclical pattern that alternates between "democratic and authoritarian 'moments'" or whether democracies face the prospects of a "slow death" (Malloy 1987; O'Donnell 1992); whereas optimists believe that the changes may be viewed as critical junctures leading to a new epoch of freedom and prosperity.

The consequence of these differences is the suggestion of contending research agendas that take off from the primacy of different dependent variables. Should we be studying, as Karen L. Remmer (1995, 114) favors, the underlying causes of the "surprising and unprecedented vitality of democracy in the region" or, instead, what she criticizes, the factors affecting the poverty of democracy and its fragilities? Given the importance of this alternative, it makes sense to explore the factors behind differences in the evaluation of democracies in Latin America.

## FACTORS INFLUENCING THE ASSESSMENT

S ocial scientists generally specialize in the study of specific institutions, policy areas, or social and political actors. The *primary angle or dimension of analysis* chosen for the study of one or more cases is one of the factors influencing the analysis of democracy. The focus on a specific actor, for example, labor, women, the military, or a specific set of institutions, such as electoral politics or issues of participation, is likely to influence the conclusion. For instance, assessment of democratization will likely be bleaker in a study that focuses on women as actors in the issue of participation than one that centers on elections or, in some cases, economic reform or social policy (Waylen 1994).[5] A focus on elite consensus (Higley and Gunther 1992) will yield different results than if attention centered on human rights or the rule of law (Ensalaco 1994; Barahona de Brito 1997; Panizza and Barahona de Brito 1997; O'Donnell 1998). Similarly, studies focusing on civil-military relations (Loveman 1994) are likely to yield different evaluations than those resulting from studies of electoral politics (Pérez and Stein 1994; Valenzuela and Siavelis 1991).

*Diachronic comparisons within countries* are also likely to influence conclusions by highlighting the degree of change attained since the democratic transition. Specific countries will look better or worse relative to their immediate past histories. It is hard, for instance, not to highlight the sea change in El Salvador, where the democratic process, now including all sectors in competitive politics, has left behind a period of violence, repression, and massive routine violations of human rights by a largely autonomous, oversized military (Seligson and Córdova Macías 1992; Montgomery 1995). The yardstick is obviously different than if the comparison were, for instance, with Costa Rica. Bolivia is another case where diachronic comparison leads to a positive evaluation. Successful institutional reforms and peaceful transfer of power through free and clean electoral procedures stand sharply in contrast with the instability and military interventionism that characterized this country in the past (Gamarra 1996; Barrios and Mayorga 1994). In the case of Brazil, on the contrary, scholars engaged in the comparison of the period immediately following the transition with the previous period of military authoritarian rule highlighted a large degree of continuity (Hagopian 1992) or pointed to the difficulties facing the *Nova República* in light of the accomplishments of military rule — what were referred to as the "paradoxes of success" (O'Donnell 1992). Later comparisons between the early years of the *Nova República* and the attainments during the Itamar Franco and Fernando Henrique Cardoso administrations yielded, in turn, more favorable evaluations (Hunter 1997) than would have obtained from a cross-national comparison.

Divergent views on the *relationship between economics and politics* in democratization and reform processes are another source of difference in assessments. For instance, Karen L. Remmer (1995, 117, 114) argues that, quite remarkably, Latin American democratization "has been sustained in the face of economic decline," a fact that, in her view, challenges "the conventional wisdom about the relationship between economic prosperity and political democracy." Indeed, the coexistence of costly economic reform with persevering democratic government has been widely verified as a trait of the post-authoritarian period.[6] Ben Ross Schneider (1995, 222), for instance, observes that ineffectual management of economic transformation does not prevent the consolidation of new democracies, and Barbara Geddes (1995a, 205) notes that democratic governments can survive the heavy costs to their populations that result from the pursuit of economic reforms. This feat tends to support, among some, a positive balance of the new democracies. Remmer, for instance, is swayed by the "surprising vitality" of democracy in the face of economic constraints. In her view, Latin American democracies became much more inclusionary than previous modal forms of political democracy had been (Remmer 1991).

Others, however, without denying the coexistence of enduring democratic government with economic reforms or even the necessity of these reforms, emphasize detrimental effects on democratic governance. In this vein, scholars have stressed that interest representation has weakened (Geddes 1995a); inequality has greatly increased, undermining the foundations of citizenship; and state capacity to act on behalf of the public interest has diminished, all of which affect the quality of the new democratic arrangements (Gamarra 1994; Smith and Acuña 1994; Oxhorn and Ducatenzeiler 1998).[7]

Critics also have noted the detrimental effects on the affirmation of democratic institutions that result from the exclusionary and technocratic *style* of formulating and executing economic reform. Small policy circles conceiving and implementing vast reforms with decree powers and little or no debate, it is argued, are not conducive to the advancement and strengthening of democratic institutions (Przeworski 1993; Przeworski et al. 1995; Conaghan and Malloy 1994; O'Donnell 1994). Others, like Remmer (1995), disagree as follows: by not succumbing to the temptations of economic populism, democracy is strengthened rather than undermined.[8] Stephan Haggard and Robert R. Kaufman, in turn, maintain that the initiation of economic reforms necessary for improved performance and, thus, for democratic legitimacy may require centralized, discretionary, personal executive authority, although they concede that in the long term this authority should "be depersonalized and made accountable if both democracy and economic reform are to be institutionalized" (Haggard and Kaufman 1995, 335).[9]

Different ways of evaluating democracy in Latin America today are also reflected in the varying *analytic weight given transitions*, specifically modes or paths of transition. Schemes used for the study of transitions naturally have influenced studies of democratization and new democracies. These schemes generally have consisted of clusters of cases brought together by varying criteria — initial conditions, facilitating factors, and starting points — according to which degrees of success or failure were to be expected. Whether the previous regimes had been successful or not or had collapsed or negotiated their exit; whether transitions were conducted by elites or from below or were negotiated or imposed; whether the outgoing elites favored or resisted change, and numerous other distinctions were held to define certain transition paths upon which outcomes and lesser or greater chances of success were said to depend.

These schemes were useful for understanding transition dynamics and their relevant factors and for comparatively addressing the different results of transitions. If, in addition, they were presented in ways that conceived transition outcomes as situations in longer sequences of change affected by newer and larger sets of variables, they would shed further light on post-transition dynamics as well. Often, however, they remained content with the specification of structural or other initial factors and modes of transition as they determined or set the likelihood of certain outcomes. Seldom were these approaches sensitive to unexpected twists or unanticipated change and their surprising consequences, which, for instance, could turn around situations previously regarded with pessimism.[10] Discrepancies between predictions from the transition models and actual outcomes often resulted in hesitation and an inability to assess progress confidently, determine failure, or outline expected future developments. Nowhere was this hesitation expressed more clearly than in the statement, meant to balance the positive with the negative, that just as important as where these countries are coming from is where they are headed ("...where one is going matters as much as where one is coming from" [Przeworski 1991, 99]). Thus, the lagging weight of the past was countered with a sort of pulling power of the future, a future seen as presenting no alternatives to democratization.

Besides the lingering and inconclusive influence of transition models, there also emerged a clearer difference in the role assigned transitions, with consequences for the views on present democratic regimes. One group of scholars reaffirmed the constraining impact of transitions, often emphasizing harmful effects on new democracies. In this view, the transition "is a founding moment the legacy of which helps to shape the new democratic regime for years" (Friedheim 1993, 482).[11] Yossi Shain and Juan J. Linz (1995, 4) underscored the importance of the transition by making the case that "the type of interim administration is crucial in determining the subsequent regime...." Linz and Alfred Stepan (1996) viewed the tasks and chances of democratic consolidation strongly influenced by prior regime type and its leadership structure as well as by who initiates and controls the transition.

Others have explicitly rejected the predictive power of transition modes or features of the previous authoritarian regime, highlighting instead the harmful weight of the pre-authoritarian past. Guillermo O'Donnell, revising his previous work, is a clear exponent of this view.[12] Problems in new democracies reveal not the modes of transition or features of the authoritarian regimes but, instead, the resurgence of an old "schizophrenia" that predates authoritarianism, on which newer problems are superimposed. Problems stem from a profound crisis of the state, infused with clientelistic features, compounded with recent economic crises (O'Donnell 1993, 1359-60). Others, in a similar vein, stress the role of an historically omnipresent "constitution of tyranny" (Loveman 1993) or the cyclical pattern "alternating democratic and authoritarian 'moments'" (Malloy 1987, 236).

Some scholars also have downgraded the role of transitions, but instead of favoring a larger weight for the past, they assigned a greater role and a constructive one to post-transition institutions. In fact, a focus on new institutions highlights their ability to erode the perverse influence of legacies, which, as Adam Przeworski argues, "can be gradually wiped away" (1991, 98). Geddes (1995b, 270), for instance, maintains that new democratic institutions "create a set of compelling incentives that structure the behavior of political elites" in ways that lead to the erosion of negative legacies. Along similar lines, Wendy Hunter (1997, 8) argues, with a focus on Brazil, that "electoral competition creates incentives for politicians to reduce the interference of a politically powerful and active military" that otherwise had been expected to operate as a hard, constraining legacy. David Pion-Berlin (1997) also de-emphasizes factors of continuity with the past, favoring a focus on strategies that may better capture actual successes in democratization.[13]

Pervading the other factors, views on democratization also differ according to the *concept of democracy* employed. The distinction between institutionalist or procedural, and substantive notions of democracy is commonplace in the democratization literature. Authors often will preface their writing with expressions of preference for either one, sometimes also referred to as minimalist or maximalist versions of democracy. There is no question that working with the more trying substantive or maximalist concept will yield a gloomier assessment of existing democracies in Latin America. However, the literature presents problems and ambiguities that go beyond this simple distinction.

The literature often fails to work with an explicit definition of democracy against which actual outcomes of democratization processes may be identified and contrasted. Democracy is simply seen as the result of the unfolding of its initial conditions — such as agreement on procedures, institutionalized uncertainty, or contestation. Once it is observed that these conditions are present, it is assumed that everything else will follow.[14] This, however, much too quickly leads to the assumption that democracy is actually fully in place, thus preempting a careful look at its corresponding institutional rights and guarantees of citizenship. An opposite approach, in which analysis proceeds with a clear definition of democracy that fully takes into account those rights and guarantees, is prepared to take on existing Latin American democracies with a critical assessment (Diamond 1996; Mainwaring 1995).

In other cases, the adoption of a procedural view of democracy in stark separation from substantive views leads to ignoring the ways in which the strictly procedural aspects are limited in their reach by failure in the substantive areas. In fact, it is difficult to believe that social and economic inequality in the forms and magnitude found in Latin America will not harm the formal procedural aspects of citizen equality that are said to define democracy (O'Donnell 1993).

The actual concept of democracy behind the procedural perspective often is paid only scant attention. Scholars rightly justify the choice of such a perspective because it allows for analytically distinguishing explanatory variables to separate democracy as an outcome from its contributing factors.[15] Usually, reference is made indistinctly to Joseph A. Schumpeter (1975) or Robert A. Dahl (1971; 1989) as a principal exponent of the procedural perspective. But this often casual reference ignores the fundamental differences between the two authors.[16] While Schumpeter's view is based on the leading notion of elite competition, Dahl's emphasizes participation and the free expression of citizens' preferences. The procedural or institutional concept taken from Dahl is far more demanding than what many of those who employ it actually acknowledge. The set of institutional guarantees that sustain participation and contestation and the free formulation and expression of preferences point to the actual realization of the principle of citizen equality, a foundation of democracy. This basic principle calls for a complex institutional edifice, involving norms, procedures, and organizations. Many authors have, in fact, attempted to expand on Dahl's definition, basically by making its complex content more explicit (for instance, Diamond, Linz, and Lipset 1989; Schmitter and Karl 1993). But the literature often overlooks these *substantive* aspects of Dahl's procedural notion and instead remains satisfied with a minimalist appreciation of it. The rigor of the concept is lost in its actual use for the assessment of existing democracies. This is precisely the problem with the uses of the concept of democratic consolidation.

## THE PROBLEMS WITH CONSOLIDATION

Concern with the completion of the transitions and the stability of the new democratic arrangements led to a focus on democratic consolidation. Important contributions highlighted the problems of authoritarian legacies and "reserve domains" (Valenzuela 1992), the institutionalization and "structuration" of democracy's component regimes (Schmitter 1995), and the role of the constitutional, attitudinal, and behavioral levels of democracy (Linz and Stepan 1996). These works were useful in providing standards against which to assess existing democracies and in highlighting weaknesses in newly established post-authoritarian regimes. But they did not help much in overcoming ambiguities in conflicting evaluations of democracy. The important conceptual contribution of Linz and Stepan (1996), for instance, leads to different conclusions on specific cases, depending on whether their concept of consolidation or their insightful notion of the five arenas of democracy (civil society, political society, economic society, rule of law, and bureaucracy) is employed.

Early critics of the democratic consolidation approach highlighted the ability of the new democracies to endure in an unconsolidated state (Hagopian 1993, 465). Stability was thus not the problem, as threats to democracy came not from "dangers of relapse" as much as from the weaknesses of representation and accountability (Hagopian 1993, 499). Schneider (1995, 216) discarded democratic consolidation as "a clumsy concept."[17] From a very different kind of analysis, Przeworski et al. (1996) concluded that consolidation was "an empty term." And O'Donnell (1996) argued that consolidation did not add to the definition of democracy and that consolidation wrongly suggested a teleological trajectory for unconsolidated regimes. More important, in O'Donnell's view, consolidation drove our attention exclusively to formal institutionalization and away from the reality of a gap between formally prescribed institutions and informal institutionalization, a point at which seemingly enduring polyarchies in Latin America are found.

The introduction of the concept of consolidation ended up diminishing the concept of democracy by approaching post-authoritarian regimes too swiftly, as if they were on their way to consolidation, that is, as if they were already clearly democratic. The post-transitions literature usually contemplated a sequence through which, first, democracy was attained and, second, a process of consolidation would presumably be initiated. Thus, consolidation comprised the idea that the democratic nature of post-transition regimes ceased to be problematic. Based on a careless use of the procedural notion, studies often led to a blurring of the rigor of the concept of democracy. Many of the problems with these studies lie with the dodging of a rigorous concept of democracy that results from the rush to a concern with consolidation. If nothing else, the discussion on democratic consolidation should be used to bring back this rigor and to replace the focus from the endurance of situations of precarious democratic credentials to the problems of becoming fully democratic (Diamond 1997; Schedler 1998).

Nonetheless, numerous elements in the consolidation approach should remain helpful in the study of new democracies, as they provide yardsticks with which to contrast existing situations against stated or desired goals and to compare across countries. The identification of legacies and enclaves from the authoritarian past; the focus on the structuration of democracy's regimes, including the constitutional; and the gauging of the evolution of attitudinal and behavioral support for democratic regimes should all remain useful as dimensions for assessment and comparison. However, improvement in these areas, even if substantial, should not lead to a sense of closure in the movement to *more* complete democracy, by awarding democracies the status of being consolidated.[18] As it becomes clear from Linz and Stepan (1996), a favorable disposition in democracy's attitudinal, behavioral, and constitutional dimensions — which constitute their notion of consolidation — does not imply that the polity has overcome major problems in the configuration of a democratic regime, as viewed from the angle of its five interacting arenas.

## FAULT LINES OF DEMOCRATIC GOVERNANCE

Conflicting assessments of democratization influence the kind of research agenda suggested for pursuit in this area. If the evaluation highlights the longevity of democracy, then this is posited as the phenomenon to explain. Remmer has articulated this view; further, she has pointed out rightly that durability and stability of democracies prove to be less problematic than with authoritarian regimes (Remmer 1996). However, an interest in stability should not be presented as a rigid alternative to a concern with the quality of new democracies (Mainwaring 1995; Kaufman 1997). While durable, new democracies also are faulty.

We, therefore, argue here for a focus on the fault lines of democratic governance in Latin America.[19] If democracy has imported noteworthy change, especially in terms of institutionalizing electoral competition and pluralism, notable problems remain in its illiberal flaws, in the ways participation and representation are reconfigured, in the control over institutionalized force and violence, and in many other ways.

The fault lines metaphor proposes a focus on the uneven development of democracy in post-authoritarian regimes. The metaphor utilizes the idea of geological fractures to suggest friction between "tectonic plates" that causes pressure to be applied in different directions, along and across democratic arrangements at different levels of depth. These "plates" or levels confront, for instance, legal formality with actual shallowness in the rule of law, leaving a rift through which corrupt and clientelistic practices sift in and through which overtly unconstitutional behavior by state officials is tolerated. These fissures also reflect the opposition of well-assembled judicial structures at the top that, although occasionally effective in basic constitutional functions, are only feebly deployed throughout society, denying access to justice to large segments of the population. Through these cracks, violations of human and individual rights find their way in. The fault lines imagery permits the visual image of a breach between the normal operation of representative national institutions and the disintegrated structure of organized interests in civil society or the weakening of participation. It also depicts the breach separating the goal of promoting universal norms and procedures in the public sector as part of state reform, with, for instance, the actual toleration of exceptionalism and autonomy for the armed forces.

Several examples of fault lines can be cited. In Colombia, alongside the visible gaps in sovereignty, shared by the state, guerrillas, and criminal organizations, there also exist fissures within the realm of law and the judiciary. While top structures of the judiciary have developed significant power to sanction or restrain the central government, courts and justices have been unable to respond effectively to the astonishing development of the *acciones o recursos de tutela* (writs) that have mobilized thousands in pursuit of their rights. Citizens who, through this resource, may become greatly empowered with a new conscience of rights and grievances, face a judiciary powerful enough to overrule government decisions but incapable of satisfying basic citizen demands (Gómez Albarello 1996). Brazil, as the chapter by James Holston and Teresa Caldeira in this volume shows, finds itself in a similar situation.

In Peru, the development of all kinds of organizations in society (nongovernmental organizations and community organizations) expresses the advancement of a long-standing aspiration for the strengthening of civil society. Yet, this development exists in total separation from actual channels of access to power, largely due to the weakness and subordination of political parties — in many cases, their nearly total disappearance — relative to the power of central technocratic rule. This separation vividly reflects the imagery of a major fault line.

In Brazil, an unprecedentedly firm and credible stance by the government on the promotion of human rights, expressed in a national plan and the creation of a special government secretariat, stands side by side with the weakness of courts to enforce it and the dubious and violent practices of the police, which actually make the human rights situation there one of the worst in the region. In Chile, the vigorous implantation of democratic institutions, with perhaps the strongest and most effective party system in the region, coexists with a gradual but significant decline in participation and a diminished prestige of government institutions and parties. Along with numerous situations of this kind, specific to individual countries, other fractures across the region are widely shared. This is the case, for instance, of the actual limitations that income disparities impose on citizenship or of the pervasive exceptionality that separates the military from the rest of state organizations and administration.

These are probably not San Andreas-type fault lines, presaging the big and final tremor that will take us back to the blatant authoritarianism of the military regimes of the recent past. Most countries do not present situations of extreme political or ideological polarization of the kind that typically precedes regime breakdown, and in most countries the military is not in a disposition to entertain such possibility. This is not to say that severe threats of regression may not surface, as Venezuela, Peru, and Paraguay have reminded us, but that the obstacles to democratic advancement lie primarily elsewhere, in fault lines underneath democratic terrains. Threats are not so much against regime stability as they are against the depth, quality, and consistency of its democratic features.

A focus on fault lines, on the fractures and unevenness of democratic development in post-authoritarian regimes, may be pursued from different angles, and the literature already offers avenues for their productive exploration. The simple suggestion of a gap between formal and informal institutionalization (O'Donnell 1996) or between different levels of state presence (O'Donnell 1993) opens up vast and rich avenues for research along these lines. At the same time, these gaps encourage more attention to areas of power and empowerment that escape central loci (Rubin 1996). Also very helpful to productive research is the conceptualization of democracy's arenas (Linz and Stepan 1996). Fault lines, from this perspective, may be viewed as expressing a disjuncture among these arenas in ways that block the actual exercise of citizenship. Disjuncture between different levels of regime structuration (Schmitter 1995) may also be viewed in this light.

Finally, a focus on fault lines of democratic governance does not assume that they are the exclusive creation of the post-transition period. Quite the contrary, this approach calls for a historical perspective that tries to discern the new from the old. Many of the problems highlighted here may well be the revival of problems of the pre-authoritarian democratic times, combined in new arrangements or strengthened, as a result of authoritarian legacy and the new challenges faced in the post-transition period. To what extent are fault lines a creation of the new regimes responding to a new context, and to what extent are they the expression of recalcitrant constraints stemming from authoritarian and pre-authoritarian legacies? Answers to these questions are essential if ways are to be found for further democratic advancement in the region.

This volume emphasizes three major areas as expressing the principal fault lines. One is the changes affecting the representation of societal interests and citizen participation, which, in turn, affect mechanisms of accountability. Another is the area pertaining to the rule of law and its connections to transformations in the judiciary. Third, there is the area of organized force and violence, which is approached through analyses of the military and civil-military relations. In the conclusion, we expand on these areas and outline avenues for future research.

# Notes

1. Remmer (1995, 104) pointed to this in clear terms: "Comparativists are very far from agreeing upon any set of models capable of addressing the new democratic realities...."

2. For different views on Argentina's democracy, see De Riz (1994); Canitrot (1994); Cheresky (1996); Quiroga (1996); Palermo and Novaro (1996); and Peruzzotti (1997). O'Donnell's views on delegative democracy are largely based on the case of Argentina under Menem (O'Donnell 1994).

3. One noteworthy area is the promotion of human rights, which has become for the first time, through a national program, an official policy of Brazil (Pinheiro and Mesquita Neto, n.d.).

4. For different views on Chile, see Garretón (1995); Moulian (1997); Ensalaco (1994); Martínez and Díaz (1996).

5. For a recent, more favorable assessment of representation of women, see Jones (1998).

6. The cases of Venezuela (Goodman et al. 1995; McCoy et al. 1995; Romero 1997) and Peru in the early 1990s challenged the view about the easy coexistence of democracy with economic reform. Haggard and Kaufman (1995, 327) emphasize the weakening effects that poor economic performance has over democratic rule.

7. Questions about the relations between economic reforms and democracy recently have led to research on the connections between these reforms and public support or public opinion. See, for instance, Stokes (1996); Kaufman and Zuckermann (1998).

8. In her view, the arguments she criticizes amount to defining "the differences between democracy and dictatorship in terms of government responsiveness to short-term group pressures — a definition that would shift many authoritarian regimes into the democratic category" (Remmer 1995, 115).

9. This debate has given rise to interesting research on policy style and policy coalitions for the pursuit of economic reforms. See, for instance, Conaghan and Malloy (1994); Weyland (1994); Roberts (1995); Gibson (1997) for the connections between neoliberalism and new forms of populism.

10. For the role of these twists and turns, see Hirschman (1971, 26-37 passim; 1992, 171-175).

11. This view was clearly part of the earlier literature, which emphasized that the manner in which the transition was carried out, the character of the main forces pushing for it and leading it, their relative strengths, and the pace of the transition were all factors affecting democratic governance in successor regimes. See, for instance, O'Donnell and Schmitter (1986); Stepan (1986); Karl (1990); Karl and Schmitter (1991); Valenzuela (1992); Bruszt and Stark (1992); Mainwaring (1992). For an excellent presentation of transition factors and their consequences, see McGuire (1995).

12. O'Donnell asserts that "...recent typologies of the new democracies based on characteristics of the preceding authoritarian regimes and/or on the modalities of the first transition have little predictive power concerning what happens after the first democratically elected government has been installed" (O'Donnell 1993, 1356).

13. A few, however, warn about problems associated with the nature of new institutions, such as presidentialism (Linz 1994; Valenzuela 1994) or the institutionalization of exclusionary and technocratic policy-making styles.

14. For instance, Przeworski (1991, 10 fn), adopting a "contestationist" view of democracy, argues that "once political rights are sufficiently extensive to admit of conflicting interests, everything else follows...." See also Di Palma (1990).

15. The choice of approaches is also influenced by the extent to which analyses are driven by domestic or international political or ideological imperatives. Social science is often affected by its embeddedness in conflicting agendas reflected in domestic politics and international organizations, as well as in divisions within the discipline itself. See Przeworski and Limongi (1993); Geddes (1991); Carothers (1996).

16. For a critique of Schumpeter, see Held (1987).

17. We had advanced similar kinds of criticism in Felipe Agüero, "Democratic Governance in Latin America: Thinking About Fault Lines," Discussion Memo, Workshop on Fault Lines of Democratic Governance, North-South Center, Miami, November 18-19, 1994.

18. For a very insightful discussion of the uses of the concept of consolidation, see Schedler (1998). In his view, "The term 'democratic consolidation' should refer to expectations of regime continuity — and to nothing else" (Schedler 1998, 103).

19. The problems we highlight are certainly not exclusively Latin American, and many see them pervading all Third Wave democracies (Carothers 1997; Zakaria 1997; Kaplan 1997; Plattner 1998), while many other problems affect old democracies as well (Maier 1994; Sandel 1996).

# References

Agüero, Felipe. 1993. "Chile: South America's Success Story?" *Current History* 92 (572).

Agüero, Felipe. 1995. *Soldiers, Civilians, and Democracy: Post-Franco Spain in Comparative Perspective*. Baltimore and London: The Johns Hopkins University Press.

Agüero, Felipe. 1998. "Chile's Lingering Authoritarian Legacy." *Current History* 97 (616).

Agüero, Felipe, Eugenio Tironi, Eduardo Valenzuela, and Guillermo Sunkel. 1998. "Voters, Parties, and Political Information: Fragile Political Intermediation in Post-Authoritarian Chile." Unpublished article, forthcoming in a publication edited by Paul Beck and John Curtice; "Votantes, partidos, e información política en el Chile posautoritario," forthcoming in *Revista de Ciencia Política*. Universidad Católica. Santiago, Chile.

Barrios, Raúl, and René Antonio Mayorga. 1994. *La cuestión militar en cuestión: democracia y fuerzas armadas*. La Paz: CEBEM.

Burton, Michael, Richard Gunther, and John Higley. 1992. "Elites and Democratic Consolidation in Latin America and Southern Europe: An Overview." In *Elites and Democratic Consolidation in Latin America and Southern Europe*, eds. John Higley and Richard Gunther. Cambridge: Cambridge University Press.

Bruszt, László, and David Stark. 1992. "Remaking the Political Field in Hungary: From the Politics of Confrontation to the Politics of Competition." In *Eastern Europe in Revolution*, ed. Ivo Banac. Ithaca and London: Cornell University Press.

Canitrot, Adolfo. 1994. "Crisis and Transformation of the Argentine State (1978-1992)." In *Democracy, Markets, and Structural Reform in Latin America: Argentina, Bolivia, Brazil, Chile, and Mexico*, eds. William C. Smith, Carlos H. Acuña, and Eduardo A. Gamarra. Coral Gables, Fla.: North-South Center Press at the University of Miami.

Carothers, Thomas. 1996. "Promoting Democracy in a Postmodern World." *Dissent* (Spring).

Carothers, Thomas. 1997. "Democracy Without Illusions." *Foreign Affairs* 76.

Chalmers, Douglas A., Carlos M. Vilas, Katherine Hite, Scott B. Martin, Kerianne Piester, and Monique Segarra, eds. 1997. *The New Politics of Inequality in Latin America: Rethinking Participation and Representation*. Oxford: Oxford University Press.

Cheresky, Isidoro. 1996. "Poder presidencial limitado y oposición activa como requisitos de la democracia." Paper prepared for the Seminar "La Democracia en Argentina: Evolución Reciente y Perspectivas," Instituto Gino Germani, Universidad de Buenos Aires, July 11-12.

Conaghan, Catherine M., and James M. Malloy. 1994. *Unsettling Statecraft: Democracy and Neoliberalism in the Central Andes*. Pittsburgh: University of Pittsburgh Press.

Dahl, Robert A. 1971. *Polyarchy: Participation and Opposition*. New Haven: Yale University Press.

Dahl, Robert A. 1989. *Democracy and Its Critics*. New Haven and London: Yale University Press.

De Brito, Alexandra Barahona. 1997. *Human Rights and Democratization in Latin America: Uruguay and Chile*. Oxford: Oxford University Press.

De Riz, Liliana. 1994. "Argentina: el enigma democrático," *Nueva Sociedad* 129 (January-February).

Diamond, Larry. 1996. "Democracy in Latin America: Degrees, Illusions, and Directions for Consolidation." In *Beyond Sovereignty: Collectively Defending Democracy in the Americas*, ed. Tom Farer. Baltimore and London: The Johns Hopkins University Press.

Diamond, Larry. 1997. "Introduction: In Search of Consolidation." In *Consolidating the Third Wave Democracies*, eds. Larry Diamond, Marc F. Plattner, Yun-han Chu, and Hung-mao Tien. Baltimore and London: The Johns Hopkins University Press.

Diamond, Larry, Juan J. Linz, and Seymour Martin Lipset, eds. 1989. *Democracy in Developing Countries: Latin America*. Boulder, Colo.: Lynne Rienner Publishers.

Di Palma, Giuseppe. 1990. *To Craft Democracies*. Berkeley, Calif.: University of California Press.

Ensalaco, Mark. 1994. "In with the New, Out with the Old? The Democratizing Impact of Constitutional Reform in Chile." *Journal of Latin American Studies* 26 (2).

Friedheim, Daniel V. 1993. "Bringing Society Back into Democratic Transition Theory after 1989: Pact Making and Regime Collapse." *East European Politics and Societies* 7.

Gamarra, Eduardo A. 1994. "Market-Oriented Reforms and Democratization in Latin America: Challenges of the 1990s." In *Latin American Political Economy in the Age of Neoliberal Reform*, eds. William C. Smith, Carlos H. Acuña, and Eduardo A. Gamarra. Coral Gables, Fla.: North-South Center Press at the University of Miami.

Gamarra, Eduardo A. 1996. "Bolivia: Managing Democracy in the 1990s." In *Constructing Democratic Governance: Latin America and the Caribbean in the 1990s*, eds. Abraham F. Lowenthal and Jorge I. Domínguez. Baltimore and London: The Johns Hopkins University Press.

Garretón, Manuel Antonio. 1995. "Redemocratization in Chile." *Journal of Democracy* 6.

Geddes, Barbara. 1991. "Paradigms and Sand Castles in the Comparative Politics of Developing Areas." In *Political Science Looking to the Future (Volume Two): Comparative Politics, Policy and International Relations*, ed. William Crotty. Evanston, Ill.: Northwestern University Press.

Geddes, Barbara. 1995a. "The Politics of Economic Liberalization." *Latin American Research Review* 30 (2).

Geddes, Barbara. 1995b. "A Comparative Perspective on the Leninist Legacy in Eastern Europe." *Comparative Political Studies* 28.

Gibson, Edward. 1997. "The Populist Road to Market Reform: Policy and Electoral Coalitions in Mexico and Argentina." *World Politics* 49 (3).

Gómez Albarello, Juan Gabriel. 1996. "Justicia y democracia en Colombia: en entredicho?" *Análisis Político* 28 (May/August).

Goodman, Louis W., Johanna Mendelson Forman, Moisés Naim, Joseph S. Tulchin, and Gary Bland. 1995. *Lessons of the Venezuelan Experience*. Baltimore: The Johns Hopkins University Press.

Haggard, Stephan, and Robert R. Kaufman. 1995. *The Political Economy of Democratic Transitions*. Princeton, N.J.: Princeton University Press.

Hagopian, Frances. 1992. "The Compromised Consolidation: The Political Class in the Brazilian Transition." In *Issues in Democratic Consolidation: The New South American Democracies in Comparative Perspective*, eds. Scott Mainwaring,

Guillermo O'Donnell, and J. Samuel Valenzuela. Notre Dame, Ind.: University of Notre Dame Press.

Hagopian, Frances. 1993. "After Regime Change: Authoritarian Legacies, Political Representation, and the Democratic Future of South America." *World Politics* 45 (3).

Held, David. 1987. *Models of Democracy*. Stanford, Calif.: Stanford University Press.

Higley, John, and Richard Gunther, eds. 1992. *Elites and Democratic Consolidation in Latin America and Southern Europe*. Cambridge: Cambridge University Press.

Hirschman, Albert O. 1971. *A Bias for Hope*. New Haven and London: Yale University Press.

Hirschman, Albert O. 1992. *Rival Views of Market Society*. Cambridge, Mass.: Harvard University Press.

Hunter, Wendy. 1997. *Eroding Military Influence in Brazil: Politicians Against Soldiers*. Chapel Hill, N.C.: University of North Carolina Press.

Huntington, Samuel P. 1994. *The Third Wave: Democratization in the Late Twentieth Century*. Norman, Okla.: University of Oklahoma Press.

Kaplan, Robert D. 1997. "Was Democracy Just a Moment?" *The Atlantic Monthly* 280 (6).

Karl, Terry Lynn. 1990. "Dilemmas of Democratization in Latin America." *Comparative Politics* 23.

Karl, Terry Lynn, and Philippe C. Schmitter. 1991. "Modes of Transition in Latin America, Southern and Eastern Europe." *International Social Science Journal* 128.

Kaufman, Robert. 1997. *The Next Challenges for Latin America*. Estudio/Working Paper 1997/108. Madrid: Centro de Estudios Avanzados en Ciencias Sociales, Instituto Juan March de Estudios e Investigaciones.

Kaufman, Robert R., and Leo Zuckermann. 1998. "Attitudes Toward Economic Reform in Mexico: The Role of Political Mediations." *American Political Science Review* 92 (2).

Kingstone, Peter R. 1997. "The Limits of Neoliberalism: Business, the State, and Democratic Consolidation in Brazil." Paper presented at the XX International Congress of the Latin American Studies Association, Guadalajara, Mexico, April 17-20.

Linz, Juan J. 1994. "Presidential or Parliamentary Democracy: Does It Make a Difference?" In *The Failure of Presidential Democracy: Comparative Perspectives,* eds. Juan J. Linz and Arturo Valenzuela. Baltimore and London: The Johns Hopkins University Press.

Linz, Juan, and Alfred Stepan. 1996. *Problems of Democratic Transition and Consolidation: Southern Europe, South America, and Post-Communist Europe*. Baltimore and London: The Johns Hopkins University Press.

Loveman, Brian. 1993. *The Constitution of Tyranny: Regimes of Exception in Spanish America*. Pittsburgh and London: University of Pittsburgh Press.

Loveman, Brian. 1994. "'Protected Democracies and Military Guardianship: Political Transitions in Latin America, 1978-1993." *Journal of Interamerican Studies and World Affairs* 36 (2).

Lowenthal, Abraham F., and Jorge I. Domínguez. 1996. "Introduction: Constructing Democratic Governance." In *Constructing Democratic Governance: Latin America and the Caribbean in the 1990s*, eds. Abraham F. Lowenthal and Jorge I. Domínguez. Baltimore and London: The Johns Hopkins University Press.

Mainwaring, Scott. 1992. "Transitions to Democracy and Democratic Consolidation: Theoretical and Comparative Issues." In *Issues in Democratic Consolidation: The New South American Democracies in Comparative Perspective*, eds. Scott

Mainwaring, Guillermo O'Donnell and J. Samuel Valenzuela. Notre Dame, Ind.: University of Notre Dame Press.

Mainwaring, Scott. 1992-1993. "Brazilian Party Underdevelopment in Comparative Perspective." *Political Science Quarterly* 107: 4.

Mainwaring, Scott. 1995. "Democracy in Brazil and the Southern Cone: Achievements and Problems." *Journal of Interamerican Studies and World Affairs* 37 (Spring).

Maier, Charles S. 1994. "Democracy and Its Discontents." *Foreign Affairs* 73 (4).

Malloy, James M. 1987. "The Politics of Transition in Latin America." In *Authoritarians and Democrats: Regime Transition in Latin America*, eds. James M. Malloy and Mitchell A. Seligson. Pittsburgh: University of Pittsburgh Press.

McCoy, Jennifer, and Andrés Serbín, William C. Smith, and Andrés Stambouli, eds. 1995. *Venezuelan Democracy Under Stress*. Coral Gables, Fla.: North-South Center Press at the University of Miami.

McGuire, James W. 1995. "Interim Government and Democratic Consolidation: Argentina in Comparative Perspective." In *Between States: Interim Governments and Democratic Transitions*, eds. Yossi Shain and Juan J. Linz. Cambridge: Cambridge University Press.

Montgomery, Tommie Sue. 1995. *Revolution in El Salvador: From Civil Strife to Civil Peace*. Boulder, Colo.: Westview Press.

Moulian, Tomás. 1997. *Chile actual: anatomía de un mito*. Santiago: Universidad Arcis.

O'Donnell, Guillermo. 1992. "Transitions, Continuities and Paradoxes." In *Issues in Democratic Consolidation: The New South American Democracies in Comparative Perspective*, eds. Scott Mainwaring, Guillermo O'Donnell, and J. Samuel Valenzuela. Notre Dame, Ind.: University of Notre Dame Press.

O'Donnell, Guillermo. 1993. "On the State, Democratization and Some Conceptual Problems: A Latin American View with Glances at Some Postcommunist Countries. *World Development* 21.

O'Donnell, Guillermo. 1994. "Delegative Democracy." *Journal of Democracy* 5 (1).

O'Donnell, Guillermo. 1996. "Illusions About Consolidation." *Journal of Democracy* 7 (2).

O'Donnell, Guillermo. 1998 (forthcoming). "Polyarchies and the (Un)Rule of Law in Latin America." In *The Rule of Law and the Underprivileged in Latin America,* eds. Juan Méndez, Guillermo O'Donnell, and Paulo Sarge Pinheiro. Notre Dame, Ind.: University of Notre Dame Press.

O'Donnell, Guillermo, and Philippe C. Schmitter. 1986. *Transitions from Authoritarian Rule: Tentative Conclusions About Uncertain Democracies*. Baltimore and London: Johns Hopkins University Press.

Oxhorn, Philip D., and Graciela Ducatenzeiler. 1998. "Economic Reform and Democratization in Latin America." In *What Kind of Democracy? What Kind of Market?: Latin America in the Age of Neoliberalism*, eds. Philip Oxhorn and Graciela Ducatenzeiler. University Park, Pa.: Pennsylvania State University Press.

Palermo, Vicente, and Marcos Novaro. 1996. *Política y poder en el gobierno de Menem*. Buenos Aires: FLACSO, Grupo Editorial Norma.

Pérez, Orlando J., and Andrew J. Stein. 1994. "The Mechanics of Counting the Vote: The Institutionalization of Elections in Central America." Paper prepared for delivery at the 1994 Annual Meeting of the American Political Studies Association, The New York Hilton, September 1-4.

Peruzzotti, Enrique. 1997. *The Legacy of the Politics of Human Rights in Post-Dictatorial Latin America: Social Movements and Cultural Innovation in Argentina.* Working Paper No. 42. Universidad Torcuato Di Tella.

Pinheiro, Paulo Sérgio, and Paulo de Mesquita Neto. n.d. "Programa nacional de direitos humanos: avaliacão do primeiro ano e perspectivas," Núcleo de Estudos da Violencia, São Paulo, Brazil.

Pion-Berlin, David. 1997. *Through Corridors of Power: Institutions and Civil-Military Relations in Argentina.* University Park, Pa.: Pennsylvania State University Press.

Plattner, Marc. 1998. "Liberalism and Democracy." *Foreign Affairs* 77 (2).

Power, Timothy J. 1997. "Why Brazil Slept: The Search for Political Institutions, 1985-1997." Paper presented at the XX International Congress of the Latin American Studies Association, Guadalajara, Mexico, April 17-20.

Przeworski, Adam. 1991. *Democracy and the Market: Political and Economic Reforms in Eastern Europe and Latin America.* Cambridge: Cambridge University Press.

Przeworski, Adam. 1993. "Economic Reforms, Public Opinion, and Political Institutions: Poland in the Eastern European Perspective." In *Economic Reforms in New Democracies: A Social-Democratic Approach*, eds. Luiz Carlos Bresser Pereira, José María Maravall, and Adam Przeworski. Cambridge: Cambridge University Press.

Przeworski, Adam, and Fernando Limongi. 1993. "Political Regimes and Economic Growth." *Journal of Economic Perspectives* 7 (3).

Przeworski, Adam et al. 1995. *Sustainable Democracy.* Cambridge: Cambridge University Press.

Przeworski, Adam, Michael Alvarez, José Antonio Cheibub, and Fernando Limongi. 1996. "What Makes Democracies Endure?" *Journal of Democracy* 7 (1).

Quiroga, Hugo. 1996. "Cómo estabilizar una democracia entrecortada?" Paper prepared for the Seminar "La Democracia en Argentina: Evolución Reciente y Perspectivas," Instituto Gino Germani, Universidad de Buenos Aires, July 11-12.

Remmer, Karen L. 1991. "New Wine or Old Bottlenecks? The Study of Latin American Democracy." *Comparative Politics* (July).

Remmer, Karen L. 1995. "New Theoretical Perspectives on Democratization." *Comparative Politics* (October).

Remmer, Karen L. 1996. "The Sustainability of Political Democracy: Lessons from South America." *Comparative Political Studies* 29.

Roberts, Kenneth. 1995. "Neoliberalism and the Transformation of Populism in Latin America: The Peruvian Case." *World Politics* 48.

Romero, Aníbal. 1997. "Rearranging the Deck Chairs of the Titanic: The Agony of Democracy in Venezuela." *Latin American Research Review* 32 (1).

Rubin, Jeffrey W. 1996. "Decentering the Regime: Culture and Regional Politics in Mexico." *Latin American Research Review* 31 (3).

Sandel, Michael. 1996. *Democracy's Discontent: America in Search of a Public Philosophy.* Cambridge: Belknap/Harvard.

Schedler, Andreas. 1998. "What is Democratic Consolidation?" *Journal of Democracy* 9 (2).

Schmitter, Philippe C. 1994. "Dangers and Dilemmas of Democracy." *Journal of Democracy* 5 (2).

Schmitter, Philippe C. 1995. "The Consolidation of Political Democracies: Processes, Rhythms, Sequences and Types." In *Transitions to Democracy: Comparative*

*Perspectives from Southern Europe, Latin America and Eastern Europe*, ed. Geoffrey Pridham. Aldershot, U.K.: Dartmouth Publishing Company.

Schmitter, Philippe C., and Terry Lynn Karl. 1993. "What Democracy Is...and Is Not." In *The Global Resurgence of Democracy*, eds. Larry Diamond and Marc F. Plattner. Baltimore: The Johns Hopkins University Press.

Schneider, Ben Ross. 1995. "Democratic Consolidations: Some Broad Comparisons and Sweeping Arguments." *Latin American Research Review* 30 (2).

Schumpeter, Joseph A. 1975. *Capitalism, Socialism, and Democracy*. New York: Harper and Row Publishers.

Seligson, Mitchell. A., and Ricardo Córdova Macías. 1992. *Perspectivas para una democracia estable en El Salvador*. San Salvador: Instituto de Estudios Latinoamericanos.

Shain, Yossi, and Juan J. Linz. 1995. "Part I: Theory." In *Between States: Interim Governments and Democratic Transitions*, eds. Yossi Shain and Juan J. Linz. Cambridge: Cambridge University Press.

Shin, Doh Chull. 1994. "On the Third Wave of Democratization: A Synthesis and Evaluation of Recent Theory and Research." *World Politics* 47 (1).

Smith, William C., and Carlos H. Acuña. 1994. "Future Politico-Economic Scenarios for Latin America." In *Democracy, Markets and Structural Reform in Latin America*, eds. William C. Smith, Carlos H. Acuña, and Eduardo Gamarra. Coral Gables, Fla.: North-South Center Press at the University of Miami.

Smith, William C., Carlos H. Acuña, Eduardo Gamarra, eds. 1994. *Democracy, Markets, and Structural Reform in Latin America*. Coral Gables, Fla.: North-South Center Press at the University of Miami.

Smith, William C., and Roberto Patricio Korzeniewicz. 1997. "Latin America and the Second Great Transformation." In *Politics, Social Change, and Economic Restructuring in Latin America*, eds. William C. Smith and Roberto Patricio Korzeniewicz. Coral Gables, Fla.: North- South Center Press at the University of Miami.

Stepan, Alfred. 1986. "Paths Towards Redemocratization: Theoretical and Comparative Considerations." In *Transitions from Authoritarian Rule: Comparative Perspectives*, eds. Guillermo O'Donnell, Philippe C. Schmitter, and Laurence Whitehead. Baltimore and London: The Johns Hopkins University Press.

Stokes, Susan C. 1996. "Public Support for Market Reforms in Emerging Democracies." Issue ed., Susan Stokes. A Special Issue of *Comparative Political Studies* 29 (5).

Valenzuela, Arturo. 1994. "Party Politics and the Crisis of Presidentialism in Chile: A Proposal for a Parliamentary Form of Government." In *The Failure of Presidential Democracy: The Case of Latin America*, eds Juan J. Linz and Arturo Valenzuela. Baltimore and London: The Johns Hopkins University Press.

Valenzuela, Arturo, and Peter Siavelis. 1991. "Ley electoral y estabilidad democrática: un ejercicio de simulación para el caso de Chile." *Estudios Públicos* 43 (Winter).

Valenzuela, J. Samuel. 1992. "Democratic Consolidation in Post-Transitional Settings: Notion, Process, and Facilitating Conditions." In *Issues in Democratic Consolidation: The New South American Democracies in Comparative Perspective*, eds. Scott Mainwaring, Guillermo O'Donnell, and J. Samuel Valenzuela. Notre Dame, Ind.: University of Notre Dame Press.

Waylen, Georgina. 1994. "Women and Democratization: Conceptualizing Gender Relations in Transition Politics." *World Politics* 46 (3).

Weffort, Francisco C. 1998. "New Democracies and Economic Crisis in Latin America." In *What Kind of Democracy? What Kind of Market? Latin America in the Age of*

*Neoliberalism*, eds. Philip D. Oxhorn and Graciela Ducatenzeiler. University Park, Pa.: The Pennsylvania State University Press.

Weyland, Kurt. 1993. "The Rise and Fall of President Collor and Its Impact on Brazilian Democracy." *Journal of Interamerican Studies and World Affairs* 35 (1).

Weyland, Kurt. 1994. "Neo-Populism and Neo-Liberalism in Latin America: Unexpected Affinities." Paper prepared for the 90th Annual Meeting of the American Political Science Association, New York, September 1-4.

Weyland, Kurt. 1996. *Democracy without Equity: Failures of Reform in Brazil*. Pittsburgh: University of Pittsburgh Press.

Zakaria, Fareed. 1997. "The Rise of Illiberal Democracy." *Foreign Affairs* 76 (6).

Zaverucha, Jorge. 1997. "The 1988 Brazilian Constitution and Its Authoritarian Legacy: Formalizing Democracy While Gutting Its Essence." Paper presented at the XX International Congress of the Latin American Studies Association, Guadalajara, Mexico, April 17-20.

# CHAPTER TWO

# The Transformations of Politics

## NORBERT LECHNER

## WHAT IS A DEMOCRATIC POLITICS?

Democracy in Latin America does not allow for complacent evaluations. Democracy is a liberty that was attained only after great sacrifice, and it is highly valued in view of the recent past. Considered against the authoritarianism predominant in the region just a few years ago, the prevalence of democracy is a crucial change. At the same time, this unavoidable contrast should not prevent a critical look at democracy as it really exists and at the challenges it faces for the future.

A survey of recent studies of democracy indicates how hard it is to evaluate the progress made and the problems pending (Agüero 1994). If the advent of democracy has strengthened the realms of liberty, civilian participation, political responsibility, civil control of the armed forces, and social equity concerns, it is no less true that a number of problems persist: authoritarian enclaves, precarious representative institutions, weak citizen rights, and intolerable levels of poverty and exclusion. As each Latin American society has gone about constructing democracy according to specific conditions, these attempts must be evaluated within a framework of fragility and diversity. Still, it remains to be seen whether the problems of analysis also arise from the inadequacy of our analytical tools.

If we use criteria drawn from a minimal definition of democracy and if we develop our analysis with a certain empathy toward the particular problems of the Latin American countries, we note that in a good part of the region there is democracy, even though this democracy may quickly be relativized as a *sui generis* democracy. However, when we perceive that the promises of democracy (Bobbio 1987) are systematically left unfulfilled, when no program takes citizen deliberation seriously, when a real plurality of options and, above all, effective accountability and transparency of power do not exist, then an analysis of Latin America based on the premises of democratic theory raises doubts. In fact, the practical value of basic notions of democratic theory — popular sovereignty, representation, participation, and general interest or collective will — was always controversial, and, now, the growing complexity of our societies definitively calls into question the "model" to be built (Von Beyme 1994; Zolo 1994). Perhaps the only consolation, according to John Dunn, is that "today, in politics, democracy is the *name* for what we cannot have — yet cannot cease to want" (Dunn 1993, 28). Thus, democracy goes beyond the political regime, pointing to a future horizon or, in Jürgen Habermas's terms, expressing the "unfinished project of modernity."

Seen in this fashion, the question of democracy, particularly in Latin America, resides fundamentally in the processes of the deliberate construction of a democratic order. Hence, we must ask ourselves about politics as the privileged realm of the regulation and channeling of social processes. Despite a vast and excellent literature on democratic transitions, there are few studies that focus on the new conditions in which political dynamics operate. The ease with which we visualize the step from impressionism to cubism or the transition from Keynesianism to neoliberalism contrasts with the static image that we have of politics. We maintain an immutable conception of politics that leaves no room for the changes that have occurred. This situation generates false expectations of what politics can do and, as a result, produces frustration with its results. Moreover, the situation and our reactions inhibit us from exploring and taking advantage of innovative ways of engaging in politics.

I begin here from an intuition: *The prevailing preoccupation with democratic transition has hidden from view that politics itself is undergoing transition.* Once certain minimum aspects of a democratic regime are achieved, democratic theory becomes oddly artless before new challenges. When our attention moves from the democratic regime to politics, we discover that the latter appears to conform to factors other than those of democratic doctrine. Democracy as a normative system of legitimation and the organization of political power is one thing, and the variegated field of interactions and constraints in which decisions are made (or not made) is another. In sum, it is not the same to have democracy as to have democratic politics. Furthermore, the judgment of democracy (in Latin America as elsewhere) depends to a large degree not on our understanding and evaluation of one policy or another but on the ways of doing politics. Democratic politics is not only a question of procedures and institutions or of by whom and how things are decided; democratic politics equally has to do with the social and historical conditions in which these processes take place. In recent years, the collapse of communism and the predominance of the capitalist market economy, the processes of globalization and social differentiation, a new cultural climate, and the very preeminence of liberal democracy in the world have shaped a new context that affects the ways of thinking about and practicing politics. A first step, therefore, consists of briefly reviewing the new frame of reference. But this is not the central point. The underlying question centers on the idea that *not only the context of politics, but politics itself is changing.* I will use most of this chapter to present this hypothesis.

First, I must clarify the limits of this endeavor. What follows is a very schematic description that attempts to highlight some general tendencies; further analysis would require introducing multiple distinctions concerning the factors analyzed and their greater or lesser presence in individual Latin American countries. Furthermore, there is no radical, total change. Instead, we find ourselves before processes of decomposition and recomposition in which old and new elements overlap and intertwine. Such changes imply risks and opportunities; they carry with them threats to the fragile democracies of the region, but they also open new options for profound reforms of social organization.

# THE NEW CONTEXT

In the last few years, a number of large-scale tendencies have crystallized to modify the status of politics. Six overarching factors shape this new context.

## The End of the Bipolar System

The fall of the Berlin Wall in 1989 not only put an end to the East-West military-political polarization, but also represented the end of the antagonism between capitalism and socialism that had structured the world scene for a good part of the century. Along with the grand ideological discourses, which held together a plurality of political opinions and choices, the political cleavages that structured collective identities and social conflicts were also weakened. Similarly, a set of classificatory axes and symbolic landmarks that structured social reality vanished. The social web was shaken, and a world that, for better or worse, was familiar collapsed. Interpretative codes crumbled, and, as a result, contemporary reality often is perceived as a great disorder. In this shifting landscape, other tendencies become visible.

## The New Social Complexity

One such tendency noted in recent years is the growing complexity of Latin American societies, at least in the larger countries. In addition to the ongoing process of social differentiation, long underway, now there is a functional differentiation of the different social fields or "subsystems" — for example, economics, law, art, and science — which are gaining increasing autonomy and are subject to specific rationalities that are hardly commensurate between and among themselves.

The new social complexity gives rise to two consequences that are crucial to our discussion. The plurality of more and more autonomous spaces, regulated by contingent and flexible criteria, divides material interests and undermines normative principles, symbols, and beliefs. In sum, it uproots the bases of collective identities. At the same time, the multiplication of specific "logics" weakens the unity of social life to the point that sociologist Niklas Luhmann (1984, 1993) warns of the advent of a society without a center to guide, coordinate, and regulate the distinct "subsystems" of social life.

In Latin America, societies already characterized by a high "structural heterogeneity" are undergoing an increasing diversification. This situation poses a fundamental problem: How can diversity be translated into democratic plurality? In other words, how can differences be articulated into an order and, thereby, avoid social fragmentation? The irreducible tension between differentiation and integration calls into question the capacity of politics to provide this synthesis, a doubt that is equally prompted by other phenomena.

## The Processes of Globalization and Segmentation

The dizzying process of globalization spans multiple aspects, including a good part of everyday life. Nevertheless, we know little about the significance of the process. Two aspects will be highlighted here. The Mexican and Asian financial crises and the immediate "tequila effect" and "Asian flu" felt in other countries have made clear one element: the disproportion between the global reach of the processes underway and the merely national domain for their immediate political management. Whereas politics continues to have a fundamentally national character, critical aspects of development (such as financial flows) remain largely outside national control, distorting the public agenda. Nevertheless, it is important to reiterate that globalization is not an external phenomenon, but a complete, although differentiated, restructuring within each country. Thus, the second element is that globalization must be considered a double process of segmentation. On the one hand, it deepens the already extremely asymmetrical participation of different countries in the world system. On the other, globalization aggravates the social distances internal to each society. This effect is especially troublesome in Latin America, which is marked already by some of the highest inequalities in the world. Especially during the crisis situations that shake the foundations of society, Latin American nations face all manner of threats of fragmentation — social, economic, territorial, and cultural. As a result, social integration arises as a priority, pointing again to the question of the integrative capacity of politics.

## Rise of the Market Society and the Redimensioning of the State

The capitalist market economy is not something new in Latin America, but the social impact that the market is having is new. The novelty in the region is the transformation of Latin American societies into true "market societies"; that is, societies with norms, attitudes, and expectations that conform to market mechanisms.

In the United States and Europe, this process matured over centuries, during which those societies counteracted and cushioned the destructive impacts of the market. In Latin America, the market is being imposed in a rapid and brutal manner that is disarticulating a good part of the existing social relations and leaving broad sectors defenseless. For Latin Americans, the violence and high social and economic costs accompanying the establishment of a market society are not a thing of the past, but an experience in the present. This situation explains the limits of the present phase of modernization: the rise of an "instrumental reason" molds new patterns of sociability that permeate and modify the political scene, but the new rationality cannot base itself upon ethical-moral forces that grant meaning to the new types of relations. Consequently, people internalize the exigencies of efficiency, productivity, and competition, at the same time refusing to subscribe to that "logic." In this manner, the market society operates effectively but without a normative framework to legitimate it. This situation brings us to another key aspect of the overall scenario — the state.

In much of the region, the state is being reformed as a function of economic liberalization. Markets are freed of political controls, and, conversely, political intervention is regulated by means of macroeconomic variables. By focusing primarily on the relationship between the state and the market, the relationship between the state and society falls from view. An overvaluation of the economic responsibilities of the state, however, results in a severe disregard for other dimensions of state activity.

## The New Cultural Climate

Even though to speak of a "postmodern culture" is controversial, some new "spirit of the age" clearly exists, with different sensibilities and values. Here, several illustrative traits will be mentioned.

In the first place, one perceives an acceleration of time. The rhythm of life is ever more heady, rendering past experiences rapidly obsolete, and simultaneously hindering any view of the future. In contrast to other epochs of rapid change, the link today between present and future is broken. The invocation of progress, which for so long legitimated political activity, vanishes into a permanent present. No time other than the present appears to exist, an omnipresent present that draws politics back to the here and now.

This ephemeral and diffuse world takes us to another aspect of the new culture: the predominance of the image. The word and, therefore, discursive argumentation are displaced by a cascade of fleeting images. The centrality of television alters the communicative structures that support both the relations of political representation and the strategies of negotiation and decisionmaking. Marketing mechanisms do not substitute for, but modify, citizen deliberation. Fragmented into thousands of unconnected instances, politics has to be reconstructed as a kaleidoscope of news flashes. There is an overabundance of information that only illuminates the absence of interpretative codes. In effect, political cultures are without "cognitive maps" capable of ordering an intelligible panorama.

A certain "crisis of direction" brings into focus the problem of meaning, but at the same time a new wave of secularization renders the question less dramatic, stripping politics of the quasi-religious aura that it could have. A "light" atmosphere prevails, marked by disposable consumption, which fosters the cult of differences, marks of distinction, and resentments of the small tribe to such an extent that the notion of society itself tends to disappear.

## Democracy

The existence of liberal democratic regimes in large parts of the planet marks a drastic change of context. Nevertheless, if the importance of the megatrends indicated is controversial, it is even more difficult to determine the present significance of democracy. The value placed upon democracy and human rights everywhere today is in itself a remarkable factor. At the same time, however, the disappearance of alternatives, the exclusionary dynamics of the market, the globalization of communications, and other aspects of the new national and world contexts appear to change the nature of liberal democracy.

The continuity of actors and democratic procedures obscures the fact that democracy has changed. Paradoxically, in the very moment that democratic regimes are most widely in place in Latin America, the meaning of democracy is uncertain. The regional processes of democratic transition and consolidation reveal again an old truth: democracy is not a point of arrival, fixed once and for all. The old invocation of a democracy that levels and harmonizes all of its tensions is no longer sufficient. Insofar as we face a "really existing democracy," we need a more complete understanding of its difficulties and challenges, and, above all, we need to update the meaning of democracy in the new context.

In short, this brief overview of megatrends points to a dual fact: we find ourselves within a new frame of reference, and this context conditions our ways of thinking and doing politics. This holds globally as well as for each of the Latin American countries. One cannot discount the specificities of each case, but Latin American societies are deeply conditioned by these global changes.

From this point, my main contention arises: *The great transformations in course imply a transformation of politics itself.* So far, there are only a few studies (Maier 1987; Benedicto and Reinares 1992; Messner 1997) that focus directly on this issue, although many discussions on democracy address it obliquely. In fact, such a focus poses a number of difficulties. It is not easy to make clear-cut distinctions between changes in politics and changes in the conditions in which politics occurs. Similarly, it is not easy to determine the degree to which these changes correspond to internal political dynamics or to the tendencies noted above. In contrast, we find ourselves at a turning point in which long-term and emerging phenomena intermingle into multiple amalgams. As a result, it is difficult to distinguish genuinely new forms from configurations specific to a period of transition. Nevertheless, the following reflections are intended to provide a survey whose main purpose is to call attention to new and important changes in political life. The new forms of politics will be approached through the examination of three traits: the decentering of politics, the informalization of politics, and the articulation of the public and the private.

## THE DECENTERING OF POLITICS

One of the most conspicuous changes evident today is the *loss of the centrality of politics*. A constitutive feature of the modern epoch — the idea that politics is the central guiding force of social development — has fallen into question.

Understanding modernity as the movement from a *received* order to a *produced* order, the production of social order was primarily (though not exclusively) rooted in politics. The organization of society was subject to the *primacy of politics* as the principal realm of representation, regulation, and direction of social life. This centrality was particularly clear in Latin America and reached its peak with "developmentalism." Toward the mid-1970s, the state-centered cycle appeared to have exhausted itself, both for internal and external reasons. For a good while, the extent of the change was not perceived, either because attention was exclusively fixed upon transitions to democracy in abstraction from the consideration of socioeconomic changes or because structural adjustments were examined without consideration of the political-institutional framework (Cavarozzi 1994).

Only in retrospect do we see that the crisis of the "developmentalist model" gave rise to a second push of modernization. Slowly, the contours of the new context — and with it the changes that politics has undergone — are emerging. A number of processes condition the decentering of politics.

First of all, recall the processes of functional differentiation that lead to the formation of relatively autonomous fields and "subsystems." Insofar as these develop specific rationalities and abide by their own canons, politics no longer manages to impose its decisions as valid and binding norms. In other words, the political capacity for vertical regulation recedes, and it must be compensated by mechanisms of horizontal coordination.

Second, the new social complexity increases the factors and respective interdependencies at play to the point that the number of variables surpasses the framework of political calculation. The effects of a particular decision are less and less predictable. Consequently, the value of political decisions and the efficacy of political management are diminished. All of this renders problematic the classical conception of politics as the deliberate construction of the future.

A third factor that must be considered is the de-territorialization fostered by the ongoing processes. This de-territorialization weakens the borders of the nation-state and, therefore, the spatial and temporal congruence between diverse areas within the national framework. Because of the visibility of the process of globalization, the divergences among different geographic spaces are clear; nevertheless, a similar disharmony occurs among different temporal phases. As a result, politics is no longer capable of representing the different overlapping social arenas nor of synchronizing the multiple rhythms of social life.

Fourth, this fact does not eliminate the nation-state, and the state continues to embody a certain unity of social life, but in the new context the protagonism of the state is weakened. Whereas the opposition of capitalism versus socialism unfolded primarily in the political and military realm (leaving economic performance as only an auxiliary instrument in the conflict), with the ending of political tensions and the lessened nuclear threat, the center of gravity shifts to the economy. The economy, in turn, abides by the dynamics of globalization, which eludes political control to a large degree.

Finally, the new cultural framework must be emphasized. The processes pointed out not only weaken institutions of systemic integration (administration, law, and the even more segmented market) but also the norms and values that contribute to social integration. In Latin America, at least within urban settings, the shared body of values and beliefs, based in sanctified religion and tradition, that formed the fragile moral-intellectual cement of social cohesion is fragmenting. The multiplication of spheres and specific logics weakens the founding principles, collective ideals, and symbolic anchors that formed collective identities. This fragmentation of collective identities undermines feelings of social belonging and connection and, therefore, also the psychosocial barriers of tolerance in the face of uncertainty. Moreover, the cultural mechanics for restraint weaken at the very moment that the changes in course accentuate uncertainties. This cultural situation casts a dramatic imprint upon the present situation: demands directed to politics in pursuit of protection and security increase precisely at the moment that the capacity of politics to satisfy them has been pared back.

These structural trends transform social organization and, as a consequence, the place of politics in social life. The resulting restrictions upon the political capacities of regulation, social penetration, and symbolic expression reveal themselves in a number of ways; however, only two will be highlighted here.

First, there are restrictions on the scope of what can be expressed politically. The rise of distinct, relatively autonomous rationalities does not limit the range of matters and choices subject to political decision; in fact, there is an increase in the number of micro-decisions (Zolo 1994). Rather, the political capacity to articulate the many day-to-day decisions into "projects" is limited, that is, into proposals that give meaning to the development of society. It seems that the capacity of politics to generate a "sense of order" is diminishing. In the past, the existing order attained meaning through the political construction of a historical tomorrow that made it possible not only to defer hopes and fears to the future, but also to find a sense of progress to legitimate the present in the project of perfecting the future. With the perceived vanishing of the future, the representation of meanings projected upon the past is also diluted. The result is a weakening of the capacity of political decisionmaking to choose among uncertainties by selecting a course of action and endowing it with a socially valid meaning.

Second, politics is weakened as a general instance of representation. In the past, politics helped to reduce social complexity in regard to some basic cleavages. Due to the segmentation of publics, politics now confronts great problems in aggregating citizen interests and opinions and in offering citizens interpretative codes or "maps" capable of structuring an intelligible panorama of social reality. Hence, one sees the loss of credibility suffered by the parties and the party system itself. The political arena contracts into a system that is more and more self-referential, oriented toward its own internal dynamics (rules and strategies of electoral competition), and facing great obstacles in developing the relationship between the political and the social.

The neoliberal offensive that has predominated in Latin America since the late 1970s is a response to these tendencies. During these years, the "neoliberal" label has been so abused that it is of little informative value. For present purposes, however, I shall speak of the neoliberal model in a dual sense.

To begin with, neoliberalism represents the first systematic proposal that attempts to make sense of the new context. Neoliberalism provides a radical reinterpretation of social development founded upon a critique of the *political production of order* in the name of a *self-regulating order*. In Friedrich Hayek's terms, order is the result of human action but not of human will. Insofar as society is no longer conceived as a produced order, but as a self-regulated one, any attempt at the deliberate construction of the future appears as an arbitrary interference with the spontaneous mechanisms of self-organization. At the theoretical level, the neoliberal critique coincides with the systems theory developed by sociologist Niklas Luhmann. When the different fields or "subsystems" of social activity (for example, economics, law, morality) acquire increasing autonomy, thereby developing specific and hardly commensurable rationalities, political intervention in social life is harmful or, at best, useless.

Nevertheless, along with offering an interpretation of the social changes underway, neoliberalism represents a political program.[1] On the assumption that politics is an unnecessary interference with processes of social self-organization, the neoliberal strategy proposes to replace politics with the market as the alternative for rational coordination under conditions of high social complexity.

The neoliberal offensive, therefore, turns the decentering of politics into a deliberate strategy. The explicit objective of reforms is to *depoliticize the economy*, thereby avoiding bureaucratic excesses and clientelistic abuses. In reality, these reforms achieve important changes: they reduce bureaucratic regulation and administrative centralism, lessen political and corporatist pressure upon the state apparatus, and limit the populist use of fiscal spending and the public sector. In sum, neoliberal reforms reduce market distortions and rationalize state regulation. Their implicit scope, however, goes further. Under the pretext of protecting economic processes from political fluctuations, these policies propose to displace power from the political system to, according to David Ibarra, "institutions immune to democratic pressures that can better defend minority rights against political whims" (1995, 40-41).

In other words, in pursuit of the goal of imposing in unrestricted fashion the rationality of the market, the neoliberal strategy seeks to withdraw the economy from all processes of democratic decision. Economic efficiency becomes the end all; rather than limit the field of political intervention, the goal is to put politics "in line" with the alleged technical imperatives of the economy. Social policy provides an illustrative example. In recent years, a profound reformulation has taken place that, along with correcting some earlier deficiencies, introduces de facto a new approach. Social policies are no longer conceived of as universal measures corresponding to rights that all citizens are legally entitled to. Rather, social policies are seen as focused measures to be aimed at specific "vulnerable sectors" (that is, those in extreme poverty), with the objective of promoting their inclusion in the market. This reorientation increases the efficiency of social spending, but its political implications should not be ignored: social policies are uncoupled from their political foundation — citizenship — and redefined as a variable of economic growth.

At least in its extreme version, the neoliberal strategy is unsuccessful for the reasons already noted by Karl Polanyi (1957). In reality, the market neither operates as a self-regulating system, nor can the organization of society be conceived in the image of the market. The recent experiences in Latin America, Central Europe, and Russia clearly illustrate that the forces unleashed by the market often tend to be self-destructive, and a well-functioning capitalist market requires the (political) creation of institutions.

Put in general terms, politics and economics obey different logics and, as a consequence, cannot be regulated by the singular code of the market. In fact, in Latin America, the more successful cases of economic liberalization were supported by strong political intervention (Smith, Acuña, and Gamarra 1994a, 1994b).

This "neoliberal paradox" reveals the present dilemma: At the same time that politics is being questioned as a central mechanism for social representation and guidance, there is no vision of an alternative means of assuring the unity of social life as a collective order. Certainly, mechanisms of systemic interdependence and integration exist, but they say nothing about the direction that social dynamics take. The capacity for guidance is in question precisely at the moment that questions about the course of development have become increasingly pressing.

## THE INFORMALIZATION OF POLITICS

The decentering of politics is accompanied by a *blurring of its institutional foundations*. Even when the institutionalized forms of the political system endure and are consolidated, they lose centrality before the process of informalization. As in the informalization of economics and law, politics increasingly overflows institutional forms, thus eroding the contours of the political system. Of course, clear, precise limits never distinguished the political from the non-political; as the apex of social organization, politics always tends to intervene in other fields of social life. In theory, however, a basic delimitation was operative through the identification of politics with the political system itself. This delimitation included the link with other social fields through the representative character of democratic institutions. In this manner, the institutionalization of politics permits the bounding of a specific rationality and, at the same time, the inclusion of mediation with other fields. This dual face of politics (specific and representative at the same time) crumbles under the new conditions.

In the late 1990s, processes of institutionalization and de-institutionalization coexist in Latin America. There are important attempts to reinforce the powers of parliament and the judiciary and to limit the discretionary powers of the executive and the armed forces. Yet, despite these advances, the fragility of representative institutions and institutionalized forms of politics is well known (O'Donnell 1991). On repeated occasions, populist electoral promises and technocratic policies of economic adjustment have formed a perverse and unstable combination. However, the tendency within vast sectors of the region toward non-institutional attitudes and behavior is founded not only on deeply rooted clientelistic structures and *caudillista* styles. The old customs are interwoven with new tendencies, and several factors undermine the traditional limits of politics.

In the first place, to return to a topic mentioned earlier, one sees the effects of the decentering of politics. As contemporary society becomes highly differentiated, the coordinating function of politics also changes. Political coordination can no longer consist of the imposition of common norms. In the face of social diversity, coordination implies the articulation of a plurality. In a "society without a center," the political realm ceases to be the central instance of coordination; certainly, it continues to be important but now as part of a polycentric coordination of social processes. As a result, political coordination must renounce its customary supremacy and seek fluid and flexible linkages with other social realms.

In this context, it is necessary to stress immediately that the very differentiation of politics itself leads to the disaggregation of its diverse aspects. In particular,

I refer to the gap that emerges between the electoral-legitimizing moment and the executive-decisional moment of politics. Paraphrasing the well-known observation of Anthony Downs (1957), it appears that parties do not win elections in order to carry out their policies, but, rather, they formulate their programs to win elections. Then, once in government, they assess from day to day which policies they can pursue. Common are the cases in Latin America in which the government executes economic reforms quite opposite to the populist promises used to win the electoral competition. Such incongruence between the electoral mandate and governmental policies has to do with the two tendencies mentioned before. One is the differentiation of specific rationalities, through which many social matters escape political control. Yet, as the political struggle also has its "logic," parties tend to mobilize any theme that might attract majority support, regardless of its programmatic viability. This takes us back to the second tendency. The relation between the present future (the options currently open) and the future present (the reality of tomorrow) vanishes to such a degree that the results of today's decisions are increasingly difficult to foresee. In other words, the anticipation of the future becomes increasingly risky. This sense of risk contributes to the search for reassurances outside of political institutions.

The acceleration of time weakens the institutional framework in another way. One of the functions of institutions is to assure the continuity and calculability of social processes, neutralizing subjective considerations and transitory political forces. Institutionalization thus serves to create a temporal horizon reaching beyond the present. To generate this time horizon, however, institutions require time; only by persisting through time can institutions generate confidence in "investing in the future." The credibility of institutions requires time for the development of ties of reciprocal trust. Time, nevertheless, is nowadays among the scarcest of resources. The acceleration of time produces a lack of time for the consolidation of institutions. The rapid pace of change does not allow emerging institutions to acquire the continuity needed to generate a foreseeable calculus of the future. The urgency of matters at hand demands immediate solutions and allows little space for the establishment of routines. The hurry to obtain results thus spurs extra-institutional arrangements. In the short run (which is the term that counts in politics), the negotiation of agreements on the margin of institutions promises to be more profitable than following institutional rules.

Finally, it appears that informalization is tied to the expansion of market society to the political sphere. This is a paradoxical situation, given that institutionalization is not only an element of the process of democratization but also a requisite for predictability within the capitalist market economy. In fact, for many analysts, the liberal dream regarding the self-regulating virtues of the market has given way to a more realistic view: A well-functioning market presupposes a solid and stable institutional framework (North 1990). Given that the spontaneous tendency of the market to generate continual increases in efficiency and capitalist profitability does not produce a sustainable economy but, on the contrary, produces certain self-destructive effects, private exchanges must be regulated and subject to oversight, according to general rules that protect the collective order. This distinction between two rationalities, the private and the social, upon which is based the relationship between economics and politics, is precarious and is permanently threatened either by an unnecessary politicization of the economy or by an unlimited expansion of the market.

Today, we face the second case: the paradox of a market that demands its insertion within an institutional framework while inhibiting institutionalization. It is no longer merely a matter of the market's tendency to escape juridical-institutional restrictions. What is new is the colonization of politics by the rationality of the market. The criteria of exchange, competition, and individual utility foster the tendency to seek political agreements by means of private accords. In actual practice, many matters of public interest are handled through informal networks that bring together government and social actors to resolve a particular matter (Marin and Mayntz 1991). Taking into account the prevalence of such private accords, it appears that the market tends to supplant democratic institutions and procedures as a mechanism of coordination.

Informalization leads to a *politicization of the social* insofar as social actors participate ever more directly in the making of political decisions, and it equally leads to a *socialization of politics*, insofar as political decisions result from quasi-private forms of negotiation and exchange. The fact is that "really existing politics" occurs on the margin of democratic institutions, which often are limited to ratifying extra-institutional accords.

We are before a dual phenomenon. On one side, there is *an institutional spillover*. Politics exceeds the limits of the political system, as it emigrates from institutions and installs itself in mutant form within informal networks. Yet, this overshooting of institutions brings with it, conversely, *an emptying of the political system*. The democratic institutional order functions more and more as a self-referential system. Politics is diluted into multiple micro-decisions that affect the everyday lives of citizens who never find out about those decisions. Similarly, democratic institutions end up ritually legitimating a decision-making process that is no longer based within them (Zolo 1994). In other words, the internal rationality of the political system is secured at the expense of its representative function; the competition of party leaders, the discussion of programs, and parliamentary deliberation cease to be the "stage" for the alternatives and decisions that confront the citizenry. Furthermore, as Luhmann notes, the stability of the system requires a certain imperviousness to external impulses (1993).

This shrinking of the political system is not the responsibility of the so-called "political class" but a structural problem. In fact, in conjunction with the erosion of relations of representation, the political capacities of regulation and management erode. More exactly, the informalization of politics responds precisely to the effort to fulfill a regulatory and coordinating function under the new conditions, at a time when this function no longer lies principally within the political system.

An analysis of this tendency cannot proceed further without more empirical antecedents. I would, however, like to call attention to one consequence of this process. The "emptying" of the political system is accompanied by a citizen de-identification. I do not refer here to expressions of political apathy, discontent with government, unhappiness over particular policies, or malaise with politics in general. Underlying all of these is a more significant phenomenon: the difficulties for the political system to crystallize collective identities. If politics implies subjectivity, informalization means externalizing the subjective dimension, removing it from the political system. It is difficult for the citizen to identify himself or herself with democratic institutions because they do not offer a place for identity. As a result, political identities tend to emigrate to "civil society," where they are reconstituted in hybrid fashion. This takes us to the third trait of the new forms of politics.

## THE ARTICULATION OF THE PUBLIC AND THE PRIVATE

A longside the transformation of institutionalized politics, the *political* itself changes; that is, the everyday experience of the collective order. The transformation of the political is no less significant, as it shapes the raw material from which institutionalized politics feeds. Indicative of this change is the restructuring or articulation of the public and the private and, above all, of the relationship between these spheres. If a historical retrospective of the distinction between the public and the private spheres — such as Hannah Arendt's masterful account — gives rise to an idealized view that ignores grey areas, today it is difficult to sketch even an approximate boundary (Arendt 1993).

The changing political realm manifests a number of characteristics. The most visible is a "structural transformation of the public sphere" (Habermas 1989) in which *public opinion dissipates as an expression of citizen deliberation that complements representative institutions*. The primacy of an "image culture," which television carries to the farthest reaches of a country, replaces the laborious reasoning of the word with the instantaneous impact of the look. The powerful influence of the image modifies (more by its internal logic than by manipulative intentions) the rhythm and the sphere of politics, as well as the role of the citizen. It affects everything, from the attention available and the information that is valued, to the aesthetic criteria with which the political spectacle is regarded (Landi 1992). The role of the consumer (strictly delimited to the freedom of choice) replaces the notion of the citizen as a rational and autonomous individual.

Under such conditions, public opinion possesses the force and impermanence of a flash. This change in the character of public opinion reflects a transformation of the public as a shared space. It is in this context that the privatization of many public services should be recalled. The evaluation of privatizations in terms of their economic efficiency usually fails to consider also how they call into question the concept of public goods equally accessible to all. The public school and public health are realms (albeit deficient) of social integration. Their privatization tends to weaken the integrative dimension of the public realm, a serious matter in Latin American countries with strong social inequalities.

The "fall of public man" (Sennet 1978) does not imply, however, his elimination. Rather, what is involved is a restructuring of the public sphere, now dominated by the *public character of the market*. Whoever travels through Latin American cities has seen the role that shopping malls now play as new symbolic *tópoi* (shared public places) of the social web. More to the point, there appears to be the redefinition of markets as a function of economic liberalization and of the image of the country or "country rating" in world competition. The development of legally accountable norms (quality control, consumer rights, environmental impacts) or of ethical criteria (such as boycotts of products from a specific country or firm) is well known. Such developments are defining a public responsibility of the market that goes beyond the usual rules of civil law. Although embryonic, this trend indicates a new notion of the public, close to the new self-understanding of the citizen as consumer. This is reflected — and counteracted — by the restructuring of the private sphere.

A principal feature of our time is the *process of privatization*, not merely of public firms but also of sociability. Whether it is because the public realm excludes them, because they sublimate disappointed political commitments, or because there is a genuine revaluation of intimacy and small immediate surroundings, in recent years individuals tend to withdraw into private life, generating a true "culture of the self" (Bejar 1993). The cultivation of the ego, of authentic emotions, of aesthetic enjoyment, and other pleasures does not mean a rejection of politics, much less democracy. Rather, it is a case of economizing one's available attention in face of the complexity of social life. It thus appears preferable to secure "negative liberty" and to shun collective actions conferring dubious gratification.

Nevertheless, the private world no longer offers a refuge secure from the uncertainties of public life. This fact profoundly alters, although unintentionally, the meaning of the private sphere. Along with privatization, we find a *politicization of the private sphere*, which derives from its colonization and its expansion (García Canclini 1990). Examples of the former are the continuous invasion of the home by the external world (for example, television) and the disciplining of personal behavior as a matter of social hygiene (for example, campaigns against smoking). Illustrative of the latter trend is the visibility recently attained by concerns traditionally kept within private life. I refer here to such issues as gender conditions, sexual preferences, ethnic identity, reproductive health, and religious confession; in other words, a set of elements of the private sphere that jump to the center of the public agenda.

The new status of sociocultural differences crisscrosses with the old structures of socioeconomic inequality to form a variegated combination — the public appears as an archipelago of unconnected minorities. Another consequence, however, is more relevant: the politicization of personal attributes or subjective preferences questions the distinction between *citoyen* (citizen) and *bourgeois* upon which liberal democracy is based. The debate not only seeks to prevent "private" differences from being a source of discrimination injurious to citizen equality; to the contrary, the goal is explicitly to incorporate subjectivity in the exercise of citizenship. This is not the place to discuss the effects of this phenomenon upon the democratic regime. It is enough to bring out the tendency to reformulate — from within the private realm — a new notion of citizenship. This experience appears to be a main motivation behind the repeated invocation of civil society (Lechner 1994).

As in a game of mirrors, the transformation of the public redefines the private sphere at the same time that the transfiguration of the private modifies the public sphere. The relation changes, and the boundaries between the private and the public steadily weaken. However, the most outstanding trait is not so much the redefinition of these spheres as the evolving political framework of the public and the private. If we consider such different and urgent tasks as consumer protection through public supervision, the oversight of state activities delegated for private initiative, the incorporation of private capital in public education policy, and the regulation of sexuality (AIDS) and health (drugs), then the unfolding articulation of the public and the private appears as a central aspect of politics in the near future.

## A PRELIMINARY EVALUATION

D rawing conclusions from a reflection that, to reiterate, must necessarily be inconclusive would be premature. I hope that the argument offered has provided a basis for the claim that, along with the political changes of the last few years, there has been a change in the nature of politics itself. It will be the task of empirical research to assess the validity of that proposition. Certainly, the phenomena discussed could have been organized in a different manner, and emphasis could have been given to other factors, such as the new structures of communication, the reorganization of society through the multiplication of collective actors, or the transnationalization of domestic policy. In any case, the argument would have to bring to the fore that traditional ideas of politics have become problematic.

The neoliberal phase (at least as originally conceived) is exhausted, and Latin America is entering a new stage of development. One of the challenges for this new phase arises from the lag of politics in relation to the dynamics of society. This situation suggests the cycle analyzed by Polanyi: with the rise of capitalism toward the middle of the nineteenth century, the market became autonomous and escaped political control, provoking an increasing disintegration of social life that culminated in the 1920s and 1930s in a vast reorganization of society. At the close of the twentieth century, we find ourselves again faced with the need to reorganize political control over economic dynamics that appear to impose themselves as natural phenomena before which there are no alternatives. There are no viable options, in point of fact, if we conceive of politics in traditional terms. Different courses of action may open up, however, if we know how to discover and take advantage of the possibilities offered by the new forms of politics. To do so, we must revise the customary conception of politics. Several ideas that emerge from our inquiry and point in this direction may be traced out in preliminary fashion.[2]

Revising the meaning of politics in today's Latin America entails asking ourselves about the deliberate construction of the social order. If it is true that Latin American society no longer corresponds to a single constitutive principle, the primacy of politics disappears in favor of polycentric forms of producing and reproducing order. This implies going from a central form of coordination to an articulation of multiple rationalities. Such articulation is neither spontaneous nor self-regulating; on the contrary, it requires deliberate action but of a different type. The management of politics no longer derives so much from hierarchical command as from interaction. This change implies new challenges, especially in Latin America, where the impulses for modernization tend to arise from variations on enlightened despotism. When the power of vertical command becomes inadequate in face of the multiplicity of social spaces and tempos, coordination becomes more horizontal. A politics of more horizontal coordination among diverse state and nonstate actors demands not only greater agility and flexibility — the principal challenge lies in interaction itself.

In large measure, the coordination of social processes depends on the political capacity to promote the constitution of collective actors and to institutionalize interaction among them. This is crucial for translating diversity into an effective and coherent plurality and to facilitate a reciprocal adjustment of preferences and expectations. Moreover, such a capacity is crucial for another basic dimension of politics: the production of meaning. When the meaning of the social order is no longer guaranteed by venerated institutions nor issues from a commonly held notion of progress, that meaning must be negotiated through collective interaction. Such a negotiation implies the permanent updating of shared perspectives of meaning, which requires a high degree of self-reflection on the part of political actors. All of this poses unheard of demands upon politics, which not only must regulate and coordinate highly differentiated processes but also must fulfill its protective function, that is to say, to endow this order with meaning. In other words, politics must acquire greater complexity, with a high degree of contingency, and, at the same time, reduce social complexity to culturally tolerable levels (Lechner 1997).

There exists, in fact, a cultural-anthropological limit to uncertainty. The human need to exorcise the uncertainties of the future is particularly strong: "The open horizon must remain open and the unimaginable must remain imaginable, but both the positive and negative effects must be known and controllable beforehand" (Nowotny 1992, 49). Politics, definitely, is about this control over social reality. In Latin America, it is well known that where men and women perceive that politics does not protect social harmony, they resort to other forms of self-defense, even at the price of sacrificing their liberties. It is against this backdrop that, in my judgment, the question of the future of democracy ought to be posed.

Sometimes the debate on the question of democracy in Latin America suggests a meeting of magicians who pull any number of resources from hats and sleeves and use them to contrive illusions that remove, recover, and even multiply the most diverse objects. Why highlight the fragility of party systems and not the impact of drug trafficking? Why analyze the role of the "mafias" and not address the administration of justice? What is the point of talking about justice, given the magnitude and scandalous proliferation of social inequalities? How can social structure be addressed without analyzing the political economy? What sense is there to studying socioeconomic dynamics without considering our fears and, why not, our dreams? The list is long and, certainly, arbitrary. What does this mean? In the final analysis, democracy contemplates and crystallizes the different aspects of social life. Each element makes up part of this open constellation of varied geometry and constant motion, which under the generic name of democracy poses anew the old question of order. Perhaps the difficulties posed by the notion of democracy today are nothing more than the difficulties that are presented by the reordering of social life in a world undergoing rapid transformation. If so, it then becomes essential to study the capacity of democratic politics to guide this reordering of Latin American societies in a conscious way.[3]

# Notes

I wish to acknowledge the helpful comments made on an earlier draft of this chapter by Terry Lynn Karl, Robert Kaufman, Phillipe Schmitter, Felipe Agüero, and Jeffrey Stark.

1. Insofar as neoliberal policies negate politics, neoliberalism is part of the contemporary trend toward a "politics of anti-politics." On this trend, see Schedler (1996).

2. This preliminary discussion owes much to conversations with René Millán and Francisco Valdés.

3. I have explored this point in more depth in Lechner (1995).

# References

Agüero, Felipe. 1994. "Democratic Governance in Latin America: Thinking About Fault Lines." Unpublished manuscript.

Arendt, Hannah. [1958] 1993. *La condición humana.* Barcelona: Paidos.

Bejar, Helena. 1993. *La cultura del yo.* Madrid: Alianza Universidad.

Benedicto, Jorge, and Fernando Reinares, eds. 1992. *Las transformaciones de lo político.* Madrid: Alianza Universidad.

Bobbio, Norberto. 1987. *The Future of Democracy*, trans. Roger Griffin. Minneapolis: University of Minnesota Press.

Cavarozzi, Marcelo. 1994. "Politics: A Key for the Long Term in South America." In *Latin American Political Economy in the Age of Neoliberal Reform*, eds. William C. Smith, Carlos H. Acuña, and Eduardo A. Gamarra. Coral Gables, Fla.: North-South Center at the University of Miami.

Downs, Anthony. 1957. *An Economic Theory of Democracy.* New York: Harper.

Dunn, John. 1993. *Western Political Theory in the Face of the Future.* New York: Cambridge University Press, Canto Book Series.

García Canclini, Néstor. 1990. *Culturas híbridas: estrategias para entrar y salir de la modernidad.* Mexico City: Grijalbo.

Habermas, Jürgen. 1989. *The Structural Transformation of the Public Sphere: An Inquiry into a Category of Bourgeois Society*, trans. Thomas Burger and Frederick Lawrence. Cambridge, Mass.: MIT Press.

Ibarra, David. 1995. "La pareja del siglo." *Nexos* 18 (206): 39-49.

Landi, Oscar. 1992. *Devórame otra vez.* Buenos Aires: Planeta.

Lechner, Norbert. 1994. "La (problemática) invocación de la sociedad civil." *Perfiles Latinoamericanos* 5.

Lechner, Norbert. 1995. "La reforma del estado y el problema de la conducción política." *Perfiles Latinomericanos* 7.

Lechner, Norbert. 1997. "Three Forms of Social Coordination." *CEPAL Review*, No. 61 (April): 7-17.

Luhmann, Niklas. 1984. *Soziale Systeme.* Frankfurt: Suhrkamp.

Luhmann, Niklas. 1993. *Teoría política en el estado de bienestar.* Madrid: Alianza.

Maier, Charles, ed. 1987. *Changing Boundaries of the Political.* New York: Cambridge University Press.

Marin, Bernd, and R. Mayntz, eds. 1991. *Policy Networks.* Boulder, Colo.: Westview Press.

Messner, Dirk. 1997. *The Network Society: Economic Development and International Competitiveness as Problems of Social Governance.* London: Frank Cass Publishers.

North, Douglass. 1990. *Institutions, Institutional Change, and Economic Performance.* New York: Cambridge University Press.

Nowotny, Helga. 1992. *Le temps a soi.* Paris: Maison des Science de l'Homme.

O'Donnell, Guillermo. 1991. "¿Democracia delegativa?" *Novos Estudos CEBRAP* 31.

Polanyi, Karl. 1957. *The Great Transformation*. Boston: Beacon Press.

Schedler, Andreas. 1996. *Antipolitics — Challenging the Boundaries of Politics*. New York: Macmillan.

Sennett, Richard. 1978. *The Fall of Public Man*. New York: Vintage Books.

Smith, William C., Carlos H. Acuña, and Eduardo A. Gamarra, eds. 1994a. *Democracy, Markets, and Structural Reform in Latin America*. Coral Gables, Fla.: North-South Center at the University of Miami.

Smith, William C., Carlos H. Acuña, and Eduardo A. Gamarra, eds. 1994b. *Latin American Political Economy in the Age of Neoliberal Reform*. Coral Gables, Fla.: North-South Center at the University of Miami.

Von Beyme, Klaus. 1994. *Las teorías políticas en el siglo XX*. Madrid: Alianza.

Zolo, Danilo. 1994. *Democracia y complejidad. Un enfoque realista*. Buenos Aires: Nueva Visión.

CHAPTER THREE

# Faulty Democracies? A Reflection on the Capitalist "Fault Lines" in Latin America

## ATILIO A. BORÓN

### THE STRAIGHT LINE AND THE PENDULUM

Diagnoses and interpretations of Latin American historical development seem to have oscillated between two polar moods: the foolish blind optimism of Pollyanna and Cassandra-like deep pessimism. These moods have prevailed alternately, neither ever completely wiping out its opposite, with the trace of the mood that has receded operating as a marginal and eccentric expression of dissent.[1] Optimism was at its best in the 1950s and 1960s: Economic development, "trickle-down" illusions, and civilian rule appeared to herald a definitive "break with the past," to use Barrington Moore's (1966) felicitous expression. Shortly afterward, Latin Americans would painfully learn that such optimism was ill founded — and that all those achievements were transient and rather artificial. Pessimism was overwhelming in the 1970s: Never in Latin American history were there so many tyrannies holding power, and never were human rights and fundamental freedoms so blatantly violated as in those anguished years. In addition, pessimism at that time was also rampant among industrialized nations, as evidenced by the somber overtones of a well-known Trilateral Commission report dealing with the prospects of democracy in advanced countries (Crozier et al. 1975).

In the late 1980s and early 1990s, optimism returned triumphant. Democracies flowered, and the United States even pressed Gen. Augusto Pinochet to open the democratic gates in Chile; in addition, a radical neoliberal program of economic reform was at last carried out with astonishing resoluteness. Latin American economies changed almost overnight, aligning themselves with the policies set off by the governments of U.S. President Ronald Reagan and British Prime Minister Margaret Thatcher and promoted by technocrats within the World Bank and the International Monetary Fund (IMF). As had occurred in the former period of optimistic euphoria, the predominant "climate of opinion" prevented the identification of potential sources of frustration.

Not surprisingly, this new disposition started to register signs of exhaustion by the mid-1990s. Throughout the region, poverty surged, and income distribution worsened. The external vulnerability of Latin American economies increased, as did their foreign debt. Democratic institutions were discredited, and citizens' hopes gave way to frustration and resentment. Several significant reversals took place. The removal of President Jean-Bertrand Aristide in Haiti was the first and most notorious case. In President Alberto Fujimori's Peru, to a large extent democracy became the facade of an increasingly authoritarian rule. Venezuela's democracy — the oldest in South America — faltered under the combined effects of orthodox stabilization policies' enormous social cost; restive, nationalistic, young military officers; and rampant governmental corruption. Finally, and to the dismay of those who exalted the figure of President Carlos Salinas de Gortari, the sweeping "market-oriented" economic reforms carried out in Mexico proved unable to prevent the collapse of the Mexican peso shortly before Christmas 1994. In contrast, the Institutional Revolutionary Party (Partido Revolucionario Institucional — PRI) leadership confirmed that it was more willing to try "free-market" economics than to expose its domination to the challenges of democratic politics, and it raised formidable obstacles of all sorts to forestall the transformation of its decaying authoritarian regime into a political democracy. The 1994 peasant and Indian insurgence in Chiapas, as well as the ensuing political murders of PRI leaders Luis Donaldo Colosio and José Francisco Ruiz Massieu, wrapped up a veritable *annus terribilis* for the legion of neoliberal ideologues, who, until these embarrassing events, had been pointing toward economically reformed Mexico as one of the models to emulate. The Mexican financial crash signaled, in a rather dramatic fashion, the end of neoliberal optimism and triggered a wave of instability — the notorious "tequila effect" — that engulfed so-called "emerging markets" world-wide.

Reflecting on the Latin American democratic experience, we see that during optimistic periods the Sisyphus-like job of building democratic institutions often has been represented as a straight line emerging from the rotten soil of caudillo rule and the ill-fated "Iberian tradition," pointing unwaveringly toward the high summits of liberal democracy and the market economy. Deprived of any sense of history, some conceive of the future as being the enduring offspring of the rosy present. The pessimistic temperament, on the contrary, has relied on a melancholy political metaphor: the pendulum eternally swinging back and forth and producing a maddening alternation between short-lived "democratic springs" and prolonged authoritarian outbursts. Despite their eloquence, these metaphors have been completely discredited by experience. Each reflects one aspect of a complex reality; yet both explanations fail to capture the real movement of Latin American history. The democratic arrow did not fly as high and straight as was hoped, nor did the pendulum swing back and forth as drastically or as widely as was feared. In both cases, the images are misleading; they miss history and real life.

In the current circumstances, it seems extremely important to avoid falling into these intellectual traps yet again. We are facing the unprecedented challenges of a new epoch that requires a careful and well-balanced combination of optimism and pessimism, of intelligence and will. One could reformulate Antonio Gramsci's classic formula by saying that what is needed in this age is the optimism of the heart tempered by the analytical pessimism of the intelligence. This seems to be sound methodological and political advice. Inspired by Gramsci's aphorism, in the following pages I will examine and discuss some problems challenging democratic governance in Latin America and, if possible, attempt to anticipate the terrain through which the future history of our region is likely to pass.

## The Shortcomings of the Schumpeterian Legacy

Latin American democratization in the 1980s ignited debate on the scope and promises of democracy.[2] A discussion of this sort could hardly have been more welcome in a continent that, as Agustín Cueva (1976) rightly observed, in its almost two centuries of independent political life was unable to know a single bourgeois revolution that culminated in the implantation of a democratic regime. Bourgeois revolutions were rare: Mexico between 1910 and 1917; Guatemala in 1944; Bolivia in 1952; and, perhaps, Brazil from 1964, and none of them — not even the Jacobin ones — concluded their "pending questions" by establishing a democratic regime (Cueva 1976; Fernandes 1975).[3] The overriding concern of those revolutions seemed to have been more an upholding of the capitalist mode of production than the introduction of bourgeois democracy. Thus, the authoritarian imprint of Latin American capitalism has very deep roots, which can be traced both to the colonial heritage and the dependent and reactionary modality of capitalist development by means of which Latin American societies were integrated into the world markets (Borón 1989).

Yet, despite the burdensome legacies of its traumatic history, at the beginning of the 1980s, Latin America seemed ready to try democracy again. This trend was reinforced by the democratic thrust that started to gain momentum in an unprecedented manner in world history. As a result, at the beginning of the 1990s, nearly 60 percent of the 187 countries in the world organized their political processes according to the democratic rules of the game; in recent years, democracies have increased from 44 in 1972 to 107 (Shin 1994, 136). Impressed by these events, some theorists argue that the world is running through a "third democratic wave" (Huntington 1991). Others, like Francis Fukuyama, see in these developments the signs of a victorious capitalism that, hand in hand with a no less triumphant liberal democracy, heralds the "end of history" (Fukuyama 1992). As a result of this democratic flood and what Norberto Bobbio called "the harsh rebuttals of history" (Bobbio 1976) — which in this case includes the resounding failure of "really existing socialisms" as well as the complete ineffectiveness of social democracy to transcend capitalism — a significant section of the left has adhered to a rather naive conception of democracy that rests on two premises: One is the supposedly linear and irreversible nature of democratic progress, something that a lucid conservative scholar like Huntington refuses to admit. The other is the belief, both historically false and theoretically wrong, that democracy is a project coterminous solely with the establishment of adequate representative and governmental institutions. The heroic enterprise of creating a democratic state is thus reduced to the establishment of a system of rules and procedures unconcerned with and unrelated to the ethical contents proper of democracy — and indifferent to the implications of deep-seated social contradictions and class inequalities in the political process. Thus (mis)understood, democracy as a set of abstract rules can only pose "technical" problems of governance and administrative efficacy (Garretón 1987; Flisfisch, Lechner, and Moulian 1985; Strasser 1990 and 1991).

It is rather puzzling how democracy, being such a simple and reasonable political program, has been able to arouse fierce passions and dogged resistance throughout history, bringing about revolutions and counter-revolutions, bloody civil wars, protracted popular struggles, and brutal repressions of all sorts (Moore 1966). Was all this drama — the drama of the West since Pericles' times — just the result of a simple *malentendu*? Wouldn't it be more reasonable to think instead that the implantation of democracy reflects a peculiar outcome of class conflicts, something that goes beyond an innocent procedural arrangement? From this perspective, looking at the historical experience of Brazil, for instance, how can we possibly account for the fact that it was much easier to abolish slavery — and the empire that rested on slave labor — than to achieve capitalist democracy?

The belated triumph of Joseph Schumpeter's ideas ([1943] 1976)), which reduced the democratic promise to its formalistic and procedural arrangements, mirrors the narrow scope and limits of capitalist democracies by ignoring both the ethical contents of democracy — as a crucial constituent element of any discourse dealing with the organization of a good society — and the practical-historical processes of the constitution of "really existing democracies" (Borón 1995b, 189-220). It is of utmost importance to realize that Schumpeter-inspired "procedural" theories of democracy imply a radical departure from the classic argument developed by the Western political tradition during 25 centuries, from Plato to Marx. Authors as diverse as Plato, Aristotle, Machiavelli, Rousseau, Marx, and de Tocqueville considered democracy something completely different from what most political scientists imagine it to be today. De Tocqueville's introductory chapter to his famous *Democracy in America*, for instance, portrays the epic nature of democratization with these moving words, "This whole book has been written under the impulse of a kind of religious dread inspired by the contemplation of this irresistible revolution advancing century by century over every obstacle and even now going forward amid the ruins it has itself created" (de Tocqueville [1835] 1969, 12).

Despite the compelling force of de Tocqueville's historical fresco, "mainstream" political science still regards democracy only in instrumental terms — as a method aimed solely at the formation of a government, no longer as a condition of civil society as well. In actuality, democracy is a unique amalgam that binds together three inseparable components. First, there is a complex set of unambiguous institutions and rules of the game that produce the "uncertain" outcomes that characterize democratic states (Przeworski 1985, 138-145).[4] The institutions and rules make up the "political condition," necessary although not sufficient, because democracy cannot flourish as a political regime if it is embedded in a society characterized by structures, institutions, and ideologies antagonistic to its spirit. Therefore, democracy also requires two further "social conditions." First, a minimum level of fundamental equality must be widespread, thus allowing for the full development of unique individuals and the full plurality of expressions in social life. Second, the citizenry must have the effective enjoyment of freedom, not only as a formal entitlement — which has been beautifully written in many dead-letter constitutions in Latin America — but also as a living and practical day-to-day experience. Like the above-mentioned political condition, these two social conditions are necessary but not sufficient to produce a democratic state by themselves. A full-fledged democracy exists only when all three conditions are met. As Adam Przeworski has observed, "[t]o discuss democracy without considering the economy in which this democracy is to function is an operation worthy of an ostrich" (Przeworski 1990, 102). In practical terms, capitalist democracies, even the most developed ones, barely meet these standards. The institutional deficits of advanced democracies are quite well known; serious doubts are raised when minimum levels of equality are not met or when the effective enjoyment of freedoms is distributed extremely unevenly among the different sectors of the population (O'Donnell 1994). By the same token, Robert Dahl's distinction between democracy and polyarchy rightly acknowledges the incompleteness of "really existing democracies," thus revealing at a theoretical level the inadequacies of a conceptualization confined to the boundaries of the political realm (Dahl 1971).

## DEMOCRACY REVISITED: THE FAULTY LINES OF DEMOCRATIC GOVERNANCE

In a recent concept paper, Felipe Agüero convincingly argued in favor of rethinking democratic governance in Latin America in terms of the "fault lines" that underlie the democratic formations in our region. His argument rightly underlined the saliency of a problem that until now has failed to receive the attention it deserved — the fact that the major threat now besieging democracy in Latin America (and, it should be added, in industrialized democracies as well) is not so much a "blatant authoritarian regression" but the loss of purpose and meaning of democracy due to its lack of depth, poor quality, unfairness, and incompleteness (Agüero 1994, 5-7). Thus, democracy suffers a process of "emptying-out" (Borón 1995b, 214-216) or institutional decay (Haggard and Kaufman 1992, 349), or it may well degenerate into "delegative democracies," as Guillermo O'Donnell has dubbed them (O'Donnell 1992). In other words, the dangers come from inside rather than from outside our embattled and faulty democracies. More often than not, democracy has been downgraded to an abstract, empty set of rules deprived of much meaning for the citizenry. Or, as in the case of "delegative democracies," they have entangled themselves in the vicious circle of messianic caudillismo, leading to institutional decay and a perverse form of endurance that should be clearly distinguished from truly democratic consolidation (O'Donnell 1992, 6-10).

Anatole France once observed that it gave little comfort to the poor to know that the rich and the poor were equally free to sleep under the bridges of Paris. Citizens' right to participate in the election of their government, granted by universal suffrage, confers to them an aura of dignity and self-respect that is one of the landmarks of democracy. However, when democratically elected governments break the "representative covenant" and unveil a total lack of compassion for the sufferings of their fellow citizens, it is highly likely that most of them will be inclined to think that democracy is just a sham. As is neatly captured by the

Lincolnian formula — government of the people, by the people, and for the people — the democratic ideal grants to the people the sovereign power formerly deposited in the hands of autocrats of all sorts. Nevertheless, in democratic capitalism, governmental actions and policies systematically disprove the supposed equality predicated in the democratic discourse, and not all societal interests have equal weight or are equally regarded by the authorities. While interests of the rich and powerful receive preferential attention and favorable responses, others are not even heard, let alone addressed. The persistent reiteration of this contradiction may well result in democracy's vanishing into thin air, especially in countries plagued by the persistent presence of a dense authoritarian political tradition. If this class selectivity of democratic governments is coupled with the institutional pitfalls that characterize current and past Latin American democratic experiences, then the prospects of a genuine democratic consolidation could be rather grim. The involution experienced by democracy in Peru; the worrying instability of Venezuela; the distressing persistence of violence in Colombia; the enduring prerogatives of the military, especially in Chile and to a lesser extent in Brazil; and the devastating impacts of "structural adjustment" programs on the very fabric of societies such as Argentina and Mexico are sobering reminders that cannot be overlooked.

In other words, once it is accepted that the classic cycle of "economic instability-military coup" seems to have been historically superseded in Latin America, there are still other sources of stress and danger, like newborn, menacing Hydra heads poised to undermine the nascent democracies in the region. In this regard, the growing "legitimacy deficits" produced by the inability of the democratic regimes to improve the lot of the citizenry or produce good governments free of the taints of corruption and selfishness are worrisome (Knight and Pope 1994, 40-43; Brooke 1994). Of course, the erosion of a government's legitimacy does not mean that democracy as a political regime will necessarily follow the same path (Linz 1978). However, if several successive governments — in many cases, from different political parties — prove unable to cope with democratic shortcomings and institutional decay, then the future of democracy in Latin America will certainly be anything but bright.

Democracies may break down for many reasons. Wars, economic depressions, ideological and communal conflicts, class struggles resulting in civil war, foreign invasions, and similar factors may bring democracies to the point of collapse (Linz 1978; Therborn 1977). A much less spectacular but nonetheless serious cause of democratic breakdowns is the protracted decline in democratic mass beliefs. Of course, not all the forms of erosion of democratic legitimacy necessarily bring about the dismissal of a democratic regime. The outcome is largely contingent on how widespread democratic disrepute and frustration are among the citizenry and how long these factors have been underway. If just a few believe, even persistently, that democracy is a sham, the outcome is not likely to have a destabilizing impact on the democratic regime. The same may happen when many people occasionally, or for short spans, are led to believe that democracy is a sham. These combinations may pose varying degrees of threat, but in general they are rather innocuous or easily countered by the democratic state. Much more dubious and worrisome is the outcome of the other possibility, when many people always believe that democracy is a sham. Of course, this depends upon how many the "many" are, how well organized they are, what their capacities for collective action are, how long they have been nurturing these kinds of sentiments, and, of course, what capacities the specific country has to absorb such a critical situation. In this regard, public opinion data for several Latin American countries are a source of serious concern.

Recently, for example, the proportion of those who felt dissatisfied with democracy ranged from 40 percent in Peru and Bolivia, to 59 percent in Brazil, and 62 percent in Colombia (Haggard and Kaufman 1995, 330-334). On this, the Western political tradition speaks with a single voice: Contrary to other, non-democratic regimes, democracy is to a large extent contingent on the citizens' beliefs. Autocracies are quite independent from their subjects' ideas and senti-ments, but one of the Achilles' heels of democracy is precisely dependency upon popular legitimacy. Seen in this light, Latin American democracies seem to be very vulnerable.

## A Seismological Metaphor

In a heuristic politico-seismological metaphor, Agüero suggests that we should ask how deep, long, and wide are the faults underlying the "really existing democracies" of Latin America; how much pressure has accumulated underground; how severe are the disjunctures; and what is likely to happen — a big earthquake or minor tremors? (Agüero 1994, 5). Having ruled out the possibility that Latin American democracies may be sitting on a San Andreas-type political fault line, Agüero mentions several other sorts of "fault lines": 1) the incompleteness of civilian supremacy over the military; 2) the weakness of the party systems or political parties, leaving the political arena open for the unchecked influence of lobbies, interest groups, and powerful corporative interests; 3) discouragement of the participation of new actors and the inclusion of new issues, given the dispropor-tionate weight of closed elites in the region's "pacted democracies"; 4) the staggering levels of poverty and the gap dividing rich and poor, negative conditions that are likely to continue into the near future; 5) crime, impunity, and a high-level violation of citizen rights; 6) discretionary powers of the bureaucracy. Obviously, not all countries are affected by these fault lines in the same way. Nor do their configurations of fault lines follow the same patterns. Military prerogatives are high in Chile, parties are weak in Brazil, crime is running high in Colombia, poverty and economic insecurity have increased everywhere, and bureaucrats and elites seem to be well entrenched and powerful in all countries.

## Looking into Two Fault Lines

In the following pages, I will explore in some detail two fault lines whose potential impacts severely jeopardize the prospects of democratization in Latin America: the so-called market-oriented reforms' effects on the capacities of democratic states and the withering-away of national sovereignty on the periphery.

## Neoliberalism and Its Difficult Relationship with Democracy

Neoliberal economic reforms have become a major obstacle in the process of democratic consolidation. Accepted as an unchallenged dogma by the ruling elites and by what, paraphrasing Antonio Gramsci, can be described as its "organic" intellectuals, the moral and ideological hegemony of neoliberalism extends over kindred reform-minded groups and political forces, engulfing even parties and organizations allegedly identified with socialism or with progressive ideas of other sorts. Economic crisis, and particularly the problem of foreign debt, was instrumental in the quite swift abandonment of time-honored ideological tenets and policies, prompting the intense adoption of the neoliberal blueprint in the diverse countries of the region. As has been discussed elsewhere, Latin America shares with Eastern Europe and Russia the dubious honor of being the part of the globe where the ideological influence of the "Washington Consensus" is felt with greatest intensity (Borón 1995a, 90-97). Some governments embraced neoliberalism with the frenzy of the converted; this was the case for the governments of Víctor Paz Estenssoro in Bolivia, Carlos Menem in Argentina, and Carlos Salinas de Gortari in Mexico. Others, like the Chilean Concertación, adopted a less sanguine approach, given that these "reforms" and their "accomplishments" were the enduring and distinctive legacies of the Augusto Pinochet regime (Cox Edwards and Edwards 1994, 217-218).

At any rate, the ideological success of neoliberalism far exceeds the modest accomplishments — with inordinate social costs — obtained in the domain of the economy (Smith, Acuña, and Gamarra 1994a and 1994b; Sader and Gentili 1995). The case of Chile, usually cited as the paradigm of neoliberal success, is particularly instructive. By 1988 (after 15 years of economic restructuring!), Chilean workers' per capita income and real wages were not much higher than they were in 1973, and immense social costs were implied by the average unemployment rate of 15 percent between 1975 and 1985, with a peak of 30 percent in 1983. Between 1970 and 1987, the percentage of homes under the poverty line increased from 17 percent to 38 percent, and in 1990 the per capita consumption of the Chileans was still less than it was in 1980 (Meller 1992). After acknowledging the "important gains" seen in urban minimum wages in Chile between 1990 and 1992, a recent CEPAL report concluded that such wages had recovered the purchasing power achieved in *1980* (CEPAL 1994, 10). As pointed out by Luiz Carlos Bresser Pereira, "The Chilean society probably would not have tolerated these transitional costs if the regime had been democratic" (1993, 38).[5]

In Mexico, the social and economic involution experienced after more than a decade of orthodox adjustments is obvious. Official data show that per capita national income fell 12.4 percent between 1980 and 1990, despite the reformist rhetoric used by PRI governments to promote neoliberal policies (Altimir 1992). Similar data indicate that in those years poverty increased significantly. Between 1982 and 1988, real wages went down by 40 percent, and they have remained very close to that level ever since. In addition, the traditionally high level of Mexican unemployment went up, while per capita consumption in 1990 was 7 percent lower than in 1980 (Bresser Pereira 1993). According to Jorge G. Castañeda (1994), the 1992 Mexican government data on income distribution (the first in 15 years) were "terrifying."

However, official optimism was not deterred by these revelations. It took the outbreak of the insurrection in Chiapas, two assassinations, a huge trade deficit, and finally the collapse of the Mexican peso in December 1994 to make local elites and their advisors realize that things were getting out of control. The new emergency package launched by President Ernesto Zedillo was bound to exact, as usual, renewed hardships from the poor, entailing a marked downward shift in the purchasing power of salaries.

In Latin America as of the late 1990s, monetary stabilization, opening of the economy, balanced budgets, deregulation, privatizations, downsizing of the state, and free rein given to the markets do not seem to be enough to ensure self-sustained growth, a more equitable income distribution, and the essential supply of other non-commodifiable values, such as justice, fairness, and well-being (Bresser Pereira, Maravall, and Przeworski 1993, 203-205; Przeworski 1992; Dahl 1992). As Western European experience since World War II clearly shows and as the experiences of Japan and Southeast Asia convincingly prove, capitalist development requires an appropriate mix of public policies that rely upon a strong (not "big" but "strong") state endowed with effective capacities of intervention in — and regulation of — the markets (Blackburn 1991). Regarding the role of the state, Richard Feinberg invites us to think in terms of a witty analogy: When the neoliberal deluge is over and the Latin American nations have to reconstruct their states, "Do we want the final product to be a sleek, high-performance Jaguar or a minimalist Yugo?" (Feinberg 1990, 22).

In this regard, it is worthwhile to remember that the accomplishments of Chilean economic restructuring — much praised by partisans of the Washington Consensus, despite their looking fairly unimpressive when compared to Southeast Asia's (until recently) or China's — have had as one of their most eccentric features the preservation of the strategic copper industry in government hands, an embarrassing relic for the neoliberal blueprint, to say the least. Nationalized during the Allende years, state-owned copper firms account for about half of all Chilean export revenues. This significant amount of cash goes directly to the fiscal treasury and not, as in Argentina, Brazil, and most Latin American economies, into the pockets of private businesspeople; thus, public finances and the capacities of the state apparatus are strengthened. In 1995, the state-owned Corporación del Cobre (Copper Corporation) transferred to the fiscal treasury US$1.76 billion in profits, a figure far higher than the total taxes paid by all private firms in Chile (IHL 1996). This economic "aberration" is disregarded by neoliberal economists, who argue that all forms of public property are inefficient or inflationary. If the lessons of the Chilean "economic success" were to be extrapolated to Argentina and Brazil, the World Bank or IMF missions would find themselves in the uncomfortable situation of having to recommend to their "clients" the nationalization of the pampas and parts of the modern export sector of Argentina or the *paulista* industry in Brazil, or both. In addition, Chilean public expenditures have been growing continuously in the last decade, as have state regulations concerning the financial markets, two features hardly compatible with the neoliberal creed. These "peculiarities" of the Chilean model have apparently passed unnoticed by the otherwise alert economists of the World Bank. In a recent official document — including a section called "Chile as a Model" — the World Bank's chief economist, Sebastián Edwards, fails to mention these facts even as a footnote (Edwards 1993, 34-35). In point of fact, Chilean economic restructuring does not seem to be a shining example of neoliberal policies (Bresser Pereira 1993, 38).

Some of the results of this "free-market fundamentalism" have been manifested quite uniformly throughout Latin America. In the two countries the World Bank and the IMF used to regard as "success" stories, Chile and Mexico, the latter at least for a while quietly removed from the list, as well as in the rest of the countries of the region, the application of neoliberal policies has increased the numbers of the poor, those living under conditions of "extreme poverty," and it has widened the gulf separating the rich and the poor. The Economic Commission on Latin America and the Caribbean (ECLAC/CEPAL), not inclined to rhetorical excesses, has commented on this connection:

> Poverty is the greatest challenge for the economies of Latin America and the Caribbean. Between 1980 and 1990 it worsened as a result of the crisis and the adjustment policies, wiping out most of the progress in poverty reduction achieved during the 1960's and 1970's. Recent estimates place the number of poor at the beginning of this decade, depending on the definition of poverty, somewhere between 130 and 196 million. . . . Recession and adjustment in the eighties also increased income inequality in most of the region. In the countries with the most highly concentrated income distribution, the richest 10 percent of the households receive 40 percent of the total income (CEPAL 1994, 1).

Of course, this does not deny the fact that "pockets of improvement" are found amidst a sea of poverty. In Chile, the Aylwin government reportedly reduced the numbers of people living under the poverty line to 28 percent, but this proportion is almost twice as much as it was in 1970. At any rate, the poor in Chile apparently have not reaped the benefits of the economic progress yet. As Pilar Vergara has convincingly shown, the bottom 40 percent of households in Greater Santiago reduced their participation in total consumption from 19.3 percent in 1969 to a meager 12.6 percent in 1988, while neoliberal economists were busy celebrating the accomplishments of the Chilean "economic miracle" (Vergara 1944, 243). In Argentina, too, the Menem government claimed to have reduced the number of the poor from the breathtaking figures resulting from the 1989-1990 hyperinflation, but recent figures have been almost four times as high as they were at the beginning of the 1970s (Borón 1995c, 219-222). To sum up, generalized poverty in the region does not cancel out the modest improvements in some small, carefully targeted sections of the popular classes. However, these gains, as welcome as they are, have been unable to change the overall negative impact of neoliberal reforms.

The impoverished, fragmented societies that resulted from the economic crisis and the conservative response to it hardly constitute the most fertile soil for the flowering of democracy. Nor are such societies positive factors in the upgrading of the quality of democratic governance. Certainly, democracy cannot be understood as only the liturgical fulfillment of certain routines and rituals completely deprived of any substantive meaning. In this regard, it should not be forgotten that national elections were held on schedule under the dictatorships of Anastasio Somoza and Alfredo Stroessner and that the legislatures in Nicaragua and Paraguay used to be scenarios of fierce — but rather inconsequential — verbal disputes between government and the "opposition."

Not only in Latin America but also in the United States and the United Kingdom, neoliberal policies have augmented the share of the very rich in national income (Krugman 1994; Phillips 1991). Further, policies aimed at deregulating markets, at privatization, and at liberalization have reinforced the bargaining power of a handful of privileged collective actors whose demands gain direct access to the upper echelons of the government and the central bureaucracy. Thus, the quality of democratic governance in Latin America is impaired not only by deterioration of the material foundations of citizenship. These fragile democratic experiments are also endangered by the fact that neoliberal policies, unresponsive to the legitimate expectations of the underlying population, magnify the strength of the dominant classes and further reinforce the role of noninstitutionalized power relations, before which the state (and not only the president) becomes increasingly impotent (O'Donnell 1992, 7, 14).

This unprecedented empowerment of private interests at the expense of everything public places Latin American democracies under the Damocles' sword of the bourgeoisie and its allied social forces, which can easily destabilize the political process. A weak democratic state can produce only a feeble and ineffective government, and this weakness in due course will tend to aggrandize the social, economic, and political weight of very rich, small, and well-organized groups of private collective actors (Przeworski 1985, 138-139). To make things worse, the capitalist economy is extraordinarily sensitive to the initiatives of entrepreneurs, and the weakened national states have very few instruments of mediation and control when the globalization of economic and financial transactions is duly taken into account. The structural dependence of democratic states on the capitalist classes and their "confidence" in the ability of local rulers to maintain a favorable atmosphere for the business community have become so acute that now in Latin America market forces "regulate" state policies, rather than the reverse, as had been the case since the Great Depression. The entrepreneurial elites' skepticism or lack of enthusiasm regarding a newly elected democratic government can trigger strategic business moves likely to have a devastating impact on the performance of the democratic state. For instance, firms may refrain from making new investments, may adopt a "wait and see" policy, may make selective disinvestments or capital transfers, or may choose full-blown capital flight. Each one of these moves may, to varying degrees, seriously upset the political and economic stability of a democratic government. In fact, such actions can be considerably more important than a general workers' strike. The impact of the "wildcat strike" launched by capitalists in Chile under Allende was devastating, while the "market coups" orchestrated by the Argentine, Brazilian, Mexican, and Venezuelan bourgeoisie were somewhat milder but still highly effective forms of "influencing" public policies. Certainly, one of the most important "fault lines" threatening the genuine consolidation of the new democracies in Latin America is caused by the structural imbalance between a handful of very powerful bourgeois actors and "market forces" reigning without adequate counterweights; large sectors of a demobilized, disorganized, mostly apathetic, and depoliticized populace; and increasingly impotent democratic states.

## The Withering-Away of the Sovereign State: Fiscal Crisis and Globalization

An intimately related problem is posed by the progressive deterioration of the capacities of nation-states in Latin America to ensure the provision of the collective goods needed for the bare reproduction of civilized life: health, education, housing, social security, food programs, retirement funds, and so on. This situation is due to a variety of causes, two of which I will examine here. First, there is the persistence of fiscal crisis and the "tax veto" still successfully wielded by capitalists throughout Latin America, and, second, there is the weakening of autonomy and state power through the effects of globalization.

Regarding the "tax veto," it must be reckoned that this aberrant social and economic tradition — dating back to colonial times, when the rich were not bothered by local tax collectors — has periodically created tremendous pressures on the national budget. Given the rigidities faced by the fiscal accounts on the "revenue" side because of legal loopholes, tax evasion, and the successful resistance of capitalists to the modernization and democratization of the tax system, policymakers have routinely tried to "solve" the fiscal crisis by cutting expenditures or, when possible, raising new indirect and socially regressive taxes. In both cases, the burden of the financial adjustment rests on the shoulders of workers and the poor.

With the debt crisis, the chronic underfinancing of the state in Latin America became a source of major national and international concern. Heavily indebted countries, especially those that signed the Brady Plan, needed a consistent budgetary surplus in order to repay the principal and interest of large external debts. Therefore, amid the severe crisis of the 1980s, Latin American states reinforced the recessive trends of the economy with a pro-cyclical fiscal policy that further depressed the purchasing power of large sections of the population and shrank the incomes of the middle classes while creating, in accordance with fashionable "supply-side" economics, new "tax incentives" for the rich. The harsh cuts in social expenditures and in public spending in general became one of the cornerstones of the neoliberal blueprint, justified by the need to "keep the numbers in the black," to reduce allegedly oversized states, and to prevent inflation from escalating into hyperinflation. It is quite clear that under this dogma the fiscal surplus becomes an end in itself that subdues policy goals such as economic growth, full employment, and national sovereignty. In the Keynesian era, the paramount goal of economic policymaking — full employment — had a clear affinity with fundamental democratic values such as equality, participation, and full-fledged citizenship. Consequently, the public budget was a flexible, anti-cyclical instrument useful to cope with both economic downturns and inflationary repercussions. The neoliberal revolution of the 1980s wiped away those Keynesian ideas and installed the fiscal surplus as public policy's supreme goal. Thus, a policy instrument became an overriding policy goal in itself (Hall 1989).

What theorists of the Washington Consensus overlook is the fact that the critical status of state accounts in Latin America is caused not by governmental expenses but by the chronic inability of governments to tax the rich. The World Bank's schizophrenia in this regard is impossible to ignore. While the research of the Bank's own experts conclusively demonstrates the strongly regressive nature of

Latin American tax systems, the policy recommendations given by the Bank's leadership have encouraged governments of the region to "reduce the tax burden" in order to attract private investment. Contrary to what neoliberal enthusiasts argue, the state's size in Latin American countries, as measured by the proportion of public expenditures to gross domestic product (GDP), is substantially lower than in the industrialized nations. Argentina, Brazil, Chile, and Mexico spend much less proportionately than France, Germany, the United States, and Canada. In more than half of the Organization for Economic Cooperation and Development (OECD) countries in 1985, state expenditures represented slightly more than 50 percent of their GDP; despite the recommendations of fiscal austerity by neoliberal economists, public expenditures in advanced economies have been growing continuously (Borón 1995b, 180-185). Data that the World Bank compiled at the beginning of the 1990s show that while the average proportion of public expenditures to GDP in less developed countries amounted to 23 percent, this figure in the industrialized market economies ran to 40 percent. Meanwhile, public expenditures were 11.8 percent of GDP in Guatemala and 14.6 percent of GDP in Paraguay (World Bank 1991, 139). Should Latin America as a whole move in the direction of France and the Netherlands or Guatemala and Paraguay? The inability to develop a modern, progressive tax system is a crucial factor in the financial crisis of the state in Latin America.

Of course, this is in no way meant to ignore that many times public expenditures are made rather inefficiently or to imply that state agencies and offices are not immune to the destructive consequences of corruption. However, inefficiency and corruption are also found in the industrialized economies, and private firms and markets have not been impervious to these calamities. The heart of the matter lies in the weakened extractive capacities of the national states in Latin America because they are unable to tax the rich. While the tax burden measured as a percent of GDP for the more developed countries of Latin America hovers around 17 percent, in the OECD countries it rises to 37.5 percent, excluding in all cases social security contributions. Even more meaningful are the figures concerning taxes on capital gains and profits. They reach an average level of 14 percent of GDP in the OECD countries. However, they are 4 percent in Brazil; 3 percent in Argentina, Chile, and Uruguay; and 1 percent in Bolivia (CEPAL 1992, 92). It is astonishing that these Latin American states, strong enough to sell or to dismantle and sell, at very low prices, large and sometimes very efficient public enterprises; shut down governmental agencies; terminate social programs; privatize all kinds of public services; destroy labor unions; overwhelm public resistance to some of these policies; and slash the public budget appear surprisingly weak-willed and feeble when faced with the task of organizing an equitable and progressive tax regime. The class selectivity of the neoliberal state is blatant: strong in promoting market forces and advancing the interests of big capital and weak in defending the public interest and responding to the needs of the poor.

The outbreak of the debt crisis in Latin America hastened the relentless disarticulation of state apparatuses and the rather disorderly retreat of governments from policy areas in which their contributions had been very positive and important for large sections of the popular classes: public health, education, housing, social security, and justice. Three decades of persistent economic growth — albeit "state-centered" — were not enough to forestall the wide, sudden, and epoch-making shift in macroeconomic policymaking from variants of "structuralism" and "developmentalism" to free-market dogma. This movement of the pendulum from a scorned public sphere to the private sphere, as well as from the state to the markets and firms, is bound to have long-lasting consequences on the quality of the region's democracies and on the overall performance of its states. In a very short span, the balance between public and private was radically altered through wholesale privatizations, deregulation, and liberalization of all sorts (Therborn 1995). These policies, joined to the obsessive pursuit of "fiscal surplus" and monetary stability as all-encompassing values, have led to a situation in which markets operate with almost no constraints, afraid that governmental interventions may upset the virtuous dynamics of unfettered free markets. The case of Russia is important to bear in mind as it has become a colossal caricature of the neoliberal model, demonstrating with unparalleled clarity the kinds of results that can be expected from capitalist markets lacking a state able to play even a nineteenth century, clearly pre-Keynesian role of umpire. I am not arguing that the unfortunate Russian case truly parallels what is going on in Latin America today. However, I strongly suggest that without changes in current policies, reconstructed Latin American capitalism will bear much more resemblance to corrupt, mafia-ridden Russia than to Switzerland or Austria.

## Globalization and External Vulnerability

In this context, the process of economic globalization has only made things worse. The "tax veto," coupled with globalization, has brought about a radical weakening of national states, the lessening of their administrative and decision-making capacities, a decline in the quality of governance, and growing levels of vulnerability in relation to an increasingly complex domestic and international environment. The enfeeblement of Latin American new democracies caused distortion in their priorities and responsiveness. First, governments in the region are responsive to the interests of foreign creditors and key sectors of international capital and its "watchdogs," the World Bank and the International Monetary Fund. Second, the governments respond to domestic "market forces," a euphemism to designate local or foreign big capital and big firms that operate within domestic markets. Third, and only later, these governments respond to the citizenry and civil society at large. The problem is that it is very hard to conceive of a solid democracy without a minimum threshold of national sovereignty, which means the ability to make autonomous decisions in crucial matters that inevitably have alternative distributional impacts. Given the formidable reach of globalization and the reinforcement of financial dependence due to external debt, a democracy resting upon a weak state increasingly deprived of decisional autonomy is likely to decay.

The globalization of economic activities caused the new Latin American democracies to surrender important margins of national sovereignty and self-determination de facto, sometimes legally transferring decision-making powers in a growing number of sensitive areas to transnational firms and international financial institutions. Today, monetary, industrial, commercial, and fiscal policies hitherto largely decided within the national boundaries of Latin America are settled primarily in New York, Washington, London, Bonn, Paris, and Tokyo — far removed from the reach, let alone the control, of the "sovereign" citizenry. Citizens cannot counter the harmful effects of the globalized economy and for the most part are unable to take advantage of the scarce opportunities that it brings to the poor. In the last 30 years, the gap between rich and poor worldwide has increased at remarkable rates, as increased global economic output has failed to be distributed according to standards of justice and fairness. Peripheral nations are much poorer and weaker than in the past. In the year 1960, the ratio of the wealth of the richest 20 percent to the wealth of the poorest 20 percent of the international economy was 30 to 1; by 1989, this ratio had reached 59 to 1 (UNDP 1992, 86).

The world has become both more "global" and more fragmented. The critique of the exclusionary impacts of globalization should not be construed as a sibylline apology for an "opting-out" strategy like those imposed by the notorious Khmer Rouge in Cambodia or by the Stalinist rulers in Albania. The catastrophic results of these unfortunate experiences are sobering reminders of what should never be done. However, the horror arising from these ruthless social experiments should not lead us to forget that neoliberal policies in a globalized economy also have produced inordinate levels of human misery, surely less apocalyptic but also extremely costly. Perhaps globalization and neoliberal policymaking are "the only game in town," but so was Keynesianism in the post-war era, as was "laissez-faire" economics before 1929. We should be aware that history always has alternative paths. There is not a unique choice: that is pure ideology.

Globalization did not occur in a political vacuum. It evolved as a part of a now-defunct hegemonic system, the Pax Americana. The post-hegemonic phase of the 1990s is witnessing the indecorous scramble of the major economic and financial powers to ensure a privileged position in the uncertain global economic system currently in the making (Borón 1994, 214-220). Yet, globalization took place according to some rules of the game — not at all democratically established — that to some extent organized the international division of labor between rich and poor and shaped the ideas and values that were enshrined as sound and reasonable "common sense" and that, therefore, predominate without counterweight. Robert W. Cox was right when he called attention to the notable degree of congruence among material power, ideology, and the institutions now prevailing in the world system (Cox 1986, 217-225).

One result of globalization has been the apparently irresistible trend to remove from nation-states, especially the weak and small ones in the periphery of the international system, some of their former strategic jurisdictions and prerogatives. The standard justification for this has been that every country has to abide by the written or unwritten rules governing the functioning of international markets. However, since the distinction between "external" and "internal" has become almost impossible to draw, international regulations and practices do, in fact, imply a dramatic interference in the sovereign powers of the democratic state. Countries may be required to adopt a given commercial policy in order to trade in overseas markets. If they want access to credit they may have to show balanced budgets (even if they are rather rare among the industrialized nations). Thus, the distinction between the "external" and the "internal" loses much of its relevance. In heavily indebted countries, the "conditionalities" imposed by the creditors are tantamount to a subtle takeover of the national economy. The case of Argentina, albeit a radical one, is quite illustrative. In formal terms, the national currency is the peso, but in real terms, it is the dollar. The Menem government has thrown monetary policy overboard; from now on it has to be removed from the menu of choices for policymakers. Although the situation is not exactly the same in other places, such detrimental impacts of globalization on national sovereignty assert themselves with varying degrees of intensity on a variety of policy areas in almost every country of the region.

Instrumental in this surrendering of sovereignty was the revealing discourse associated with the "new economic thinking" actively promoted by the Bretton Wood institutions and echoed by "mainstream" economists all around the world. According to this discourse, everything public or governmental is "inefficient," corrupt, and wasteful, while private initiative is held up as the neat sphere of efficiency, honesty, quality, and rationality. Yet, these Manichean images of the public and the private do not survive even the most perfunctory analysis. The other side of the corrupted official and state inefficiency is the private entrepreneur who bribes the public servant. Corruption is a dialectical process, in which one side cannot exist without the other. Corrupted officials need private corrupters.

This process of state enfeeblement was not neutral in its distributional impacts. Local capitalists and their international partners gained from the dramatic "downsizing" of the old developmentalist state in three ways. First, their economic predominance was significantly reinforced when the public control of markets and economic activities established in previous times was drastically reduced, which undermined both the consistency and the scope of the public sphere itself. Latin American societies themselves have become "privatized." As the state retreated to minimal functions, former collective goods — health, nutrition, education, housing, and occupational training — have became individual problems that must be solved according to the self-interested rules of the marketplace. The name of the game is the survival of the fittest; the poor, the elderly, children, the sick, the homeless, the unemployed, and the unemployable are the new clients of the Red Cross and a host of non-governmental organizations. Private charity and altruistic associations substitute for supposedly cost-ineffective social policies.

Second, the withering away of national states and the wholesale privatization of state-owned enterprises and state-administered services transferred highly profitable monopolies to capitalists and granted the repayment of the foreign debt that had been contracted in Argentina, Brazil, Chile, Uruguay, and elsewhere by irresponsible, corrupt authoritarian rulers. Neoliberalism supplied the general justification for the transfer of public assets and state-owned enterprises paid for with public savings — even in areas considered "taboo" and untouchable until a few years ago, such as electricity, oil, and telephones.

Third, these reforms tipped the balance between state and markets in favor of the latter. Given the weakening of the public sphere, a government sensitive to popular demands or inspired by a reformist vocation may find that it lacks some of the most elementary instruments of public policymaking as well as efficient administrative personnel to carry out these tasks. One of the most urgent tasks facing

Latin American societies once the neoliberal deluge is over will be to correct this "fault line" and proceed to reconstruct the state. A former minister of industry in Venezuela rightly observed that by the end of the 1990s, "Washington may encounter some surprises to the south. Latin America, which has spent the last 10 years demolishing the state, will spend the next 10 rebuilding it" (Naim 1993, 133).

## CIVIL SOCIETY AND DEMOCRATIC GOVERNANCE IN PERIPHERAL CAPITALISM

In the foregoing discussion, I focused on the detrimental impact that some "fault lines" exert on an essential feature of any government — the capacity to govern. A government can be right-wing or left-wing, progressive or conservative. It can rule the country well, not so well, or badly. But a government must at least govern. This analysis suggests that most Latin American states have diminished possibilities of setting up governments able to run effectively. In this concluding section, I will make a few complementary remarks on these issues.

Theoretically, the type of society that democracy requires is well known by all. The question for Latin American democracy, therefore, is this: To what extent are the Latin American societies that have been transformed by 15 years of neoliberal ideological hegemony suited to the development and consolidation of our nascent democracies? It does not seem that a fragmented and heterogeneous society, crisscrossed by deep and profound inequalities and cleavages of all sorts — ethnicity, class, gender, region — can offer the best terrain for an enterprise as demanding as building a democracy in peripheral capitalism. Yet, the problem is not exclusively an attribute of Latin American societies. Examining these matters from a wider theoretical perspective, Ellen Meiksins Wood asked in a magnificent essay, "Is it possible to conceive of a form of democratic citizenship that reaches into the domain sealed off by modern capitalism? Could capitalism survive such an extension of democracy?" (Meiksins Wood 1995, 237).[6] So far, the answer seems clearly negative. In Western Europe, the social involution resulting from the relative rolling back of the gains made during the heyday of the welfare state has prompted some scholars to talk about a "two-thirds" society. In the conservative capitalist societies of the late 1980s and 1990s, a wide sector, one composing roughly one-third of the population, has been progressively excluded from the benefits of material progress, doomed to become an underclass or a marginal and decaying segment of modern society, unable to be "reconverted" and reinserted into the formal labor markets of advanced capitalism (for example, Gorz 1989).

This concerns more than the immorality of social exclusion. Another enduring legacy of neoliberalism is a society whose social integration has been debilitated by the upsetting impacts of unfettered market dynamics; this weakening has crystallized the tremendous cleavages and inequities that characterize our "really existing capitalism." We may expect different conditions in Latin America than those emerging in European societies. In Latin America, contrary to neoliberal interpretations, the benefits of the welfare state arrived belatedly — and in homeopathic doses — to the underlying population. The "two-thirds" in the case of

Latin America are more likely to comprise those condemned to exclusion and marginality, while only the remaining one third — a section of the bourgeoisie extending as far down as the upper sections of the middle classes — would enjoy the niceties of economic well-being and "postmodernity." A "society" of this type is a mere juxtaposition of "social universes," and Latin American societies are quickly approaching this. Classes and social groupings may be almost completely disconnected and, as Meiksins Wood has argued, scarcely adequate for the sustenance of a democratic order.

Paradoxically, slave-owner Brazil and colonial Mexico were far more integrated as societies than their late twentieth-century capitalist successors. In those precapitalist modes of production, the exploitation of the subordinated classes demanded forms of sociability, structural integration, and interclass relationships that are largely absent in Brazil or Mexico today. The *fazendeiro* and the slaves, as the landowner and the indigenous peasants, were antagonistic poles, but both belonged to the same society. Their contradictions developed within a single social and economic structure, unified by the exploitative bonds of slavery and servitude and by a host of other social relations. In contrast, at the end of the twentieth century, the Latin American bourgeoisie (and its associated social groups and sectors) belong to an entirely different social universe than that of the marginal masses living in appalling poverty. The perverse fragmentation of modern capitalism and its ever growing tendency to create social apartheids has created dual societies in which people coexist only in an illusory manner, thanks to the vicarious influence of television. In fact, two societies live socially, culturally, economically, and ecologically in worlds apart. Referring to the United States, Robert Reich, former secretary of labor in the first Clinton administration, has remarked that as a result of neoliberal policies, people in America are living in the same society but in two completely different economies (Rifkin 1995, 180).

Reich's assertion is even truer in Latin America, where the bourgeoisie and the "winners" in this game of capitalist restructuring have sought refuge in exclusive residential districts, protected by sophisticated surveillance systems and by small armies of all sorts of security guards. Their children go to private schools and bilingual institutes along with others of the same social condition, and afterward they are sent to continue their education in U.S. colleges and universities. When they become ill, they travel to Houston or Miami to see a doctor. For entertainment, they prefer New York, London, or Paris. The source of their wealth is a global process of capital accumulation undertaken in a broad array of highly diversified economic activities, where physical contact with a member of the laboring masses is an extraordinary and highly unlikely event.

What economic and social relationship, if any, can exist between this social creature, the "end-of-the-century bourgeois," and the millions of "wretched of the earth" who make their livings selling candy, chewing gum, and other cheap goods in the busiest intersections of our decaying cities, as fire-eaters or ragged clowns on downtown sidewalks, as occasional windshield cleaners at congested traffic lights, or as precarious informal workers without any skills, barely speaking the language of the country, with no formal education, never having seen a doctor and living in tin and cardboard shacks? As Darcy Ribeiro once noted, these people have a fervent desire to be exploited because that would mean that they were at least given an entrance ticket, albeit an expensive one, to the lower echelons of the system. In order for this to be possible, they first have to acquire the qualifications that may convert them into a "usable" and exploitable labor force, an almost impossible task at a time when neoliberal restructuring is destroying the state and dismantling social services, including public education and health — and when there is no other place where these masses may obtain the minimum training needed for entering the labor market. For these growing sections of Latin American societies, class exploitation or oppression is not their immediate problem. Their handicap is precisely the inability to become an exploitable labor force. It should be noted that in all the previous modes of capitalist accumulation, the exploitability of the masses was universal. It was so much taken for granted that even children were regarded as able to meet the conditions that capitalist production set forth to produce surplus value. In addition, in those bygone times, there existed at least a common ground for the bourgeois and the worker — the factory. Today, that shared space has almost vanished as a result of deindustrialization, the replacement of live labor by intelligent machinery, the rise of the "service" economy, and financial speculation.

Thus, the problems of governance within new democracies and weak states are compounded in Latin America by the deep, long, and wide "fault lines" running through the very fabric of its civil societies. As we have seen, democratic states have to face a whole series of problems that in themselves raise serious concerns regarding the possibilities of effective democratic governance. The situation grows worse when these governments have to deal with dual and fragmented civil societies — and with large masses of marginal people unable to be incorporated by the capitalist economy. Yet, those people still live within the nations, and, in one way or another, formally enjoy citizenship rights.

Democratic governance, the art of the good government, brings us back to Plato's classic metaphor of the statesman as the helmsman. Is a good helmsman likely to be elected by these sorts of boat passengers? Reacting to this question, conservative thinkers would argue in favor of some more or less subtle form of popular disenfranchisement in order to prevent the "underclass" from gaining influence in the political process and to allow the "responsible" people to conduct the business of government without the interference of the rabble. John Kenneth Galbraith has dealt insightfully with this problem in the case of the United States, disposing of the conservative arguments underlying some of the political right's proposals for tackling the problem (Galbraith 1992). However, refuting the arguments of the right does not solve the problem. From a progressive standpoint, it is quite clear that the decay in the quality of the citizenry in peripheral states — and not only there, of course — results from deep-seated and structural tendencies of capitalist societies. Discussing the governability crisis of the early 1970s in the United States, Samuel P. Huntington wrote that the problems besieging industrialized countries were not the fault of capitalism but the consequence of democracy's excesses (Crozier et al. 1975, 73, 106-113). His thesis was wrong then, and as far as new democracies are concerned, it is wrong again today. The main problem undermining democratic governance at the end of the century lies in the ways in which capitalist production and bourgeois societies have evolved — and not in supposedly built-in, self-destructive tendencies of democracy.

To address appropriately the challenges posed by governance takes much more than an adequate institutional setting, a reasonable compromise among the elites, improvement in the quality of political leadership, and the betterment of the public policies carried out by the emerging democracies. All these are good but not enough. Much deeper fundamental changes are required in the very structure of capitalist societies, and to this effect a radical program of social and economic reform is badly needed. Improved democratic governance must always be welcome as an asset, but it would be naive to expect from it the miraculous cure for the deeply ingrained ills of Latin American capitalism. Political reform must go hand in hand with economic reform, but not in the chaotic way we see today — politics moving in the direction of a procedural democracy and formal entitlements while the economy heads toward more exclusion. Political and economic reforms must work together, but structural reforms aimed at the transformation of capitalist formations must take precedence (Borón 1995b, 152-168).

Democracy and liberty are higher and more cherished values than markets and profits. Political liberty is a necessity, while economic liberty is a convenience, John Stuart Mill wrote. The goal of a reform-minded democratic leadership in Latin America should be first of all to make our countries safe for democracy and freedom — nothing more but also nothing less. The fulfillment of this mission will be the great task of the years to come, and there is no doubt that many will join efforts to move in this direction. Marx believed that democracy would, at the end, prevail over capitalism. De Tocqueville, within the class boundaries of his aristocratic condition, expressed a concern with what for Marx was the possibility of a victorious and liberating outcome. Returning to Meiksins Wood's questions, if democracy is, in de Tocqueville's words, that "irresistible revolution advancing century by century over every obstacle and even now going forward amid the ruins it has itself created," will it respectfully stop at the gates of the present capitalist mode of production? It does not seem likely at all. Ironically, while many around the world are celebrating the final triumph of capitalism, its obscure and anonymous democratic grave diggers may well be beginning to assemble in preparation for a burial even more important than the one performed two centuries ago with the demise of aristocratic rule.

# Notes

1. This paper was written mostly while I was Visiting Faculty Fellow at the Kellogg Institute of the University of Notre Dame. I want to thank Guillermo O'Donnell, Carlos Acuña, and María Alicia Gutiérrez for the opportunity I had to discuss some of the ideas in this paper with them. I also thank Jeffrey Stark and Felipe Agüero for their careful and thoughtful comments on an earlier version of this paper. Of course, the usual disclaimer applies.

2. This section of the paper relies, by and large, on Borón 1995b, where these issues are discussed at length.

3. The Brazilian case is rather dubious and controversial, a bourgeois revolution "from above" at best. At any rate, Fernandes provides an interesting discussion on this issue.

4. We should stress the "relative" nature of these guarantees, because in bourgeois democracies some political games — certainly not all — are played with "loaded" dice. Additionally, there is no country in which capitalists have called a popular plebiscite to decide whether the economic system has to be organized on the basis of private property or publicly owned enterprises. Not only are some games played with "loaded" dice; other games are not played at all.

5. More data on these issues are available in Manuel Délano and Hugo Traslaviña (1989); Eugenio Tironi (1988); and Xabier Arrizabalo Montoro (1993).

6. A discussion of this key matter, the relationship between democracy and capitalism, exceeds the scope of this paper. In addition to Meiksins Wood's book, Bobbio 1976, Borón 1995a and 1995b, O'Donnell 1994, and Przeworski 1990 offer discussions of the topic.

# References

Agüero, Felipe. 1994. "Democratic Governance in Latin America: Thinking about Fault Lines." Unpublished manuscript. Coral Gables, Fla.: North-South Center at the University of Miami.

Altimir, Oscar. 1992. *Cambios en las desigualdades de ingreso y en la pobreza en América Latina*. Buenos Aires: Instituto Torcuato Di Tella.

Arrizabalo Montoro, Xabier. 1993. *Resultados económicos de la dictadura en Chile (1973-1989)*. Madrid: Instituto Internacional del Desarrollo.

Blackburn, Robin. 1991. "Socialism after the Crash." *New Left Review*, No. 185 (January-February): 5-66.

Bobbio, Norberto. 1976. "Esiste una dottrina marxista dello stato?" In *Il Marxismo e lo Stato*, ed. Federico Coen. Rome: Quaderni di Mondoperaio.

Borón, Atilio A. 1989. "Authoritarian Ideological Traditions and Transition Towards Democracy in Argentina." Occasional Paper No. 8, The Institute of Latin American and Iberian Studies, Columbia University, New York.

Borón, Atilio A. 1994. "Towards a Post-Hegemonic Age? The End of Pax Americana." *Security Dialogue* (Oslo) 25 (2): 211-221.

Borón, Atilio A. 1995a. "A sociedade civil depois do dilúvio neoliberal." In *Pos-Neoliberalismo. As políticas sociais e o Estado democrático*, eds. Emir Sader and Pablo Gentili. Rio de Janeiro: Paz e Terra.

Borón, Atilio A. 1995b. *State, Capitalism, and Democracy in Latin America*. Boulder, Colo., and London: Lynne Rienner Publishers.

Borón, Atilio A. 1995c. "Argentina's Neoliberal Reforms: Timing, Sequences, Choices." In *Conversations on Democratization and Economic Reform*, ed. Leslie Elliott Armijo. Los Angeles: Center for International Studies, University of Southern California.

Bresser Pereira, Luiz Carlos. 1993. "Economic Reforms and Economic Growth: Efficiency and Politics in Latin America." In *Economic Reforms in New Democracies: A Social-Democratic Approach*, eds. Luiz Carlos Bresser Pereira, José María Maravall, and Adam Przeworski. Cambridge and New York: Cambridge University Press.

Brooke, James. 1994. "A Vast Scandal is Shaking Brazilians' Faith in Democracy." *The New York Times*, January 4, A1, A2.

Castañeda, Jorge G. 1994. *Utopia Unarmed: The Latin American Left after the Cold War*. New York: Vintage Books.

CEPAL (Comisión Económica para América Latina y el Caribe). 1992. *Equidad y transformación productiva. Un enfoque Integrado*. Santiago: CEPAL.

CEPAL. 1994. *Panorama social de América Latina*. Santiago: CEPAL.

Cox Edwards, Alejandra, and Sebastián Edwards. 1994. "Markets and Democracy: The Lessons From Chile." *The World Economy* 15: 2 (March): 203-219.

Cox, Robert W. 1986. "Social Forces, States and World Orders: Beyond International Relations Theory." In *Neorealism and Its Critics*, ed. Robert Keohane. New York: Columbia University Press.

Crozier, Michel, Samuel P. Huntington, and Joji Watanuki. 1975. *The Crisis of Democracy: Report on the Governability of Democracies to the Trilateral Commission*. New York: New York University Press.

Cueva, Agustín. 1976. *El desarrollo del capitalismo en América Latina*. Mexico City: Siglo XXI.

Dahl, Robert. 1992. "Why Free Markets Are Not Enough." *Journal of Democracy* 3 (3): 82-89.

Dahl, Robert. 1971. *Polyarchy: Participation and Opposition*. New Haven, Conn., and London: Yale University Press.

Délano, Manuel, and Hugo Traslaviña. 1989. *La herencia de los Chicago-boys*. Santiago: Ornitorrinco.

DePalma, Anthony. 1995. "Mexicans Ask How Far Social Fabric Can Stretch." *The New York Times*, January 10, A1, A10.

Edwards, Sebastián. 1993. *América Latina y el Caribe. Diez años después de la crisis de la deuda*. Washington, D.C.: World Bank.

Feinberg, Richard. 1990. "Comment." In *Latin American Adjustment: How Much Has Happened?* ed. John Williamson. Washington, D.C.: Institute for International Economics.

Fernandes, Florestán. 1975. *A revoluçao burguesa no Brasil. Ensaio de interpretação sociológica*. Rio de Janeiro: Zahar Editores.

Flisfisch, Angel, Norbert Lechner, and Tomás Moulian. 1985. "Problemas de la democracia y la política democrática en América Latina." In *Democracia y Desarrollo en América Latina*, eds. Angel Flisfisch, Norbert Lechner, and Tomás Moulian. Buenos Aires: GEL.

Frenkel, Roberto. 1995. "Macroeconomic Sustainability and Development Prospects: Latin American Performance in the 1990s." UNCTAD Discussion Paper No. 100. Geneva: UNCTAD.

Fukuyama, Francis. 1992. *The End of History and the Last Man*. New York: The Free Press.

Galbraith, John Kenneth. 1992. *La cultura de la satisfacción*. Buenos Aires: Emecé Editores.

Garretón, Manuel Antonio. 1987. *Reconstruir la política. Transición y consolidación democrática en Chile*. Santiago: Editorial Andante.

Gorz, André. 1989. *Critique of Economic Reason*. London: Verso.

Haggard, Stephan, and Robert R. Kaufman, eds. 1992. *The Politics of Economic Adjustment: International Constraints, Distributive Conflicts, and the State*. Princeton, N.J.: Princeton University Press.

Haggard, Stephan, and Robert R. Kaufman. 1995. *The Political Economy of Democratic Transitions*. Princeton, N.J.: Princeton University Press.

Hall, Peter, ed. 1989. *The Political Power of Economic Ideas: Keynesianism Across Nations*. Princeton, N.J.: Princeton University Press.

Huntington, Samuel. 1991. *The Third Wave: Democratization in the Late Twentieth Century*. Norman, Okla.: University of Oklahoma Press.

*IHL* (Interlink Headline News). 1996. No. 432, April 6.

Knight, Robin, and Victoria Pope. 1994. "Back to the Future: Democratic Regimes Have Stumbled, Opening the Door to a Communist Political Comeback." *U.S. News and World Report,* May 23, 40-43.

Krugman, Paul. 1994. *Peddling Prosperity: Economic Sense and Nonsense in the Age of Diminished Expectations*. New York and London: W.W. Norton and Co.

Linz, Juan. 1978. *The Breakdown of Democratic Regimes: Crisis, Breakdown and Reequilibration.* Baltimore: Johns Hopkins University Press.

Lustig, Nora. 1993. "Measuring Poverty in Latin America: The Emperor Has No Clothes." Paper presented at the Conference on Social Development and Poverty, Oaxaca, Mexico.

Lustig, Nora, ed. 1994. *Coping with Austerity: Poverty and Income Distribution in Latin America.* Washington, D.C.: The Brookings Institution.

Meiksins Wood, Ellen. 1995. *Democracy Against Capitalism: Renewing Historical Materialism.* Cambridge: Cambridge University Press.

Meller, Patricio. 1992. "Latin American Adjustment and Economic Reforms: Issues and Recent Experience." Unpublished manuscript. Santiago: CIEPLAN.

Moore, Barrington. 1966. *Social Origins of Dictatorship and Democracy: Lord and Peasant in the Making of the Modern World.* Boston: Beacon Press.

Naim, Moisés. 1993. "Latin America: Post-Adjustment Blues." *Foreign Policy,* No. 92 (Fall): 133-150.

O'Donnell, Guillermo. 1992. *Delegative Democracy?* Working Paper No. 172. Notre Dame, Ind.: Kellogg Institute, University of Notre Dame.

O'Donnell, Guillermo. 1994. "The State, Democracy, and Some Conceptual Problems." In *Latin American Political Economy in the Age of Neoliberal Reform,* eds. William C. Smith, Carlos H. Acuña, and Eduardo A. Gamarra. Coral Gables, Fla.: North-South Center at the University of Miami.

Phillips, Kevin. 1991. *The Politics of Rich and Poor.* New York: Harper Perennial.

Przeworski, Adam. 1985. *Capitalism and Social Democracy.* Cambridge: Cambridge University Press.

Przeworski, Adam. 1990. *The State and the Economy Under Capitalism.* London and New York: Harwood Academic Publishers.

Przeworski, Adam. 1992. "The Neoliberal Fallacy." *Journal of Democracy* 3 (3): 45-59.

Rifkin, Jerome. 1995. *The End of Work: The Decline of the Global Labor Force and the Dawn of the Post-Market Era.* New York: G.P. Putnam and Sons.

Sader, Emir, and Pablo Gentili, eds. 1995. *Pos-Neoliberalismo. As políticas sociais e o Estado democrático.* Rio de Janeiro: Paz e Terra.

Schumpeter, Joseph. [1943] 1976. *Capitalism, Socialism, and Democracy.* London: George Allen & Unwin Publishers.

Shin, Doh Chull. 1994. "On the Third Wave of Democratization: A Synthesis and Evaluation of Recent Theory and Research." *World Politics,* No. 47, 135-170.

Smith, William C., Carlos H. Acuña, and Eduardo A. Gamarra, eds. 1994a. *Latin American Political Economy in the Age of Neoliberal Reform.* Coral Gables, Fla.: North-South Center at the University of Miami.

Smith, William C., Carlos H. Acuña, and Eduardo A. Gamarra, eds. 1994b. *Democracy, Markets, and Structural Reform in Latin America.* Coral Gables, Fla.: North-South Center at the University of Miami.

Strasser, Carlos. 1990. *Para una teoría de la democracia posible. Idealizaciones y teoría política.* Buenos Aires: GEL.

Strasser, Carlos. 1991. *Para una teoría de la democracia posible. La democracia y lo democrático.* Buenos Aires: GEL.

Therborn, Göran. 1977. "The Rule of Capital and the Rise of Democracy." *New Left Review,* No. 103 (May-June).

Therborn, Göran. 1995. "A crise e o futuro do capitalismo." In *Pos-Neoliberalismo. As políticas sociais e o Estado democrático*, eds. Emir Sader and Pablo Gentili. Rio de Janeiro: Paz e Terra.

Tironi, Eugenio. 1988. *Los silencios de la revolución*. Santiago: La Puerta Abierta.

Tocqueville, Alexis de. [1835] 1969. *Democracy in America*. New York: Doubleday/Anchor Books.

United Nations Development Program (UNDP). 1992. *Desarrollo Humano. Informe 1992*. Bogotá: UNDP.

Varas, Augusto. 1995. "Latin American Democratization: Citizenship, Empowerment, and Accountability." Unpublished paper presented at the Conference on Fault Lines of Democratic Governance in the Americas, North South Center, University of Miami, Coral Gables, Florida.

Vergara, Pilar. 1994. "Market Economy, Social Welfare, and Democratic Consolidation in Chile." In *Democracy, Markets, and Structural Reform in Latin America*, eds. William C. Smith, Carlos H. Acuña, and Eduardo A. Gamarra. Coral Gables, Fla.: North-South Center at the University of Miami.

World Bank. 1991. *World Development Report: The Challenge of Development*. Oxford: Oxford University Press.

CHAPTER FOUR

# Globalization and Democracy in Latin America

## JEFFREY STARK

Globalization is a phenomenon of such scope and diversity that it is inevitably discussed in very different ways by scholars working in different disciplines. As in the parable of the blind men describing an elephant by prodding its various parts, highly divergent accounts emerge as to the nature of the beast. From international relations theory, international political economy, sociology, economics, cultural theory, and political geography, as well as other disciplines, one now encounters a burgeoning collection of book-length characterizations and analyses (Featherstone 1995; Featherstone, Lash, and Robertson 1995; Jones 1995; Waters 1995; Boyer and Drache 1996; Hirst and Thompson 1996; Kofman and Youngs 1996; Mato, Montero, and Amodio 1996; Mittelman 1996; Spybey 1996; Baylis and Smith 1997; Greider 1997; Rodrik 1997; Jameson and Miyoshi 1998). At the same time, a general trend exists in which scholars, activists, and policymakers often extract, interpret, evaluate, and combine various and sundry aspects of globalization to assert that it is in some way, shape, or form either good news or bad news — either the harbinger of greater peace and prosperity or the herald of growing conflict and inequality.[1] Of course, enough evidence is at hand to be deployed on a selective basis to support either point of view. Yet, trying to reach a dichotomous or "balance sheet" assessment of globalization — which is still a relatively new and contested concept in the social sciences — is bound to produce less than satisfactory results. Globalization is a moving target, both empirically and conceptually, and because of this, perhaps the relevant challenge is less to assess than to try to understand globalization in a more comprehensive way.

This holds true even within the more limited domain of the relationship between globalization and democratic governance in the Americas. Here, too, the connections are so numerous and the implications so disparate that any grand evaluation is almost certain to be open to telling objections. Globalization, a term with connections to many referents, is often used as a kind of vague shorthand to make a point or advance an argument (typically in the form, "as a result of globalization," x or y is occurring), but such stylized or notional assertions do not provide much clarity to the term itself. What is clear, however, is that globalization and its meaning for democracy is increasingly a topic of conversation and concern for citizens and democratic governments in Latin America. There is a strong sense of globalization as a challenge and possibly a threat, especially in relation to economic forces. For example, in 1996, Brazil's most prominent news magazine,

*Veja,* devoted its front cover and a lengthy article to the topic.[2]  Beneath a depiction of three businessmen striding across the globe on the cover, a caption read, "Unemployment, anxiety, wealth, and other promises of the revolution that is knocking down borders and propelling capitalism with an unprecedented velocity" (*Veja,* April 3, 1996). After more than 15 years of harsh economic reforms and far-reaching social change in Latin America, such sentiments are understandable and widespread. One must remember that it was in the context of exhortations by foreign banks, governments, and international financial institutions to slash public spending, service debts, privatize, and deregulate that Latin America experienced between 1980 and 1990 a decline in average per capita income of 7 percent, a drop in consumption of 6 percent, and a fall in investment of 4 percent (UNDP 1996, 17).

At the same time, the austerity of the "lost decade" of the 1980s paradoxically was accompanied by a wave of democratization that saw many Latin American countries shift from military to democratic rule. While the principal forces for these democratic transitions were home-grown, it cannot be overlooked that they were part of a global "third wave" of democratization whose wellsprings included the promotion of human rights by powerful states and non-governmental organizations (NGOs), the proliferation of new social movements, increased community activism within the Catholic Church, and demonstration effects (for example, the turn toward democracy in Spain), channeled through media outlets and other forms of international communication (Huntington 1991, 40-46). Here, the globalization of norms directly or indirectly supporting the idea of human rights and democratic governance played an important role (Sikkink 1996). For better or worse, the trajectories of what have arguably been Latin America's two principal dynamics in recent years — persistent economic crisis and the restoration or advent of democratic regimes — have been inscribed within global trends.

Concurrent with the deepening of globalization have been changes that have narrowed some of the qualitative differences between democracy in Latin America and in North America.[3]  The transition to and gradual consolidation of democracy in Latin America have coincided with declining levels of participation and growing disenchantment with the two-party system in the United States (Lipset 1994). Discussions concerning democracy in Latin America have generally moved from a preoccupation with coup possibilities to more complex analyses of the scope, depth, and quality of existing democratic regimes, while the lack of trust in public officials in the United States has produced debates about its root causes (Dionne 1991; Putnam 1995). Allowing for the obvious differences of past history and present wealth between North and Latin America, the two-steps-forward-one-step-back process of democratization in Latin America and the slippage of standard indicators of democratic health in the United States place the respective discussions in a shared "democracies with problems" mode that reveals a fair degree of overlap in such noteworthy areas as representation and participation.[4]  Canada's situation with respect to the politics of identity and social welfare embedded in the Quebec and indigenous peoples questions brings it, too, within the ambit of fundamental questions about democratic governance (Black 1995; DePalma 1998). Overall, it is a plausible working hypothesis that, over time, the phenomena resulting from globalization will contribute toward making hemisphere-wide comparisons increasingly possible, but for the purposes of this chapter, the discussion is limited to Latin America.

Globalization is now an important, unavoidable frame of reference for contemporary discussions of democratic governance in Latin America. Inhabiting the economic, social, cultural, and political spheres of every country, globalization adds a new and problematic level of complexity in understanding and assessing democratic rule. Globalization produces effects of insecurity, instability, inequality, and inflexibility that inevitably have ramifications for the legitimacy, accountability, representation, participation, and justice normally associated with democratic life. At the same time, the global circulation of democratic values, norms, and ideas — as well as certain often-ignored aspects of economic liberalization — offer paths to citizen empowerment. In the shaping and reshaping of both the aspirations of citizens and the capacities of democratic governments, one can observe an accelerating process of change that leads to new problems and uncertainties and a rapid scramble to adapt.

The discussion that follows is in four parts. First, the most salient aspects of globalization are explicated further with some empirical referents and qualitative observations. Second, these are related to global economic processes and a number of important problems for the democracies of Latin America. Third, the sometimes overlooked but still powerful social and cultural aspects of globalization are elaborated. Fourth, some final observations on the implications of globalization for Latin American democracies are combined with suggestions for further research.

## CONCEPTUALIZING GLOBALIZATION

As a term or concept, globalization has been defined and used in myriad ways. To facilitate the discussion that follows, I offer a working definition, building upon the usages of Roland Robertson (1992, 8) and Malcolm Waters (1995, 3).

> Globalization as a concept refers both to the compression of the world and the intensification of consciousness of the world as a whole. It is a social process in which the constraints of geography on political, economic, social, and cultural arrangements and practices recede and in which people become increasingly aware that they are receding.[5]

Four categories can be given to encompass the most important examples of these shifts in practices and perceptions: 1) the world economy, where finance, production, and trade networks are increasingly globally integrated (or exist in relation to such global networks) and where labor often competes on a worldwide basis;[6] 2) a communications and information revolution that has collapsed previously existing space-time boundaries — for example, the electronic media (now including global newspapers), high-technology transportation and satellite systems, and the growing use of the Internet; 3) products and behaviors associated with a global consumerism that encompasses mass advertising, videos, music, clothing, food products, and so on; and 4) a wide assortment of new political cultures and subcultures,[7] both cosmopolitan and parochial, that constitute an expanding sociopolitical or sociocultural realm of discourse and action that aggregates identities and loyalties not only on the basis of nationality or territory but also in relation to such themes as religion, gender, ethnicity, and the environment. These four categories are obviously highly interrelated, overlapping, porous, and should by no means be thought of as neat distinctions. In their interstices flourish such diverse and significant phenomena as transnational crime cartels, transborder migratory flows, and international tourism.[8]

Globalization cannot be understood if thought of as a homogenizing process. Rather, it is a dynamic set of interactions between world-as-a-whole processes, ideas, and sensibilities and the local practices, responses, and adaptations of individuals in lives constituted by and expressed through particular societies and cultures, as well as local, national, regional, and international associations and institutions. It is important to keep in mind that two of the principal features of globalization are to be found in its reflexivity and its effects of relativization. Once the world has been perceived and experienced in various ways as "one place," one's own cultural locale and social systems inevitably are framed in relation to the larger whole. Even when the response to this situation is to seek to reject or deny it, the act of rejection carries within it an awareness of the global, thereby bringing about a persistent commingling of the near and the far. Similarly, as the world is compressed, one witnesses "the disembedding of social systems . . . and the *reflexive ordering and reordering* of social relations in the light of continual inputs of knowledge affecting the actions of individuals and groups" (Giddens 1990, 17, italics in the original). In the end, as Robertson (1995) notes, globalization is not a matter of either homogeneity or heterogeneity, but both at once, a state of affairs captured in the unwieldy but apt term, "glocalization."[9]

A pair of initial propositions are in order. First, a main feature of globalization is a diffusion of power away from the nation-state toward other arenas of human activity. With increasingly liberalized economies oriented toward export and enmeshed in ramifying and often largely autonomous global networks of finance, production, and exchange, the capacity of national policymakers to manage domestic economies has been attenuated in many ways. Functions once central to the conception of the state in Latin America have been shifted to the market in order to streamline the public sector. Through increasingly sophisticated business practices and the rise of new groups in civil society, technological, organizational, and administrative networks have developed to create new centers of power and influence. "Risk managers" in insurance and credit rating agencies, professionals in large and influential accounting firms, and the practitioners of international commercial arbitration engage in actions that must be taken into account by state authorities (Sassen 1996). Further, in recent years in Latin America, the implementation of International Monetary Fund (IMF) austerity packages and World Bank structural adjustment loans have diminished the range of available and badly needed compensatory social policies. Paradoxically, as the citizens of Latin American democracies increasingly look toward their elected officials for the provision of effective policies and minimum levels of public goods, the forces attendant to globalization have reduced in important respects the capacity of governments to provide them.

Second, and very much related to this paradox — given globalization's market-driven wellsprings — is an increasingly observable trend whereby complex forms of economic life are ascendant and conventional or traditional forms of political life are in retreat. New economic phenomena, including aspects of post-Fordist production such as subcontracting, flexible specialization, intra-firm trade, and global commodity chains are accompanied by the loss of effectiveness of political parties and the disappearance of familiar, state-centric guideposts in the making of foreign policy. As economic globalization leads to market segmentation, functional differentiation divides formal and informal workers, reconfigures categories of skilled and unskilled workers, and — through the increasing participation of women in the workforce — even affects roles and responsibilities within the family. At the same time, the economic bases for political solidarities (unions, professional associations, business organizations) shift, and, as a result, political party allegiances and party composition are disrupted, and customary political practices are altered.

These two developments, the diminished centrality of the nation-state and the spread of the new "economic polity" (Wolin 1989) or "market civilization" (Gill 1995), pose dilemmas for democratic governance in Latin America. They can be detailed further through a discussion of the four categories mentioned above: world economy, communications, consumerism, and new political cultures.

# WORLD ECONOMY

Ultimately, the driving force behind globalization in nearly all its manifestations is the capitalist world economy. Because of the profound economic crisis experienced throughout Latin America in the 1980s, the linkages among democratic governance, economic stabilization and adjustment programs, and the entire process of neoliberal economic restructuring have been the subject of extensive scholarship over the past decade (Nelson 1989; Stallings and Kaufman 1989; Frieden 1991; Bresser Pereira, Maravall, and Przewzorski 1993; Smith, Acuña, and Gamarra 1994a; Smith, Acuña, and Gamarra 1994b; Nelson et al. 1994; Haggard and Kaufman 1994; Bulmer-Thomas 1996; Chalmers et al. 1997). Rather than revisiting those discussions, the question here relates to the demands and dynamics of the contemporary global economy and the capacity of democracies in the Americas to respond to them.

## The Trade Push

Delinking from the world economy is no longer discussed as a serious option. As a result of the debt crisis of the 1980s — which, despite multiple external causes, also derived from serious flaws in the "state-centered matrix" associated with import-substitution industrialization — Latin American countries had to confront the need for a new development model. In doing so, they were forced to face the fact that they were "embedded in a worldwide trading and financial system, from whose rigid rules there was no easy escape" (Morley 1995, 5). At the outset of the 1990s, with high levels of urbanization (roughly 75 percent of the population);

youthful unemployed populations (Table 1); and extensive poverty (approximately 40 percent of the urban population and 60 percent of the rural population), Latin American nations required a development strategy that placed primary emphasis on economic growth and was capable of receiving the backing of key international financial institutions.[10] This entailed restoring macroeconomic equilibrium; adopting a strong export orientation (often through the promotion of nontraditional exports); and the gradual lowering of trade barriers. With the partial exception of Cuba, all of the countries of the hemisphere have responded to the exigencies of the world economy by pursuing, to one degree or another, strategies of economic liberalization and export-led growth. From the limited standpoint of establishing a baseline of macroeconomic equilibrium, these strategies have been partially successful. Inflation, long the bane of the region's economies, was reduced from an average of nearly 200 percent in 1991 to just over 10 percent in 1997 (ECLAC 1997, 51).

**Table 1.**

**Latin America (8 Countries): Percentage of Unemployed Population Between Ages 15 and 34, 1992**

| Country | Age 15-34 |
|---|---|
| Mexico | 83.2 |
| Panama | 80.0 |
| Colombia (eight major cities) | 79.0 |
| Costa Rica | 75.1 |
| Venezuela | 74.8 |
| Chile | 74.1 |
| Bolivia | 64.9 |
| Argentina (Greater Buenos Aires) | 56.1 |

Source: Adapted from *Social Panorama of Latin America 1994*, ECLAC, 145.

Regional trade agreements proliferated in the Western Hemisphere in the first half of the 1990s, and the rapidity of the expansion of trade was impressive. Twenty-seven bilateral and multilateral free trade agreements were signed in Latin America between 1990 and 1996, and total trade in Latin America and the Caribbean increased by 70 percent between 1991 and 1995. From 1990 to 1995, U.S. trade with Latin America and the Caribbean increased by 72 percent (Bamrud 1996).[11] However, although trade contributes to economic growth, as part of a larger, skills-based restructuring process, it widens the wage differential between literate and illiterate workers, and it displaces workers unable to compete in a global marketplace (for example, small-scale farmers in Mexico or post-NAFTA textile workers in the Caribbean). Studies of the overall effects of trade on income inequality are mixed, with some claiming the jury is still out (Wood 1994) and others saying income inequality has been worsening (Fitzgerald 1996). According to a study published by the Economic Commission for Latin America and the Caribbean

(Alcorta and Peres 1996, 7), "Although most Latin American and Caribbean countries have greatly increased their exports during the early 1990s, the goal of moving towards higher value-added products in their export structure is proving as elusive as during the import substitution industrialization period" (see Table 2 for a cross-regional comparison).

**Table 2.**

**Exports of High Value-Added Technology by Percentage**

|      | Latin America and the Caribbean | G-7 Countries | East Asian Tigers[a] |
|------|----------------------------------|---------------|----------------------|
| 1990 | 19.4 | 55.0 | 42.9 |
| 1991 | 20.6 | 55.2 | 44.8 |
| 1992 | 23.1 | 55.9 | 47.4 |
| 1993 | 25.2 | 56.3 | 51.2 |

[a] Hong Kong, Korea, Singapore, Taiwan.

Source: Adapted from Ludovico Alcorta and Wilson Peres, 1996, *Sistemas de innovación y especialización tecnológica en América Latina y el Caribe*, CEPAL, 15.

These concerns notwithstanding, trade integration indisputably remains at the top of the inter-American policy agenda. As a result of the December 1994 Summit of the Americas in Miami, an agreement was reached among the 34 signatory nations to begin preparatory discussions for the formation of a Free Trade Area of the Americas (FTAA) by the year 2005 — a trade grouping whose commercial exchanges would exceed in value those of the European Union. Summit initiatives concerning democratization made only modest progress (Agüero 1998), as did those relating to sustainable development, until they were reaffirmed and supplemented by actions taken at a follow-up (and poorly attended) summit in Santa Cruz, Bolivia, in December 1996 (Scherr and Watson 1998). However, summit provisions having to do with trade integration received, at least at the bureaucratic level, fairly sustained attention. Trade ministerials were held in Denver, Cartagena, and Belo Horizonte in 1995, 1996, and 1997, respectively. At the April 1998 Summit of the Americas II in Santiago, Chile, negotiations for the FTAA were formally launched, and negotiating groups were created to deal with trade issues in nine separate areas (market access; investment; services; government procurement; dispute settlement; agriculture; intellectual property rights; subsidies, antidumping, and countervailing duties; and competition policy). Ironically, it is at this technical and less visible level that certain procedural norms and legal practices spread through globalization may make some of their more important contributions to democratic governance and political institutionalization in Latin America.

An important example of this is competition policy, an area of acute need for many if not most of the governments of the region. The recent wave of privatizations in Latin America, which often were motivated by the need to finance deficits rather than as a result of careful planning intended to achieve real efficiency gains, led in a number of instances to the mere conversion of public enterprises into private monopolies. Once governments committed themselves to privatizing, the brokering of actual transactions became intensely politicized. With oversight mechanisms either nonexistent or weak, newly privatized enterprises entered a regulatory vacuum devoid of accountability. The FTAA, which is concerned with the discriminatory effects of anticompetitive practices on trade, at least opens the possibility for redress of this problem.

A lack of transparency and frequent corruption in the state's dealings with the private sector mar democratic governance in many countries of the region. The prevalence of political clientelism meant that kickbacks and bribes accompanied a number of the major privatization transactions (Manzetti 1994; Saba and Manzetti 1997). An important provision resulting from the Miami Summit, however, led in March 1996 to the signing by 21 countries of the hemisphere of the Inter-American Convention Against Corruption, which prohibits illegal enrichment and the payment of bribes by foreign companies. These measures require ratification by national legislatures, and they will have to be backed up by revamped and strengthened judiciaries in order to come to fruition, but they further bolster democratic accountability. More generally, as Hugo Frühling points out in his chapter in this volume, much-needed legal reforms in the region often find supporters among businesspeople concerned with the inadequacies of national legal systems in an era of global integration. These little-noted yet significant influences of economic liberalization on issues related to accountability and justice serve as reminders that globalization's effects on democracy are often to be found in the seams of larger processes.

Economists and other analysts of world trade sometimes call into question the "claims of globalization" by pointing out that 1) trade is clustered around regional trading blocs (for example, NAFTA, MERCOSUR, the European Union, and Japan and East Asia); 2) there are relatively few truly transnational corporations (nationally based multinationals still predominate); and 3) "the internationalization of economic relationships . . . is not in itself proof of the emergence of a distinctly 'global' economic structure" (Hirst and Thompson 1996, 195). These objections miss the mark in relation to the definition of globalization offered earlier, which emphasizes the intensifying compression of the world and the growing collective awareness that such a process is underway. Seen from that point of view, regional trading blocs are clearly an expression of globalization, insofar as they are conscious responses to worldwide economic competition. Even when structures of production and exchange are "international" and not global, the more fundamental point remains that they, nevertheless, operate according to globalized norms and practices that constitute the rules of the game for the modern world economy.

## The Volatility of Capital Flows

Latin American countries are not blessed with high rates of domestic saving. While the Inter-American Development Bank noted in 1997 that ". . .the average rate of saving in Latin American countries other than Brazil rose from a low of 15.3 percent to 18 percent in 1996," the saving rate of prominent East Asian economies (for example, South Korea, Malaysia, Singapore, and Thailand) ranged from 30 percent to 40 percent of gross domestic product (GDP) over the same time frame (IDB 1997, 16). The Secretary-General of the Organization of American States, César Gaviria, was one among many to identify this problem as *the* principal obstacle to economic growth in the region. There are various reasons for the low rate of saving, including lack of small-saver confidence, weak banking systems, large-scale government borrowing, and erratic economic performance (Edwards 1997). Given the urgent need for economic growth in Latin America and the centrality of the rate of investment in achieving it, acquiring additional investment capital has been imperative.

**Table 3.**
**Net Foreign Direct Investment in Latin America[a]**
**(Millions of Dollars)**

| 1991 | 1992 | 1993 | 1994 | 1995 | 1996 | 1997[b] |
|------|------|------|------|------|------|---------|
| 10,679 | 13,228 | 11,386 | 23,603 | 25,174 | 35,386 | 44,021 |

[a]Based on estimates from 19 countries.                    [b]Preliminary figures.

Source: *Preliminary Overview of the Economy of Latin America and the Caribbean 1997,* ECLAC, 57.

Table 3 shows that the restructured Latin American economies have been successful in attracting steadily increasing foreign direct investment (FDI) in the 1990s. From 1991 to 1997, FDI more than quadrupled from just under $11 billion to slightly over $44 billion. In the early 1990s, however, as global capital and repatriated flight capital surged into "emerging market" funds, there was a sharp increase in portfolio investments, particularly in Mexico, Brazil, and Argentina. Over the period 1990 to 1994, this amounted to $50 billion of equity capital and $43 billion in bond issues.[12] About half of this money went into Mexico in the form of short-term investments. With a seriously overvalued exchange rate, a very large current account deficit, a lax monetary policy, and a year's worth of cumulative, back-to-back political crises (the guerrilla uprising in Chiapas, the assassination of presidential candidate Luis Donaldo Colosio, and the killing of José Francisco Ruiz Massieu, secretary-general of the ruling political party), the ground gave way in December 1994 beneath the new government of President Ernesto Zedillo. Investors withdrew their money en masse, and a radical devaluation of the peso (65 percent in five weeks) ensued. After the inevitable austerity package that followed, Mexican citizens faced a massive drop in real wages.

The collapse of the Mexican peso sent shock waves throughout world capital markets via the so-called "tequila effect," exerting severe pressures on other Latin American countries (most notably Argentina) and impacting countries as far away as Thailand. In the fall of 1997, the process was reversed, as financial crises and currency devaluations in Thailand, South Korea, and Indonesia produced havoc in capital markets, sending reverberations of the "Asian flu" back to Latin America. Brazil, in response to a speculative attack on the *real* in November 1997, was forced to double interest rates to 43 percent. To reduce the public sector deficit and maintain investor confidence (and to the consternation of unions and some business sectors), the Fernando Henrique Cardoso government followed shortly thereafter with an $18 billion package of spending cuts, civil servant layoffs, and tax increases.[13] These episodes have raised serious questions about the globalization of finance and its relationship to and effects on democracy. Now that severe financial problems and massive devaluations have hit both Latin America and East Asia, with huge financial bailouts for Mexico and then South Korea, even investment bankers and money managers have become alarmed at the bandwagon effects of electronically connected global capital markets (Uchitelle 1997). The challenge to national policymakers is double: not only must they hold macroeconomic variables, current account balances, and exchange rates within the parameters of conventional wisdom, they also must be attuned to the perceptions of fund managers who may see real or imagined affinities between geographically distant and politically distinct national situations (Krugman 1997).

For the Latin American democracies, the constraints imposed by the need to maintain an attractive investment climate — which in turn depends on the endorsement of economic policies by the major international financial institutions — are substantial. It appears that the window of opportunity for progressive social policies in Latin America, which some saw opening with the end of Cold War geopolitics, has turned out in the new era of geoeconomics to be quite a narrow aperture. The potential decoupling of the relationship of legitimacy and consent existing between democratic leaders and citizens by virtue of policy vetoes or sanctions imposed by global financial markets hovers like a dark cloud over the democratic process. This is not to say that there are not better and worse ways for governments to manage and monitor capital flows. For example, at the time of the Mexican peso crash, Chile was protected from the tequila effect by a law requiring equity capital to stay in the country for at least one year. Yet, while such policies may work well when foreign exchange reserves are high and a nation's investment possibilities are seen as attractive, they may at other times deter badly needed capital inflows. Ultimately, sound domestic financial systems with strong supervisory and regulatory regimes are required — and even these may not preclude periodic crashes.[14]

Whereas economic growth and investment were directly tied to the production of goods and services in the past, the rise of securitization through stock and bond issues shifts the focus to "wealth creation." As John C. Edmunds (1996, 118) puts it, this "new approach requires that a state find ways to increase the *market value* of its stock of productive assets" (italics in original). Moreover, "The world financial market feeds on rumors, sound bites, and video clips," and "[i]t is essential that investors have a positive image of a country" (Edmunds 1996, 131-132). In the Mexican case, of course, these very forces produced perverse effects, as the fear of losing the country's "positive image" held back policymakers from undertaking necessary economic reforms. Thus, government officials are placed in the sometimes untenable position of trying to project an "everything's fine" image abroad, simultaneously demonstrating to their citizens an appreciation of the seriousness of socioeconomic problems at home. This very real conundrum places strains upon the political credibility of leaders and erodes the coherence of the democratic process.

## Inequality

The global economy is marked by increased inequality not only in Latin America but also in countries such as Russia, France, Italy, Japan, Holland, Sweden, the United Kingdom, and the United States (United Nations 1994, 31). In fact, while inequality is nothing new in the Americas, the absolute increase in the poor populations of Latin America took off on an accelerating trajectory in the 1980s. Samuel Morley found that "...between 1980 and 1989 there was an increase of almost 40 million in the number of Latin Americans living on less than $2 per day" (1995, 189). Victor Bulmer-Thomas (1996, 10-13) refers to the principal characteristics of the recent economic reforms in Latin America as the region's "New Economic Model" (NEM); however, in its main features the model is not merely regional but global. In relation to Latin America, data ". . .show quite clearly that the NEM is not a sufficient condition for the reduction in poverty and an improvement in income distribution. . . . [T]here are cases where equity is in fact made much worse" (Bulmer-Thomas 1996, 308). Reviewing recent data from a dozen Latin American countries, Nora Lustig (1998, 1) found declines in poverty in more than half the countries, but "In more than half the episodes, the trends in the distribution of income were neutral (that is, there was no change) or countered the positive impact of growth on poverty reduction (that is, income became more concentrated)."

It should be noted, however, that despite the fact that poverty and inequality are logical starting points for any discussion of problems of governance in Latin America, their exact meaning in terms of political outcomes is often elusive. As long as citizens express their dissatisfaction with poor economic performance by simply voting particular governments out of office, the political tremors are minor. Perhaps of more concern is the potential for social outbursts of the sort seen in Chiapas, Mexico; Santiago del Estero, Argentina; or among the landless in Brazil. Other possibilities include the ascent to power of charismatic political figures from the left or right who promise strong actions to relieve socioeconomic suffering quickly. The tracing of citizens' expectations along the spectrum from a sense of hopelessness to an indignant or even explosive sense of "relative deprivation" is difficult, and such subjective responses are inscribed within a constellation of other contextual variables. However, in their subterranean, political unpredictability, the problems of persistent poverty and inequality fit well the image of a "fault line" for Latin American democracies.

Of course, it has often been observed that socioeconomic polarization produces less than optimum democratic outcomes, and this has been historically the case in Latin America. Clearly, market relations are also power relations, and those who are powerful in the market fare better than those who are weak or completely sidelined from participation in it. As David Held cogently puts it, "If the rule of law does not involve a central concern with distributional questions and matters of social justice, it cannot be satisfactorily entrenched, and the principle of autonomy and democratic accountability cannot be realized adequately" (1995, 248). Moreover, widening social divides may place in peril the sorts of tenuous "class compromises" described as pivotal in much of the literature on democratization (cf. Rueschemeyer, Stephens, and Stephens 1992). The essential point here is not that globalization has caused socioeconomic disparities in the Americas, but simply that recent evidence indicates that those disparities are apt to persist even as globalization deepens, bringing in tow all of the negative effects that they entail.

## Competition

How can we then summarize the main characteristics of the global economy and the demands they place upon the Latin American democracies? Jeffrey Sachs, who has been a well-placed "participant-observer" in the economic policy reform process in a number of Latin American countries and elsewhere, proposes six main characteristics of contemporary globalization: 1) open international trade; 2) currency convertibility; 3) private ownership as the main engine of economic growth; 4) corporate ownership as the dominant organizational form for large enterprises; 5) openness to foreign investment; and 6) membership in key international economic institutions, including the International Monetary Fund, World Bank, and World Trade Organization (Sachs 1995, 51).

By these standards, Latin America has been on a path of deepening immersion in the process of economic globalization.[15] In the early 1990s, the standards for Latin America's effective participation in the world economy were posed in quite formulaic terms, such as the "ten commandments" of the Washington Consensus, which elaborated a series of market-based reforms.[16] Overall, the environment produced by the globalization of market forces acted to reshape countries into "competition states" (Cerny 1996), a description echoed in endless discussions of international competitiveness in Latin America and elsewhere. However, in Latin America, the scope of the restructuring process of the late 1980s and early 1990s reduced state capacities to levels that may inhibit future competitiveness and growth (O'Donnell 1994).

By the mid-1990s, it was becoming increasingly clear that the region's market reforms demanded in many ways stronger (and more democratic) states, for post-liberalization economies require clear regulatory frameworks, widely shared market information, confidence in the rule of law, and institutional monitoring and accountability. A "new paradigm of systemic competitiveness" for Latin America was emerging (Bradford 1994), and the elements of this paradigm entailed the redefinition and reprovisioning of the state. In brief, this vision of competitiveness sketches out an ambitious strategy linking knowledge-intensive inputs, organizational innovations, educational support, and social programs.[17] Furthermore, according to Colin I. Bradford, Jr.:

> The new paradigm is systemic because it incorporates new understandings about the microeconomic foundations of competitiveness, based on a different theory of production which is consistent with a new concept of innovation processes. This notion of innovation in turn meshes with a rebalancing of macroeconomic and trade policy to emphasize real-side variables such as investment, employment, output growth, production for export, and productivity change. These are consistent with a redefined state capable of supporting initiative, innovation, and investment in the private sector by providing a strategic framework for investment decisions, channels for interaction between the public and private sectors, and supportive policies for economic growth (1994, 58).

By the end of the 1990s, the need for such a set of "second generation reforms" (or variants thereof) reached the level of conventional wisdom, echoed in government ministries and international financial institutions (Bresser Pereira 1997; Stiglitz 1998).

However, accepting the reasonableness of and even necessity for such an approach in today's world economy, fundamental questions arise about how one gets "there" from "here" as a matter of policy. First, the creation of such a redefined state is a daunting prospect certain to require sizable revenues, not simply as a means to stock market-friendly bureaucracies with reasonably compensated employees but also in support of education and training initiatives. The starting point for the scale of the proposed transition is reflected in Table 4. At the outset of the decade of the 1990s, the existing base of research and development as a share of gross national product (GNP) in Latin America and the Caribbean was far behind that of Asian competitors and not all that dissimilar from that of African countries.

**Table 4.**
**Forging Ahead and Falling Behind in the New Competition:**
**Research and Development as a Share of Gross National Product**
**1970, 1980, and 1990**

| REGION | 1970 | 1980 | 1990 |
|---|---|---|---|
| World | 2.04 | 1.85 | 2.55 |
| Developed Countries | 2.36 | 2.22 | 2.93 |
| Europe | 1.70 | 1.81 | 2.21 |
| North America | 2.59 | 2.23 | 3.16 |
| Developing Countries | 0.32 | 0.52 | 0.64 |
| Africa | 0.33 | 0.30 | 0.29 |
| South, East, and Southeast Asia | 1.02 | 1.14 | 2.08 |
| Western Asia | 0.31 | 0.97 | 0.76 |
| **Latin America and the Caribbean** | **0.30** | **0.44** | **0.40** |

Source: Adapted from *World Investment Report 1994: Transnational Corporations, Employment and the Workplace,* 157.

A recent task force on "Education, Equity, and Economic Competitiveness in Latin America and the Caribbean," organized by the Partnership for Educational Revitalization in the Americas (PREAL 1998, 6), concluded that, in terms of education, Latin America's labor force "appears to be steadily falling further behind" its Asian competitors. Teaching is poor, investment in primary and secondary education is too low (nearly one-third of primary school students repeat whatever grade they are in), and schools lack authority and accountability. The task force further concluded, "Good public education cannot be provided at the present levels of expenditure" (PREAL 1998, 19).[18] Recalling the evidence presented earlier (Table 1), which showed that the overwhelming majority of unemployed people fall into the 15 to 34 age bracket, it appears that second generation reforms to boost competitiveness — or at least to improve education and training — have to be undertaken with some rapidity, or democratic governments will face large numbers of youthful citizens with few prospects for betterment. In the meantime, as can be seen in the 1998 world competitiveness rankings of 53 countries, issued by the World Economic Forum (Table 5), Latin American nations (with the exception of Chile) still score poorly when their competitiveness is compared with that of other countries.

**Table 5.**
**World Competitiveness Ranking, 1998**

| Country | 1998 rank | Country | 1998 rank |
| --- | --- | --- | --- |
| Singapore | 1 | **Peru** | **37** |
| Hong Kong | 2 | South Africa | 42 |
| United States | 3 | **Venezuela** | **45** |
| **Chile** | **18** | **Brazil** | **46** |
| China | 28 | **Colombia** | **47** |
| **Mexico** | **32** | Ukraine | 53 |
| **Argentina** | **36** | | |

Source: World Economic Forum, *Global Competitiveness Report, 1998,* cited in *Business Latin America,* June 22, 1998.

Both the well-known high levels of unemployment and underemployment in the wake of restructuring (open unemployment was over 10 percent in 10 countries in the mid-1990s) and the weakened and disorganized condition of labor unions are of concern for Latin American democracies, especially given the historically important role of unions as mechanisms of political representation.[19] Adding to the instability and uncertainty of the current labor scenario are qualitative changes, varying over national and subnational settings, that have affected the structure and composition of sectors in the labor market, increasing the proportion of precarious and informal employment, altering the territorial distribution of employment, and shifting upward the substance and scope of women's participation in the formal and informal labor force (Tardanico 1995). Cumulatively, these shifts have acted to disarticulate previously existing networks of political representation, with still uncertain effects on democratic performance.

The creation of the resources and institutions that are necessary for the jump from stabilization to sustained growth poses serious difficulties for Latin American nations. With a narrowing of potential policy choices, large-scale social transformations, and scarce resources, the region's democratic leaders face huge challenges in navigating the world economy. For these reasons and because those on the left of the political spectrum appear to lack a compelling post-Cold War alternative political discourse, serious discussions of redistributionist schemes are rare.[20] The principal anti-poverty programs of the region, such as those in Chile and Mexico, have addressed problems of poverty in modest increments. Even those most concerned with Latin America's socioeconomic inequalities appear to have lowered their sights. For example, Mexican political scientist Jorge G. Castañeda has speculated, albeit unenthusiastically, that it may be enough to shift the extreme poor into the next-higher category — just poor, period — ". . .in order for the virtuous cycle of democracy and justice to be set in motion" (Castañeda 1995, 235). Even reaching this goal would be a significant accomplishment for most Latin American countries.

## COMMUNICATIONS

Very much linked to the world economy as both cause and consequence are accelerating technological changes in electronic media, transportation, and communication networks. The profusion of these changes has resulted in the unprecedented circulation of news, norms, beliefs, images, persons, and ideas. Although there is great diversity in terms of the intensity with which such messages and projections are distributed among various regions, provinces, communities, and groups in Latin America, they are now more or less ubiquitous. In the global context of commerce, many informational and symbolic exchanges, even those ostensibly for other purposes, are forms of mass advertising. Jean Baudrillard (1981), characteristically mixing hyperbole with insight, has suggested that capitalism is now less oriented toward the production of material commodities than the production of signs and images. In the intensely urban settings of many Latin American metropolises, where mass culture flourishes in myriad forms, there is resonance to this assertion.

The globalization of communications and information not only produces effects compressing space and time; it also alters somewhat the relationship between state and citizen. First of all, while hardly powerless, the state cannot effectively control the range or content of the cognitive universes of citizens. Normative assertions, implicit or explicit criticisms, or simply other ways of life filter into the mental life of the nation in innumerable ways. Second, the net effect of this input — good, bad, or indifferent — is to produce citizens with expanded terms of reference, who are able to envision more complex scenarios in relation to their lives (Rosenau 1990). (See Table 6 for a schematic representation of such changes.) Whether this is invariably a positive development for social well-being or democratic governance is unlikely, but it seems probable that over time it works to engender a better understanding of, and perhaps tolerance for, a plurality of viewpoints. Third, the diffusion of pictures and stories of other ways and other lives may also weaken traditional territorial identities and lead to a somewhat different affective geography. It bears repeating, however, that the creation of new intersubjective realms under the force of globalization is ultimately a local and indeterminate process that can just as easily lead to resistance and the construction of intensely parochial identities as to universal values and cosmopolitan solidarities (Scholte 1995). The fast-growing evangelical Christian movements in Latin America in some ways represent attempts to ward off the destabilizing cultural and social effects produced by late-modern capitalism. The communications and information revolution serves to fashion and refashion citizens' perspectives in diverse ways that tend to expand the political agendas and challenge the "carrying capacity" of democratic institutions. With overt forms of coercion generally now seen as outside the realm of acceptable political practices, power accrues to those able to make effective use of the media and crafted images. Thus, the calculated framing of political issues and their discourse take on heightened importance in the democratic process.

**Table 6.**
**Changes in Analytical Aptitudes and Attitudes Under Globalization**

| Attribute | From | Toward |
|---|---|---|
| Learning | Habitual | Adaptive |
| Cognitive maps | Less complex | More complex |
| Role scenarios | Brief | Elaborate |
| Empathetic dispositions | Dormant | Active |
| Compliance orientations | Accepting | Questioning |
| Legitimacy sentiments | Traditional criteria | Performance criteria |
| Political loyalties | Focused on nation-state | Variable foci |

Source: Modified from James N. Rosenau, 1990, *Turbulence in World Politics: A Theory of Change and Continuity* (Princeton, N.J.: Princeton University Press), 211.

Political scientists have studied for some time the use of focus groups, strategic polling, and media consultants during the course of political campaigns, a set of practices originating in the United States but now common to most countries of the Western Hemisphere. However, as messages and viewpoints broadcast via the electronic media proliferate, elected officials increasingly struggle to perpetuate stable images that serve to uphold their aura of legitimacy and power. Here, globalization makes more acute a central problem of politics perhaps best described by Clifford Geertz:

> At the political center of any complexly organized society . . . there is both a governing elite and a set of symbolic forms expressing the fact that it is in truth governing. No matter how democratically the members of the elite are chosen . . . or how deeply divided among themselves they may be . . . they justify their existence and order their actions in terms of a collection of stories, ceremonies, insignia, formalities, and appurtenances that they either inherited or, in more revolutionary situations, invented. It is these — crowns and coronations, limousines and conferences — that mark the center as center and give what goes on there its aura of being not merely important but in some odd fashion connected with the way the world is built (1983, 124).

The growing multivocality of the media in many Latin American countries, as well as the bright spotlight brought to bear upon the peccadilloes, dissimulations, and corrupt presidential practices of Fernando Collor and Carlos Andrés Pérez, Ernesto Samper and Carlos Menem, Carlos Salinas and Alberto Fujimori, have not only tarnished, albeit deservedly, such auras but may have contributed at times to levels of voter disbelief and cynicism that constitute a serious problem for democratic governance. Moreover, with political life unfolding in "real time," and both the media and elected officials hypersensitive to the projection of images and symbols of power, democratic politics edge toward becoming a self-referential shadow play whose patent (and often perceived) lack of authenticity may further alienate electorates.

Yet, studies of the impact of television coverage on recent presidential elections in Argentina, Brazil, Chile, and Mexico have found that — despite the frequently disproportionate control of the medium by specific commercial interests or the state — television provided important and useful information that helped voters in making their choices (Skidmore 1993). Whether and in what ways television affects democratic practices positively or negatively is a crucial question because television reaches vast audiences and absorbs a high percentage of leisure time. For example, in Brazil, the market research firm Marplan found in 1992 that 77 percent of the population watches television "habitually," and daily household viewing exceeds five hours (Straubhaar 1996).

In Robert Putnam's influential discussion of democracy and deficiencies in social capital (that is, the networks, norms, and trust that help people work cooperatively) in the United States, he identifies the main culprit as probably television. "The technological transformation of leisure" (read "television") is said to be "privatizing" the use of leisure time and making what citizens experience as communities "wider and shallower," as well as contributing to political passivity (Putnam 1995a). A large body of literature, according to Putnam, "suggests that heavy watchers of TV are unusually skeptical about the benevolence of other people — overestimating crime rates, for example." He further quotes Ithiel de Sola Pool to the effect that the communications revolution "will promote individualism and will make it harder, not easier, to govern and organize a coherent society" (Putnam 1995b, 679-680). While some dispute these claims (for example, Norris 1996), television is the cultural medium par excellence in the present phase of globalization — it collapses one's experiences of time and space, provides the simulacra of real experiences, relies upon a vast but generally thin cultural repertoire, and, commodity itself, contributes to the commodification of its content. Television is clearly a powerful instrument of political intermediation in modern Latin America, and its effects on political participation and citizens' attitudes need to be better understood.

## CONSUMERISM

Communications, the media, and consumer culture are entwined in complex ways. News, entertainment, sales, and marketing overlap and sometimes exist in hybrid forms. The centrality of consumerism — capitalism's leading edge — to globalization and the effects of global consumerism on the socialization of wants have been subjects of attention in sociological literature (Sklair 1995). These wants find their way in some fashion into the political arena, although their impact and meaning are not obvious.

In the context of globalization, there are two fundamental aspects of consumer culture. First, one of the underlying dynamics of globalization is the "production" of wants through the ubiquitous framing and display of goods, linked to a view of consumption that equates "more" or different with "better." Notably, Argentina, Brazil, and Mexico are among the top 20 advertising markets in the world (Sklair

1995, 167). Second, the range and rapid turnover of choices, fads, and fashions pose the possibility of the adoption of changing ways of life and views of the self. These characteristics lend to consumer culture its protean qualities. According to Terry Eagleton, "The logic of the market-place is one of pleasure and plurality, of the ephemeral and discontinuous, of a great decentered network of desires of which individual consumers are the passing functions" (Eagleton 1994). In Latin America, even the poor can and do participate in this marketplace in the sense that much of it is manifested through publicly shared signs and symbols. In the informal sector, a common practice is the cheap production of ersatz versions of popular, mass-market articles and celebrity or famous-maker goods.

Increasingly, it is culture itself (understood as a shared set of symbols and meanings) that is consumed. But the interplay of "local" and "foreign" brings to the Latin American context influences that tend to destabilize identities as well as fracture and reconstitute communities. As José Joaquín Brunner puts it:

> . . .our identities no longer appear as such but rather as sectors of the international market, especially in the area of culture. There subsist infinite local cultural exchanges that form the framework of our daily life, that mass of more or less direct interactions in which customs, use values, images, and beliefs accumulate. But through and above this framework — can we still call it national? — flow and are articulated messages and institutions and circuits fully incorporated into a modernity whose heart is far from the heart of "our" culture (Beverly et al. 1995, 40-41).

As consumerism leads to changes in citizens' perspectives on individual well-being, it brings with it assumptions and expectations that have direct or indirect political consequences. Further, within consumer culture is a process of commodification that can turn not only material products but ideas and people into commodities. Some worry about the effects of this on the quality of democratic life in the sense that "citizenship . . . tends to be confused with consumerism" (Kaldor 1995, 80). That is to say, candidates for office and their public statements are perceived in the same way as are product choices. This is not far off Joseph Schumpeter's parsimonious "democratic method . . . in which individuals acquire the power to decide by means of a competitive struggle for the people's vote" or his assertion that "the role of the people is to produce a government" ([1942] 1976, 269). This strictly procedural, consumerist approach to democracy, with its distancing effects between citizens and representatives, echoes fairly closely the divide between state and civil society so often condemned in contemporary Latin America. In addition, consumer-style voting in the context of high-tech political advertising pushes citizens toward making judgments on the basis of criteria other than substantive political considerations.

Similarly disconcerting is the possibility that, as consumerism increasingly transforms the "citizen" into *homo economicus*, "market civilization" is, in effect, enveloping and smothering the minimum notion of the public good requisite to the maintenance of healthy democracies. If one compares the "great decentered network of desires" embodied in consumer culture with the anemic, embattled, and much criticized state that is the legacy of years of restructuring in Latin America, the relative appeal of each is clear. In this sense, the rehabilitation of the state and the strengthening of democratic participation may require salesmanship as well as political vision.

# NEW POLITICAL CULTURES

In the reordering of socioeconomic life produced by global imperatives for macroeconomic adjustment and market liberalization, in the far-reaching effects of transnational media images and ideas, and in the ever-changing displays of consumer culture and the marketplace, individuals encounter an intricate mix of opportunities and constraints. Attached to these possibilities are socially established meanings and potentially new forms of self-understanding. Within this field of possibilities, identities are expressed or modified in ways that interact with and are influenced by prevailing political practices. In contemporary Latin America, existing political institutions and parties often have been inadequate for the representation of citizens' concerns, especially those related to new issues or the "politics of identity." In these instances, new social movements and other associations and non-governmental organizations (some transnational and some not) have increasingly filled the void.

In Latin America, these movements, associations, or simply gatherings are remarkably diverse and may be "political" in a conventional sense because they engage institutions and public authorities with specific demands, or they may be forging survival strategies in relation to daily life, or they may alternatively be pursuing "democratic spaces for more autonomous action" in relation to self and identity (Escobar and Alvarez 1992). At times, they may have substantive or symbolic linkages with other groups that transcend national boundaries, especially in the cases of movements dealing with environmental issues, indigenous peoples, and feminism. To understand such movements often is as much a hermeneutical undertaking as it is a simple matter of the framing of groups' interlocution or lack thereof with political systems. Yet, their local concerns, elusive qualities, and eclectic agendas are often linked in mediated ways with the larger forces of globalization.

Concerns that were previously "private" — especially those having to do with matters of identity — now enter the public realm of politics. The proliferation of items on the political agenda during a time of weak political representation and institutionalization in Latin America reinforces the search for new sites of political practice above and below the state (international organizations, community groups, NGOs). With the significant strengthening of civil societies across Latin America over the past 20 years and the diminution of resources available to governments, the question of how to produce effective dialogue and cooperation between non-governmental organizations (often with international linkages or support) and governments has become central to the deepening and performance of democracy. However, despite pledges by heads of state and a growing consensus among international organizations and multilateral lending institutions in support of government-NGO consultation and collaboration, rhetoric has so far exceeded reality. In actual practice, Latin American government officials often raise questions about the legitimacy and accountability of NGOs, thereby marginalizing them. In somewhat similar fashion, political parties in Latin America have frequently failed to accommodate the participation of grassroots popular organizations. Nonetheless, continuing international support for non-governmental organizations can be expected to help chip away at such bottlenecks in the democratic process.

The socioeconomic and sociocultural dislocations produced by globalization, however, not only spark constructive and new democratic departures but also contribute to destructive social energies. Throughout the hemisphere, crime, violence, and social pathologies are at high levels. Politicians and editorialists periodically sound the alarm for a return to the values of a world that no longer exists. Calls for strong action and — in some countries such as Brazil and El Salvador — still unclear divisions of labor between the police and the military threaten to open a serious fault line for democracy. Further complicating matters are the sporadic interventions of vigilante groups, off-duty police, and private security firms, all of whom contribute to the ad hoc "privatization" of justice. As a matter of urban geography, the climate of insecurity is made manifest by the spatial segregation of rich and poor, with the former inhabiting walled, often guarded enclaves and the latter shantytowns. Bringing together a diverse blend of social classes and foreign and local influences, public spaces form ambivalent "interstitial zones of transition," as in the description of Brazilian anthropologist Antonio Arantes:

> In São Paulo's Cathedral Square, the violation of the civil rights of the great majority of the city's population is publicly demonstrated by the high incidence of robbery, drug dealing and open consumption of marijuana and glue, the construction of 'invisible' houses, along with a general underemployment, begging and the pedlars of the illusion of a better life through lotteries, magic medicines and religious preaching. At the same time, several political and humanitarian institutions bring to this scenario their words and rituals of salvation (1996, 82).

Globalization both marginalizes and empowers. As a sometimes destructive and threatening economic and cultural force, it provokes resistance and elicits attempts to construct lives based on "localization"; as a cosmopolitan market of ideas, it offers a multitude of potential paths to social, political, or personal emancipation. Several well-known social scientists and commentators have tried various ways of scooping up and encapsulating the dynamics of globalization — for example, Immanuel Wallerstein's (1991) never quite stable "geoculture," Samuel Huntington's (1993) "clash of civilizations" between "the West and the rest," and Peter Drucker's (1994) knowledge-intensive and organization-based "age of social transformation." All of these analyses, whatever their merits or shortcomings, indicate that major shifts are going on, and these interrelated transformations are of a scope difficult to encompass through any one analytic approach.

The constant, rapid, intersubjective shifts that today are creating and eliminating social actors in Latin America mean that we need to know much more not just about "who governs?" but also about "who is being governed?" In emphasizing the "governance" dimension of democratic governance, we need to keep in mind that "governance . . . is a more encompassing phenomenon than government. . . . Governance is thus a system of rule that is as dependent on intersubjective meanings as on formally sanctioned constitutions and charters" (Rosenau 1992, 4). By focusing on the intersubjective basis of democratic governance, one is better positioned to grasp the sociopolitical effects of globalization. After nearly two decades of comprehensive economic and political restructuring processes in the Americas, research is badly needed on the cognitive universes of citizens and the "intersubjective underpinnings" of the region's democracies.

## CONCLUSION

In this chapter, I have sketched out one account of the effects of globalization on democracy in Latin America. Somewhat fragmented in its scholarly treatment to date, the concept of globalization remains more multidisciplinary than interdisciplinary. Substantial advances in integrated approaches to globalization — especially those synthesizing international political economy and sociology — will be required to make globalization the "new paradigm of the social sciences" some wish it to be (Ianni 1994). Nevertheless, it is an intellectual enterprise worth undertaking, as no other single approach holds as much promise for examining and understanding in mutual relation the global economic, political, and social influences that interact with state and society in Latin America and elsewhere. These influences produce a complex, shifting matrix that is interwoven with national realities and the prospects for democratic practices.

The competitive demands of the world economy weigh particularly heavily upon Latin American democracies. To date, the results of economic reform are quite mixed, with improved macroeconomic performance, uneven spurts of growth, and greatly expanded levels of trade, but also still intractable levels of poverty and inequality, new forms of corruption, and high levels of unemployment and under-employment. At the same time, the dynamics and vagaries of international capital markets have increased the "structural power" of capital, thereby narrowing the parameters of domestic policy options. The Latin American democracies here face a paradox: Although there is a growing international consensus among government officials and multilateral financial institutions that there needs to be a rethinking of the state's capacity to invest in human resources and regulatory capacity in order to ameliorate socioeconomic inequalities that represent a drag on democratic participation and accountability, some of the forces of globalization call into question the very possibility of being able to implement such reforms. Expressed in another way, the discussion offered in this chapter lends support to the claim that "there is a new disjuncture between institutional capacity to provide public goods and the structural characteristics of a much larger-scale, global economy" (Cerny 1995, 598). This disjuncture represents a key area for future research.

That being said, it remains just as important not to lose sight of the fact that careful research is also needed on the democratic *opportunities* contained within related phenomena of globalization, especially with respect to international standards of transparency and accountability in business and finance, judicial strengthening and legal reforms, equitable labor practices, enhanced environmental protection, and the deepening of civil society participation. The international commitments and negotiations initiated and reaffirmed by the 1994 and 1998 hemispheric summits in Miami and Santiago — accords inscribed within other networks of global commitments undertaken by the nations of the region — represent an opportunity for the monitoring and analysis of issues crucial to democratic governance. Fundamentally, such reforms are about developing the political institutions needed to cope and interact productively with the emerging global economy, while assuring civil society participation in a democratic process. In the clear absence of any compelling alternative political discourse to pose a fundamental challenge to the tenets of the present phase of (hoped-for) second generation reforms in Latin America, this sort of "post-neoliberal reform-monger-ing" may be among the most realistic and effective paths to improved democratic performance.

Chief among the effects of globalization on the Latin American democracies is the reconfiguration of the state. This goes far beyond fiscal austerity and shrinking the size of the state. The new competitive, global environment requires the organization and coordination of diverse public and private actors in support of efforts to make the state work effectively with the market. Formal and informal networks of national and municipal government agencies, business organizations, universities, research institutes, trade unions, export associations, and non-govern-mental organizations must be cultivated and maintained in order to maximize economic performance and assure social participation (Lechner 1997). As a practical matter, this also requires new, more effective channels of communication to provide access to information. Additionally, the withdrawal of the state from the production of goods and services for the market and the logic of the "new public administration" being implemented in the region are likely to lead to decentraliza-tion, outsourcing, and competitive bidding on an unprecedented scale (Bresser Pereira 1997). Taken together, the multiple tasks associated with state reform in Latin America constitute a daunting agenda of intense political coordination and public administration. This will require institution building and legislation designed to create and maintain the conditions for impartial regulatory oversight, transparent transactions, and public and private accountability. At present, in most of Latin America's democracies, these conditions are very far from being in place.

In the meantime, globalizing trends in communications, consumerism, and new political cultures will continue to alter the intersubjective domains of Latin American societies. It can be expected that for the foreseeable future these trends will tend to strengthen civil society, constructively expanding the political agenda but making more difficult distinctions between the public and private as well as between the political and the nonpolitical. In a similar vein, addressing issues of gender and ethnicity will require new understandings of how to reconcile diversity and common purpose. To understand the effects of these developments on democ-racy in the hemisphere, students of Latin American comparative politics will need not only to continue to explore international political economy but also to venture into what might be called "international political culture."

The phenomena of globalization bring a contradictory amalgam of democra-tizing and de-democratizing forces. While I have identified a number of the most important of these forces and their general effects, how they play out in the democratic life of Latin American countries is highly indeterminate. I have sought to emphasize that such forces cannot be ignored, but they remain subject to the deep variability brought about by specific national histories, distinctive political cultures, diverse institutional arrangements, and actual policy choices. Thus, a final and indispensable area of research is the systematic study of how individual Latin American democracies respond and adapt to globalization.

# Notes

I am grateful for the comments and suggestions of Ralph Pettman, Felipe Agüero, and Max Castro on an earlier version of this chapter.

1. This general trend, of course, has its exceptions. A noteworthy example is Rodrik's (1997) careful and balanced discussion of the tensions between economic globalization and the maintenance of forms of social insurance.

2. For the text of the article, see Nascimento (1996).

3. Early in President Bill Clinton's first term, Richard Feinberg, the Special Assistant to the President for Inter-American Affairs on the U.S. National Security Council, wrote of "substantive symmetry in hemispheric relations" based on "a similar agenda rooted in . . . common participation in the one-world economy," and a need in the United States to rebuild "a sense of community and social inclusion," while "Latin America is turning to its own social agenda" (Feinberg 1994).

4. Touching upon the same point in a slightly different sort of way, Thomas Carothers has noted that "little attention has been given to the surprising and in some ways paradoxical fact that the United States, and to a lesser extent Western Europe, have moved into a particularly active phase of promoting democracy in other countries precisely at a time when the health of their own democratic systems is clouded with doubt." See Carothers (1996).

5. The first sentence is from Robertson, and the second is from Waters. I have modified Waters' by adding the words, "political, economic," and the phrase, "and practices."

6. One noteworthy aspect of the worldwide trading and financial system is that while capital, technology, goods, and services move freely, labor does not.

7. Here, "political culture" is used in the sense given by Lucian W. Pye: "Involving both the ideals and the operating norms of a political system, political culture includes subjective attitudes and sentiments as well as objective symbols and creeds that together govern political behavior and give structure and order to the political process." See Pye (1993, 712-713).

8. Somewhere under the heading of "globalization" there obviously also exists a category having to do with more formal institutions such as the United Nations, the International Monetary Fund, the World Bank, and the World Trade Organization. For the purposes of this essay, which principally focuses on the socioeconomic and sociocultural dimensions of globalization, I have mostly set them aside.

9. Perhaps fittingly, the word "glocalization" finds its etymological roots in the Japanese term *dochakuka*, itself a product of globalization, referring to the Japanese practice of "global localization," in which global sales proceed through micromarketing and the creation of products designed for local markets.

10. Data for poverty in 1990 are from estimates for 19 countries from the Economic Commission for Latin American and the Caribbean (ECLAC) in ECLAC (1994), which

provides a good picture of the conditions at the beginning of the decade. In 1997, using a broader set of figures, ECLAC stated: "In Latin America, the poverty rate declined from 41 percent to 39 percent in the first five years of the 1990s." However, this was not enough "to make any headway in eradicating the structural poverty characteristic of the region." See the news announcement, "Economic Growth in Latin America Has Reduced Poverty But Not Inequality" at <http://www.eclac.cl/english/ news/Cronicaseng/ICC97161.html>.

11. In 1996, Latin America's total trade increased by an additional 10.8 percent. See Bamrud (1997).

12. See "A Survey of Latin American Finance," 1995, *The Economist*, December 9.

13. In combination, the interest rate hike and fiscal reform measures were expected to reduce Brazil's economic growth significantly in 1998. See "Toughing It Out," 1997, *Latin American Economy and Business*, December, 2-3.

14. In the view of economist Lester Thurow, "Sooner or later, most economies experience a crash. Generalized claims that the Asian countries were stupidly or badly run will not adequately explain the crash or predict the future. The relevant question is which governments are going to be good at cleaning up the mess. The big losers will be those without effective governments to do it" (Thurow 1998, 23).

15. In addition to the patterns of expanding trade and investment discussed earlier, Latin American countries have undertaken numerous privatizations over the past decade. Between 1990 and 1996, five Latin American countries (Mexico, Argentina, Brazil, Peru, and Venezuela) totaled over $75 billion in privatizations (*Business Latin America*, May 18, 1998, 8). In July 1998, Brazil realized $19 billion from one privatization auction alone, that of the Telebrás telecommunications group (*Financial Times*, July 30, 1998, 1).

16. These measures include fiscal discipline, the elimination of subsidies to provide money for health and education expenditures, tax reform, market-driven interest rates, market-based exchange rates, trade liberalization, foreign direct investment, privatization, deregulation, and respect for property rights (Williamson 1990). Whatever the exact provenance of these reform recommendations — whether Washington as some say, or from Latin America itself, as others claim — they remain perhaps better understood as rooted "in structural change in technology, production, finance, and beliefs" (Strange 1994, 215), than simply as the policy preferences of the United States and other industrialized countries and international financial institutions.

17. There are, of course, variations in the exact policy mix offered by analysts who emphasize the need to make Latin American economies globally competitive, although the basic measures tend to be similar in broad outline. Interestingly, John Williamson, who was the author who originally dubbed the late 1980s' wave of reforms the "Washington Consensus," is among those who see the need for a rethinking of economic reform in Latin America. Williamson's new "Washington Consensus Revisited" includes policy recommendations for bank supervision, independent central banks, strong budget offices, and better education. See these points and a short review of new development thinking in Samuel Silva (1996). For Williamson's article, see Williamson (1997).

18. However, one member of the PREAL task force, former Argentine Finance Minister, José María Dagnino Pastore, added in his supplemental comments: "[Education] is becoming more costly over time. But globalization forces efficiency on governments, which limits the expenditures that they can make, and places serious restrictions on social policies. . . . The only question is whether change will come from without, through inadequate

financing, segmentation, and de facto privatization, or from within, through proposals that respond to the demands of globalization" (PREAL 1998, 21).

19. Data on employment can be found in IDB (1997). Also, see Lustig (1998).

20. Yet, Nora Lustig, chief of the Poverty and Inequality Unit at the Inter-American Development Bank, asserts that "growth alone may not be enough . . . at yearly growth rates of 3 percent per capita, it could take close to 50 years to over a century — depending on the country — to completely eradicate poverty as measured by the proportion of individuals living below US$2 per day" (Lustig 1998, 4).

# References

Agüero, Felipe. 1998. "Democracy and Human Rights Since the 1994 Summit of the Americas." Working Paper. *Monitoring the Summit of the Americas Series.* Coral Gables, Fla.: North-South Center at the University of Miami.

Alcorta, Ludovico, and Wilson Peres. 1996. *Sistemas de innovación y especialización tecnológica en América Latina y el Caribe.* Desarrollo Productivo No.33. Santiago: CEPAL.

Arantes, Antonio A. 1996. "The War of Places: Symbolic Boundaries and Liminalities in Urban Space." *Theory, Culture, and Society* 13 (4).

Bamrud, Joachim. 1996. "Uniting Forces: The Integration of the Hemisphere." *Latin Trade* (March): 2A-20A.

Bamrud, Joachim. 1997. "Setting the Agenda: From Miami to Brazil." *Latin Trade* (June): 3A-12A.

Baylis, John, and Steve Smith, eds. 1997. *The Globalization of World Politics.* New York: Oxford University Press.

Beverly, John, Michael Aronna, and José Oviedo, eds. 1995. *The Postmodernism Debate in Latin America.* Durham, N.C.: Duke University Press.

Black, Conrad. 1995. "Canada's Continuing Identity Crisis." *Foreign Affairs* 74 (2).

Boyer, Robert, and Daniel Drache, eds. 1996. *States Against Markets: The Limits of Globalization.* London: Routledge.

Bradford, Jr., Colin I. 1994. *The New Paradigm of Systemic Competitiveness: Toward More Integrated Policies in Latin America.* Paris: OECD.

Bresser Pereira, Luiz Carlos. 1997. "State Reform in the 1990s: Logic and Control Mechanisms." *Cadernos MARE da Reforma do Estado.* Brasília: Ministério da Administração Federal e Reforma do Estado.

Bresser Pereira, Luiz Carlos, José Maria Maravall, and Adam Przeworski, eds. 1993. *Economic Reforms in New Democracies: A Social-Democratic Approach.* New York: Cambridge University Press.

Bulmer-Thomas, Victor, ed. 1996. *The New Economic Model in Latin America and Its Impact on Income Distribution and Poverty.* New York: St. Martin's Press.

Carothers, Thomas. 1996. "Promoting Democracy in a Postmodern World." *Dissent* (Spring): 35-40.

Castañeda, Jorge G. 1995. *The Mexican Shock: Its Meaning for the United States.* New York: New Press, distributed by W.W. Norton.

Cerny, Philip. 1995. "Globalization and the Changing Logic of Collective Action." *International Organization* 49:4 (Autumn).

Cerny, Philip. 1996. "What Next for the State?" In *Globalization: Theory and Practice*, eds. Eleonore Kofman and Gillian Youngs. London: Pinter.

Chalmers, Douglas A., Carlos M. Vilas, Katherine Hite, Scott B. Martin, Kerianne Piester, and Monique Segarra, eds. 1997. *The New Politics of Inequality in Latin America.* New York: Oxford University Press.

DePalma, Anthony. 1998. "Canada Pact Gives a Tribe Self-Rule for the First Time." *The New York Times*, August 5, A1, A10.

Drucker, Peter F. 1994. "The Age of Social Transformation." *The Atlantic Monthly* (November).

Eagleton, Terry. 1994. "Discourse and Discos." *Times Literary Supplement*, July 15.

Economic Commission for Latin America and the Caribbean (ECLAC). 1994. *Social Panorama of Latin America*. Santiago: United Nations.

ECLAC. 1997. *Preliminary Overview of the Economy of Latin America and the Caribbean*. Santiago: United Nations.

Edmunds, John C. 1996. "Securities: The New World Wealth Machine." *Foreign Policy* (104): 118-133.

Edwards, Sebastian. 1997. "Why Are Latin America's Saving Rates So Low?" In *Pathways to Growth: Comparing East Asia and Latin America*, eds. Nancy Birdsall and Frederick Jaspersen. Washington, D.C.: Inter-American Development Bank.

Escobar, Arturo, and Sonia Alvarez, eds. 1992. *The Making of Social Movements in Latin America*. Boulder, Colo.: Westview Press.

Featherstone, Mike, Scott Lash, and Roland Robertson, eds. 1995. *Global Modernities*. London: Sage.

Featherstone, Mike. 1995. *Undoing Culture: Globalization, Postmodernism and Identity*. London: Sage.

Feinberg, Richard. 1994. "Substantive Symmetry in Hemispheric Relations." Remarks delivered to the Latin American Studies Association, Atlanta, March.

Fitzgerald, E. V.K. 1996. "The New Trade Regime, Macroeconomic Behaviour and Income Distribution in Latin America." In *The New Economic Model in Latin America and Its Impact on Income Distribution and Poverty*, ed. Victor Bulmer-Thomas. New York: St. Martin's Press.

Frieden, Jeffry A. 1991. *Debt Development and Democracy: Modern Political Economy and Latin America, 1965-1985*. Princeton, N.J.: Princeton University Press.

Geertz, Clifford. 1983. *Local Knowledge: Further Essays in Interpretive Anthropology*. New York: Basic Books.

Giddens, Anthony. 1990. *The Consequences of Modernity*. Stanford, Calif.: Stanford University Press.

Gill, Stephen. 1995. "Globalization, Market Civilization, and Disciplinary Neoliberalism." *Millennium* 24 (3): 399-423.

Gill, Stephen R., and David Law. 1989. "Global Hegemony and the Structural Power of Capital." *International Studies Quarterly* 33 (4).

Greider, William. 1997. *One World, Ready or Not: The Manic Logic of Global Capitalism*. New York: Simon & Schuster.

Haggard, Stephan, and Robert Kaufman. 1994. "The Challenges of Consolidation." *Journal of Democracy* 5 (4).

Hirst, Paul, and Grahame Thompson. 1996. *Globalization in Question*. Cambridge, U.K.: Polity Press.

Huntington, Samuel P. 1993. "The Clash of Civilizations?" *Foreign Affairs* 72 (3).

Ianni, Octávio. 1994. "Globalização: Novo paradigma das ciências sociais." *Estudos Avançados* 8 (21).

Inter-American Development Bank (IDB). 1997. *Latin America After a Decade of Reforms: Economic and Social Progress 1997 Report*. Washington, D.C.: Inter-American Development Bank.

Jameson, Fredric, and Masao Miyoshi, eds. 1998. *The Cultures of Globalization*. Durham, N.C.: Duke University Press.

Jones, Barry R.J. 1995. *Globalisation and Interdependence in the International Political Economy: Rhetoric and Reality*. London: Pinter.

Kaldor, Mary. 1995. "European Institutions, Nation-States and Nationalism." In *Cosmopolitan Democracy,* eds. Daniele Archibugi and David Held. Cambridge, U.K.: Polity Press.

Kofman, Eleonore, and Gillian Youngs, eds. 1996. *Globalization: Theory and Practice*. London: Pinter.

Krugman, Paul. 1997. "Seven Habits of Highly Defective Investors." *Fortune* (December 29).

Lechner, Norbert. 1997. "Three Forms of Social Coordination." *CEPAL Review* 61 (April).

Lipset, Seymour Martin. 1994. "Democracy in the United States: A Status Report." In *A New Moment in the Americas*, ed. Robert S. Leiken. Coral Gables, Fla.: North-South Center at the University of Miami.

Lustig, Nora. 1998. "Poverty and Inequality in Latin America and the Caribbean: The Challenge Remains in Place." Paper prepared for the Inter-American Dialogue, Sol M. Linowitz Forum.

Manzetti, Luigi. 1994. "Economic Reform and Corruption in Latin America." *North-South Issues* III (1). Coral Gables, Fla.: North-South Center Press at the University of Miami.

Mato, Daniel, Maritza Montero, and Emanuele Amodio. 1996. *América Latina en tiempos de globalización: Procesos culturales y transformaciones sociopolíticas.* Caracas: Centro Regional para la Educación Superior en América Latina y el Caribe (CRESALC).

Mittelman, James H., ed. 1996. *Globalization: Critical Reflections*. Boulder, Colo.: Lynne Rienner Publishers.

Morley, Samuel A. 1995. *Poverty and Inequality in Latin America: The Impact of Adjustment and Recovery in the 1980s*. Baltimore: The Johns Hopkins University Press.

Nascimento Neto, Atenor. 1996. "A roda global." *Veja* (April 3): 80-89.

Nelson, Joan, ed. 1989. *Fragile Coalitions: The Politics of Economic Adjustment*. New Brunswick, N.J.: Transaction Publishers.

Nelson, Joan, Jacek Kochanowicz, Kálmán Mizsei, and Oscar Muñoz. 1994. *Intricate Links: Democratization and Market Reforms in Latin America and Eastern Europe*. New Brunswick, N.J.: Transaction Publishers.

Norris, Pippa. 1996. "Does Television Erode Social Capital? A Reply to Putnam." *PS: Political Science & Politics* XXIX:3 (September): 474-479.

O'Donnell, Guillermo. 1994. "Some Reflections on Redefining the Role of the State." In *Redefining the State in Latin America*, ed. Colin I. Bradford, Jr. Paris: OECD.

Przeworski, Adam. 1991. *Democracy and the Market*. New York: Cambridge University Press.

Putnam, Robert D. 1995a. "Bowling Alone: America's Declining Social Capital." *Journal of Democracy* 6 (1).

Putnam, Robert D. 1995b. "Tuning In, Tuning Out: The Strange Disappearance of Social Capital in America." *PS: Political Science & Politics* XXVIII (4): 664-683.

Pye, Lucian W. 1993. "Political Culture." In *The Oxford Companion to Politics of the World*, ed. Joel Krieger. New York: Oxford University Press, 712-713.

Robertson, Roland. 1992. *Globalization: Social Theory and Global Culture*. London: Sage.

Robertson, Roland. 1995. "Glocalization: Time-Space and Homogeneity-Heterogeneity." In *Global Modernities*, eds. Mike Featherstone, Scott Lash, and Roland Robertson. London: Sage.

Rodrik, Dani. 1997. *Has Globalization Gone Too Far?* Washington, D.C.: Institute for International Economics.

Rosenau, James N. 1990. *Turbulence in World Politics: A Theory of Change and Continuity*. Princeton, N.J.: Princeton University Press.

Rosenau, James N. 1992. "Governance, Order, and Change in World Politics." In *Governance Without Government: Order and Change in World Politics*, eds. James N. Rosenau and Ernst-Otto Czempiel. New York: Cambridge University Press.

Rueschemeyer, Dietrich, Evelyne Huber Stephens, and John D. Stephens, eds. 1992. *Capitalist Development and Democracy*. Chicago: University of Chicago Press.

Saba, Roberto P., and Luigi Manzetti. 1997. "Privatization in Argentina: The Implications for Corruption." *Crime, Law, and Social Change* 25 (4).

Sachs, Jeffrey. 1995. "Consolidating Capitalism." *Foreign Policy* (98).

Sassen, Saskia. 1996. *Losing Control? Sovereignty in an Age of Globalization*. New York: Columbia University Press.

Scherr, S. Jacob, and Robert K. Watson. 1998. "Implementing the Miami Summit of the Americas: Partnerships for Sustainable Development." Working Paper. *Monitoring the Summit of the Americas Series*. Coral Gables, Fla.: North-South Center at the University of Miami.

Scholte, Jan Aart. 1995. "Constructions of Collective Identity in a Time of Globalisation." Paper presented at the International Studies Association Conference, Chicago, February.

Schumpeter, Joseph. [1942] 1976. *Capitalism, Socialism and Democracy*. New York: Harper and Row.

Sikkink, Kathryn. 1996. "The Emergence, Evolution, and Effectiveness of the Latin American Human Rights Network." In *Constructing Democracy: Human Rights, Citizenship, and Society in Latin America*, eds. Elizabeth Jelin and Eric Hershberg. Boulder, Colo.: Westview Press.

Skidmore, Thomas E., ed. 1993. *Television, Politics, and the Transition to Democracy in Latin America*. Baltimore: The Johns Hopkins University Press.

Silva, Samuel. 1996. "Latin America Looks to the 21st Century." *The IDB* (Sept.-Oct.).

Sklair, Leslie. 1995. *Sociology of the Global System*. 2d ed. Baltimore: The Johns Hopkins University Press.

Smith, William C., Carlos H. Acuña, and Eduardo A. Gamarra, eds. 1994a. *Latin American Political Economy in the Age of Neoliberal Reform*. Coral Gables, Fla.: North-South Center at the University of Miami.

Smith, William C., Carlos H. Acuña, and Eduardo A. Gamarra, eds. 1994b. *Democracy, Markets, and Structural Reform in Latin America*. Coral Gables, Fla.: North-South Center at the University of Miami.

Spybey, Tony. 1996. *Globalization and World Society*. Cambridge, U.K.: Polity Press.

Stallings, Barbara, and Robert Kaufman, eds. 1989. *Debt and Democracy in Latin America*. Boulder, Colo.: Westview Press.

Stiglitz, Joseph. 1998. "More Instruments and Broader Goals: Moving Toward the Post-Washington Consensus." The 1998 WIDER Annual Lecture, Helsinki, Finland, January 7.

Strange, Susan. 1994. "Wake up Krasner! The World *Has* Changed." *Review of International Political Economy* 1 (2).

Straubhaar, Joseph D. 1996. "The Electronic Media in Brazil." In *Communication in Latin America: Journalism, Mass Media, and Society*, ed. Richard R. Cole. Wilmington, Del.: Scholarly Resources Inc.

Tardanico, Richard. 1995. "From Crisis to Restructuring: Latin American Development and Urban Labor Markets in World Perspective." Paper presented for XIX PEWS Conference, North-South Center, Miami, April.

Thurow, Lester. 1998. "Asia: The Collapse and the Cure." *The New York Review of Books* (February 5): 22-26.

Uchitelle, Louis. 1997. "A Bad Side of Bailouts: Some Go Unpenalized." *The New York Times*, December 4, C6.

United Nations. 1994. *World Investment Report 1994: Transnational Corporations, Employment and the Workplace*. New York and Geneva: United Nations.

United Nations Development Program (UNDP). 1996. *Human Development Report 1996*. New York: Oxford University Press.

Wallerstein, Immanuel. 1991. *Geopolitics and Geoculture: Essays on the Changing World-System*. New York: Cambridge University Press.

Waters, Malcolm. 1995. *Globalization*. London: Routledge.

Williamson, John, ed. 1990. *Latin American Adjustment: How Much Has Happened?* Washington, D.C.: Institute of International Economics.

Williamson, John. 1997. "The Washington Consensus Revisited." In *Economic and Social Development into the XXI Century*, ed. Louis Emmerij. Washington, D.C.: Inter-American Development Bank.

Wolin, Sheldon S. 1989. *The Presence of the Past*. Baltimore: The Johns Hopkins University Press.

Wood, Adrian. 1994. *North-South Trade, Employment and Inequality: Changing Fortunes in a Skill-Driven World*. London: Clarendon Press.

World Economic Forum. 1998. *Global Competitveness Report*, cited in *Business Latin America*. June 22.

# Part II

## Participation, Representation, Empowerment, and Accountability

# CHAPTER FIVE

# Democracy and Political Representation in Latin America in the 1990s: Pause, Reorganization, or Decline?

## FRANCES HAGOPIAN

For a decade after authoritarian leaders in Brazil, Peru, and the Dominican Republic promised political liberalization and the eventual abdication of power, students of Latin American politics doggedly — even obsessively — researched and pondered nearly every angle of transitions to democracy.[1] What could launch them? What could sustain them before democracy's enemies? How could democracy spread throughout society? Almost as soon as the transitions to democracy in Latin America had safely taken root, however, scholars shifted the focus of their study of democratization in the region to the subject of democratic consolidation, and their main concern became the institutionalization of new democratic regimes. It now appears that the field is undergoing another seismic shift. Beginning in 1994, a call was sounded to focus research about the current state of Latin American democracy on "the capacity of institutions within democratic regimes to govern effectively and accountably in response to the expressed concerns of the electorate,"[2] and scholars accordingly have started to turn their attention away from the question of how fragile democracies can be consolidated to how their governance can be improved.

If the earlier shift was occasioned by the sense that the first stage of democratization had been successfully achieved, the more recent shift is perhaps born of failure or, more accurately, frustration over not being able to find the Holy Grail of what will keep the region's democracies safe from their military and civilian enemies. The shift to "quality of democracy" issues, however, should not be viewed as a strategic retreat into a less worthwhile endeavor. Rather, it is the logical conclusion to the dilemma of how to understand why so many democracies in the region have limped along but still cannot comfortably be declared "consolidated." It also perhaps stems from a recognition that the weaker democracies in the region are less vulnerable to the threat of a military coup than they are to potential corrosion emanating from their own internal weaknesses.

Arguably, the most glaring of these weaknesses to date has been in the area of democratic accountability. Key institutions of democracy that are badly in need of reform lack and are further losing legitimacy (Domínguez and Lowenthal 1994, 4). Citizens in new and established democracies evaluate poorly the quality and performance of democratic institutions, and while the lack of public support for judicial systems, national and subnational legislatures, and the politicians and parties that serve them is understandable in many cases, it is, nonetheless, alarming for the future of democratic governance. In this context, the central question that any single study or broader project should hope to answer about the quality and efficiency of democratic institutions in a particular country or set of countries is to what extent and in what ways they are fulfilling, or failing to fulfill, their mission to represent the political interests of citizens. This chapter does not pretend to answer a question of such immense scope. Its narrower and more realistic ambition is to offer a tentative assessment of the current state of political representation in Latin America today. More specifically, it attempts to sketch out the extent to which citizens are attached either to networks of representation that served them in the past or to new alternatives that may have emerged with redemocratization.

Preliminary indications are that representative institutions in the region are weak. Citizens joining the political arena for the first time since redemocratization are not being successfully incorporated into existing or new networks, and those who were once anchored to networks structured by traditional political parties or state-sponsored labor unions are becoming disjoined from them. Speaking specifically of Chile, with one of Latin America's most firmly entrenched party systems, Manuel Antonio Garretón recently observed, "We are witnessing a process of disarticulation of the classical socio-political matrix without a clear emergence or consolidation of a new one."[3] In countries with weaker party systems, well functioning networks of political representation are even rarer. Based on the results of a political culture survey in Brazil that he directed, José Alvaro Moisés concluded, "The strongest links between citizens and their representative institutions are dissolving or are proving difficult to forge" (Moisés 1993b, 576). Catherine Conaghan has characterized the Ecuadorian party system as populated with "floating politicians and floating voters" (Conaghan 1995, 450-453).

The question raised by these observations and the phenomena underlying them is whether or not the weakness of representation is temporary. If it is, then existing channels of representation should resuscitate themselves quickly (in which case, we might speak of a "pause" in representation). However, if this weakness is not merely ephemeral, then we would want to know whether the decay of existing networks of interest mediation will pave the way for the emergence of new and better forms of representation in the near future (a "reorganization") or whether it is part of a secular trend toward the decline of political representation and the diminished accountability of many democracies in the region.

This chapter, unfortunately, cannot definitively answer this question. On the basis of the scant evidence available, it argues that the networks of political representation that link citizens to political institutions on the whole have decayed since the period of transition to democracy at a faster rate than new alternatives have been organized or existing ones energized. Nevertheless, while the decline in the density and intensity of political representation is generally visible across the region, one "Latin American" answer to this question does not necessarily exist. The "decline" of political representation is more advanced in Ecuador, Brazil, and Peru than it is in Costa Rica and Uruguay. There are, moreover, exceptional cases of resilience and realignment of old networks of political representation (identified in the penultimate section of this chapter). More research is clearly needed to illuminate why these national differences exist, as well as along what lines the reorganization of interests might take place, if at all.

## POLITICAL INSTITUTIONS AND THE TRANSFORMATION OF POLITICAL REPRESENTATION

With redemocratization and the staging of regular elections, students of Latin American politics have refocused their research on political institutions, especially systems of government, executive-legislative relations, and laws governing elections. Concerned over how best to bring about democratic stability, scholars working within the tradition of the "new institutionalism" have identified the structural deficiencies of the region's democracies that led to their breakdowns in the past, and they have sought institutional designs that can improve the effectiveness of democratic institutions and make democracy work better.[4] In particular, they have contended that parliamentary systems of government might prevent democratic breakdowns and that closed list proportional representation can provide badly needed incentives for political parties to become stronger, more disciplined entities that can participate in responsible governance.[5]

The focus of this body of scholarship on political institutions may, however, be inadequate for illuminating either whether democracies are accountable or how the quality of political representation can be improved in the future. If there is reason to be skeptical that the glaring flaws of democratic governance in the region are all due to institutional design,[6] it is even less likely that a decline of public faith in political institutions can be attributed to institutional designs that have not varied.[7] A shift in the research agenda from democratic consolidation to democratic accountability more generally calls into question the adequacy of a strategy of studying political institutions without a serious consideration of the aspirations of citizens and the way in which they engage democratic institutions. The study of political representation today requires a focus on citizen perceptions of political institutions and the linkages among citizens, the intermediate (voluntary and otherwise) organizations in which they associate politically and have their interests mediated before the state, and the formal institutions of government where their interests are translated into policy.

The most obvious intermediate body, and the one from which any discussion of democratic institutions and political representation must begin, is political parties. As Scott Mainwaring and Timothy Scully have recently insisted, following a distinguished tradition,[8] parties are the main agents of political representation and virtually the only actors with access to elected positions in democratic politics. They provide access to government and, by taking positions on key issues rending a society, put order into what would otherwise be a cacophony of dissonant conflicts, reducing the information costs of voting and making it easier for citizens with little time and political information to participate in politics. Parties organize groups and encourage groups to organize (Mainwaring and Scully 1995a, 3-4).

Of course, a complete investigation of political representation cannot be limited to political parties. Other organizations and networks can also represent citizens, as long as these groups eventually engage the formal institutions of political society. During the era of "populist" democracy, labor unions that were organized along corporatist lines to mediate a broad range of interests of their members in a public, political space fulfilled such a role. They differed qualitatively from those organized spontaneously at the workplace to defend the jobs, wages and benefits, and rights of their members to participate in production decisions with employers in the private sector (such unions more often than not do not engage those institutions). Also, voluntary civic associations, organized along residential or ethnic lines, and non-governmental organizations (NGOs), established to inform and influence public policy, might operate as effective mediating agents in new arenas of political representation. Of particular concern should be how and to what degree these associations and organizations are linked to decision-making arenas in the legislative and executive branches of the state, either directly or through political parties.

## THE ELUSIVE STANDARD OF POLITICAL REPRESENTATION

A ny inquiry into political representation requires that a standard be established against which the current condition of representation can be assessed. The immediate problem is that there is no obvious menu of specific, desirable features, organizational forms, or procedures against which political parties and other representative institutions can be measured for their "representativeness," nor is there a single model for how these institutions should represent their constituents accountably. Party representatives, for example, may either frame and widely publicize a program of government meant to appeal to constituents on a group basis or may act as brokers who deliver patronage to their voters. Parties may even behave in radically different ways in different regions of a country or at different levels of the political system.[9] Programmatic parties more often inspire intense party identification in the electorate than do clientelistic ones, but even clientelistic parties such as the Conservatives and Liberals in Colombia and the Blancos and Colorados in Uruguay have structured stable representative networks for decades.

The legitimate debate over which networks of political representation — programmatic or clientelistic political parties, social movements, and NGOs — are the most effective and accountable mediators between citizens and states cannot be resolved here. I proceed on the assumption that there does exist consensus around the notion that parties and other institutions should act on the purpose of advancing the interests of their members and constituents, and not merely on those of their own leaders or the states before which they are commissioned formally or de facto to mediate. Parties and other organizations should also give voice to and be accountable to those they claim to represent. I also concede that some networks or institutions of representation might be more effective for some members of the population than others and that multiple institutions and forms of representation can coexist simultaneously in any body politic.

More often than measuring the efficacy of political representation against an objective standard, however, institutions and networks of political representation here and elsewhere are implicitly or explicitly measured against the standard of the past. In fact, the road toward achieving fair and effective systems of political representation has been bumpy and winding. While elite interests were well served in this century by both corporatist and voluntary associations such as the Federation of Industries of the State of São Paulo (Brazil) and the National Agricultural Society (Chile), popular political representation was long denied. Across Latin America when aspiring citizens finally succeeded in gaining the chance to participate in political life in the aftermath of economic ruin precipitated by the Great Depression, they found their energies and aspirations harnessed politically into vertically organized state- or party-controlled networks. During the postwar era of populist government, corporatist labor unions and political parties more often controlled and co-opted their constituents and members than genuinely represented their interests before the state. The segments of the lower classes who were "included" in the populist bargain could, nonetheless, expect state policies to protect their livelihoods and communities. In exchange for forfeiting their autonomy, they gained recognition for their unions, job security, retirement and health benefits, and generous wage settlements. Others were excluded altogether. Political parties, by and large, mobilized only Spanish- and Portuguese-descended urban males; they neglected to represent women and peasants (except in Mexico), and in many countries, the exclusion of the rural poor also meant that indigenous groups and racial minorities lacked political representation altogether. Oligopolistic parties in Colombia and several other countries hardly competed. In countries where populism did not take root and political systems were more closed, the basis for political representation was even narrower.

Since the wave of redemocratization that has swept the region, male and female citizens of previously underrepresented classes, regions, and ethnic origins have been socially and politically mobilized and enfranchised. At the same time, postwar networks of political representation appear to be crumbling, and some observers might appropriately question whether their decay is a necessary precondition to the construction of a genuinely democratic political and civic culture. Dealignment could conceivably lead to the incorporation of new interests and policy alternatives via new parties. The emergence of the Workers' Party (Partido dos Trabalhadores — PT) in Brazil and the Great Front (Frente Grande) in Argentina; the insertion of the Broad Front (Frente Amplio) and Radical Cause (Causa R) in less competitive systems in Uruguay and Venezuela, respectively; and the addition of the Party of the Democratic Revolution (Partido Revolucionario Democrático — PRD) and the Democratic Alliance (Alianza Democrática — AD/M-19) to previously noncompetitive party systems in Mexico and Colombia could well enhance the prospects for both the representativeness and accountability of political parties. If such parties emerge to capture and articulate new interests and define positions on new sets of issues, then we may indeed be witnessing a mere "pause" in political representation.

What if, on the other hand, new parties do not emerge that develop strong roots in the electorate and instead parties themselves are experiencing a sort of secular decline? For some observers, the past monopolization of organizing initiatives by political parties was undesirable; therefore, expanding the alternative, potentially competitive avenues of political representation is seen as only beneficial to political consumers. Within this camp coexist the most rabid critics of parties and those who see the potential for new and diverse forms of political association to augment party representation. Both would expect political interests to reorganize soon, if they have not already done so. One of the more compelling conceptions of a brave new world of political representation has been portrayed by Douglas Chalmers, Scott Martin, and Kerianne Piester, for whom "associative networks," which link societal actors to decision-making centers in the state through interpersonal, media, and/or interorganizational ties in multiple networks that "process and reshape contending political claims through relatively open-ended and problem-focused interactions," have perhaps taken the place of such familiar representative structures and organizational forms as corporatism, clientelism, and populism (Chalmers, Martin, and Piester 1997, 545). Associative networks can reconfigure themselves relatively rapidly, and despite a plague of "substantial fragmentation and social disembeddedness" across the region, Chalmers, Martin, and Piester (1997, 545-546) conclude that "there is far more movement in the direction of recomposition of popular representation through the novel forms [of associative networks] than is perceived conventionally." If this and related analyses are correct, then political representation could be in a process of "reorganization," perhaps even accompanying a shift in the modalities as well as arenas for representation.

For other scholars, the decay of party networks that has loosed former "subjects" from their moorings in the postwar matrix of political representation has left a growing void in political representation, which the principal alternatives to parties to emerge in the past two decades — social movements and NGOs — may not be able to fill. Exploiting this void, enterprising "neopopulist" political leaders such as Fernando Collor de Mello, Carlos Menem, and Alberto Fujimori rose to the presidency in Brazil, Argentina, and Peru.[10] The success of populist leaders in these countries and elsewhere in Latin America stems from their solemn promises, made directly to the people, to solve national problems virtually single-handedly and without political parties. These appeals have resonated with mass publics that have, to at least some degree, lost confidence in political institutions. Emblematic of the neopopulist phenomenon, Fujimori, in claiming his reelection victory in Peru in 1995, pronounced an end to the *partidocracia* that had been stifling Peru, offering instead, "order, discipline, and progress" (*The Economist* 1995, 40). The impact of the rise of populist chief executives on democratic institutions has been devastating. As Guillermo O'Donnell has masterfully sketched out, when presidents who present themselves above parties and who claim a mandate to govern as they see fit treat political institutions such as the congress and courts as nuisances, the real and perceived effectiveness of these institutions is further diminished in a self-reinforcing cycle (O'Donnell 1992). These pessimists might conclude that political representation is in decline, to the detriment of the mass citizenry.

To the extent that the current flaws or "gaps" in political representation have deleterious consequences for political institutions and for the representation of interests, then, they are cause for alarm. If we are to know whether interests are reorganizing themselves to respond to shifting institutional arenas for decisionmaking or, alternatively, their capacity to respond is steadily declining, we require an accurate map of the state of existing and new networks of representation and an answer to the question of what has brought about the current disarray. First, the hypotheses that might explain "temporary" versus "secular" declines in political representation are considered; then, in turn, evidence for a decline in political representation and for its reorganization are examined.

## EXPLAINING THE DECLINE IN POLITICAL REPRESENTATION

The reason for citizens having become disjoined from traditional networks of political representation in Latin America is often attributed to public dissatisfaction with short-term economic performance. Faced with rising inflation and declining living standards in the 1980s, citizens in several countries, including Mexico, Peru, Brazil, and Argentina, categorically rejected incumbents and their parties at the polls.[11] After living standards had fallen by 40 percent in Mexico in the years after the 1982 crisis, for example, the vote for the presidential candidate of the Institutional Revolutionary Party (Partido Revolucionario Institucional — PRI), Carlos Salinas de Gortari, plummeted in 1988 to barely more than 50 percent. In Peru, the Popular Action (Acción Popular — AP) party of incumbent President Fernando Belaúnde Terry garnered only 7.3 percent of the vote in 1985 in the election for his successor; similarly, the vote for the American Popular Revolutionary Alliance (Alianza Popular Revolucionaria Americana — APRA) fell from 53.1 percent in 1985, when it elected Alan García president, to 22.5 percent in 1990. In the 1990s, both parties continued to decline to the advantage of Alberto Fujimori's upstart Cambio Noventa-Nueva Mayoría (Change 90-New Majority): in 1995, the two traditional parties combined received less than 6 percent of the vote.[12] Similarly in Brazil, the two major parties that supported the administration of José Sarney (1985-1990), the Party of the Brazilian Democratic Movement (Partido do Movimento Democrático Brasileiro — PMDB) and the Party of the Liberal Front (Partido da Frente Liberal — PFL), enjoyed a crushing majority in the Congress and controlled most state governments in 1986 but saw their fortunes plummet in the presidential election of 1989: in the first round of those elections, their two candidates combined did not receive 5 percent of the vote. In Argentina, the incumbent Radical Party also suffered a stunning defeat in congressional and provincial elections in 1987 and in the presidential election of 1989.

Another reason for the vitiation of political parties may be the impact of television, which is alleged to have assumed the function of disseminating political information once performed by political parties (Skidmore 1993). In the past three decades, the number of homes reached by television across Latin America has increased exponentially. By 1985, according to one estimate, 60 to 70 percent of Brazilians, Cubans, and Mexicans; 80 percent of Venezuelans; and 90 percent of Colombians, Argentines, and Uruguayans had regular access to television (Oxford Analytica 1991, 72). In the mid-1980s, at least three-quarters of Brazilian homes had a television set, and 95 percent of the population watched TV regularly (de Lima 1993, 102). To some extent, people do rely more on television for political information than in the past. In Brazil in October 1989, 34 percent of respondents to a poll conducted by the Brazilian Institute for Public Opinion and Statistics (IBOPE) reported that the free political advertising hour on radio and television was one of the three information sources they used most to choose a candidate in the presidential election; 26 percent cited candidate debates on television; 20 percent, television news about candidates; 15 percent, newspapers; and 10 percent, radio news.[13] In Chile in 1991, 19 percent of 1,500 survey respondents in nine large urban centers claimed to be politically informed frequently by TV or the press and 50 percent some of the time.[14] In 1966, by contrast, only 10.8 percent of the population surveyed in Greater Santiago by Eduardo Hamuy had a radio and television set, 78.7 percent had just a radio, and 10.6 percent had neither (Hamuy 1966). The rising influence of broadcast networks is also signaled by the fact that 60 percent of Latin Americans responding to a July 1993 poll expressed trust in the mass media, whereas only 17 percent placed the same faith in political parties.[15] Responding to these trends, parties have poured energy and resources into mastering television and deciphering public opinion polls, as Conaghan reports for the case of Ecuador, to the detriment of the programmatic dimension of party life (Conaghan 1995, 454).

Adherents of the "declining living standards" or "rise of television" theses might be skeptical of a notion of a "decline" in political representation. After all, if citizen disillusionment with politicians and political institutions is largely a function of the publicity surrounding corruption, while ordinary folk are bearing the deep if temporary pain of economic adjustment, then this disillusionment could not only be circumstantial but very possibly easily reversed with new leadership and economic recovery. In other words, the more rapid the loss of political faith, like weight loss resulting from a crash diet, the more quickly it can, in principle, be regained. If, alternatively, the trend toward partisan or electoral dealignment is linked to the rise of new communication technologies, then it would not be unique to Latin America, and we should see a comparable decline wherever television viewing has increased. This hypothesis would suggest that it is perhaps no longer even reasonable to expect citizens to be tightly associated with political parties in the modern age.

There is little doubt that the electorate holds governing parties accountable for economic downturns. The question is whether short-term economic conditions alone can shake the foundations of the political order. Just as democratic governments survived the Great Depression in Sweden and the United States but collapsed in Weimar Germany, so, too, the National Liberation Party (Partido Liberación Nacional — PLN) was reelected to government in Costa Rica in 1986 after implementing a harsh austerity program, whereas the government of Carlos Andrés Pérez in Venezuela, which also applied shock therapy to an ailing economy, could not count on public support during two military coup attempts in 1992. The Venezuelan case is all the more striking because the dramatic decline in public confidence became manifest *after* economic growth rates had rebounded to an impressive degree. It is no less true that political parties have changed their campaign styles to take advantage of the broad access to voters afforded by television. But the question is whether the rising importance of television is a *cause* of the decline of parties in Latin America or merely a *reflection* of the state of their decay.

Against the backdrop of these plausible scenarios, there may be several reasons, on the other hand, to believe that political representation is in the process of a profound transformation brought on by more structurally rooted variables. One possibility, suggested by Chalmers, Martin, and Piester (1997, 555-560), is that the dispersion of political decision-making activity away from the centralized state of the postwar era toward multiple decision-making centers, including subnational governments, more or less autonomous centers in the central government, and external arenas, has precipitated the recomposition of popular representation into associative networks. These networks, even when those they represent are only loosely attached to them, are particularly well suited to influencing public policy in an era when many policy spheres and political arenas have become either internationalized or decentralized.

An alternative view, developed here, is that whether political representation is undergoing a process of secular decline or will recover in a reorganized form in the near future, it is at least temporarily disorganized to a greater extent than it has become reconfigured. This decline, however temporary or permanent, is best explained by the underlying collapse of the political and economic matrix (called the "state-centered matrix" by Marcelo Cavarozzi) in which postwar networks of representation were formed (Cavarozzi 1992, 24). The matrix was first weakened in the 1960s and 1970s, when strains in the economic model of the postwar era caused many of the region's democracies to buckle and give way to military regimes with ambitions not only to stabilize and restructure their economies but also to restore political order. The repression enforced by dictators exerted corrosive effects on political representation. Banning political party activity and detaining, exiling, or killing party leaders severely damaged party organizations and, even more destructive to those organizations, severed the links between party leaders and activists and between parties and voters. In repressing various organizations of civil society, and labor organizations in particular, military dictatorships also eroded the legitimacy and effectiveness of corporatist bodies in the region.[16] These networks could not easily be repaired with redemocratization; to the contrary, political transitions more often reinforced the tendencies toward their fragmentation. Today, the structural design, internal organization, and cultural practices of political parties and other representative institutions in the region that evolved under conditions of restricted franchises in less participatory democracies may be ill-suited to mass democracies.[17]

With redemocratization, civilian governments discovered that the economic order on which contemporary systems of political representation were founded was terminally ill. Pressured by galloping inflation and unprecedented levels of foreign debt, Latin American governments in the 1980s followed Chile's earlier lead and successively abandoned state-protected import-substituting industrialization in favor of market-oriented development strategies premised on a liberal trade regime and a reduced scope for state intervention. This transition to economic liberalism has engendered a good deal of political disarray, partly, it is claimed, as the result of elite efforts to weaken those organized sectors of society most likely to oppose trade liberalization and privatization of state enterprises, in order to minimize dissension and political opposition to economic liberalization. To build support for their reform programs, elites tailor their campaign appeals to, but do not mobilize, the unorganized poor in the informal sector (Weyland 1996, 10). However, most of the disorganization, I would contend, has been triggered by the retreat of the state from its extensive involvement in production, regulation, and distribution and the accompanying transformation of political constituencies. These changes have stirred the political waters on which vessels of political representation in the postwar era were custom-built to navigate.

In brief, economic reform has created compelling incentives for political parties, labor unions, employers' associations, and other interest groups to reorganize themselves and their constituents and members away from the incentives created by state intervention (Nelson 1994, 150-157). In the postwar era when states intervened broadly and routinely in economic life, political demands throughout Latin America coalesced around what the state had to offer and how it was to be distributed. With the end of the promise of the expansion of the state's role in production, regulation, and distribution, the traditional ideological appeals of center-left programmatic parties ring hollow and fail to inspire electors. These parties that once raised the banner of a thoroughly revised and more just social order must now frame different sorts of programs of government and electoral strategies.[18] At the moment, they feebly grope for such bland, if vote-winning, campaign themes as anticorruption. The potential of nonprogrammatic political parties to compete electorally and mediate interests via the traditional channels of corporatism and clientelism is also diminished by the reduction in the scope of state regulatory and distributive activity. Corporatist institutions that were put in place by state authorities in order to control the incipient mobilization of labor will, by design, be less effective mediators for more mature labor movements in open economies. The deregulation of labor markets and the restructuring of labor benefits, objectives on the agenda of every neoliberal reformer in Latin America, in fact have weakened corporatist unions and union-party alliances. The reduction in state patronage, too, potentially threatens parties that successfully competed and governed on the basis of delivering state patronage to individuals and communities.

Party constituencies have also been transformed by economic change. The primary constituency of parties of the left — the working class — has been reconfigured by trade liberalization. In Chile, economic restructuring provoked a series of changes in the nature of work: unemployment rose sharply; the number of industrial workers declined; production was transferred from large to small factories; and a shift occurred in the status of many workers from wage-earners to self-employed (30 percent of urban Chileans worked in the informal sector in the late 1980s). Jobs disappeared from traditional industries such as coal mining and textiles, which included some of the best organized and most militant segments of the Chilean working class, and new ones were created in importing companies and financial services (Barrera 1994). Although the sharp decline in general union membership of the 1970s and early 1980s has been reversed with sustained economic recovery, the decline in union membership in manufacturing industries has not.[19] Parties of the left, in short, can no longer rely on the votes of organized workers concentrated in large factory settings; instead, they must now reach out to new constituents in commercial and banking establishments, as well as among the self-employed poor. James McGuire describes much the same trends in Argentina.[20]

If the argument is correct that the electoral volatility, disengagement of citizens from political institutions, and general disorganization of representation of the late 1980s and early 1990s have deeper underlying political and economic reasons than declining living standards and rising television access and influence, then representative networks will not be resuscitated easily. Rather, they will succumb to advanced decay or will have to reinvent themselves in ways that are unclear at the present time.

# THE DECLINE OF POLITICAL REPRESENTATION?

To restate the central argument of this chapter, in the aftermath of the processes of democratization and marketization that have gripped Latin America in the past decade, societal interests have become disorganized and disjoined from the networks of political representation that buttressed populist democracies and hybrid regimes in the past. This disorganization manifests itself in two specific, significant ways. First, corporatist unions are either losing their monopoly of representation over their members or undergoing structural changes that divert their attention away from the political arena. Second, at the same time, citizens are failing to identify with parties and often do not even vote.

## *The End of the Century of Corporatism? Preliminary Evidence*

Since the emergence of labor as a political actor in Latin America around the time of the Great Depression, corporatism has served as a system of interest representation, one that organized societal interests along functional lines. Where corporatism was practiced, the state regulated labor markets through complex legal codes and institutions, primarily state labor courts. Labor leaders forfeited union autonomy in exchange for favorable wage settlements and the prerogative to distribute state social welfare benefits. Bypassing elected legislatures, these quasi-legal, "associationally organized interests of civil society" pressed their influence directly to the "decisional structures of the state" in the executive branch, to which they were formally linked (Schmitter 1974, 86, 100). Corporatist networks also spilled over into the electoral arena. In Brazil, the system erected in 1943 by the dictator Getúlio Vargas worked well for two decades in marshaling the support of labor for the electoral alliance of the elite-dominated Social Democratic Party (Partido Social Democrático — PSD) and the mass-based Brazilian Labor Party (Partido Trabalhista Brasileiro — PTB). In Argentina, corporatist unions provided the electoral basis for Peronism, and in Mexico, urban and rural unions were primarily responsible for sustaining the electoral hegemony of the PRI for six decades.

Since the 1980s, corporatism has been decaying across Latin America. This process of decay has its origins in the attacks on labor organizations undertaken by military regimes bent on dismantling populism, and it has been accelerated by economic reformers seeking to liberalize the functioning of labor markets. In Brazil, the military government straightaway used corporatist laws to remove labor leaders and repress union organizations. From 1964 to 1973, Brazilian labor reeled from the harsh measures of the dictatorship, but urban labor regrouped in the second decade of military rule to emerge stronger and more independent of the state than it had ever been, with radically altered orientations toward the state and new strategies for representing the interests of members. In Schmitter's 1965 survey of local union leaders, 59 percent agreed very much and 35 percent a little with the statement, "The government should act as arbitrator between employers' associations and workers' syndicates in the interest of social harmony" (Schmitter 1971, 101). By the late 1970s, a new generation of labor leaders rejected the strategy of relying on the intermediation of state labor courts and state support for their organizations. They instead strengthened their own organizations and struck for higher wages and the right to engage in face-to-face, collective bargaining with employers. The two most important central labor organizations in Brazil today, the Central Workers' Union (Central Unica dos Trabalhadores — CUT) and the Union Power (Força Sindical — FS), differ in their degree of militancy vis-à-vis employers, but the underlying philosophies of both — the "new unionism" and the "unionism of results," respectively — no longer tie the fortunes of their organizations and members to state largesse (Antunes 1991, 43-70). Thanks to key victories won by labor representatives in the Constituent Assembly of 1987-1988, unions in Brazil today enjoy more freedom from the state to maneuver than ever before.

These changes in perception and law have contributed to a decline in corporatist "practice." In 1990, 70 percent of the more than 28,000 collective bargaining processes initiated by urban, rural, and professional workers' unions were settled directly, either at the firm level or with employers' associations, and more than half of all unions relied on the state-collected *imposto sindical* (union tax) for less than 20 percent of their total revenues (only 7 percent reported that it represented more than 80 percent of their finances). By contrast, in 1965, 99 percent of confederation, 92 percent of federation, and 70 percent of local union income derived from the *imposto sindical* (Schmitter 1971, 101). This contrast is all the more impressive when the fact of rural unionization since 1965 is taken into account. In 1990, 66.8 percent of urban but only 5.3 percent of rural workers' unions (whose members are much poorer) reported that between 80 and 100 percent of their members had paid dues.[21] Employers were traditionally less constrained by corporatist representation than were workers, but employers embraced government intervention in the labor market just as fervently as workers did. In 1965, 63 percent of employers agreed very much and 17 percent a little that the government should act as an arbitrator between employers' associations and workers' syndicates in the interest of social harmony (Schmitter 1971, 101). In recent years, employers have been slower to disengage from corporate group-based politics than labor. From 1987 to 1988, 70 percent of industrialists interviewed by Leigh Payne judged the lobbies of their associations as serving business interests well, whereas only 29 percent rated congressional representatives and 12 percent political parties as similarly effective.[22]

The extent to which corporatism in Mexico has decayed is a more open question, but evidence is mounting that corporatist structures there, too, will not survive in their postwar form indefinitely. In the 1980s in the face of a serious decline in living standards, the corporatist Confederation of Mexican Labor (Confederación de Trabajadores de México — CTM) maintained its monopoly of representation and played a major role in the negotiations with capital and the state in 1987 that led to the "economic solidarity pact" (Pacto de Solidaridad Económica — PSE) to hold down wages during a prolonged period of economic adjustment. Within the framework of the PSE, the CTM negotiated a series of continuing agreements over the course of the next five years governing the minimum wage, public sector prices, and public finances (Whitehead 1989; Zapata 1994). After 1992, the CTM even conceded changes in the nature of work, compensation, and factory-level participation, and above all, de facto labor flexibility through collective contracts, in order to resist reforming the Federal Labor Law. More significantly, the CTM ended its resistance to privatizations in "nonstrategic" sectors in 1993 and accepted the reform of social security and the government-subsidized worker housing fund in exchange for maintaining its privileged position in the governing party.[23] Despite proposals to transform the structure of the PRI from a "party of organizations" to a "party of citizens," the Sixteenth Assembly of the PRI in 1993 returned the corporatist structure to the National Executive Committee (Murillo 1996, 10; Teichman 1995, 177). Even in Mexico, however, corporatist unions and structures may now be decaying (Oxhorn 1994). Ann Craig and Wayne Cornelius have observed that beginning in the mid-1970s, the PRI failed to incorporate a large number of dissident movements that emerged among the urban poor, campesinos, and trade unions, a process accelerated by the Mexico City earthquake of 1985. By jealously guarding their autonomy, they claim, these organizations "undermined PRI-affiliated sectoral organizations as intermediaries with government agencies and as institutions representing popular interests" (Craig and Cornelius 1995, 280). At minimum, if Mexican *unions,* and particularly the central CTM, have to date maintained a privileged organizational position due to skillful concessions to government authorities eager to accelerate economic liberalizing measures, the configuration of corporatism and the types and range of benefits administered by corporatist unions to citizens are clearly in the process of profound transformation.

In Argentina, traditional corporatism has been under attack for nearly a decade by economic reformers who have argued that economic competitiveness depends upon democratizing the union structure (allowing more than one union per activity or per region), decentralizing labor negotiations to the firm level, and eliminating the government's role in binding arbitration in conflicts between labor and management (de la Balze 1995, 110). Toward the goals of reducing employer contributions to unemployment, pension, and social assistance funds and liberalizing labor markets, the Argentine government has enacted by decree and through negotiation with legislators a series of reforms that have partially privatized social security, ended the monopoly distribution by unions of medical services and other forms of social assistance to their approximately 17 million members, and moved in the direction of decentralizing labor negotiations. As in Mexico, the terms of Argentina's postwar state-labor bargain are being renegotiated. Some unions (notably those representing electrical, railroad, and oil workers) have turned to entrepreneurial activities in order to extend their organizational resources to gain autonomy vis-à-vis the state and perhaps eventually to survive the de facto erosion of their representational monopoly in centralized collective bargaining.[24]

Thus, in Brazil, Mexico, Argentina, and elsewhere, corporatism is collapsing. The market price for labor is increasingly being set not by state regulators and labor courts, but by a series of collective bargaining transactions in the private sector. Social welfare is being administered, moreover, not by union organizations, which in the future will play a diminished role in delivering state-funded medical care and pensions, but increasingly by targeted assistance programs being administered by the president's office. The decline of corporatism will have an ambiguous effect on interest mediation. On the one hand, the erosion of corporatist controls has undeniably created the possibility of stronger, more independent unions. By financing their own activities through member dues and entrepreneurial activities, more unions across the region are loosening the yoke of dependence on state authorities. At the same time, unions are increasingly gaining the recognition of employers as bargaining agents.

The end of the century of corporatism that is enhancing the effectiveness of Latin American labor unions in securing their members' economic interests in the marketplace may, however, paradoxically be weakening the unions' role in *political* representation. With the expansion of the role of markets in allocating labor and social services in Latin America today, the negotiating channels once open between unions and the "decisional structures of the state" are being rendered obsolete. Whatever the desirability or necessity of the reform process, the breakdown of corporatism and the concomitant migration of the representation of one huge slice of labor interests from nonelected (and nonaccountable) arenas of the state — labor courts, the ministries of labor and social security — to elected (and accountable) institutions will pressure formal and informal institutions of representation such as political parties, voluntary associations, social movements, and NGOs to fill the void left by decaying corporatist labor organizations.

## FROM CORPORATISM TO PARTIES? PRELIMINARY EVIDENCE

That parties in Latin America have not thus far responded with aplomb to the challenges of representing the interests of citizens being discarded by decaying networks of representation as well as those of new entrants into political life — youth, women, illiterates — is neither damning nor surprising. To expect parties to represent effectively a broader array of interests than they ever have, modernize their ideologies, reform their organizations, and deliver a quality democracy for which they can be held accountable, particularly during a period of profound economic transformation such as the present time, would be unrealistic. In less trying circumstances, parties in much richer countries with long-established democracies have been largely unable to deliver effective and ultimately satisfactory public policy that generates loyalty and good will among citizens. In the 1970s, when citizens across Western Europe perceived that parties had failed to protect the environment and had diminished rather than enhanced national security through their nuclear weapons policies, scores of new social movements proliferated, in some cases spawning new parties that registered electoral breakthroughs in the 1980s in Germany, Belgium, France, and elsewhere.[25] Even well-established parties in advanced democracies that have experienced being the opposition as well as controlling the government struggle today to satisfy mass publics, recruit candidates that "look like the country," and provide political information to electorates largely socialized politically by the mass media. While parties in Bolivia and Brazil struggle to find ways to represent the interests of underrepresented ethnic and racial majorities, we should take note that the Labour Party in Britain endured more than a decade of debate and internal party reform until it apparently found a formula in the parliamentary election of 1997 for increasing the candidacies to local councils and Parliament of women and ethnic and racial minorities (Norris and Lovenduski 1995).

In these times of major economic change, the flux and confusion in Latin American party systems caused by the formidable challenges of incorporating new interests and rewriting programs of government are understandable. The formation of new parties to reflect new identities and interests and the passing of old ones, along with disappearing classes and the salience of old cleavages, are part and parcel of the normal, if rare, process of electoral realignment. Nonetheless, continuity in party organization and programs provides an essential basis for citizens to make rational and informed electoral decisions, while excessive party system discontinuity and electoral volatility threaten the capacity of parties to fulfill their mission of political representation. If parties do not have well-established organizations and if their representatives are not disciplined and faithful to policy courses proposed during electoral campaigns,[26] parties not only will become mere ephemeral vehicles to satisfy the personal ambitions of politicians (who can and will frequently change parties) but also will be unaccountable to their electors. Politicians themselves, amid such uncertainty, can be held accountable at best only for their constituency service, not for their votes on issue-based legislation.

In some Latin American countries with notably weak parties, recently party consistency has been sacrificed not often because of a necessary reexamination of party program and revision of party policy, but to permit the circulation of party elites struggling to escape the brand of their party's failures. In Brazil once the opposition elected the president in 1985, state and local politicians deserted the promilitary Social Democratic Party (Partido Social Democrático — PSD) en masse for the ranks of the newly created PFL and the former opposition party, the PMDB; in the early 1990s, the fortunes of the Party of National Reconstruction (Partido de Reconstrução Nacional — PRN) similarly rose and fell with the star of Fernando Collor de Mello. In Ecuador, according to Anita Isaacs, by April 1994 one-third of those elected to Congress in 1992 had deserted the party for which they ran (Isaacs 1996, 45). Analysts of parties in both countries have employed the same metaphor of "shirt changing" to describe the frequency with which politicians move from one party to another (Isaacs 1996, 45; Fleischer 1987, 5). In Guatemala, eight of 17 parties contesting the 1984 elections had been created less than one month before the elections, and another five were less than one year old. In 1990, one of Guatemala's traditionally most important parties, Christian Democracy, lost half of its core electorate (Torres-Rivas 1996, 55).

Parties, often in these same countries, also lack discipline and cohesion. The most disciplined party in Brazil is the PT, whose delegation in the 1987-1988 Constituent Assembly voted unanimously in favor of agrarian reform and against a five-year term for President Sarney. By contrast, 59 percent of PMDB deputies voted for agrarian reform and 33 percent against (with 8 percent absent or abstaining), and in the vote on the five-year term for Sarney, 60 percent voted with the president, a PMDB member, and 39 percent opposed the extension of his mandate.[27] Scott Mainwaring has calculated the average Rice Index on 11 controversial issues in the Constitutional Assembly to be 100 for the PT and 86 for the Democratic Labor Party (Partido Democrático Trabalhista — PDT) but only 58 for the PFL, 47 for the PSD, 41 for the PTB, and 33 for the PMDB.[28] Although in Colombia it is difficult to assess party discipline because few congressional votes are recorded, it is illustrative that in 1990 around 80 percent of members in each chamber were elected from factional lists that elected no other candidate, up from 45 percent of deputies and 58 percent of senators in 1974 (Archer and Shugart 1997, 138, 134).

In those countries where parties have only short life spans and suffer from infidelity on the part of their leaders and representatives, it is also often the case that party-citizen links will fray or at minimum be unstable. To ascertain the degree to which citizens have become disjoined from political parties in Latin America, we must turn our attention to evidence of partisan and electoral dealignment.

## Partisan Dealignment?

When students of political parties speak of the attachment or detachment of citizens to parties, they speak of realignment and dealignment. Electoral realignment signifies a significant and permanent shift of electors from one party to another and implies a successful reorganization of interests. Partisan and electoral dealignments, in contrast, imply that the loyalty of citizens to their preferred party erodes but is not replaced with loyalty to a competitor. Partisan dealignment is often signaled by declining levels of voter identification with parties and is a prelude to electoral dealignment. Electoral dealignment is marked by volatile voting patterns and rising rates of voter abstention.

Partisan dealignment is indicated by the increasing unwillingness on the part of voters to identify with standing parties. In several countries in the region, especially those lacking established party systems, the percentage of the population that identifies with these parties has visibly declined in recent years (see Table 1). In Ecuador, the percentage of survey respondents in Guayaquil and Quito, respectively, who failed to identify themselves as "militants" or "supporters" of any party rose from 47 and 38 percent in 1989 to 67 and 88 percent in 1993 (Issacs 1996, 45). In Brazil, partisan identification is weak and eroding. For a while during the military dictatorship it appeared that Brazilians may have been developing attachments to one or the other of the two parties created by the military, but this trend was erased by the move to a multiparty system after 1979 that permitted parties to form and reorganize with great ease. In 1976, in the municipality of Presidente Prudente in the western part of the state of São Paulo, Bolívar Lamounier found 80 percent of those surveyed to have a partisan preference. Thirteen years later, at the close of the presidential campaign in 1989 in the same community, Maria D'Alva Gil Kinzo found only 23 percent of those interviewed declared a preference for a party (Kinzo 1993b, 320). The same trend is visible in the city of São Paulo and on the national level: only 19 percent of respondents in 1974 but 64 percent in 1987 and 52 percent in 1990 expressed no party preference.[29] Julio Cotler has claimed that the attachments of citizens to political parties have eroded in Peru, although regrettably he does not provide numeric confirmation of what he calls the "decomposition of party identities" in the years from 1980 to 1987 and the "disintegration of political identities" from 1987 to 1992 (Cotler 1995, 337, 346).

In traditionally more stable party systems, similar trends have taken shape. In Mexico, the proportion of the population *not* identifying with parties rose from 38 percent in July 1987 to 51 percent in April 1990 (Craig and Cornelius 1995, 262). In Chile, which had one of the highest rates of party identification in Latin America (80 percent) in 1988, party identification has weakened considerably in the short time span since the restoration of democratic governance. In 1996, 50 percent of survey respondents did not identify with a party (Tironi 1997, 7). These rates contrast sharply with those in the period preceding the military coup of 1973. In May 1967, 88.5 percent of 299 residents surveyed in Greater Santiago (10 percent of the total respondents in Chile) either belonged to or identified with (78.4 percent) a political party.[30] Slightly less than one-quarter of total respondents (23.4 percent) could not recall the name of the person they had voted for in the 1967 municipal elections — they reported voting for their party. In Argentina, party identification declined sharply in the five-year period from 1989 to 1994, from 44.4 to 24.6 percent. Of those not identifying with a party in 1989, 40 percent claimed to vote for the best party, 22 percent expressed no interest in parties, and 22 percent claimed the parties had deceived them. Partisan identification was stronger in older age cohorts (50.9 percent of those over 65) than in the younger (41.1 percent among 17-29 year-olds) (Sofres-IBOPE 1989; Sofres-IBOPE 1995). In the Patagonia region of Argentina, an Argentine researcher discovered that of the 40 persons he interviewed in depth, "very few" identified themselves as sympathizers with a party (Fara 1994, 8).

## Electoral Dealignment?

The first sign of electoral dealignment is electoral volatility. Electoral volatility is a measure of the net change in the vote shares of all parties from one election to the next. One difficulty in measuring the full extent of electoral dealignment in Latin America with respect to earlier decades is that the voting population has not remained constant but has changed and grown considerably over time. Natural population growth and the enfranchisement of youths and particularly of illiterates have expanded the electorate in Brazil from 19 million in 1960 to 95 million in 1994 and from 2 million in 1979 to 5 million in 1992 in Ecuador.[31] "Realignment," strictly speaking, is a phenomenon that is meant to apply to a rather static voting population, not one that has expanded rapidly.

Mainwaring and Scully have calculated mean electoral volatility in 12 Latin American countries (see Table 2). While some of these figures are inflated, due to the appearance of new parties after dictatorships, the degree to which electors in the region have scattered their votes among *existing* parties since the mid-1980s, especially in Ecuador, Peru, and Brazil, is striking. Of course, these three countries are among those with the most weakly institutionalized party systems in Latin America, and they stand in stark contrast to Costa Rica, Chile, and Uruguay, where citizens identify with parties, vote, and evaluate the performance of democratic institutions reasonably favorably. Nonetheless, well-established party systems that have deep and long roots in the electorate do not provide immunity from the contagion of dealignment. In Colombia, the volatility index rose from 11.4 in the period from 1986 to 1990 to 21.9 from 1990 to 1991. In Venezuela, after a lengthy period of party system stability (the volatility index for 1973-1983 was 11.6 and for 1983-1988, 6.9), volatility soared to 42.3 from 1988-1993 (Hartlyn 1994b, 34),

## Table 1.
## Party Identification in Latin America and Western Europe

| | Year | Percent Identifying with a Party |
|---|---|---|
| *Latin American Cases* | | |
| Argentina | 1989 | 44.4 |
| | 1995 | 24.6 |
| Brazil | 1974 | 19.0 (no party) |
| | 1987 (June) | 34.0 |
| | 1989-1990 (avg.) | 51.3 (no party) |
| Chile | 1967 | 88.5 |
| | 1988 | 80.0 |
| | 1991-1994 (avg.)[1] | 75.0 |
| | 1996 | 50.0 |
| Colombia | 1970s | 70.0 |
| | 1980s (late) | 60.0 |
| Ecuador[2] | 1989 | 47.0, 38.0 (no party) |
| | 1993 | 67.0, 88.0 (no party) |
| Mexico | 1987 (July) | 62.0 |
| | 1990 (April) | 49.0 |
| *Comparative Cases* | | |
| Britain | 1964-1970 (avg.) | 81.6 |
| | 1974-1979 (avg.) | 75.0 |
| | 1983-1992 (avg.) | 70.3 |
| Germany | 1972-1980 (avg.) | 82.3 |
| | 1983-1987 (avg.) | 75.0 |
| Italy | 1976-1981 (avg.) | 72.7 |
| | 1982-1989 (avg.) | 62.9 |
| Sweden[3] | 1968-1985 (avg.) | 90.0 |
| | 1988 | 64.0 |

1 = Never less than one-third, and an average of 25 percent, declared not to be identified with right, center, and left lines or not to have sympathy for any political party.
2 = For Guayaquil and Quito, respectively, in 1989 and 1993.
3 = Includes strong and weak identification and expressions of party preference.
Sources: Argentina: Sofres-IBOPE 1989, 1995. Brazil: Mainwaring 1995, 385; Moisés 1993b, 595. Chile: Hamuy 1967a; Garretón 1994, 8; Tironi 1997, 7. Colombia: Archer 1995, 178. Ecuador: Isaacs 1996, 45. Mexico: Craig and Cornelius 1995, 262. Britain: Messina 1995, 34. Germany, Italy, Sweden: Katz and Mair 1992, 330, 477, 790-791.

when Andrés Velásquez received 22 percent of the vote representing Causa R in the presidential election and the party's parliamentary candidates captured one-fifth of the seats in Congress (López Maya 1997, 130-131). Similarly, although Argentina was less volatile from 1991 to 1993 than it had been in previous years, its volatility rates surely surged after the electoral ascendency of the Frente Grande and the FREPASO coalition and the decline of the Radicals in the 1994 and 1995 elections.

Electoral volatility is also manifest in a trend toward increasing competitiveness in previously "safe" electoral districts. In Argentina, the electoral hegemony of the Radical Civic Union (Unión Cívica Radical — UCR) in the predominantly middle-class districts of the federal capital of Buenos Aires was broken in the elections of 1994 and 1995, and even previously safe Peronist districts in the province of Buenos Aires have been penetrated by the Frente Grande. In Mexico, where electoral support for the PRI has sharply eroded in recent years, the percentage of the vote obtained by PRI candidates for president plummeted from an average of 83.5 percent in the years from 1952 to 1982 to 50.7 percent in 1988.[32] Patterns of electoral competition in Mexico's 300 federal electoral districts are perhaps even more illuminating. As Craig and Cornelius have shown, the proportion of electoral districts in which the PRI had a monopoly, strong electoral hegemony, or weak electoral hegemony dropped from 85 percent in 1964 to 35 percent in 1988, while PRI candidates in the latter year were subjected to multiparty competition in 34 percent of districts and electoral defeat in 23 percent (Craig and Cornelius 1995, 260-261).

A second sure sign of electoral dealignment is an increase in voter abstention. The evidence presented in Table 3 suggests that rates of voter abstention in Latin America vary widely by country. In Costa Rica, abstention levels actually *declined* from 32.8 percent in 1953 to 18.2 percent in 1990. At the opposite end of the spectrum, in El Salvador absenteeism rose from 31.5 percent in 1984 (its lowest level in the decade of the 1980s) to 67.4 percent in 1989. In Venezuela, levels of abstention rose from a low of 3.5 percent in 1973 to 18.3 percent in 1988. In Colombia, rates of participation have been low since the 1950s; with the exception of the presidential election of 1970, they fell within the range of 34 to 50 percent of the electorate. However, in March 1994, the rate of electoral abstention rose to the staggering level of 70 percent (Kline 1996, 24). Turnout declined in Mexico between 1982, when 66 percent of eligible adults voted, and 1988, when 49 percent did so (Craig and Cornelius 1995, 258). Historically, abstention rates in Brazil hovered around 20 percent (the election of 1955, for which 40 percent of the electorate stayed home, was atypical). In 1990, the turnout rate for the gubernatorial and legislative election was 70 percent, and of those who voted, 31.5 percent cast blank or spoiled ballots, approximately the same proportion as in 1970 during the height of the Médici dictatorship (Moisés 1993b, 581). From 58 to 69 percent of survey respondents during the 1989 presidential campaign reported that they would not vote were it not mandatory (Moisés 1993b, 596). In Peru, Fujimori's apparently decisive 1995 reelection victory was less impressive on closer examination than first appears. Although he polled 64 percent of the vote, he received the endorsement of only 35 percent of

## Table 2.
## Mainwaring and Scully's Index of Electoral Volatility
## in Twelve Countries

| Country | Time Span | Mean Volatility[1] (Percent) |
|---|---|---|
| Uruguay | 1971-1989 | 9.1 |
| Colombia | 1970-1990 | 9.7 |
| Costa Rica | 1970-1990 | 16.3 |
| Chile | 1973-1993 | 16.5 |
| Venezuela | 1973-1993 | 18.8 |
| Argentina | 1982-1993 | 20.0 |
| Mexico | 1982-1991 | 27.3 |
| Paraguay | 1983-1993 | 31.4 |
| Bolivia | 1979-1993 | 36.1 |
| Ecuador | 1978-1992 | 37.9 |
| Peru | 1978-1990 | 54.2 |
| Brazil | 1982-1990 | 70.0 |

1 = Combined mean volatility for lower-chamber and presidential votes held during the time span indicated for each country. They calculate the electoral volatility index by adding the net change in percentage of seats (for the lower chamber) or votes (for president) gained or lost by each party from one election to the next, then dividing by two.
Source: Mainwaring and Scully 1995, 8.

the total electorate: 28 percent did not vote, and 17 percent cast blank or spoiled ballots (Palmer 1995, 19).

Underlying this trend toward declining levels of voter turnout has been a rising tide of citizen disinterest, disillusion, and disaffection. Although in El Salvador turnout was obviously depressed by the cumbersome registration process for aspiring voters in areas that formerly supported the guerrilla insurgency, the United Nations believed that by 1993 a lack of citizen mobilization was the largest obstacle to electoral participation (Córdova Macías 1996, 39). Similarly in Guatemala, Torres-Rivas attributes to a "manifest lack of interest of the population" a rise in the abstention rate from 39 percent in the first democratic election in 1985 to 84 percent in the January 1994 referendum on constitutional reform, following the political crisis spawned by President Serrano's *autogolpe*, and 79 percent in the congressional elections held later that year (Torres-Rivas 1996, 60, 62). In Chile, the rate of electoral participation among the 299 residents of Greater Santiago surveyed by Eduardo Hamuy in 1967 was only 71 percent, but nearly 16 percent of these eligible voters were not registered (the vote to illiterates was awarded in 1970).

Two percent were registered elsewhere, and 2 percent had problems with their registration; only 2 percent of respondents expressed disinterest in what was a municipal election (Hamuy 1967a). By contrast, over the three-year period from 1987 through 1989 that constituted Chile's transition to democracy, when one might reasonably expect interest in politics to surge, an average of 37 percent of respondents to panel surveys expressed no interest in politics and 34 percent only a little.[33] Moreover, between 1988 and 1996, the percentage of 18- to 21-year-olds registered to vote declined from 21 to 9 percent (Tironi 1997, 6).

Confidence in political institutions has also eroded. In Chile, public opinion in the first years after democratic governance had been restored and was ambivalent toward but respectful of parties. In the panel study conducted in 1987, 1988, and 1989, 54 percent of respondents agreed and 39 percent disagreed with the statement that echoed a claim heard often from the military regime, "The parties only divide people." But 68 percent agreed with the statement, "The parties are necessary to defend social and class interests," and only 21 percent disagreed (Baño et al. 1991). In another poll, 53 percent of respondents viewed politicians favorably, while 56 percent rated deputies and senators in particular with approval (CERC 1992, 4). In 1993 LatinBarometer surveys, however, only approximately 13 percent of respondents expressed confidence in parties, as compared with 65 percent for the church and 70 percent for the police (Hartlyn 1994). In Colombia in 1988, only 21 percent of more than 1,800 respondents rated the quality of Congress as "good," about half the proportion (41 percent) who rated it as "bad." Colombian parties fared worse (16 percent good and 53 percent bad), and politicians were rejected by approximately a two-thirds majority (61 percent found "traditional politicians" bad, and 67 percent found politicians of the left bad) (Archer 1995, 195). In Guayaquil and Quito, Ecuador, more than 80 percent of respondents in 1989 believed that parties did not care about people's problems, a similar percentage that, in 1994, felt that political parties did not serve the public interest.[34]

The public judges political parties far more harshly than it does other institutions. In the comparative surveys of public opinion in 11 Latin American countries, citizens expressed the greatest confidence in the Catholic Church and the mass media (63 and 60 percent, respectively), substantially less in the justice system and the police (approximately 31 percent), and least of all in political institutions — most notably, parties and congresses. Fewer than 20 percent of Latin Americans on the whole and 10 percent of Guatemalans and Venezuelans had confidence in political parties (Hartlyn 1994b, 27-32).

## THE HYPOTHESES CONFRONTED

What have these data told us about the causes and likely duration of the "decline" in political representation? First, they suggest that electoral dealignment is in a fairly advanced state and is not likely to reverse itself at any time soon. Not only is the rate of voter abstention significantly higher than it was in the 1960s, but the reasons for its sharp rise augur poorly for the ability of parties to recover quickly their bases of steady support. In the 1960s, voter abstentions were more often due to problems with registration than to the sentiment that parties had deceived voters (only 2 percent of nonvoters in Chile in 1967 stayed home from the

## Table 3.
## Dealignment? Voter Abstention

| Country | Years | Voter Turnout/Abstention Rates |
|---|---|---|
| *Modest Decline or Increase:* | | |
| Argentina | 1983 | 85.6 |
| | 1995 | 80.2 |
| Costa Rica | 1953 | 32.8 (abstention) |
| | 1990 | 18.2 (abstention) |
| Dominican | 1978-1986 (avg.) | 26.0 (abstention) |
| Republic* | 1990 | 40.0 (abstention) |
| | 1994 | 14.0 (abstention) |
| *Steady-Moderate Decline:* | | |
| Venezuela | 1958 | 7.9 (abstention) |
| | 1973 | 3.5 (abstention) |
| | 1978 | 12.4 (abstention) |
| | 1988 | 18.3 (abstention) |
| *Precipitous Decline:* | | |
| Mexico | 1982 | 25.2 |
| | 1988 | 49.7 |
| Colombia | 1958-1990 | 34.0-50.0 (except 1970 presidential election) |
| | 1994 | 70.0 (abstention) |
| Brazil | pre-1964 avg. | 20.0 (abstention) |
| | 1990 | 70.0 ([turnout], 31.5 blank or spoiled ballots) |
| Guatemala | 1985 | 39.0 (abstention) |
| | 1991 | 57.1 (abstention) |
| | 1994 | 84.0 (abstention) |
| El Salvador | 1984 | 31.5 |
| | 1989 | 67.4 |
| Ecuador | 1984 | 25.0 (abstention) |
| Peru | 1995 | 28.0 ([abstention], 17.0 blank or spoiled ballots) |
| *Comparative Cases:* | | |
| Britain | 1983-1992 | 76.9 |
| Germany | 1980-1994 | 83.7 |

* = Electoral registry (excluding foreigners, military, criminals).
Sources: Argentina: Fara 1995. Costa Rica: Yashar 1995, 82. Dominican Republic: Hartlyn 1994a, 103. Venezuela: Kornblith and Levine 1995, 56. Mexico, El Salvador, Ecuador: Wilkie, Contreras, and Weber 1993, 326, 305, 301. Colombia: Archer 1995, 508. Brazil: Moisés 1993b, 582. Guatemala: Torres-Rivas 1996, 60. Peru: Palmer 1995, 19. Britain, Germany: Messina 1995.

polls because they were discontented with parties). Today, rising voter abstentions and electoral volatility are consistent with poor evaluations of politicians and legislatures in much of the region.

Second, partisan and electoral dealignment is occurring faster in several Latin American countries than in Western Europe. Even after two decades of decline, 70 percent of British and 75 percent of German citizens still identify with political parties, and an even higher percentage turn out to vote (76.9 and 83.7 percent, respectively; see Tables 1 and 3). Although the percentage of citizens failing to identify with parties is higher in Italy, its slide is less precipitous than in the other European cases. Only in Sweden have levels of voter discontent apparently slipped into the Latin American range.[35] The comparative data suggest that the origins of the Latin American crisis of political representation run deeper than increased television viewing, and this crisis cannot easily be dismissed as no worse than elsewhere. The political dislocation in Latin America caused by the move from state-sponsored industrialization to economic liberalism may parallel that precipitated by economic adjustment and monetary union in Western Europe, but its scope and intensity are far greater.

The evidence, however preliminary, also casts doubt on the hypothesis that the decline in political representation is a mere temporary phenomenon born of a period of acute economic downturn that will reverse itself with economic recovery. In Mexico, general expectations about the economy's future were important in shaping the vote for the PAN in 1988 but not for the PAN in 1991 or the left in either election (Domínguez and McCann 1995, 46). More vividly, the Argentine example shows that partisan dealignment can proceed at an alarming rate even during an economic recovery: indeed, it was precisely between 1989 and 1995, when inflation rates were reduced from 3,079 percent to 3.9 percent (de la Balze 1995, 71, 76) and the gross domestic product grew by 40 percent, that party identification eroded precipitously from 44.4 to 24.6 percent. Most dramatically, Venezuela's recovery of growth rates to 10 percent in 1992 did not arrest the erosion of support for the government of Carlos Andrés Pérez. If these cases are generalizable, then we must reject the hypothesis that the weakness of political representation today represents a mere "pause" in a longer trajectory of expanded avenues for political mediation.

Perhaps more ominous with respect to the prospects for reorganization of interests, once voters become detached from political parties to such an extent that only one-quarter of the population identifies with them, the reattachment of citizens to the available alternatives is neither rapid nor automatic. Jorge I. Domínguez and James A. McCann have recently demonstrated that despite the elevated protest vote for Cuauhtémoc Cárdenas in Mexico in 1988, parties of the left failed to mobilize voters in both 1988 and 1991 who had chosen to abstain in previous elections (Domínguez and McCann 1995, 46). But this is admittedly a thin basis upon which to dismiss the broad hope for a reorganization of political representation; a closer examination of the alternatives is warranted.

# THE REORGANIZATION OF REPRESENTATION?

If it has been demonstrated that corporatism is eroding as a principal means of interest representation in Latin America and that electoral dealignment is significantly advanced in many countries in the region, the alternative scenarios sketched out in the beginning of this chapter need to be considered. Is it possible that electoral realignment might be on the horizon after dealignment, and that old systems of political representation, such as clientelism, are more resilient than might at first appear? Alternatively, is there sufficient evidence to conclude that new networks of political representation based on social movements and/or NGOs are supplementing or supplanting the representative functions once performed by corporatist institutions and political parties?

## Realignment and Resilience

While the overarching trend described in this chapter is toward disorganization and dealignment, there also emerge puzzling cases of realignment, resilience, and possible reorganization of political interests and representation. In Uruguay and Costa Rica, two countries that have the region's most respected democratic traditions and well-established party systems, it may be possible to speak of an electoral realignment in the making. In Uruguay, in two successive elections (1989 and 1994), the parties of the Broad Front (Frente Amplio) and the New Space (Nuevo Espacio) gained nearly 30 percent of the vote (up from 18 percent in 1971 and 1984). In Costa Rica, as Deborah Yashar has suggested, attacks on the welfare state have shifted voter loyalties from the social democratic PLN to the center-right United Social Christian Party (Partido Unidad Social Cristiana — PUSC) in municipal, legislative, and presidential elections (Yashar 1995, 97-98).

It is also true that some existing networks of representation have shown surprising resilience. Although we might expect a decrease in state budgets and regulatory authority to produce a corresponding reduction in the exercise of patronage, in many countries political clientelism has survived the initial phases of redemocratization and market-oriented reform, and in some it even flourishes. It is widely acknowledged that free-spending politicians have dispensed state patronage at staggering rates in Brazil, but it is perhaps less well understood that they do so not indiscriminately but through well-established networks brokered by local bosses. Barry Ames has found that outside the metropolitan capitals of southeast Brazil, party endorsements and the mobilizational commitments they represent had a powerful impact on the fortunes of the major candidates in the 1989 presidential elections (Ames 1994, 96). One reason clientelism is not disappearing as fast as corporatism may be that it is being used in negotiations over economic change. In Brazil, the temporary gains made by politicians who trade votes on pieces of an economic liberalization program in exchange for state resources to distribute and manipulate for electoral purposes in the short term are bolstering their electoral position in the longer term, even as their parties lose presidential elections (Hagopian 1995).

New forms of clientelistic state mediation are also surfacing in the region, primarily through targeted assistance programs meant to cushion the most vulnerable population from structural adjustment policies. The Mexican National Solidarity Program (Programa Nacional de Solidaridad — PRONASOL) was the prototype. According to Denise Dresser, it redefined members of corporatist organizations as consumers of state benefits (electricity, scholarships, and paved streets), which in turn came to substitute for the traditional forms of state protection. PRONASOL also took over previously autonomous organizations. Perhaps most salient for our purposes, PRONASOL was constructed (and managed) by the office of the president as a giant patronage operation to circumvent the long-standing network of patron-client relationships that were manipulated by *caciques* (party bosses) with relatively autonomous local power bases.[36] Perhaps impressed with the political utility of targeted assistance, after 1993 Alberto Fujimori invested more heavily in Peru in comparable funds — FONCODES (National Development and Social Compensation Fund), FONAVI (National Housing Fund), and PRONAA (National Nutritional Assistance Program) — with much the same success as that enjoyed by the Mexican PRI (Kay 1995, 20-24).

Juan Molinar and Jeffrey Weldon have claimed that by allocating resources according to electoral outcomes through PRONASOL in Mexico, the federal government was responding to the population's politically expressed demands (Molinar Horcasitas and Weldon 1994, 140). They, like many others, believe that targeted assistance programs, even managed on a clientelistic basis, can be an effective means of representation in a neoliberal economy. Even if clientelism permits executives to proceed with the liberalization of trade and foreign investment, the delivery of patronage by parties is not an adequate formula for representing the interests of voters in the long term. Clientelism practiced in the extreme robs parties of identities and coherence and crowds out other forms of interest representation. Most important, it deprives citizens of their capacity to hold parties and politicians accountable for the policies they pursue in office.

## Alternatives to Parties: Preliminary Evidence

When military regimes closed legislatures and declared recesses on political party activity, new social movements arose in many countries to fill the representational void. Although party activists moved into leadership roles in some of these organizations,[37] by and large the new social movements of the 1970s mobilized sectors of the population, especially poor women, that had never been politically mobilized before (Alvarez 1990). This was especially true of the grassroots movements of the Catholic Church known as ecclesial base communities (comunidades eclesiales de base (Sp.)/comunidades eclesiais de base (Pg.) — CEBs), neighborhood associations, and other gender, ethnic, and neighborhood-based groups that formed to defend the material interests of communities neglected by authoritarian rulers. These movements proved to be at least as effective at gaining a sewer or a school for local communities or legal protection for women as parties had been — perhaps even more so. Even before enthusiasm for new social movements waned, the activities of home-grown and transnational NGOs in Latin America have expanded. NGOs have been praised for their ability, often in conjunction with transnational organizations, to protect communities in myriad ways. The largely unanticipated growth and initial success of these movements and organizations have led some scholars to question whether the decline of parties and partisan loyalties and the commensurate rise of social movements and NGOs represent at minimum nothing more than a change in the arenas and mechanisms of representation, while other, more optimistic scholars view these new sites for political representation as actually having more democratizing potential than the crusty and decaying political institutions they are apparently replacing.[38]

Civil associations have indeed proliferated since the previous period of democratic governance on the continent. Where associational life existed previously, net gains in membership in voluntary organizations were perhaps more modest than generally believed. In Chile, for example, surveys conducted in Greater Santiago in 1967 revealed that about one-third of the population belonged to a labor union, political party, or religious, sporting, or neighborhood association. Most belonged to only one (Hamuy 1967b). In 1993, participation in such organizations had increased slightly: 44 percent of survey respondents in Greater Santiago reported participating in religious, sport, philanthropic, local, culture, union, and other organizations (Garretón 1994, 8). But where civil society was weaker, the proliferation of new civic associations was impressive. In Peru in the 1960s, only 7 percent of the economically active population and 10 percent of rural families were unionized, and only approximately 5 percent of peasants in various communities considered themselves members of a political party (McClintock 1989, 355). As part of its project of national incorporation, the Peruvian military spurred popular sector mobilization; paradoxically, a dense network of teachers' unions and shantytown neighborhood organizations sprang up that the military ultimately could not control (Stokes 1991, 91-93). Perhaps nowhere in Latin America was the "resurrection of civil society" more dramatic and the rise of new social movements more pronounced than in Brazil. In the years following the military coup of 1964, approximately 80,000 CEBs regularly brought together one-quarter of a million people for political and spiritual reflection. During the 1970s and 1980s, as many as 400 feminist organizations injected into the national political debate several issues that had previously been considered private — reproductive rights, violence against women, and day care (Alvarez 1990, 66). The most explicitly political of all social movements in the waning years of the military dictatorship were neighborhood associations. In 1982, there were approximately 8,000 in Brazil, with about 550 in the city of Rio de Janeiro alone, and 900 in São Paulo (Boschi 1987, 180).

Despite their promise, there may be a number of reasons to temper our enthusiasm for the representative potential of what are generally still called the new social movements. First, whether or not social movements can grow independently, apart from political parties, and therefore eventually supplant the functions of parties is debatable. Philip Oxhorn (1995) found that popular organizations in Chilean shantytowns flourished during the dictatorship when political parties were proscribed and that these organizations contributed positively to the development of a new collective identity. However, Susan Stokes reported a very different result in Peru. After the Velasco years, she writes, "The Left and the new movements of the urban poor developed in symbiosis with one another: the Left benefited from the movements' spread, and the movements drew institutional support and protection from the Left" (Stokes 1995, 133-134). Because local activists were inspired by and thrived under the protection of municipal governments of the United Left, they became vulnerable when the national United Left coalition fell apart in 1989 and the partisan Left faltered. After Alberto Fujimori's relentless attack on political parties, waged beginning in 1990 with rhetoric and changes in electoral rules, the partisan

Left became debilitated, and the social movements that it had protected floundered. Second, despite the expansion of social movements in the 1980s, social movements and voluntary associations still do not reach most of society. In Brazil, where these organizations flourished during the dictatorship, only 4 percent of the electorate were affiliated with neighborhood associations in 1988, and only 10 percent were trade union members (Kinzo 1993a, 150).

A third qualifier on the political representation afforded by the surge in social movements of the 1980s stems from the fact that, as one student (and member) of Brazil's neighborhood associations has pointed out, even in the best circumstances, voluntary associations, organized around specific and therefore transitory demands, do not enjoy permanent channels of access to the state (Boschi 1987, 189-190). Yet, in order to be effective mediators for their members, voluntary associations should have regular access to decision-making arenas in Congress or the executive branch. In practice, social movements do not even enjoy regular contacts with individual political representatives in Congress who must approve ordinary legislation and constitutional reform. More than two-thirds (68.5 percent) of the 700 state deputies across Brazil in the period from 1987 to 1990 had no links with either unions or professional/employer, neighborhood, sport, religious, or other associations. Of the major party representatives, 67.9, 64.7, and 71.5 percent of the deputies of the Brazilian Social Democratic Party (Partido Social Democrático Brasileiro – – PSDB), PFL, and PMDB, respectively, had no links with civic associations; 51.5 percent of PT deputies — a party reputed to have more links with social movements than any other — had none (Kinzo 1993a, 151).

Perhaps because of these constraints on the representational capacity of social movements, and because they can and do link themselves directly to policy-making networks, NGOs proliferated in Latin America during the late 1980s and 1990s. In Ecuador, whereas prior to the 1980s there were little more than a handful of NGOs that provided social services or focused on policies to address the issue of land reform, there were well over one thousand registered NGOs by 1994, spurred on by the withdrawal of the state from social service provision, rising levels of university-trained professionals who could no longer be absorbed by the state, and the increasing attention and resources channeled to NGOs by international organizations (Segarra 1997, 492, 499-500). NGOs in Ecuador have contributed positively to political representation on a range of issues from health care provision to income generation, Monique Segarra contends, by widening "the range of voices in social policy" and "by inserting their interpretation of popular needs, social problems, and methods of addressing those problems into traditionally circumscribed policy arenas" (Segarra 1997, 493-495). She is quick to admit, though, that the question of whether NGOs represent popular sector interests as the interventionist state is reformed is more problematic because "NGOs are not sanctioned by elections to represent the poor in deliberations about social policy and state reform," and, therefore, "if the direct consultation and linkage of NGOs to particular groups of popular sectors are the criteria for representation, then many NGOs will fail the test" (Segarra 1997, 494).

In sum, if democracy in the 1990s is more *inclusive* than ever before in Latin America, it is not necessarily more *representative*. New social movements may have *mobilized* broader segments of the citizenry than parties did in the past (and in so doing they have broadened the bases for political association), but they have not necessarily *represented* them as effectively. NGOs may voice the interests of the poor in policy arenas as they understand them but offer few if any mechanisms of accountability to the citizenry. When citizens are represented largely by social movements or NGOs, they are detached from the political institutions whose function it is to aggregate interests in a democratic society. This divorce may leave citizens unrepresented on such salient issues as monetary and trade policy, social security reform, and consumer protection. Although social movements and voluntary organizations can effectively *supplement* party networks of representation, there is no evidence that they work well as *substitutes* for them and, at this time, no basis for concluding that the breakup of old networks is a necessary prelude to broader and more genuine future forms of political representation.

## POSSIBLE ALTERNATIVES AND DIRECTIONS FOR FUTURE RESEARCH

This chapter has raised many questions with respect to the nature of political representation in Latin America in the 1990s. The only answer it can provide with certainty is that the nature of political representation is changing. Whether this change amounts to no more than a metamorphosis in form and arena or whether the change is for better or for worse simply cannot at this time be concluded definitely. Below, I briefly summarize the major findings of this chapter, suggest some possible lines along which interests might reorganize, and mention some avenues where scholars might seek answers.

Among the most important findings of this chapter are that in Latin America today, 1) corporatism is in decline, 2) partisan and electoral "dealignment" has proceeded farther and faster in more countries than has "realignment," and 3) there is not yet evidence that voluntary associations and NGOs have mobilized many more citizens than when they "first" appeared in the 1970s and 1980s, respectively. While disengagement from some networks of representation (such as stifling state corporatism and traditional clientelism) might conceivably signal an advance toward the formation of new and better forms of political representation, it has more often contributed to a growing gap in representation. Although there are scattered indications of a reorganization of political representation in the 1990s to date, we do not yet know, and cannot yet explain, why the process of electoral realignment is occurring faster, if at all, in some countries than in others, nor when a regime is able to develop a new means for mediating societal interests to replace ones in decay. At the moment, we urgently require a framework for understanding when, how, and why the reorganization of societal interests and their reattachment to political institutions take place.

How interests might reorganize in the coming decade is as yet unclear, but one possibility is that the nature of political representation could become more decentralized. Even programmatic parties might turn to organizing constituents in local units along territorial lines. Corresponding to the decentralization of governmental structures, financing, and decisionmaking begun under Augusto Pinochet, parties across the ideological spectrum in Chile are decentralizing their party organizations. Even the Socialist Party, according to one leader, needs to think about "reaching its constituents not at their place of work but where they live."[39] Already, survey evidence reveals that citizens are taking their problems to local governments, along with churches and neighborhood groups (Juntas de Vecinos), and most are satisfied that their requests for help have been well received. The most frequent demands made to local governments are for education and health services (Garretón 1994, 8).

The likely effect of political decentralization on democratic representation is unclear and potentially ambiguous. A long tradition in social theory celebrates the virtues of democracy at the local level, where decisionmakers are close to their electors and a great degree of popular participation is obviously possible. Recently, Deborah Yashar has argued effectively in a similar vein that greater transparency in decentralized democracies will also help the political representation of ethnic minorities in Central America and the Andes (Yashar 1996). However, traditional elites are almost always stronger in local areas, and the prospects for implementing progressive agendas are often better in national arenas, where their power is diluted. Decentralization could also conceivably encourage the practice of clientelism.

Just as political representation could become more localized, it might also conceivably go "global." "Transnational issue alliances" between indigenous communities in Brazil and non-governmental environmental and human rights organizations in the developed countries have proved effective in augmenting the influence of both partners.[40] What may especially spark the development of transnational forms of interest representation is economic integration at the regional and subregional levels. If the European example is instructive, the Southern Cone Common Market (Mercado Común del Sur — MERCOSUR), the Association of Caribbean States, and the projected expansion of the North American Free Trade Agreement will open up profound and genuine possibilities for supranational political representation.[41]

In order to illuminate more fully the current state of political representation in Latin America and which of the numerous possibilities for the reorganization of those interests might come to pass, a collective research agenda is needed.[42] In particular, we need to clarify what drives the loyalty of citizens, how the process of political decentralization will affect the reorganization of political representation, and the nature of links between social movements and the halls of political power and decisionmaking. Toward this end, researchers might consider an extended use of survey research. Surveys of public opinion can provide a snapshot of how citizens evaluate the performance of particular representatives (politicians and organizations), whether or not they belong to or identify with political parties, unions, and voluntary organizations, whether they have faith in or are cynical about democratic institutions, and for whom they are likely to vote. With the Latin American field currently undergoing a delayed behavioral revolution, students of Latin American politics have a wider array of excellent surveys of public opinion at their disposal than at any previous time. The results of these surveys can be crucial for determining the current state of the linkages between voters and parties, and I have obviously relied heavily upon such data in preparing this chapter.

Surveys may, however, be less suggestive of the overarching framework in which individuals make decisions about who should represent them. They are less able to predict where a disillusioned Mexican voter in 1989 or 1991 will turn in 1998 than to record the fact of that voter's disillusion. Manuel Garretón's surveys of a new Chilean political culture struggling to be born may constitute an exception, and more work like this needs to be done.[43] Even when surveys are well designed, however, not all studies of political representation should be situated at the individual level. It is also important to understand the dynamic interaction among political parties, citizen groups, and political institutions. Systematic yet in-depth interviews will be needed to complement large-number surveys if we are to discover these qualitative patterns of interaction, which in turn are important for understanding the basis for the realignment of political interests in the region.

Finally, in order to evaluate in a comprehensive manner the *quality* of political representation in Latin America, the links between political representatives and centers of decisionmaking in the state must be mapped out and the results of political mediation delineated. Studies seeking to illuminate the process by which various political mediators influence public policy ideally could target a range of programs and policies across levels of government (for example, from basic sanitation, usually delivered by local authorities, to economic policy, formulated by central governments). Beyond the transformative effect that new forms of social and political organization are claimed to have on political identities and political culture, any study of democratization in Latin America that has as a core concern the quality of democratic representation and accountability must identify the contributions of these new and old channels of political mediation to representing the interests of a new generation of citizens.

# Notes

1. I would like to acknowledge the financial support of the joint program of the Social Science Research Council and American Council of Learned Societies, the Fulbright-Hays Faculty Research Program, and the Heinz Endowment of the University of Pittsburgh's Latin American Studies Center that made initial research for this chapter possible. For their excellent comments on the preliminary version of this chapter, I wish to thank Felipe Agüero, Jonathan Hartlyn, Scott Mainwaring, Tony Messina, Jeffrey Stark, and Juan Manuel Villasuso. Finally, I am also grateful to the participants in the "Conference on the *Fault Lines of Democratic Governance*" that spawned this volume, at whose spirited urging I have attempted to clarify that the paradise of political representation in Latin America lies ahead of, not behind, us.

2. See Jorge I. Domínguez and Abraham F. Lowenthal, 1994, "The Challenges of Democratic Governance in Latin America and the Caribbean," Policy Brief, Inter-American Dialogue. Such a focus, they point out, leads us away from sometimes futile exercises in categorizing democracies and makes our focus on democracies' weaknesses meaningful.

3. Manuel Antonio Garretón, 1994, "The Political Culture of Democratization in Chile," paper presented to the annual meeting of the American Political Science Association, New York (September), 5.

4. A very useful synthesis of the literature of the new institutionalism can be found in Peter A. Hall and Rosemary Taylor, 1994, "Political Science and the Four New Institutionalisms," paper presented at the annual meeting of the American Political Science Association, New York (September). Hall and Taylor highlight that at least four relatively distinct schools of thought have developed under the broad rubric of the "new institutionalism": historical institutionalism, rational choice institutionalism, economic institutionalism, and sociological institutionalism. Despite their differences, each school shares the view that institutions matter in shaping political behavior. Among a spate of works in recent years in the Latin American field are Larry Diamond, Juan J. Linz, and Seymour Martin Lipset, eds., 1989, *Democracy in Developing Countries: Latin America* (Boulder, Colo.: Lynne Rienner Publishers); Matthew Soberg Shugart and John M. Carey, 1992, *Presidents and Assemblies: Constitutional Design and Electoral Dynamics* (Cambridge, U.K.: Cambridge University Press); Barbara Geddes, 1994, *Politician's Dilemma: Building State Capacity in Latin America* (Berkeley: University of California Press); and Scott Mainwaring and Matthew Soberg Shugart, 1997, *Presidentialism and Democracy in Latin America* (Cambridge, U.K.: Cambridge University Press).

5. The most persuasive case for parliamentarism has been presented by the contributors to Juan J. Linz and Arturo Valenzuela, eds., 1994, *The Failure of Presidential Democracy* (Baltimore: The Johns Hopkins University Press). The strongest case for reform has been made for Brazil by Bolívar Lamounier, 1989, "Brazil: Inequality Against Democracy," in Linz, Diamond, and Lipset 1989, 150-153; and Scott Mainwaring, 1991, "Politicians, Parties, and Electoral Systems: Brazil in Comparative Perspective," *Comparative Politics* 24 (1): 21-43.

6. One review of the recent literature on democratic institutions suggests that studies of political institutions cannot agree on whether presidential or parliamentary systems are more stable, two-party or multiparty systems are more representative, and unicameral or bicameral legislatures are more effective. See George Tsebelis, 1994, "Decision-Making in Political Systems: Veto Players in Presidentialism, Parliamentarism, Multicameralism and Multipartism," paper presented at the annual meeting of the American Political Science Association, New York (September).

7. Of course, in instances where institutional design *has* varied, such as when countries have enacted permissive party legislation during democratic transitions, institutional change can contribute to less effective governance and hence more public disillusionment with government.

8. Among the classic works on political parties, see Maurice Duverger, 1964, *Political Parties: Their Organization and Activity in the Modern State*, translated by Barbara and Robert North, 3rd ed. (London: Methuen); Walter Dean Burnham, 1970, *Critical Elections and the Mainsprings of American Politics* (New York: W.W. Norton); and Giovanni Sartori, 1976, *Parties and Party Systems: A Framework for Analysis* (Cambridge, U.K.: Cambridge University Press).

9. For the case of the United States, see Martin Shefter, 1977, "Party and Patronage: Germany, England, and Italy," *Politics and Society* 7 (4): 403-451. Arturo Valenzuela, 1977, *Political Brokers in Chile: Local Government in a Centralized Polity* (Durham, N.C.: Duke University Press), also claims this was true of Chilean parties before 1973.

10. See Graciela Ducatenzeiler, Philippe Faucher, and Julián Castro-Rea, 1990, "Back to Populism: Latin America's Alternative to Democracy," paper presented at the annual meeting of the American Political Science Association, San Francisco (August 30-September 2); Carina Perelli, 1991, "The New *Caudillos* and Democracy without Parties," paper presented at the conference on "Political Parties and Political Representation in the Post-Authoritarian Era," Woodrow Wilson Center for Scholars, Washington, D.C. (November 8-9); and Kurt Weyland, 1996, "Neopopulism and Neoliberalism in Latin America: Unexpected Affinities," *Studies in Comparative International Development* 31: 3 (Fall): 3-31. All these authors clamor rightly for a political definition of populism as a form of political representation in order to disassociate it from the postwar economic model, and Weyland in particular distinguishes "neopopulists" from populists by their constituents. Classical populists had their primary following among urban workers and the provincial lower middle classes, whereas neopopulists of the 1980s and 1990s have sought support in the urban informal sector and among the rural poor.

11. For an exposition of the idea that citizens vote to reward or punish incumbent performance, see Morris P. Fiorina, 1981, *Retrospective Voting in American Elections* (New Haven, Conn.: Yale University Press).

12. Electoral results are from Bruce H. Kay, 1995, "Fujipopulism and the Liberal State in Peru, 1990-1995," paper presented at the International Congress of the Latin American Studies Association, Washington, D.C. (September), 28. APRA received 4.1 percent of the vote and AP only 1.7 percent.

13. Joseph Straubhaar, Organ Olsen, and Maria Cavaliari Nunes, 1993, "The Brazilian Case: Influencing the Voter," in Skidmore 1993, 123, 127-128, 133. Also frequently cited were family and friends (41 percent) and conversations with colleagues at work and school (27 percent), while relatively few respondents reported being influenced by neighborhood associations (6 percent), the Catholic Church (5 percent), union activists (5 percent), and public opinion polls (5 percent).

14. Garretón 1994, 8. Between 14 and 17 percent of those sampled reported speaking about politics frequently with family and friends, from 34 to 38 percent some of the time, and 49 percent not at all.

15. Jonathan Hartlyn, 1994b, "Democracies in Contemporary South America: Convergences and Diversities," paper presented at the Segundo Encuentro de Estudios Políticos sobre el Mundo Andino, Villa de Leyva, Colombia (April), 9. Hartlyn's figures are from a public opinion survey in 11 Latin American countries (Brazil, Peru, Colombia, Venezuela, Chile, Uruguay, Bolivia, Ecuador, El Salvador, Guatemala, and Mexico) plus Spain (the second "Barómetro de Opinión Iberoamericana") reported in *La República* (Lima, Peru).

16. I have explored these ideas further in my 1993, "After Regime Change: Authoritarian Legacies, Political Representation, and the Democratic Future of South America," *World Politics* 45 (3): 464-500.

17. Julio Cotler, 1995, "Political Parties and the Problems of Democratic Consolidation in Peru," in Mainwaring and Scully 1995b, 340, has argued that both "bourgeois" parties and parties of the Left in Peru lost support in the 1980s because they continued to be plagued by personalized leadership, authoritarian structures, segmentary recruitment methods, and rigid ideological positions.

18. While some parties in the region such as the Chilean Socialist Party have struggled to redefine party programs in a coherent way that resonates with their underlying philosophical foundations, many have not. I have examined the ideological evolution of Chilean parties in my 1994, "State Retreat and the Reformulation of Political Representation in Latin America," paper presented at the annual meeting of the American Political Science Association, New York (September).

19. Union membership declined from a peak of 679,910 in 1973 (the year of the military coup) to 627,217 in 1977; it dropped sharply to 386,910 in 1980, largely as a result of trade liberalization; and after the deep recession of 1981-1983, it dipped again to 320,903. It recovered modestly to 446,194 in 1988 and then rapidly after the transition to democracy with the reform of labor laws and economic prosperity to 606,812 in 1990 and 701,355 in 1991. By contrast, the unionized population in manufacturing fell from 280,143 in 1973 to 128,419 in 1988 but recovered only to 179,192 in 1991. Guillermo Campero and José A. Valenzuela, 1984, *El movimiento sindical en el régimen militar chileno, 1973-1981* (Santiago: Instituto Latinoamericano de Estudios Transnacionales [ILET] and Labor Department).

20. See James W. McGuire, 1995, "Political Parties and Democracy in Argentina," in Mainwaring and Scully 1995b, 232. The number of public sector workers declined.

21. IBGE, *Annuário Estatístico 1993*, 2-252. Rural laborers, whose organizations were previously repressed, were organized into state-sponsored unions beginning during the first decade of military rule. By 1974, rural unions had 2.9 million members; by 1990, 7.8 million.

22. Leigh Payne, 1994, *Brazilian Industrialists and Democratic Change* (Baltimore: The Johns Hopkins University Press), 118. Industrialists were offered the opportunity to provide multiple responses.

23. For three excellent accounts of the transformation of state-union relations in Mexico, see M. Victoria Murillo, 1996, "A Strained Alliance: Continuity and Change in Mexican Labor Politics," Working Paper #96-3 (Cambridge, Mass.: David Rockefeller Center for Latin American Studies, Harvard University); Kevin Middlebrook, 1995, *The Paradox of Revolution: Labor, the State, and Authoritarianism in Mexico* (Baltimore: The

Johns Hopkins University Press); and Judith Teichman, 1995, *Privatization and Political Change in Mexico* (Pittsburgh: University of Pittsburgh Press).

24. M. Victoria Murillo, 1994, "Union Responses to the Economic Reform in Argentina: Organizational Autonomy and the Marketization of Corporatism," paper presented at the annual meeting of the American Political Science Association, New York (September).

25. For a representative sampling of the vast literature on the rise of new social movements and political parties in Western Europe, see Peter Merkl and Kay Lawson, eds., 1988, *When Parties Fail* (Princeton, N.J.: Princeton University Press); Ferdinand Müller-Rommel, ed., 1989, *New Politics in Western Europe: The Rise and Success of Green Parties and Alternative Lists* (Boulder, Colo.: Westview Press); Herbert Kitschelt, 1989, *The Logics of Party Formation: Ecological Politics in Belgium and West Germany* (Ithaca, N.Y.: Cornell University Press); Martin A. Schain, 1990, "Immigration and Politics," in *Developments in French Politics*, eds. Peter A. Hall, Jack Hayward, and Howard Machin (New York: St. Martin's Press); and Russell J. Dalton and Manfred Kuechler, eds., 1990, *Challenging the Political Order: New Social and Political Movements in Western Democracies* (Oxford, U.K.: Oxford University Press).

26. Some executives who have embarked on radically different policy courses than those promised during electoral campaigns, such as Carlos Menem, have survived unscathed, but others, such as Carlos Andrés Pérez, have not.

27. Calculated from DIAP (Departamento Intersindical de Assessoria Parlamentar), 1988, *Quem foi Quem na Constituinte nas Questões de Interesse dos Trabalhadores* (São Paulo: OBORE/Cortez), 261-318.

28. Scott Mainwaring, 1995, "Brazil: Weak Parties, Feckless Democracy," in Mainwaring and Scully 1995b, 379. The Rice Index is calculated by taking the percentage of party members voting with the majority, subtracting the percentage voting against the majority, and dropping the percent sign. An index of 100 means that all party members voted together; an index of 0 means that the party split down the middle.

29. Data for 1974 and 1990 are from José Alvaro Moisés, 1993a, "Democratization and Political Culture," in *Brazil: The Challenges of the 1990s*, ed. Maria D'Alva Gil Kinzo (London: The Institute of Latin American Studies, University of London), 170; and for 1987 from Mainwaring 1995, 385. The results of the June 1987 nationwide poll conducted by IBOPE are very similar to ones conducted in March 1988 in the city of São Paulo and in June 1988 in the cities of São Paulo, Rio de Janeiro, Belo Horizonte, Recife, and Curitiba.

30. Eduardo Hamuy, 1967a, "Investigación post-electoral," Survey #23 (May). Approximately one-half of the respondents identified with the centrist Christian Democratic Party (PDC) (5 percent as members and 45.2 as sympathizers); nearly one-fifth (18.7 percent) as members and sympathizers of the Socialist and Communist Parties; and just under 10 percent with the rightist National Party (PN).

31. Conaghan 1995, 451. Also cited as a factor in the growth of the electorate in Ecuador were registration drives.

32. The National Action Party (PAN) first ran a candidate for president in 1952. I averaged the vote in presidential elections in this 30-year period because of the atypical 1976 election, in which the PAN did not run a candidate. Data are from Craig and Cornelius 1995, 258.

33. Rodrigo Baño, Fernando Bustamante, and Hernán Gutiérrez, 1991, "Conformación de opiniones sobre los partidos políticos en el desenlace de la transición," FLACSO Political Studies Series, Working Paper #10 (Santiago: FLACSO) (April), 16. The panel included 3,084 respondents from metropolitan Santiago, 567 from the city of Concepción, and 455 from Temuco.

34. Data for 1989 are from Conaghan 1995, 451, and for 1994 from Isaacs 1994.

35. Although electoral alignments have been characterized as weakening and party systems as experiencing increased fragmentation and electoral volatility across advanced industrial democracies, party instability and electoral dealignment appear to be most pronounced in The Netherlands, Britain, Scandinavia, and Spain. Russell J. Dalton, Scott C. Flanagan, and Paul Allen Beck, 1984, "Political Forces and Partisan Change," in *Electoral Change in Advanced Industrial Democracies: Realignment or Dealignment?* eds. Dalton, Flanagan, and Beck (Princeton, N.J.: Princeton University Press). Leading British scholars, too, characterize the 1970s in Britain as the "decade of dealignment." For a now classic statement of electoral dealignment in Britain, see Bo Särlvik and Ivor Crewe, 1983, *Decade of Dealignment: The Conservative Victory of 1979 and Electoral Trends in the 1970s* (Cambridge, U.K.: Cambridge University Press).

36. Denise Dresser, 1994, "Bringing the Poor Back In: National Solidarity as a Strategy of Regime Legitimation," in *Transforming State-Society Relations in Mexico: The National Solidarity Strategy*, eds. Wayne A. Cornelius, Ann L. Craig, and Jonathan Fox (La Jolla: University of California, San Diego, Center for U.S.-Mexican Studies), 147-157. The characterization of the *cacique*-led clientelistic network is from Susan Kaufman Purcell, 1981, "Mexico: Clientelism, Corporatism and Political Stability," in *Political Clientelism, Patronage, and Development*, eds. S.N. Eisenstadt and René Lemarchand, *Contemporary Political Sociology*, Volume 3 (Beverly Hills, Calif.: Sage), 200.

37. This is evident in Chilean shantytowns. See Philip D. Oxhorn, 1995, *Organizing Civil Society: The Popular Sectors and the Struggle for Democracy in Chile* (University Park, Pa.: The Pennsylvania State University Press), 28; and Cathy Lisa Schneider, 1995, *Shantytown Protest in Pinochet's Chile* (Philadelphia: Temple University Press).

38. Such arguments are consistent with a long tradition in the social sciences that leads back to Alexis de Tocqueville. Recently, Robert D. Putnam, 1993, *Making Democracy Work: Civic Traditions in Modern Italy* (Princeton, N.J.: Princeton University Press), has popularized once again the view that the denser the cluster of voluntary associations in civil society, the better for democracy. For Putnam, networks of civic engagement provide the social capital that enables democratic institutions to operate more effectively.

39. Author's interview with Marcelo Schilling, Santiago, August 13, 1992.

40. See Kathryn Sikkink, 1993, "Human Rights, Principled Issue-Networks, and Sovereignty in Latin America," *International Organization* 47 (3): 411-441; and Margaret Keck and Kathryn Sikkink, 1998, *Activists Beyond Borders: Advocacy Networks in International Politics* (Ithaca, N.Y.: Cornell University Press).

41. For a view on the transformation of political representation in the European Union, see Wolfgang Streeck and Philippe C. Schmitter, 1991, "From National Corporatism to Transnational Pluralism: Organized Interests in the Single European Market," *Politics and Society* 19 (2): 133-164.

42. Here I endorse Robert Kaufman's call to scholars in the planning session for the conference that spawned this volume to build collective knowledge that is truly comparative and cumulative. See Felipe Agüero, et al., 1994, "Fault Lines of Democratic Governance in the Americas: Workshop Report" (Coral Gables, Fla.: North-South Center) (November).

43. Garretón (1994) describes the surveys he has directed or codirected since 1989.

# References

Agüero, Felipe, Mark Everingham, Julie Diehl, and Rebecca Wisot. 1994. "Fault Lines of Democratic Governance in the Americas: Workshop Report." Coral Gables, Fla.: North-South Center at the University of Miami. December.

Alvarez, Sonia E. 1990. *Engendering Democracy in Brazil: Women's Movements in Transition Politics*. Princeton, N.J.: Princeton University Press.

Ames, Barry. 1994. "The Reverse Coattails Effect: Local Party Organization in the 1989 Brazilian Presidential Election." *American Political Science Review* 88 (1): 95-111.

Antunes, Ricardo. 1991. *O Novo Sindicalismo*. São Paulo: Brasil Urgente.

Archer, Ronald P. 1995. "Party Strength and Weakness in Colombia's Besieged Democracy." In *Building Democratic Institutions: Party Systems in Latin America*, eds. Scott Mainwaring and Timothy R. Scully. Stanford, Calif.: Stanford University Press.

Archer, Ronald P., and Matthew Soberg Shugart. 1997. "The Unrealized Potential of Presidential Dominance in Colombia." In *Presidentialism and Democracy in Latin America*, eds. Scott Mainwaring and Matthew Soberg Shugart. Cambridge, U.K.: Cambridge University Press.

Baño, Rodrigo, Fernando Bustamante, and Hernán Gutiérrez. 1991. "Conformación de opiniones sobre los partidos políticos en el desenlace de la transición." FLACSO Political Studies Series, Working Paper #10. Santiago: FLACSO (April).

Barrera, Manuel. 1994. "El ajuste macroeconómico en Chile y la política de los sectores populares." Paper presented at the conference, "What Kind of Market? What Kind of Democracy?" McGill University, Montréal, Canada (April).

Boschi, Renato R. 1987. "Social Movements and the New Political Order in Brazil." In *State and Society in Brazil: Continuity and Change*, eds. J.D. Wirth, Edson de Oliveira Nunes, and Thomas E. Bogenschild. Boulder, Colo.: Westview Press.

Burnham, Walter Dean. 1970. *Critical Elections and the Mainstream of American Politics*. New York: W.W. Norton.

Campero, Guillermo, and José A. Valenzuela. 1984. *El movimiento sindical en el régimen militar chileno, 1973-1981*. Santiago: Instituto Latinoamericano de Estudios Transnacionales (ILET).

Cavarozzi, Marcelo. 1992. "Beyond Transitions in Latin America." *Journal of Latin American Studies* 24 (3): 665-684.

Centro de Estudios de la Realidad Contemporánea (CERC). 1992. "Informe de prensa: el segundo año del gobierno democrático." Santiago (March),

Chalmers, Douglas A., Scott B. Martin, and Kerianne Piester. 1997. "Associative Networks: New Structures of Representation for the Popular Sectors?" In *The New Politics of Inequality in Latin America: Rethinking Participation and Representation*, eds. Douglas A. Chalmers, Carlos M. Vilas, Katherine Hite, Scott B. Martin, Kerianne Piester, and Monique Segarra. Oxford, U.K.: Oxford University Press.

Conaghan, Catherine M. 1995. "Politicians Against Parties: Discord and Disconnection in Ecuador's Party System." In *Building Democratic Institutions: Party Systems in Latin America*, eds. Scott Mainwaring and Timothy R. Scully. Stanford, Calif.: Stanford University Press.

Córdova Macías, Ricardo. 1996. "El Salvador: Transition from Civil War." In *Constructing Democratic Governance: Latin America and the Caribbean in the 1990s*, eds. Jorge I. Domínguez and Abraham F. Lowenthal. Baltimore: The Johns Hopkins University Press.

Cotler, Julio. 1995. "Political Parties and the Problem of Democratic Consolidation in Peru." In *Building Democratic Institutions: Party Systems in Latin America*, eds. Scott Mainwaring and Timothy R. Scully. Stanford, Calif.: Stanford University Press.

Craig, Ann, and Wayne Cornelius. 1995. "Houses Divided: Parties and Political Reform in Mexico." In *Building Democratic Institutions: Party Systems in Latin America*, eds. Scott Mainwaring and Timothy R. Scully. Stanford, Calif.: Stanford University Press.

Dalton, Russell J., and Manfred Kuechler, eds. 1990. *Challenging the Political Order: New Social and Political Movements in Western Democracies*. Oxford, U.K.: Oxford University Press.

Dalton, Russell J., Scott C. Flanagan, and Paul Allen Beck, eds. 1984. "Political Forces and Partisan Change." In *Electoral Change in Advanced Industrial Democracies: Realignment or Dealignment?* eds. Dalton, Flanagan, and Beck. Princeton, N.J.: Princeton University Press.

de la Balze, Felipe A.M. 1995. *Remaking the Argentine Economy*. New York: Council on Foreign Relations.

de Lima, Venicio A. 1993. "Brazilian Television in the 1989 Presidential Election: Constructing a President." In *Television, Politics, and the Transition to Democracy in Latin America*, ed. Thomas E. Skidmore. Baltimore/Washington, D.C.: The Johns Hopkins University Press/Woodrow Wilson Center.

Departmento Intersindical de Assessoria Parlamentar (DIAP). 1988. *Quem Foi Quem na Constituinte nas Questões de Interesse dos Trabalhadores*. São Paulo: OBORE/Cortez.

Diamond, Larry, Juan J. Linz, and Seymour Martin Lipset, eds. 1989. *Democracy in Developing Countries: Latin America*. Boulder, Colo.: Lynne Rienner Publishers.

Domínguez, Jorge, and Abraham F. Lowenthal. 1994. "The Challenges of Democratic Governance in Latin America and the Caribbean." Policy Brief, Inter-American Dialogue (September).

Domínguez, Jorge I., and James A. McCann. 1995. "Shaping Mexico's Electoral Arena: The Construction of Partisan Cleavages in the 1988 and 1990 National Elections." *American Political Science Review* 89 (March): 34-48.

Dresser, Denise. 1994. "Bringing the Poor Back In: National Solidarity as a Strategy of Regime Legitimation." In *Transforming State-Society Relations in Mexico: The National Solidarity Strategy*, eds. Wayne A. Cornelius, Ann L. Craig, and Jonathan Fox. La Jolla: University of California, San Diego, Center for U.S.-Mexican Studies.

Ducatenzeiler, Graciela, Philippe Faucher, and Julián Castro-Rea. 1990. "Back to Populism: Latin America's Alternative to Democracy." Paper presented at the annual meeting of the American Political Science Association, San Francisco (August 30- September 2).

Duverger, Maurice. 1964. *Political Parties: Their Organization and Activity in the Modern State*. Translated by Barbara and Robert North, 3rd ed. London: Methuen.

*Economist*. 1995. "Peru: Fujimori Takes All," April 15.

Fara, Carlos. 1994. "La sociedad de Pico Truncado: informe sobre las entrevistas cualitativas," unpublished paper (August), 8.

Fara, Carlos. 1995. "Observaciones sobre los resultados del 14 de mayo de 1995," unpublished paper (May).

Fiorina, Morris P. 1981. *Retrospective Voting in American Elections*. New Haven, Conn.: Yale University Press.

Fleischer, David V. 1987. "O Congresso-Constituinte de 1987: Um Perfil Socio-Econômico e Político," unpublished paper, Universidade de Brasília.

Garretón, Manuel Antonio. 1994. "The Political Culture of Democratization in Chile." Paper presented at the annual meeting of the American Political Science Association, New York (September).

Geddes, Barbara. 1994. *Politician's Dilemma: Building State Capacity in Latin America*. Berkeley: University of California Press.

Hagopian, Frances. 1993. "After Regime Change: Authoritarian Legacies, Political Representation, and the Democratic Future of South America." *World Politics* 45 (April): 464-500.

Hagopian, Frances. 1994. "State Retreat and the Reformulation of Political Representation in Latin America." Paper presented at the annual meeting of the American Political Science Association, New York (September).

Hagopian, Frances. 1995. "Negotiating Economic Transitions in Liberalizing Polities." Paper presented at the annual meeting of the American Political Science Association, Chicago (September).

Hall, Peter A., and Rosemary Taylor. 1994. "Political Science and the Four New Institutionalisms." Paper presented at the annual meeting of the American Political Science Association, New York (September).

Hamuy, Eduardo. 1966. "Jornada única, leche, y aprendizaje político." Surveys 18-19 (October-November).

Hamuy, Eduardo. 1967a. "Investigación post-electoral." Survey 23 (May).

Hamuy, Eduardo. 1967b. "Encuesta Política." Survey 24 (November).

Hartlyn, Jonathan. 1994a. "Crisis-Ridden Elections (Again) in the Dominican Republic: Neopatrimonialism, Presidentialism, and Weak Electoral Oversight." *Journal of Interamerican Studies and World Affairs* 36 (4): 91-144.

Hartlyn, Jonathan. 1994b. "Democracies in Contemporary South America: Convergences and Diversities." Paper presented at the Segundo Encuentro de Estudios Políticos sobre el Mundo Andino, Villa de Leyva, Colombia (April).

Instituto Brasileiro de Geografia e Estatística (IBGE). 1993. *Annuário Estatístico 1993*. Rio de Janeiro: IBGE.

Isaacs, Anita. 1996. "Ecuador: Standing the Test of Time?" In *Constructing Democratic Governance: Latin America and the Caribbean in the 1990s*, eds. Jorge I. Domínguez and Abraham F. Lowenthal. Baltimore: The Johns Hopkins University Press.

Katz, Richard, and Peter Mair, eds. 1992. *Party Organizations: Data Handbook on Party Organizations in Western Democracies, 1960-1990*. London: Sage.

Kay, Bruce H. 1995. "Fujipopulism and the Liberal State in Peru, 1990-1995." Paper presented at the International Congress of the Latin American Studies Association, Washington, D.C. (September).

Keck, Margaret, and Kathryn Sikkink. 1998. *Activists Beyond Borders: Advocacy Networks in International Politics*. Ithaca, N.Y.: Cornell University Press.

Kinzo, Maria D'Alva Gil. 1993a. "Consolidation of Democracy: Governability and Political Parties in Brazil." In *Brazil: The Challenges of the 1990s*, ed. Maria D'Alva Gil Kinzo. London: The Institute of Latin American Studies, University of London.

Kinzo, Maria D'Alva Gil. 1993b. "The 1989 Presidential Election: Electoral Behavior in a Brazilian City." *Journal of Latin American Studies* 25 (May): 313-330.

Kitschelt, Herbert. 1989. *The Logics of Party Formation: Ecological Politics in Belgium and West Germany*. Ithaca, N.Y.: Cornell University Press.

Kline, Harvey F. 1996. "Colombia: Building Democracy in the Midst of Violence and Drugs." In *Constructing Democratic Governance: Latin America and the Caribbean in the 1990s*, eds. Jorge I. Domínguez and Abraham F. Lowenthal. Baltimore: The Johns Hopkins University Press.

Kornblith, Miriam, and Daniel H. Levine. 1995. "Venezuela: The Life and Times of the Party System," In *Building Democratic Institutions: Party Systems in Latin America*, eds. Scott Mainwaring and Timothy R. Scully. Stanford, Calif.: Stanford University Press.

Lamounier, Bolívar. 1989. "Brazil: Inequality Against Democracy." In *Democracy in Developing Countries: Latin America*, eds. Larry Diamond, Juan J. Linz, and Seymour Martin Lipset. Boulder, Colo.: Lynne Rienner Publishers.

Linz, Juan J., and Arturo Valenzuela, eds. 1994. *The Failure of Presidential Democracy*. Baltimore: The Johns Hopkins University Press.

López-Maya, Margarita. 1997. "The Rise of Causa R in Venezuela." In *The New Politics of Inequality in Latin America: Rethinking Participation and Representation*, eds. Douglas A. Chalmers, Carlos M. Vilas, Katherine Hite, Scott B. Martin, Kerianne Piester, and Monique Segarra. Oxford, U.K.: Oxford University Press.

Mainwaring, Scott. 1991. "Politicians, Parties, and Electoral Systems: Brazil in Comparative Perspective." *Comparative Politics* 24 (1): 21-43.

Mainwaring, Scott. 1995. "Brazil: Weak Parties, Feckless Democracy." In *Building Democratic Institutions: Party Systems in Latin America*, eds. Scott Mainwaring and Timothy R. Scully. Stanford, Calif.: Stanford University Press.

Mainwaring, Scott, and Timothy R. Scully. 1995a. "Introduction: Party Systems in Latin America." In *Building Democratic Institutions: Party Systems in Latin America*. Stanford, Calif.: Stanford University Press.

Mainwaring, Scott, and Timothy R. Scully, eds. 1995b. *Building Democratic Institutions: Party Systems in Latin America*. Stanford, Calif.: Stanford University Press.

Mainwaring, Scott, and Matthew Sobert Shugart. 1997. *Presidentialism and Democracy in Latin America*. Cambridge, U.K.: Cambridge University Press.

McClintock, Cynthia. 1989. "Peru: Precarious Regimes, Authoritarian and Democratic." In *Democracy in Developing Countries: Latin America*, eds. Larry Diamond, Juan J. Linz, and Seymour Martin Lipset. Boulder, Colo.: Lynne Rienner Publishers.

McGuire, James W. 1995. "Political Parties and Democracy in Argentina." In *Building Democratic Institutions: Party Systems in Latin America*, eds. Scott Mainwaring and Timothy R. Scully. Stanford, Calif.: Stanford University Press.

Merkl, Peter, and Kay Lawson, eds. 1988. *When Parties Fail*. Princeton, N.J.: Princeton University Press.

Messina, Anthony. 1995. "Are West European Parties in Crisis? Select Evidence from the British and German Cases." Paper presented at the conference "Party Politics in the Year 2000," Manchester, U.K. (January).

Middlebrook, Kevin. 1995. *The Paradox of Revolution: Labor, the State, and Authoritarianism in Mexico*. Baltimore: The Johns Hopkins University Press.

Moisés, José Alvaro. 1993a. "Democratization and Political Culture." In *Brazil: The Challenges of the 1990s*, ed. Maria D'Alva Gil Kinzo. London: The Institute of Latin American Studies, University of London.

Moisés, José Alvaro. 1993b. "Elections, Political Parties, and Political Culture in Brazil: Changes and Continuities." *Journal of Latin American Studies* 25 (October): 575-611.

Molinar Horcasitas, Juan, and Jeffrey A. Weldon. 1994. "Electoral Determinants and Consequences of National Solidarity." In *Transforming State-Society Relations in Mexico: The National Solidarity Strategy*, eds. Wayne A. Cornelius, Ann L. Craig, and Jonathan Fox. La Jolla, Calif.: University of California, San Diego, Center for U.S.-Mexican Studies.

Müller-Rommel, Ferdinand, ed. 1989. *New Politics in Western Europe: The Rise and Success of Green Parties and Alternative Lists*. Boulder, Colo.: Westview Press.

Murillo, M. Victoria. 1994. "Union Responses to the Economic Reform in Argentina: Organizational Autonomy and the Marketization of Corporatism." Paper presented at the annual meeting of the American Political Science Association, New York (September).

Murillo, M. Victoria. 1996. "A Strained Alliance: Continuity and Change in Mexican Labor Politics." Working Paper #96-3, David Rockefeller Center for Latin American Studies, Harvard University.

Nelson, Joan. 1994. "Labor and Business Roles in Dual Transitions: Building Blocks or Stumbling Blocks?" In *Intricate Links: Democratization and Market Reforms in Latin America and Eastern Europe*, ed. Joan Nelson. Washington, D.C.: Overseas Development Council nd New Brunswick, N.J.: Transaction Publishers.

Norris, Pippa, and Joni Lovenduski. 1995. *Political Recruitment: Gender, Race and Class in the British Parliament*. Cambridge, U.K.: Cambridge University Press.

O'Donnell, Guillermo. 1992. "Delegative Democracy?" Kellogg Institute Working Paper (March).

Oxford Analytica. 1991. *Latin America in Perspective*. Boston: Houghton Mifflin.

Oxhorn, Philip. 1994. "Is the Century of Corporatism Over? Neoliberalism and the Rise of Neopluralism." Paper presented at the conference, "What Kind of Market? What Kind of Democracy?" McGill University, Montréal, Canada (April).

Oxhorn, Philip D. 1995. *Organizing Civil Society: The Popular Sectors and the Struggle for Democracy in Chile*. University Park, Pa.: Pennsylvania State University Press.

Palmer, David Scott. 1995. "Peru's 1995 Elections: A Second Look." *LASA Forum* 26 (Summer): 17-20.

Payne, Leigh. 1994. *Brazilian Industrialists and Democratic Change*. Baltimore: The Johns Hopkins University Press.

Perelli, Carina. 1991. "The New *Caudillos* and Democracy Without Parties." Paper presented at the conference, "Political Parties and Political Representation in the Post-Authoritarian Era," Woodrow Wilson Center for Scholars, Washington, D.C. (November 8-9).

Purcell, Susan Kaufman. 1981. "Mexico: Clientelism, Corporatism, and Political Stability." In *Political Clientelism, Patronage, and Development*, eds. S.N. Eisenstadt and René Lemarchand, *Contemporary Political Sociology* 3. Beverly Hills, Calif.: Sage.

Putnam, Robert D. 1993. *Making Democracy Work: Civic Traditions in Modern Italy.* Princeton, N.J.: Princeton University Press.

Särlvik, Bo, and Ivor Crewe. 1983. *Decade of Dealignment: The Conservative Victory of 1979 and Electoral Trends in the 1970s.* Cambridge, U.K.: Cambridge University Press.

Sartori, Giovanni. 1976. *Parties and Party Systems: A Framework for Analysis.* Cambridge, U.K.: Cambridge University Press.

Schain, Martin A. 1990. "Immigration and Politics." In *Developments in French Politics*, eds. Peter A. Hall, Jack Hayward, and Howard Machin. New York: St. Martin's Press.

Schilling, Marcelo. 1992. Interview by author. Santiago, Chile, August 13.

Schmitter, Philippe C. 1971. *Interest Conflict and Political Change in Brazil.* Stanford, Calif.: Stanford University Press.

Schmitter, Philippe C. 1974. "Still the Century of Corporatism?" In *The New Corporatism: Social-Political Structures in the Iberian World*, eds. Frederick B. Pike and Thomas Stritch. Notre Dame, Ind.: University of Notre Dame Press.

Schneider, Cathy Lisa. 1995. *Shantytown Protest in Pinochet's Chile.* Philadelphia: Temple University Press.

Segarra, Monique. 1997. "Redefining the Public/Private Mix: NGOs and the Emergency Social Investment Fund in Ecuador." In *The New Politics of Inequality in Latin America: Rethinking Participation and Representation*, eds. Douglas A. Chalmers, Carlos M. Vilas, Katherine Hite, Scott B. Martin, Kerianne Piester, and Monique Segarra. Oxford, U.K.: Oxford University Press.

Shefter, Martin. 1977. "Party Patronage: Germany, England, and Italy." *Politics and Society* 7 (4): 403-451.

Shugart, Matthew Soberg, and John M. Carey. 1992. *Presidents and Assemblies: Constitutional Design and Electoral Dynamics.* Cambridge, U.K.: Cambridge University Press.

Sikkink, Kathryn. 1993. "Human Rights, Principled Issue-Networks, and Sovereignty in Latin America." *International Organization* 47 (3): 411-441.

Skidmore, Thomas E., ed. 1993. *Television, Politics, and the Transition to Democracy in Latin America.* Baltimore/Washington, D.C.: The Johns Hopkins University Press/ Woodrow Wilson Center.

Sofres-IBOPE. 1989. "Estudio electoral nacional." (February).

Sofres-IBOPE. 1995. "Estudio de opinión pública-nacional." (April).

Stokes, Susan C. 1991. Politics and Latin America's Urban Poor: Reflections from a Lima Shantytown." *Latin American Research Review* 26 (2): 75-101.

Stokes, Susan. 1995. *Cultures in Conflict: Social Movements and the State in Peru.* Berkeley: University of California Press.

Straubhaar, Joseph, Organ Olsen, and Maria Cavaliari Nunes. 1993. "The Brazilian Case: Influencing the Voter." In *Television, Politics, and the Transition to Democracy in Latin America*, ed. Thomas E. Skidmore. Baltimore/Washington, D.C.: The Johns Hopkins University Press/Woodrow Wilson Center.

Streeck, Wolfgang, and Phillipe C. Schmitter. 1991. "From National Corporatism to Transnational Pluralism: Organized Interests in the Single European Market." *Politics and Society* 19:2 (June): 133-164.

Teichman, Judith. 1995. *Privatization and Political Change in Mexico*. Pittsburgh: University of Pittsburgh Press.

Tironi, Eugenio. 1997. "Discontinuidades en el 'paisaje político' chileno." Paper presented at the XX International Congress of the Latin American Studies Association, Guadalajara, April 17-19.

Torres-Rivas, Edelberto. 1996. "Guatemala: Democratic Governability." In *Constructing Democratic Governance: Latin America and the Caribbean in the 1990s*, eds. Jorge I. Domínguez and Abraham F. Lowenthal. Baltimore: The Johns Hopkins University Press.

Tsebelis, George. 1994. "Decision Making in Political Systems: Veto Players in Presidentialism, Parliamentarism, Multicameralism and Multipartism." Paper presented at the annual meeting of the American Political Science Association, New York (September).

Valenzuela, Arturo. 1977. *Political Brokers in Chile: Local Government in a Centralized Polity*. Durham, N.C.: Duke University Press.

Weyland, Kurt. 1996. "Neopopulism and Neoliberalism in Latin America: Unexpected Affinities." *Studies in Comparative International Development* 31 (3): 3-31.

Whitehead, Laurence. 1989. "Political Change and Economic Stabilization: The 'Economic Solidarity Pact.'" In *Mexico's Alternative Political Futures*, eds. Wayne A. Cornelius, Judith Gentleman, and Peter H. Smith. La Jolla: Center for U.S.-Mexican Studies, University of California, San Diego.

Wilkie, James, Carlos Alberto Contreras, and Christof Anders Weber, eds. 1993. *Statistical Abstract of Latin America* 30 (Part 1). Los Angeles: University of California, Los Angeles, Latin American Center Publications.

Yashar, Deborah J. 1995. "Civil War and Social Welfare: The Origins of Costa Rica's Competitive Party System." In *Building Democratic Institutions: Party Systems in Latin America*, eds. Scott Mainwaring and Timothy R. Scully. Stanford, Calif.: Stanford University Press.

Yashar, Deborah J. 1996. "Indigenous Protest and Democracy in Latin America." In *Constructing Democratic Governance: Latin America and the Caribbean in the 1990s*, eds. Jorge I. Domínguez and Abraham F. Lowenthal. Baltimore: The Johns Hopkins University Press.

Zapata, Francisco. 1994. "Sindicalismo y régimen corporativo en México." Paper presented at the conference "What Kind of Market? What Kind of Democracy?" McGill University, Montréal, Canada (April).

# Acronyms and Definitions

| | | |
|---|---|---|
| AD/M-19 | Alianza Democrática (Colombia) | Democratic Alliance M-19 |
| AP | Acción Popular | Popular Action (Peru) |
| APRA | Alianza Popular Revolucionaria Americana | American Revolutionary Popular Alliance (Peru) |
| | Cambio Noventa-Nueva Mayoría | Change 90 - New Majority (Peru) |
| Causa R | Causa Radical | Radical Cause (Venezuela) |
| CEBs | comunidades eclesiales de base/comunidades eclesiais de base | ecclesial base communities |
| CUT | Central Unica dos Trabalhadores | Central Workers' Union (Brazil) |
| CTM | Confederación de Trabajadores de México | Confederation of Mexican Workers  (Mexico) |
| FONAVI | Fondo Nacional de Vivienda | National Housing Fund (Peru) |
| FONCODES | Fondo Nacional de Compensación y Desarrollo | National Development and Social Compensation Fund (Peru) |
| FS | Força Sindical (Brazil) | Union Power |
| | Frente Amplio | Broad Front (Uruguay) |
| | Frente Grande | Grand Front (Argentina) |
| FREPASO | Frente para el País Solidario | Coalition of Frente Grande, País, and other small parties (Argentina) |
| IBOPE | Instituto Brasileiro de Opinão Pública e Estatística | Brazilian Institute of Public Opinion and Statistics (Brazil) |
| M-19 | | Nineteenth of April Movement (Colombia) |
| MERCOSUR | Mercado Común del Sur | Southern Cone Common Market |

| | Nuevo Espacio | New Space (Uruguay) |
|---|---|---|
| PAN | Partido Acción Nacional | National Action Party (Mexico) |
| PDC | Partido Democrático Cristiano | Christian Democratic Party (Chile) |
| PDT | Partido Democrático Trabalhista | Democratic Labor Party (Brazil) |
| PFL | Partido da Frente Liberal | Party of the Liberal Front (Brazil) |
| PLN | Partido Liberación Nacional | National Liberation Party (Costa Rica) |
| PMDB | Partido do Movimento Democrático Brasileiro | Party of the Brazilian Democratic Movement (Brazil) |
| PN | Partido Nacional | National Party (Chile) |
| PRD | Partido Revolucionario Democrático | Democratic Revolutionary Party (Mexico) |
| PRI | Partido Revolucionario Institucional | Institutional Revolutionary Party (Mexico) |
| PRN | Partido de Reconstrução Nacional | Party of National Reconstruction (Brazil) |
| PRONAA | Programa Nacional de Asistencia Alimentaria | National Nutritional Assistance Program (Peru) |
| PRONASOL | Programa Nacional de Solidaridad | National Solidarity Program (Mexico) |
| PSD | Partido Social Democrático | Social Democratic Party (Brazil) |
| PSDB | Partido Social Democrático Brasileiro | Brazilian Social Democratic Party (Brazil) |
| PSE | Pacto de Solidaridad Económica | Economic Solidarity Pact (Mexico) |
| PT | Partido dos Trabalhadores | Workers' Party (Brazil) |
| PTB | Partido Trabalhista Brasileiro | Brazilian Labor Party (Brazil) |
| PUSC | Partido Unidad Social Cristiana | United Social Christian Party (Costa Rica) |
| UCR | Unión Cívica Radical | Radical Civic Union (Argentina) |

CHAPTER SIX

# Democratization in Latin America: A Citizen Responsibility

## AUGUSTO VARAS

### INTRODUCTION[1]

The struggle for democratization in Latin America simultaneously confronts three basic challenges. First, it must resolve conflicts generated by the clash between historical trends that propel these societies toward modernity and by the resistance to change based in pre-modern political and cultural relations. Second, it must establish, in some instances for the first time, minimal rules of the democratic game and, in others, reestablish democratic institutions destroyed by de facto governments, while at the same time confronting powerful oligarchic or authoritarian structures and groups. Third, it must generate broad agreements on urgent economic and political institutional reforms capable of adapting existing democratic institutions to the demands of globalization. The end of the Cold War and a sort of postmodern wariness toward systemic proposals also means that these processes must take place within a context marked by a relative absence of global democratizing visions and programs that encompass both development and efficient administration of the new democratic institutions.[2]

In light of these difficulties, as well as a variety of other historical and economic obstacles, efforts to recover democratic regimes and traditions in the region have been successful. The 1990s as a decade of democratization contrasts with the authoritarian decades of the seventies and the eighties and reveals the democratizing potential existent in the region. Nevertheless, the number of challenges and the relative absence of new perspectives and attractive ideas to guide the deepening of democracy are limiting the possibilities of Latin American political systems at a crucial moment in their development. Even though most countries in the region respect the minimal rules of the democratic game, citizenship and citizen participation have remained immobilized by procedural visions of democracy.[3] Citizens and the very notion of citizenship have been trapped and absorbed by the market. This phenomenon hinders the emergence of new democratic perspectives, which can only be broadened by interested citizens themselves.

First, this chapter will define the democratizing dynamic in terms of the notion of citizenship, which once again assumes strategic importance. Second, it will explore demands for broader participation arising from an increasingly hetero-geneous mass of citizens. This will be explained in reference to the new organization of production as shaped by technological progress. Third and last, the present situation of some Latin American countries will be examined, and new perspectives on democratization in the region will be explored.

## A CONCEPTUALIZATION OF DEMOCRACY

Democratic processes are characterized by being intrinsically unending with uncertain results. [4] The present inadequacy of our conceptual approaches to these problems makes the analytical task even more difficult. To advance toward appropriate conceptual tools, the evolution of democratization in Latin America may be examined in terms of the development of the notions of citizenship and citizen rights. In order to do this, it is necessary to analyze theoretically the dynamic relationship between democracy and democratization.

### Democracy and Democratization

A number of conceptual limitations constrain both the study and the develop-ment of new democratizing perspectives. One has been the predominance of procedural definitions that conceive of democracy only as a political form of government (Diamond 1990, 228). This definition of democracy in a *narrow sense* (Dahl 1989, 130), as a set of rules and functional procedures, faces three major difficulties. First, contemporary democracies are more than the sum of their rules of operation. Philippe C. Schmitter and Terry Lynn Karl (1993, 40) have argued that "democracy does not consist of a single unique set of institutions." Socioeconomic conditions, as well as state structures and practices, are equally decisive ingredients of a democratic system. Thus, Schmitter and Karl append two major additional conditions to the classical list of basic characteristics of a polyarchy, as defined by Robert A. Dahl: elected officials must be able to govern without being subject to overriding pressures from unelected officials, and the polity must be free from external domination by another overarching political system.

A second, further analytical limitation of procedural definitions of democracy is their tendency to explain democratic development outside of the bounds of politics, directly or indirectly associating democracy's evolution with structural variables.

Third, there is the "teleological bias" often found in the analysis of democ-racy. This appears in conceptions of democracy as a continuous process of gradual installation and progressive perfecting of the minimum norms of democratic functioning which, through a series of stages, leads to a final state of democratic grace. From this procedural perspective, the breakdown of democracies, demo-cratic transitions, and the consolidation of democracies appear as three stages in a continuum that proceeds from the absence of minimal rules of democratic operation to a completely perfected democracy. Regarding this purposive bias, Dahl recog-nizes that "... in the real world, no system will fully meet the criteria for a democratic process. At best, any actual polity is likely to achieve something of an approxima-tion to a fully democratic process. My guess is that any approximation will fall pretty far short of meeting the criteria" (1989, 131). And Dahl further notes, "Surely we

... must reject the complacent view that the democratic idea has finally reached the highest feasible level of attainment with the institutions of polyarchy in the nation-state" (1989, 231). This perspective is shared by Latin Americanists such as Samuel Valenzuela, who criticizes the "...tendency to push the conception of democracy in discussions of democratic consolidation towards an ideal, well-structured and comprehensive institutional system that can hardly be attained. Even long established democracies rarely have all the attributes that can ideally be associated with such regimes" (1992, 60). This teleological view of democracy is reinforced when democratic consolidation is limited to the existence and stability of minimal rules of the functioning of democracy. Thus, democratic development becomes reduced to the functioning of pre-established minimal conditions. Nevertheless, as a number of authors indicate, democratic developments are far from having come to an end, even in the most developed democracies.[5]

Thus, it may be asserted that democracy is not only the functioning of political systems, but basically a *continuous process that is permanently driven by the constant need to extend and institutionalize the rights of citizens in the face of existing or emerging absolute powers*. Consequently, democratization efforts must confront both the entrenched absolute powers that resist their eradication, as well as new forms of absolutist power.

## Representative Democracy and Citizenship

From this perspective, democracy has been a historical process of political change that, by its very nature, has no end. In this process, previous democratic developments have conditioned and created new historical perspectives for the next democratizing phases. As Norberto Bobbio has indicated, "The different forms of government do not only constitute different forms of organizing the political life of a social group, they are also different and at successive stages — generally one concatenated with another, one completely derived from the development of the other — of the historical process" (1987, 13). The dynamic element in this long process of democratization has been the permanent social and conceptual expansion of citizenship and the materialization of a growing number and quality of citizen rights, such as protection from absolute powers stubbornly opposed to social control.[6]

The centrality of the concept of citizenship was underlined half a century ago by T.H. Marshall in his inaugural class at the London School of Economics.[7] On this occasion, Marshall extended the Aristotelian concept of citizenship — full participation of the community (the basic condition of citizen happiness, see Oscar Godoy 1995) — noting, "Civil rights gave legal powers whose use was drastically curtailed by class prejudice and lack of economic opportunity" (1964, 105). As the twentieth century comes to a close, Marshall's confidence that citizens would reach increasing levels of equality contrasts sharply with the present socioeconomic condition of the vast world population. Although Marshall's analysis has been criticized (Zolo 1993, 256), the assertion that citizen rights might "alter patterns of social inequality" can still be upheld. The existence of new rights and the expansion of citizenship have been instrumental in overcoming ascriptive inequalities in modern industrial societies and, to a lesser extent, in Latin America. The growth and development of the middle classes throughout the world and, less forcefully, in Latin America is evidence supporting this expectation. In fact, empirical information shows that liberal democracy, structured around civil liberties, is the form of organizing public power that best guarantees and protects human rights.[8]

As the dynamic element in democratizing processes, the expansion of citizenship gives democratization both form and content. The substantive content of democracy has been and continues to be liberty as a supreme value. This value is expressed in social struggles against various forms of concentrating and centralizing power in the hands of military, entrepreneurial, bureaucratic, ideological, or religious minorities. To maintain and protect these gains, democratizing processes are the product of long-standing efforts to put into practice the minimal rules of democratic functioning. From this perspective, democracy is also a methodology, a set of procedures suitable for organizing society (Kelsen 1988, 211).

Unilateral approaches to democratizing processes drastically limit their analysis. Recent elaborations on democracy by Alain Touraine demonstrate that democracy is an interdependent and indivisible combination of respect for human and civil rights and citizen representation. From this perspective, democracy is more than a political project; it is also a moral-ethical project. According to Touraine, "Democracy is the subordination of the organization of society — and of political power in particular — to one objective that is not social but moral: the liberation of everyone" (1994b, 44, 262). Therefore, to characterize democracy in terms of only one of its components makes the adequate study of democracy impossible.

Democracy, then, is a historical process of combining institutionalized rules — the minimal or irreducible democratic rules — with a substantive, ethical content, which holds freedom as the uppermost value. In this process, the expansion of citizenship is the key element for understanding both specific democratizing processes and the distance that separates these processes from the minimal universal rules of democratic functioning.

## Citizenship and Social Differentiation

Democracy has been and is a struggle of citizens against absolute powers — and their contemporary heirs — for greater degrees and realms of freedom and respect for diversity.[9] This capacity to assure economic, political, and social freedoms to an ever-growing number of citizens demonstrates democracy's potential for absorbing and putting into practice a broad set of rights, as they have emerged over time, under changing social and economic conditions. From this perspective, the concept of citizenship makes it possible to shed new light on social dynamics and collective actions.

The concept of citizenship helps capture the social dynamic insofar as citizen rights expand along with economic development and social differentiation. According to Ernesto Laclau and Chantal Mouffe (1985, 168), new democratizing struggles are being driven by a displacement of the egalitarian ideal, formerly centered around the liberal-democratic discourse, to new areas of social life. Moving from the political order to other social and economic areas, democratic discourses, and the egalitarian ideal confront old and new relations of domination.

Simultaneously, this displacement reveals new inequalities. In this view, the multiplicity of antagonisms and egalitarian demands may be articulated within a unified discourse, which absolutely respects the autonomy of each confrontation, while constituting the center of the new democratic revolution.[10] The democratizing process has "to be extended and applied elsewhere.... The task is to assure that no group is excluded by virtue of its peculiarities and position, and that equal citizenship is extended to all" (Phillips 1993, 79, 81).

From a very different conceptual perspective and with a less radical proposal, Dahl asserts that in addition to the minimal rules that he himself systematized, *the strong principle of equality* is central to democracy. This principle fundamentally aims at "the reduction of the remediable causes of gross political inequalities" (1989, 323). This is an operation that opens new horizons for democratization and expands the notion of citizenship beyond its traditional political setting.

To the extent that in liberal representative democracies "the private autonomy of citizens with equal rights can only be guaranteed to the beat of their own socio-political mobilization" (Habermas 1994, 9), this broadening of the notion of citizenship facilitates the understanding of collective action insofar as it "account[s] for the different struggles that groups, movements and classes have waged against specific forms of discrimination, social stratification and political oppression" (Zolo 1993, 257).

Thus, democratization, citizenship, and social movements are indivisible. The last are fundamental for giving support to the demand for and the defense of greater degrees of liberty for excluded social sectors.[11] Consequently, increasing citizen power — both of individuals and organized social groups — will be crucial in making effective old and new civil rights (Lechner, 1994, 18) and in opening new spaces for diversity, thereby granting support to the democratizing processes themselves.

In this approach, the concept of citizenship should not be confused with public opinion, which is so easily manipulated.[12] This false transmutation is especially dangerous for democratizing processes in societies where social fragmentation, generated by economic liberalization policies, prevails over principles of community and solidarity. In these contexts, the collective social actor — the potential agent of transformation of their objective surroundings[13] — turns from citizen into social monad. In this process, the very notion of citizenship and community are eroded.

## Democracy, Civic Culture, and Economic Development

This complex relationship is not new. During the 1940s, Marshall insisted, "In the twentieth century, citizenship and the capitalist system have been at war" (1965, 93). Forty years later, from a different line of thought, once again the positive impact and contribution of non-political factors, such as economic development, upon democratization are being questioned. Thus, Ralf Dahrendorf recognizes, "The experience of recent decades shows that it was wrong to believe that the wealth of the few will in due course trickle down or filter through. The *filter is impenetrable* or can be made so by a privileged class bent on defending its position rather than allowing the basis of its privilege to be shifted." Insisting that it is necessary to link democratizing processes to political factors such as citizenship, Dahrendorf further notes, "Civil rights are a key part of the entitlements needed to enable people to take part in the modern economic process..." (1990, 101, emphasis added).

Nevertheless, procedural visions of democracy tend to associate democratization with non-political or structural factors, such as levels of economic development. Despite the abundant literature on this topic, attempts to establish causal or probabilistic explanations upon the association of democracy and a broad range of independent or intervening variables still have not generated convincing conclusions (Huntington 1991; Agüero and Torcal 1993). In the same manner, estimates of the positive impact of democracy upon levels of economic development have not been conclusive (Przeworski and Limongi 1993). Each of the sets of explanations established between, for example, democracy and civic culture,[14] income distribution,[15] economic development, or other structural factors have subsequently been questioned by new empirical findings, none of which have yet to provide valid answers to explain the diversity of levels of democratization.[16]

Studies of the impact of government economic performance upon democracy have also produced unclear findings.[17] In contrast to earlier claims, Weil (1989, 68) has demonstrated that poor economic performance may lead to a low level of confidence in democratic governments but may not weaken support for democracy. For their part, Seymour Martin Lipset, Kyong-Ryung Seong, and John Charles Torres (1993) have indicated that the relationship between economic growth and democratization is not curvilinear but has the shape of an "N." Even when levels of economic development and government economic performance are important factors in the analysis of processes of democratization, these are not the only factors, nor necessarily the most pertinent. Albert O. Hirschman (1994) provides a more fine-grained analysis of the relation between economic factors and democracy. Working with an "on-and-off" or "disengagement" approach, he argues that in some periods political institutions "disengage" or become autonomous from economic determinants, which allows them to have an independent political life.

The difficulty in clearly associating economic factors and intervening variables with democratization has been partially explained by the use of nonpolitical factors in a framework in which democracy is essentially defined from a procedural perspective. In this manner, the ongoing processes of accommodation of economic, social, and political structures with the changing interaction of national and international power factors — essentially political elements — usually ends up lost.

Insofar as no society can claim that its democratizing process has been completed, it is important to try to better understand the factors that actually are operative. In this context, the central role is played by the struggle for the expansion of existing citizen rights and the protection of those that are emerging. All of this occurs in a context of radical changes in the social organization of production. To paraphrase one of Dahrendorf's arguments, allowing people to take part in the modern economic process is essential to turning their social and political rights into realities.

## CITIZENSHIP AND TECHNOLOGICAL REVOLUTION

A n effective entitlement and provision of economic rights in Dahrendorf's sense presents even greater challenges. To the extent that in the post-Cold War era the expansion of citizenship is being affected by the new technological revolution, this latter process demands that contemporary democracies reform their institutions to adapt them to the new international conditions and their imperatives. According to James Rosenau, the present period of economic growth at a world level is characterized by

> ... the shift from an industrial to a post-industrial order and focuses on the dynamics of technology, particularly on those technologies associated with the micro-electronic revolution.... the emergence of issues ... that are the direct products of new technologies or of the world's greater interdependence ... the reduced capability of states and governments to provide satisfactory solutions to the major issues on their political agendas.... Subsystems have acquired a correspondingly greater coherence and effectiveness, thereby fostering tendencies to decentralization.... Finally, there is the feedback of the consequences of all the foregoing for the skills and orientations of the world's adults who ... have had to cope with the new issues of interdependence and adjust to the new technologies of the post-industrial order... (1990, 12-13).

Thus, technological progress, the new organizing principle at the global level, and economic globalization are affecting democratic developments at four different levels. First, by increasing and diversifying the number of potentially eligible citizens, the rights of these new citizens must be defined, accepted, and implemented. Second, globalization erodes the legitimacy of central governments by weakening central state systems through effective processes of decentralization. Third, access to the new centers of economic dynamism is increasingly difficult for the poorest sectors of society. And, finally, new technological developments help create and consolidate new absolute powers.

### Citizens' Rights and New Technologies

Greater social diversification, that is, the emergence of new social roles and functions, is creating the conditions for an increase in the demand for citizen rights. As has been indicated, "The transformation of the industrial order into its postindustrial successor involves a transition from a reliance on action-centered skills, in which workers use their brains to coordinate their bodies, to a dependence on intellective skills, in which they use their brains to coordinate observations, concepts, and patterns" (Rosenau 1992, 263). The most outstanding example of this has been the demand for the full integration of women in society and, in particular, in the labor market on equal terms with men (Kennedy 1993, 339-343), as was evidenced in September 1995 during the "IVth World Conference on Women" in Bejing, China. The massive use of new technologies in production has made labor markets less manual and more abstract; this change has also redefined the demographics of labor markets. The dependence on an intensive use of energy in industry, services, and the most dynamic sectors of the economy has lessened. In this context, says José Felix Tezanos, "We note a more general societal demand regarding the new status of women and their incorporation to work, which causes a number of functions and tasks previously realized by women to be organized differently ... the available empirical evidence demonstrates that during the 1980s women have filled the largest share of new jobs in non-agricultural sectors" (1992, 67, 76). These new positions are basically concentrated in the service sector. Nevertheless, women are not getting the best jobs created during this period, despite possessing qualifications equivalent to their male counterparts. This phenomenon indicates the importance of sociocultural and institutional obstacles to full citizenship of women (Abramo 1995).[18]

Expanding diversity, resulting from technological developments and the growing need for more sophisticated individual skills, has generated a new social demand for full citizen integration. The appropriation of social capital by the emerging strata will permit them to accede to and perform these new jobs (Bourdieu 1994).[19] Social appropriation and integration can only be *guaranteed* by the formalization of new rights within the framework of a broadened notion of citizenship. Nevertheless, these trends clash with political, social, and economic structures that are resistant to such changes.

Along with the increase in social differentiation, previously disregarded situations of social inequality are becoming more apparent to lawmakers and citizens alike. Nevertheless, the codification of new rights and mechanisms to implement them develop according to a slower rhythm than the process of social differentiation. In this context, the post-Cold War period can be seen as the beginning of a new cycle of social struggles to achieve respect for traditional rights that are being threatened and to define and put into practice new rights. In a context of considerable legal gaps, this process is forcing the modernization of representative democracies. Gender equality is again a good example of how emergent sectors have to confront traditional groups and structures to achieve full citizenship (Guzmán and Todaro 1995). For these reasons, the very notion of citizenship tends to expand along with the growing social differentiation — with its rich gamut of new roles and rights.

## The Legitimacy of the State

Technological changes and globalization are associated with a demand for more "political autonomy and self-governance.... global aspirations for more democracy, ... redefined criteria for legitimacy" and a relocation of authority which has "evolved in two directions, 'upwards' toward transnational organizations and 'downwards' toward subnational groups"... (Rosenau 1992, 254). The present trends toward decentralization and corresponding public policies are closely related to this phenomenon. The "bifurcation" of authority makes it more difficult for states in the post-Cold War period to create institutional conditions that allow for full citizen participation in these restructured societies.

Even more complicated is the situation in developing countries: as they construct representative democratic institutions, they must reform their institutional structures, while their central governments are losing traditional prerogatives.[20] In these societies, civil, political, and social rights have not been fully institutionalized, as can be seen in some countries in the hemisphere that still have not reached full modernity (Hopenhayn 1995; Brunner 1994). To make matters worse, amid a profound process of economic restructuring, with the market replacing the *mobilizing state* (Touraine 1994a), social and political institutions are incapable of assimilating and protecting the new rights of an expanding citizenry. This is further aggravated by the persistent vulnerability of specific social sectors, who face increasing levels of marginalization amid a crisis of representation, while new absolute powers emerge.

This crisis of the democracies is expressed in the loss of centrality of the public as a legitimate realm for resolving societal problems. The present bifurcation of authority has undermined the state as a political space in which the citizenry was traditionally venerated and strengthened. At the same time, new forms of global and transnational government — as well as subnational authorities — are not fully developed or are still incapable of playing their new roles and replacing state functions and, thus, incapable of providing citizenship to emergent and marginalized sectors. The social demand for more democracy, embodied in the growing mass of marginals, therefore finds no appropriate response at the state level, generating anomic or radically antisystemic political reactions. To summarize, social demands for more democracy and full citizenship are directed at central governments that cannot provide the goods and services demanded, whether material or symbolic, nor can they assure respect for the social and political rights promised in the egalitarian ideal.

## EXCLUSION

Globalization; the new, expansive role of the market; and the redefinition and reduction of the state's mobilizing role have weakened central governments. Coupled with this are the present political institutions' and public spaces' incapacities to respond to the demand for broadened citizenship. In this manner, consumption has become a skewed expression of full citizenship and citizen participation. Nevertheless, both the markets and the global economy are incapable of fully integrating the entire citizenry so that they can enjoy any of the benefits of citizenship. On the contrary, ongoing structural transformations have spawned the structural exclusion of broad social contingents.[21] According to Dahl (1989, 326), only with difficulty can *inclusion* — the basic condition for a real democracy — be reconciled with markets under present conditions of capitalism.[22] This raises two key questions: how can all citizens, regardless of income, be equal politically, and can democracy survive?

The majority of developing societies are trying to respond to demands for greater citizen integration by placing their hopes in the market, that is, by promoting "economic citizenship" via consumption. Nevertheless, insofar as these economies are incapable of fulfilling this role and meeting egalitarian expectations, the legitimacy crisis of the state deepens. According to the United Nations (Sachs 1995, 12), one-third of the worldwide labor force does not have productive work; one-fifth suffers famine; one-fourth lacks potable water; one-third lives in extreme poverty; and the poorest quintile of the worldwide labor force receives 1.4 percent of the world's gross product, while the richest quintile receives 84.7 percent. Such statistics (with differing intensities, similar statistics are available for the Latin American countries) eloquently reveal how a technology-intensive organization of production excludes those groups with the frailest cultural capital from the benefits of social and economic development and, as a result, from political participation. Thus, these underclasses remain definitively outside the social fabric organized by present economic development (Tezanos 1992, 80).

The tension between centrifugal forces that broaden social exclusion and centripetal forces that demand full participation in society may generate critical situations. Possible negative outcomes might be authoritarian formulas, *democraduras*, neo-fascist reactions similar to those seen in Europe, or possibly anti-modern conservative reactions supported by secular or religious fundamentalist ideologies.[23] Nevertheless, this situation also creates a more conducive environment for the development of new social movements and proposals to deepen democracy in the region.

## New Absolutist Powers

Representative democracy in both developing and industrialized countries is being challenged by the emergence of new absolutist powers. Not only has the profile of citizenry been altered by the impact of technological developments, these new technologies have also effected changes in structures and forms of power. The control and use of technological developments tend to concentrate power beyond representative institutions' control, thereby challenging the modern, democratic concept of citizenship. In an era of expanding new communication technologies and globalization, at the moment when participation empirically risks being replaced by consumption, the concept of citizenship tends to be supplanted by that of public opinion. In turn, consumers and voters face the challenge posed by state and private techno-bureaucracies: the media and mass entertainment that are molding cultural development, the advertising agencies that dominate consumer choices, the political propaganda that organizes political alternatives, and the state techno-bureaucracies that control coercion and threaten to penetrate private lives (Ramonet et al. 1996).

Global corporate control of communications, driven by the economic rationality of the market (Keane 1993), calls into question the possibility of any continuous democratizing dynamic.[24] Insofar as the traditional representative and deliberative functions of political parties have been diminished and representation has become more fragmented and diversified, political life has assumed more plebiscitary forms.[25] In this context, the corporate owners of the means of communication have begun to alter the nature of politics in post-Cold War societies. Recent mega-mergers among these firms are defining new challenges for citizen capacity to scrutinize and hold these entities accountable, as well as to defend civil rights.

Even though democratic institutions have exerted a certain control over traditional powers, these new absolutist powers are not as subject to control as their predecessors. National regulations are insufficient or difficult to apply against them to protect citizen rights. Furthermore, advocacy of organized citizen participation and intervention in the decision-making processes of these firms is not very realistic. Likewise, there is the risk that the new absolutist powers may control public and private life by manipulating public opinion. For these reasons, existing and potential forms of social vulnerability have increased.

In short, politics in developed and developing countries is characterized by old and new demands for citizen rights, which are now linked to new technological developments and an increasingly definitive urbanization of society. At the same time, new absolutist powers, which are less and less subject to scrutiny and accountability, assert themselves at the expense of political democratic structures and spaces. In this manner, conflict over citizenship emerges as the central theme amid the tensions presently observed in Latin American democratization, as well as in the industrialized countries.[26]

## LATIN AMERICAN DEMOCRATIZATION: A CITIZEN RESPONSIBILITY

The persistence of institutional weaknesses and obstacles to modernizing representative, democratic institutions has caused skepticism among some scholars. Juan L. Linz and Arturo Valenzuela's criticisms of presidentialism (1994), along with criticisms of parliamentary systems, illustrate this disenchantment[27] and have identified a series of problems that beset democracies: an ongoing decline in electoral participation; low levels of union affiliation; a deterioration in public perceptions of politicians and of citizen interest in public affairs; a decline in the role of legislatures and judiciaries; and the narrow coverage and intensity of party identifications, resulting in unstable party preferences (Schmitter 1995). Similarly, intrinsic dilemmas of democratic systems have been highlighted, such as oligarchic tendencies, individualism, public policy cycles, institutional and functional autonomy, limited and interdependent sovereignty, along with extrinsic limits, such as complex national identities, economic rigidities, overburdened policies, social ungovernability, corruption, and threats to internal order and external security (Schmitter 1994).

The overwhelming variety and complexity of situations underlying present Latin American democracies[28] has led to somber predictions. Laurence Whitehead notes, "At least for the near future the norm will be a more provisional and unsatisfactory form of constitutional rule — 'democracy by default'" (1993, 323). The scant private sector commitment to democracy and the reappearance of confrontational politics, which can be seen with differing intensities in Venezuela, Chiapas, and the Argentine provinces, would tend to support this analysis and casts doubts upon the democratic future of some countries. In others, basic structural limitations also appear to condition the viability of democracy (Nuñez del Prado 1990). As a result, present democratic political systems in Latin America have been described with a variety of qualifiers: "by default" and "delegative" (O'Donnell 1994a); "incomplete" (Garretón 1995b); "incoherent" (Wiarda 1995); and as "hybrid regimes" (Karl 1994).

In addition to the problems inherent in all democracies, Latin America must also confront problems inherited from its past. As Schmitter points out, "The politicians and citizens of FNDs (fledgling neodemocracies) may come to recognize the intrinsic dilemmas that are plaguing the ELDs (established liberal democracies) and begin to experiment with new arrangements" (1995, 16). Furthermore, this experimentation must address the three principal tasks pending in the region:

the introduction of modernity, overcoming persistent pre-modern traditions and relations; the introduction or re-installation of democratic fundamentals in oligarchical or authoritarian contexts; and the implementation of reforms that accommodate present structures and institutions to the requirements of globalization. The combination of these tasks in a single, tangled process reveals at least two major sets of problems: how to legitimate democratic representative institutions and how to develop and respect citizen rights.

The state, the arena in which public goods and services are organized and distributed in Latin America, is undergoing a severe legitimacy crisis, which is exacerbated by the drastic implementation of liberal market policies and opening to global markets.[29] These transformations were introduced by military dictatorships or authoritarian governments. In some cases, democratically elected governments with a low level of citizen participation in decisionmaking led this process. Such concentration of power was the result of an erroneous assumption that these reforms bestow governments with greater political-economic efficacy, enabling them to confront crises associated with structural transformations more effectively (Ducatenzeiler and Oxhorn 1994, 31).[30] This was the case in Chile during the military dictatorship, in Mexico under the rule of the Institutional Revolutionary Party (Partido Revolucionario Institucional — PRI), in Peru after Fujimori's 1992 autogolpe, and in Argentina during Menem's democratic government, which enjoyed an absolute majority in Congress until 1995, when it lost its majority in the Senate. Likewise, the presidencies have concentrated power and depend upon specialized techno-bureaucracies, which, even after regime transitions, are increasingly autonomous and free from existing mechanisms of scrutiny and accountability. This concentration of power in presidencies has weakened parliaments and political parties.[31]

Both presidentialism and parliamentary systems face the central problem of how to develop and maintain political coalitions, structured around substantive accords to provide stability (Horowitz 1992, 206). The hyper-presidentialist regimes, however, are more likely to intensify structural transformation crises because the regimes themselves are attractive sources of spoils and purposely do not create incentives for coalition formation among parties and groups, which could shape a broad consensus (Valenzuela 1993, 7, 14). The Latin American parliaments, in contrast, have been increasingly marginalized from decisionmaking as a result of de jure and de facto reductions of their institutional powers, as well as by their limited capacities to develop and strengthen coalitions.

The ongoing crisis has affected the credibility of representative democratic institutions. In the Andean countries, Catherine Conaghan (1994) has noted low levels of public trust in their congresses, an imbalance of powers between presidents and parliaments, and great dissatisfaction with political parties. These trends indicate a gap between the parties and the people they are supposed to represent. The crisis is exacerbated by lack of effective mechanisms and a civic culture that ensures accountability. According to Guillermo O'Donnell (1994a), delegative democracy, as seen in Latin America, is a persistent form of weakly institutionalized democracy: it displays majoritarian and plebiscitarian biases; is structured around high risk, acute situations; relies on leaders to maintain unity; consolidates strong technocratic groups within decision-making processes; is free of horizontal scrutiny; and is prone to clientelism, patrimonialism, and corruption.

The weakened credibility of representative and governmental institutions is exacerbated by the ongoing corporatization and increasing functional autonomy of the principal state institutions (Sanz Menéndez 1994). This is seen with the Latin American armed forces (Varas 1989; Johansen 1993), the police, and the judiciary. The historical tradition of permanent regimes of exception (Loveman 1994) only reinforces these trends. In hyper-presidentialist systems, without stable substantive accords, decision-making processes are normally in the hands of techno-bureaucratic elites.

In summary, radical structural changes, political resources concentrated in the executive, weakly legitimated democratic institutions, autonomous state bodies, and the lack of substantive accords regarding the continued democratization of politics and society give rise to a syndrome of crisis for representative institutions. The future of democracy in Latin America is going to depend on overcoming these weaknesses and on the role of active citizenship in strengthening democracy. The new democratic challenges are accountability[32] and citizen power.

Existing limits on democratic systems increase the vulnerability of citizenship to new, absolute powers. Now techno-bureaucratic government agencies control coercion, and private corporations overwhelmingly influence mass culture, consumption, and electoral choices. All of these forces operate through increasingly technified bureaucracies managed by elites that are not easily held responsible.

Max Weber viewed rational bureaucratic government as the characteristic trait of modern societies. This form of government inhibited patrimonialist tendencies among political groups and limited the power of functionaries. Consequently, Weber distrusted active citizen participation in bureaucracies and maintained that its absence was a condition for stable democracy (1944, 739).[33] Nevertheless, the functional autonomy of the techno-bureaucracies, managed by a caste of elites who control public policy decisionmaking (Dahl 1989, 345), obstructs citizens from exercising their right to control complex organizations in the security, cultural, political, and economic fields. Rather than setting up obstacles to patrimonialist tendencies, bureaucratization generates new political oligarchies. Thus, neo-patrimonialism, that is, the combination of encapsulated elites who monopolize the design of public policies along with the techno-bureaucracies that implement their policies, form one of the major threats to modern democracies. Given that some form of representative democracy is inevitable[34] in complex mass societies,[35] introducing some direct democratic mechanisms might mitigate the elitist and undemocratic elements of existing representative democracies (Budge 1993, 154).

## Accountability: A Necessary Condition for Democratization

Across the political-ideological spectrum, it is broadly agreed that accountability is a key mechanism for protecting and granting force to citizen rights.[36] Accountability, the link between bureaucracy and democracy (Lipsky 1970), creates possibilities for greater citizen control and participation, grants transparency to public affairs, and inhibits neo-patrimonialist tendencies. Scrutiny of public functionaries and agencies is equally fundamental for controlling corruption and state coercion against citizens.[37] The same is true of organized state coercion and nihilistic or endemic social violence (Enzensberger 1994), which are culpable of mega-deaths (Brzezinski 1993) and can only be stopped and prevented through social control over coercive state apparatuses and individual violent actions. Scrutiny and accountability are also critical for containing the private techno-bureaucracies that influence culture, consumption, and political choices. For these reasons, scrutiny and accountability — and the transparency that they permit[38] — have become a cardinal theme in post-Cold War democratizing processes.

According to O'Donnell (1994a, 61), representation requires accountability. Accountability works vertically by holding elected officials responsible to the voting box and horizontally through the network of relatively autonomous entities that are empowered to demand information and even discipline specific function-aries when they fail to respond appropriately.

Since representative democracy and citizenship also rest upon participation (Barber 1984, 155), non-governmental organizations and citizen associations have an important role to play in overseeing private and state techno-bureaucracies. Therefore, democracies should develop mechanisms of participation complemen-tary to and compatible with representative institutions (Barber 1984, 262). Empiri-cal evidence reveals the importance of the existence of an organized society, with a dense network of intermediate groups and voluntary associations independent of the state (Diamond 1990, 235). In this context, a broadened concept of citizenship would include the notion of the "active citizen." This concept requires opportunities for "those affected by the decision-making structures of their communities to participate in the latter's regulation" (Held 1993, 25). Given that "the power to make decisions must be free of the inequalities and constraints which can be imposed by an unregulated system of private capital" (Held 1993, 24), the strengthening of organized society's political capacity is an important element in the "double democratization" of the state and society. Thus, amid contemporary social crises, the associational impulse is fundamental not only for purposes of accountability but also for confronting urgent, severe economic and social problems (Sachs 1995, 12-13).

In a cosmopolitan democracy, the transparency created by scrutiny and accountability also should extend to international financial institutions and other international multilateral organizations. Considering the development of proto-institutions of world government over recent decades, such as the International Monetary Fund (international finances), the World Trade Organization (interna-tional trade), United Nations peacekeeping operations (world policing), as well as other pre-existing organizations in health, justice, and education, these bodies' accountability appears to be an extremely important emergent theme.[39]

In this manner, empowering citizen capacity — citizen power — to oversee and hold accountable public and private techno-bureaucracies is one of the corner-stones of post-Cold War democratization. As Paul Hirst (1993, 131-32) notes, "The associational principle can democratize and reinvigorate societies as a supplement to and a healthy competitor to the currently dominant forms of social organization: representative mass democracy, bureaucratic state welfare and the big corporation." The associational principle is "a pattern of organizing social relations that can be generalized across sectors and domains of social activity, which is not a localized institution or pattern of customary action." And according to Hirst, "Associationalists have to rely on the multiplication of diverse efforts.... The role of legislation must be permissive and gradual, not prescriptive and peremptory" (Hirst 1993, 131-132).

## CITIZEN POWER:
## A SUFFICIENT CONDITION FOR DEMOCRATIZATION

If scrutiny and being held accountable are necessary conditions for democratization, then the increase in citizen capacity to hold elected and appointed public officials and institutions responsible is the sufficient condition for democratization.

Citizen capacity for scrutiny is essential to assuring the installation and stable functioning of the minimal rules of democratic operation. These rules are not always fully re-established following authoritarian breakdowns. In some cases in which democratic rules have been re-established, their full force is nonetheless seriously restricted. The 1993 Peruvian Constitution is an example. To provide greater latitude for market reforms, the Constitution restricted the scope of constitutionally guaranteed basic rights and eliminated or lowered the constitutional rank of some of the social and economic rights contained in the 1979 charter. In the same way, among other restrictions, the Constitution lessened municipal government powers and reduced the oversight role of Congress (Comisión Andina de Juristas 1993). As a result, the concentration of power in the presidency increased substantially. In this way, the crisis of representative, democratic institutions may endure despite the force of the minimal rules of democracy.[40] The full application of democracy is thus a central theme on the contemporary agenda of democratic mobilization in Latin America (Adrianzén 1994).

In this context, one positive dimension of the new wave of democratizations in the region is the concern with putting into practice measures that assure the transparency of private and public affairs, oversee government agencies, and introduce new norms aimed at guaranteeing full respect for civil rights. In addition to consolidating the minimal rules of the democratic game, these new procedures provide a potential basis for further democratization. The realization of this potential will depend on the utilization of these new instruments by a citizenry with a strengthened capacity for political action. The cases of Colombia, Argentina, Peru, and Chile allow us to illustrate this new and regionally diverse situation.

The 1991 Colombian constitutional reform, an example of this new trend, represents the broadest attempt to confront the issues of democratic governability and citizen scrutiny in the region. By the end of the 1980s, Colombia's democratic institutions, social fabric, and economy were confronting powerful tensions and threats (Hartlyn 1989; Archer 1990). The traditionally weak central government was increasingly incapable of confronting social and political problems, such as rural-urban migration, urban crime, narco-terrorist violence, guerrilla movements, and corruption. In response to this critical situation, then President César Gaviria's Liberal Party began an ambitious process of political recuperation, economic liberalization, and modernization of public affairs. The efforts of the Gaviria government made possible the enactment of the 1991 Constitution.

The new Colombian Constitution reaffirms individual and collective rights, and, at the same time, introduces mechanisms to integrate and protect social and political groups that had traditionally been marginalized from decisionmaking and justice. Article 103 establishes participatory democratic mechanisms such as the vote, the plebiscite, the referendum, the popular consultation, the open town council meeting, the legislative initiative, and the recall of officials (Frühling 1995). Additionally, the Constitution provides for institutions of control, such as the controller general of the republic and the public prosecutor of the republic. It also empowers the Senate and the Chamber of Deputies to scrutinize public functionaries and institutions. Similarly, Article 88 allows individuals to initiate class actions to defend individual and collective rights referring to the national wealth, public space, security, administrative morality, environment, and consumer quality. The Constitution foresees reforms to the civil and penal codes to permit class actions as remedies for infringements of rights. To this end, the Constitution creates two new writs, the *recurso de tutela* (a writ of protection, similar to an injunction) and the *recurso de cumplimiento* (a writ of execution, essentially a court order to execute the law). Citizen use of the *tutela* writ has strengthened these new constitutional mechanisms; to date, some 30,000 petitions are filed per year.

What effects these exceptional legal opportunities will have depend upon how Colombians respond to the new possibilities. Such notions as law and public interest, as they are understood in the Anglo-Saxon tradition, have been dormant in Colombian legal culture and structure. Other challenges arise out of Colombia's weak — though no less patrimonialist — centralized state structure, the concentration of powers in the executive, and a weary civil society. Consequently, government and non-government efforts at strengthening the new mechanisms of scrutiny and accountability have focused on assuring state compliance with its own norms, informational campaigns to educate citizens about their rights, as well as efforts to promote the active use of the mechanisms now available. To sum up, in Colombia, overcoming the crisis of legitimacy entails strengthening through citizen action these new mechanisms of scrutiny and accountability.

With less pronounced features, the 1994 Argentine constitutional reform introduced new mechanisms to increase the political capacity of citizens. These eventually will serve to control public powers more effectively.[41] This typical delegative democracy established such mechanisms as popular legislative initiative (article 39), the popular referendum (article 40), and the *habeas data* (article 43). Each of these mechanisms is available to the citizenry (although some first require additional legal regulation), who may demand the full implementation and utilization of these mechanisms of horizontal accountability now existent in Argentina.[42]

In Peru, the 1993 Constitution strengthened the presidential system. The introduction of the referendum also points in this direction. Yet, at the same time, the new Constitution introduces new mechanisms for citizens, such as popular legislative initiative, the rendering of accounts by public functionaries, the *habeas data*, and the petition of unconstitutionality. Nevertheless, all of these innovations require further legal regulation before they can go into practice. In the Peruvian post-electoral context, with a government majority in a Congress with fewer oversight powers than it had before, the making of these legal regulations has been a subject of bitter political disputes.

Chile in this regard is the least developed case.[43] In addition to the writ of protection, the 1980 Constitution only provides for such public interest mechanisms as the municipal plebiscite and indirect citizen participation in the Economic-Social Councils.[44] Similarly, horizontal accountability is limited to the controller general of the republic and the weak oversight role of the Chamber of Deputies (Aravena Bolívar 1995).

## Crisis of Political Representation

The increase in citizen capacity for accountability under the new structural conditions resulting out of the radical transformation and globalization of our societies may help redistribute economic and political power after a period of extreme concentration and centralization. Such an effect may stabilize the system as a whole. Nevertheless, this possibility is hindered by radical structural changes, that, in a context of economic crisis, have weakened social movements by transforming the traditional constellation of interests and political alignments associated with the import substitution model of industrialization. Thus, for example, the trade union movement has been profoundly affected by changes in sectoral organization, as a result of restructuring toward an export-oriented model of growth. The prior social and associational fabric has weakened, and the representative capacity of political parties and institutions has fragmented and diversified.[45]

The simultaneous and combined effects of the legitimacy crisis of representative institutions and the radical transformations in the interests of the citizens to be represented alter traditional party alignments. These changes assume, at least, three different forms: the *disappearance of parties*, when citizen interests change but their representatives and institutions do not equally follow suit, as in Peru in 1998; the *representational hiatus*, when representatives insulate themselves and citizen interests fragment, as in Chile from 1990 to 1997; and the *blurring of party boundaries*, when intra-party rivalries and divisions that have dominated the party give way and interparty alignments are re-formed in a context of changed citizen interests. Only after the development of new coalitions and formal alliances — such as the recently successful Alianza — could this crisis be overcome, as in Argentina in 1995 and 1997.[46]

Authoritarian democracies (*democraduras*) are a suboptimal solution to these crises, and, as exemplified in Peru, these regimes occur within a framework of party system crisis.[47] In the Argentine case, the transition from ideological party identities toward more pragmatic identifications tends to reinforce the character of political parties as lobbies by distancing them from citizen associations. This process strengthens the position of technocrats among party cadre and, as a result, increases the distance between the political parties and the electorate (García Delgado 1994). In the Chilean case, the prospects for continuing democratization, driven by a complex, multi-dimensional agenda and substantive accords, are difficult. This situation is largely due to the limits of existing democratic, representative institutions (Cortés Terzi 1994). These limits are aggravated by Chile's unfair and peculiar binominal electoral system and its unrepresentative Senate, as well as by changes within citizen organizations and their government counterparts. As established in the 1980 Constitution, the Chilean Congress has reduced powers, which limit the representative function of parties. The modernization of the political parties, which paradoxically began under the military dictatorship, has not gone far enough to overcome the resulting gap. As a result, Chilean political parties must also increase their representative capacities. In addition, the concentration of power in the executive has, as a lamentable corollary, the tendency to pursue and effect elite political accords outside the legislative. This practice bolsters the role of the techno-bureaucracies, presidential commissions, and the so-called "de facto powers" (*poderes fácticos*).[48] Though in different forms, the erosion of indirect citizen capacity to scrutinize government acts also can be seen in other countries of the region.

The Latin American crisis of political representation has penetrated all social movements and has been intensified by the implementation of deregulation policies. The social fragmentation associated with this radical restructuring, coupled with globalization, has weakened social movements and collective identities, thereby frustrating social mobilization (Guerra Rodríguez 1994). The fragmentation of interests capable of representation erodes public interest and political space, as well as identities formed around common national interests. As Juan Carlos Portantiero notes in reference to Argentina (though his comments apply equally to all of Latin America), there is a situation marked by a "loss of autonomy by the actors and the decadence of the public realm, ... a situation of 'every man for himself' and a moral climate that only rewards individual success attained through business or lawbreaking. In the ethic of defensive reclusion, politics, the realm of the *polis* is transformed into a spectacle ... and the *agora* where the spectacle takes place is the television screen, as a form of illusory community. In the kingdom of alienation, politics is video politics" (Portantiero 1994, 30).

In this situation, only the development of new identities capable of expressing new social demands can assure the full force of traditional and new rights and the democratic procedural minimum (O'Donnell 1994b). Opening the political space so that these social movements may emerge will contribute to the governability of democracy and not to its destabilization.[49]

The means of mass communication play a central role in the process of strengthening democracy through the mobilization of new social identities. In a context of fragmented political interests and an institutional crisis of representation, emergent collective identities and actions will depend heavily upon access to the mass media. Such access is a key element in strengthening the political capacity of citizens, in generating citizen power.[50] The new absolutist powers that have been mentioned — the mass media, advertising, and political marketing — rely upon new communications technologies. Thus, government regulations that grant citizens access to the media, the setting of ethical and cultural standards for advertising, and public financing of political campaigns form a basic part of any agenda of democratization. Alongside the scrutiny and accountability of public agents and agencies, such regulations could provide some control over absolute powers, old and new.

Simultaneously, to achieve greater degrees of democracy, the system of representation needs to be restructured. It is no longer feasible to assign all possible functions of representation to the political party system. Along with increasing their political capacities, parties ought to coexist alongside a dense network of representative social organizations that participate in decisionmaking.[51] Particular attention must be given to institutional design to achieve these objectives. The creation of democratic institutions should be a more interactive process. To be successful, the process must be developed from "above" and "within," with results equally reflecting pressures from "below" and "without." A strong democratic state should be capable of both processes, as well as able to regulate the new absolute powers, while being responsible and accountable.

To summarize, increases in citizen capacity to demand greater degrees of democracy more effectively depend upon the formation of new social identities capable of projecting themselves in collective actions that actively involve the citizenry in scrutinizing public and private bodies, thereby contributing to the development of democratic institutions.

## CONCLUSION

Profound regional and global structural changes are redefining the economic, social, and political profile of Latin American countries. These transformations are driving demands for new and greater citizen rights and setting a much broader citizen agenda: the respect for citizens' rights and their codification, the recognition of emergent groups, the qualitative expansion of these rights, and the internationalization of rights (Squella 1995). Paradoxically, the transformations are also generating "negative political externalities." These take the forms of increasing socioeconomic exclusion and an increased concentration and centralization of power and wealth, which threaten the very expansion of citizenship.

To avoid the negative impact of contemporary political and economic changes in Latin America and to make possible a new democratic agenda, political power must be responsible and accountable. To this end, the citizens in the most vulnerable sectors of each society need to be empowered to exercise their rights. Even though some citizen oversight mechanisms exist in the region, their implementation and efficacy will depend upon how forcefully organized citizens demand their use. To the extent that citizen power increases, citizens may hold state institutions and agencies responsible: by scrutinizing the state's actions, citizens will protect and assure their own rights and, in this manner, help redistribute political power. The increase in citizen capacity through scrutiny and institutional responsibility is a key element for the stability and continuity of the democratizing process in Latin America.

# Notes

The ideas and opinions expressed in this document are the exclusive responsibility of the author and do not represent those of the Ford Foundation.

1. I thank Felipe Agüero, Claudio Fuentes, Jonathan Hartlyn, Iván Jaksic, Enrique Silva, and Jeffrey Stark for their valuable help, comments, and suggestions on earlier versions of this essay.

2. As Touraine (1994a) indicates, this deficiency can be seen in domestic Latin American politics.

3. On the theoretical limitations of procedural approaches to the analysis of democratization, see Ben Ross Schneider (1995).

4. As Phillips (1993, 1) has indicated, "There are two stories of democracy that circulate today, and, like most tales of political endeavor, they allow us to choose between a happy ending and a future that is still unresolved." On the predictability of democratic outcomes, see Przeworski (1988).

5. As Beetham (1993, 71) points out, "The history of liberal democracy, in conclusion, has not yet come to an end. The struggle for democratization both will, and should, continue."

6. This is especially so in Latin America, where, as it has been recently recognized (Cauffignal 1993, 67), "it is not possible to speak of democracy without considering the construction of citizenship."

7. In February 1946, T.H. Marshall (1964, 78) asserted, "... the modern drive towards social equality is ... the latest phase of an evolution of citizenship which has been in continuous progress for some 250 years." The renewed influence of the concept of citizenship and of theoretical elaborations centered on it can be seen in Seligman (1992), Beiner (1995), and Cohen and Arato (1995).

8. For an attempt to support this assertion empirically, see Poe and Tate (1994).

9. According to Touraine (1994b, 24-25), democracy "is the struggle of the subjects, in their culture and their freedom, against the dominant logic of the systems...[it is] the form of political life that grants the greatest freedom to the greatest number of people, [it is democracy] that protects and recognizes the greatest diversity possible." Nevertheless, this concept of citizenship is open to criticism. Some authors maintain that radical multicultural differentiation and the cult of diversity may erode social unity when, taking the argument to the extreme, all of the different activities, beliefs, preferences, or habits aspire to validation through public sanction. In these cases, the very notion of citizen and citizenship may be distorted by removing civil rights from their original context — full participation in society — and using them publicly to legitimate individual private worlds. On this, see Elshtain (1995, 54). For other authors, this radicalization of the displacement of citizenship toward private realms even calls into question the concept of nationality. See, for example, Schlesinger (1992) and Lasch (1995).

10. On the role of this "expansion" of citizenship in the democratic project, see Leal (1994).

11. As Touraine (1994b, 88, 262) notes, "A social movement always rests upon the liberation of a social actor," and can only be defended by social movements. Thus, "if democracy is nothing more than a system of institutional guarantees, who will defend them when they are threatened?"

12. For an attempt to respond to this problem in the form of "dynamic representation," see Stimson, Mackuen, and Ericksen (1995).

13. This concept is also central to Catholic thought. See, for example, Mounier (1968).

14. Regarding civic culture, a key independent variable for explaining democratizations, Muller and Seligson (1994, 646-647) have recently noted that many of the civic culture attitudes have no significant impact upon changes in democracies.

15. Weede (1989) notes that the relation between democracy and income distribution is not robust and that the available data do not allow for a clear evaluation of the relationship between years of democracy and income inequality. In Chile, according to the CASEN survey, the distribution of income worsened between 1992 and 1994.

16. Other studies (Huntington 1991, 106-107) indicate that intervening variables, such as literacy, education, urbanization, a broad middle class, democratic values, the role of the Catholic Church, and international factors, are key elements in democratization.

17. Some studies (Alcántara Sáez 1994, 12) indicate that governability is assured when governments simultaneously maintain legitimacy and promote socioeconomic development. Or it is argued (Burkhart and Lewis-Beck 1994) that economic development, directly or indirectly, "produces" democracy.

18. The importance of the legal rehabilitation of women appears even more clearly in the comments of the Norwegian Prime Minister, Gro Harlem Brundtland (1994). She notes that women will not gain more power just because they desire it; they will gain it through legislative changes, greater information, and a reallocation of resources. On the nature of women's rights, see Thomas (1995).

19. For an empirical analysis of this situation in the developed countries, see Buckberg and Thomas (1995).

20. This phenomenon is not limited to the developing countries. It is more general and affects the range of national governmental organizations. See, for example, Claval (1995, 306).

21. The present minister of culture of Brazil (Weffort 1994) characterizes these democracies as "democracies of apartheid." On exclusion, see Rodgers, Gore, and Figueiredo (1995).

22. From a different perspective, Lasch (1995, 22) illustrates this contradiction when he notes that when money talks, everyone is condemned to listen.

23. These tensions can take the form of "clash of civilizations" (Huntington 1993). A less dramatic approach (Schutz and Slater 1990) shows how modernization has awakened anti-Western attitudes, as can be seen in the principal anti-modernizing revolutions in the Third World. For an analysis of modernizing alternatives within Islam, see Varas, Mewes, and Caro (1994).

24. This disenchantment with democratic institutions may even erode the supposed pacifist mission of democracies. On this, see Russett (1993) and Weart (1994). For the argument that democracies are pacifist, see Lake (1992).

25. See Robert Dahl's commentaries in Castañeda (1994, 20). Fishkin (1991) presents a proposal for institutional correctives to narrow the gap between the electorate and the elected.

26. On the problems of democracy in the United States, see Castañeda (1994).

27. At the same time as parliamentary crises were being seen in some European and Asian countries, Sartori (1994, 110) recommended a pragmatic, intermediate choice, "semipresidentialism can improve presidentialism and, similarly, that semiparliamentary systems ... are better than plain parliamentary ones." He concludes, "That political form is best that best applies."

28. Despite the obvious differences among Latin American countries, some common problems are shared. On this, see Garretón (1994a, 1995a). The same is true of other developing areas (Pusic 1994).

29. Mainwaring (1992, 307) has argued, "the notion of legitimacy is easily plagued by a tautology." Nevertheless, the empirical evidence of levels of support for authoritarian experiences indicates a crisis, either in the works or one that as yet has not ended. See *Latinobarómetro, La Epoca*, August 29, 1995, 12.

30. On the need for participation as a pre-condition for the success of public policies, see Bradford (1994).

31. On the Argentine case, see Cheresky (1995).

32. The term accountability (*fiscalización*) does not exist in Spanish. We are including here the dimensions of responsibility and transparency, as well as their realization through both juridical and non-juridical means.

33. In addition to bureaucratically controlled parliamentary supervision, Weber (Gerth and Mills 1958, 235) thought that bureaucracies could be subject to external controls only in regard to economic matters; only in the world of business was the expert knowledge of private economic interests superior to that of bureaucracy.

34. For this reason, Beetham (1993, 71) points out, "representation, despite the limits it imposes on autonomy, is an irreducible necessity.... Within these limits, however, there remains a large scope for further extending and equalizing the opportunities for popular control."

35. On the problems faced by densely populated democracies, see Le Roy (1995).

36. Multilateral entities such as the World Bank (1994) also consider this to be a key dimension. For an academic perspective, see Buchanan (1982) and Beetham (1993). Scrutiny is also key to the implementation of economic policies (Haggard and Kaufman, 1994). Worldwide, public interest legal action is an increasingly used instrument for defending the rights of women (Jethmalani 1995).

37. In fact, as the Italian case demonstrates (Salvi 1994), the encapsulation of decisionmaking and the lack of any separation between these processes and the bureaucratic administration of decisions lead inevitably to corruption.

38. On forms of accountability and the need for transparency, see Wood and Waterman (1994).

39. On the practice of evaluating programs with the participation of those affected, initiated by the World Bank in 1993, see Salmen (1994) and Banco Inter-Americano de Desarrollo (1994).

40. On Eastern Europe, see Pusic (1994). On the Peruvian case, see Shifter (1995).

41. For an analysis of this reform process, see Feijoó (1994), Sain (1994), and de Riz (1995).

42. On the importance of participatory and representative institutions for democratization in Argentina, see Botana (1995) and Gargarella (1995).

43. For a sharp criticism of the present Chilean political situation, see Cassen (1995). Also see Ruiz Schneider (1993).

44. On attitudes toward citizen participation in Chile, see Garretón (1994b).

45. For a regional analysis of these phenomena, see Mainwaring and Scully (1995), Cansino (1995), and Cantón (1995). For a knowledgeable political opinion on the Chilean case, see the interview with the President of the Chilean Chamber of Deputies, Jaime Estévez (*La Epoca,* December 26, 1995).

46. On this case, see Novaro (1995).

47. See Grompone (1995). For an analysis of the long crisis of representation in Peru, see Panfichi and Sanborn (1995).

48. This insulation of decisionmakers creates opportunities for and, hence, dangers of corruption. In Chile the government created a presidential commission on ethical conduct within the public administration as a first response to this renewed threat.

49. As Mainwaring (1994) notes, civil society is an important source for democratic innovations. On national cases, see López Jiménez (1993), Revilla (1994), dos Reís Vellos (1994), and González (1995).

50. Conaghan (1994) has argued that civic competence requires that the people possess the necessary skills to acquire and process relevant political information. In this sense, changes in journalistic practices, public information, and freedom of the press are crucial to the consolidation and expansion of citizenship.

51. For an argument along these lines, see Nogueira (1995).

# References

Abramo, Laís. 1995. "Política de recursos humanos y modernización productiva." In *El trabajo de las mujeres en el tiempo global*, eds. Rosalba Todaro and Regina Rodríguez. Santiago: ISIS-CEM.

Adrianzén, Alberto. 1994. "Gobernabilidad, democracia y espacios locales." *Pretextos* 6.

Agüero, Felipe, and Mariano Torcal. 1993. "Elites, factores estructurales, democratización (Una discusión de aportes recientes en la literatura)." *Revista de Estudios Políticos* 80.

Alcántara Sáez, Manuel. 1994. "De la gobernabilidad." *America Latina* 8.

Aravena Bolívar, Pamela. 1995. "Las penurias de la oposición. Fiscalizar, un acto imposible." *El Mercurio*, October 15.

Archer, Ronald P. 1990. *The Transition to Broker Clientelism in Colombia: Political Stability and Social Unrest*. Working Paper No. 140. Notre Dame, Ind.: Helen Kellogg Institute for International Studies, University of Notre Dame.

Banco Inter-Americano de Desarrollo (BID).1994. *Elementos para la modernización del estado*. Washington, D.C.: IDB.

Barber, Benjamin. 1984. *Strong Democracy: Participatory Politics for a New Age*. Berkeley, Calif.: University of California Press.

Beetham, David. 1993. "Liberal Democracy and the Limits of Democratization." In *Prospects for Democracy: North South East West*, ed. David Held. Palo Alto, Calif.: Stanford University Press.

Beiner, Ronald, ed. 1995. *Theorizing Citizenship*. Albany: State University of New York Press.

Bobbio, Norberto. 1987. *Teoría de las formas de gobierno en la historia del pensamiento político*. Mexico City: Fondo de Cultura Económica, 13.

Botana, Natalio R. 1995. "Las transformaciones institucionales en los años del menemismo." *Sociedad* (April).

Bourdieu, Pierre. 1994. *Raisons Pratiques*. Paris: Édition du Seuil.

Bradford, Colin I. 1994. "Redefining the Role of the State: Political Processes, State Capacity and the New Agenda in Latin America." In *Redefining the State in Latin America*, ed. Colin I. Bradford. Paris: Organization of Economic Cooperation and Development.

Brzezinski, Zbigniew. 1993. *Out of Control: Global Turmoil on the Eve of the 21st Century*. New York: Macmillan Publishing Company.

Brundtland, Gro Harlem. 1994. "The Solution to the Global Crisis." *Environment* 36:10 (December).

Brunner, José Joaquín. 1994. *Bienvenidos a la modernidad*. Santiago: Planeta.

Buchanan, James. 1982. "Democracia limitada o ilimitada." *Estudios Públicos* 6.

Buckberg, Elaine, and Alun Thomas. 1995. "Wage Dispersion and Job Growth in the United States." *Finance and Development* 32:2 (June).

Budge, Ian. 1993. "Direct Democracy: Setting Appropriate Terms of Debate." In *Prospects for Democracy: North South East West*, ed. David Held. Palo Alto, Calif.: Stanford University Press.

Burkhart, Ross E., and Michael S. Lewis-Beck. 1994. "Comparative Democracy: The Economic Development Thesis." *American Political Science Review* 88 (4).

Cansino, César. 1995. "Party Government in Latin America: Theoretical Guidelines for an Empirical Analysis." *International Political Science Review* 16 (2).

Cantón, Santiago A. 1995. "Partidos políticos en las Américas: desafíos y estrategias." Unpublished manuscript. Washington, D.C.: National Democratic Institute for International Affairs.

Cassen, Bernard. 1995. "Au Chili, les sirènes de l'oubli et les dividendes du libéralisme." *Le Monde Diplomatique* (February): 8-9.

Castañeda, Jorge G. 1994. *Three Challenges to U.S. Democracy: Accountability, Representativeness, and Intellectual Diversity*. Working Paper No. 3. Notre Dame, Ind.: Helen Kellogg Institute for International Studies, University of Notre Dame.

Cauffignal, Georges. 1993. "La question de l'état en Amérique Latine." *Cahiers des Ameriques* 16.

Chersky, Isidoro. 1995. "La declinación del compromiso político y la cuestión republicana en las nuevas democracias latinoamericanas: el caso argentino." *Agora* 3.

Claval, Paul. 1995. "Communication and Political Geography in a Changing World." *International Political Science Review* 16 (3).

Cohen, Jean L., and Andrew Arato. 1995. *Civil Society and Political Theory*. Cambridge, Mass.: The MIT Press.

Comisión Andina de Juristas. 1993. *Del golpe de estado a la nueva constitución*. Lima: Comisión Andina de Juristas.

Conaghan, Catherine. 1994. *Democracy That Matters: The Search for Authenticity, Legitimacy, and Civic Competence in the Andes*. Working Paper No. 1. Notre Dame, Ind.: Helen Kellogg Institute for International Studies, University of Notre Dame.

Cortés Terzi, Antonio. 1994. *Estado, institucionalida y gobernabilidad*. Working Paper No. 46. Santiago: Programa de Estudios Prospectivos.

Dahl, Robert A. 1989. *Democracy and Its Critics*. New Haven, Conn.: Yale University Press.

Dahrendorf, Ralf. 1990. "Adam Smith Was an Optimist." In *The New Democracies. Global Challenges and U.S. Policy*, ed. Brad Roberts. Cambridge, Mass.: MIT Press.

de Riz, Liliana. 1995. "Reforma constitucional y consolidación democrática." *Sociedad* (April).

Diamond, Larry. 1990. "Beyond Authoritarianism and Totalitarianism: Strategies for Democratization." In *The New Democracies: Global Challenges and U.S. Policy*, ed. Brad Roberts. Cambridge, Mass.: The MIT Press.

dos Reís Vellos, João. 1994. "Governance, the Transition to Modernity and Civil Society." In *Redefining the State in Latin America*, ed. Colin I. Bradford. Paris: Organization of Economic Cooperation and Development.

Ducatenzeiler, Graciela, and Philip Oxhorn. 1994. "Democracia, autoritarismo y el problema de la gobernabilidad en América Latina." *Desarrollo Económico* 34 (133).

Elshtain, Jean Bethke. 1995. *Democracy on Trial*. New York: Basic Books.

Enzensberger, Hans Hagnus. 1994. *Civil Wars: From L.A. to Bosnia*. New York: The New Press.

Feijoó, María del Carmen. 1994. "Una mirada sobre la Convención Nacional Constituyente." *Revista de Ciencias Sociales* (November).

Fishkin, James S. 1991. *Democracy and Deliberation: New Directions for Democratic Reform.* New Haven, Conn.: Yale University Press.

Frühling, Hugo. 1995. "Fiscalización y control ciudadano en un régimen político democrático: los casos de Argentina, Colombia, Chile, y Peru." Unpublished manuscript.

García Delgado, Daniel. 1994. *Estado y sociedad. La nueva relación a partir del cambio estructural.* Buenos Aires: FLACSO and Tesis Grupo Editorial Norma.

Gargarella, Roberto. 1995. "El ideal de la democracia deliberativa en el análisis del sistema representativo. Algunas notas teóricas y una mirada sobre el caso de la Argentina." *Sociedad* (April).

Garretón, Manuel Antonio. 1994a. "New State-Society Relations in Latin America." In *Redefining the State in Latin America*, ed. Colin I. Bradford. Paris: Organization of Economic Cooperation and Development.

Garretón, Manuel Antonio. 1994b. "Tres aproximaciones a la problemática actual de la participación ciudadana en Chile." *Temas de Participación* 1.

Garretón, Manuel Antonio. 1995a. *Hacia una nueva era política.* Santiago: Fondo de Cultura Económica.

Garretón, Manuel Antonio. 1995b. "Redemocratization in Chile." *Journal of Democracy* 6 (1): 146-158.

Gerth, H.H., and C. Wright Mills. 1958. *From Max Weber.* New York: Oxford University Press.

Gibson, Edward. 1994. "Democracy, Conservatives, and Party Politics: From Lost Decade Mobilizations to Governing Coalitions." Paper presented at the Inter-American Dialogue Project on Democratic Governance in the Americas, Washington, D.C., April.

Godoy, Oscar. 1995. "La felicidad aristotélica: Pasado y presente." *Estudios Públicos* 57.

González, Raúl. 1995. "Apuntes para una democracia mejor." In *Economía y Trabajo en Chile*, ed. Programa de Estudios del Trabajo. Santiago: PET.

Grompone, Romeo. 1995. "El incierto futuro de los partidos políticos." In *Perú, 1964-1994: economía, sociedad y política*, ed. Julio Cotler. Lima: Instituto de Estudios Peruanos.

Guerra Rodríguez, Carlos. 1994. "Crisis y construcción de identidades en Santiago de Chile." *Revista Latinoamericana de Ciencias Sociales* 2.

Guzmán, Virginia, and Rosalba Todaro. 1995. "La discriminación laboral ingresa a la agenda pública." In *El trabajo de las mujeres en el tiempo global*, eds. Rosalba Todaro and Regina Rodríguez. Santiago: ISIS-CEM.

Habermas, Jurgen. 1994. "Luchas por el reconocimiento en el estado democrático de derecho." *Estudios Internacionales: Revista del IRIPAZ* (Instituto de Relaciones Internacionales y Investigaciones para la Paz, Guatemala).

Haggard, Stephen, and Robert Kaufman. 1994. "Democratic Institutions, Economic Policy and Performance in Latin America." In *Redefining the State in Latin America*, ed. Colin I. Bradford. Paris: Organization of Economic Cooperation and Development.

Hartlyn, Jonathan. 1989. "Colombia: The Politics of Violence and Accommodation." In *Democracy in Developing Countries: Latin America*, eds. Larry Diamond, Juan J. Linz, and Seymour Martin Lipset. Boulder, Colo.: Lynne Rienner Publishers.

Held, David. 1993. "Democracy: From City-States to Cosmopolitan Order." In *Prospects for Democracy: North South East West*, ed. David Held. Palo Alto, Calif.: Stanford University Press.

Hirschman, Albert O. 1994. "The On-and-off Connection between Political and Economic Progress." *American Political Science Review* 82 (2).

Hirst, Paul. 1993. "Associational Democracy" In *Prospects for Democracy: North South East West*, ed. David Held. Palo Alto, Calif.: Stanford University Press.

Hopenhayn, Martín. 1995. *Ni apocalípticos, ni integrados. Aventuras de la modernidad en América Latina*. Santiago: Fondo de Cultura Económica.

Horowitz, Donald L. 1992. "Comparing Democratic Systems." In *Parliamentary Versus Presidential Government*, ed. Arendt Lijphart. New York: Oxford University Press.

Huntington, Samuel. 1991. *The Third Wave*. Norman: University of Oklahoma Press.

Huntington, Samuel. 1993. "The Clash of Civilizations?" *Foreign Policy* 72:3 (Summer).

Jethmalani, Rani. 1995. "Public Interest Litigation in India: Making the State Accountable." In *From Basic Needs to Basic Rights*, ed. Margaret A. Schuler. Washington, D.C.: Women, Law & International Development.

Johansen, Robert C. 1993. "Military Policies and State Systems as Impediments to Democracy." In *Prospects for Democracy: North South East West*, ed. David Held. Palo Alto, Calif.: Stanford University Press.

Karl, Terry Lynn. 1994. "Hybrid Regimes of Central America." *Journal of Democracy* 6 (3): 72-86.

Keane, John. 1993. "Democracy and the Media — without Foundations." In *Prospects for Democracy: North South East West*, ed. David Held. Palo Alto, Calif.: Stanford University Press.

Kelsen, Hans. 1988. *Escritos sobre la democracia y el socialismo*. Madrid: Editorial Debate.

Kennedy, Paul. 1993. *Preparing for the Twenty-First Century*. New York: Random House.

Laclau, Ernesto, and Chantal Mouffe. 1985. *Hegemony and Socialist Strategy*. London: Verso.

Lake, David A. 1992. "Powerful Pacifists: Democratic States and War." *American Political Science Review* 86 (1).

Lasch, Christopher. 1995. *The Revolt of the Elites*. New York: W.W. Norton.

Leal L., Antonio. 1994. *La política en el fin del siglo: Democracia y ciudadanía*. Working Paper No. 47. Santiago: Programa de Estudios Prospectivos.

Lechner, Norbert. 1994. *"La (problemática) invocación de la sociedad civil. Cuestión de Estado* 2 (11).

Le Roy, Michael K. 1995. "Participation, Size, and Democracy: Bridging the Gap between Citizens and the Swedish State." *Comparative Politics* 27 (3).

Linz, Juan L. 1994. "Presidential or Parliamentary Democracy: Does It Make a Difference?" In *The Failure of Presidential Democracy*, eds. Juan L. Linz and Arturo Valenzuela. Baltimore: The Johns Hopkins University Press.

Lipset, Seymour Martin, Kyong-Ryung Seong, and John Charles Torres. 1993. "Análisis comparado de los requisitos sociales de la democracia." *Revista Internacional de Ciencias Sociales* 136.

Lipsky, Michael. 1970. *Street-Level Bureaucracy: Dilemmas of the Individual in Public Services*. New York: Russell Sage.

López, Juan J. 1992. *Business Elites and Democracy in Latin America.* Working Paper No. 185. Notre Dame, Ind.: Helen Kellogg Institute for International Studies, University of Notre Dame.

López Jiménez, Sinesio. 1993. "Perú: La democratización es ancha y ajena." *Revista Peruana de Ciencias Sociales* 3 (3).

Loveman, Brian. 1994. *The Constitution of Tyranny.* Pittsburgh: University of Pittsburgh Press.

Mainwaring, Scott. 1992. "Transition to Democracy and Democratic Consolidation: Theoretical and Comparative Issues." In *Issues in Democratic Consolidation: The New South American Democracies in Comparative Perspective*, eds. Scott Mainwaring, Guillermo O'Donnell, and J. Samuel Valenzuela. Notre Dame, Ind.: University of Notre Dame Press.

Mainwaring, Scott. 1994. *Democracy in Brazil and the Southern Cone: Achievements and Problems.* Working Paper No. 2. Notre Dame, Ind.: Helen Kellogg Institute for International Studies, University of Notre Dame.

Mainwaring, Scott, and Timothy R. Scully. 1995. *Building Democratic Institutions: Party Systems in Latin America.* Stanford, Calif.: Stanford University Press.

Marshall, T.H. 1964. *Class, Citizenship and Social Development.* New York: Anchor Books.

Montecinos, Verónica. 1993. *Economic Policy Elites and Democratic Consolidation.* Working Paper 191, Helen Kellogg Institute for International Studies, University of Notre Dame.

Mounier, Emmanuel. 1968. *El personalismo.* Buenos Aires: EUDEBA.

Muller, Edward N., and Mitchell A. Seglison. 1994. "Civic Culture and Democracy: The Question of Causal Relationships." *American Political Science Review* 88 (3).

Nogueira, Marco Aurelio. 1995. "Gobernabilidad y democracia progresiva." *Análisis Político* (May-August).

Novaro, Marcos. 1995. "Crisis de representación, neopopulismo y consolidación democrática." *Sociedad* (April).

Nuñez del Prado, Arturo. 1990. "Las economías de viabilidad difícil." *Revista de la Cepal* (42).

O'Donnell, Guillermo. 1994a. "Delegative Democracy." *Journal of Democracy* 5 (1): 55-69.

O'Donnell, Guillermo. 1994b. "Some Reflections on Redefining the Role of the State." In *Redefining the State in Latin America*, ed. Colin I. Bradford. Paris: Organization of Economic Cooperation and Development.

Panfichi, Alo, and Cynthia Sanborn. 1995. "Democracia y neopopularismo en el Perú contemporáneo." *Márgenes* 7 (13-14).

Phillips, Anne. 1993. *Democracy and Difference.* University Park, Pa.: Pennsylvania State University Press.

Poe, Steven C., and C. Neal Tate. 1994. "Repression of Human Rights to Personal Integrity in the 1980s: A Global Analysis." *American Political Science Review* 88 (4).

Portantiero, Juan Carlos. 1994. "Revisando el camino: Las apuestas de la democracia en Sudamérica." *Sociedad* 2.

Przeworski, Adam. 1988. "Democracy as a Contingent Outcome of Conflicts." In *Constitutionalism and Democracy*, eds. Jon Elster and Rume Slagstad. Cambridge, Mass.: Cambridge University Press.

Przeworski, Adam, and Fernando Limongi. 1993. "Political Regimes and Economic Growth." *Journal of Economic Perspectives* 7 (3).

Pusic, Vesna. 1994. "Dictatorship with Democratic Legitimacy: Democracy Versus Nation." *East European Politics and Society* 8 (3).

Ramonet, Ignacio, et al. 1996. *Les nouveaux maitres du monde*. Paris: Le Monde Diplomatique.

Revilla, Marisa. 1994. "Gobernabilidad y movimientos sociales, una relación difícil." *América Latina* (8).

Richani, Ignacio. 1995. "El divorcio entre la democracia y el capitalismo." *Análisis Político* 26.

Rodgers, Gerry, Charles Gore, and José B. Figueirido. 1995. *Social Exclusion: Rhetoric, Reality, Responses*. Geneva: International Labour Organization.

Rosenau, James. 1990. *Turbulence in World Politics. A Theory of Change and Continuity*. Princeton, N.J.: Princeton University Press.

Rosenau, James. 1992. "The Reallocation of Authority in a Shrinking World." *Comparative Politics*.

Ruíz Schneider, Carlos. 1993. *Seis ensayos sobre teoría de la democracia*. Santiago: Universidad Nacional Andrés Bello.

Russett, Bruce. 1993. *Grasping the Democratic Peace: Principles for a Post-Cold War World*. Princeton, N.J.: Princeton University Press.

Sachs, Ignacy. 1995. "Contre l'exclusion, l'ardente obligation du codévelopment planétaire." *Le Monde Diplomatique* (January).

Sain, Marcelo Fabián. 1994. "El contexto político de la reforma constitucional del 1994." *Revista de Ciencias Sociales* (November).

Salmen, Lawrence. 1994. "Escuchando al pobre." *Finanzas & Desarrollo* 31:4 (December).

Salvi, Giovanni. 1994. "Aspectos de la corrupción en Italia." *Estudios Públicos* 56.

Sanz Menéndez, Luis, ed. 1994. "Representación de intereses y políticas públicas: ¿corporatismo o pluralismo?" *Zona Abierta* 67-68.

Sartori, Giovanni. 1994. "Neither Presidentialism Nor Parliamentarism." In *The Failure of Presidential Democracy*, eds. Juan L. Linz and Arturo Valenzuela. Baltimore: The Johns Hopkins University Press.

Schlesinger, Jr., Arthur M. 1992. *The Disuniting of America*. New York: W.W. Norton.

Schmitter, Philippe C. 1994. "Dangers and Dilemmas of Democracy." *Journal of Democracy* 6 (1): 15-22.

Schmitter, Philippe C. 1995. "More Liberal, Preliberal, or Postliberal?" *Journal of Democracy* 5 (2).

Schmitter, Philippe C., and Terry Lynn Karl. 1993. "What Democracy Is ... and Is Not." In *The Global Resurgence of Democracy*, eds. Larry Diamond and Marc F. Plattner. Baltimore: The John Hopkins University Press.

Schneider, Ben Ross. 1995. "Democratic Consolidations: Some Broad Comparisons and Some Sweeping Arguments." *Latin American Research Review* 30 (2).

Schutz, Barry M., and Robert O. Slater. 1990. *Revolution and Political Change in the Third World*. Boulder, Colo.: Lynne Rienner Publishers.

Seligman, Adam B. 1992. *The Idea of Civil Society*. Princeton, N.J.: Princeton University Press.

Shifter, Michael. 1995. "Now the Hard Part." *Hemisfile* 6 (3).

Squella, Agustín. 1995. "¿Qué derechos humanos habrá en el próximo milenio?" *La Epoca* 16 (April).

Stimson, James A., Michael B. Mackuen, and Robert E. Erikson. 1995. "Dynamic Representation." *American Political Science Review* 89 (3).

Tezanos, José Felix. 1992. "Transformaciones en la estructura de clases en la sociedad tecnológica avanzada." *El Socialismo del Futuro* 6.

Thomas, Dorothy Q. 1995. "Acting Unnaturally: In Defense of the Civil and Political Rights of Women." In *From Basic Needs to Basic Rights*, ed. Margaret A. Schuler. Washington, D.C.: Women, Law & International Development.

Touraine, Alain. 1994a. "From the Mobilizing State to Democratic Politics." In *Redefining the State in Latin America*, ed. Colin I. Bradford. Paris: Organization of Economic Cooperation and Development.

Touraine, Alain. 1994b. *Qu'este-ce que la démocratie?* Paris: Fayard.

Valenzuela, Arturo. 1993. "Latin America: Presidentialism in Crisis." *Journal of Democracy* 4.

Valenzuela, J. Samuel. 1992. "Democratic Consolidation in Post-Transitional Settings: Notion, Process, and Facilitating Conditions." In *Issues in Democratic Consolidation: The New South American Democracies in Comparative Perspective*, eds. Scott Mainwaring, Guillermo O'Donnell, and J. Samuel Valenzuela. Notre Dame, Ind.: University of Notre Dame Press.

Varas, Augusto, ed. 1989. *Democracy under Siege: New Military Power in Latin America*. New York: Greenwood Press.

Varas, Augusto, Pamela Mewes, and Isaac Caro. 1994. *Democracia y mercado en el post-socialismo. Rusia y las repúblicas del Asia Central*. Santiago: FLACSO.

Weart, Spencer R. 1994. "Peace among Democratic and Oligarchic Republics." *Journal of Peace Research* 31 (3).

Weber, Max. 1944. *Economía y sociedad*. Mexico City: Fondo de Cultura Económica.

Weber, Max. 1958. *From Max Weber*, eds. H.H. Gerth and C. Wright Mills. New York: Oxford University Press.

Weede, Erich. 1989. "Democracy and Income Inequality Reconsidered." *American Sociological Review* 54.

Weffort, Francisco C. 1994. "Nuevas democracias. ¿Que democracias?" *Sociedad* 2.

Weil, Frederick D. 1989. "The Sources and Structure of Legitimation in Western Democracies: A Consolidated Model Tested with Time-series Data in Six Countries since World War II." *American Sociological Review* 54.

Wiarda, Howard J. 1995. "The Future of Political Reform in the Southern Cone: Can Democracy Be Sustained?" *The Washington Quarterly* 18 (3).

Whitehead, Laurence. 1993. "The Alternatives to 'Liberal Democracy': A Latin American Perspective." In *Prospects for Democracy: North South East West*, ed. David Held. Palo Alto, Calif.: Stanford University Press.

Wood, B. Dan, and Richard W. Waterman. 1994. *Bureaucratic Dynamics: The Role of Bureaucracy in a Democracy*. Boulder, Colo.: Westview Press.

World Bank. 1994. *Governance — the World Bank's Experience*. Washington, D.C.: World Bank.

Zolo, Danilo. 1993. "Democratic Citizenship in a Post-Communist Era." In *Prospects for Democracy: North South East West*, ed. David Held. Palo Alto, Calif.: Stanford University Press.

# CHAPTER SEVEN

# Fault Lines of Democratic Governance: A Gender Perspective

## MARYSA NAVARRO AND SUSAN C. BOURQUE

S ince the eighteenth century, the exclusion of women from the political system and their relegation to a status of second-class citizens have been vital issues for feminists; however, with a few notable exceptions, these issues have had little relevance for political philosophers or political scientists. When addressing the "woman question," political philosophers have accepted women's exclusion from the public realm as a given. At the same time, they have long recognized the family as central among the institutions that undergird and frame political life. Beginning with Plato and Aristotle, philosophers have pointed out the need for resonance between the structure of the family and the desired ends in the political system. Less apparent has been an argument by democratic theorists for a relation between gender equity and democratic polities. Jean-Jacques Rousseau, the great exponent of participatory democracy and social equity, found no inconsistency in excluding women from citizenship and, therefore, from political rights. As Susan Okin and Carole Pateman have demonstrated, philosophical discussions of political democracy have been carried on largely in the absence of a discussion of women's rights or the impact of gender inequities on the function of a democratic political order.[1]

Historically, democracy has been an exclusionary political system with regard to women. Everywhere, it has resisted ending the exclusion of women and their inferior status. Significantly, other political systems have not been more inclusive, even when they have granted political rights to women. However, women have persisted in imagining themselves as part of the political community that resists their inclusion. Women throughout the world have recognized a fundamental, albeit at times problematic, link between feminism and democracy. In Latin America as elsewhere, women have fought for what they determined to be their rights, with the stubborn belief that democracy should be inclusive, even when the laws written by men were not.

Democracy carries with it a promise of equal access and popular control that has not been fulfilled in Latin America. In a region more accurately characterized as one where democratic impulses are at war with longstanding authoritarian patterns, the claim to a "return to democracy" should be accompanied by important qualifications on what is meant by "democracy." The major fault lines of democratic governance are found in the tentative commitment to its principal assumptions among large groups of the public and the weakness of democratic practice in the social and cultural norms that underpin political institutions.

Equal access to political participation and leadership remain distant goals for women in the region's newly reconstituted democracies. Yet, close examination of events and trends in the 1980s and 1990s suggests some significant changes in women's political action and political space. Furthermore, we argue in this essay that key components of the Latin American cultural context have been altered, a transformation that holds out hope for democracy and for greater political access and leadership for women.

We note at the outset that there are important variations throughout the region. Just as political scientists have posited that the pattern of redemocratization is influenced by the nature of the preceding authoritarian regime and the conditions of its "exit," so, too, scholars have argued that the degree of gender equity and level of women's political participation that occur with redemocratization depend on the nature of the regime under which women mobilized and the democratic alternative, with its particular contours, that emerges (Jaquette 1994; Waylen 1994; Basu 1995; Bourque 1989).

This essay is a contribution to an ongoing discussion about the long-term impact of women's mobilization on democratic politics in Latin America. Simply put, the central question is: Will the mobilization of women associated with the emergence of second wave feminist movements, the opposition to the military regimes of the 1970s and 1980s, and the transformations of national liberation movements in Central America be short-lived and ephemeral? Or, will women's involvement in social movements and political activism lead to long-term expansion of their political participation, changes in the behavior of political elites toward them, and a shift in the contours of political life to include women? Those who argue that the impact of women's mobilization will be limited remind us that women's participation in formal politics and political office has not increased markedly in the past 20 years. Furthermore, these observers stress the vulnerability of social movements in which women play leading roles during the transition to democracy only to disappear when competitive party politics return to dominate political discourse. Those who argue for the lasting impact of women's mobilization have emphasized the heightened level of political consciousness and efficacy among individual women as a result of their political participation, and at the national level, an altered political discourse in which gender issues have become concerns shared by a broad spectrum of political groups.

In this chapter, we argue that any judgment on this central question should include a broader assessment of the history of women's struggle for civil and political rights and the changing nature of democratic politics and practices in contemporary Latin America. Similarly, mindful of the wide variety of women's groups in Latin America and the particular circumstances of each country, we find it essential to identify the significant widespread changes in the region's cultural context that result from transformations in the Roman Catholic Church, in the political "left," in the international nature of contemporary feminism, and in women's expanded educational and employment opportunities.

# THE STRUGGLE FOR FRANCHISE AND PATTERNS OF EARLY POLITICAL ACTIVISM

Obtaining the franchise, the fundamental aspect of democratic citizenship, was a slow process for Latin American women. It began in Ecuador in 1929 and ended in Paraguay in 1961. Only four countries granted political rights to women before 1940;[2] the rest did so in the 1940s[3] and 1950s.[4]

Throughout most of the continent, suffrage proved a limited asset, given the prevalence of military regimes, the weakness of democratic institutions, and the absence of a democratic political culture. In most countries, the vote was initially restricted to educated women. Thus, in countries with a large indigenous population, such as Bolivia and Guatemala, these restrictions were particularly severe for a very high percentage of women, and illiterate women could not vote until the 1980s (Valdés and Gomariz 1995). In Chile, suffrage was extended in stages; women voted first in municipal elections in 1934, and they obtained the franchise for national elections in 1949.

In many cases, the vote was *not* the result of women's mobilization or the culmination of a long campaign waged by groups of committed feminists. Ecuador, the first country to give women the franchise, is a case in point. In May 1924, Dr. Matilde Hidalgo de Prócel, one of Ecuador's first female professionals, registered to vote at the electoral board of Machala on the grounds that the Constitution did not stipulate that only men had the right to vote (Estrada 1981). The board agreed but requested a confirmation from the Ministry of Interior. The ministry confirmed the decision, but as criticism spread, the issue was brought to the attention of the State Council. Once again the decision was ratified, this time unanimously. The Liberals then mounted a campaign against women's suffrage and postponed the decision until 1929, when a Conservative-backed bill gave adult, literate Ecuadorian women the right to vote — if they so chose. Women's vote was not declared mandatory until 1967. The Liberals' main concern was women's allegiance to the Catholic Church and their fear that women would follow the directives of priests at election time. The same argument against women's suffrage was advanced in several other countries.[5]

Mexico offers another unusual example. Women fought alongside men during the 1910 Revolution and provided important logistical support for the revolutionary armies. Feminists agitated for the vote and petitioned the constitutional convention, but to no avail. The convention received three different proposals for women's suffrage but did not discuss the question. When the 1917 Constitution was finally adopted, it gave illiterate adult males the right to vote, but it excluded all adult women. In the following decades, women obtained the right to vote in several Mexican states, and the Institutional Revolutionary Party (Partido Revolucionario Institucional — PRI) gave its female members the right to vote in internal elections. Nevertheless, Mexican women had to wait until 1953 to obtain the franchise and voted for the first time in a national election in 1958.

Even without the vote, feminists were active in several countries after the turn of the century. They published magazines and newspapers and created women's parties. In Brazil, it was the Women's Republican Party (Partido Republicano Femenino) (1910); in Argentina, the Women's Party (Partido Feminista) (1918); in

Chile, the Women's Civic Party (Partido Cívico Femenino) (1922) and the Chilean Women's Party (Partido Femenino Chileno) (1946); and in Panama, the National Women's Party (Partido Feminista Nacional) (1924). They also organized congresses. In 1910, some 200 women from Argentina, Chile, Peru, Uruguay, and Paraguay attended the First International Feminine Congress in Buenos Aires. Mexican feminists met in Mérida in 1916, and Colombian women organized another international congress in 1930 (Luna and Villareal 1994). Representatives from several Latin American countries attended the Pan American Women Congresses, held in Chile in 1922 and in Peru in 1924, and participated in the founding meeting of the Inter-American Commission of Women that took place in Havana, Cuba, in 1930 (Miller 1990).

In a few cases, women received the franchise as part of a particular government's attempt to broaden the social base of its support. This occurred in Argentina, Bolivia, Colombia, Costa Rica, Cuba, Guatemala, and Venezuela. In several instances, women were incorporated into the political process by authoritarian regimes with little respect for democratic ideals and practices: women obtained the franchise in Brazil under Getúlio Vargas (1932), in Peru under Gen. Manuel A. Odría (1956), in the Dominican Republic under Rafael Leonidas Trujillo (1942), in Nicaragua under Anastasio Somoza (1955), and in Paraguay under Gen. Alfredo Stroessner (1961). Frequently, voting was mandatory, and elections were neither free nor regularly held. The vote in such contexts was little more than an additional arrow in the quiver of the dictator, used to confirm the international legitimacy of the regime. Under these circumstances, women's access to the vote had little impact on increased popular control.

Political parties also bear a major responsibility for the lack of women's participation; they acted as gatekeepers intent on either controlling or excluding women. Women did not join political parties in massive numbers, and the parties did not elaborate new platforms to respond to women's right to vote, attract them to the parties' ranks, or put them forth as candidates for elected office. Except for the occasional rhetorical declarations exalting the role of women in the family and their crucial participation in pro-natalist policies, women's presence in political parties from left to right was largely ignored, and party leadership remained male. When women did participate, they were relegated to "auxiliary sections," women's committees, or secretariats that worked dutifully at election time to secure the election of male candidates. The PRI in Mexico is a particularly good example of this pattern.

Chile and Argentina are two of the exceptions to women's limited political participation. In Chile, interest in women's suffrage began in the nineteenth century. In 1873, the writer Martina Barros de Orrego published an article on John Stuart Mill's ideas in *Revista Santiago* and also lectured on women's suffrage. Women joined political parties in the 1920s and 1930s and created organizations like Movimiento Pro Emancipación de la Mujer (MEMECH), founded by left-wing women. According to one of its founders, Elena Caffarena, it encompassed women of all classes, and it was composed of local committees that sprang up in cities, communes, and neighborhoods. When they were given the right to vote in municipal elections, Chilean women became candidates, and a few were elected, especially from conservative parties. In 1947, in the last stages of the campaign for suffrage, María de la Cruz founded the Partido Femenino Chileno, which she allied with Carlos Ibáñez del Campo. In 1953, she became the first female senator, two years after the election of Inés Henríquez as a deputy for the Radical Party.[6]

Argentine women have a long tradition of political activism in the Anarchist Movement and the Socialist Party, dating back to the nineteenth century. By the turn of the century, women such as Gabriela L. de Coni already occupied leadership positions in the Socialist Party. Argentina's most important suffragist, Alicia Moreau de Justo, was a party leader and a socialist from 1910 until her death at the age of 100 in 1986. Deeply committed to democratic politics, during the years of the Proceso (1976-1983), she became involved in the human rights movement. She was co-founder and president of the Asamblea Permanente de Derechos Humanos (1975), and she publicly participated in activities in defense of human rights.

On several occasions in the 1930s, Moreau de Justo and other feminists obtained the support of Radical and Socialist congressmen for the passage of female suffrage. Unfortunately, all attempts died in the Senate due to the domination of the Conservative Party. Following the military coup of June 1943, to the dismay of feminists, socialists, and others, Col. Juan Domingo Perón announced his support for women's suffrage (Gaviola et al. 1978). Soon after he was elected president in February 1946, he reiterated his position and included a suffrage bill in his first Five Year Plan. With the Conservatives no longer in control of the Senate and a Peronist majority in both houses, women were granted the right to vote in September 1947.

Contrary to Peronist mythology, Evita was not responsible for women obtaining the vote in Argentina, but she did play a crucial role in their massive entrance into politics (Navarro 1997). Shortly after the passage of the suffrage bill, she selected a group of women who traveled across the country to explore support for a women's organization and to oversee the drive for female voter registration. In 1949, she founded the Partido Peronista Femenino (PPF) or Rama Femenina, the women's branch of the Peronist Party. Evita ran the PPF with an iron hand, and in the November 1951 elections, she delivered the vote to President Perón. He received 63.9 percent of the women's vote. Furthermore, thanks to Evita's insistence, Argentines also voted for a total of 29 women candidates for Congress, an unusually high number, even by today's standards. After the 1955 congressional elections, the numbers increased to 45 (37 deputies and 8 senators), representing 16 percent of the Chamber of Deputies and 25 percent of the Senate.

Evita was never formally part of Perón's government and was forced to give up her only attempt to be a candidate for elected office. In August 1951, she allowed her name to be placed in nomination for vice-president on the Peronist ticket but had to withdraw because of opposition from the armed forces. Her transformation into a major political figure in the Peronist hierarchy, second only to Perón, was a process that began to take shape in 1947. By 1950, at the height of her power and influence, she was Evita, the charismatic *abanderada de los descamisados* (the standard bearer of the shirtless ones) or, as she preferred to be called, "the bridge of love between Perón and the *descamisados*." As such, she was Perón's personal liaison with the General Labor Confederation (Confederación General de Trabajo — CGT), the rank and file access to Perón, and Perón had in her an indefatigable speechmaker and a one-woman propaganda machine, always ready to extol the greatness of Perón and chastise his enemies (the oligarchy, imperialists, communists, and socialists). She was also Eva Perón, Argentina's first lady, the only woman member of the superior Council of the Peronist party, president of the Rama Femenina, and president of the Fundación Eva Perón, a wealthy social welfare organization, whose funds she controlled.

Until her death at the age of 33, in July 1952, Evita was a crucial figure in Perón's first government. Her impact on Argentine women was significant. After Perón was deposed in 1955, all political parties, including the most conservative, sought to attract the women's vote, although they did not imitate the Peronists in terms of organization and did not open their leadership ranks to women candidates. However, except for the creation of the Rama Femenina and the candidacy of 45 women, admittedly important achievements, Evita did not use her considerable influence to support the advancement of women. As "standard-bearer" of the workers, she demonstrated little interest in the specific conditions of women workers and did not champion their cause or that of all wage-working women. Furthermore, she did not help women achieve leadership positions, even in those unions whose membership was largely female, and the secretariat of the CGT remained an all-male institution.

The myths surrounding Evita increased during the 1960s and 1970s, those long years of off-and-on military rule and anti-Peronist hysteria when Perón was living in exile. She was instrumental in the support that young women gave to the Peronist guerrillas in the 1970s. In an ironic twist, she paved the way for the election to the vice-presidency of Perón's third wife, María Estela Martínez de Perón (Isabel). After Perón died in office in 1974, Isabel succeeded him and became Argentina's first woman president.[7]

## REWRITING THE CIVIL CODES AND THE CONSTITUTIONS

One key element that is generally ignored in discussing women's suffrage is that most Latin American women obtained the vote and went to the polls while their citizenship was still limited by regulations that rigidly subjugated them to their fathers or their husbands. The erosion of women's codified second-class citizenship has been very slow — and it is still unfinished. In a few countries, challenges to secondary legal status began in the late nineteenth century. At the time, marriage transformed a woman into a creature incapable of performing legal acts, such as signing a contract. By some extraordinary phenomenon, left unexplained by jurists, philosophers, theologians, or politicians, a woman, even one no longer a minor, underwent a metamorphosis the minute she married. She automatically suffered a loss of "mental ability," a phenomenon that the jurists called in all seriousness *"capitis diminutio,"* a diminution of her capacity. Interestingly, this diminished, infantilized creature, in a contradiction familiar throughout the West, was given the exalted role of Mother, in charge of reproducing and educating future generations.

Redressing Latin American women's second-class citizenship began in Chile with an 1877 decree that allowed women to register at the university. Similarly, in other countries, middle-class women began to challenge their de facto exclusion from higher education during the nineteenth century. Once admitted to the university, they went on to demand the right to practice their professions. In several countries, working-class women organized unions and declared strikes over demands that were ignored by male-led unions. In Argentina, they joined the socialist unions that proclaimed adherence to the principle of equal salary for equal work and included this principle in their initial party platform. Yet, neither socialist labor leaders, nor anarchists, communists, or Peronists ever called a strike in support of equal pay for equal work.

The legal status of women was timidly altered in the early decades of the twentieth century in many countries, and a number of reforms were gradually undertaken in the next decades, especially following the rebirth of feminist movements in the 1980s. Nevertheless, there are still discriminatory measures on the books. Although in most countries women now have full legal capacity, in Bolivia and Guatemala, husbands can forbid their wives from exercising specific trades or professions.[8] In Nicaragua and the Dominican Republic, the marital domicile is not established by mutual consent (as it is in other Latin American countries) but by decision of the husband.

In Brazil, while the 1988 Constitution guarantees equality before the law to men and women and includes several measures to end discrimination against the latter, the Brazilian Civil Code, originally drafted in 1884 and approved by Congress in 1916, still retains discriminatory articles. For example, articles 178 and 219 establish that a husband can seek annulment if, within ten days following his marriage, he is able to prove that his wife has been "deflowered" by another man. Article 233 gives the responsibility *(chiefia)* of the couple to the husband. Article 380 grants the *poder pátrio* (parental authority) to the couple, but in yet another example of exquisite nineteenth-century liberal gobbledygook, its exercise rests with the husband. In Argentina, it was not until 1985 that women succeeded in sharing the *patria potestad* (parental authority). In Chile, the mother can exercise it only if the father is not available.

In Peru, the Constitution of 1978 included important revisions and improvements in women's status, guaranteeing to women rights no less than those available to men. Nevertheless, the civil code still contained outmoded distinctions.

Turning to reproductive rights, with the exception of Cuba, abortion is a crime in all countries, unless it is therapeutic or when the pregnancy is the result of rape or statutory rape. In most countries, punishment for an abortion (as well as for infanticide) is reduced if the woman interrupts her pregnancy to cover up her dishonor (abortion *honoris causa;* infanticide *honoris causa).* In several countries, adultery is not a crime, but in others it is a crime only for married women. In still others, the definition of adultery for a woman is different from that for a man. For instance, a married woman who has sexual intercourse with any man other than her husband commits adultery and can be punished, but a married man commits adultery only if he has sexual intercourse with a mistress or a concubine. In addition, in Venezuela, Mexico, and Guatemala, the adultery must take place in his home for it to be considered an actionable offense.

Thus, despite access to the vote, significant discrimination continues to exist in the legal codes. The law continues to reflect differences between men's and women's status, and it explicitly exercises control over women's sexuality.

# FROM SOCIAL MOVEMENTS TO WOMEN'S MOVEMENTS

In the flurry of scholarly works on redemocratization in Latin America, and more specifically on the subject of democratic consolidation, relatively little attention has been paid to the question of women's participation. In most studies, women remain invisible, and in others they are barely mentioned in passing as part of the new social movements. The most generous dedicate a chapter to women (frequently written by a woman) and then proceed to ignore the issues raised in it. Similarly, women scholars have written relatively little about this topic.[9]

This lack of attention means that we have only begun to analyze how the link between feminism and democracy became a vital force in the Latin American feminist movements that developed in the 1970s and 1980s. We do, however, find the individual country studies in Jane Jaquette's volume, *The Women's Movement in Latin America,* to be excellent contributions to our understanding of this link, as are the essays on Latin America in *The Challenge of Local Feminists,* edited by Amrita Basu. While we will not summarize those studies here, we wish to highlight several overlapping themes found in those volumes and then turn to our major points on the changing cultural context.

The link between women's mobilization and democracy was certainly highly visible in the Southern Cone, in countries where the armed forces ousted elected leaders in the 1960s and 1970s to restructure the state and society in accordance with the doctrine of national security. The armed forces created right-wing authoritarian and exclusionary regimes that outlawed labor unions and suppressed political parties, disbanded parliaments, suspended constitutions, dispensed with civil liberties, and trampled on fundamental human rights. All means for redress were shut off, and all forms of protest were forbidden, thus freeing the military to begin an initial round of neoliberal policies. Because the nation was threatened by an internal enemy — subversion or terrorism — the military was allowed to combat those they defined as enemies with assassinations, the systematic torture of those held in hidden concentration camps or barracks, and the forced abductions or disappearances of men, women, entire families, elderly persons, and babies.

One common denominator of the Southern Cone military dictatorships is that they produced the unexpected mobilization of women. The *movimiento de mujeres* (women's movement), as this mobilization is known in Latin America, was at times massive.[10] It was largely centered in the capitals and engaged women workers, recent rural migrants, middle-class and professional women, and women of varying racial and ethnic origins, as well as those from the poorest sectors. Interestingly, contrary to what occurred in the United States, where elite, middle-class, and professional women have been active and sometimes prominent members of the second wave of the feminist movement from its inception, in Latin America and the Caribbean, elite women generally have not been involved.

One sector of the *movimiento de mujeres* was composed of women from the popular sectors who lived in shantytowns and were compelled to act in order to survive unemployment and inflation. Women from these densely populated sectors defined themselves as mothers because of their domestic role. They organized deafening pot-banging sessions in Montevideo and marched in the streets of

Santiago, São Paulo, and Buenos Aires to protect the welfare of their families when public expressions of political activity were not permitted. To survive economically, they did laundry, cooking, and ironing for wages, traded or bartered, and prepared food to sell in the streets. In Santiago, they created *organizaciones económicas populares* that set up hundreds of soup kitchens and created organizations such as the Committee for the Defense of the Rights of Women (Comité de Defensa de Derechos de la Mujer — CODEM), Women of Chile (Mujeres de Chile — MUDECHI), and Movement of Shantytown Women (Movimiento de Mujeres Pobladoras — MOMPO) to respond to the basic needs of their families. They also created artisan workshops where women knitted sweaters or sewed tapestries depicting daily life, made with bright colored scraps of cloth on a burlap backing. And, when political conditions barely permitted it, they organized protests against the absence of urban infrastructure in their neighborhoods, against inflation, and against price increases of basic foodstuffs. These grassroots neighborhood block associations and popular economic organizations were created by women who saw their lives anchored in the home, not the workplace. The issues that mobilized them were issues of survival, but they were private, domestic, and not related to paid employment. In Brazil, encouraged by the Catholic Church, they created Mothers' Clubs in the 1970s and participated in large numbers in the Movement Against the Rising Cost of Living.

The mobilization of women was not restricted to the Southern Cone countries. In Peru, several types of organizations emerged in the shantytowns and poor neighborhoods of the city: "mothers' clubs," funded by the state welfare program; "people's kitchens," which received support from the Catholic Church and international non-governmental organizations (NGOs); "glass of milk committees" sponsored by the Lima city government; and networks of grassroots health and legal aid promoters (Blondet 1995; Navarro 1992). In 1984, they began coordinating their activities, holding the First Meeting of Free Meal Programs of Lima and Callao, later on creating the national Commission of Free Meal Programs.

The *movimiento de mujeres* also involved working-class and middle-class women organized in newly created or reactivated human rights organizations. In Brazil, women flocked to the Movement for Amnesty founded in 1972 to denounce human rights violations. In fact, there were so many human rights organizations, from the Confederación de Viudas de Guatemala to the Bartolinas Sisa in Bolivia and COMADRES in El Salvador, that in 1980 they joined together in FEDEFAM, the Latin American Federation of Relatives for the Defense of Missing Persons. Those who participated in these new organizations had one thing in common: the search for disappeared relatives, victims of the brutal repression unleashed by the military. Because military repression was largely directed toward men, though a substantial number of women also "disappeared," it was left to mothers, grandmothers, wives, and sisters to search for those who had been taken away. In Santiago, in the aftermath of the September 11, 1973, coup, women from all walks of life found themselves searching for their loved ones in police stations, courthouses, jails, the morgue, the curia, the soccer stadium, army depots, as well as the army, navy, and air force ministries. Drawn together by their anguish, by the realization that many others were undergoing the same horror, and by the desperate need to obtain information, they soon developed a strong sense of solidarity. On October 1, 1973, less than three weeks after the coup, five women founded the Democratic Women's Group (Agrupación de Mujeres Democráticas) to help political prisoners and their families.

The Agrupación was the first of many Chilean groups formed by women seeking the whereabouts of detained relatives or concerned about human rights violations. Founded under the aegis of the Catholic Church, their activities initially consisted of providing vital humanitarian support and solidarity to political prisoners and their relatives, as well as to those of the disappeared. By 1978, they began to undertake other kinds of actions. On March 8, one of these groups organized a celebration of International Women's Day, an event which became the first post-coup political demonstration. In the following year, 1979, several members belonging to the Association of Relatives of Detained and Missing Persons carried out a public hunger strike. With photographs of their missing relatives pinned on their clothes, they chained themselves to the fence that surrounds the Congress building and were arrested. Their action was the first political protest against the Pinochet regime.

In contrast, in Argentina, the Madres de la Plaza de Mayo, the best internationally known mothers' organization, adopted a defiant, militant stance from the moment the group was founded in April 1977, 13 months after the military deposed President Perón and launched its "holy war" or "dirty war." The Madres was not the first Argentine human rights organization, but it was the only one exclusively composed of women, and it was the first one to decide that its work on behalf of the disappeared required weekly public demonstrations. Overcoming their fears, the members of the Madres were the first to demonstrate against the military junta, and, for a quite a long time, the only ones. In a context in which all traditional forms of political expression, resistance, or action were illegal and extremely dangerous, every Thursday afternoon, in an extraordinary act of defiance and courage that no other human rights group or political or religious organization dared to undertake, they went to the Plaza de Mayo, a square in downtown Buenos Aires where the Casa Rosada (the President's residence), the Ministry of Interior, the Cathedral, and the old Cabildo stand, to ask a simple question: "Where are our children?" Their heads covered with white kerchiefs and carrying signs bearing photographs of their disappeared, the Madres marched silently for an hour around the Mayo pyramid, right in front of the isolated and closely guarded Casa Rosada. They did this week after week, year after year, with very few interruptions, despite threats, persistent harassment, forceful removals from the plaza, raids by the police, and the murder of their first leader, Azucena Villaflor. As the end of the military regime approached, after the disaster of the Malvinas/Falklands war, the Madres had become the symbol of opposition to the junta. When large-scale mobilizations began exerting pressure on the military for the return to democracy, Argentines took to the streets, led by the Madres and other human rights organizations. They stood their ground and maintained that the issue of the disappeared was a non-negotiable question when the military attempted to urge the nation to forget it and the politicians seemed inclined to accept some kind of compromise. Instead, to their old quest for information on their loved ones, they added a demand, *"justicia a los culpables"* (justice for the guilty).

A final facet of the mobilization of women during the military dictatorships in the Southern Cone was the rebirth of a feminist movement. Feminism was slow to take root in Latin America, as Ana María Portugal says below:

> Habitantes en un continente marcado por el lastre del subdesarrollo y la dependencia, la primera consigna con el puño en alto fue la lucha antiimperialista, y cuando el uniforme verde olivo de los barbudos de la Sierra Maestra se convirtió en el santo y seña en las luchas de liberación nacionales, las mujeres no pudimos sustraernos a los cantos de sirena y ahí acudimos en contingente para adherirnos a una causa que por ser la de "todos," creimos también propia. . . . En 1970 el feminismo parecía como un enlatado made in USA y sus ecos llegados a través de los cables de las agencias de prensa internacionales, nos sonaban ajenos por ser equívocos. Que las mujeres del país más poderoso del planeta se quitaran los "brassiers" para protestar contra el machismo, se nos antojaba una humorada propia de gringas aburridas.[11]

In 1971, a group of young women marked the founding of MAS (Mujeres en Acción Solidaria), the first Mexican feminist group, with a public protest against the celebration of Mother's Day. That same year, in Argentina, still in the throes of the Peronist/anti-Peronist dichotomy, a small group of women founded the Unión Feminista Argentina (UFA). Until the 1976 military coup, the UFA sponsored consciousness-raising groups, lectures, and discussions on sexuality, feminism, and abortion — despite censorship, political restrictions, and increasing violence. In 1973, a protest against the Miss Universe Pageant by a group of Peruvian women in front of the Lima Sheraton Hotel signaled the founding of ALIMUPER, Alianza para la Liberación de la Mujer Peruana, and the rebirth of feminism in Peru. But the number of organizations created in the 1970s was small.

In Brazil, still under military rule, the feminist movement began while the new policy of *distensão* (reduction of tensions) inaugurated by Gen. Ernesto Geisel gradually took hold and preparations for the United Nations International Women's Year were under way. Women's groups began to meet to elaborate gender-specific demands. Their celebration of International Women's Day on March 8, 1975, was the first public gathering since 1968. They went on to create the Centro da Mulher Brasileira in Rio de Janeiro and the Centro de Desenvolvimento da Mulher Brasileira in São Paulo. As opposition to the military dictatorship grew, feminists and women involved in neighborhood clubs, church groups, and various political parties flocked to the organizations that began to emerge. They were central participants in the Movement for Amnesty, the Campaign Against the Cost of Living, and other struggles for the redemocratization of Brazil that led to the triumph of the opposition in the 1982 elections.

The first Chilean feminist organization was the Círculo de Estudios de la Mujer, a study group whose members began to meet in 1977 and, until 1983, developed research on women, activities with grassroots women, consciousness raising, and courses on women's history, all under the protection of the Academy of Christian Humanism, an institution of the Catholic Church. Feminists participated in the protests organized in the early 1980s by the *movimiento de mujeres* (women's movement), which had a strong connection with left-wing political parties. They joined in the two main umbrella organizations created in 1983 to lead the opposition movement, MEMCH 83 (Movement for the Emancipation of Chilean Women — Movimiento por la Emancipación de la Mujer Chilena), named for their feminist foremothers, and Mujeres por la Vida. On May 7, 1987, they adopted a document entitled "Women's Demands from Democracy," which included, among other things, ratification of the UN Convention on the Elimination of All Forms of Discrimination Against Women by the new government, the creation of a Ministry for Women, an evaluation of the educational system to eliminate inequalities between the sexes, and the appointment of women to 30 percent of all government jobs.

Under very difficult circumstances, the feminist groups in the Southern Cone created *espacios de reflexión* (study groups). There they could discuss translations of feminist texts sent to them by women who had escaped prison or a worse fate and gone into exile in Europe, where they had discovered feminism. They reread history while asking new questions, devised non-hierarchical forms of interaction based on respect for democratic principles, and elaborated a critique of hierarchy and authoritarianism that was fundamental to their utopian project. Living under regimes whose economic policies produced unemployment and impoverishment; whose armed forces killed, exiled, tortured, and "disappeared" citizens; and whose civil societies were cowed into silence and formal acquiescence, feminists were pressed by the need to participate in oppositional politics. They were thrown into activism, while they sought to reveal and dismantle the discriminatory and anti-democratic principles and practices of the state, the law, the family, and political parties. They organized around gender issues, debating among themselves whether or not to become *feministas autónomas* or *militantes de partido* (autonomous feminist organizations or affiliated with political parties). In any case, they joined the opposition movements against the military regimes and worked with women who belonged to traditional political parties or to grassroots organizations that had ties with parties or the Catholic Church. These interactions, shaped during very difficult times, engaged feminist organizations in acts of fundamental solidarity and opposition politics. They also committed feminist groups to widening the political spaces to bring back democracy and created trust and a process of collaboration that resulted in a solid bond between feminists and the *movimiento de mujeres.*

In the Southern Cone, as in Peru, Brazil, and Mexico, the new feminist movement initially attracted young, educated, middle-class women. They were the first generations to benefit from the 1960s' expansion of secondary and university education. Access to public primary schools and high schools for most Latin American women was a post-World War II phenomenon, and in many nations free public high schools were not available to women until the 1960s. They entered universities in increasingly large numbers to study humanities, nursing, and teaching — the so-called feminine professions. In a decade of intense student agitation, women also became *militantes* and joined newly formed organizations. They broke down old sexual restrictions, and, as Portugal recalls, many heard the siren call of revolution, participating in guerrilla organizations, especially with urban guerrillas. In the late 1970s, disenchantment with left-wing parties and organizations led them to feminism. In the context of an international feminism that insisted on the primacy of gender equity, they began to lose patience with their comrades' refusal to discuss feminist ideas seriously. They gradually came to accept the facts that, as feminists insisted, the right to vote does not necessarily mean access to political power, that the right to be paid a fair wage and not "a woman's wage" was a long way off, that traditions have a way of constituting a much heavier burden on women than on men, and that, while sisterhood is powerful, patriarchy is much older. Some became convinced by the feminists' arguments and walked out of their organizations, but others were unable to do so and became advocates of *doble militancia* (Stromquist 1992; Bourque 1993).

Feminist disenchantment with the radical left was accelerated by the experience of those who had participated in urban guerrilla organizations and had turned their backs on armed struggle because of the sexism of their "comrades." That sexism was expressed in numerous ways — from the belief that women had to bear children "for the revolution" to men's unwillingness to accept women in positions of leadership, notwithstanding rhetorical declarations. Even in countries like Nicaragua, where women served in guerrilla organizations, represented some 30 percent of the Sandinista National Liberation Front (Frente Sandinista de Liberación Nacional —FSLN) combat forces, and rose to positions of military leadership, after the insurrectional stage ended and the construction of a revolutionary society began, women found themselves at odds with their *compañeros*. As a consequence of the mobilization of Nicaraguan women and the emergence of a feminist movement, the Sandinista government was confronted with issues traditionally dismissed by the left as minor bourgeois feminist concerns, such as sexism, abortion rights, and violence against women (Criquillion 1995).

The rejection of left-wing parties by feminists did not imply abandoning a commitment to radical social change. For many, it meant that part of their activities as feminists would be directed to women from the poorest sectors. Therefore, besides creating collectives, magazines, radio programs, health and research centers, and *casas de la mujer* (women's centers), they also founded groups (usually NGOs) whose activities were directed toward women in poor neighborhoods or shantytowns. The funding for these organizations came from international agencies and was used to establish the NGOs that developed special programs for women, provided legal and psychological assistance to them, mounted efforts to denounce violence against them, operated halfway houses for battered women, and organized programs in support of women's rights. Many NGOs were explicitly feminist, and others were institutions with research agendas centered on women, which produced important data that have been used to alter public policies.

## ASSESSING THE ROLE OF THE CATHOLIC CHURCH

A nother significant development during those years was the growing disenchantment of Catholic women with the church, despite the transformation of the church and the disposition of Catholics to support democracy. The changes in the church begun by Pope John XXIII, the writings of liberation theologians, and the Latin American Bishops' pronouncements of Medellín (1968) and Puebla (1979) altered the church's teachings about the poor. All Catholics, both men and women, were rallied to work for social and economic justice. In some countries, the construction of the new "People's Church" compelled members of the hierarchy to speak out against military regimes and support campaigns for social and human rights; in others, to work with *comunidades eclesiales de base* (ecclesial base communities), "small face-to-face gatherings of Christians who read the scriptures and celebrate the liturgy together in the context of reflection and action on behalf of justice for their people" (Ruether 1995, 93-104). These experiences committed important sectors of Latin America's Catholic leadership to democracy, although in countries such as Argentina, the Church hierarchy stood by the military juntas and was cool if not hostile to human rights groups.

According to some observers, the changes that have taken place in the Catholic Church have also affected its views on women. In many countries, the progressive clergy actively encouraged women to participate in the new ecclesial base communities or in the neighborhood organizations created to resist or adjust to the economic policies of the authoritarian governments. In Chile, the church provided shelter and support to feminists and other women's groups during their struggles against the Pinochet regime. They point out that since John XXIII, Papal pronouncements on the proper relations between men and women have unexpectedly democratic and egalitarian elements within them — in his encyclical, *Pacem in Terris,* John XXIII noted women's increased participation in public life and that as they become "ever more conscious of their human dignity, they will not tolerate being treated as mere material instruments, but demand rights befitting a human person both in domestic and public life." These observers are aware that Pope John Paul II's 1987 encyclical, *On the Dignity of Women,* stresses the complementarity of male and female roles and the primacy of women's roles as mothers (a problematic position at best), but they underscore his emphasis on the equal importance of the female role.

All this, it is argued, has the potential to challenge the tradition of unquestioned male dominance within the family, which has been a key element in women's acceptance of a subordinate status. In an interesting convergence, Latin American women's use of "militant motherhood" as the justification for their foray into the public realm is both, as Jaquette notes, culturally astute and politically sensitive, but it also resonates with trends in Latin American Catholicism. Thus, in a rather unexpected fashion, one of the chief cultural impediments to democracy and women's equality, the resistance of the Catholic Church, has been reshaped.

To other observers, this assessment is much too generous. It is true that important sectors of the Latin American church have changed their traditional support for the status quo and openly sided with democratic processes. But the church as a whole insists that women's primary role should be that of wives and mothers and thus ignores the fact that most women cannot stay home — they need to earn a salary to make ends meet. The church's stance exalts the home and family without acknowledging that domestic violence is pervasive. It, therefore, overlooks the dangers posed to women in patriarchal family structures. Furthermore, the church has made very clear that it refuses to change its position on such matters as sexuality, birth control, and the ordination of women. Additionally, encouraging women to participate in the ecclesial base communities or in neighborhood organizations was not really a departure from tradition; women have long been the backbone of the church and central to many of its social activities. Participation in reproduction (Mazzotti et al. 1994). Taken together, their activities signal a central fault line in the new contours of Latin American democracy. While there are significant differences among women on these issues (particularly in the area of reproduction and ordination), the presence of this line of questioning within the Latin American Catholic Church and its link to democratic experiments among the population may come to represent a chasm of significant proportions.

## THE STRUGGLE FOR NEW POLITICAL FORMS: AUTONOMY, THE STATE, AND THE INTERNATIONAL CONTEXT

While second-wave feminism in the Southern Cone developed with a dual commitment to oppositional politics and democracy, the same pattern emerged as the movement expanded throughout Latin America and Central America.[13] Everywhere suspicious of any authority, especially male authority, fearing co-optation, and unwilling to jeopardize their autonomy, feminists initially distanced themselves from the state, and their relations with political parties, when they existed, were strained. Most sought to retain their autonomy as feminist organizations while participating in joint activities with the *movimiento de mujeres* and together attempting to develop a new form of *"hacer política."* The new form of politics was to be broadly based, non-hierarchical, respond to grassroots needs, recognize community leadership, and, at the same time, be capable of using existing structures to advance its objectives. The theory somehow seemed to work better than the practice because it failed to have a major impact on the political culture. Some political parties did take notice of the changes affecting women, and during electoral campaigns male candidates learned to address women as well as men, but the majority did not change their position toward women. In Chile, where women participated centrally in the redemocratization process, Patricio Aylwin admitted during the presidential campaign that Chilean women had been the first to fight against the military regime and to work in defense of human rights — Chilean women also coined the best slogans, since then adopted by feminists throughout the continent: *si la mujer no está, la democracia no va* (without women's participation, democracy cannot go forward) and *queremos democracia en el país y en el hogar, sí* (yes, we want democracy in our country and in our homes). Yet, when Gen. Pinochet finally stepped down, and the country returned to its sui generis democratic rule, no woman was elected to parliament.

In the aftermath of the military dictatorships throughout the hemisphere, there was concern that the politicians of some established parties would attempt to turn back the clock and reclaim their traditional hegemonic share of power and representation. But the return to past practices was no longer possible. In Chile, President Alywin had to agree to implement a Programa de Gobierno Para la Mujer, elaborated by a coalition of feminists and *políticas* (politically active women) prior to his election, and also created the National Women's Service (Servicio Nacional de la Mujer — SERNAM), which they requested. In Argentina, the debate over affirmative action, called *discriminación positiva*, began during the presidency of Raúl Alfonsín. In 1991, under his successor, the Ley de Cuotas (Quota Law) was passed. It compels political parties to compose their lists of candidates with at least the ecclesial base communities can be seen as part of that tradition. Fii liberation theology discourse addressed women from a patriarchal perspectiv in no way dealt with the social roles assigned to women. The democratic im stemming from the new theology, as it was elaborated by male theologians, to a halt on the question of women. It did not include them in its most pro transformations. As Sonia E. Alvarez has pointed out, "liberation theology a Christian-base community have made women more aware of themselves as c but not as *women*. When empowerment as citizens triggers women's conscio of their gender specific oppression," as occurred in two cases she documen church has intervened to discourage this process of change" (Alvarez 199( And when female theologians began to develop a feminist critique of lib theology, they were rebuffed with arguments reminiscent of those advancee left against feminists a few years earlier.

Notwithstanding its commitment to democracy and social justice, tl See has found itself increasingly at odds with policies specifically addresse women's subordination and foster their empowerment, both nationally and tionally. It has opposed these policies since 1975 at all the UN Women' Conferences, the 1992 Earth Summit in Rio de Janeiro, and the 1994 Intei Conference on Population and Development held in Cairo. In the past five y Holy See has been the main force behind the concerted opposition to adopted by UN world conferences with respect to women, policies affe family, sexual preference, and reproductive rights.

While the Holy See does not find a contradiction between its su democracy and social justice and its opposition to reproductive right ordination of women, a growing number of Latin American Catholic won the contradiction (Fabella and Oduyoye 1988). Many have left the chi vinced that it will not change with respect to women, but others have decie and to confront the theologians. According to Rosemary Radford Rue only had male liberation theologians ignored the distinct and additional women are oppressed — sexual violence, lack of right to control reprodt but all too many liberation theologians collaborated with these sexist sti ignoring them and resisting women's efforts to educate them" (Ruether

At present, Catholic women in Latin America read the writings theologians such as North Americans Rosemary Radford Ruether and I and the Brazilian Ivonne Gebara, a nun and member of the Congrega Lady. They have formed groups like the Círculo de Feministas Cristia Cumi in Lima, the Urdimbre de Aquehua in Buenos Aires, and Espacio Cristianas in Mexico. In several countries, they participate in activitie by organizations such as Catholics for a Free Choice (Católicas por e Decidir), an international network of feminist Catholic groups witl Washington, D.C., Mexico City, Montevideo, and São Paulo. They pi like *Del cielo a la tierra. Una antología de teología feminista* and *Sor* and edit magazines like *Con-spirando, Conciencia Latinoame Mandrágora*. In numerous communities, they have been interpreting t from their own experience as women, and, similar to women in the I or Europe, they do not follow church teachings on matters of s

30 percent women. In addition, the women are to be listed in positions alternating with men, so as not to give absolute preference to male candidates.

Furthermore, in the mid-1980s, in response to unexpected opportunities for collaboration with the state, a significant sector of the feminist movement gradually changed its oppositional stance. Forsaking their fears of co-optation, some feminists decided to advance their agenda *desde el estado* (from within the state) and cooperate in the elaboration of public policies for women. This first occurred in São Paulo, Brazil, in the early 1980s, when feminists were able to create a State Council on the Status of Women. The Council's most famous measure was to create women-staffed police stations to combat violence against women. This 1985 initiative was so successful that it was replicated in 140 Brazilian cities and was widely adopted throughout the continent.

Two factors contributed to the changed relationship between Latin American feminists and the state: 1) the impact of international support for democracy and 2) the creation of global feminist networks focused on women's rights, human rights, women's empowerment, and political participation. International support for both efforts came from a series of international women's meetings sponsored by the United Nations that have been held over the past 25 years and stand as benchmarks to measure the expansion of feminism and the growth of women's organizations. The women's meetings have also benefited from other UN-sponsored world meetings that were not centered on women, yet included them in their Plans of Action: for example, the Rio de Janeiro Earth Summit; the Cairo International Population Conference; the World Conference on Human Rights, held in Vienna in June 1993; and the World Summit on Social Development, held in Copenhagen in 1995.

In each case, resolutions and recommendations were adopted that were specifically addressed to women. The Cairo Program for Action, for example, had a specific chapter on women that underscored the need to foster 1) women's autonomy; 2) the implementation of their political rights; and 3) the improvement of their economic, social, and health conditions. The chapter also clearly established women's right to make decisions on questions of reproduction and sexuality. Through the international conversations of the past 25 years, something akin to a common agenda has emerged. That agenda seeks, among other things, to empower women, eradicate violence against them in the public and domestic spheres, eliminate sexual harassment, eliminate the trafficking of women, and eliminate gender discrimination in the law as well as in traditions, cultural prejudices, and religious extremism. These conferences and the four UN World Conferences on Women in Mexico City (1975), Copenhagen (1980), Nairobi (1985), and Beijing (1995) have produced an international consensus concerning gender inequity and the measures needed to eradicate it. The Platform for Action adopted in Beijing addresses 12 areas of concern that are obstacles to women's advancement: poverty (60 percent of the poor in the world are women), lack of political representation, illiteracy, and domestic violence, among others.

Each of the world meetings hosted a parallel forum of non-governmental organizations. The participation of women in the NGO forums tracks the expansion of the women's movement internationally. The Mexico meeting involved some

6,000 participants; 10,000 attended the forum in Copenhagen; 15,000 went to Nairobi; and the numbers jumped to 30,000 in Beijing/Huairou, making it the largest UN world conference and the largest women's conference.[14] The first two forums were held when feminism was primarily centered in the United States and a few European countries. They took place while the Cold War was raging, at a time when discussions of women's issues were frequently drowned out by heated disputes over imperialism, colonialism, communist aggression, U.S. interventions in Latin America, the Palestinian question, apartheid, and the appropriateness of feminism for developing or newly independent nations. Nairobi (1985) was the real turning point for women's global organizing and the creation of networks like DAWN and the International Women's Health Coalition. By 1985, international tensions had begun to ease off, and in Latin America the military were negotiating their retreat to the barracks. Serious global networking began during the Nairobi NGO Forum, and participants returned to their countries, committed to "Think Globally and Act Locally," ready to create global, national, and local organizations.

The new global networks produce basic statistical information on women, position papers, and strategies for addressing the obstacles they face. In the past decade, network representatives have also attended international meetings and developed effective lobbying techniques to advocate for specific policies. Their actions have been crucial for the introduction of a strong feminist content in the UN agenda.

Latin American women have been prominent at the UN meetings. While 300 participated in the Beijing Conference, some 2,000 attended the Huairou Forum. In addition, for more than a decade, Latin American feminists have been celebrating regional *encuentros* approximately every two years.

While organized for and by feminists, the *encuentros* are open to all women and are generally attended by large numbers of activists from the *movimiento de mujeres*. They are usually chaotic affairs where participants discuss common concerns, clarify ideological differences, outline common strategies, and create networks (Sternbach et al. 1992). The political debates that have taken place in the *encuentros* have shaped Latin American feminism because the topics discussed in the international meetings are taken up in Encuentros Nacionales. These national meetings multiplied after the Nairobi Conference.

Since its founding, the United Nations has granted NGOs a relevant role in its structure and in its world conferences. The United Nations has also exerted increasing pressure upon member governments to incorporate NGOs into their decisions, especially in matters pertaining to the UN agenda, and official delegations to world conferences are expected to include NGO representatives. Latin American governments have reacted very differently to the idea of cooperating with NGOs, especially when the latter advocate controversial positions on questions of sexuality or reproductive rights. Not all Latin American official delegations to the UN World Conferences in the past five years had feminist or women's NGO representatives among their members. At the Beijing Conference, the most open to NGOs were perhaps the Mexican and the Brazilian delegations, while the Argentine, Peruvian, and Guatemalan were the most exclusionary. However, in all countries, the importance of NGOs has grown enormously.

It would be hard to overstate the importance of UN world conferences. They have provided women throughout the world with access to resources, both intellectual and material, that did not exist previously or were not available to them. Since 1975, as governments prepared to send delegations to international meetings, they have had to gather information on their female population and report on women's advancement, as mandated by the United Nations. This has given an unexpected legitimacy to feminists' demands and helped to focus the attention of national leaders on inequities, income disparities, and lack of political rights. The mandate also has brought to light long submerged issues such as domestic violence and sexual trafficking.

Furthermore, the documents resulting from the world conferences have altered public policies toward women, pushing some governments to offer feminist NGOs the opportunity to cooperate with the state. In many instances, feminists used UN position papers and action programs to exert pressure on political parties and governments, and (after bypassing the opposition of the church) compelled them to adopt measures they would normally refuse to enact. A good example of this process is the consensus that has developed on reproductive rights and reproductive health agreed upon by the international community in successive meetings, culminating in the Cairo conference.

Another example of the United Nations' leadership on women's rights is the Convention on the Elimination of All Forms of Discrimination Against Women, adopted by the General Assembly in 1979. This document established, in binding form, internationally accepted principles on the rights of women and prescribed measures to ensure that women could enjoy their rights. In the Southern Cone, as democratization proceeded, one of the feminists' demands was the ratification of this Convention. It has been ratified by almost all Latin American nations. Among the measures prescribed by the document is the creation of a national mechanism to ensure the advancement of women. With the exception of Colombia and Mexico, all other Latin American countries have created such an institution. The offices for women mandated by the convention vary greatly among countries in rank, resources, power, location in the government bureaucracy, origin, and legitimacy. In Argentina, the Consejo Nacional de la Mujer (CONAMU), established in 1992, is attached to the presidency, as are its counterparts in the Dominican Republic, El Salvador, Honduras, Paraguay, and Venezuela; in Chile, the Servicio Nacional de la Mujer (SERNAM), founded in 1991, is located in the Ministry of Planning and Cooperation; in Brazil, the Conselho Nacional dos Direitos da Mulher is in the Ministry of Justice as is the Peruvian Consejo Permanente de los Derechos de la Mujer y el Niño [sic].

The new generations of women who participate in international conferences and staff government agencies, global networks, and NGOs are examples of the continuing changes in women's education and employment taking place in Latin America and the Caribbean. Women's access to education has continued the trend begun in the 1960s and has increased markedly in the last two decades. The change is most notable at the university level, where women's enrollment has gone from less than 10 percent of the student body to over 30 percent (as in Mexico and Peru), and in a few exceptional cases such as Argentina and the Dominican Republic, women now represent 50 percent of university students. Academic field selection is still highly sex stereotyped, as women tend to follow service-related professions in education or health. In the field of education, women predominate on the bottom rungs of the hierarchy; teaching at the preschool and primary levels is almost exclusively a female profession. Women are a majority at the secondary level, but make up less than one third of university instructors. However, there is some growth in nontraditional fields, such as mathematics, law management, and computer science.

As indicated earlier, many female university graduates have found employment in the expanding number of non-governmental agencies that direct their activities toward women. Thus, the impact of widening access to higher education has had a secondary impact on the quality of nonformal education and literacy programs available to women previously excluded from the educational system. Perhaps most important, research on gender and women's studies programs have become part of Latin American universities, despite initial resistance to curriculum changes. These study centers have documented women's contributions to economic productivity and petitioned government agencies to reflect these contributions in public policies. The universities can be expected to continue producing new knowledge about women and to pose challenges to the traditional curriculum of Latin American universities, much as they have done in the United States and Europe.

Women's educational achievements have led to demands for more equitable compensation and access to a fuller range of labor force opportunities. Combined with the demands of the economic crisis in Latin America, cultural barriers to women's paid employment have been altered by the necessity of their contribution to the family income. Women have joined the labor force in trade and services in such high numbers that, according to a study published in Chile, "Undoubtedly, this is one of the most spectacular and significant changes experienced by Latin America in recent decades" (Valdés and Gomariz 1995, 63). In 19 Latin American countries, the percentage of women in the economically active population rose from 19.1 percent in 1960 to 28.1 percent in 1990. In the same period, the number of economically active women increased 211 percent, that is, more than three times in the same decades (from 18 to 57 million), although the number of economically active men only grew 84 percent (from 80 to 147 million). Some of the growth in women's employment comes from the expansion of offshore and maquiladora enterprises. In addition, the informal sector absorbs a large number of women. Nevertheless, a substantial proportion are paid housekeepers, teachers, retail clerks, and secretaries. Similarly, the number of women employed in technical, professional, and trade areas has also increased substantially (Valdés and Gomariz 1995, 63-64). If paid employment is linked to more personal and domestic power and control, the patterns of increased education and workforce participation are welcome trends. However, the link to political institutions and power is still critically missing. This is particularly problematic when we recall that women's employment and education exist within a social system that still assigns women the majority of the domestic and child-rearing responsibilities.

## CONCLUDING REMARKS: THE RESEARCH AGENDA

In the past 20 years, Latin American feminists have worked energetically to bring about democracy where it was suppressed; throughout the continent they have sought to transform, deepen, and make it more inclusive. They have reformed legal codes; created equal opportunity plans, especially in employment and education; devised new institutional mechanisms to implement public policy initiatives; and, with differing degrees of success, they have participated in the framing of new constitutions in Brazil, Colombia, Argentina, and Peru. They have also legitimized a new discourse that encompasses women from diverse social classes and varied ethnicities and sexualities. Feminists are to be found in large and well-funded NGOs; small lesbian collectives; organizations of black women, indigenous women, and ecofeminists; *casas de la mujer;* human rights associations; and groups that publish magazines or produce videos. Some avoid joining any kind of organization because they are *feministas independientes* (independent feminists). Feminists are young and middle-aged; teach or study in universities; work in soup kitchens, grassroots organizations, government offices, and neighborhood centers; and practice law in battered women's shelters. They have changed the representation of women in advertisements and the depiction of heroines in soap operas. In some countries, feminists have challenged women's lack of power in labor unions, even those that have an overwhelmingly female membership. In the long run, they may have an impact on the contours of Latin American political culture.

From a formal point of view, much of the success achieved by Latin American women activists and feminists has taken place since they began creating NGOs and abandoned their reluctance to work with the state. In general, their participation in the elaboration of public policies has not been the result of changes in the platforms of political parties, nor has it stemmed from internal debates within those parties. The changes were brought about by government decisions largely predicated on national and international needs. Feminists were approached because they had developed an expertise on gender matters.

The emergence of international networks and NGOs has had a significant impact on Latin American feminism. To a large extent, the new NGOs institutionalized the feminist movement, or at least much of it, although there are still feminists who maintain their distance from the state. In their structures and operating principles, NGOs resemble nonfeminist organizations much more than traditional feminist groups or collectives. While feminist groups are usually shoestring operations with few resources, often donated by their members, NGOs are often relatively wealthy organizations, generally funded by international funding agencies or U.S. and European foundations.

Ironically, in the age of downsizing, privatization, and curtailing the social functions of the state, feminist NGOs have multiplied in most Latin American countries. Today, they are ready to educate legislators on questions of gender, offer them the wording of new laws that put an end to discrimination, mount efforts to denounce violence against women, operate halfway houses for battered women, and undertake campaigns to decriminalize abortion and implement government programs.

Bypassing formal national political structures because of the availability of international funding may solve immediate problems for governments, but it does not represent a long-term solution or structural change in the practice of Latin American democracy. Thus, political representation, a problem in the past, continues unresolved into the present. While some political parties tolerate the new breed of women activists, even when they are feminists, most have not changed their platforms and continue to be overwhelmingly male institutions. As a member of the Nicaraguan National Feminist Committee explained in 1994, "We believe that the political parties of this country have a very fractured and rhetorical concept of democracy. In this country democracy is seen from the perspective of men, and in some cases, from the perspective of machos" (*mujer/fempress* 1994).

The gatekeeper role of the political parties has not been challenged. The occasional presence of women in parliament, as heads of ministries, or as mayors of small towns or even large cities does not dispel the fact that parties constitute a barrier to women's participation.[15] Until recently, there has been relatively little incentive for political parties to reassess their stance toward women because, with few exceptions, feminists have either given up on the parties or have sought their aims in arenas other than competitive electoral contests. Of course, some ties and collaborations remain, especially with the left. However, buried in a deep crisis since the collapse of the Soviet Union and unable to develop a viable leftist alternative in the hemisphere, the left has not taken notice of the changes affecting women. A singular exception is the Zapatista National Liberation Army (Ejército Zapatista de Liberación Nacional — EZLN) in Mexico. The emergence of a new left coalition that includes a feminist or even a strong woman's component is not yet on the horizon in the rest of the continent.

Furthermore, traditional longstanding political parties throughout the hemisphere have been challenged as never before by the electoral success of individuals not affiliated with traditional parties. The weakness of parties has been noted frequently by students of Latin America politics. But in the 1980s and 1990s, even the exceptions to the dominant pattern of party weakness, such as the Popular American Revolutionary Alliance (Alianza Popular Revolucionaria Americana — APRA) in Peru and the PRI in Mexico, have been surprised and shaken by new claims upon the allegiance of voters. To date, that experience has not led the parties to think about new overtures to women. Nor have feminists been effective in translating their new willingness to work with the state into a similar ability to reorient the willingness of political parties to respond to women's needs. That this has not occurred is no doubt a reflection of the fact that neither feminists nor political parties have identified an incentive for the political parties to do so.

In Mexico, Brazil, Bolivia, and several others countries, feminists have been willing to establish a dialogue with political parties. For example, in the 1994 and 1996 presidential elections in the Dominican Republic, the Research Center for Women's Action (Centro de Investigación para la Acción Femenina — CIPAF), one of the oldest NGOs in the nation, coordinated the preparation of an Equal Opportunity Plan for Women, which was presented to all the candidates.

In El Salvador, as war gave way to peace and elections, women joined in Mujeres 94, composed of some 40 different women's organizations, and elaborated a platform for feminist demands. Throughout the continent, however, women's congressional representation continues to be low. In those countries that have a bicameral system, women tend to be concentrated in the Chamber of Deputies. Brazil did not have a woman senator until 1980. The exception in this pattern of slow growth is Argentina, where despite resistance to the Ley de Cuotas, there were 28 women deputies and three women senators as of 1997. The executive branch (with very few exceptions) continues to be a male bailiwick .

Notwithstanding the changes brought about by women in the last decades, from a more macro level we would concur with the assessment of Georgina Waylen, who writes, "Relatively few women are active in institutional politics, partly because democratization has not been accompanied by moves toward wider social and economic equality that would enable women to participate in greater numbers" (Waylen 1994, 353).

If things have been hard in the past, there is little reason to believe that they are going to be easier in the future. As we emphasized at the outset, democracy in Latin America is fragile. Further, as Waylen notes, the economic climate has not been auspicious for women seeking to expand their foothold in the economy or for democracy. Neoliberal policies may not ease the way for democracy, especially if those policies lead to impoverishment and frustration among those seeking empowerment. While there is some evidence of efforts by working women to address the "feminization of labor," the growth of the informal sector, and the erosion of social security through international labor organizations, nevertheless, the resistance of labor unions to women's leadership and full participation remains.

In assessing the positive impact of the Catholic Church's new alignment with democratic impulses, we must note that with regard to the control of sexuality, the church's position has not changed. If anything, it has become more entrenched, and some governments have taken similarly rigid positions. To the extent that democratization of the family depends upon new levels of personal responsibility and freedom in the area of sexuality, there has not been notable success in many nations, and the Catholic Church continues to be a major factor in resistance to change. Of course, not all governments have similarly rigid positions, and there are notable instances of successful resistance to church dictates, as in the case of President Alberto Fujimori of Peru, who successfully confronted the church on reproductive rights. The stance of each nation will vary, depending upon the history of its church-state relations, the strength of the women's movement, and the saliency of the population issue for the government. Finally, we would note that many of the newly popular fundamentalist groups proselytizing in Latin America have similarly conservative positions on women and on sexuality.

Most of the topics we have addressed deserve further examination. For instance, to what extent will family life become more democratic and egalitarian? To what degree will labor leaders promote the democratization of the labor movement and include women in their ranks? To what extent will political elites respond positively to women's increased political participation? In a larger sense, we need to ask the question, to what degree has the political culture of Latin America been altered in a fashion that would invite greater political leadership for women? Certainly the experience of the growth of women's organizations and the use of those organizations by the state to address gender-specific concerns would suggest important changes. The degree to which there will be long-term cultural shifts as a result of this activity is a research project well worth further attention. We also need to keep a close eye on political parties and the possibility for women's expanded participation within formal political structures. A full-scale study of Latin American female legislators, their attitudes, commitments, and self conceptions is long overdue. All of these are fruitful arenas for further research, much of which we hope will be conducted by women and men in Latin American universities and research institutes who will understand the significance of these questions for the future of democracy in their societies.

# Notes

1. John Stuart Mill and Mary Wollstonecraft stand as splendid exceptions. See Susan Moller Okin, 1979, *Women in Western Political Thought* (London: Virago); Carol Pateman, 1988, *The Sexual Contract* (Stanford, Calif.: Stanford University Press); Carol Pateman, 1989, *The Disorder of Women* (Stanford, Calif.: Stanford University Press); and Anne Phillips, 1991, *Engendering Democracy* (Pennsylvania Park, Pa.: The Pennsylvania State University Press).

2. Ecuador, 1929; Brazil, 1932; Uruguay, 1932; and Cuba, 1934.

3. Dominican Republic, 1942; Guatemala, 1945; Panama, 1946; Argentina, 1947; Venezuela, 1947; Chile, 1949; and Costa Rica, 1949.

4. El Salvador, 1950; Bolivia, 1952; Mexico, 1953; Colombia, 1954; Honduras, 1955; Nicaragua, 1955; Peru, 1955; Haiti, 1959; and Paraguay in 1961.

5. While conservatives generally did not advocate women's suffrage, a recent paper by Erika Maza Valenzuela demonstrates that in nineteenth century Chile, Catholic and Conservative leaders were among the first to advocate granting women the right to vote. See Erika Maza Valenzuela, 1994, *Catholicism, Anticlericalism and the Quest for Women's Suffrage in Chile,* The Helen Kellogg Institute for International Studies, University of Notre Dame, Working Paper No. 214, December.

6. The first woman elected in the region, in 1932, was the Brazilian deputy, Carlota Queiroz. She was followed by Bertha Lutz, also a deputy, in 1936. Lutz, a leader of the Brazilian suffrage movement, was also one of three women signatories of the 1945 UN charter.

7. Eva Perón is the most prominent Latin American example of the complexity of the "first lady" role and the particular problems posed for women in politics by the fears conjured up by the powerful non-elected first lady. While Evita has become the subject of TV movies, films, plays, novels, essays, various kinds of biographies, and even a Broadway musical, she is generally ignored as a political figure in the scholarly literature written on Peronism. This failure to subject Eva Perón's life to serious political analysis is an important lacuna in the literature, and it needs to be addressed in future research.

8. See Valdés and Gomariz (1995). For Peru, see the discussion of constitutional change in Susan C. Bourque, 1985, "Experiments with Equality: Complexities in Peruvian Public Policy," *Journal of Asian and African Studies* 20:3 (July-October).

9. See, however, Sonia E. Alvarez, 1994, "The (Trans)formation of Feminism(s) and Gender Politics in Democratizing Brazil," in *The Women's Movement in Latin America: Feminism and the Transition to Democracy,* 2nd edition, ed. Jane Jaquette (Boulder, Colo.: Westview Press), 13-63; Georgina Waylen, 1994, "Women and Democratization: Conceptualizing Gender Relations in Transition Politics," in *World Politics* 46:3 (April): 327-354; and Susan C. Bourque, 1989, "Gender and the State: New Perspectives from Latin America," in *Women, Development, and the State,* eds. Sue Ellen Charlton, Jana Everett, and Kathleen Staudt (Albany, N.Y.: State University of New York Press).

10. In Mexico, the name for the movement is *Movimiento Amplio de Mujeres*. See Marta Lamas, 1994, "Algunas características del movimiento feminista en Ciudad de México," in *Mujeres y participación política: avances y desafíos en América Latina*, ed. Magdalena León (Bogotá: TM Editores).

11. "Inhabitants of a continent marked by the weight of underdevelopment and dependency, the first cry to battle was the anti-imperialist struggle, and when the olive green uniform of the bearded men of Sierra Maestra became the symbol of the national liberation battles, we women could not avoid the siren calls and we went together to join a cause that for being 'everyone's' cause, we believed also our own. . . . In 1970, feminism seemed a product made in the USA and its echoes, arriving via the international press agencies, sounded foreign and equivocal to us. That the women of the most powerful country of the world would remove their brassieres to protest against male dominance seemed to us a joke typical of bored gringas." See Ana María Portugal, 1986, "Qué es ser feminista en América Latina?" in *Movimiento feminista balance y perspectivas*, ediciones de las mujeres, No. 5 (Santiago: Isis Internacional).

12. Mary Judith Ress, Ute Seibert-Cuadra, and Lene Sjorup, eds., 1994, *Del cielo a la tierra: una antología de teología feminista* (Santiago: Sello Azul, Editorial de Mujeres); and 1996, *Somos Iglesia* (Mexico City: Católicas Por el Derecho a Decidir). The first magazine appears in Santiago de Chile, the second is published in Montevideo, and the third is produced by NETMAL (Núcleo de Estudios Teológicos de la Mulher en América Latina) in São Paulo.

13. For Peru, see the essay by Maruja Barrig, 1994, "The Difficult Equilibrium Between Bread and Roses: Women's Organizations and Democracy in Peru," in *The Women's Movement in Latin America: Participation and Democracy,* ed. Jane S. Jaquette (Boulder, Colo.: Westview Press), 151-175; the essay by Susan C. Bourque, 1985, "Urban Activists: Path to Political Consciousness in Peru," in *Women Living Change*, eds. Susan C. Bourque and Donna Robinson Divine (Philadelphia: Temple University Press), 25-56; and one by Cecilia Blondet, 1995, "Out of the Kitchens and onto the Streets: Women's Activism in Peru," in *The Challenge of Local Feminisms: Women's Movements in Global Perspective*, ed. Amrila Basu (Boulder, Colo.: Westview Press), 251-275. For Mexico, see the essay by Carmen Ramos Escandón, 1994, "Women's Movements, Feminism, and Mexican Politics," in *The Women's Movement in Latin America*, ed. Jane S. Jaquette (Boulder, Colo.: Westview Press), 199-221; and Marta Lamas et al. 1995, "Building Bridges: The Growth of Popular Feminism in Mexico," in *The Challenge of Local Feminisms*, ed. Amrita Basu (Boulder, Colo.: Westview Press), 324-347.

14. The Fourth United Nations World Conference on Women took place in two sites: the NGO Forum met in Huairou, a resort some 50 kilometers north of Beijing, and the official conference took place in the center of Beijing. The latter encompassed more than 4,000 NGOs and played a crucial role in the Cairo Population Conference. The sites for these meetings were Bogota, Colombia (1981); Lima, Peru (1983); Berlioga, Brazil (1985); Taxco, Mexico (1987); San Bernardo, Argentina (1990); and Costa del Sol, El Salvador (1993). The last meeting, in a country that was barely emerging from a bloody civil war and was part of a geographic area with a very different recent history from the rest of Latin America, signaled the presence of a growing number of Central American women anxious to discuss feminist issues, including the process in Nicaragua.

15. For an interesting exception, see the plan of Izquierda Unida, "Reconocimiento de la Igualdad y Dignidad de la Mujer," issued for the 1985 elections in Peru. That year, Izquierda Unida also invited two well-known feminists to join its list of candidates for deputies. Both were defeated.

# References

Alvarez, Sonia. 1990. "Women's Participation in the Brazilian People's Church: A Critical Appraisal." *Feminist Studies* 16:2 (Summer).

Alvarez, Sonia. 1994. "The (Trans)formation of Feminism(s) and Gender Politics in Democratizing Brazil." In *The Women's Movement in Latin America*, 2nd edition, ed. Jane Jaquette. Boulder, Colo.: Westview Press.

Barrig, Maruja, and Andy Wehkamp, eds. 1994. *Engendering Development: Experiences in Development Planning*. Lima: NOVIB.

Barrig, Maruja, and Andy Wehkamp. 1994. "The Difficult Equilibrium Between Bread and Roses: Women's Organizations and Democracy in Peru." In *The Women's Movement in Latin America: Participation and Democracy*, ed. Jane S. Jaquette. Boulder, Colo.: Westview Press.

Basu, Amrita, ed. 1995. *The Challenge of Local Feminisms: Women's Movements in Global Perspective*. Boulder, Colo.: Westview Press.

Blondet, Cecilia. 1995. "Out of the Kitchens and onto the Streets: Women's Activism in Peru." In *The Challenge of Local Feminisms: Women's Movements in Global Perspectives*, ed. Amrita Basu. Boulder, Colo.: Westview Press.

Bourque, Susan. 1985. "Experiments with Equality: Complexities in Peruvian Public Policy." In *Journal of Asian and African Studies* 20:3-4 (July-October).

Bourque, Susan. 1985. "Urban Activists: Paths of Political Consciousness in Peru." In *Women Living Change*, eds. Susan C. Bourque and Donna Robinson Divine. Philadelphia: Temple University Press.

Bourque, Susan. 1989. "Gender and the State: Perspectives from Latin America." In *Women, Development and the State*, eds. Sue Ellen Charlton et al. Albany, N.Y.: State University of New York Press.

Bourque, Susan C. 1993. "Citizenship and Education in Peru and Mexico." In *The Politics of Women's Education*, eds. Susan C. Bourque and Jill Ker Conway. Ann Arbor, Mich.: University of Michigan Press.

Criquillion, Ana. "The Nicaraguan Women's Movement: Feminist Reflections from Within." In *The New Politics of Survival: Grassroots Movements in Central America*, ed. Minor Sinclair. New York: Monthly Review Press.

Escandón, Carmen Ramos. 1994. "Women's Movements, Feminism, and Mexican Politics." In *The Women's Movement in Latin America*, ed. Jane S. Jaquette. Boulder, Colo.: Westview Press.

Estrada, Jenny. 1981. *Una mujer total: Matilde Hidalgo de Prócel*. Guayaquil: Imprenta de la Universidad de Guayaquil.

Fabella, Virginia, and Mercy Oduyoye. *With Passion and Compassion: Third World Women Doing Theology*. Maryknoll, N.Y.: Orbis Press.

Gaviola, A. Edda, Ximena M. Jiles, Lorella Lopresti, and Clauda Rojas M. 1978. "Queremos votar en las próximas elecciones." In *Historia del movimiento femenino Chileno 1913- 1952*, eds. Paz Covarrubias and Rolando Franco. Santiago: Mujer y Sociedad.

Gonzales Moutes, Soledad, ed. 1993. *Mujeres en relaciones de género en la antropología latinoamericana*. Mexico City: El Colegio de México.

Henríquez, Narda, ed. 1996. *Encrucijadas del saber: los estudios de género en las ciencias sociales*. Lima: Pontificia Universidad Católica del Peru.

Jaquette, Jane, ed. 1994, *The Women's Movement in Latin America: Participation and Democracy*, 2nd edition. Boulder, Colo.: Westview Press.

Lamas, Marta. 1994. "Algunas características del movimiento feminista en Ciudad de México." In *Mujeres y participación política: avances y desafíos en América Latina*, ed. Magdalena León. Bogota: TM Editores.

Lamas, Marta, Alicia Martínez, María Luisa Tarrés, and Esperanza Tuñón. 1995. "Building Bridges: The Growth of Popular Feminism in Mexico." In *The Challenge of Local Feminisms*, ed. Amrita Basu. Boulder, Colo.: Westview Press.

Luna, Lola G., and Norma Villareal. 1994. *Historia, género y política. Movimientos de mujeres y participación política en Colombia, 1930-1991*. Barcelona, Spain: Seminario Interdisciplinario Mujeres y Sociedad.

Mazzotti, Mariella, Graciel Pujol, and Carmen Terra. 1994. *Una realidad silenciada. Sexualidad y maternidad en mujeres católicas*. Montevideo: Trilce.

Miller, Francesca. 1990. "Latin American Feminism and the Transnational Arena." In *Women, Culture and Politics in Latin America*, ed. Francesca Miller. Berkeley and Los Angeles, Calif.: University of California Press.

*mujer/fempress*. 1994. No.151 (May): 22.

Navarro, Marysa. 1997. *Evita*. Buenos Aires: Planeta.

Okin, Susan M. 1979. *Women in Western Political Thought*. London: Virago.

Pateman, Carol. 1988. *The Sexual Contract*. Stanford, Calif.: Stanford University Press.

Pateman, Carol. 1989. *The Disorder of Women*. Stanford, Calif.: Stanford University Press.

Phillips, Anne. 1991. *Engendering Democracy*. University Park, Pa.: The Pennsylvania State University Press.

Portugal, Ana María. 1986 "Qué es ser feminista en América Latina?" In *Movimiento feminista balance y perspectivas*. Ediciones de las mujeres, No. 5. Santiago: Isis Internacional.

Ress, Mary Judith, Ute Seibert-Cuadra, and Lene Sjorup. 1994. *Del cielo a la tierra: una antología de teología feminista*. Santiago: Sello Azul, Editorial de Mujeres.

Ruether, Rosemary Radford. 1995. "The Crisis of Liberation Theology: Does God Opt for the Poor?" In *God and the Nations*, eds. Douglas John Hall and Rosemary Radford Ruether. Minneapolis: Fortress Press.

Sternbach, Nancy Saporta, Marysa Navarro Aranguren, Patricia Chuchryk, and Sonia E. Alvarez. 1992. "Feminisms in Latin America: From Bogotá to San Bernardo." In *SIGNS: Journal of Women in Culture and Society* 17 (21).

Stromquist, Nellie. 1992. "Feminist Reflections on the Politics of the Peruvian University." In *Women's Education in Latin America*. Boulder, Colo.: Lynne Rienner Publishers.

Valdés, Teresa, and Enrique Gomariz, coordinators. 1995. *Latin American Women: Compared Figures*. Santiago: Instituto de la Mujer and FLACSO.

Valenzuela, Erika Maza. 1994. *Catholicism, Anticlericalism, and the Quest for Women's Suffrage in Chile*. The Helen Kellogg Institute for International Studies, University of Notre Dame, Working Paper no. 214, December.

Waylen, Georgia. 1994. "Women and Democratization: Conceptualizing Gender Relations in Transition Politics. In *World Politics* 4:3 (April).

CHAPTER EIGHT

# Ethnicity and Democratic Governability in Latin America: Reflections from Two Central Andean Countries

## CARLOS IVÁN DEGREGORI

It has become common to note the crisis of national states, besieged from above by the exigencies of globalization and from below by regional, ethnic, linguistic, or religious claims that express growing, often exclusionary, local identities at the expense of citizen or national identities. Ethnic movements frequently have been seen as the spearhead of this assault from below. Using the Bolivian and Peruvian cases as examples, this essay explores the nature and dimensions of this siege, discusses the conditions under which ethnic movements arise, and analyzes the extent to which such movements, when they do arise, obstruct governability or, rather, favor the consolidation of citizenship and the deepening of democracy in the Andean region.

In recent years, ethnic movements in Latin America generally have been studied from the perspective of new social movements. Most scholars who have tackled the political dimension of ethnicity have been more interested in such topics as the construction/deconstruction of national states in multiethnic countries, the dialectic between domination and resistance, or the human rights of indigenous peoples than in themes such as democracy and governability.[1] Recent works have begun to reverse this trend (Van Cott 1994; Yashar 1996). Nevertheless, extended reflection on the consolidation of democracy in multi-ethnic countries remains pending.

This essay seeks to contribute to such efforts, while attesting to the centuries of subordination and resistance of the indigenous populations in Bolivia and Peru and to the inequity that banishes the majority of Indians to statistical reservations in the poorest deciles of income pyramids. Nevertheless, it attempts to go further by shunning the construction of homogenous ethnic subjects — usually construed as radically distinct and counterpoised against the West — whose only attitude tends to be resistance to a state that, in some studies, does not appear to have changed since the Conquest. Such an approach is necessary because when confrontation alone is emphasized, many other interactions between indigenous and nonindigenous populations are lost from view. Although asymmetric, these interactions have created common spaces that are also contested terrain in relation to hegemony and the negotiation of power. Furthermore, a unilateral emphasis on difference carries with it the danger of viewing indigenous populations solely as victims or as peoples fundamentally closed in upon themselves, whose energy is concentrated upon reproducing nearly immutable ways of life. In other words, scholars run the risk of not noticing that it may be the hegemonic elites who are more engaged in reproducing differences and that the subordinate groups, in this case indigenous, may be interested instead in breaking the barriers of exclusion, not to acculturate themselves nor to construct an inverted mirror image of the hegemonic culture. Alternatively, indigenous groups may seek to penetrate the political and symbolic spaces of the elites, universalizing their own particularities within national states, striving implicitly or explicitly for citizenship and, by attaining it, manage to broaden the realm and even redefine the very concept of citizenship.[2]

A look at Peru and Bolivia confirms that movements that define themselves in ethnic terms do not arise automatically. When such movements do develop, they do not always arise in the same manner, present the same characteristics, or evolve in the same way. Thus, while ethnic movements exist in Bolivia, they do not in Peru. Nevertheless, the Peruvian case allows one to see how ethnicity influences politics even in the absence of ethnic movements. Such a comparison also makes it possible to observe more sharply other forms of action among indigenous populations, including the appropriation of the elite's instruments of power (such as the dominant language) or the invasion of economic spaces that correspond economically, politically, and symbolically to the criollo or mestizo elites within the "spatialization of power" (Alonso 1994, 393).

This work concentrates on the Quechua and Aymara peoples of the Andes[3] and seeks to answer the following questions: Why do important ethnic movements arise in some countries and not in others? From what perspective do these movements — and the emergence of the Andean populations onto the political stage more generally — question the national state, if indeed they do? In what way do these movements affect governability and democratic consolidation? Answering these questions requires a historical approach that takes into account the long and complex interrelations between each state and its indigenous populations. Within this approach, it is important to highlight the role of new intellectual sectors in imagining communities (Anderson 1983), [re]inventing traditions (Hobsbawm and Ranger 1982), and formulating new projects.

# PERU

At the moment of the European invasion, the Incas ruled over a multi-ethnic and multilingual empire called Tawantinsuyu in Quechua. Beginning in 1532, the Spanish imposed two processes of social organization. The first was the construction of "Indian" as a generic term to homogenize the former subjects of Tawantinsuyu.[4] The second was the construction of a deep dividing line separating the inhabitants of the new viceroyalty into the Republic of Spaniards and the Republic of Indians, by which the colonizers sought to bar fluidity between these two worlds.

However, the Spaniards' success was not total. In the interstices between the two republics grew a mass of *forasteros* (outsiders) and mestizos. The "republic of

Indians" did not come to be a homogenous whole on either the socioeconomic level or in terms of politics and culture. Even though the imperial elite was disarticulated between 1532 and 1570, local and regional elites, the *curacas,* survived. The *curacas* retained their privileges and served as the nexus between the two republics. Often the *curacas* were biologically mestizo and, having been educated in "schools for *curacas,"* may have at times felt themselves to be culturally closer to the Spaniards. Yet, throughout the eighteenth century, a number of factors contributed to the rise of what John Rowe (1955) has termed the "Inca national movement." A sector of *curacas,* reinventing traditions and recovering symbols, proceeded to the reconstruction of an idealized image of the Tawantinsuyu (Flores Galindo 1987). Before the era of the great national revolutions, the *curacas* managed to "imagine a community" and a certain new common identity, where prior to the conquest there had been a plurality of kingdoms and domains. The movement culminated in 1780 with the great rebellions of Túpac Amaru among the Quechua and Túpac Katari among the Aymara. Their defeat proved fatal for the intermediary elite. "Through fault of the rebel," as the royal edict stated, the use of Quechua was prohibited, and from then on the privileges of the *curacas* were nullified.

In 1821, as part of a process that spanned the whole continent, the criollos declared independence. José de San Martín then stated, "In the future the aborigines shall not be called Indians or natives; they are children *and citizens* of Peru and they shall be known as Peruvians" (quoted in Anderson 1983, 49-50). As Henri Favre (1996, 26) asserts, for the liberal elites in charge of the new countries of the region, "the Indian becomes a citizen and ceases to exist" after independence.

Nevertheless, despite the liberal statutes promulgated by Simón Bolívar around 1825, the old colonial barriers were intermittently raised once again, this time to exclude the indigenous population from citizenship. First, there was the indigenous tribute, which was in effect until 1854. Later, toward the end of the nineteenth century and the beginning of the twentieth century, there was the expansion of large landholding in the Andes and the consolidation of what was called *gamonalismo* in Peru. The term alludes to the configuration of local powers, which included, at the top of the social pyramid, large landowners and judges, lawyers, police, merchants, priests, and teachers, among others. Located in the urban centers, these local powers were composed of mestizos, or *mistis,* to use the Quechuized version of the term, who almost always were bilingual. The distinguishing feature of this *gamonalismo misti* as a system of domination was its high degree of privatization of power, akin to what Andrés Guerrero (1993), referring to the Ecuadorean case, termed "ethnic administration."

At its peak, *gamonalismo* marked the culmination of the long process of destroying the *curaca* elites, who had practically ceased to exist by the beginning of the twentieth century. The place they left as intermediaries between the two colonial republics now was occupied by the *mistis,* who stood as intermediaries between the Andean rural hinterland and the coastal urban centers, especially Lima. The difference is important because whereas the *curacas* were an endogenous elite, the *mistis,* even though biologically very much indigenous and culturally much like Indians, tended to form a sector of intermediaries exogenous to the Andean peoples.

The title of Ciro Alegría's novel, *El mundo es ancho y ajeno* (Broad and Alien Is the World), expresses rather graphically the situation of these peoples during the zenith of latifundio expansion at the beginning of the twentieth century — they were strangers in their own land.

## The Twentieth Century:
## The State, Social Movements, and New Identities

The situation, nevertheless, was not static. Beneath the surface of this asphyxiating order, which threatened to suffocate the Andean peoples, profound modifications began to occur. From the beginning of the century, with the expansion of the market and the modernization of the state, inter-ethnic boundaries began to become more porous. At this point, a phenomenon began that has intensified over recent decades. As ethnic identities became less distinct, the lower levels of the ethnic pyramid began to erode and disintegrate (Mayer 1970; Fuenzalida 1970). "Indian" as an ethnic identity increasingly appeared to be something from the past (Bourque and Warren 1978). To put it bluntly, nobody wanted to be an Indian.

Here, I do not wish to "naturalize" a phenomenon full of painful, cruel oppression. I note a fact and ask, why? From one perspective, that of the *longue durée*, Abercombie (1991, 96) provides an answer for Bolivia that also illuminates the Peruvian historical background: "the stigma attached long ago by Europeans to 'Indianness' has worked its way into 'Indian' self-consciousness as well." Nevertheless, a number of questions remain. How and why did this stigma come to be internalized? Why is it that in Bolivia and Ecuador — but not in Peru — a moment arrived when this stigma became a resource? However, the Peruvian case indicates that the persistence of this stigma associated with 'Indianness' does not necessarily imply resignation to subordination or a lack of identity or identities. As hypotheses, three additional reasons may explain why even today social movements or political representations that fundamentally define themselves in ethnic terms do not arise in the Peruvian Andes.

1. Throughout the nineteenth century, particularly after the expansion of latifundios, "Indian" was gradually converted into a synonym for poor peasant and, in many cases, serf.[5] The struggle of the Quechua and Aymara peoples against this servitude led to organizing efforts, which occurred first during the 1920s and then extended massively during the 1950s and 1960s. These organizations had as central goals: the recovery of the lands usurped by the expansion of latifundios and the struggle for education, understood as learning Spanish and the basic elements of the "national culture." The object of education was to appropriate one of the most conspicuous instruments of criollo-mestizo domination and, thereby, break the *mistis*' monopoly of intermediation (Degregori 1986). In other words, ending servitude implied tearing down the inter-ethnic barriers that *gamonalismo* was determined to keep watertight. The *mistis* were the ones most interested in maintaining the social equation Indian = serf = other, so as to maintain a monopoly on ethnic administration, along with its high quotas of privatized power. This meant that, in the Peruvian case, the demand for citizenship also came from below and, to a certain extent, combined with the discourse of "national integration" that the state

began to use, thereby imbuing this demand with democratizing and anti-landowner tones.

2. Since the beginning of the twentieth century, the state began to distance itself from *gamonalismo* and oligarchic discourse, increasingly adopting an *indigenista* policy. According to Favre (1996, 2), *indigenismo* represents the privileged form that nationalism assumes in twentieth-century Latin America. At the same time, an *indigenista* politics would be part of a more general policy of the modernization of society and also the means whereby states, whose roles were being redefined and whose field of action was widening, sought to convert their societies into nations (Favre 1996, 78). With this objective, as part of a homogenizing conception of nation, states developed policies of national integration that implied a cultural "whitening" of the original populations, and these were to culminate in homogenization around the criollo or mestizo culture. Nevertheless, given the historic context of a predominance of traditional, large agrarian property, tied to exclusionary oligarchical domination and a *hispanista* ideology, at that time *indigenismo* played a progressive role as a current of opinion and as an ideological movement. Similarly, *indigenista* state policies represented a passage to new, more modern, hegemonic forms of domination. Thus, after almost a century in limbo, the 1920 Constitution gave legal recognition to the indigenous communities. Even though "indigenous" was an ethnic label and although this recognition was part of a much broader "tutelary legislation," which implicitly treated the Indians as minors, the channels opened by legal recognition were not used to process strictly ethnic-cultural demands. Rather, demands that had a strong peasant dimension, especially the right to land, were recognized. Insofar as the recognition of the communities implied the recognition of their boundaries, there began a long, legal struggle for the recuperation of the lands usurped in the preceding decades by *gamonalismo*.

During the 1940s, *indigenismo* ceased to be merely an intermittent policy of the state because the state more explicitly embraced the discourse of "national integration" as the center of building a national state. The Plan Nacional de Integración Aborigen (National Plan of Aboriginal Integration) was created. Absent a revolution and typically administered by rather conservative governments, the program never had the budget or force that similar programs attained in Mexico. Nevertheless, these programs marked the passage from an exclusionary form of oligarchic domination to new political dynamics. The process was neither unambiguous nor unilinear; yet, a more or less sustained trend was under way. Thus, between 1958 and 1964, important peasant movements took place in Peru. Hundreds of thousands of hectares of land were seized by tens of thousands of peasants grouped together in communities, unions, and federations. Contrary to the Guatemalan experience, the Peruvian peasant movement was surprisingly bloodless, as the Peruvian state did not go all out in defending traditional, large agrarian property.

In Peru in 1969, the so-called Revolutionary Government of the Armed Forces, headed by Gen. Juan Velasco (1968-1975), began an extensive process of agrarian reform and promulgated such measures as the Law of Peasant Communities and the Law of Native Communities that involved the Andean and Amazon peoples. In 1979, a new Constitution gave voting rights to the illiterate, who by that time consisted almost entirely of indigenous populations. With a century and one-half delay, the proclamation of San Martín at last materialized — however, this did not mean that the reproduction of differences and ethnic and racial discrimination had come to an end.

Nevertheless, the policy of the Velasco government already was proving difficult to square with the classic paradigm of "national integration." During these years, even though the term "Indian" was eliminated from the official vocabulary and replaced by "peasant," there was at the same time a strong push by the state toward cultural pluralism. Among other measures, this included the recognition of Quechua as an official language. If this step was not effective, it was due not only to governmental neglect — the linguistic demand was not the top priority on the agenda of Quechua populations themselves. In the interval between the Velasco government and the 1979 Constitution, certain ethnic-cultural grievances that had been implicit in the great mobilizations of the Andean peasantry in previous decades acquired a *national* dimension. These grievances left the realm of "tutelary legislation" to become part of a more universal, citizen sphere. The state, nevertheless, did not finish redefining its role before the Andean peoples. From the early 1970s through the 1990s, Peru may be seen as a history of successive frustrations in the consolidation of a post-oligarchic, national state, a state that would, among many other necessary changes, replace the paradigm of national integration with another model containing a central place for respect for diversity. Yet, there remains one more reason why in Peru almost no one wants to be identified as Indian or some equivalent term.[6]

3. When groups of Quechua or Aymara origin emerged who were capable of imagining communities, they imagined these communities along class lines. In effect, the expansion of the market and means of communication, the multiplication of peasant organizations, the recovery of lands, and various great migrations once again made the Andean peoples complex and differentiated. In recent decades, they ceased to be overwhelmingly serfs or poor peasants. New, educated strata appeared, who were capable of elaborating discourses and projects. Among these were the leaders of the peasant unions and federations that proliferated during the 1960s and 1970s and the youth of both sexes — children or grandchildren of peasants — who gained access during these years to Spanish in primary schools and to secondary and university education.[7] These indigenous groups came to two realizations.

First, the criollos and later the mestizos had appropriated from them a good part of the mechanisms and symbolic capital upon which they might construct an Indian *we*. Since the nineteenth century, there had been a noticeable, incipient process of appropriation of the Inca imperial elite by the criollo elite, which left to flesh and blood Quechuas and Aymaras the tradition of the servile Indian (Méndez 1993). During the first half of the twentieth century, to compete with the criollo elite, who sprinkled their *hispanismo* with sporadic references to the glorious Inca past, sectors of mestizos even more determinedly appropriated the Inca imperial heritage and also the communitarian indigenous tradition.[8] Valued positively at first by *indigenismo* and socialism, this communitarian tradition began to be incorporated into the symbolism of the state long before Velasco. This happened first, ephemerally, during the initial term of office of President Augusto B. Leguía (1919-1923) and later, more systematically, during the first presidency of Fernando Belaúnde Terry (1963-1968).

Second, the parties of the Peruvian Marxist left — the most peasant-oriented left in the region and at the time overwhelmingly Maoist — offered these groups an alternative project. The Quechua and Aymara peasant leaders met the small left parties, which during those years expanded forcefully into the countryside. The 1970s saw the apogee of the class-oriented Peasant Confederation of Peru (Confederación Campesina del Perú — CCP), which had its principal bastions of strength in the Andean Trapeze, an area where the highest percentage of the Quechua and Aymara populations are concentrated.[9] For their part, the youth who gained access to secondary education encountered highly politicized teachers who spread among them what Gonzalo Portocarrero and Patricia Oliart have called "the critical idea": a radical and authoritarian conception of Peruvian society, in which class contradictions play a central role. Individuals arriving in the university encountered what I (Degregori 1990) have referred to as "the revolution of the manuals": the diffusion of the highly schematic, dogmatic version of Marxism contained in the manuals of historical and dialectical materialism published by the Soviet Academy of Sciences and the Foreign Languages Editions of Peking.[10]

The second half of the 1970s is key to this history. In 1975, Gen. Velasco was overthrown, and during the same year an economic crisis was unleashed, which continued until the collapse of the populist state toward the end of the following decade. The beginning of the crisis coincided with the development of the most important social movements in contemporary Peruvian history. Regional movements, land takeovers, and teachers' and union strikes culminated in 1977 and 1978 in two virtually total national strikes that significantly contributed to the democratic transition (1978-1980). Yet, precisely during these years — when the exhaustion of the populist state and the paradigm of national integration allowed the opening of spaces for an ethnic-cultural discourse — the alliance between the most organized, radicalized sectors of the social movements and the Marxist left was sealed. This moment was reflected in the strong vote for the left throughout the 1980s,[11] especially in the Andean Trapeze and in the districts of Lima with the highest concentration of Andean migrants.

## Constructing Peruvian Citizenship: The Intersection of Class, Region, and Ethnicity

According to Carlos Franco (1991), migration is the most important life experience shared by a majority of Peruvians. In fact, over the past half century, Peru ceased to be a predominantly rural country, and today over 70 percent of the population live in cities. If migration has played such an important role, it is appropriate to leave the countryside and note the experience of Andean migrants to understand the redefinition of identities and the continued absence of ethnic movements.

Due to adverse circumstances at the beginning of the "Andean counteroffensive," at the cultural level a "strategy of dissimulation" or the Trojan Horse initially prevailed. Language and dress, the two most visible ethnic markers, were hidden to avoid being stigmatized in the cities. However, two events made it possible to go beyond this first strategy. Through kinship networks linking city and countryside, the migrants consolidated ever more solid and extensive footholds in the urban centers without losing their rural, Andean roots (Golte and Adams 1987). Yet, with the expansion of the market, one sector of peasants was becoming ever more differentiated from the rest. Along with the social leaders and the educated youth, these "rich peasants," who were increasingly tied to the cities to which their children had migrated, formed another important group that neither imagined communities nor elaborated discourses but did reformulate behavior, social relations, and cultural patterns. One sector among them branched out toward the cities, where they swelled the ranks of the successful micro-entrepreneurs celebrated by Hernando de Soto (1987), a sector similar to the group in Bolivia referred to by Carlos Tornanzo (1991) as a "*cholo* bourgeoisie."[12]

These different sectors constituted the critical mass for the formulation of a set of cultural manifestations in the countryside and the cities. In many cases, language and dress were lost, but the networks of cooperation based on extended kinship, for example, extended to the urban centers. In this way, other characteristics of the stigmatized identity came to be converted into resources used in the economic realm, such as when forming informal enterprises (Steinhauf 1991; Adams and Valdivia 1991), and in the cultural realm. For example, the Andean festivals — which need not be understood only as manifestations of the persistence of traditional lifestyles and symbolism, but also as reaffirmations of social group cohesion, rural-urban networks, and a means of conferring legitimacy upon leaders — underwent a strong expansion toward the cities. Simultaneously, these festivals were also transformed in the countryside in the very places where they had originated on the basis of the influences picked up in the cities. While migrants ceased to be Indians, they did not become acculturated. Some scholars (Quijano 1980; Nugent 1992) speak of the emergence of a *cholo* or *chicha* culture in Peru. Neither term is free of pejorative connotation. To avoid bias, we might use descriptive terms and speak of the cultures of the population of Quechua and Aymara origin that develop primarily in the cities and increasingly influence the Quechua and Aymara who remain in the countryside.

These contingents of migrants are constructing through their city-countryside networks a fragile, embryonic identity of *Peruvian citizens*. This new Peruvian identity, distinct from the "official" identity, is arising from the intersection among gender, regional, class, and ethnic identities.[13] In a study of migrants, we (Degregori, Blondet, and Lynch 1986) found that the inhabitants of one Lima neighborhood identified themselves as belonging to the popular sector or as workers (and to a lesser extent as poor) in opposition to the upper classes; they also defined themselves as provincial as opposed to *limeños* (natives of the capital); as highlanders as opposed to coastal dwellers; as *cholos* in opposition to the traditional criollos; or simply as Peruvians.[14] The terrain in dispute is no longer only the right to land or to education; now it is the very country, the imaginary community called Peru.

This identity change became possible because during the twentieth century, the Peruvian state moved from an exclusionary, oligarchic domination to a state that is embryonically hegemonic. Although it sounds paradoxical, perhaps the more precise adjective is *weakly* hegemonic. In contrast to Mexico, where the assimilationist paradigm of national integration was so thoroughly consolidated that in recent years when Indian movements reappeared they did so as "ethnic minorities," in Peru efforts at integration and acculturation were less effective, so the Andean/popular/ provincial majorities proceeded to appropriate the concept of Peru itself and gave it another content.[15] This is what has come to be called "the new face of Peru" (Matos 1984), a profile deeply transformed by the Andean/provincial eruption into all realms of national life. This new situation should have been taken into account in the new institutional framework resulting from the democratic transition, but it did not occur to a sufficient degree. Despite the abundant literature on the democratic regression in Peru since 1992,[16] it remains to be seen whether and to what extent the present crisis of institutions, especially of the political parties, is due to their incapacity to transform themselves to take into account this new reality.

In any case, with political institutions in crisis, the new cultural correlation has made itself felt in the political arena. Even in the vote for the left, beyond the discourse of class, ethnic elements were expressed.[17] With the left dividing in 1989, its voters gave a majority of their votes to Alberto Fujimori, whose strongest vote was precisely in the Andean Trapeze. In this election, the Fujimori vote contained a noticeable rejection of the white/criollo elite surrounding his contender, the writer Mario Vargas Llosa, and an identification with the *nikkei* candidate. Insofar as Fujimori was the son of non-white migrants, he appeared closer to the aspirations of these ethnic majorities than the cosmopolitan writer. They placed more value in Fujimori's campaign tractor than in Vargas Llosa's elegant pen.[18] In the 1995 elections, virtually every presidential candidate sought to include the new social actors in their campaign formulas: *cholos*, provincials, women, and successful micro-entrepreneurs. However, by 1995, another alliance (fragile, but real) had been established between Fujimori and important rural and urban Andean sectors.[19] In addition to successes in the struggles against inflation and Sendero Luminoso, the systematic use of specific cultural symbols played a role in this alliance. Accordingly, Fujimori might be nicknamed "the man of a thousand suits," since there was not a poncho, *chullo cushma*, hat, or other ethnic garb that he did not wear during his constant trips throughout the country.[20]

Thus, a pending task for democratic consolidation in Peru is to translate into concrete demands and to incorporate into institutions what today appears mostly at the level of symbols and gestures. Although the Trojan Horse strategy made possible important advances for the Andean populations, it did not tear down the symbolic walls of the oligarchic *ancien régime*: it ate into them, cracked them, and pushed them back to the *habitus* and everyday life. Yet, there persisted a pecking order whereby individuals who have penetrated the walls, or think that they have, feel themselves to be superior to those who remained on the doorstep, either because they were incapable or unwilling to enter. Nevertheless, both groups are strongly interconnected via dense rural-urban networks.[21]

Perhaps, in this sense, the interaction of different identities — of region, class, ethnicity, citizenship, and gender — among a citizenry respectful of diversity would provide a better basis for achieving democratic rights. By including such themes as linguistic and cultural pluralism, as well as struggles against ethnic and racial discrimination, such a program might avoid the dead ends that unilateral preeminence of ethnic identities has produced in other parts of the world. As Michael Walzer has noted, when identities multiply, passions divide. Given the Sendero Luminoso experience and the violence prompted by its extreme "class reductionism," such words seem appropriate for the Peruvian case.

## BOLIVIA

The historical similarities between Peru and Bolivia are many. Nonetheless, notable differences have been present from early on. In the sixteenth century, the Aymara people, living in what is today the southernmost part of Peru and the Bolivian Altiplano, secured special treatment from the Spanish monarchy, whereby the crown ordered that the Aymara receive their indoctrination in their own language and not in the "general language," which was how the Spanish then referred to Quechua (Remy 1994, 127). This privilege contributed to the survival of the Aymara language and the Aymaras as a people distinct from the Quechua.

After the independence of South America and the creation in 1825 of Bolivia, the politics of both countries remained intimately linked until the 1840s. During the first decades of republican life, some colonial institutions persisted in both countries. The indigenous tribute, for example, was suppressed in Peru only in 1854 and in Bolivia in 1866, when the revenue stemming from, first, guano (seabird dung used for fertilizer) and nitrates and, later, silver and tin rendered the tribute dispensable (Klein 1982). But whereas in Peru the tribute was charged individually, in Bolivia, the community continued to be the unit taxed. This practice contributed to the survival of the *ayllus mayores* (larger communal lands) and attenuated or delayed their fragmentation into ever smaller units as occurred in Peru. Toward the end of the nineteenth and the beginning of the twentieth century, an expansion of large landholdings began in both countries. Nevertheless, due, among other reasons, to the better preservation of the old communal structures and hierarchies in Bolivia, in many parts of the Bolivian Altiplano, descendants of *curacas* came out in defense of their communities, showing their private colonial titles (Rivera 1984, 43-44).

At the turn of the century, both countries possessed fundamentally agrarian and extractive economies, a dominance of traditional latifundios in rural areas, an oligarchical political structure with less than 10 percent of the adult population qualified to vote, and an indigenous majority viewed as a dead weight by the criollo elite. Nevertheless, before the expansion of the market and the modernization of the state had advanced significantly, two events decisively marked the course of Bolivian history. The first was the Chaco War (1932-1935), which set Bolivia against Paraguay in the bloodiest twentieth-century conflict in South America and ended in a debacle for Bolivia. The second was the national revolution of 1952.

The war laid bare the corruption and incompetence of government elites and the armed forces, producing a process of radicalization among mining workers, the urban middle classes, sectors of the army, and the peasantry. In addition to a significant *indigenista* current, the modern political parties of the center and the left emerged at this time — most notably, the Nationalist Revolutionary Movement (Movimiento Nacionalista Revolucionario — MNR), whose orientation was nationalist and populist.[22] For the Quechua and Aymara peasants who had been forcibly taken to fight in a war that was not their own, at the behest of a country that they did not feel was theirs, the Chaco turned out to be an encounter that led to the broadening of horizons. In Peru, the expansion of the market and means of communication, the modernization of the state, and, above all, the great migrations to the cities were the structural factors that opened the possibilities for breaking down localism, expanding organizational networks, and assuming a national perspective. In Bolivia, the Chaco was an early and violent immersion into these processes. In the post-war years, peasant organizations extending beyond the community multiplied, especially among the Quechua from the inter-Andean Cochabamba valleys, who had a more developed mercantile economy and were less constrained by traditional latifundios (Dandler 1969).

For its part, the state, which since 1880 had consolidated around the mining and landholding oligarchy, underwent an accelerated process of splitting apart. Between 1936-1939 and 1943-1946, during short-lived military governments led by officials from the so-called Chaco Generation, the state made its first attempts to incorporate the Quechua and Aymara populations into political life. In 1942 and 1943, the first two Congresos Indígenas de Habla Quechua (Congresses of Quechua-Speaking Indians) took place, with the support of various labor unions and university organizations (Rivera 1984, 63). In May 1945, the government of Gen. Gualberto Villaroel convoked the Primer Congreso Indígena Nacional (First National Indigenous Congress). The event took place in La Paz and brought together over 1,000 leaders (Klein 1982, 219). The citizenry of the capital was "visibly affected and frightened by the eruption of hundreds of *mallkus, jilaqata*, and Indian mayors from all over the country, who for the first time since the beginning of the century freely entered the Plaza Murillo chanting hurrahs to *tata*[23] Villaroel and his leaders. . ." (Rivera 1982, 64). One year later, however, Villaroel was lynched by a furious mob in the same plaza, and the parties representing the old order, united in the "Concordance," for the last time regained power (Klein 1982, 221). It was not the decrees that Villaroel promulgated after the Indigenous Congress (these were not a mortal threat to the latifundio system) that allowed the conservative parties to take power with the support of a popular uprising in La Paz. Rather, it was the sudden eruption of the "Other" into a city that perceived itself to be historically under siege, long before the market, migrations, and new paths of communication would bring the city and the countryside closer and would change attitudes and perceptions.[24] As Silvia Rivera (1982, 67) asserts:

> The most outrageous thing of all was the presence of the President of the Republic within the Indian mob, as it prefigured a new state project in which the Indian peasantry would occupy a privileged position. . . . The oligarchy was set on edge by this ever more overwhelming and palpable presence, whose demands now even appeared reasonable and worthy of consideration, whereas previously it was sufficient to invoke the stigma and idea of barbarism to resolve by arms any conflict unleashed in the countryside.

## The Revolution of 1952

Six years later, this project became a reality with the triumph of the 1952 Revolution, the most important revolution in Latin America since the 1910 Mexican Revolution. The insurrection, which culminated with the collapse of the oligarchic state and its armed forces, was led by the MNR in alliance with the Bolivian Workers' Union (Central Obrera Boliviana — COB) and with the support of a broadly mobilized peasantry, especially in the Quechua zones of Cochabamba.[25]

For every social sector in Bolivia, the 1952 Revolution signified a radical turning point. The new government nationalized large mining operations, which had been the source of the bulk of the country's foreign exchange earnings and was the fundamental power base for the so-called "tin barons," who until 1952 exercised hegemony over the state. For the indigenous peasantry, which made up the majority of the population, the revolution meant unionization, citizenship, and land. In the preceding decade, peasants had won the right to unionize, but after 1952 the unions became part of the new power structure. At the same time, from this point on, an overwhelmingly illiterate peasantry held the right to vote, an expansion that produced a fivefold increase in the number of voters (Klein 1982, 232). In 1953, the law of agrarian reform was promulgated, which eventually would result in the demise of the traditional latifundios.

From 1952 on, the official language of the state began to refer to Indians as peasants. This change in terminology reflected the program of the two other forces victorious in 1952. For the MNR, the goal was to constitute a homogeneous, mestizo nation, a conception embedded within the then dominant paradigm of "national integration," principally exemplified by post-revolutionary Mexico. For the COB, which had been strengthened by the nationalization of mining, the goal was to construct a worker-peasant alliance that would transform the national revolution into a socialist one. Yet, the change in terminology was not merely a change of name or a manipulation. Today, when respect for diversity is valued and recognized, the homogenizing goals of the national integration policy may appear in retrospect to be not only unjust but archaic. However, during the epoch of the tin barons and the "semifeudal" latifundios, the 1952 Revolution opened new horizons for the Quechua and Aymara peoples. Additionally, even though the Bolivian Revolution was conceived within the domain of national revolutions, it underwent an initial, extremely intense period of class-based creativity that lasted until about 1956. According to Rivera, "Unionization on a massive scale and worker and peasant militia [were] the predominant forms of the new power of the masses in the post-revolutionary political arena" (1984, 88).

In following years, the MNR drifted toward more moderate positions, reinforced by the reconstruction of the armed forces and the support of the United States (Klein 1982). At the same time, it was still capable of consolidating its alliance with the peasantry and isolating the COB. It did so by taking advantage of the union organization's exclusively class approach and its underestimation of the peasantry, which was viewed by the COB as a "petty bourgeois" force. The key to the alliance between the government and the peasantry, however, was the handing over of lands within the framework of the agrarian reform.

In 1964, tensions between the MNR and the COB as well as divisions within the MNR itself precipitated a military coup. However, it was not the old army that had been defeated and dismantled in 1952 that took power, but another army that situated itself within the perspective of the national revolution and which, in recognition of the new strategic importance of the indigenous peasantry, took great pains to continue promoting the agrarian reform. Furthermore, Gen. René Barrientos, the populist general who came to power in a coup in 1964, was a Quechua-speaking mestizo from Cochabamba. By means of populist rhetoric and an intensified distribution of lands, Barrientos managed to seal the Military-Peasant Pact (Pacto Militar-Campesino — PMC), which continued even after his death in an air accident in 1969. The PMC survived during left-wing military governments (1969-1971) and even during the first years of Gen. Hugo Banzer's rightist government, which took power in 1971.

Not until two decades after the 1952 Revolution did Gen. Banzer think it possible to dispense with peasant support. The economic situation was very favorable — mineral prices were on the upswing in the international market, newly discovered gas deposits in the east permitted exports to Brazil and Argentina, the eastern region of Santa Cruz developed a vigorous commercial agriculture and a modernizing bourgeoisie, and a manufacturing sector even began to take shape in La Paz (Klein 1982, 254). Just as the state during the 1860s could do without the indigenous tribute because of revenue from guano, nitrates, and the Altiplano mines, during the 1970s, the government decided to dispense with peasant support. At the beginning of 1974, the government, among other measures, decreed price increases for essential goods. These increases significantly affected the peasantry, which was by then much more linked to the market as a result of agrarian reform. In Cochabamba, both the bastion of the PMC and the most commercial Andean zone, peasants blocked highways, demanding talks with the president. Yet, times had changed. This time the army and the air force responded to the protest, bombarding the mobilized peasants.[26]

## Katarismo

The Cochabamba massacre marked the beginning of the end of the Military-Peasant Pact. Yet, this split did not translate into an opportunity for the COB and the left to win the peasantry over to their side, as might have been expected. Rather, it laid the basis for the emergence of a new protagonist onto the Bolivian political and union scene: el katarismo. Named in honor of Túpac Katari, the eighteenth-century Aymara rebel, katarismo evolved after the late 1960s, primarily in the city of La Paz. The movement emerged among Aymara migrants, particularly teachers and students sensitive to the discrimination that persisted despite two decades of integrationist preaching in the loftiest city in the world, which began to be dotted with skyscrapers during the bonanza years of Banzer.[27]

To a significant degree, katarismo is a child of the 1952 Revolution and cannot be explained without reference to it. With the revolution, the peasantry won land, education, and the right to vote. In conjunction with migrations and the expansion of the market, these gains made it possible for "sectors capable of imagining communities" to arise, again invoking the words used to refer to the Peruvian case. In contrast to Peru, however, when the 1952 Revolution reached its limits, the urban Aymara intellectuals did not face indigenous social scenarios and symbolic spaces densely populated with nonindigenous discourses and actors.

Thus, even though significant, particularly during the Chaco post-war, *indigenismo* — understood as an urban discourse about the "original peoples" — did not achieve in Bolivia at this point the overwhelming presence that it came to have in Bolivia's northern neighbor, where pro-indigenous organizations, literary groups, magazines, artists, writers, lawyers, and agronomists proliferated. A Peruvian party, the American Popular Revolutionary Alliance (Alianza Popular Revolucionaria Americana — APRA), was one of the sources of ideological inspiration for the MNR. Yet, whereas the APRA located *indigenista* symbolism at the center of its identity,[28] the MNR, perhaps because from 1952 on it had become a governing party, preferred to focus on concrete political measures, such as agrarian reform, rather than on conquering the indigenous symbols. *Tiwanakota* symbols appear in the MNR's discourse, but Túpac Katari, for example, does not occupy a prominent place in the pantheon of the 1952 Revolution. In contrast, Túpac Amaru was converted into the foremost symbol of the revolutionary government headed by Gen. Velasco in Peru.

Whereas José Carlos Mariátegui (1895-1930), the central figure of the socialist left in Peru, was posthumously accused by the Third International of being an *indigenista* and a "populist," due to his emphasis on the then-called "Indian problem," in Bolivia events rather than persons occupied center stage in the symbolism of the left. The first event was the drafting of the Pulacaya Theses, adopted by the mining proletariat in 1946, which contained a strong emphasis on the construction of the worker-peasant alliance and a strong Trotskyist influence. The second event was the Popular Assembly that functioned in the Congress, which grew between June 1970 and August 1971 during the government of Gen. Juan José Torres, described as "one of the most extraordinary governments in Bolivian history" (Klein 1982, 250). The Assembly, nonetheless, was "brutally working-class based."[29] During the 1970s, when *katarismo* grew, Maoism was a marginal force in Bolivia, whereas in Peru the majority of the left embraced Maoism.[30]

Thus, when populism headed toward its final crisis, its relationship with indigenous populations differed in both countries. In Bolivia, the breaking up of the PMC expressed the state's desire to distance itself from the indigenous populations, whereas the emerging criollo-mestizo radical groups were indifferent to them. In Peru, in contrast, the state's *indigenista* discourse and policy intensified, while on its left flank new radical groups threw themselves into political work among the Andean peasantry.

As a result, the new Aymara intellectuals encountered a relatively unclouded "air space" and elaborated their discourse with the support of sectors of the Catholic Church, non-governmental institutions, and Basque and Catalán priests (Calla 1993, 61), who came from regions where ethnic-cultural grievances are central. In November 1973, leaders of Aymara associations moved to the ruins of what had been the capital of the first Andean empire and launched the Manifiesto Tiwanaku.[31] Even though a balance was sought between a class and an ethnic perspective, the

Manifiesto placed ethnic-cultural grievances in a central position: "They have neither respected our virtues nor our vision of the world and life. . . . Our culture has not been respected, nor have our ways of thinking been understood" (Rivera 1984, 133).[32]

During the following years, when the Banzer government entered its most repressive phase, the *katarista* discourse legitimated itself in the anti-dictatorial struggle, and *katarismo* grew rapidly among peasant organizations, displacing the discredited MNR leaders. Nevertheless, even though the COB did not monopolize the symbolic realm, its presence on the social and political scene was too overwhelming to be ignored. The most dynamic sectors took care to move between ethnic and class grievances to "look with two eyes" and "to walk with two feet,"[33] trying to commit the COB to an alliance, but on their own terms. The peasant unions were the arenas in which this process of unity and struggle was fought out, with the left making progress as the organizations linked to the PMC fell apart. The split between the peasantry and the government culminated in 1979 with the creation of the Sole Labor Confederation of Bolivian Peasant Workers (Central Sindical Única de Trabajadores Campesinos de Bolivia — CSUTCB). Its name alone reveals the deep imprint of class within the peasant movement. The *kataristas* respected the name and the form of union organization, but they steeped it with ethnic-cultural content in an open polemic with Marxist discourse:

> There are those that accuse us of being "petty bourgeois" because we are owners of our plots or *chacos*, and therefore establish class differences among us; they divide us into owners and have-nots, into peasants and laborers. There are also those who define us as a class in the process of disappearing, destined to swell the ranks of the proletariat. We do not agree with these opinions . . . we peasants do not consider ourselves to be a marginal or decadent class, destined to disappear. We continue being a majority of the population of the country. Even less are we petty bourgeoisie because we own plots of land. The land for us is principally a condition of production and an inheritance from our ancestors, rather than a means of production (Rivera 1984, 189).[34]

The *kataristas* thus embarked upon a hegemonic cultural strategy, which educated the left, the labor movement, and Bolivians in general. With an ease of manner that must have struck orthodox Marxists as insolence, those who had been predestined to play the role of chorus or second fiddle to the vanguard proletariat rebelled and demanded an equal or greater role as a historical protagonist.

During the years of democratic transition (1978-1982) and during the first years of the center-left Democratic Popular Unity (Unidad Democrática Popular — UDP) government (1982-1985), *katarismo* found itself at its peak as a social movement, but it failed when it attempted to make inroads into the new political scene. Weakened by successive divisions, its different candidates never won more than 3 percent of the vote. To explain these results, Xavier Albó (1996, 334) stresses the lack of financial resources, weak organization, internal divisions, and localism. Without denying these factors, it is, however, worth mentioning others as follow:[35]

First, the movement was marked by an excessively ideological slant. When moving from union/communal demands and cultural discourse to its national program, *katarismo* revealed itself to be overly ideological. This slant was shaped by the strong intellectual presence in the movement, which was reinforced by relations with NGOs, as well as leftist and Christian influences, with a propensity to "hard ideologies." Albó speaks of the need to move "from utopian dream to the prosaic political clash" (1994, 72).

Second, the movement was marked by a social base and, above all, a symbolism and "utopian horizon" that were overly rural social base of *katarismo*, precisely when not only the country in general but the Quechua and Aymara peoples themselves were becoming increasingly urban and beginning to develop other needs and other ideals.[36] Even in the countryside, important currents within *katarismo* pulled out of the unions and concentrated their work on strengthening the *ayllus* and the communities, just at the moment when the very reality of the countryside itself was becoming increasingly complex, and, in addition to the established unions, cooperatives and mothers' clubs were popping up, as were civic committees in the small and medium-sized towns (Urioste 1989, 233-234).

Third, the *kataristas* underestimated the challenges of representative democracy and the enormous difficulties of acting within the new political framework opened up by the democratic transition. During the preceding decade, almost all of the currents active within the CSUTCB — not only *katarismo* — thought that the dictatorship would fall as a result of a revolutionary push. Even during the UDP government, the hesitant democracy appeared as a mere turn on the road to imminent revolution. Afterward came hyperinflation, the crisis of the UDP government, which had to convoke early presidential elections in 1985, the triumph of a recycled MNR that presented itself as a neoliberal alternative, and the subsequent economic adjustment. These events marked the end of the 1952 populist state and the consolidation of another model that involved the reduction of the role of the state, economic privatization and informalization, elections, and representative democracy.

*Katarismo*, and the CSUTCB in general, then collapsed into political abstentionism. At the First Extraordinary Congress of the CSUTCB held in 1988, Ricardo Calla, for example, warned, "Not a single document pays attention to the political situation posed by the imminent national electoral contest of May 1989" (1989, 70-72). According to Calla, "To not think about defeating the neoliberal model at the polls [means] being left out of the real political struggle." This is what was happening. In the debate around the Congress, Jorge Lazarte indicated some of the characteristics of the new political scene: the formation of a new collective, citizen subject; the emergence of public opinion; the passage from confrontation to negotiation as the method for handling conflicts; the decline of ideology; and a focus on concrete results (in Pinelo 1989, 157). But this new scene did not enter the delegates' discussion. The document presented by the Grassroots Peasant Movement (Movimiento Campesino de Bases — MCB), the group receiving the most votes in the Political Commission of the First Extraordinary Congress, was the only one that touched the issue of democracy. It said:

> We peoples who make up the different nationalities aspire to implant a complete democracy that guarantees equal rights, not only those of individuals, but also equality of national rights. We speak of the establishment of a new democracy, distinct from and superior to the present pseudo-democracy, which is sustained

by the exploitation of workers and the oppression of various popular sectors (Calla, Pinello, and Urioste 1989, 183).

For its part, the Túpac Katari Revolutionary Movement Liberation (Movimiento Revolucionario Túpac Katari-Liberación — MRTK-L), the most important *katarista* faction within the peasant movement, limited itself to proposing to "constitute a Confederation of *Ayllus* and Communities" in contrast to the CSUTCB, which already "has fulfilled its historic role (Calla 1989, 49)." According to Miguel Urioste, sectors of the Catholic Church and NGOs contributed to peasant abstentionism, since they tend "to have basically anti-statist or non-statist criteria; in other words, they dispense with any relation with the state on the assumption that this tie automatically will turn into oppression, domination, and exploitation" (1989, 243).

The distance between utopian dreams and prosaic politics could be clearly noted in the proposals for an Assembly of the Nationalities (Asamblea de las Nacionalidades), which confronted the "pseudo democracy" of the "bourgeois criollo state" with a "complete democracy" of the original peoples and proposed a multinational state with a new territorial division based upon administrative units defined by ethnicity.[37] The Assembly of the Nationalities developed over a long period of time, and it was intended to come to full realization during the symbolic year of 1992. Yet, by this date, seven years of neoliberalism had already transpired, and the political life of the country had taken other paths.

Fourth, *katarismo* had problems in penetrating the world of "informality." If politics had changed, this was not only because of the democratic transition but also the social transformations produced after the collapse of the populist state and structural adjustment. Massive layoffs and privatization weakened the unions and facilitated an explosive growth in the "informal sector." In this sense, *katarismo* is also a child of the 1952 Revolution, which gave Bolivia a minimally defined class structure: the *kataristas* knew how to move about in the world of communities and unions; they knew how to confront the welfare state and cultural imperialism. But it was hard for them to understand the apparently chaotic world that grew with the informal sector.

## From Social Movement to Cultural Horizon

Paradoxically, at the moment of *katarismo*'s greatest union and political weakness, the *katarista* discourse, nonetheless, came to have its greatest influence among broad sectors of the country. The country had been prepared for this message by migration, urbanization, the expansion of the market, and the mass media, all of which had not homogenized the country but had *articulated* it, bringing its different components closer without making them all uniform. In this manner, during the 1990s, the whole of society was penetrated by the central grievances raised by *katarismo*: cultural diversity, inclusion of the original populations on the political scene, and the redefinition of the Bolivian state. The path cleared by the *kataristas* opened like a fan, and the issues on their agenda advanced through sometimes unexpected channels.[38]

Thus, for example, the ethnic groups of least demographic weight, grouped together in the Indigenous Confederation of the East, Chaco, and Amazon of Bolivia (Confederación Indígena del Oriente, Chaco, y Amazonia de Bolivia — CIDOB), took the baton from the Aymara and Quechua to spearhead indigenous social movements. Already, the Assembly of the Guaraní People (Asamblea del Pueblo Guaraní), set up in 1987, had served as the inspiration for the proposal of an Assembly of the Nationalities. But the turning point was the March for Territory and Dignity, organized by the Coordinator of the Beni Indigenous Peoples (Coordinadora de Pueblos Indígenas del Beni — CPIB). In 1991, the march traveled over 700 kilometers to reach La Paz. The Amazon and Guaraní peoples adopted as their own a large part of the *katarista* cultural discourse and, at the same time, contributed their own symbols and grievances, such as respect for ancestral lands.

New *cholo* parties erupted onto the political stage and grew rapidly, especially among urban migrants of Aymara and Quechua origin. The collapse of the populist state around 1985 and the effects of economic adjustment dragged the COB down with it as well as, to a certain extent, *katarismo*, which proved unable to occupy the spaces opened by the shrinking of the left. At that point, but from the other extreme of the ideological spectrum, two new parties emerged, Conscience of the Homeland (Conciencia de Patria — CONDEPA) and the Solidarity Civic Union (Unión Cívica Solidaridad — UCS).[39]

In 1968, when the cultural centers that would become the precursors of *katarismo* were formed, a folk singer, Carlos Palenque, began a radio program with music, greetings, letters, and expressions of opinion from the public (Saravia and Sandoval 1991, 46). Sixteen years later, Palenque owned the television and radio stations most popular among the popular sectors of La Paz. In September 1988, amid the very same ruins of *Tiwanaku*, where the *kataristas* had launched their first manifesto, Palenque founded CONDEPA, which emerged as the fourth political force in the country in the 1989 elections and the strongest in the department of La Paz.

In October 1969, an employee of Gulf Oil, Max Fernández, decided to leave the firm after its nationalization and to become a beer distributor in Santa Cruz. Later, his activities branched into shipping and the manufacture of plastic packaging. In mid-1987, he moved into the national spotlight when he became president of the board of directors of the Bolivian National Brewery (Cervecería Boliviana Nacional), controlling a majority of its shares (Mayorga 1991, 114). One year later, Fernández founded UCS, which grew by using beer distributors as activists and by investing the firm's profits into public works throughout the country. His was a new type of clientelism, more akin to Andean reciprocity than to classical Latin American patronage (Mayorga 1991). UCS was prevented from participating in the 1989 national elections, but in the December municipal elections of the same year, it placed mayors in four of the nine department capitals in the country.

CONDEPA and UCS had their greatest successes among the new "post-class" sectors: freight haulers; small, informal merchants; peasants; and the unemployed. Fernández's discourse had national coverage, whereas Palenque's strength was concentrated in La Paz.[40] The former spoke Quechua, the latter Aymara. Aside from his use of Quechua at public rallies, Fernández did not resort to indigenous symbolism. His presence as a "triumphant *cholo*" was sufficient to turn him into a frame of reference and a model for upward social mobility.[41] Palenque approached the ethnic-cultural question from the angle of everyday life (Saravia and Sandoval 1991, 208) through his open-mike radio shows in which an informal relationship was established with listeners. In the 1993 national elections, each received 13 percent of the vote.

*Katarismo* had a hard time calibrating the importance of these parties. Although each appealed to a similar social base, their profiles could not be more different: the *kataristas* were intellectual, institutional, and ideological, whereas the *cholo* outsiders were pragmatic, personalistic, and entrepreneurial, operating with the explicit goal of participating in elections. These differences gave rise to the difficulties the *kataristas* faced in penetrating the urban, informal world, as well as their reticence before cultural intermingling — what Nestor García Canclini (1990) would call "hybrid cultures" or what Carlos Toranzo (1991, 13), referring specifically to Bolivia, calls a sociocultural *ch'enko*.[42] Fernández and Palenque were populists, demagogues, and paternalists; they lacked coherent programs, but they did take up a number of symbols and themes first promoted by *katarismo,* and they incorporated other issues that arose out of the experiences of urban migrants. Furthermore, amid the social upheavals that accompanied the collapse of the populist state and the pains of neoliberal adjustment, Fernández embodied possibilities of social advancement, and Palenque offered an identity with Andean roots to individuals who could not readily feel represented by the Confederation of Communal Lands (Confederación de Ayllus), which was then proposed by important *katarista* sectors.

In 1993, Víctor Hugo Cárdenas, one of the historic leaders of *katarismo* and a leader of MRTK-L, was elected vice president of Bolivia in an alliance with the MNR. Cárdenas' election marked a double turning point: that of those sectors of *katarismo* who decided to move from the "utopian dream to political clash" and that of the traditional parties who intensified their opening to ethnic-cultural demands.

This opening was already noted during the government of the Patriotic Accord (Acuerdo Patriótico), headed by Jaime Paz Zamora (1989-1993), which supported bilingual, intercultural education; engaged in talks with the participants of the 1991 March for Dignity and Territory; insisted upon the cultural value of the coca leaf; recognized some indigenous lands in the East; ratified Covenant 169 of the International Labor Organization (ILO) on the rights of indigenous peoples; and succeeded in seeing that Bolivia would be the seat of the Indigenous Development Fund, created by the Inter-American Development Bank (Albó 1996, 337). The MNR, after evaluating new sensibilities expressed among broad sectors of Bolivians in the 1989 electoral growth of the *"cholo"* parties, was simply taking one more step when it entered into an alliance with the MRTK-L. The same was true of the MNR governmental alliance with the UCS following its victory. Yet, it was an extremely important, symbolic step that brought to a head the surprisingly abrupt switch of the MNR, which moved from leading a populist, statist revolution with a project of national integration in 1952; to becoming the spearhead of a privatizing, neoliberal revolution from 1985 to 1989; to being a base of support for a multicultural country beginning in 1993.

When he ran as a presidential candidate in 1989, Cárdenas received very few votes. It might be thought that, apart from his symbolism, Cárdenas' electoral contribution to the alliance with the MNR was nil. Nevertheless, the figures presented by Xavier Albó (1994) for the 1993 election are fairly impressive. The MNR's Gonzalo Sánchez de Losada-Cárdenas ticket obtained 34 percent of the vote — an exceptional result in Bolivia, some 14 percentage points more than the next strongest candidate among a field of 14 candidates. Furthermore, the MNR, in alliance with MRTK-L, won in La Paz for the first time since the 1982 democratic transition, defeating even CONDEPA.

The 1993 results proved that Miguel Urioste had been right when, critical of certain NGOs' tendencies to avoid any relationship with the state, he noted, "Many peasants want to be a part of the structure of state power: even within this anti-peasant state..." (1989, 243). The MNR-MRTK-L alliance was able to take up this need for participation and representation among peasant and migrant sectors, which neither component of the alliance alone was able to satisfy. Using one of Víctor Hugo Cárdenas' own metaphors, it might be said that to interpret today's Bolivian reality, it is necessary to have a "third eye" — in addition to ethnicity and class, one needs the "citizen's eye." In Bolivia, as in Peru, the demand for citizenship came from below and was not only a state imposition.

According to Eduardo Gamarra, "Coalition building [is] the only strength of the Bolivian system" (1996, 94). On the basis of what has occurred since 1982, it is clear that another of Bolivia's strengths is its inclusion of the new demands of Indians and *cholos*. If we look at what happened with indigenous rights during the four years of Sánchez de Lozada's government (1993-1997), the results appear promising, given internal political configurations and the international context. The government promulgated fundamental legislation, especially the Educational Reform, which supports bilingual intercultural education, and the Law of Popular Participation, which incorporates the traditional organizations and authorities, including the *ayllus*, into the new structure of local power. This reform multiplied the number of municipal authorities elected by universal suffrage and increased the number of peasant and indigenous town councilors to over 400 in 1995.[43] This demonstrates the extent to which the elites have had to take into account the grievances and symbolism of the original peoples, whether due to conviction, expedience, or the demographic, political, cultural, and social importance of these sectors.

## Plurinational or Multicultural?

As the MNR moved from a statist and integrationist position to one advocating privatization and open to diversity, the MRTK-L also modified its proposals in this complex game of interrelationships. In his 1993 inauguration speech, delivered in Spanish, Aymara, Quechua, and Guaraní, Cárdenas declared:

> After 500 years of colonial silence and 168 years of republican exclusion, we have come forward to tell our truth. Ours has been a history of permanent struggle for freedom and justice, for multicultural and multi-ethnic democracy. Today, we are entering the age of a new *pachakuti*, a fundamental change. We Bolivians, united,

are beginning to transform those 500 years of exclusion and marginality (cited in Albó 1994, 68).

As Albó (1994) notes, Cárdenas at the time avoided the term "multinational." According to Albó, Cárdenas did so to avoid causing bad will among the dominant sectors. Yet, might it also have been that the proposal of a multinational country also would have alienated broad popular sectors? Would not the proposal of a multicultural and multi-ethnic country better reflect the reality of a Bolivia that has moved forward in the process of national articulation? This process, distinct from the classical process of "national integration," does not necessarily have as its destination point "the traditional criollo politics" or a mythical West but a different Bolivia. Such a country would be distinct from that imagined by the proponents of the Assembly of Nationalities. It would not be a Bolivia with clearly delimited "sub-state nations" (Cárdenas as cited in Albó 1996, 350), which would require laying down boundaries where they do not exist, as well as entailing the many risks of conflict that are clearly suggested by the present international situation. Establishing boundaries would only seek to separate what is inextricably interpenetrated, not only territorially but culturally.

Looking toward the future, it might be that ethnic-cultural grievances will be expressed not only through the organizations of the original peoples but also through diverse channels, including the struggle for the implementation or improvement of the laws promulgated by the MNR-MRTK-L government. Perhaps for the Quechua and the Aymara, the essentially ethnic moment of their grievances has passed, and they have entered a new period that combines ethnic-cultural demands with citizen demands, class grievances in the struggle against inequity, and local and regional demands. And perhaps the subjects that pursue these grievances will not be solely the ethnic movements that reached their zenith during the 1970s and 1980s, but more plural subjects.

## CONCLUSION

On the basis of the analysis of Peru and Bolivia, it appears that the expression and recognition of ethnic-cultural diversity precedes and transcends specifically ethnic movements as well as strictly indigenous subjects. The specific case of the Andean region includes, for example, strata referred to as "*cholos.*" When ethnic movements develop in the region,[44] they question the nation-state in some of its most obsolete dimensions: centralism, the ideology of national integration, and the ideology of national security. Generally, ethnic movements question the state from the perspective of what can be called "the other modernity" (Franco 1992). In other words, the national states, which were considered to be the bearers of modernity and civilization, find themselves questioned by peoples who until recently were considered "archaic" or primitive. This challenge arises from a "post-modern" context and sensibility, through movements that find support in specific aspects of the present process of globalization (Brysk 1994).

Consequently, if the ethnic movements threaten governability, it will be because of the inflexibility and incapacity of the states to restructure themselves effectively, rather than a powerful inclination toward radical confrontation. Such restructuring has to extend beyond declarations. The state has to restructure itself to assume its role as the representative of "unity in diversity," as well to reverse the persistent economic inequity that keeps the majority of Indians in poverty. Nevertheless, the states are beginning to incorporate some indigenous demands, perhaps in part because they "have learned to practice international appeasement more than democratic accountability" (Brysk 1994, 45) or because such incorporation does not conflict with the presently hegemonic neoliberal model (Favre 1996, 123).

For their part, although some *indigenista* ideologues counterpose communitarian democracy against formal democracy, the ethnic movements in general have taken advantage of the recent wave of democratic transitions, which "has created the legal space for the expression of new identities as the resort to repression has become more problematic, although certainly not altogether absent" (Yashar 1996, 98). For some, this has meant moving from "utopian dream to the prosaic political clash" (Albó 1994, 72). In this passage, the road to be traveled is still very long and combines ethnic-cultural grievances with others, especially the struggle against poverty and inequality, which can be driven by coalitions that extend beyond indigenous subjects while still including them prominently.

Thus, in contrast to other parts of the world, in the Andean region, ethnic movements and the visible expression of ethnic diversity play, in general, an important role in broadening and consolidating democracy.

# Notes

1. On new social movements, see, among others, Escobar and Alvarez (1992). On national states and indigenous peoples, see Smith (1990), Urban and Sherzer (1991), Stavenhagen (1992), and González Casanova and Roitman (1996). On indigenous peoples and human rights, see Stavenhagen (1988).

2. In a very suggestive article, Guerrero (1993) speaks of ethnic citizenship. For the same concept in the Peruvian context, see Montoya (1992).

3. The indigenous peoples of Peru and Bolivia exhibit considerable demographic, social, and political heterogeneity. The demographically small peoples living in the Amazon regions of both countries and in the Bolivian Chaco, who are mentioned only tangentially here, contrast sharply with the large Andean Quechua and Aymara peoples, who, if the Quechua in Ecuador are included, account for around 45 percent of the total indigenous population of Latin America (percentage calculated from Yashar 1996, 92). Even though the situation is fluid, it can be said that the Andean peoples are — or until very recently were — indigenous peasants in the majority; the Amazon and Chaco peoples are not. At the same time, the Andean peoples exhibit marked differences. On the differences between Quechuas and Aymaras in Bolivia, see, for example, Rivera 1984. Among the Quechua, in addition to differences in dialect, there are marked cultural variations, which arise from distinct national — and even regional — histories.

4. The use of Quechua as the "general language" for Christian indoctrination, the "extirpation of idolatry," the *reducciones de indios*, and the Christian settlements that facilitated the impositions of tributes and religious indoctrination as well as demographic catastrophe all contributed to this homogenization by weakening prior organizational forms and linguistic-cultural particularities, increasingly blurring ethnic identities.

5. This equation did not hold during the colonial period. The "Republic of Indians" was socially stratified and complex. Túpac Amaru was a muleteer, and his mule trains covered the route between Lima and Buenos Aires. "Indian" was not a synonym for poor. However, it remains to be seen to what extent the stigma associated with "Indianness" crystallized in the nineteenth century with the appearance of "scientific racism," the expansion of positivism, and the idea of progress, all of which classified the Indians as archaic, backwards, obstacles to development, and so on.

6. In Bolivia, Quechuas and Aymaras prefer to call themselves "original peoples," whereas the Guaraníes accept the term "indigenous" (Albó 1994). In Ecuador, the stigma was also converted into a resource with the adoption of terms such as "Indian" or "indigenous," whereas in Guatemala the indigenous population refers to itself as "Mayan peoples."

7. The law of free secondary education in state schools was promulgated in 1953. The total number of university students went from approximately 30,000 in 1960 to 100,000 in 1970, 350,000 in 1980, and over 500,000 in the 1990s.

8. De la Cadena (1995) has studied how the urban *mistis* of Cuzco, the former capital of Tawantinsuyu, expropriated important symbols of the Inca tradition from the Quechua

peasants. Around 1944, for example, they (re)invented a tradition: the celebration of *Inti Raymi*, the most important religious festival of the imperial epoch. Around the same time, the Real Academia de la Lengua Quechua (Royal Academy of the Quechua Language) was created. It was made up of bilingual mestizo writers and lawyers, according to whom the Quechua spoken by peasants was not pure.

9. The Andean Trapeze extends over the departments of Huancavelica, Ayacucho, Apurímac, Cuzco, and Puno.

10. Galo Ramón notes the contrast with the Ecuadorean case: "Whereas in Peru the process of school expansion took place amid the impetuous emergence of the *clasista* left, in Ecuador it took place amid a powerful process of ethnic revitalization, whose most finished product has been the generation of an alternative, globalizing discourse that discusses the construction of a multinational Ecuador" (1991, 370).

11. In the elections for the 1978 Constituent Assembly, leftist groups attained about 30 percent of the vote, ten times what they had received in the last presidential elections that took place in 1963. In 1980, they formed the United Left (Izquierda Unida) coalition, which, until its division in 1989, constituted itself as the second political force in the country, fluctuating between 25 percent and 30 percent of the national vote.

12. Since the 1950s, terms such as "*cholo*," "*cholo* culture," and "process of cholification" have given rise to an abundant sociological and anthropological literature. In very simple terms, *cholos* are the sons and daughters of Quechuas and Aymaras who have gone to school and who have had an urban experience. On this basis, they are culturally "mestizo" but maintain Indian cultural characteristics that modify and combine with criollo-mestizo or directly transnational traits. In ordinary language, *cholo* can have a pejorative connotation, but it can also convey pride and affection, depending on who is using it and in what context. In recent decades, the term often has been used as a synonym for "Peruvian."

13. In one of the few comparative studies of Peru and Guatemala, Bourque and Warren (1978) noticed rather early how ethnic identities in some Andean communities were being redefined as regional identities. Members of rural land communities ceased to consider themselves Indians and identified themselves as *serranos* (highlanders).

14. In another more recent study, we (Degregori 1996a) saw that people displaced by political violence during the 1980-1993 period who returned to their communities of origin in Ayacucho did not reestablish the old pattern of dispersed households but grouped together in small towns, not only to defend themselves better but also to enjoy basic urban utilities such as running water, electricity, and satellite dish antennas. More recently, the most important communities are leading efforts to transform themselves into municipalities. These efforts may be viewed as state co-optation or as a pragmatic choice, since as municipalities the dwellers can have access to state resources. Though there is some truth to this interpretation, it also seems that the conversion into municipalities might be pursued as representative units to deal with the political structure of the state, allowing residents to go beyond what they might attain as indigenous communities or peasants for the first time without the intermediation of exogenous local powers.

15. A comparison with Mexico illustrates what is meant by "weak hegemony." Florencia Mallon (1995, 282) relates how in 1943 an official of Puebla invited the Indians of Xochiapulco — who had participated in the May 5, 1862, battle against the French invasion — to take part in the parade commemorating this victory. The official from Puebla wrote to a functionary in Xochiapulco and asked him, "If it is possible for you to organize for us a group of [Indian] natives with their typical costumes . . . so that they can come to the city of Puebla this Fifth of May to march in the parade. . . . I beg you let us know, for they will need

to learn how to march correctly...." Mallon points out how the state "created spaces in which previous local history could be remembered" but at the same time "set the discursive boundaries within which such remembering could take place." The people of Xochiapulco even had to learn how to march! In Peru, in contrast, a dance that arose in the Central Andes commemorating the resistance against the Chilean invasion, *Los Avelinos*, spread in Lima without any invitation. It was taken there by migrants from the region. It began to be danced at festivals in the peripheral neighborhoods where these migrants settled, then penetrated into the center of the city as some migrants rose into the middle class. Since the beginning of the 1980s, *Los Avelinos* has even become part of official commemorations, without ever having been standardized from above.

16. See, among others, Cotler (1995) and Stokes (1996).

17. The strong vote for the left in the Andean Trapeze and among migrants in the cities has already been mentioned. In 1978, the leader receiving the most votes for the Constituent Assembly was Hugo Blanco, a Quechua-speaking *cholo* from Cuzco. Through the 1980s, the presidential candidate of the left was Alfonso Barrantes; he won the mayor's office in Lima in 1983 and stressed his provincial highland origin and mestizo features.

18. On the ethnic factor in the 1990 elections, see Degregori (1991).

19. Fujimori also included in his slate two people who can be portrayed as *cholos*. The nominee for the first vice presidency was the president of the National Assembly of University Deans (Asamblea Nacional de Rectores). For the second vice presidency, the president of the Association of Small and Medium Businessmen (Asociación de Pequeños y Medianos Empresarios) was a candidate. Both were individuals of Andean extraction who had become chief representatives of the two pillars undergirding the myth of progress: education and "the other path" of success in the market.

20. Certainly, this tactic was part of a transformative hegemonic strategy (Alonso 1994) in the literal sense of the term. Yet, it is also true that power has to recognize diversity and incorporate it at the symbolic level, even if only subordinately. Beyond symbols, it remains to be seen to what extent this strategy translates into greater social policies or rights in favor of these sectors. *Chullo* is a wool cap with earflaps, very common in the Andes. *Cushma* is a type of gown worn by the Asháninka people of the Amazon.

21. Ethnic hierarchies and racism can erupt into political life in the most unexpected and brutal ways, as occurred during the recent period of political violence in Peru. During the first years of the violence, the old racist reflex flourished within the armed forces, which in 1983-1984 unleashed a genocidal offensive in Ayacucho. Yet, surprisingly, despite the absence of the ethnic theme in its documents, it was in the activity of the Partido Comunista del Peru-Sendero Luminoso (Communist Party of Peru-Shining Path) that this reflex most brutally blossomed. Nevertheless, the violence of Shining Path was not an indigenous violence, but one principally of provincial *misti* sectors who felt they were oppressed and discriminated against by the creole elites of Lima. At the same time, however, they felt themselves to be superior to the indigenous peasants because of their education (Degregori 1996). The Shining Path's violence against the Andean peasantry, especially the Quechua, and against the Asháninkas of the Amazon thus had as its backdrop the ethnic contempt that the *mistis* traditionally felt for the Indians (Coronel 1996).

22. At this time, the Trotskyist Revolutionary Workers Party (Partido Obrero Revolucionario — POR) and the Stalinist Party of the Revolutionary Left (Partido de Izquierda Revolucionaria) were formed. Young officers, for their part, formed nationalist lodges, some of which converged with the MNR years later.

23. *Mallkus* and *jilakatas* are traditional authorities of the *ayllus*. *Tata*, the word for "father" in Quechua, was the nickname the peasants gave President Villaroel as a result of his pro-Indian policy.

24. On a number of occasions throughout its history, indigenous armies laid siege to La Paz, especially during the 1781 Túpac Katari and the 1899 Zarate Willka rebellions. After the latter, Indians were prohibited from circulating freely through the chief plazas and streets of the cities, especially the Plaza Murillo, which was the seat of the governmental palace and other official buildings.

25. The COB was organized during the years following the Chaco War from among mining workers grouped in the Bolivian Workers Union Federation (Federación Sindical de Trabajadores Bolivianos — FSTMB). It was officially formed in 1952.

26. Rivera (1982, 136) recounts how the peasants' trust in the government was so high that when they were warned that troops were approaching on the highway, they believed it was the president's escort and not troops that were about to massacre them.

27. Toward the end of the 1960s, Aymara students in La Paz founded the November 15th Movement (Movimiento 15 de Noviembre), the date of Túpac Katari's execution. Around the same time, the Julián Apaza University Movement (Movimiento Universitario Julián Apaza) emerged in the Universidad San Andrés of La Paz. In 1969, the Mink'a Center for Peasant Advancement and Coordination (Centro de Promoción y Coordinación Campesina Mink'a) was founded. The Center was dedicated to education and organization in rural and urban areas. In 1971, the Centro Campesino Túpac Katari began radio broadcasts and a newspaper in Aymara in La Paz. One of the first acts of the Aymara cultural centers was to erect a monument to Túpac Katari in his birthplace, Ayo-Ayo. The monument was inaugurated in 1970 (Rivera 1982, 127-8).

28. The APRA's rainbow-colored flag was the flag of Tawantinsuyu, and the party's coat of arms was the Condor of Chavín, an emblematic figure drawn from this pre-Hispanic culture (seventh to second century B.C.). During the years of clandestine party activity (1933-1945), the secret safe houses where the leadership hid were generically referred to as Incahuasi, which in Quechua means "house of the Inca."

29. As Klein (1982, 252) notes, "Ultimately made up of some 218 delegates, the Assembly counted only twenty-three representatives of the peasant confederations, as against 123 delegates from the labor unions, of which the FSTMB alone had thirty-eight. It also contained all the major left groupings...." Gonzalo Rojas (in Calla, Pinello, and Urioste 1989, 193) uses the term *brutalmente obrerista* to refer to the Assembly.

30. In Bolivia, new left currents were strongly influenced by the Cuban revolution and the presence and death of Ernesto "Ché" Guevara in Bolivia. The most radicalized criollo-mestizo youth formed groups such as the Army of National Liberation (Ejército de Liberación Nacional — ELN) and the Movement of the Revolutionary Left (Movimiento de Izquierda Revolucionaria — MIR). The Peruvian versions of the MIR and the ELN launched guerrilla *focos* in 1965, but these were rapidly defeated. In the following years, the bulk of the Peruvian "New Left" changed track and to a greater or lesser extent oriented itself toward Maoism. Sendero Luminoso was the most extreme case.

31. The institutions attending were the Centro Campesino Túpac Katari, the Centro Mink'a, the National Association of Peasant Teachers (Asociación Nacional de Profesores Campesinos), the Association of Peasant Students of Bolivia (Asociación de Estudiantes Campesinos de Bolivia), and the Puma Cultural Center (Centro Cultural Puma). The Manifesto was signed amid the ruins of what had been the capital of the first pan-Andean

state, Tiwanaku, between the second and ninth centuries A.D. *Katarismo* was always stronger among the more communitarian Aymara (who were on the frontier of the transformations unleashed by the 1952 Revolution) than among the Quechua (who are more commercial, more individualized, and more inclined to political diversity).

32. Around the same time in Peru, the decisive IVth Congress of the Confederación Campesina de Perú took place, marking the beginning of the accelerated growth of this organization. At the Congress, an orthodox Maoist faction was displaced from the leadership by "new left" groups, who were more flexible ideologically but generally pro-peasant and Maoist with a clear class discourse. Around 1979, a short-lived Federación Aymara arose in Puno (a department bordering on Bolivia) and was stigmatized by the leadership of the CCP as promoting divisions.

33. "See reality with two eyes" is a phrase used by the *katarista* leader Víctor Hugo Cárdenas. In 1993 Cárdenas became vice president of the republic (Albó 1996, 327).

34. These statements were approved at the Second Congress of the CSUTCB in 1983.

35. Events such as the triumph of Alberto Fujimori in 1990 in Peru or the success of the National Confederation of Indians of Ecuador (Confederación Nacional de Indígenas del Ecuador — CONAIE) render Albó's first two reasons insufficient.

36. In his excellent article, Albó (1996, 336) indicates these two points: the *cataro* (purist) character of the *kataristas* and their utopian program in which "the Andean is also the final end" and whites continue being the "other." However, Albó does not make these points to explain the political limits of *katarismo*, but to contrast them with the "hybrid and shifty, character of the so-called *"cholo* parties," which are seen as being "open to all of the typical deceits of criollo politics." The *cholo* parties will be discussed later.

37. On the new territorial division along ethnic lines, see CIPCA (1991). On the Asamblea de las Nacionalidades, see CIPCA (1991); and Calla, Pinelo, and Urioste (1989).

38. Among the factors that facilitate the diffusion of *katarista* ideas, Albó (1996, 329-340) mentions the general crisis of the Left, the rise of new indigenous organizations and new international currents supporting indigenous rights, the appearance of the new *"cholo"* populism, the opening up of the traditional parties to the ethnic issue, and especially the MNR's "half turn." In this article, we adopt three of these factors but approach the last two from a different perspective.

39. On CONDEPA, see Saravia and Sandoval (1991). On UCS, see Mayorga (1991).

40. Both Max Fernández and Carlos Palenque met premature deaths. Fernández died in an air crash in 1996, dealing a harsh blow to the UCS. Palenque died of a heart attack in March 1998, and the leadership of CONDEPA was taken over by Remedios Loza, a party deputy known as "La Chola," who had worked with Palenque on his radio shows.

41. Silvia Rivera (cited in Albó 1996, 336) notes, "It is on the basis of the beer distribution networks, his relationship to ritual and holiday consumption, that Fernández most explicitly articulates the *cholo*-indigenous aspects of his political practice." Albó (1996) points out that Fernández himself gets annoyed at being taken as *cholo*. It is his opponents and political analysts who stressed this connection. For Toranzo (1991), Fernández and, to a certain extent, Palenque represented a *"cholo* bourgeoisie."

42. In Aymara, *Ch'enko* means "bundle, tangle, the variegated made more heterogenous" (translation by Toranzo himself). The *kataristas* tend to take a very hard position regarding identities that lack clearly defined shape. Thus, for example, the Manifiesto

Tiwanaku (Rivera 1982, 133) asserted that education "not only seeks to convert the Indian into a kind of *mestizo*, without definition and personality, it equally seeks to assimilate them to Western, capitalist culture." It is beyond the scope of the present chapter to discuss why this same tension in relation to "intermediary" identities also can be found among many NGOs and academics from the north.

43. Until 1985, the mayors of the departmental capitals were appointed by the executive. Beginning in 1985, mayors were elected in the nine departmental capitals (La Paz, Santa Cruz, Cochabamba, Sucre, Oruro, Potosí, Tarija, Trinidad, and Cobija) and in cities with over 15,000 inhabitants — no more than a dozen in the whole country. Additionally, the municipal jurisdiction of these places ended at the urban city limits. With the Law of Popular Participation, 308 new municipalities were created, many of which were rural, thus also breaking the sharp separation between the rural and the urban (Urioste and Baldomar 1996).

44. The characteristics that follow appear to be valid also for the Ecuadorean case, but the limits of the present work prohibit an in-depth discussion of that country.

# References

Abercombie, Thomas. 1991. "To Be Indian, to Be Bolivian: 'Ethnic' and 'National' Discourses of Identity." In *Nation-States and Indians in Latin America*, eds. Greg Urban and Joel Shrezer. Austin: University of Texas Press.

Adams, Norma, and Néstor Valdivia. 1991. *Los otros empresarios. Ética de migrantes y formación de empresas en Lima*. Lima: IEP.

Adrianzén, Alberto, ed. 1993. *Democracia, etnicidad y violencia en los países andinos*. Lima: IEP/IFEA.

Albó, Xavier. 1994. "And from Kataristas to MNRistas? The Surprising and Bold Alliance Between Aymaras and Neoliberals in Bolivia." In *Indigenous Peoples and Democracy in Latin America*, ed. Donna Lee Van Cott. New York: Inter-American Dialogue/St. Martin's Press.

Albó, Xavier. 1996. "Nación de muchas naciones: nuevas corrientes políticas en Bolivia." In *Democracia y estado multiétnico en América Latina*, eds. Pablo Gonzales and Marcos Roitman. Mexico City: La Jornada Ediciones and Centro de Investigaciones Interdisciplinarias en Ciencias y Humanidades, UNAM.

Alonso, Ana María. 1994. "The Politics of Space, Time and Substance: State Formation, Nationalism, and Ethnicity." *Annual Review of Anthropology* (23): 379-405.

Anderson, Benedict. 1983. *Imagined Communities: Reflections on the Origin and Spread of Nationalism*. New York: Verso.

Bourque, Susan, and Kay Warren. 1978. "Denial and Reaffirmation of Ethnic Identities: A Comparative Examination of Guatemalan and Peruvian Communities." Occasional Papers Series, Program in Latin American Studies, University of Massachusetts at Amherst.

Brysk, Alison. 1994. "Acting Globally: Indian Rights and International Politics in Latin America." In *Indigenous Peoples and Democracy in Latin America*, ed. Donna Lee Van Cott. New York: Inter-American Dialogue/St. Martin's Press.

Calla, Ricardo. 1989. "Apuntes para una lectura crítica de los documentos del I Congreso extraordinario de la CSUTCB." In *CSTUCB: Debate sobre documentos políticos y asamblea de nacionalidades*, eds. Ricardo Calla, José Enrique Pinelo, and Miguel Urioste. La Paz: CEDLA.

Calla, Ricardo, José Enrique Pinelo, and Miguel Urioste, eds. 1989. *CSTUCB: Debate sobre documentos políticos y asamblea de nacionalidades*. La Paz: CEDLA.

CIPCA (Centro de Investigación y Promoción del Campesinado). 1991. *Por una Bolivia diferente: Apuntes para un proyecto histórico popular*. La Paz: CIPCA.

Coronel, José. 1996. "Violencia política y respuestas campesinas en Huanta." In *Las rondas campesinas y la derrota de Sendero Luminoso*, ed. Carlos Iván Degregori. Lima: IEP/UNSCH.

Cotler, Julio. 1994. *Política y sociedad en Perú: Cambios y continuidades*. Lima: IEP.

Dandler, Jorge. 1969. *El sindicalismo campesino en Bolivia: Los cambios estructurales en Ucureña*. Mexico City: Instituto Indigenista Interamericano.

de la Cadena, Marisol. 1995. "Race, Ethnicity and the Struggle for Indigenous Self-Representation (1919-1992)." Ph.D. Dissertation, Department of Anthropology, University of Wisconsin-Madison.

de Soto, Hernando. 1987. *El otro sendero*. Buenos Aires: Sudamericana.

Degregori, Carlos Iván. 1986. "Del mito de Inkarri al 'mito' del progreso. Poblaciones andinas, cultura e identidad nacional." *Socialismo y Participación* (36): 49-56.

Degregori, Carlos Iván. 1990. "La revolución de los manuales. La expansión del marxismo-leninismo en las ciencias sociales y el surgimiento de Sendero Luminoso." *Revista Peruana de Ciencias Sociales* 2 (3): 103-126.

Degregori, Carlos Iván. 1991. "El aprendiz de brujo y el curandero chino. Etnicidad, modernidad y cuidadanía en las elecciones de 1990." In *Elecciones 1990. Demonios y redentores en el nuevo Perú*, eds. Carlos Iván Degregori and Romeo Grompone. Lima: IEP.

Degregori, Carlos Iván. 1993. "Identidad étnica. Movimientos sociales y participación política en el Perú." In *Democracia, etnicidad y violencia en los países andinos*, ed. Alberto Adrianzén. Lima: IEP/IFEA.

Degregori, Carlos Iván. 1996. "Cosechando tempestades. Las rondas campesinas y la derrota de Sendero Luminoso en Ayacucho." In *Las rondas campesinas y la derrota de Sendero Luminoso*, ed. Carlos Iván Degregori. Lima: IEP/UNSCH.

Degregori, Carlos Iván, ed. 1996. *Las rondas campesinas y la derrota de Sendero Luminoso*. Lima: IEP/UNSCH.

Degregori, Carlos Iván, Cecilia Blondet, and Nicolás Lynch. 1986. *Conquistadores de un nuevo mundo. De invasores a ciudadanos en San Martín de Porres*. Lima: IEP.

Domínguez, Jorge, and Abraham Lowenthal, eds. 1996a. *Constructing Democratic Governance: Latin America and the Caribbean in the 1990s, Themes and Issues*. Baltimore: The Johns Hopkins University Press.

Domínguez, Jorge, and Abraham Lowenthal, eds. 1996b. *Constructing Democratic Governance: South America in the 1990s*. Baltimore: The Johns Hopkins University Press.

Escobar, Arturo, and Sonia Álvarez, eds. 1992. *The Making of Social Movements in Latin America: Identity, Strategy and Democracy*. Boulder, Colo.: Westview.

Favre, Henri. 1996. *L'indigénisme*. Paris: Presses Universitaires de France.

Flores Galindo, Alberto. 1987. *Buscando un Inca. Identidad y utopía en los Andes*. Lima: IAA.

Franco, Carlos. 1992. *La otra modernidad. Imágenes de la sociedad peruana*. Lima: CEDEP.

Fuenzalida, Fernando. 1970. "Poder, raza, y etnia en el Perú contemporáneo." In *El indio y el poder en el Perú*, ed. Fernando Fuenzalida. Lima: Moncloa-Campodónico Editores.

Gamarra, Eduardo. 1996. "Bolivia: Managing Democracy in the 1990s." In *Constructing Democratic Governance: South America in the 1990s*, eds. Jorge Domínguez and Abraham Lowenthal. Baltimore: The Johns Hopkins University Press.

García Canclini, Néstor. 1995. *Hybrid Culture: Strategies for Entering and Leaving Modernity*. Minneapolis: University of Minnesota Press.

Golte, Jürgen, and Norma Adams. 1990. *Los Caballos de Troya de los invasores: Estrategias campesinas en la conquista de la Gran Lima*. Lima: IEP.

González Casanova, Pablo, and Marcos Roitman, eds. 1996. *Democracia y estado multiétnico en América Latina*. Mexico City: La Jornada Ediciones/Centro de Investigaciones Interdisciplinarias en Ciencias y Humanidades.

Guerrero, Andrés. 1993. "De sujetos indios a ciudadanos-étnicos: de la manifestación de 1961 al levantamiento indígena de 1990." In *Democracia, etnicidad y violencia política en los países andinos*, ed. Alberto Adrianzén. Lima: IFEA/IEP.

Hobsbawm, Eric, and Terence Ranger. 1984. *The Invention of Tradition*. Cambridge: Cambridge University Press.

Huber, Ludwig. 1995. *"Después de Dios y la Virgen está la ronda." Las rondas campesinas de Piura*. Lima: IEP/IFEA.

Isaacs, Anita. 1996. "Ecuador: Democracy Standing the Test of Time?" In *Constructing Democratic Governance: South America in the 1990s*, eds. Jorge Domínguez and Abraham Lowenthal. Baltimore: The Johns Hopkins University Press.

Klein, Herbert. 1982. *Bolivia: The Evolution of a Multi-ethnic Society*. New York: Oxford University Press.

Mallon, Florencia. 1995. *Peasant and Nation: The Making of Postcolonial Mexico and Peru*. Berkeley, Calif.: University of California Press.

Matos Mar, José. 1984. *Desborde popular y crisis del estado. El nuevo rostro del Perú en la década de 1980*. Lima: IEP.

Mayer, Enrique. 1970. "Mestizo e indio: el contexto social de las relaciones interétnicas." In *El indio y el poder en el Perú*, ed. Fernando Fuenzalida. Lima: IEP.

Mayorga, Fernando, ed. 1991. *Max Fernández: La política del silencio*. La Paz: ILDIS/ Universidad Mayor de San Simón.

Méndez, Cecilia. 1993. *Incas sí, indios no. Apunte para el estudio del nacionalismo criollo en el Perú*. Lima: IEP.

Montoya, Rodrigo. 1992. *Al borde del naufragio. Democracia, violencia y problema étnico en el Perú*. Lima: Sur.

Nugent, Guillermo. 1992. *El laberinto de la choledad*. Lima: Fundación Ebert.

Pinelo, José Enrique. 1989. "Asamblea de nacionalidades." In *CSTUCB: Debate sobre documentos políticos y asamblea de nacionalidades*, eds. Ricardo Calla, José Enrique Pinelo, and Miguel Urioste. La Paz: CEDLA.

Portocarrero, Gonzalo, and Patricia Oliart. 1989. *El Perú desde la escuela*. Lima: IAA.

Quijano, Aníbal. 1980. *Dominación y cultura. Lo cholo y conflicto cultural en el Perú*. Lima: Mosca Azul Editores.

Rivera, Silvia. 1984. *Oprimidos pero no vencidos: Luchas del campesinado Aymara-Quechua 1900-1980*. La Paz: CSUTCB/Hisbol.

Remy, María Isabel. 1994. "The Indigenous Population and the Construction of Democracy in Peru." In *Indigenous Peoples and Democracy in Latin America*, ed. Donna Lee Van Cott. New York: Inter-American Dialogue/St. Martin's Press.

Rowe, John. 1955. "Movimiento nacional inca del siglo XVIII." *Revista Universitaria del Cuzco* (107): 3-33.

Saravia, Joaquín, and Godofredo Sandoval. 1991. *Jach'a uru: ¿la esperanza de un pueblo?* La Paz: ILDIS/CEP.

Selverston, Melina. 1994. "The Politics of Culture: Indigenous Peoples and the State in Ecuador." In *Indigenous Peoples and Democracy in Latin America*, ed. Donna Lee Van Cott. New York: Inter-American Dialogue/St. Martin's Press.

Smith, Carol. 1990. *Guatemalan Indians and the State: 1540-1988*. Austin: University of Texas Press.

Stavenhagen, Rodolfo. 1988. *Derecho indígena y derechos humanos en América Latina.* Mexico City: Instituto Interamericano de Derechos Humanos/El Colegio de México.

Stavenhagen, Rodolfo. 1992. "Challenging the Nation-State in Latin America." *Journal of International Affairs* 34 (2): 418-439.

Steinhauf, Andreas. 1991. "Diferenciación étnica y redes de larga distancia entre migrantes andinos: el caso de Sanka y Colcha." *Boletín del Instituto Francés de Estudios Andinos* 20 (1): 93-114.

Toranzo, Carlos. 1991. "A manera de prólogo: burguesía chola y señorialismo conflictuado." In *Max Fernández: La política del silencio*, ed. Fernando Mayorga. La Paz: ILDIS/ Universidad Mayor de San Simón.

Urban, Greg, and Joel Sherzer, eds. 1991. *Nation-States and Indians in Latin America.* Austin: University of Texas Press.

Urioste, Miguel. 1989. "Provocaciones para continuar la discusión." In *CSTUCB: Debate sobre documentos políticos y asamblea de nacionalidades*, eds. Ricardo Calla, José Enrique Pinelo, and Miguel Urioste. La Paz: CEDLA.

Van Cott, Donna Lee, ed. 1994. *Indigenous Peoples and Democracy in Latin America.* New York: Inter-American Dialogue/St. Martin's Press.

Yashar, Deborah. 1996. "Indigenous Protest and Democracy in Latin America." In *Constructing Democratic Governance: Latin America and the Caribbean in the 1990s, Themes and Issues*, eds. Jorge Domínguez and Abraham Lowenthal. Baltimore: The Johns Hopkins University Press.

# Part III

## Justice, Law, and the Judiciary: Citizenship and Democracy

CHAPTER NINE

# Judicial Reform and Democratization in Latin America

## HUGO FRÜHLING

## INTRODUCTION

Democratic theory is based on the notion that individuals should enjoy a degree of autonomy that is best ensured by being able to participate in the governance of their communities and by freely choosing their representatives. The government that emerges from popular will is a limited government, restrained by procedural checks as well as by the constitutional rights that it must respect (Murphy 1993).

One of the most relevant limitations on governmental power is that which distinguishes between administration and adjudication. The final authority to determine what the law means rests on the judge, who should be independent from the administrator, so as to ensure the impersonal interpretation of legal rules.[1] The distinction between administrators and judges is not only associated with democratic regimes, as it can survive even under very oppressive governments. However, it is a necessary although insufficient condition for democracy, for judges play a key role in upholding constitutional rights and freedoms (Hilbink 1995).

Latin American lawyers would agree that an independent and effective judicial system is a central feature of a democratic society. Yet, the problems of justice and of the state institutions charged with administering it are deep and pervasive in Latin America, and most of the judicial systems in existence are neither independent nor effective. With some exceptions, they have failed to ensure citizens' proper enjoyment of constitutional rights, suffered from political manipulation by both democratic and military governments, and lacked adequate funding to perform their functions efficiently. The political standing of judges vis-à-vis the government has always been very weak.[2] Moreover, time delays and corruption are common in many Latin American judiciaries, and the judicial systems are not accessible to all who want justice done.

Judicial reform depends to a great extent on the functioning of a democratic system. However, some authors have pointed out that political violence has always played a key role in the evolution of Latin American societies, and they have blamed the constant recurrence of authoritarianism and repression both on a prevailing cultural tradition antagonistic to democracy in important sectors of the elite and on the fragility of political pluralism.[3] Thus, this poses the question as to whether the democratic ideal of the rule of law can, in fact, take hold in such a social and cultural context. While an authoritarian political culture is deeply rooted in Latin America, it has been more prevalent in some countries than in others that have enjoyed long periods of democratic stability. Recent events in the region seem hopeful, such as the rise of freely elected civilian governments and the increasing consensus on economic policies, creating environments more favorable to the strengthening of democratic institutions than in the past. This change in the political context has created conditions for a new concern with improving the operation of judicial and legal systems. However, these legal reform efforts still face considerable obstacles.

This chapter examines current efforts to transform the judiciary in Latin America. It explores the factors that have contributed to these efforts as well as the impact they may have for strengthening the rule of law and the improved accountability of political authorities. It posits that these changes are only the beginning of a long process whose success is by no means certain. The first part of this chapter analyzes the problems that Latin American legal and judicial systems have faced since the 1960s, both in terms of advancing economic development and ensuring the right to justice. It gives a brief history of reformist attempts to change the prevailing South American legal culture, looking at the law and development movement of the late 1960s and early 1970s in South America. The second part describes the problems confronted by the judiciary as well as the efforts that began in the early 1980s to reform the judicial systems of the hemisphere. The concluding section analyzes the obstacles that these efforts are meeting, suggesting that progress will be gradual and full of contradictions.

## Socio-legal Reform Attempts During the 1960s and Early 1970s

The advancement of democratization in Latin America calls for very profound legal and social changes to ensure respect for human rights, access to justice, and the accountability of civil and military authorities. As James Holston and Teresa P.R. Caldeira point out in their chapter in this volume, the rule of law, access to justice, and the protection of civil rights are not the automatic by-products of the institutionalization of competitive politics. In order to assess the impact of legal and political reforms that are currently being implemented, as well as their chances for success, I will compare reform attempts made in the 1960s and 1970s with those taking place today. The comparison will begin by describing the issues that were addressed by these reforms, the forces that supported them, and the reasons for their partial successes and failures.

### The Crisis of Law and the Ideal of Modernization

The policies of the most developed Latin American countries from the 1940s onward showed at least some concern for social equality. However, only some of the most egregious forms of social inequality were addressed by government intervention in the market. This situation perpetuated problems of political polarization and unrest. By the end of the 1950s, the symptoms of a social malaise were quite apparent in such major problems as poverty, inflation, and the inherent limitations of primary export economies.

Many social scientists and political leaders defined the process of underdevelopment as one caused by the uneasy coexistence of Western and traditional traits and institutions. In law, there was a juxtaposition of different types of legal life. There was a formal central legal order that imitated foreign models; however, there also was an informal system of customs, values, and codes of procedure that influenced the operation of that legal order, rendering it ineffective (Unger 1976, 228). Even more important than this gap between law and reality was the growth of a body of law that regulated the economy and that showed little concern for the more established methods of legal reasoning, creating conflicts between the law of the lawyers and the law enacted by regulatory agencies. This contradiction stimulated the notion that the legal system was experiencing a crisis; that is, substantial reforms of the legal system were required to foster economic growth and social equality, and it was not just a matter of amending particular areas of the law (Frühling 1984a, 291; Novoa 1965, 229).

In Chile, Eduardo Novoa stressed the notion that there existed a crisis in the legal system. The crisis was the result of a lack of harmony among the system's different components. Novoa stated that the new economic role of the state had resulted in the emergence of law whose principles were contradictory to those embodied in the traditional, individualistic, nineteenth-century codes (Novoa 1965, 230-231). Novoa thought that the lack of concern for the growth of public law shown by jurists was the consequence of training that was excessively concerned with the concepts of private law. Thus, lawyers and, particularly, judges were ill-prepared to systematize and interpret the public legislation enacted after the 1930s or to deal with new collective needs (Novoa 1964, 563-564).

The perception that the legal system was confronting a crisis comprised several elements. The first was the notion that there was a widening gap between law on the books and law in reality. The reality in many countries was that formal law was totally disregarded, which called into question the validity of state-made rules as instruments for economic development. The second element was that there existed serious contradictions between the central legal system inspired by the European codification movement of the nineteenth century and the regulatory rules enacted after the 1930s. The third element was widespread discontent with the Latin American legal education system. During the 1960s and early 1970s, the region underwent significant movements toward the reform of legal education designed to produce lawyers and judges better equipped to deal with global social change.

The ideal of social planning associated with modernization policies created a new demand for specific expertise in planning, accounting, and the drafting of development projects. These skills had been mastered by economists and sociologists but were not taught to law students (Fuenzalida 1977). The movement toward the reform of legal education in Latin America came from the region's own law schools, and it was supported by relatively young law professors and students. Thus, the Conferences of Latin American Law Schools, which addressed the need to promote active and practical teaching, as well the learning of social and economic facts in areas regulated by the legal system, were held in different countries in the region in 1959, 1961, 1963, 1964, and 1965 (Wilson 1989, 393-394).

Another source of support for these changes came from the law and development movement, which was an outgrowth of U.S. assistance to developing countries. U.S. institutions such as law schools, foundations, and government agencies concerned with development in the Third World were involved in this effort (Gardner 1980, 6-12). Substantively for Latin America, the effort consisted of promoting the reform of legal education and initiating an inquiry into the role of law in development.

Law and development scholars saw the U.S. model of the lawyer as a problem solver as particularly useful for developing countries (Lowenstein 1970, 65-74). Therefore, they thought that Latin American lawyers and judges should assume the role of modernizers who would deal with new problems, devise solutions for them within the framework of the law, and see that the appropriate solutions were applied. This view, in turn, encouraged the use of the case method to confront students with the very problems they would face in professional practice (Frühling 1984a, 297-298). The stress on teaching methodology was based upon the model of the lawyer and the judge as social engineers, and it reflected an instrumental conception of the law as open to various interpretations and as a tool to be used for the shaping of new relations and social processes.

Programs to support research and the training of law professors were launched in Costa Rica, Brazil, Chile, Colombia, and Peru. In Colombia, the Association for Reform in the Teaching of Law (Asociación para la Reforma de la Enseñanza del Derecho — ARED) was formed, and in Chile, the Institute of Legal Teaching and Research (Instituto de Docencia e Investigaciones Jurídicas) was created. By the end of 1972, ARED was moribund, and the Instituto de Docencia disappeared after the 1973 coup d'état in Chile. Thus, the movement for reform from within the law schools created a new interest in the analysis of the role of law in society. However, it lost its momentum in a few years, leaving little enduring effect (Wilson 1989, 394).

A few points may be given to explain the reform movement's failure. First, the political context in some of the countries where the new programs were launched was not conducive to the experience. During the second half of the 1970s, Chile, Brazil, Peru, Argentina, and Uruguay experienced political changes and increased repression that ended experiences of social change in which law could play an important role. Second, these reform efforts were largely resisted by the bar and the most established academics of the law schools. Third, it is questionable whether mere changes in legal training could have modified the internal ideology and outlook of lawyers and judges, whose values and practices were also shaped by factors such as the professional market, the internal power structure of the judiciary, and the place of the judiciary within the political system.

# THE LEGAL REFORM MOVEMENT AND THE JUDICIARY

The legal reform movement inspired the first socio-legal studies of the Latin American judiciary (Frühling 1984b; Pásara 1984). Most writings by followers of the movement that referred to judges emphasized the ideological content of their interpretation of the law, distinguishing those judges who showed an innovative approach to interpretation of rules from those who strictly adhered to the textual analysis of the law (Gutiérrez 1973; Pásara 1984). However, apart from a few exceptions, little attention was given to the judiciary as an organization, the principles and rules that governed the exercise of authority within it, its independence from the executive branch, its relationship to politics, and other institutional aspects that defined the ideology of the judges and their approach to the law. Strictly speaking, the reformers of the 1960s and early 1970s put very little effort into working with the judges themselves, given that they had defined law professors as their target group.[4] Thus, for the most part, the impact of their criticism of traditional legal thought never went beyond the academic legal community.

In the 1980s and 1990s, public policies to ensure an independent, impartial, and effective judicial system have become the focus of intellectual and political debate. Judicial reform has gained an important place on the public agenda because the events that took place in Latin America during the 1970s and early 1980s deepened many of the problems that the judiciary had faced for some time. The quality of justice diminished as repression intensified, and equal access to the justice system deteriorated even further. Concern with reforming the judiciary was also the fruit of a convergence of forces and causes, to which I will refer in the following sections.

## The Administration of Justice Reform Efforts

Throughout Latin America, the transition to democratically elected civilian governments made simultaneously with the implementation of free market policies have contributed to current concerns regarding judicial reform. The expansion of democratization, which began in Ecuador during the late 1970s, continued in Peru in 1980, and spread from there to Uruguay, Argentina, Brazil, Paraguay, and Central America, created the conditions for a new concern with improving the judicial system, particularly in those countries where gross and systematic violations of human rights had taken place. The re-establishment of civilian rule focused attention on the judiciary as a safeguard against human rights abuses. As we will see, this process has not been entirely consistent throughout the region.

A second element that explains the new importance of judicial reform on the region's political agenda is the rising pattern of criminal violence in a number of countries such as El Salvador, Colombia, Brazil, Guatemala, and Peru. Increased criminality has created a demand for reforms in the criminal justice system to enhance the investigation and enforcement capabilities of the police, the courts, and prosecutors. This is not an easy task, given that in many of these countries the police have been key participants in criminal acts.

A third and more recent factor to consider is that properly functioning judiciaries are necessary for the economic reforms taking place in Latin America to be successful. A stable institutional environment with institutions that apply the law in a consistent and predictable manner is very important to private investors. Investors' concerns have focused attention on the need to improve the administration of the courts, organize continuing training programs for judges, and provide for alternative dispute resolution mechanisms.

A key factor in the promotion of judicial reform has been the U.S. policy of support for governments willing to build and strengthen democratic institutions. The United States Administration of Justice Program, designed to improve the functioning of judiciaries, government prosecutors, and police, has supported periodic meetings among Latin American legal experts to discuss problems of justice, evaluations of judicial systems by legal and public administration consultants, and training programs for judicial personnel.

During the 1990s, the Inter-American Development Bank (IDB), the Organization of American States, and the World Bank have given their support to judicial reform projects within the context of programs aimed at modernizing the state and promoting development. In April 1998, the *Plan of Action* of the Summit of the Americas II held in Santiago, Chile, called for the establishment of a "judicial studies center" to facilitate training of personnel, information exchange, and technical support.

# LATIN AMERICAN JUDICIARIES

There is a widespread belief throughout Latin America and the international community that some of the basic characteristics of an independent, democratic, and efficient judicial system are missing in many of the countries of the region. Some of the symptoms of judicial malfunctioning include the following: 1) the judiciary has supported or has refrained from restraining the repressive policies of security forces; 2) the criminal justice system is bound by a criminal procedure that is not efficient for the investigation of common crime; 3) the adjudication process is suffering from increasing time delays and uncertainty associated with the anticipated time frame for the decision of cases (Buscaglia and Dakolias 1995, 12); and 4) corruption and public distrust for the judiciary are reaching very high levels.

## The Judiciaries and Human Rights

During the 1970s and part of the 1980s, Latin America experienced a rise in political violence and a deteriorating human rights situation. Military repression reached unprecedented levels in Chile, Argentina, Brazil, Colombia, Guatemala, and El Salvador.

In Chile, after the seizure of power by the military in 1973, the Supreme Court accepted that the adjudication of political cases be transferred to military courts and showed extreme deference toward the authoritarian state by refusing to challenge the emergency legal powers invoked by the government. Despite conclusive proof that human rights abuses were taking place, the courts delayed the investigation of disappearances requested by the church and by relatives of the victims.[5] Only during the latter part of the 1980s did a few judges display more independence in pursuing cases of human rights abuse.[6]

Many analysts see the judiciary's attitude as rooted in the pre-coup era, arguing that it was due to two factors: first, the high level of conflict that existed between President Salvador Allende (1970-1973) and the Supreme Court, which exacerbated the judges' conservatism, and, second, the fact that judges operated within corporate autonomy and did not renew their legal thinking in line with social and political evolution. Thus, they abdicated their duty to interpret and develop the law to uphold democratic principles (Frühling 1984b; Hilbink 1995). A partial consequence of the courts' attitude regarding human rights is the negative perception of the judiciary held by public opinion. For example, a survey among the urban poor in Chile showed that 46.5 percent of those interviewed thought that the judiciary was bad or very bad, 43.5 percent thought it was mediocre, and only 9.1 percent rated it as good or very good (Correa Sutil and Barros Lazaeta 1993, 136).

Guatemala presents an even more extreme case, as the judiciary has sought to remain on the sidelines in the face of decades of military repression. With some exceptions, the judiciary played almost no part in the defense of human rights during the military regimes of the 1980s (Anderson 1989, 9-10). Over the same period of time, its legitimacy to adjudicate legal disputes in other areas of the law was considerably weakened, rendering it virtually ineffective. Only with the September 1996 signing of the "Accord on the Strengthening of Civilian Power and the Role of the Army in a Democratic Society," as part of the Guatemalan peace accords, did provisions emerge to reform the judicial system and eliminate pervasive impunity (Jonas 1998, forthcoming).

As Holston and Caldeira indicate in their chapter on Brazil, the delegitimation of the justice system that has taken shape in that country is partly due to the fact that the judicial system is not seen by working class people as a reliable resource to defend them against abuses by the police and other public officials. Thus, the feeling that the judiciary has not been a forceful defender of human rights is widely shared by many in Latin American societies, weakening its legitimacy and that of the rule of law.

## The Criminal Justice System and Its Response to Common Crime

During the past decade, common crime — as expressed by rampant street crime, narcotrafficking, and corruption — has become an important issue in most Latin American countries. The sources of this phenomenon are many.

Common crime has increased after the end of civil strife in El Salvador and Nicaragua due to the demobilization of military and guerrilla personnel who lacked the training for civilian life and who began to earn their living through criminal acts. It was within this social context that the Peace Accord between the government of El Salvador and the Farabundo Martí National Liberation Front (Frente Farabundo Martí para la Liberación Nacional — FMLN) addressed judicial reforms as well as the organization of a new civil police force to protect human rights and investigate criminal actions (Popkin 1994; Costa 1994).

In other cases, such as Colombia by the end of the 1980s, the social order itself was threatened by the increase of crime and by changes in the type of criminality, which became more organized and violent. The criminal justice system was simply unable to deal with the situation. As early as June 1982, 1,397,800 cases were pending before the courts, which amounted to an 85 percent increase in cases since 1971 (Instituto SER de Investigación 1983).

Even in Chile, where violent crime was less prevalent, the main concern of the population, as measured by different surveys, became the rise in street crimes, as well as the increase in drug trafficking and drug consumption. In 1989, the Carabineros (police) had recorded 1,556 crimes per 100,000 inhabitants; in 1990, 1,681; and by 1991, the crime rate had risen to 1,711. Most remarkable was the increase in assaults with firearms reported to the police (Blanco and Frühling 1995).

Many Latin American justice systems are not able to confront such crime situations because they share a number of common weaknesses. The justice systems' agencies lack the resources and the motivation to conduct criminal investigations. At times, they are not sufficiently independent from the military. Lack of technical competence is a problem in the police forces. Prosecution mechanisms are inadequate because the office of the prosecutor does not exist or has little impact on the delivery of justice. Additionally, the criminal procedure is formalistic and written with almost no opportunity for oral hearings, cross examination of witnesses, and the like.

In response to this situation, several countries, such as Guatemala, Peru, and Ecuador, have drafted new codes of criminal procedure, and a similar process is underway in Chile. These new codes are introducing oral and adversary proceedings into the criminal justice system. Public trials and adversary proceedings are faster than procedures under the old codes, and they ensure the direct participation of the judge in proceedings that in Latin America usually are delegated to administrative officers of the courts. The publicity surrounding the trial strengthens the accountability of the judges, and the procedure itself is more efficient in controlling and discovering false testimonies, since it allows for the cross-examination of witnesses (Maier 1993; Binder 1993). Even more important, the adversary system ensures that a real trial takes place, in which the accused has full access to the evidence gathered by the police, and all the rights of the defense are fully guaranteed.[7]

## Economic Reform, Corruption, and Timely Adjudication

Latin America is experiencing an important socioeconomic transformation that is affecting cultural values, patterns of political and social conflict, the role of the state, and the place of the judiciary in society (Calderón and Dos Santos 1991).

From 1930 onward, the state played a major role in the economic development of the region, establishing high import tariffs to protect national entrepreneurs, fixing prices, subsidizing certain products, and discouraging the production of others. This had a strong impact upon the regulation of important social and legal conflicts, which, in many cases, were resolved by administrative and political officers and did not reach the courts.[8] Important labor conflicts were mediated by the government, land invasions rapidly evolved into political rather than legal conflicts, and diffuse interests, such as those of consumers, were defended by regulatory agencies. In a society of this kind, access to administrative agencies was more relevant than access to the courts. Naturally, this is a generalization, for the data show that the case load of the courts expanded quite rapidly during this period. However, most of the cases dealt with particular limited matters, such as the recovery of bad debts and criminal prosecution for robbery, assault, and battery (Pérez Perdomo 1993, 140-141).

Recent economic changes have tended to reverse this reality. New policies generally pursue the opening of internal markets, the expansion of the role of the market, the lessening of the influence of administration in the allocation of economic benefits to different parties, and an increase in the importance of external markets for internal producers. Rogelio Pérez Perdomo (1993) and Carlos Peña (1994) point out that these changes will tend to result in more complex and more numerous demands for judicial adjudication. More numerous transnational legal transactions necessarily will result in more complex cases being adjudicated by the courts, even if the parties write arbitration clauses into their contracts. Pérez Perdomo also points out that increased transnational business transactions have resulted in an explosion of new suits being filed before the courts in countries such as the United States and Spain (Pérez Perdomo 1993, 146).

The emergence and growth of markets is a complex process requiring that legal rights be enforced in a consistent, objective manner, within reasonable lengths of time, and by institutions that are accessible to the parties in conflict (Buscaglia and Dakolias 1995, 6-7). A court system affected by excessive delays, whose personnel is corrupt or incompetent, injects an additional element of uncertainty into economic transactions. Unfortunately, the quality of justice in the region is perceived to be very poor. In the 1994 *World Competitiveness Report*, for example, which provided a comparison of public confidence in the judicial systems of 35 countries, all of the listed Latin American countries, with the exception of Chile, ranked in the bottom 20 percent of the confidence index ranking (World Economic Forum 1994).

The belief that the judiciary is not effective or honest is also reflected in national public opinion polls (with the exception of those in Costa Rica). In the case of Peru, after the 1992 governmental intervention in the judicial branch, 95 percent of the people interviewed stated that they agreed with such a reorganization. A public poll taken in August 1992 in Buenos Aires reported the following results: 23 percent of the people surveyed thought that there were many cases of corruption among judges, 43 percent thought corruption existed in a good number of cases, 24 percent said it occurred in just a few cases, and only 2 percent responded "none" (Garrido 1994, 77). Further, time delays seem to be increasing within Latin American justice systems. For example, the 1993 median times for settlements within civil jurisdictions in Argentina, Ecuador, and Venezuela were 2.5, 1.9, and 2.4 years, respectively (Buscaglia and Dakolias 1995, 13). In this context, the growth of market economies is a source of pressure for undertaking the reform of judicial institutions.

# THE ACTORS THAT SUPPORT JUDICIAL REFORM

## International Support

International support for judicial reform in Latin America originated in the United States. Despite initial distrust of democratic development assistance, the Ronald Reagan administration launched a number of political development projects in the early 1980s. These programs included an extensive judicial assistance program, called the Administration of Justice Program, that became the main recipient of development funding.[9]

This program was carried out by the United States Agency for International Development (USAID), the State Department, the Justice Department, and the U.S. Information Agency. The main emphasis was on assistance to Latin American courts, judges, prosecutors, and law commissions to improve the administration of justice, particularly criminal justice. A secondary component of the program was assistance to police forces in Latin America for skill development in criminal investigations.

Initially, the Administration of Justice Program focused on El Salvador as an immediate response to denunciations of the Reagan administration by congressional Democrats for not pressing El Salvador to bring right-wing criminals to justice. The State Department responded with the idea of an assistance program for the judiciary in that country. The growth of USAID activities in the area of judicial reform in Central America was the target of criticism, as many within and outside the United States questioned whether some of the governments being assisted were in fact democratic and whether they had the will to prosecute human rights violations and establish the rule of law. In fact, technical assistance to judiciaries that sidestepped any serious response to governmental terror and to police forces that committed many of the crimes that they were supposedly investigating was doomed to fail.[10]

However, after a peace accord was reached in El Salvador and a new police force was created, the debate over the program subsided. Under President George Bush, the Administration of Justice Program in Latin America expanded to approximately US$40 million per year. The emphasis on regional projects diminished and was replaced by bilateral agreements that provided for assistance to individual justice ministries, courts, and non-governmental organizations (NGOs) working on judicial reform. In 1985, USAID established the Regional Administration of Justice Project, based in Costa Rica at the United Nations Institute for the Prevention of Crime and Treatment of Offenders (ILANUD). ILANUD offered assistance to the judicial systems of Central America, including training courses for judges and technical assistance on issues such as judicial administration, case management, and legal databases.

In 1986, project funding was increased to support programs in Guatemala, Bolivia, Colombia, Peru, Ecuador, and Venezuela. Funding was provided for assessments of the judicial sector, research, training programs, grants to both Latin American and U.S.-based organizations, and other activities (WOLA 1990, 12). The new program had definite differences from the law and development movement of the 1960s and 1970s. It was addressed to state institutions, for the most part, within the judiciary. The non-governmental sector was called upon to provide technical assistance in this effort, but it was not the target of the program.

As a consequence of this new approach, one of the themes of the judicial reform program was the improvement of the administrative capabilities of the court system. This included handling of case load, keeping a sound statistical system, planning adequate responses to the increasing flux of cases, and maintaining adequate databases on the evolution of the cases. The reasoning behind this concern with administrative management was that substantive changes of the law could not be sustained by an inefficient court administrative structure (Davis 1993, 203-212). A second aspect emphasized by the program was the institutionalization of training for magistrates and administrative personnel. While no model of training was specifically advocated, one essential component was the teaching of skills needed to handle the administration of the courts.[11]

Within the context of judicial reform programs, concern with devising alternative dispute settlement methods outside the judiciary has grown. The rationales for such new interest include the need to divert conflicts from the judiciary that can be solved by methods other than formal adjudication and the fact that many minor conflicts could be resolved more efficiently by methods other than adjudication (Pérez Perdomo 1994). For instance, in Colombia, as a net result of the need to reduce the burden of the courts, the settlement of a number of legal conflicts was transferred from the court system to administrative agencies. At the same time, centers for conciliation and arbitration were created by several social organizations (Giraldo 1994).

In recent years, the reform of the justice system has also become part of the agenda of multilateral organizations, such as the IDB and World Bank. In the mid-1990s, the IDB strongly emphasized that the process of economic reform through-out Latin America also required the reform of the state. A new state was needed, one capable of analyzing, devising, and implementing the new, market-oriented economic policies and at the same time capable of controlling and supervising those business areas that had been deregulated not long before.[12] According to IDB President Enrique Iglesias, such state reforms would not succeed if the new legal norms were not efficiently applied by an independent judiciary. An agenda for change in the judiciary required that four main areas be addressed: 1) the efficient management of the court system; 2) the training of judges and maintenance of respect for the professional career; 3) new issues that demand judicial action (prevention of crime, protection of the family, women's rights, and so on); and 4) the relationship between law and the globalization of the economic system, which implies changes in international economic law and its application by the judiciary (Iglesias 1993, 10-11).

Pursuant to this policy statement, the IDB has supported the development of conciliation and arbitration mechanisms to resolve foreign investment and financial disputes and has supported projects aimed at the improvement of administrative management in the judicial system (Martínez 1993). The World Bank has also funded some projects designed to strengthen the judicial sector in Venezuela and Argentina and is supporting judicial training in Peru.

Two points seem to explain the new interest in judicial reform within international organizations. First, it is increasingly clear that national development depends on a stable and legitimate system of government, which includes an independent judiciary. Second, in the context of liberalizing market economies, economic growth depends on the establishment of a predictable and reliable legal system.

## Domestic Support

Judicial reform efforts are closely connected to the strengthening of civilian rule and of constitutional government that have taken place within the hemisphere in recent years. This process has lent credibility to the reform efforts and has meant that proper drafts of legislation have been submitted to congresses. Moreover, democratization has eased the way for international cooperation with the countries that have begun the transition to civilian rule.

In the case of Chile, the judicial reform package presented to Congress by the Patricio Aylwin administration was based on the implicit view that the courts had done very little to investigate human rights violations during the military government, despite the courts' not having suffered a massive political intervention, as had taken place in other countries.[13] President Aylwin's proposals were designed to reduce the corporatist and isolated outlook of the Supreme Court by creating a National Council of Justice with representatives from the Supreme Court, the Courts of Appeals, the Senate, the President, and representatives from law schools. The Council would set standards for nomination and promotion, formulate judicial policy, and be responsible for the administrative management of the judiciary. The purpose of this reform was to create a plural institution, composed of people with different legal and political views and independent from the executive branch, which would be in charge of proposing policies to address the judicial needs of the country. The new Aylwin government also proposed a reform of criminal procedures and the establishment of a judicial school, among other projects (Verdugo 1992). The proposal to create the Council of Justice was not passed by Congress, while some of the others, such as the creation of a judicial school to train judges, were passed after long debate.

Though Colombia did not endure a military government, congressional approval of a new Constitution in 1991, which strengthened a consensus on the political system and ended the monopoly of all political power by the two traditional parties, had an important impact upon the reformist agenda (Dugas 1993). The new Constitution created the Public Prosecutors' Office (Fiscalía General de la Nación), in charge of investigating all crimes; it recognized the participation of administrative authorities, as well as lay people, in the settlement of legal disputes; it reinforced the economic and administrative autonomy of the judiciary; and it created a new public organization, Defensoría de Derechos Humanos, charged with investigating human rights abuses (Giraldo 1994).

The peace accords reached in Central America have given new force to the ideas of judicial reform, as they have focused new attention on the need to establish a functioning system of law (Hernández 1993). The expansion of democratization has also created a new concern with political corruption and governmental account-ability among Central American countries, reinforcing the movement for judicial reform in the region (Weyland 1993).

The political process is not the only internal force that puts the reform of the judiciary on the public agenda. Another is the impacts that free market economics and the full integration of Latin American economies into the world market are having upon the demands placed on the judiciary. Grappling with these changes is fueling justice system reform in the region, because for the first time leaders of certain business sectors of countries such as Colombia, Venezuela, and Mexico are advocating reform.[14] However, these reformist leaders are by no means representa-tive of the entire region's business sectors, some of whom might well continue to benefit from the state's discretionary practices.

Thus, a varied constituency for judicial reform is defending it as a result of the combination of political liberalization processes, internationally funded justice reform projects, and socioeconomic integration into the global economy. The coalition includes defenders of human rights and the rule of law who perceive the need for a strong and independent judiciary; businesspeople and members of the bar concerned with the institutional weaknesses of the judiciary and the need to establish alternative dispute settlement mechanisms; and a sizable number of politicians who are aware that an inefficient or corrupt legal system is unable to enforce the law, which undermines political legitimacy.

However, judicial reform entails costs for groups that continue to gain from the present situation. Therefore, the questions remain: What kind of reform can this be, and what are the obstacles that such a reform effort must surmount before it can succeed?

# THE OBSTACLES FACED BY JUDICIAL REFORM EFFORTS

Some recent evaluations of the return to civilian government in the region have pointed out that this has been a return to minimalist democracy, as the transition to elected government has not eliminated the existing impediments to consolidating civilian-controlled constitutional democracy.[15] Even if one is less pessimistic, it is clear that in the Latin American tradition, judicial branches have lacked constitu-tional clout — this will not change overnight (Frühling 1993). A more independent judiciary with budget autonomy might also be opposed by executives and legisla-tors who may have less ability to control judicial activities. Thus, building judicial branches that are willing and able to uphold the rule of law requires some fundamental changes in the relationship between the judiciary and the rest of the political system. Such changes are not easy to achieve in the present situation and will require a long evolution, along with considerable thought and political debate.

A second consideration is that judicial reform requires much more than simply changing legal procedures and focusing on archaic judicial structures.

Judges require the collaboration of several other state institutions to proceed with their work quickly and efficiently. They need the collaboration of the police, political authorities, and forensic institutions, to name just a few. Thus, judicial change involves the reform of other parts of the state apparatus that might be even more reluctant than judges to change their values and approaches.

Third, many of the critics of the present state of affairs point out that a more active judicial approach to legal conflicts, embedded in the defense of human rights, in which the courts protect the rights of minorities and disadvantaged groups is required. However, it is not clear whether such a role will be supported by all reformers and whether the courts of many countries enjoy the legitimacy required to undertake a critical interpretation of rules passed by their legislatures. An additional concern is that a socially oriented interpretation and application of the law needs the active participation of a society willing to explore new legal strategies in order to hold large political and economic interests accountable. A passive populace, lack of knowledge of their rights, or other barriers to the access to justice might prevent this from happening.

Thus, reform strategies will probably have to proceed slowly to forge coalitions needed for change. This means that justice system reform is a long-term goal that must be achieved in societies whose politicians usually work in a world of short-term policy.

## The Place of the Judicial Branch within the Political System

Historically, the relationship between the courts and the political system has developed in ways that have weakened the courts. In many Latin American countries, the courts have had no real independence from political power. This lack of independence may be a by-product of the long historical tradition of political instability, which has nearly always ended by undermining the career continuity of judges. A few examples might support this view. In Argentina in 1946, a Juan Perón-dominated Congress impeached all but one of the members of the Supreme Court. In 1957, following President Perón's ouster, the new provisional government cashiered the entire Supreme Court, an action that was repeated in 1966. In 1973, when a return to civilian government took place, the entire Supreme Court resigned (Rosenn 1974). Similar forms of intervention occurred under the military government that assumed power in 1976. In Peru, three political interventions of the government in the judiciary have taken place since 1968. In April 1992, President Alberto Fujimori suspended all judicial activities for 10 days. Claiming that the judiciary was corrupt and politically infiltrated, he fired members of the Supreme Court, members of the National Council of the Magistracy (Consejo Nacional de la Magistratura), the National Criminal Prosecutor, members of the Courts of Appeal, judges, and other judicial officers (Zolezzi Ibárcena 1994). In April 1993, a newly elected Congress appointed five people to screen candidates who would occupy all vacant positions (De Trazegnies 1994).

In past decades, governments favoring recent political and economic reforms have intervened in the courts to ensure that their policies are implemented. For example, in 1990, President Carlos Menem of Argentina ensured majority support in the Supreme Court through the addition of four members to stop challenges to market reforms his administration introduced in Congress. Thus, political expediency continues to undermine the constitutional autonomy of the courts even under elected governments.

Chile traditionally has been an alternative model of relations between politics and the judicial branch. The 1925 Constitution established judicial professionalism through an agreement among the political parties that judicial power must not be politicized. This agreement influenced the Chilean judiciary in two different ways: it allowed the judiciary to develop internal autonomy, which favored the weight of superior courts and their hierarchic principles, but it also implied a relative marginalization of the judges vis-à-vis the course of social life. In Chile, the political stability between 1932 and 1973 helped crystallize a traditional, conservative judicial ideology marked by judges who perceived themselves as merely applying the law. The public considered judges to be relatively irrelevant until the political crisis of 1973 erupted (Peña 1994b).

As a consequence of political dependence or an excessively bureaucratic career pattern, Latin American judicial branches have been reluctant to build a constitutional jurisprudence that would augment their influence. This situation has resulted in judicial branches that, except in Costa Rica, have traditionally been understaffed and underfunded. For example, in Colombia, the budget of the judicial branch was 4 to 4.5 percent of the annual national budget in the years 1982-1984. Over the next decade, it diminished to 1.5 percent of the total budget (Giraldo 1994). In Chile, the budget of the judicial branch was never larger than 0.2 percent of the total national budget between 1977 and 1989 (Peña 1994b). In Peru, the judicial branch received an average of 0.48 percent of the national budget between 1965 and 1990 (Zolezzi 1994).

The reform of the judiciary must address its weak role within the political system, a circumstance that has many different causes. Certainly, a fundamental cause is the judiciary's lack of real independence from partisan politics and government in societies for which a truly democratic government is more a goal than a reality. The organizational and financial deficiencies noted earlier also affect the status of the institution, which is unable to respond to the existing demands for justice. Another cause of the judiciary's weakness is the bureaucratic and hierarchical organization of the judicial branch in Latin America, in which judges lack the necessary autonomy from their superiors. This model encourages conformity among judges to the jurisprudencial thought of the higher courts and discourages originality and self-improvement, contributing to the consolidation of a judicial branch composed of bureaucrats fearful of the power that the Supreme Court, the government, or the army holds over their promotions (Zaffaroni 1993).

Therefore, some authors have pointed out that an agenda for the modification of the present role of the judicial branch in Latin America requires that at least the following five issues be addressed:

- The formal independence of the judiciary should be ensured through budget autonomy and a more transparent judicial appointment process. All judicial positions should be filled through a public system where all candidates are evaluated on their merits.

- Internal governance and administration of the courts should be granted to a council composed of a majority of judges, in combination with a minority of law professors selected by the Congress, so that the council is not monopolized by the Supreme Court or influenced by the government. This would prevent both an extreme isolation from politics and political intervention in the careers of judges.

- Legal training for judges and court officers would enhance the value of their human capital by increasing their professional qualifications.

- The budget for the judiciary should be increased.

- Access to justice for all people should be guaranteed.

This reform agenda will probably be opposed by many, including some politicians and other power holders — the military in some cases — who have enjoyed the loyalty of the judges whose appointments they supported and the Supreme Court judges who will not willingly accept the reallocation of all their administrative and disciplinary powers over the court system to a different organization. Also, many judges may feel that a system of appointments based exclusively on merit could disrupt the stability of their careers. Such an agenda would require changes in budget priorities that could be resisted by some government officials.

## The Reform of the Judicial System as a Whole

The judicial system as a whole involves much more than the court system and the codes of civil and criminal procedure that dictate the legal steps of adjudication. The functioning of the courts is intrinsically related to auxiliary organs such as the public prosecutor's office, the police, forensic offices, and the penitentiary system. A properly functioning court system should also ensure that an efficient public defense system exists to protect the rights of those who cannot afford to hire lawyers. Modern civil and criminal laws should be in place and be applied by the courts.

Recently, a German legal expert who visited Chile estimated that reform of the Chilean criminal justice system would take 15 years. Among the necessary tasks recommended were replacement of the Penal Code, new legislation dealing with the criminal responsibility of minors, creation of an Office of the Public Prosecutor, and retraining of the police to collaborate more fully with the judiciary and to respect civil rights (*El Mercurio*, March 29, 1995, C15). A Chilean analysis of 100 cases of robbery and larceny showed that the time the police took in complying with the orders of the criminal judges had an important influence on judicial delays. In 77.4 percent of the cases, the police took between one and four months before verifying and informing the court that the crime being investigated had actually taken place (Barros et al. 1994). With respect to orders to capture people free on bail who had been sentenced, the results were equally disturbing: In 54.2 percent of the cases, these people could not be found by the police. In most Latin American countries, the police are attached to the Ministry of the Interior or the Ministry of Defense. Therefore, judges have very little influence on the case management procedures that the police follow, on the allocation of available time for different cases, or even on the control of corruption within the institution.

The coordination of police efforts is always a difficult task for the civil authority assigned to that task. In the case of Colombia, the public prosecutor's office has its own police force that attempts to coordinate and direct the other police forces when investigating crimes. However, in a November 1994 interview, the public prosecutor told me that his office lacked the administrative capability to implement such coordination. The task of controlling and directing police efforts becomes all the more difficult when there are multiple police forces that share some overlapping tasks, are directed by different authorities, and tend to compete for the same resources. In Colombia, for instance, crimes can be investigated by the National Police, which is overseen by the Minister of Defense; by the Technical Corps of Investigation, which is part of the public prosecutor's office; or by the Administrative Security Department (DAS), which is attached to the presidency. In Chile, the Carabineros and the Policía de Investigaciones are overseen by the Minister of Defense; Investigaciones is subject to civil jurisdiction, and the Carabineros are subject to military courts.

In many Latin American countries, the level of crime is such that the army directly participates in the repression of common crime, which renders judicial control over criminal investigations even more difficult. Of course, this also shows that there is no coherent and efficient civilian strategy to eradicate crime from the streets.

As shown by the Colombian experience, any reform of existing criminal justice systems might result in important improvements in the present situation.[16] However, without full police collaboration with the judiciary and complete respect for the rights of the accused, a truly adversarial justice system will not be possible. Again, it is clear that judicial reform necessarily involves reform efforts in other public institutions, without which the success of judicial reforms cannot be more than partial.

## The Judiciary in Democracy

In a democracy, judges play a key role in upholding constitutional law and principles, and, for this reason, they should be independent from governmental interference. However, judges have their own beliefs that affect their decisions. Judges face the need to judge in accordance with certain values. In most democratic societies, a critical, activist role of the courts is accepted by politicians and theorists alike. This is not so in Latin America, where a trend toward a more explicitly political role for the judiciary might be opposed even by those who favor certain judicial reforms.

The issue of the social and political role of judges in a democracy is important to the process of advancing judicial reform. Some groups will simply advocate bureaucratic rationalization and better legal training for the judges, hoping to confine the reforms to the areas of corporate law and civil litigation, while others will press for a judicial system concerned with the protection and development of democratic citizenship. The debate over these rival viewpoints will be an important factor in decisions about the pace and extent of the reforms to be implemented.

## *The Impact of Access to Justice on Institutional Change*

The actual functioning of Latin American legal systems depends not only on legal and institutional reform, but also on access to justice. Only if the system is accessible to all those who want justice and if the legal system is used to make the rights of ordinary people real is the machinery of justice likely to establish its legitimacy. Until now, most people have tended to avoid legal conflicts, for the barriers to effective justice are too high. Thus, the judiciary is not fully used as an effective channel for addressing social and legal grievances.

Among the barriers to justice that should be overcome in Latin American legal systems are the costs in terms of money and time involved in litigation and the relative capacities of the parties involved in litigation (Cappelletti and Bryant 1978). The main costs involved in litigation are attorneys' fees and the time required to obtain an enforceable judicial decision. In Latin America, the poor can obtain only very deficient legal assistance, which in criminal cases amounts to almost none (Barros et al. 1994). Some parties possess considerable financial resources that can be utilized in litigation that give them substantial advantages in defending claims. No reform to the justice system can be complete without real improvement in the legal assistance programs supported by the state. During the 1970s and 1980s, innovative legal assistance organized by NGOs emerged throughout Latin America, aimed at promoting legal, economic, and political changes in the region (Thome 1983; Rojas 1986). However, recent decreases in international funding for these services have weakened their institutional presence, especially in the Southern Cone. At the same time, the cost in terms of time involved in litigation is especially high in countries whose judicial systems are overloaded with cases they are incapable of handling expeditiously.

A second major obstacle to justice is the fact that certain parties enjoy advantages that are not shared by weaker parties. These advantages consist of knowledge of their enforceable legal rights. This is a barrier that is extremely serious for the poor, but it also confronts the majority of the population. Many people may not recognize that a legal right exists, and they may lack knowledge regarding the actual workings of the legal system.

A more intense use of the judiciary for claiming legal rights seems essential to the promotion of a functioning democratic legal system. If the barriers to access to justice remain too high, this goal will be delayed, notwithstanding other reforms that may be implemented. This suggests that institutional reforms of the judicial branch must be complemented with a more energetic mobilization of the law by those who seek justice and the public accountability of elected authorities.

## CONCLUSION

For the first time in decades, Latin America is experiencing the emergence of a relatively strong movement toward judicial reform. The forces that have combined to advocate these changes are diverse, including defenders of human rights and of the rule of law who were critical of previous authoritarian governments, foreign governments, and international institutions interested in the maintenance of internal order and economic stability, and local businesspeople concerned with the inadequacies of national legal systems in the face of global integration.

So far, the judicial reform movement's members have agreed on a number of reforms, although some differences remain among its supporters.[17] Themes addressed through these efforts are 1) the improvement of the administrative capabilities of the judicial branch to reduce inefficiency, case delays, and corruption; 2) the promotion of judicial training centers to convince judges of the need for reform and to teach them administrative as well as legal skills for their profession; 3) the introduction of oral and adversary criminal procedures in the criminal justice system, so as to increase the percentage of convictions while improving the enjoyment of human rights by the accused; and 4) the implementation and promotion of alternative dispute settlement procedures aimed at diverting from the judiciary those conflicts that could be best resolved by methods other than formal adjudication.

The implementation of these changes truly could mean an improvement in the quality of recently installed democratic systems, as they might create a more active and open judicial branch. However, the difficulties of the task are inescapable. First, the real reform of the judiciary requires changing the place of the judiciary within Latin American political systems. The judiciaries have lacked political independence from the government or from the parties or have been composed of judges who lack the independence from their superiors needed to apply creative principles in the interpretation of the law. Second, the reform of the judicial system involves the reform of other public institutions, such as the police, without which legal amendments will be mainly cosmetic. Third, the development of a strong and autonomous judicial branch requires a social agreement on the proper role of the judiciary in a democracy. Fourth, most of what will happen within the judicial branch will depend upon the existence of active non-governmental groups willing to use the law to defend civil rights and enforce legal claims.

The reasons for the emergence of this new movement are quite clear. The judicial reform movement has arisen through a combination of international and national concerns, among which may be included a long-standing dissatisfaction with the judiciary; the impact of political democratization, which has resulted in reform initiatives being sent to the congresses of several countries; the far-reaching processes of economic liberalization and market reform, which have created the need for legal structures in support of transparency and accountability; and sustained international interest in these political and economic reforms, which has resulted in increased funding for their study and implementation. Yet, everything seems to suggest that institutional changes will be gradual and slow in coming and that the most extensive reforms are to be expected in countries where a high degree of effective governance is evident, market reforms are in place, and the legal system is used effectively to defend the disadvantaged.

# Notes

1. Even an authoritarian view of the rule of law requires the differentiations of the procedures of legislation, administration, and adjudication. In the democratic ideal of the rule of law, however, each person must participate in the law-making process, and the main role of the judges becomes protecting constitutional rights. See Roberto Mangabeira Unger, 1976, *Law in Modern Society: Towards a Criticism of Social Theory* (New York: The Free Press), 54, 176-178.

2. For a comparative analysis of the judiciary in Latin America, see Jorge Correa, ed., 1994, *Situación y políticas judiciales en América Latina* (Santiago: Escuela de Derecho, Universidad Diego Portales); Rogelio Pérez Perdomo, 1987, "La administración de justicia en Venezuela: evaluación y alternativas," *Revista de Derecho Privado*, 2-4; Luis Pásara, 1984, "Perú: administración de ¿justicia?" in Javier de Belaúnde, ed., *La administración de justicia en América Latina* (Lima: Consejo Latinoamericano de Derecho y Desarrollo); Keith Rosenn, 1987, "The Protection of Judicial Independence in Latin America," *Interamerican Law Review* 19(1): 1-35; and Joel G. Verner, 1984, "The Independence of the Supreme Court in Latin America: A Review of the Literature," *Journal of Latin American Studies* 16: 463-506.

3. Some authors have interpreted the recurrence of human rights violations as the by-product of an authoritarian political culture. See Howard J. Wiarda, ed., 1982, *Politics and Social Change in Latin America: The Distinct Tradition* (Amherst, Mass.: University of Massachusetts Press). Brian Loveman has stressed the fact that the constitutional foundations for repression and intolerance are still present in most Latin American nations. See Brian Loveman, 1993, *The Constitution of Tyranny. Regimes of Exception in Spanish America* (Pittsburgh: University of Pittsburgh Press).

4. A clear exception took place in Peru, where a Commission of Judicial Reform was created in 1975, which organized training seminars for judges in collaboration with the Latin American Council for Law and Development.

5. For a good account of the human rights situation in Chile, see Organización de los Estados Americanos (OEA), Comisión Interamericana de Derechos Humanos, 1985, *Informe sobre la situación de los derechos humanos en Chile* (Washington, D.C.: OAS).

6. One such case was that of Judge Carlos Cerda, who conducted an investigation into the disappearance of 12 communist leaders in 1976. He charged 38 members of the armed forces and carabineros. Ultimately, the case was closed by the Supreme Court, which applied an amnesty law enacted by the military junta in 1978.

7. Alberto Binder, 1994, "La reforma procesal penal en América Latina," in Corporación de Promoción Universitaria y Fundación Paz Ciudadana, "Proyecto para la Reforma del Procedimiento Penal Chileno" (Santiago: Corporación de Promoción Universitaria), 36-67. A recent Chilean study in which 100 judicial files were examined shows that most of the people charged with a crime were finally found guilty and their appeals rejected. See Luis Barros, Hugo Frühling, Gonzalo García, Augusto Quintana, and Domingo Sánchez, 1994,

"El proceso penal chileno y su protección de los derechos del imputado," in *Proceso penal y derechos fundamentales* (Santiago: Corporación Nacional de Reparación).

8. For an analysis of the operation of the legal system under a Latin American regulatory state, see Hugo Frühling, 1984, *Law in Society*. For a comparative analysis with the present-day situation, see Carlos Peña González, 1994, "América Latina: ¿una justicia emergente?" in *Boletín Comisión Andina de Juristas* 41 (June), 9-17; and Rogelio Pérez Perdomo, 1993, "La justicia en tiempos de globalización: demandas y perspectivas de cambio," in *Justicia y desarrollo en América Latina y el Caribe* (Washington, D.C.: Inter-American Development Bank), 137-151.

9. In this section I am following closely Thomas Carothers, 1994, "The Resurgence of United States Political Development Assistance to Latin America," unpublished manuscript.

10. In 1990, a USAID judicial aid program to Guatemala, administered by the Criminal Justice Center at Harvard Law School, was terminated on grounds that the government had made no effort to investigate political assassinations. *El Habeas Corpus en Centro América*, Serie Jurídica No. 2 (San José: CODEHUCA), 49-51.

11. Jorge Correa Sutil, 1992, "Formación y perfeccionamiento de jueces," in *El poder judicial en la encrucijada*, Carlos Peña et al. (Santiago: Escuela de Derecho, Universidad Diego Portales), 115-116. With funding from USAID, research on comparative experiences of judicial training was carried out in Chile. See María Josefina Haeussler, 1993, *Experiencias comparativas de formación judicial* (Santiago: CPU).

12. See, for example, the essays produced for the IDB seminar on justice in Latin America held in Montevideo, Uruguay. These appear in *La política de la reforma judicial*, 1996 (Washington, D.C.: Inter-American Development Bank).

13. See Carlos Peña G., 1992, "Poder judicial y sistema político. Las políticas de modernización," in *El poder judicial en la encrucijada. Estudios acerca de la política judicial en Chile*, Carlos Peña et al. (Santiago: Escuela de Derecho, Universidad Diego Portales, 1992), 48. My interviews with government officials at the time convinced me that the Aylwin government thought of the judicial reform legislative package as a proper response to the report of the Rettig Commission, which documented human rights violations that had taken place in Chile under the military government.

14. Rogelio Pérez Perdomo, 1993, 147. Pilar Domingo, in a paper presented at the 1995 LASA conference, argued that certain business sectors more in tune with economic liberalization are likely to support an increasingly independent judiciary. As evidence, she cites the discourse of the business elite of Chihuahua. See Pilar Domingo, 1995, "The Judiciary and the Rule of Law in Latin America," unpublished manuscript; and Yemile Mizrahi, 1994, "Rebels Without a Cause? The Politics of Entrepreneurs in Chihuahua," in *Journal of Latin American Studies* 26: 137-158.

15. According to this view, the transition consolidated protected democracy, in which regimes of exception are basic elements of the constitutions, the armed forces maintain an internal security and a political role, and they have partial autonomy. See Brian Loveman, 1994, "Protected Democracies and Military Guardianship: Political Transitions in Latin America, 1978-1993," in *Journal of Interamerican Studies and World Affairs* 36 (2): 105-188.

16. A recent evaluation of the criminal justice system in Colombia shows that two years after the 1991 constitutional reform, the number of criminal cases that had not been resolved remained very similar. However, the percentage of cases in which someone was accused of

committing the crime was larger. See "La justicia dos años después de la reforma constitu-cional," 1994, in *Coyuntura Social* 11 (November 1994): 36-39.

17. See, for instance, the criticism against some of the criminal procedure reforms already implemented by Juan Enrique Vargas Viancos, 1994, "Reforma procesal penal en América Latina: la adecuación de las legislaciones al programa de los derechos humanos," in Corporación Nacional de Reparación y Reconciliación, 275-316. See also my previous reference in this chapter to the two visions regarding the role of the courts in the protection and promotion of democratic citizenship.

# References

Anderson, Kenneth. 1989. "Maximizing Deniability: The Justice System and Human Rights in Guatemala." Washington, D.C.: International Human Rights Law Group.

Ayala Carao, Carlos M. 1993. "El enjuiciamiento del Presidente de Venezuela: suspensión y suplencia." *Boletín Comisión Andina de Juristas* 37: 49-52.

Barros, Luis, Hugo Frühling, Gonzalo García, Augusto Quintana, and Domingo Sánchez. 1994. "El proceso penal chileno y su protección de los derechos del imputado." In *Proceso penal y derechos fundamentales*. Santiago: Corporación Nacional de Reparación y Reconciliación.

Binder M., Alberto. 1993. "Crisis y transformación de la justicia penal en Iberoamérica." In *Reformas procesales en América Latina. La oralidad en los procesos*. Santiago: CPU.

Binder M., Alberto. 1994. "La reforma procesal penal en América Latina." In "Proyecto para la reforma del procedimiento penal chileno." Corporación de Promoción Universitaria and Fundación Paz Ciudadana, unpublished manuscript.

Blanco, Rafael, and Hugo Frühling. 1995. "Proposiciones de políticas públicas en materia de seguridad ciudadana." In *Seguridad ciudadana. Políticas públicas*, eds. Rafael Blanco, Hugo Frühling, and Eugenio Guzmán. Santiago: Universidad Nacional Andrés Bello, CED, ILD.

Buscaglia, Edgardo, and María Dakolias. 1995. "Judicial Reform in Latin America. Economic Efficiency vs. Institutional Inertia." Unpublished manuscript.

Calderón, Fernando, and Mario Dos Santos. 1991. *Hacia un nuevo orden estatal en América Latina. Veinte tésis sociopolíticas y un corolario*. Mexico City: Fondo de Cultura Económico.

Cappelletti, Mauro, and Bryant Garth. 1978. "Access to Justice: The Newest Wave in the Worldwide Movement to Make Rights Effective." *Buffalo Law Review* 28: 181-196.

Carothers, Thomas. 1994. "The Resurgence of United States Political Development Assistance to Latin America." Unpublished manuscript.

Correa Sutil, Jorge. 1992. "Formación y perfeccionamiento de jueces." In *El poder judicial en la encrucijada*, Carlos Peña et al. Santiago: Escuela de Derecho, Universidad Diego Portales.

Correa Sutil, Jorge, ed. 1994. *Situación y políticas judiciales en América Latina*. Santiago: Escuela de Derecho, Universidad Diego Portales.

Correa Sutil, Jorge, and Luis Barros Lazaeta, eds. 1993. *Justicia y marginalidad. Percepción de los pobres*. Santiago: CPU-Dirección de Estudios Sociológicos de la Universidad Católica.

Costa, Gino. 1994. "La reforma policial en El Salvador." Unpublished manuscript.

Davis, William. 1993. "Administración del proceso de introducción de reformas en los tribunales." In *Reformas procesales en América Latina. La oralidad en los procesos*. Santiago: CPU.

De Trazegnies, Fernando. 1994. "El jurado de honor de la magistratura: Balance de cierre." *Ideele* 71-72: 99-103.

Domingo, Pilar. 1995. "The Judiciary and the Rule of Law in Latin America." Unpublished manuscript.

Dugas, John. 1993. "La constitución política de 1991, ¿un pacto político viable?" In *La constitución política de 1991: ¿un pacto político viable?* ed. John Dugas. Bogota: Departamento de Ciencia Política, Universidad de los Andes.

"El Habeas Corpus en Centro América." 1992. San José: CODEHUCA.

Frühling, Hugo. 1984a. *Law in Society. Social Transformation and the Crisis of Law in Chile. 1830-1970.* S.J.D. Thesis submitted to Harvard Law School.

Frühling, Hugo. 1984b. "Poder judicial y político en Chile." In *La administración de justicia en América Latina,* ed. Javier de Belaúnde. Lima: Consejo Latinoamericano de Derecho y Desarrollo.

Frühling, Hugo. 1993. "Human Rights in Constitutional Order and in Political Practice in Latin America." In *Constitutionalism and Democracy: Transitions in the Contemporary World,* eds. Douglas Greenberg, Stanley N. Katz, Melanie Beth Oliviero, and Steven C. Wheatley. New York: Oxford University Press.

Fuenzalida, Edmundo. 1977. "The Role of Legal Experts in the Process of Development. The Case of Chile." Unpublished manuscript.

Gardner, James A. 1980. *Legal Imperialism: American Lawyers and Foreign Aid in Latin America.* Madison, Wis.: University of Wisconsin Press.

Garrido, Carlos Manuel. 1994. "Informe sobre Argentina." In *Situación y políticas judiciales en América Latina,* ed. Jorge Correa. Santiago: Escuela de Derecho, Universidad Diego Portales.

Giraldo Angel, Jaime. 1994. "Informe sobre Colombia." In *Situación y políticas judiciales en América Latina,* ed. Jorge Correa. Santiago: Escuela de Derecho, Universidad Diego Portales.

Gutiérrez, Carlos José. 1973. "Los jueces de Costa Rica." *Revista de Ciencias Jurídicas* 22: 77-113.

Haeussler, Josefina. 1993. *Experiencias comparativas de formación judicial.* Santiago: CPU.

Hernández Valiente, René. 1993. "La justicia en Centroamérica en la década de los noventa." In *Justicia y desarrollo en América Latina y el Caribe.* Washington, D.C.: Inter-American Development Bank.

Hilbink, Lisa. 1995. "What is the Role of the Judiciary in a Democracy? The Judicial Reform Debate in Chile and Proposals for Future Research." Unpublished manuscript.

Holston, James, and Teresa P.R. Caldeira. 1998. "Democracy, Law, and Violence: Disjunctions of Brazilian Citizenship," in this volume.

Iglesias V., Enrique. 1993. "Derecho, justicia y desarrollo en América Latina en la década de los noventa." In *Justicia y desarrollo en América Latina y el Caribe.* Washington, D.C.: Inter-American Development Bank.

Instituto SER de Investigación. 1983. "Justicia penal, juicio y reforma." Bogota: FESCOL.

Interviews by author in Chile in 1992 (see note 13) and in Colombia.

Jonas, Susanne. Forthcoming 1998. *The Mined Road to Peace in Guatemala.* North-South Agenda Paper. Coral Gables, Fla.: North-South Center Press at the University of Miami.

Loveman, Brian. 1993. *The Constitution of Tyranny. Regimes of Exception in Spanish America*. Pittsburgh: University of Pittsburgh Press.

Loveman, Brian. 1994. "Protected Democracies and Military Guardianship: Political Transitions in Latin America. 1978-1993." *Journal of Interamerican Studies and World Affairs* 36: 105-188.

Lowenstein, Steven. 1970. *Legal Education and Development: An Examination of the Process of Reform in Chile*. New York: International Legal Center.

Martínez Neira, Néstor Humberto. 1993. "El BID y la administración de justicia." In *Justicia y desarrollo en América Latina y el Caribe*. Washington, D.C.: Inter-American Development Bank.

*El Mercurio*, 1995, March 2, C15.

Mizrahi, Yemile. 1994. "Rebels Without a Cause? The Politics of Entrepreneurs in Chihuahua." *Journal of Latin American Studies* 26: 137-158.

Murphy, Walter F. 1993. "Constitutions, Constitutionalism, and Democracy." In *Constitutionalism & Democracy: Transitions in the Contemporary World*. eds. Douglas Greenberg, Stanley N. Katz, Melanie Beth Oliviero, and Steven C. Wheatley. New York: Oxford University Press.

Novoa, Eduardo. 1964. "La crisis del sistema legal chileno." *Mensaje* 13: 563-564.

Novoa, Eduardo. 1965. "La crisis del sistema legal chileno," *Revista de Derecho Jurisprudencia y Ciencias Sociales* 62: 229.

Pásara, Luis. 1984. "Perú: administración de ¿justicia?" In *La administración de justicia en América Latina*, ed. Javier de Belaúnde. Lima: Consejo Latinoamericano de Derecho y Desarrollo.

Peña, Carlos. 1992. "Poder judicial y sistema político. Las políticas de modernización." In *El poder judicial en la encrucijada. Estudios acerca de la política judicial en Chile*. Santiago: Escuela de Derecho, Universidad Diego Portales.

Peña, Carlos. 1994a. "América Latina: ¿una justicia emergente? In *Boletín Comisión Andina de Juristas* 41: 9-17.

Peña, Carlos. 1994b. "Informe sobre Chile." In *Situación y políticas judiciales en América Latina*, ed. Jorge Correa. Santiago: Escuela de Derecho, Universidad Diego Portales.

Pérez Perdomo, Rogelio. 1987. "La administración de justicia en Venezuela: evaluación y alternativas." *Revista de Derecho Privado*, 2-4.

Pérez Perdomo, Rogelio. 1993. "La justicia en tiempos de globalización: demandas y perspectivas de cambio." In *Justicia y desarrollo en América Latina y el Caribe*. Washington, D.C.: Inter-American Development Bank.

Pérez Perdomo, Rogelio. 1994. "Informe sobre Venezuela." In *Situación y políticas judiciales en América Latina*. ed. Jorge Correa. Santiago: Escuela de Derecho, Universidad Diego Portales.

*Plan of Action*. 1998. Second Summit of the Americas. Santiago, Chile. April 19.

Popkin, Margaret. 1994. *Justice Delayed. The Slow Pace of Judicial Reform in El Salvador*. Washington, D.C.: Hemisphere Initiatives and Washington Office on Latin America.

Rivera Cira, Tirza. 1994. "Informe sobre Costa Rica." In *Situación y políticas judiciales en América Latina*, ed. Jorge Correa. Santiago: Escuela de Derecho, Universidad Diego Portales.

Rojas, Fernando. 1986. "A Comparison of Change-Oriented Legal Services in Latin America with Legal Services in North America and Europe." Working Paper, Institute for Legal Studies, School of Law, University of Wisconsin.

Rosenn, Keith S. 1974. "Judicial Review in Latin America." In *Ohio State Law Journal* 35: 509.

Rosenn, Keith S. 1987. "The Protection of Judicial Independence in Latin America." *Interamerican Law Review* 19 (1): 1-35.

Thome, Joseph. 1983. "New Models for Legal Services in Latin America." In *Human Rights Quarterly* 6: 521-538.

Unger Mangabeira, Roberto. 1976. *Law in Modern Society*. New York: The Free Press.

Vargas Viancos, Juan Enrique. 1994. "Reforma procesal penal en América Latina: la adecuación de las legislaciones al programa de los derechos humanos." In *Proceso penal y derechos fundamentales*. Santiago: Corporación Nacional de Reparación y Reconciliación.

Verdugo, Mario. 1992. "Alternativas de la reforma del poder judicial." In *El poder judicial en la encrucijada. Estudios acerca de la política judicial en Chile*. Santiago: Escuela de Derecho, Universidad Diego Portales.

Verner, Joel G. "The Independence of the Supreme Court in Latin America: A Review of the Literature." *Journal of Latin American Studies* 16: 463-506.

Weyland, Kurt. 1993. "The Rise and Fall of President Collor and Its Impact on Brazilian Democracy." *Journal of Interamerican Studies and World Affairs* 35 (1).

Wiarda, Howard J., ed. 1982. *Politics and Social Change in Latin America: The Distinct Tradition*. Amherst, Mass.: University of Massachusetts Press.

Wilson, Richard J. 1989. "The New Legal Education in North and South America." *Stanford Journal of International Law* 25 (2): 375.

WOLA (Washington Office on Latin America). 1990. "Elusive Justice: The U.S. Administration of Justice Program in Latin America." Washington, D.C.: WOLA, 12.

World Economic Forum. 1994. *World Competitiveness Report 1994*. Geneva: EMF Foundation.

Zaffaroni, Eugenio Raúl. 1993. "Dimensión política de un poder judicial democrático." *Boletín Comisión Andina de Juristas* 37: 9-40.

Zolezzi Ibárcena, Lorenzo. 1994. "Informe sobre Perú." In *Situación y políticas judiciales en América Latina,* ed. Jorge Correa. Santiago: Escuela de Derecho Universidad Diego Portales.

CHAPTER TEN

# Democracy, Law, and Violence: Disjunctions of Brazilian Citizenship

JAMES HOLSTON AND TERESA P.R. CALDEIRA

M any of the world's emerging democracies are experiencing a similar disjunction: Although their political institutions democratize with considerable
success, the civil component of citizenship remains impaired as citizens suffer
systematic violations of their rights. In such uncivil democracies, violence, injustice, and impunity are norms. As a result, the institutions of law and justice lose
legitimacy, the principle of legality is obstructed, and the realization of democratic
citizenship remains limited. Narrowly political definitions of democracy miss these
dilemmas. In this essay, we consider the disjunctive development of democracy
such problems entail. We focus on the case of Brazil to emphasize both the lived
consequences of these problems and their theoretical significance for understanding
democratic change.[1]

Studies of democratization in Latin America usually ignore the civil component and its constituent elements of justice, law, and citizenship in the real lives of
citizens and states. Instead, most studies focus on the transformation of political
systems, especially on regime change, electoral competition, and their precondi-
tions. Such considerations are certainly fundamental. They establish that most
countries in the region have indeed become democratic in the sense that they are
*political* democracies. However, their problematic and at times perverse democratizations demonstrate that the consolidation of democracy requires social and
cultural changes that escape the analysis of this narrow political perspective. This
indication becomes even more compelling if we consider similar problems in the
new democracies of Eastern Europe and Africa, as well as recent challenges to
established democracies in North America and Western Europe. All of these
difficulties strongly suggest that, although necessary, political democracy is not
enough to ensure a meaningfully democratic society, that is, one in which citizens
widely and habitually exercise their citizenship and in which this realization of the
substance of formal membership frames the negotiations and practices of social life
in significant ways. In the United States as in Brazil, it is increasingly evident that
without such conditions, democratic politics loses its legitimacy and efficacy. It
loses not only as a means to frame social interactions but also as a mode of
governance.

Our broader aim in this essay is to argue, therefore, that democracy cannot stand alone, either conceptually or actually, as a kind of political regime or political method in the context of social and cultural conditions hostile to democratic citizenship. Rather, we stress that democracy is as much a qualification of society as it is of politics. This is not to adopt a maximal definition of democracy or to make a particular political culture its precondition. It is rather to insist that the extension of democracy to the social sphere is as central to the concept as its extension to the political and that both of these colonizations (of society by the state and the state by society, to summarize the process in this way) constitute the contemporary and enabling form of democratic development. Although there are several key elements of this process, this essay focuses on the one we identify as the civil component of citizenship. In the first two sections, we examine the condition of the civil from several perspectives in the context of Brazil's current political democracy. In the last, we analyze its importance more theoretically, developing the concept we call disjunctive democracy.

By civil, we refer not to the classic liberal separation between state and non-state, political society and civil society, public and private, or to any such dichotomies that typically derive from the state/non-state divide. Rather, developing T.H. Marshall's (1977) analytic framework, we distinguish civil from the political, socioeconomic, and cultural components of citizenship. We use civil to refer to the sphere of rights, practices, and values that concerns liberty, both negative and positive, and justice as the means to all other rights. With regard to liberty, the civil component of citizenship not only secures its negative meanings in the sense of guaranteeing the autonomy of private individuals against the abuses of the state. It also secures liberty in the positive sense of rights to associate, assemble, and communicate among private individuals who thus become associated individuals and who thereby create the public sphere of society. As the component of citizenship concerned with justice, moreover, its rights, practices, and values ground the democratic rule of law, discussed later in terms of the four conditions of fairness, access, universality, and legality. Through these principles of liberty and justice, the civil component relates and regulates both society and the state as one of society's legally constituted agents. This regulation creates a not unambiguous mediation between society and state: The civil differentiates society from the political system by defending the former from the abuses of the latter; however, it also integrates the two by utilizing state power against the relations of inequality and domination within society itself. In this sense, our use embraces the paradox of modern democracy: Although society needs protection from the state, it is only within the framework of a state that this is possible. Thus, the notion of civil is used here to emphasize the complex imbrication and mediation of state and society, especially by means of law and citizenship.

To some, the argument that political democracy is not enough may seem obvious. Indeed, one of the most astute analysts of contemporary democracy, Guillermo O'Donnell, writes that consolidation requires "the extension of similarly democratic ... relations into other [not just political] spheres of social life" (O'Donnell 1992, 49). However, we would suggest that the means and modes of this extension (and not infrequent retraction) and their consequences for the theory of democracy remain inadequately investigated or conceptualized. This is especially the case because most contemporary observers use a political definition of democracy that neglects to consider that the social conditions of citizenship are constitutive of its political possibilities. This definition excludes, therefore, democracy's extension to the social sphere out of hand. Furthermore, we argue that the democratization of state and society are mutually defining in a consolidated democracy; that is, democratic extensions are reciprocal, not only between state and society but also between society and state. In an important sense, consolidation means that the state does not monopolize, in fact or claim, the sources of democracy — or of citizenship or law, for that matter. Our aim is to make these suggestions by stressing the importance of the civil component of citizenship in democratic processes. We consider the significance of this component by looking at what happens when it is systematically violated, not under dictatorship but under political democracy.

The empirical basis of this investigation derives from ethnographic research in the metropolitan regions of São Paulo and Brasília, which we have, at various times, conducted separately and together. It derives especially from an anthropological concern with the performative dimension of social and institutional relations — that is, with the representative practices and exemplary particulars through which these relations are enacted, as well as with the scripts, like democracy, that are supposed to provide a calculus for many sets of relations and that people must perform to gain the prescriptive effects. Our intention is, in this sense, not just to criticize the strictly political definition of democracy but also to suggest an anthropological perspective in its study. We do not insist on this intention by calling attention to it throughout the discussion. Rather, we try to demonstrate its force by focusing on the civil component of citizenship and the lived consequences of its violation and by letting these social practices lead to a theoretical argument about the disjunctive nature of democratization. We speak of Brazil because democratization is a specific process embedded in specific conditions. But our case could also be made, mutatis mutandis, with respect to other countries in the Americas because our subject, the civil sphere of democracy, is at the same time specific and comparable. That is, it depends upon comparable social, cultural, and economic conditions that not only make a democratic political order viable and meaningful but also constitute its legitimating purpose.

We begin with an important contradiction of democratic rule in Brazil: As Brazilians succeed in institutionalizing democratic politics, they also experience the delegitimation of many institutions of law, resulting in the privatization of justice, escalation of both violent crime and police abuse, criminalization of the poor, and massive support for illegal and/or authoritarian measures of control. We then analyze the discredit of the Brazilian justice system under political democracy with respect to the civil component of citizenship and the principle of legality. We conclude with a discussion of some of the theoretical implications of these democratic disjunctions.

## DEMOCRACY AND VIOLENCE

In recent years, Brazilian society has produced numerous events that indicate a disjunctive democratization. Two of these events happened in the last months of 1994. The first was the October election of Fernando Henrique Cardoso as president. He received 54.3 percent of the vote, the second highest percentage of any presidential candidate in Brazilian history. Many things are impressive in Cardoso's election. Not the least is the fact that a man with a background of exile and consistent opposition to the military could even become a presidential candidate. Moreover, Cardoso's main opponent in the presidential race was Luiz Inácio Lula da Silva, leader of the Workers' Party (Partido dos Trabalhadores — PT). As is well known, the PT under Lula contributed significantly to the organization of new social movements throughout Brazil during the late 1970s and 1980s. These movements changed the political scene considerably: For the first time in Brazilian history, members of the working classes constituted themselves as political agents without the mediation of leaders from the elites. Thus, the 1994 presidential campaign exhibited new democratic options and new political styles. Furthermore, the campaign relied mostly on the mass media, to which all parties had free access and in which candidates freely engaged all types of themes. In sum, the 1994 campaign indicates just how much Brazil had changed since the time when the military and its civilian allies considered any person voicing social democratic ideals a serious threat to order.

However, if the electoral campaign represents the successful institutionalization of democratic procedures in the political system, a second type of event exposes its insufficiencies. One month after the 1994 election, in what was named Operação Rio, the Army was called into the city of Rio de Janeiro in an effort to control violent criminality. This operation was articulated at the federal level and required the creation of a special juridical formula (an agreement of cooperation between the federal government and the state of Rio de Janeiro) because, in principle, it constituted an illegal federal intervention into state affairs. However, at that point, the state authorities were ready to recognize their incapacity to control a situation of widespread criminal violence in the city, from street mugging to kidnapping to homicide. Much of this crime was associated with drug trafficking that constituted, together with weapons smuggling, the main reason federal authorities used to justify their intervention.[2]

Yet what makes Rio's situation particularly difficult is that the forces of law and order are themselves one of the main agents of its violence. The city's military police are particularly plagued by corruption, entangled with organized crime, and accustomed to violent and illegal methods of action. Caught up in drug trafficking and police violence, the city has witnessed a series of shocking massacres: During the night of July 23, 1993, eight boys sleeping on the street in the central Candelária neighborhood were summarily killed. Military policemen were accused of having committed the atrocity. In the early hours of August 30, 1993, a group of about 40 masked men, armed with heavy weapons, killed 21 residents of the *favela* (squatter settlement) Vigário Geral. Among the victims was an entire Evangelical family with absolutely no criminal record. In fact, most of the 21 victims were sleeping and had no criminal records. The men accused of that massacre were, once again, military police who were allegedly avenging the death of four other military police officers killed during a conflict with drug dealers from Vigário Geral. This sort of revenge killing of civilians has been escalating, especially in conflicts related to drug trafficking. On October 18, 1994, for example, around 150 military policemen invaded another favela, Nova Brasília. The attack followed the death of a detective in a conflict with drug dealers. Seventeen civilians died that day in Nova Brasília.

Rio de Janeiro holds no monopoly on either violent criminality or violent police. In fact, incidents of violence and of human rights abuses throughout Brazil have grown dramatically *after* the institutionalization of democratic rule. This dismal record of violence against mostly innocent and unarmed civilians includes the massacre of indigenous populations, peasants, rural leaders (Chico Mendes, for example), street children, prisoners, and adolescents in poor urban neighborhoods.[3] In other words, violence, crime, abuse of human rights, and extralegal actions of the police are increasingly widespread in Brazilian society under democratic rule. Thus, we are confronted with a conjunction of contradictory events. Some indicate an expansion of democratic citizenship and others its erosion and degradation. Some indicate the strengthening of democratic state institutions and others the dismantling or "illegalization" of the state. Such conjunctions are not exceptional. We have only to remember, for example, the first week of October 1992: A few days after the National Congress voted in exemplary democratic fashion to suspend President Fernando Collor de Mello from office and to send him to ultimate impeachment in the Senate, the military police massacred 111 prisoners at São Paulo's Casa de Detenção (House of Detention). The media graphically presented the event and its carnage to the public who, as many polls and street demonstrations indicated at the time, supported the police assault in significant numbers.

The public's increasing fear of violence generated by violent criminality and a widespread disbelief in the justice system fuels broad support for various types of extraordinary measures to deal with violence and crime. As a result, people welcome appeals to the army, as in the case of Operação Rio, as well as illegal and private "acts of justice." In all these cases, the invention of some episodic order puts aside concerns for the institutional order of democratic legal norms and procedures. Moreover, the use of the army to control crime confuses the boundaries of established authorities and institutions. It also crystallizes the notion that the criminal is an internal enemy, a notion akin to ideologies of national security during the military years. Although people are ready to defend democratic procedures in the political system, consistently supporting trials of corrupt politicians at all levels and defending free elections and political organization, they also overwhelmingly welcome actions such as Operação Rio. In the context of crime, fear, and the failure of the institutions of law, people consider discussions about the legitimacy of the military occupation in Rio or of the prison assault in São Paulo and the threat they pose to the consolidation of democratic rule largely irrelevant. In what follows, we look more closely at two of the key elements that define this perversity of violence under political democracy.

## Violent Police and the Reproduction of Violence

In contemporary Brazil, violence — particularly of a criminal sort — is the domain in which the disrespect of civil rights and the failure of democratization strongly shape everyday social interactions. Since the mid-1980s, Brazilians have perceived violent criminality as the main problem affecting their cities. Not only has crime increased, but the type of criminality has also changed in this period. Crime has become more organized and more violent, as the example of São Paulo demonstrates. São Paulo is not the Brazilian city with the highest rates of violent crime; that honor goes to Rio de Janeiro. Yet compared to many cities around the world, São Paulo's rates are significantly high. In the early 1980s, violent crime represented around 20 percent of the total crime reported in the metropolitan region of São Paulo.[4] Since the mid-1980s, this percentage has been higher than 30 percent. One of the crimes that increased the most in the period 1981-1993 is murder (average annual variation of 8.54 percent). In 1990, the rate of murder per 100,000 population reached 37.2, before dropping to 33.9 in 1993. These rates are significantly higher than the 1981 rate of 14.62.[5] This pattern is not specific to São Paulo; murder rates and violent crime are increasing worldwide. According to FBI reports, in the United States the number of violent crimes per capita grew by 355 percent between 1960 and 1990. The number of rapes multiplied by four. In 1993, murder rates per 100,000 population in several U.S. cities were higher than or comparable to those of São Paulo.[6] Since 1993, however, large U.S. cities such as New York have experienced a decrease in murder rates. Nevertheless, this decrease has not prevented an increase in the fear of crime and its transformation into a central issue in U.S. national and local politics.

In spite of some similarities in patterns of rising violence between São Paulo and the United States, there are very significant differences. The most important concerns the institutions of order. A dramatic indication of these differences is the data on the relationship between the number of people killed by the police and the total number of murders. From 1986 to 1990, the police committed 10 percent of the total number of murders in the metropolitan region of São Paulo; in 1991, the percentage jumped to 15.9 percent, and in 1992 it rose to 27.4 percent. In New York City in the 1990s, the average percentage of killings by the police has been 1.2 percent, and in Los Angeles, 2.1 percent. Although since 1993 police violence has diminished in São Paulo with rates back to the level of the late 1980s, no other city in the Americas outside of Brazil has a comparable record of police abuse in the use of deadly force (Chevigny 1995). In Brazil, the police constitute part of the problem of violence.

From its creation in the early nineteenth century, the Brazilian police's practices of violence, arbitrariness, discrimination, and disrespect of rights have been well-known. Although the degree of police abuse has varied under various political regimes, during this entire period the police have never abandoned the practices of unsubstantiated arrests, torture, and battering. Frequently, they have understood that punishment and correction were part of their duties. Moreover, these practices have not always been illegal, and often they have been exercised with the support of the citizenry, even of members of social groups who have been the preferential victims of the police. Throughout this period, different governments issued various "laws of exception" to accommodate existing delinquent police practices or to cover them up. Although these laws were usually issued under dictatorships, they frequently survived under democratic rule. Thus, the legal parameters framing police work have often shifted, making the boundaries between the legal and the illegal unstable and creating conditions for the continuation of a routine of abuses. In addition, the repression of crime has targeted the working classes in particular and has frequently merged with political repression. The formula that the elites of the Old Republic made famous has remained in place: "The social question is a matter of the police." Consequently, the poorer sectors of the population in particular have unremittingly suffered various forms of police violence and legal injustice. As a result, the poor have learned to fear the police and to distrust the justice system.

It is not necessary to review the entire history of the Brazilian police to make these points. However, discussing a few of its contemporary aspects will demonstrate the complicated relationship between the police and the legal order. The military regime that took power in 1964 reorganized the police. Decree 667 of 1969 unified all preexisting state uniformed police into state military police (MP), subordinated to the army and charged with uniformed street patrolling. The objective was to train and organize this new police force according to a military model. At the same time, the civil police continued to exist, comprised of the administrative and the judiciary police. Both the civil and the military police forces are organized at the state level and are under the jurisdiction of the secretary of public security. However, they have different hierarchies, training, and recruitment procedures. In spite of their unified authority, this dual organization of police forces generates constant rivalries and conflicts between them. The two also seem to specialize in different types of abuses. As many human rights organizations have shown, the civil police, who are in charge of investigations, tend to torture people under arrest, while the military police are more likely to kill suspects.[7]

Rules governing the current military police include some laws of exception that put them above the civil justice system. Until 1977, the Brazilian justice system considered that illegal acts committed by military police in civilian functions should be judged by civilian justice. The repression of crime is such a civilian function. During the process of political liberalization, however, this understanding changed, supposedly as a way of protecting from prosecution those who had used illegal force under the military regime. Constitutional Amendment 7 of 1977 (the so-called April Package) and some subsequent interpretations of the Supreme Court (see Pinheiro 1983) established that all offenses committed by military bodies should be considered military offenses and judged by special military courts, even if they were committed in peacetime and in civilian functions. In other words, from 1977 on, there has been a special justice for the military police. This exception became the norm with the "Citizens' Constitution" of 1988. Written under democratic rule by a freely elected Congress, the 1988 Constitution maintained the dual structure of the police, the military police as the institution in charge of "ostensible policing and the preservation of public order" (art. 144, par. 5) and its special military courts.

Various human rights groups have amassed considerable evidence demonstrating that the military justice overwhelmingly acquits (or dismisses charges against) military police accused of crimes against civilians. This evidence confirms that the military justice is rigorous as far as internal discipline is concerned but not as tough if the question is the murder of civilians.[8] The conclusion is clear: This record of acquittal or dismissal stimulates an explicit sense of impunity among the police and therefore perpetuates the continuation of abuses associated especially with excessive use of force. As Paul Chevigny (1995) demonstrates in his analysis of police abuse in six cities in the Americas, a decrease of abuse is directly related to the enforcement of systems of accountability. When the police are not made accountable for their extralegal or illegal behavior, violence and abuse escalate. The legal exception that removes the Brazilian military police from the civilian justice system of accountability increases their impunity and their use of violence in dealing with civilians and indirectly assures them a wide margin for arbitrary behavior.

These consequences also can be demonstrated *a contrario*, by analyzing the cases in which accountability provoked a decline in police abuse. There are two recent examples. During the 1970s, members of São Paulo's civil police organized a famous death squad called the Esquadrão da Morte. Because they were under the jurisdiction of the civil police, judges and public prosecutors were able to bring them to trial — even under military dictatorship — and ultimately to dismantle the squad. In recent years, judges and prosecutors also have been able to enforce the article of the 1988 Constitution that considers torture a crime not subject to bail or executive clemency. They have brought civil police officers to trial, and there are indications that torture has diminished somewhat in São Paulo's civil police precincts (Americas Watch Committee 1993, 21).

In sum, although under democratic rule, the organization of current police institutions largely maintains that of the military regime. This institutional framework in large measure assures the impunity of extralegal actions of the police, especially the military police, the principal repressive police force of the state. In this sense, instead of helping to curb arbitrariness and violence, the current structure allows space for these practices to proliferate. This situation reveals an especially significant point: Usually, people associate abuses such as unsubstantiated arrests, torture of prisoners, and killing of suspects with authoritarian regimes. In Brazil, however, not only do police abuses continue to exist, but all data indicate that they have reached unprecedented high levels under the present political democracy.[9]

There is, by now, a mountain of data on police torture, battering, degradation of prisoners, and excessive use of deadly force. They show that the worsening of police violence in São Paulo — and in other Brazilian cities — coincides with the consolidation of political democracy. The number of civilians who died in confrontations with the military police in São Paulo increased considerably in the late 1980s: It surpassed 500 in 1989 and 1990, reached 1,171 in 1991, and 1,470 in 1992 (including the 111 prisoners of the Casa de Detenção). A special division of the military police called ROTA — Rondas Ostensivas Tobias de Aguiar — commits a significant number of these killings. Not surprisingly, ROTA was created during the military regime (1969) to fight terrorist attacks, especially bank robberies, in the metropolitan region of São Paulo. A few comparisons highlight the absurdity of these numbers of killings. In 1991, the military police in São Paulo killed 1,171 civilians, the New York City police killed 27 people in confrontations, and the Los Angeles police killed 23. In 1992, the numbers were 1,470 in São Paulo, 24 in New York City, and 25 in Los Angeles (Chevigny 1995, 46, 67). The São Paulo killings suggest something more like a civil war or a regime of terror than anything resembling a democracy.

These civilian deaths in São Paulo cannot be considered as accidental or as resulting from the increased violence of criminals, as the military police claim. If the latter were the case, then it would be expected that the number of police killed would also increase. But this has not happened. Rather, although high when compared to U.S. statistics, the number of military police killed in confrontations has stayed more or less stable during the 1980s and 1990s, on average 39 per year. Moreover, the proportion of civilians killed in São Paulo in relation to those wounded is completely abnormal. Usually, the police wound many more than they kill. During the 1980s and 1990s, for each civilian killed in New York City, an average of three are wounded; in Los Angeles, the ratio is 1 killed to 2 wounded. Yet in the metropolitan region of São Paulo, 4.6 were killed for each civilian wounded in 1992 by the police; in 1991, the ratio was 3.6 killed to 1 wounded; for other years in the 1980s and 1990s, there was an average of more than two deaths for each person injured. These data indicate that the police in São Paulo and in other Brazilian cities, such as Rio de Janeiro and Recife for which there are similar data, shoot to kill rather than to subdue. As shown below, shooting to kill not only has broad popular support but is also "accepted" by the "tough talk" of official policy.

Probably no single event more tragically exemplifies the routine association of these components of police violence than the massacre of 111 prisoners at Casa de Detenção in October 1992. Not a single police officer died; none was wounded seriously. Yet prisoners were randomly shot and summarily executed after surrendering. Many were beaten, attacked by dogs trained to bite the genitals, and stabbed with knives. Naked, many of the survivors were forced to watch the executions, carry the bodies of the dead, and wash away the rivers of blood because the police were terrified at the prospect of being contaminated with AIDS. In a country in which human rights violations coexist with a free press, images of the massacre ended up in the mass media: piles of bullet-riddled bodies on the prison floor, naked inmates carrying corpses, and rows of open wooden coffins arranged side by side along the corridors of the Institute of Legal Medicine, revealing the autopsied bodies with big black numbers scrawled on their legs — a concentration camp vision. Although a civilian criminal prosecutor presented charges against one of the commanders of the operation and a military prosecutor presented charges against 120 officers and soldiers for various crimes, including homicide, not a single one has been brought to trial almost six years after the massacre. Most of the accused continue to hold their jobs in the military police and to participate in public life. A few have even run for elected office on the basis of their performance in the assault.[10]

The massacre at the Casa de Detenção is an egregious example of what has become an accepted, if not encouraged, routine of police abuse. Some of this violence is no doubt associated with corruption. Possibly, some violence may be accounted for in terms of Brazilian judicial procedures. For example, especially in the precincts of the investigative civil police, the prevalence of routine torture may be related to the fact that confession is still the central piece of judicial evidence. The hellish condition of prisons surely has something to do with restricted state budgets. Police violence has, however, even more to do with official policy and with popular support. We can see the effect of the former through a contrasting experience. São Paulo's first governor after the end of military dictatorship, Franco Montoro (1983-1987), was particularly determined to cut down the abuses of the police, improve human rights generally, and enforce the rule of law. For that commitment, he suffered strong opposition not only from the police but also from right-wing politicians and the population at large. Nevertheless, Montoro was able to institute some measures, such as dismantling ROTA and accounting for police handguns and bullets, which succeeded in diminishing the number of police killings.

However, his two successors, Orestes Quércia (1987-1991) and Luiz Antonio Fleury Filho (1991-1995), adopted the opposite policy. They believed that only a "tough" (meaning violent) police force would be able to curb the rising rates of crime, and they reversed all Montoro's measures aimed at controlling police abuses. The most important of them was the reorganization of ROTA that Montoro had neutralized. When the number of deaths perpetrated by the military police started to rise considerably in 1989, Fleury, at that point Quércia's secretary of public security, declared, "The fact that this year there were more deaths caused by the MP means that they are more active. The more police in the streets, the more chances of confrontations between criminals and policemen…. From my point of view, what the population wants is that the police act boldly" (Interview in *Folha de São Paulo*, November 28, 1989). This statement indicates that advocating for "tough" police was a state policy. Yet the following events show that it was a policy possible to reverse. After the massacre at the Casa de Detenção, Fleury was forced to substitute his own secretary of public security and change his "tough" policy. As a result, the number of people killed by the MP dropped to 409 in 1993 and 453 in 1994, compared to 1,470 in 1992. Yet these numbers are still extraordinarily high, and if they indicate a certain measure of reform, they also indicate a deep resistance to it.

Resistance to reform is ultimately grounded in broad popular support for a "tough" police force. In this sense, it is sobering to realize that it was Montoro, not Quércia or Fleury, who misjudged its appeal. The hard fact is that a significant part of the population of São Paulo supports violent police action. For example, depending on the poll, between 29 percent and 44 percent of the residents of São Paulo supported the police in the massacre of prisoners at the Casa de Detenção, according to various newspaper surveys conducted at the time. Every serious study of popular sentiment shows widespread approval of violent police actions in dealing with criminals, including torture and killing. Thus, the police have continued to be violent, not only because of an assured impunity but also because of the support of the population. Paradoxically, even the main victims of police violence, the working classes, support some of its forms. Given this widespread approval, it is not surprising that the majority of the population are hostile to the notion of human rights and to campaigns launched by human rights groups to enforce a rule of law that respects individual rights. Elsewhere, Teresa P.R. Caldeira (1991) has analyzed this hostility and the failure of human rights campaigns to deal with it adequately. The point we wish to suggest here is that the population's support for police violence indicates the existence not only of an institutional dysfunction but also of a pervasive cultural pattern that associates order and authority with the use of violence and that, in turn, contributes to the delegitimation of the justice system and of the rule of law.[11]

This cultural identification generates a whole series of ambiguous and confusing practices because most Brazilians — particularly the poor and/or black ones — also fear the police.[12] Most poor people have histories of police mistreatment and abuse to tell, and their narratives are full of indignation. On the one hand, they consider that the police routinely mistake "workers" for "criminals" (these two being opposed local categories) and are therefore violent with them. On the other, they believe that the police are soft with real criminals, who can bribe them, but hard with honest and poor workers who cannot. In this triangular relation, people tend to express a confusion among all vertices: The police treat workers as criminals, workers view the police as corrupt, and in some cases workers even consider criminals as protecting them against the discrimination of the police. Moreover, when both rich and poor describe the police as workers, they mean to emphasize that they are not well prepared for their jobs because they come from the lower classes and are therefore necessarily without the requisites of education, leadership, good judgment, and so forth. Even when expressed by the poor, such criticism of the police tends to combine with prejudice against the poor.

In this context of confusion, in which police violence is both praised and feared, desired and distrusted, people do not easily associate the police with the rule of law. The synecdoche, "Here comes the law," used to refer to the arrival of the police in U.S. English, does not exist in Brazilian Portuguese. The Brazilian identification is instead with "authority" and then with abusive and often violent use of it. That the phrase "Here comes the authority" (*Lá vem a autoridade*) is often deliberately mispronounced is another indication of these deeply ambiguous relations. People do not consider the police in terms of law, rights, and citizenship — not to mention justice and fair treatment — but rather in terms of the rule of naked force.

## DEMOCRACY AND JUSTICE

Caught in this conjunction of political democracy and violence, the vast majority of Brazilians are resigned to an undemocratic fate: They cannot rely on the institutions of state to secure their civil rights, either as positive protections or as negative immunities. Moreover, once their rights have been violated, it is equally unlikely for Brazilians to expect redress through the courts. Although police abuse has received considerable attention in the evaluation of Brazil's democratization, the judiciary's similarly scandalous failures with respect to a democratic rule of law have received scant consideration. We analyze some of the theoretical implications of this neglect later. In the following section, our aim is to register the discredit of the justice system and its consequences for the development of Brazilian democracy.[13]

## Judicial Discredit

Just as the police do not embody or represent the law-as-right for most people, the judiciary is so remote as a reliable resource that many residents of São Paulo did not even mention it in our interviews about violence and crime. In fact, nationally, 72 percent of all Brazilians involved in criminal conflicts do not use the justice system to resolve their problems (PNAD statistics for 1990, cited in Adorno 1994, 136). Rather, the universe of crime and its fear seems to include only criminals, police, and powerless and insecure workers. The widespread feeling is that the justice system is extremely biased and does not offer workers any possibility of justice. Moreover, in interviews with people of all social classes, the most common response to a question about the judiciary was some version of "It's a joke!" (*É uma brincadeira, uma piada*). Frequently, people resisted explaining what they meant. It was just too obvious.

The judiciary's overwhelming failures to secure and communicate a sense of effective justice, fair and timely treatment, and reasonable access for all Brazilians render it an isolated and even irrelevant institution for most people. Beyond a very narrow professional circle, remarkably little is known about its personnel and organization. Even for educated Brazilians, the judiciary is a closed, conservative, enigmatic institution, protected by practically impenetrable bureaucratic formalities and fiercely defended corporate privileges. For the rich, when needed, the judicial system has been a reliable means of manipulation. For the poor, it has been little more than a source of humiliation.[14] This abusive rule of law embodies a double discrimination which is a "rule of thumb" in Brazil: The poor suffer criminal sanctions from which the rich are generally immune, while the rich enjoy access to private law (civil and commercial) from which the poor are systematically excluded. This double bias pollutes the entire field of law, normatively divided into public (including criminal) and private, discrediting the judiciary and the law generally as a means to justice. Thus, the courts do not provide a genuine forum within which contemporary social conflicts can be engaged with a sense of fairness and equality befitting a democracy. They remain especially ineffective in arbitrating social relations in ways that would impose sanctions on the offenses of the powerful and protect citizens from abuse by the state and its agents. These incapacities produce generalized expectations of either impunity or abuse from the justice system.

Confirmations of these expectations abound in the field of every social problem. Since the mid-1960s, for example, Americas Watch has registered the murder of 1,681 rural workers. Of these cases, there have been only 26 trials and 15 convictions (Americas Watch Committee 1991). The conclusion is certain: Hired guns murder with impunity in rural land conflicts. Or, consider child labor. The Constitution outlaws the employment of those younger than 14 years of age. Yet, the 1991 national census shows that there are more than three million children below 14 employed in the formal and informal economy. Conclusion: The legislature makes laws that the courts cannot or will not enforce, employers operate with impunity in blatant violation of the law, and workers are abused. Or, consider urban crime. Of all the crimes reported by the civil police for the municipality of São Paulo in 1993 (389,178 *boletins de ocorrência*), only 20.4 percent resulted in the police fact-finding proceedings (*inquéritos instaurados*) necessary for judicial action of any sort. For the last decade, that rate has varied between 17 and 21 percent. In 1993, for crimes of murder, it was a low 73.8 percent, though for drug dealing, it reached 94.4 percent (Seade, unpublished data). Once a crime gets to trial, however, the conviction rate is likely to be high — though it would appear that both conviction and sentencing patterns are affected by racial biases. In his study of 297 criminal jury trials in São Paulo, Sérgio Adorno found a conviction rate of three blacks to one white (Adorno 1994, 140). The overwhelming problem is that so few conflicts get to court for resolution.

The courts have a special responsibility in every democracy to protect citizens from the abuses of arbitrary executive action. Such protection is surely among the foundational and legitimating virtues of democracy. One of the most important barriers to this abuse is the constitutional requirement that the state may deprive an individual of "life, liberty, and property" only on the basis of law and its due process. Some form of this principle of legality appears as a fundamental guarantee in every democratic constitution. However, the *application* of this principle is the greater hallmark of democracy. Historically, consolidated democracies have depended on the judiciary — especially the high court — to interpret the norms of legality so that they have application to real social problems in ways congruent with their intent. Most important, this application has depended on the judicial interpretation of liberty. In the development of Western democracy, this interpretation has entailed expanding the category of liberty to include not only freedom of contract and other classically liberal economic liberties but also, and more fundamentally, the civil liberties of speech, assembly, personal security, and so forth, consistent with due process. To give constitutional norms utility and relevance, the courts must grapple with what sort of procedure due process requires and what liberty entails. As David P. Currie (1988) shows in his study of the U.S. Constitution, for example, the U.S. Supreme Court has tended to equate due process with fairness, going beyond common law procedure to meet that standard. It has interpreted liberty broadly to give civil rights not only the protection of due process but also "First Amendment liberties a 'preferred position' entitling them to greater judicial protection than ordinary economic liberties" (Currie 1988, 49).[15]

In Brazil, every democratic constitution since the first Republican charter of 1891 has contained adequate provisions for due process and the fundamental rights of life, liberty, and property — provisions directly inspired, in fact, by the U.S. Constitution. In reality, however, Brazilian courts have only consistently protected property and only certain kinds at that.[16] When tested, they have not given life and liberty rigorous judicial protection against the infringements of the state. It is not just that citizens have not used the High Court to protect their noneconomic constitutional rights. It is also that the Brazilian courts do not invite such use because they do not have a tradition of defending them. Rather than forbidding the state to deprive persons of their rights, the courts tend to acquiesce to that deprivation when they consider it at all — as the failed challenges to government censorship or illegal detention or coerced confessions, for example, illustrate. Often civil rights cases simply languish for years with no resolution until they become moot. What has been consistently missing from Brazil's judicial tradition is the sense that courts protect the rights of citizenship and the principle of legality, even though these norms have been written into every democratic constitution.

Especially indicative of this judicial discredit is that even the new social movements of the 1970s and 1980s, which did so much to generate a new conception of Brazilian citizenship, ignored the courts as an arena of redress. These movements were unprecedented in large part because they created new kinds of rights outside the normative and institutional definitions of the state and its legal codes. In particular, these rights addressed new collective and personal spaces of daily life in the city, especially in the residential neighborhoods of the peripheries. As these "rights to the city" expanded citizenship to new social bases, they also created new sources of citizenship rights. Yet, until very recently, even these social movements bypassed the judiciary in their struggles. Instead, the movements have mostly worked with models of rights that tend to limit the concept of citizenship to one of political participation and thus to political rights on the one hand and, on the other, to insertion into the system of government services and thus to socioeconomic rights. With some exceptions (such as minority and feminist movements), they have largely disregarded the courts as means of change and focused instead on securing entitlements directly from the executive and, secondarily, from the legislative institutions of government.

In sum, the new developments of Brazilian citizenship have been very uneven. Neither civil rights, nor access to justice, nor due process of law has become a prominent concern for the principal forces of democratization in the new social movements, unions, or universities. Human rights organizations defend these concerns but with little real success. Even though systematically violated, the civil component of citizenship is largely ignored. To use T.H. Marshall's (1977) typology, this disjunction means that in comparison with social and political rights, civil rights have not been effectively woven into the fabric of Brazilian citizenship. Instead, the protections and immunities civil rights are intended to ensure as constitutional norms are generally perceived and experienced as privileges of elite social statuses and thus of limited access. They are not, in other words, appreciated as common rights of citizenship.

Why civil rights are so impracticable and disregarded in Brazil is particularly difficult to analyze without being historically reductive or culturally simplistic. It requires understanding an intersection of cultural formulations about law, citizenship, and individual autonomy that is too complex to explore here. It must suffice to suggest that historically this cultural formation constitutes law and citizenship as principles of distance that remove people from what they consider socially important and, therefore, turns them into principles of disadvantage. It defines the citizen as an unrelated "other" and the law as what such people "get." As developed in the tradition of liberal constitutionalism, the concept of civil rights is at fundamental odds with this culture.

What we want to emphasize here are the consequences of this problem for the democratic rule of law: Not only are civil rights generally unenforced within the justice system, but they are also skewed by the double bias of impunity and exclusion with respect to criminal and civil law, as discussed earlier. From the perspective of most citizens, therefore, the right to justice, as a key civil right and matter of law, lacks both personal commitment and institutional consolidation. From the perspective of the courts, this neglect of the right to justice and of the civil component of democracy generally means that the judiciary has not had to confront the transformations of contemporary society. Of the branches of government, it has remained the most resistant to democratic transformation. The development of Brazilian citizenship thus remains strikingly disjunctive almost a decade after the successful institution of political democracy.

## The Privatization of Justice

One of the most important consequences of judicial discredit is the privatization of justice.[17] The combination of fearing the police and distrusting the justice system leaves people feeling terribly vulnerable. Some resign themselves to this feeling. Others seek alternatives. Usually, these are outside the boundaries of legality and may be of two types. In one alternative, people consider reacting privately and taking justice into their own hands. It is important to add that such vigilantism is usually an alternative more at the level of discourse than of practice, although lynchings have, in fact, increased considerably in the 1990s. People express their discontent by defending personal vengeance, which does not mean that they act that way, at least not as frequently and vehemently as they defend it. In the other alternative, people support the use of deadly force against alleged criminals. Both are extremely paradoxical reactions to a delegitimated justice system, for people are usually asking the police, whom they fear and accuse of being violent, to be violent "toward the side that deserves it" even though they know that the police routinely aggrieve innocent people. The intent of their request is nevertheless clear: Once dead, criminals cannot threaten them anymore. However, the paradox remains. By supporting violent police action, people are only helping to spread violence and greatly increasing their own chances of victimization.

Our research indicates that people from all classes in Brazil generally think it is too risky to take justice into their own hands because doing so may lead to a lot of trouble. However, they are more likely to argue that if this kind of justice were carried out by the "right" institution, such as a police force that defends innocent people, it would constitute an effective solution to crime. This type of institutional reasoning leads people from all classes to support summary executions by the police and to evaluate police violence and illegality positively. It is in this context that ROTA and the Esquadrão da Morte — a death squad formed by members of the civil police during the 1970s — are widely admired. Poor people see these two organizations as "tough" with criminals and as not corrupt. Moreover, they tend to believe that these organizations kill "the right people" — even against evidence to the contrary — and therefore carry out justice. Poor people perceive these organizations as more efficient than a justice system in which the death penalty does not exist and the judicial process takes forever. This same reasoning leads them to resort to and admire vigilantes, called *justiceiros* (literally justice makers). In an interview conducted by Teresa Caldeira, a young man who lives in a working-class neighborhood said the following about a famous police death squad:

> I wish the Esquadrão da Morte still existed. The Esquadrão da Morte is the police that only kills; the Esquadrão da Morte is justice done by one's own hands. I think

it should still exist. It's necessary to take justice into one's own hands, but the people who should do this should be the police, the authorities themselves, not us. Why should we get a guy and kill him? What do we pay taxes for? For this, to be protected.... It's not worth it for us to lynch. They should have the right, they have the duty, because we pay taxes for this.... The law must be this one: If you kill, you die.

People from the upper classes also defend summary executions and may use exactly the same arguments about the failure of the justice system and the need to "kill the right person," to "solve the problem definitively." However, in a country with huge social inequalities such as Brazil, the way in which justice does not work for the upper classes is not the same way as for the working classes. In fact, for the upper classes, the nonfunctioning of the justice system may be just another privilege.[18] In contrast to the working classes, who are frequently victims of police violence, constantly run the risk of being mistaken for criminals, and suffer accordingly, the upper classes are rarely victims of police abuse or of the justice system. Rather, they have the luxury of choosing to disrespect the law. They can rely on their perception that the law does not work, or works only for them, and have the privilege of bypassing it or of manipulating it.

One of the areas in which the upper classes increasingly disregard the law with impunity is traffic. Although the legal age for driving is 18, a large contingent of upper-class adolescents get cars and drive well before that age. In the last few years, people have developed a discourse to justify this transgression for security reasons: It would be safer to break the law and drive without a license than to take public transportation, they say. Without entering into a discussion about the growing social segregation in Brazilian cities that equates public services with poverty, we should observe that driving without a license is only one of the many domains in which the upper classes explicitly disrespect the law without consequences. As an upper-class woman said ironically in an interview conducted by Caldeira:

> Normally, laws are "respected for" [i.e., enforced against] the lower classes, the classes of small purchasing power. For them, the laws are well "respected." They make them follow the law, obey the law. We from the middle class, from the upper class, we don't need to respect the law because with money we pay for it. I don't think this is just.

Thus, among all social classes, the everyday experience of violence and of the institutions of law leads to a pervasive and comprehensive delegitimation of the rule of law. Poorer people are victims of arbitrariness, violence, and injustices committed by law institutions. As a result, they feel that they are left without alternatives inside the law. In contrast, the rich find it in their best interest to take advantage of the failures of legal institutions. They have the privilege of being able to choose to ignore the law and do what they think is personally more appropriate. What is similar for both groups, however, is that their reactions tend to be framed in private and frequently illegal terms. In both cases, the rule of law is discredited.

If we consider the performance of the police and the justice system in a context of growing rates of violent crime, it is not difficult to understand why São Paulo's residents increasingly adopt private measures to protect themselves and to deal with violence. Because these measures are private and several are violent, they can only contribute further to the delegitimation of the rule of law and to the reproduction of violence. Moreover, given the structure of inequality that characterizes Brazilian society, such private measures emphasize social discrimination.

Private measures to deal with crime and to carry out justice are of various sorts. The most visible are the ubiquitous walls and bars people put up in front of their houses and apartment buildings. These barriers are dramatically changing the landscape of Brazilian big cities as well as the social interactions of their public spaces. In these cities of walls, residents have high levels of suspicion and change their habits to avoid interactions in public, especially with people perceived as different. The walls not only separate residences but also create semi-public enclaves, such as shopping centers and office complexes, where entrances can be controlled and social homogeneity guaranteed. In this sense, fear of crime legitimates practices of segregation and considerably changes the character of public space. In as society where people from different social groups tend not to interact or even encounter each other in public, the chances for the propagation of democratic practices are surely diminished.[19]

The walls do not stand alone. They are part of a complex of measures including various technologies of security, from video cameras to identification of visitors, from electronic fences to all kinds of alarms. These measures also include the hiring of doormen and private guards. As in many other countries, they help to multiply the profits of the rapidly growing industry of private security — of private justice, in effect. This industry has various faces in Brazil, as it adapts to serve different social classes. At various levels, however, it mixes with the illegal actions of the police, as a significant number of private guards are off-duty police officers, frequently working with police guns. For the working classes, however, these organized private services and technologies are mostly unaffordable. At times, they may benefit from the vigilance of *justiceiros* hired by a local merchant, but they are also just as likely to suffer the adverse consequences.

The sum of all these measures of private security and justice causes deep transformations in the way people carry on their daily affairs, interact with others, and move around the city. It is possible to observe new gestures, new body postures, and new instinctive reactions of suspicion and distancing. We might call this a new culture of fear, using an expression that has referred to everyday life under authoritarian regimes for many years. In the present Brazilian case, however, there is no political repression, and police violence is routine and uncensored news. Thus, this new culture of fear takes shape in the context of a democratic political system with a free political organization and press. Its development is contemporary with the transition to democracy.

The conjunction of political democracy, violence, and judicial discredit we have described — including the abuses of the police, the delegitimation of the justice system, the private measures of justice and security, the generalized disrespect for law, the culture of fear, and the related transformations of public space — constitutes a significant obstacle to the consolidation of a democratic society in Brazil. To the contrary, this conjunction results in the reproduction of violence, injustice, and inequality. When the state is asked to react to crime by using violence outside of the boundaries of law and does so, when the population supports this illegal and violent action, when many people use the services of private guards and vigilantes and increasingly transform their residences into fortified enclaves, and when even the police deal with violent crime by private vengeance, society turns away from legality and citizenship. It also jeopardizes the possibility of demanding that public institutions of order mediate conflict and restrain violence. Such a society is, in fact, in a cycle of private and illegal vengeance that results in the spread and proliferation of violence. By entering into the cycle of vengeance instead of counteracting it, the institutions of law and order contribute to this proliferation. Their illegal, private, and violent practices undermine civil rights and the very possibility of justice. And without civil rights and justice, it would seem impossible to institute a rule of law that could break the cycle of violence and sustain democratic citizenship.[20]

## DISJUNCTIVE DEMOCRACY

What sense can we make of the conjunction of political democracy, injustice, and violence we have described? How can we account theoretically for a democracy in which the civil component of citizenship is systematically violated? What sense does it make to call this Brazil a democracy? It only does so if we recognize that these combinations of contradictory developments reveal a fundamental characteristic of democratization itself, namely, that it is disjunctive. By calling democracy disjunctive, we want to emphasize that it comprises processes in the institutionalization, practice, and meaning of citizenship that are rarely uniform or homogeneous. Rather, they are usually and normally unbalanced, irregular, heterogeneous, temporally and spatially arrhythmic, and even contradictory. The concept of disjunctive democracy stresses, therefore, that at any one moment citizenship may expand in one area of rights as it contracts in another. The concept also means that democracy's distribution and depth among a population of citizens in a given political space is uneven. It is in this arrhythmic and uneven sense that contemporary Brazil exemplifies a disjunction typical of many emerging democracies: Although the political component of its democratization is relatively strong (that is, there are respected political rights, free elections, and functioning elected institutions), its civil component is fragile and ineffective. As a result, the development of Brazilian democracy emerges as a process in which this disjunction impairs the exercise of citizenship and legality and thus limits the realization of a more substantive rather than a merely formal democracy.[21]

The notion of disjunction we suggest is different from but complementary to several other considerations of temporal and spatial issues in the study of democratization. For example, in the work of Barrington Moore (1966), Eric Nordlinger (1971), and Leonard Binder et al. (1971), arguments about timing focus on the sequences of various crises of national identity, state formation, modernization, and social structure as historical prerequisites of democracy. Central to other studies of political development is the problem of the "penetration" of the state as a central authority throughout a society and territory (for example, Joseph LaPalombara's contribution to Binder's volume cited above). Guillermo O'Donnell and Philippe Schmitter's (1986) seminal work considers regime transition as an unfolding historical process of analytically distinct sequences, patterns, and stages. In addition, dependency theory analyzes the importance of both the timing and the spatial referents of a region's insertion into the international market as factors that relate capitalist development and democratization on a world scale. All of these studies consider time and space as dimensions of change between different kinds of political regimes, systems, or stages, which they treat as more or less comprehensive wholes.

By contrast, our notion of disjunction is specifically internal to democracy. It emphasizes that democracy entails more of a complexity of shifting processes of citizenship, usually confusing and uncertain, always becoming and unbecoming, than a set stage of institutions, actors, social structures, and cultural values. This perspective has two conceptual requisites. First, it depends on conceiving of both democracy and citizenship as necessarily and inherently connected — for the democratic state exists only through the political participation of citizens and citizenship only through the state's application of the principle of legality and its defense of equality, liberty, and dignity. Second, it depends on thinking of both democracy and citizenship as extending beyond the political to encompass the social, economic, and cultural.[22] The notion of disjunction thus engages the dynamism and particularism of political, social, and cultural systems by suggesting that although there are rules of the game that might define a democracy ideally, such a regime has never existed. Rather, there are always various and often contradictory sets of rules and games in play in any democracy at the same time and in the same space, some of which may be considerably less democratic than others. All contemporary democracies are strongly marked by such disjunctions, albeit of different kinds. Thus, in the United States, the socioeconomic component of citizenship is generally weak, while the civil is strong for most but definitely not all segments of the population.

By contrast, Brazil exemplifies the democratic disjunction of a pervasively weak civil component: Brazilians vote in generally free and fair elections, have their basic rights embodied in constitutional principles, and benefit from a minimum of socioeconomic rights well-grounded in public demands. However, the vast majority cannot rely on the institutions of state — particularly on the courts and the police — to respect or guarantee their individual rights, arbitrate their conflicts justly, or stem escalating violence legally. In this sense, the slaughter of "marginals" described earlier is an extreme expression of the everyday marginalization in Brazilian society of the very notion of the anonymous individual as citizen, bearer of civil rights. This kind of disjunctive democratization inevitably brings new forms of violence and injustice. Significantly, they are forms specific to a democracy with a discredited civil sphere. As we have shown, when the civil component is discredited, social groups at all levels come to support the privatization of both justice and security and illegal or extralegal measures of control by state institutions, particularly the police.

As we have tried to demonstrate in the case of Brazil, emphasizing the disjunctive nature of democratization brings greater analytic precision to the relation between democracy and citizenship than a more homogeneous or strictly political view of either. Attention to the disjunctive separates spheres of institutions, actors, practices, and meanings that, though related, have different characteristics and potential perversions. Let us consider the elements of the civil sphere from this point of view and ask how they sustain an exercise of citizenship and legality that we can call democratic. It becomes evident that the rights and immunities that give meaning to the civil sphere require more than formal legislation or an independent legislature to become effective. Just as the extension of political rights does not by itself secure the integrity or development of a democracy's civil sphere, it is also clear that civil rights do not depend only on legislatures to draft laws. More than executive and legislative initiatives, civil rights depend on the institutions of the justice system to secure their performance both between government and citizen and among citizens in their everyday interactions.

From this perspective, the justice system includes the courts, with their bureaucratic and administrative apparatuses, the bar, and the police (even though the latter is normally part of the executive branch of government). Basic to all these elements is the right to justice — the right to have rights in Hannah Arendt's sense. As such, justice is the most fundamental civil right. Because the justice system comprises the institutions most directly associated with the exercise of this right, it is the defining element of the civil sphere of democracy. Within the justice system, the courts have the ultimate responsibility to guarantee the right to justice. That responsibility legitimates the entire justice system. There are, no doubt, other means of enforcing rights, through executive order, for instance. And in Brazil, the Public Ministry is certainly important in maintaining access to legal services for the indigent. However, if the courts do not regularly and consistently exercise the power of law to that end, then the opposites of justice — impunity and injustice — dominate because people and institutions consider themselves immune from legal vulnerabilities. Hence, the courts constitute the crucible of the democratic rule of law without which there is no democracy.

The bar and the police are also indispensable to that rule. Without reasonable and affordable access to qualified legal representation, justice becomes less a right than a remote and estranged privilege reserved for the wealthy. If the police do not enforce the law, impunity also reigns, for justice requires a force to make all people vulnerable to the power of the courts. By enforcing that liability, the police empower the innocent and protect their rights. If the police act illegally or abusively, they disable the justice system. Moreover, some police — such as the Brazilian civil police — investigate for the courts. They initiate the inquests that result in court cases and without which courts cannot adjudicate. Thus, even though policing is an executive function of government, the performance of the police is absolutely crucial to the justice system.

Each in its own way, these various agents of the justice system establish a reciprocity between the power of law at their disposal and the capacity of people and institutions to act according to expectations about the rule of law and their right to justice. In emphasizing this reciprocity, however, we do not mean to say that the rule of law per se legitimates democracy or indeed is its prerequisite. It is sufficient to note that many nondemocratic regimes subscribe to the rule of law. We have only to think of England's constitutional monarchy, France's physiocratic despotism, Nazi Germany's legally constituted government, and even Brazil's military dicta-torship, all of which went to great efforts to promulgate constitutions and laws to ensure their institutionalization and rule. In each case, the executive exercised a considerable amount of legislative power and privilege, to such an extent that one may doubt that the commitment to constitutionalism was anything more than cosmetic. Yet each promoted and indeed legitimated itself in terms of its rule of law. Thus, on the one hand, we see that although law may secure conditions for democracy, it often does not. On the other hand, it is one of the principal arguments of this essay that the practice of political democracy does not automatically produce a democratic rule of law. The contrary is easily verifiable, as in the case of Brazil. As Norberto Bobbio observes, arguing that political democracy is not enough, "It is perfectly possible to have a democratic state in a society where most institutions, from the family to school, and from the firm to public services, are not governed democratically" (Bobbio 1989, 156). Indeed, such a disjunctive democracy is all too common.

Our point is that democracy requires a *democratic* rule of law, which in turn needs the development of a strong civil component of citizenship to sustain a rule of law infused with justice. No doubt, there is a circular causality here: A strong civil component sustains a democratic rule of law that sustains a strong civil component. However, it could not be otherwise in so far as *a democracy must secure the legitimacy of the laws or itself become discredited.* How does a democracy do this? At minimum, it must maintain a justice system in which citizens are confident of fair and equitable treatment, to which they have reasonable access, to which all are liable, and which regulates according to the due process of law not only the practices of citizens but also those of the state as a legally constituted and accountable entity. These four conditions — fairness, access, universality, and legality — characterize a democratic rule of law. Its citizens participate in free elections and various forms of political organization as well as in a justice system that they consider available for the arbitration of conflict and for protection against the abuses of both state and society. That a democratic rule of law has never existed in such perfection does not lessen the importance of an approximation.

That importance becomes apparent as soon as people perceive that their right to justice lacks institutional consolidation, above all in the courts. When this is the case, a disastrous chain reaction occurs, as in Brazil, Colombia, or Venezuela in the late 1990s, for example: The justice system and those who defend it become discredited, impunity and violence prevail, and, largely as a result, a culture of vigilantism, exceptionalism, and privatized power predominates. These conditions decisively impair the exercise of citizenship and legality and, with them, the legitimacy of political democracy. One does not need to attribute this incapacitation to the persistence of "archaic" and authoritarian forms of patrimonial society, as many authors do, to find a more immediate (and probably more easily counteracted) cause in a discredited justice system.[23] Moreover, where the civil is impaired and the right to justice ungrounded institutionally and culturally, the judiciary is not challenged to confront the dynamic social and economic changes that democratization inevitably brings. Instead, the courts sink even further in reactionary isolation, often mistaking isolation for independence. Even a cursory look at the performance of justice systems in the history of Latin America's unstable democracies reveals these draconian consequences.

Although the fundamental role of the civil component of citizenship in sustaining democracy — and of law and the justice system, in particular — would thus seem indisputable, it is surprising that most of the literature on Latin American democratization neglects them. It is worth considering this puzzle to help clarify the kinds of shifts in research agenda and theoretical perspective we advocate. We do so by briefly reviewing the problem in three bodies of relevant work, namely, studies of law, human rights violation, and democratization. Our objective is not a comprehensive review of the literature, which is impossible here, but rather the demonstration of a problem.

There are numerous studies by legal scholars on the modern institution of law in Latin America (in English, for example, Karst 1966; Karst and Rosenn 1975; Merryman and Clark 1978; Rosenn 1990; and Salas and Rico 1993). These studies, however, tend to be technical and often designed for courses in comparative law. Though important in these terms, they are not focused specifically on the problem of democracy. In each national literature on law, however, there are exceptions. For example, in Brazil, the several volumes authored and edited by José Eduardo Faria and his colleagues at CEDISO (Centro de Estudos de Direito e Sociedade) of the Law School of the University of São Paulo focus on law and democracy and consider especially the role of the judiciary. Under the direction of Rogelio Pérez Perdomo, researchers at IESA (Instituto de Estudios Superiores de Administración) in Caracas, Venezuela, have produced studies of similar concerns. In Argentina, there is the work of the Center of Legal Studies at the University of Buenos Aires; in Colombia, that of Mauricio García Villegas of CIJUR (Centro de Investigación Jurídica) at the University of the Andes; and in each of the other countries of Latin America, there are similar studies and institutions. In the English-language literature of legal scholarship, Irwin Stotzky's 1993 collection of essays is an important contribution and the only sustained treatment we have found on the role of the judiciary in the transition to democracy in Latin America.[24] Unfortunately, the vast social science literature on Latin American democratization has yet to engage these law studies and carry them beyond a narrow circle of legal scholars. Conversely, the legal studies have generally not incorporated the empirical, historical, or case methodologies of the social sciences in their analyses of law. What is missing is a sustained interchange between the two.

The many works about human rights violations and police abuse focus, of course, on the failure of legal systems to protect citizens from state and civilian violence under both dictatorship and democracy (for example, Archdiocese of São Paulo 1986; Chevigny 1995; and Pinheiro 1983, 1994, 1996). However, their often lifesaving denunciations have been less concerned with the impact of democracy on specifically legal change, or of the latter on democratization, than with exposing violence and its social causes and consequences. The recent work of Paulo Sérgio Pinheiro at the Núcleo de Estudos da Violência of the University of São Paulo is a case in point. Focusing on police abuse after the end of Brazil's military regime, Pinheiro distinguishes political transitions to democratic regimes from the democratization of society, which, in his view, has not occurred in Brazil: "The political transition of the authoritarian regime is not necessarily a democratic transition: it does not affect hierarchy in society, the illegality of state violence, or the control of the autonomy of repressive apparatuses enlarged during dictatorship" (Pinheiro

1994, 240). Rather, he attributes the gap between Brazil's political democracy and its violent society to the continuity of an authoritarian culture deeply rooted in colonial history and in the micro-practices of class relations.

Without doubt, Pinheiro's pioneering research has been crucial in directing attention to the performance of the state's apparatus of repression as a fundamental indicator of a society's democratic condition. However, because he attributes this violence to a legacy of authoritarianism, his argument tends to render current transformations less important than we think they are. Certainly, we agree with Pinheiro that this legacy shapes the present, as all significant historical formations do. Giving it primary importance, though, shifts analysis away from what we think is the inevitably disjunctive nature of democratization itself to an overdetermining past. This shift leaves us wondering how to relate the recent increase in new kinds of violence with the considerable evidence of simultaneous democratic change, such as the vast expansion of the political and social rights of the working classes, the end of censorship, freedom of association, new policies toward the respect of human rights, the new Constitution with its numerous citizen rights and guarantees, and the organization of social movements and independent trade unions. It leaves us wondering also about what changes in the culture of law and justice might accompany these new citizen rights and what transformations they might force the judiciary to make. Like other kinds of structures, cultural formations are historically dynamic and subject to change.

Considering the literature on democratization per se, the neglect of law generally and the judiciary specifically becomes more striking as the focus shifts from the liberalization and transition of authoritarian regimes to the consolidation of democracy. This gap in the literature is especially notable when we realize that the reigning Schumpeterian insistence on procedural conceptions of democracy could perfectly well include judicial process but doesn't. On the whole, the earlier studies had very little, if anything, to say on the matter. Perhaps it made little sense to study the "law-ways" of military dictators who cooked constitutions, packed or sacked supreme courts, operated their own tribunals, issued arbitrary decrees, implemented secret laws, and committed massive human rights violations. Yet, even under these circumstances, research into the performance of the judiciary would be quite revealing. It would tell us not only about the relation of dictatorship to the rule of law but also about the dynamics of democratic change, because in many Latin American countries most judges remained on the bench before, during, and after dictatorship. Moreover, they cooperated with it, in many cases fully.

In Argentina, for example, the military junta appointed its own Supreme Court but left the lower courts in place.[25] The Chilean case is even more sobering because scholars have often lauded the independence and integrity of its courts as a mainstay of the supposedly strong tradition of democracy prior to the military coup in 1973. In Chile, Augusto Pinochet did not intervene in the Supreme Court or lower courts when he overthrew Salvador Allende. Ultimately, he shaped the Supreme Court but not by coercion. Rather, over the course of a decade and a half, he expanded the number of Supreme Court justices from 12 to 17 and filled five seats that became vacant due to retirement with his appointees. In fact, Pinochet's Supreme Court was made up overwhelmingly of justices appointed during democratic regimes who did nothing to protect human rights during the early and darkest years of his dictatorship. Rather, throughout the entire period, the judiciary accepted the junta's claim that a "state of war" and later "states of exception" existed and that, therefore, its civilian enemies were subject to the authority of military tribunals. Giving new meaning to the idea of blind justice, the Chilean Supreme Court rejected all but 10 of the 5,400 writs of habeas corpus that the church-based human rights organization, Vicaría de la Solidaridad, filed between 1973 and 1983 (Constable and Valenzuela 1991, 122). The Court routinely had two responses: Either it accepted at face value the government's denial that it had detained the individual in question, or it declared the detention legal by rejecting the writ on the grounds that the Code of Military Justice did not allow civilian courts to intervene in martial law cases. Not surprisingly, in Argentina, the High Court followed the same routine.[26]

In Brazil, the situation is perhaps more surreal. During the whole period of military dictatorship, the courts routinely heard *and recorded* testimonies and accusations of torture and other sorts of illegal procedures such as unsubstantiated arrest. The project "Brasil Nunca Mais" finally made these court records public, basing its denunciations of human rights abuses exclusively on the archives of the military justice (Archdiocese of São Paulo 1986). Yet, in spite of careful recording in the courts, no action was ever taken either to prevent the violations or to punish those responsible for them.

As research has turned to the problem of consolidation, the question of how democracy should be defined has become central to how it should be measured. Our intention here is not to become embroiled in debates about competing definitions of "democratic-ness" (see Karl 1990 for an enlightening discussion), for, as Bobbio has wryly remarked, "Every regime is democratic according to the meaning of democracy presumed by its defendants, and undemocratic in the sense upheld by its detractors" (Bobbio 1989, 158). Rather, our intention is to suggest why the study of the civil component of citizenship, with its attributes of law and justice, does not seem to fit the predominant conceptualization of democracy or, put in another way, to suggest that current approaches generally fail to relate their conceptions of democracy to the real extent and exercise of citizenship and that this dissociation is a serious problem.

For the last 25 years or more, Joseph Schumpeter's definition has dominated the study of both new and established democracies: "The democratic method is that institutional arrangement for arriving at political decisions in which individuals acquire the power to decide by means of a competitive struggle for the people's vote" (Schumpeter 1947, 269).[27] This definition privileges political democracy and the procedural minimums necessary to achieve it. When interpreted narrowly, this view holds that democracy is fundamentally a means of governance, a method or technical instrument of politics, and democratization, therefore, primarily a question of establishing adequate governmental institutions. In this minimalist version, the locus of the democratic project is exclusively the modern state. Some studies in this tradition extend this locus to cover the networks of the state as they reach into civil society. However, the extensions are short and, in any case, of secondary importance because grounding this perspective is the classic dichotomy between state and civil society (and associated divides, such as public and private) that locates the realm of the political in the former and distinguishes it from the social relations of the latter. Thus, as we argued in the introduction, if democracy is conceived narrowly as a political method, this dichotomization means that it cannot *also* be a condition of society. Therefore, the literature derived from this perspective dissociates democracy from society and its conditions of citizenship.

This dissociation has a number of important consequences for our problem. In its narrowest interpretation, the political definition of democracy focuses on the mere presence of elections and thereby eliminates concern for the exercise of anything other than some aspects of political citizenship. For the same reason, even though the political definition emphasizes institutions, it does not consider the effectiveness of the justice system or the extent of the rule of law, even in the latter's more restrictive form as state law or the state-as-law. Terry Lynn Karl (1986) has convincingly criticized this view as "electoralism" and argued that Schumpeter himself would not have supported it because he considered civil rights necessary for the operation of democracy. Many current studies agree and go beyond mere electoral competition to include in their definitions of democracy guarantees for civil liberties through the rule of law as well as two forms of accountability, namely, that of the governors to the governed and of the military to the civilian.[28] Nevertheless, even though the emphasis of many of these studies is institutional, none that we could find actually analyzes the legal system and its relation to democracy.

In other words, what is meant by the shibboleth "the rule of law" is seldom investigated, and the crucial question of the performance of the justice system is seldom posed. Rather, even the wider political definitions of democracy tend to suppose that the institutionalization of competitive politics and more independent legislatures will produce rule of law, access to justice, and protection of civil rights as more or less automatic byproducts of formal regime change (see note 28). Thus, it is very generally presumed that political democracies guarantee a greater respect for law and human dignity than their authoritarian predecessors. Indeed, in many Latin American countries, this supposition grounded political arguments for the replacement of dictatorship with democracy. When political democracy finally came, it was burdened with an expectation in this regard that it could not meet, and many inaugural democratic governments suffered disappointments. For, as we have shown, political democracies do not necessarily produce a democratic rule of law. And, as we have discussed, the rule of law does not necessarily secure democratic citizenship. In fact, political democracies can be more murderous than their authoritarian predecessors. In Brazil, there is no doubt that violence against civilians and disrespect for law and human dignity have increased dramatically after the formal transition to democracy.

Furthermore, the deeper dissociation of democracy from society means that these theories tend to study only the political and formal component of citizenship. The principal reason given in the literature for avoiding the other, more substantive aspects is commonly the claim that to study them, and therefore the real texture of social life, would open the door to ideological and evidentiary confusion. Thus, the social complexity in which every democratic government must survive and with which it must come to terms to act democratically falls outside the definitional scope. To make, as we suggest, the legal, ethical, and performative dimensions of citizenship fundamental to the conception of democracy seems to make it difficult for many observers "to find any actual democracies to study" (Karl 1990, 2) or "to assign a reasonable closure to the second transition process" (Valenzuela 1992, 60) because in these terms no democracy is really consolidated. But this apparent difficulty is an artifact of a classificatory scheme that insists on homogeneous categories and terminal processes. If we accept that even consolidated democracies are disjunctive, the difficulty evaporates, and we are compelled to study the full experience of democratic citizenship to understand the development of democracy.

This full experience is so unbalanced and heterogeneous in contemporary democracy that its traditional definition in terms of political membership in the nation-state is as unconvincing theoretically as it is unfaithful to its new empirical conditions. Divided from the social, the traditional political definition generally treats citizenship in terms of abstract and uniform rights of membership in the nation-state. This treatment assumes an even distribution of these rights across national space and society. However, we know that actual democracies behave very differently. We know that there are vast substantive differences of citizenship between social groups and regions at subnational and transnational levels, even when participatory political rights are effective nationally. If formal citizenship refers to membership in the territorial nation-state and substantive citizenship to the array of political, civil, socioeconomic, and cultural rights people possess and exercise, much of the turmoil in contemporary democracies (both emerging and established) derives from the disjunctive relation between the formal and the substantive. That is, although in theory full access to rights depends on membership, in practice that which constitutes citizenship substantively is often independent of its formal status. Hence, formal membership in the nation-state is increasingly neither a necessary nor sufficient condition for substantive citizenship. That it is not sufficient is obvious to many poor citizens who have formal membership and may vote regularly but are excluded in fact or law from exercising many of the rights of citizenship. This condition also applies to other kinds of citizens in various ways. In fact, as many observers are beginning to realize, the condition of formal membership without much substantive citizenship is characteristic of many of the societies that have experienced recent transitions to democracy in Latin America, Asia, and Eastern Europe.[29]

Focusing on such characteristics, O'Donnell (1993) makes a similar argument in his discussion of "low-intensity citizenship" in the "brown areas of new democracies." Moreover, he stresses the importance of an effective rule of law and the state's legal responsibility to extend and enforce citizenship rights universally. The extent to which the state does not do so curtails citizenship and compromises democracy. Although he maintains a political definition of democracy, his analysis is close to our own understanding of democracy's disjunctive nature and of the importance of studying it from this perspective. As he argues (O'Donnell 1993, 1361), "Even a political definition of democracy (such as that recommended by most contemporary authors, and to which I adhere) should not neglect posing the question of the extent to which citizenship is really exercised in a given country." We would only disagree with his limiting the concept of low-intensity citizenship "specifically to the political sphere, to the *political* theory of political democracy" — a limitation that leads him to the dubious argument that "the denial of liberal rights to (mostly but not exclusively) the poor or otherwise deprived sectors is analytically distinct from, and bears no necessary relation to various degrees of social and economic democratization" (O'Donnell 1993, 1361). But, as O'Donnell admits in the same discussion, the two "go hand in hand" empirically. Hence, the argument of "no necessary relation" seems driven more by the need to maintain the political definition than to account better for the nature of real democracies.

If we agree that contemporary democracies are significantly disjunctive in the political, civil, social, and cultural components of citizenship and that such disjunctions can delegitimate political democracy, then it seems right to insist that the extension of democracy to the social sphere is as central to the concept of democracy as its extension to the political. It seems right to argue that these extensions are reciprocal and mutually defining. It then becomes unnecessary to argue that democracy's disjunctions are incidental or extraneous to the theory. That which has the power to delegitimate democracy — as do the extreme and violent disjunctions of the civil component we have analyzed in Brazil — cannot be external to its construction. In many places, these disjunctions are exhausting the project of national democracy. In some, the nation itself is no longer a successful arbiter of democratic citizenship. In others, although it maintains the envelope of citizenship, the substance and distribution are radically challenged by new social morphologies. In both circumstances, citizenship becomes so unbalanced that profound uncertainties arise about many aspects of democracy that only recently seemed secure: uncertainties about the community of allegiance, location of sovereign power, singularity and universality of membership, distribution of rights, basis of enforcement, and role of cultural identities, to name a few. A conception of democracy that encompasses the social and cultural conditions of citizenship and considers these conditions as inherently and disjunctively linked to the political is, therefore, bound to be more effective in understanding its contemporary forms of development.

# Notes

1. We originally presented this paper at the conference "Fault Lines of Democratic Governance in the Americas," sponsored by the North-South Center at the University of Miami. We would like to thank the participants of the meeting, particularly Felipe Agüero, for their many useful comments. We are especially grateful to the organizers of both the conference and the resulting volume for encouraging us to bring together our research. Aspects of the analysis presented here of violence, crime, the police, and the privatization of justice may be found in Teresa P.R. Caldeira (forthcoming) and the concept of disjunctive democracy and the analysis of law, civil citizenship, and the justice system in Holston (forthcoming).

2. César Caldeira (1995, 15). His paper presents a detailed analysis of Operação Rio.

3. Through a series of publications on various aspects of the Brazilian case, institutions such as Amnesty International and Human Rights Watch have abundantly documented the widespread disrespect for human rights in Brazil.

4. Although there is no official definition of violent crime, for purposes of statistical evaluation, we consider it to include murder, attempted murder, rape, attempted rape, assault and battery, robbery, and felony murder (*latrocínio*).

5. Rates of murder refer to the civil police records of reported crimes (*boletins de ocorrência*).

6. According to the FBI's *Uniform Crime Report for the United States* for 1993, some of the highest rates were 80.3 in New Orleans; 78.5 in Washington, D.C.; 56.7 in Detroit; 50.4 in Atlanta; 34.1 in Miami; 30.5 in Los Angeles; and 26.5 in New York City.

7. See, for example, Americas Watch Committee 1993.

8. Centro Santos Dias, a human rights defense group associated with the Archdiocese of São Paulo, analyzed 380 trials at the courts of the military justice from 1977 to 1983 (unpublished data). For these years, it found that of 82 police officers accused of murder, only 14 were found guilty (15.9 percent). Among 44 police officers accused of crimes against property, 14 were found guilty (31.8 percent). Finally, among 53 police officers who faced trials for matters of discipline, 28 were found guilty (52.8 percent). More recently, another study by the Núcleo de Estudos da Violência from the University of São Paulo found that in 1995, from a total of 344 cases that reached the third Auditoria da Justiça Militar of São Paulo, 58 resulted in conviction (16.9 percent), 190 in acquittal (55.2 percent), while 96 (27.9 percent) were dismissed before going to trial (unpublished data).

9. One might argue that this increase is artificial because censorship was effective under military dictatorship and curtailed information about police abuse. Under democratic rule, this information is readily available in the everyday media. It is true that much more of this kind of information is accessible today and that statistics are better, though still far from reliable. However, according to every available comparative index, it is indisputable that not only have the victims of police abuse changed from political opponents to alleged criminals but also that the numbers of victims have risen dramatically in recent years. Moreover,

frequent media exposure of violent police actions has not generated condemnation but usually support among the population at large.

10. For example, in 1994, MP Colonel Ubiratan Guimarães, the commander of the Casa de Detenção operation, ran for a seat in the state assembly. Among the many shocking aspects of his campaign was his choice of the number 111 to identify himself as a candidate on the ballot, exactly the number of prisoners killed in the assault. Although he received 26,156 votes, it was not enough to be elected. More recently, in May 1996, the Eighth House of Public Law of the Court of Justice of the State of São Paulo judged the police action "legitimate" and absolved the state of all civil and financial responsibilities. The superior judge who heard the case, Raphael Salvador — also vice-president of the Paulista Association of Judges — justified his decision by blaming the prisoners for the massacre: "They started the rebellion, destroyed the prison block, and forced society, through its police, to defend itself" (*O Estado de São Paulo*, May 4, 1996). Other courts are also hearing the case, and the decision is under appeal.

11. This cultural pattern is quite complex. One of its main elements, which we cannot analyze here, is a certain dominant conception of the body that Caldeira (forthcoming) calls the unbounded body. It is a concept with two complementary aspects. First, the unbounded body is one around which there are no clear boundaries of separation and avoidance, a body that is permeable and open to intervention and that can and even should be manipulated by others. Second, the unbounded body is unprotected by individual rights and indeed results historically from the lack of their reinforcement. Thus, in Brazil, where the judicial system is openly discredited, the body (and the person) are generally not protected by a set of rights that bind it, in the sense of establishing barriers and setting limits to interference, intervention, or abuse by others. In Brazil, the unbounded body is evident not only at Carnival but also in the extraordinarily high rates of cesarean births, cosmetic surgery, and physical punishment of children by parents.

12. This discussion about the population's view of the police and the justice system is based on research conducted by Teresa Caldeira among residents of all social classes in São Paulo. The research used in-depth interviews with residents, focusing primarily on their perception of violence and on the transformations of social interactions, spatial segregation, and everyday habits due to the increase in fear. The study also included interviews with public authorities and analyses of crime statistics, policies of public security, and changes in the pattern of urban segregation. The complete study is presented in Caldeira (forthcoming).

13. The following discussion of the Brazilian justice system is drawn from Holston (forthcoming). It is based on research conducted both in the poor periphery of the city of São Paulo and in the civil courts of the state of São Paulo. In the periphery, the research involved working with neighborhood associations and residents, many of whom are engaged in land conflicts of various sorts. In the courts, the research included working closely with judges and their cartorial bureaucracies, especially those involved in cases of land conflict.

14. The one exception for the working poor is the labor tribunals for peculiar historical reasons; see Santos 1979.

15. Thus, to ensure a fair trial, the U.S. Supreme Court decided in 1932 that "due process entitles indigent defendant[s] to counsel at state expense though common law did not" (Currie 1988, 124). In Roe v. Wade (1973), the Supreme Court invalidated state statutes banning abortion by ruling that they deprived pregnant women of liberty without due process. To reach this decision, the Court expanded the category of fundamental liberties beyond those listed in the Bill of Rights by concluding that a woman's interest in having an abortion was "fundamental" and therefore could only be restricted for a compelling and not merely

reasonable purpose. By this more exacting standard of liberty, the ban failed. See Currie 1988, 44-55.

16. For example, in a case of land dispute involving millions of poor families in the periphery of São Paulo, the Supreme Federal Tribunal was petitioned in 1957 (Ação Cível Orginária 164-A) to sort out the property interests of the federal government, the state of São Paulo, and various kinds of private parties. By law, the Court has to hear all cases brought before it. Although this particular case involves constitutional issues that directly affect the well-being of countless citizens, it has simply languished in the court system without decision for almost 40 years. See Holston 1991.

17. See Caldeira (forthcoming) for a fuller discussion of this problem.

18. See Holston 1991 for an analysis of this "privilege-at-law."

19. See Caldeira 1996 for a discussion of how the proliferation of fortified enclaves transforms the character of public life both in São Paulo and in Los Angeles.

20. It would be wrong to end this discussion of the justice system's discredit without mentioning that there are some noteworthy signs of change with respect to the isolation of the judiciary, its abuses, and its estrangement from popular demands for rights and justice. These changes are developing out of the intersection of two forces — the mobilization of grassroots movements for democracy in the 1970s and 1980s and the framing of a new constitution in 1988 — neither of which would have had that effect alone. It is this combination that transforms the paper norms and remedies of the new Constitution into possible opportunities for significant judicial reform. Although we are skeptical about prospects in the foreseeable future for dramatic improvements in the realization of civil rights, it is important to draw attention to the possibilities of judicial change to emphasize that the problems of justice and legality are fundamental to Brazilian democracy.

21. The concept of disjunctive democracy is further developed in Holston (forthcoming).

22. Our conception of democratic citizenship as encompassing more than the political derives from T.H. Marshall's pioneering studies in the 1940s, in which he analyzed the relations among three spheres of citizenship, namely, the political, civil, and socioeconomic. See Holston and Appadurai 1996 for a fuller discussion. Most modern literature on citizenship already incorporates this broader conception. More recent work considers its extension to the cultural as well. Throughout Latin America, and especially in the Andean countries, questions of indigenous rights, sovereignties, and legal pluralism often turn on issues of cultural citizenship.

23. For example, O'Donnell 1992 and Pinheiro 1994.

24. The essays in Stotzky 1993 concentrate on Argentina and Chile, with some comparative comments on the United States. The volume's overarching concern is the protection of citizens from state violence. In these terms, it addresses more the issue and legacy of human rights abuse under military dictatorship than violence under democracy. However, many of the essays are also unusually interesting because of their attempts to understand the relationship between the structure of judicial process and the transition to democracy through an exploration of four major themes: judicial independence versus judicial isolation; the Latin American inquisitorial system of criminal justice (in comparison to the adversarial system in common law countries) as a possible paradigm of authoritarian norms and coercive state action; the role of the prosecution in a post-authoritarian government, especially in cases of human rights violation; and the development of judicial review and constitutionalism.

25. This discussion of the judiciary in Argentina and Chile is drawn from Constable and Valenzuela 1991; Correa Sutil 1993; Fiss 1993; and Frühling 1984.

26. Pamela Constable and Arturo Valenzuela (1991, 125), like most other researchers, attribute the failure of Chile's justice system to protect its citizens to a combination of three factors, the last being the most important: the "innate conservatism" of judges, their traumatic relation with Allende's Popular Unity, and "a system of legal training that confined them to a literal interpretation of the law and taught them to apply it without regard to the motives of the lawmakers or the political context of the times." Whereas Allende collided head-on with this legal positivism, the junta manipulated it ruthlessly. In part, no doubt, because he could not get the laws he wanted passed in Congress, Allende argued that the existing laws were subject to new interpretations in light of new social realities. Rejecting this charge, the courts demanded that he submit new laws to the legislature for passage. The junta avoided this impasse because it only needed four signatures to create or change a law (Constable and Valenzuela 1991, 126-127). Thereby, it issued a torrent of decree-laws to give its rule legal legitimacy. Thus, judges could claim that in applying the law strictly, they were not only doing their job but doing so in the finest Chilean legal tradition. Obviously, it is not the mere rule of law that is fundamental to democracy.

27. As Samuel Huntington (1991, 6-7) observes, "By the 1970s the debate was over, and Schumpeter had won. Theorists ... concluded that only [Schumpeter's procedural definition of democracy] provided the analytical precision and empirical referents that make the concept a useful one. Sweeping discussions of democracy in terms of normative theory sharply declined, at least in American scholarly discussions."

28. For example, see the essays in Mainwaring, O'Donnell, and Valenzuela 1992. Earlier, O'Donnell and Schmitter (1989, 8) defined a broader democratic minimum as "secret balloting, universal adult suffrage, regular elections, partisan competitions, associational recognition and access, and executive accountability." Similarly, for her "middle-range specification" (that is, neither minimal nor maximal), Karl (1990, 2) identifies contestation, participation, and accountability of rulers and adds civilian control over the military. Curiously, neither definition specifies rule of law or civil rights. Although accountability and associational participation presume fundamental civil rights, there are many others, such as the right to justice, that are not so obviously included.

29. See Holston and Appadurai 1996 for a fuller discussion of current theoretical and empirical problems of citizenship in the nation-state. See Holston (forthcoming) for a study of the spread of this kind of uncivil democracy.

# References

Adorno, Sérgio. 1994. "Crime, justiça penal e desigualdade jurídica: As mortes que se contam no tribunal do júri." *Revista USP* 21: 132-151.

Americas Watch Committee. 1991. *Rural Violence in Brazil.* New York: Americas Watch Committee.

Americas Watch Committee. 1993. *Urban Police Violence in Brazil: Torture and Police Killings in São Paulo and Rio de Janeiro after Five Years.* New York: Americas Watch Committee.

Archdiocese of São Paulo. 1986. *Torture in Brazil.* New York: Vintage Books.

Binder, Leonard, James S. Coleman, Joseph LaPalombara, Lucian W. Pye, Sidney Verba, and Myron Weiner. 1971. *Crises and Sequences in Political Development.* Princeton: Princeton University Press.

Bobbio, Norberto. 1989. *Democracy and Dictatorship: The Nature and Limits of State Power.* Minneapolis: University of Minnesota Press.

Caldeira, César. 1995. "Operação Rio e cidadania: as tensões entre o combate à criminalidade e a ordem jurídica." Paper presented at Anpocs XIX, Caxambu, Brazil.

Caldeira, Teresa Pires do Rio. 1991. "Direitos humanos ou 'privilégios de bandidos?'" *Novos Estudos Cebrap* 30: 162-174.

Caldeira, Teresa P.R. 1996. "Fortified Enclaves: The New Urban Segregation." In *Cities and Citizenship*, 303-328. ed. James Holston. Special issue of *Public Culture* 8 (2).

Caldeira, Teresa P.R. Forthcoming. *City of Walls: Crime, Segregation, and Citizenship in São Paulo.* Berkeley: University of California Press.

Chevigny, Paul. 1995. *The Edge of the Knife: Police Violence and Accountability in Six Cities of the Americas.* New York: New Press.

Constable, Pamela, and Arturo Valenzuela. 1991. *A Nation of Enemies: Chile under Pinochet.* New York: W.W. Norton.

Correa Sutil, Jorge. 1993. "The Judiciary and the Political System in Chile: The Dilemmas of Judicial Independence During the Transition to Democracy." In *Transition to Democracy in Latin America: The Role of the Judiciary*, ed. Irwin P. Stotzky. Boulder, Colo.: Westview Press.

Currie, David P. 1988. *The Constitution of the United States: A Primer for the People.* Chicago: University of Chicago Press.

*O Estado de São Paulo.* May 4, 1996.

Fiss, Owen M. 1993. "The Right Degree of Independence." In *Transition to Democracy in Latin America: The Role of the Judiciary*, ed. Irwin P. Stotzky. Boulder, Colo.: Westview Press.

*Folha de São Paulo.* November 28, 1989. Interview of Secretary of Public Security Luiz Antonio Fleury Filho.

Frühling, Hugo. 1984. "Repressive Policies and Legal Dissent in Authoritarian Regimes: Chile 1973-81." *International Journal of the Sociology of Law* 12.

Holston, James. 1991. "The Misrule of Law: Land and Usurpation in Brazil." *Comparative Studies in Society and History* 33 (4): 695-725.

Holston, James. Forthcoming. "Citizenship in Uncivil Democracies."

Holston, James, and Arjun Appadurai. 1996. "Cities and Citizenship." In *Cities and Citizenship*, ed. James Holston. Special issue of *Public Culture* 8 (2): 187-204.

Huntington, Samuel P. 1991. *The Third Wave: Democratization in the Late Twentieth Century.* Norman, Okla.: University of Oklahoma Press.

Karl, Terry Lynn. 1986. "Imposing Consent? Electoralism versus Democratization in El Salvador." In *Elections and Democratization in Latin America, 1980-1985*, eds. Paul W. Drake and Eduardo Silva. San Diego: Center for Iberian and Latin American Studies, University of California.

Karl, Terry Lynn. 1990. "Dilemmas of Democratization in Latin America." *Comparative Politics* 23 (1): 1-21.

Karst, Kenneth L. 1966. *Latin American Legal Institutions: Problems for Comparative Study.* Los Angeles: UCLA Latin American Center.

Karst, Kenneth L., and Keith S. Rosenn. 1975. *Law and Development in Latin America: A Case Book.* Berkeley: University of California Press.

LaPalombara, Joseph. 1971. "Penetration: A Crisis of Governmental Capacity." In *Crises and Sequences in Political Development.* Leonard Binder et al. Princeton: Princeton University Press.

Mainwaring, Scott, Guillermo O'Donnell, and J. Samuel Valenzuela, eds. 1992. *Issues in Democratic Consolidation: The New South American Democracies in Comparative Perspective.* Notre Dame, Ind.: University of Notre Dame Press.

Marshall, T.H. 1977 [1950]. "Citizenship and Social Class." In *Class, Citizenship, and Social Development.* Chicago: University of Chicago Press.

Merryman, John Henry, and David S. Clark. 1978. *Comparative Law: Western European and Latin American Legal Systems — Cases and Materials.* Indianapolis: Bobbs-Merrill.

Moore Jr., Barrington. 1966. *Social Origins of Dictatorship and Democracy.* Boston: Beacon Press.

Nordlinger, Eric. 1971. "Political Development, Time Sequences and Rates of Change." In *Political Development and Social Change*, 2nd ed., eds. Jason L. Finkle and Robert W. Gable. New York: John Wiley.

O'Donnell, Guillermo. 1992. "Transitions, Continuities, and Paradoxes." In *Issues in Democratic Consolidation: The New South American Democracies in Comparative Perspective*, eds. Scott Mainwaring, Guillermo O'Donnell, and J. Samuel Valenzuela. Notre Dame, Ind.: University of Notre Dame Press.

O'Donnell, Guillermo. 1993. "On the State, Democratization and Some Conceptual Problems: A Latin American View with Glances at Some Post-Communist Countries." *World Development* 21 (8): 1355-1369.

O'Donnell, Guillermo, and Philippe C. Schmitter. 1986. *Transitions from Authoritarian Rule: Tentative Conclusions About Uncertain Democracies.* Baltimore: Johns Hopkins University Press.

Pinheiro, Paulo Sérgio. 1983. "Violência sem controle e militarização da polícia." *Novos Estudos Cebrap* 2 (1): 8-12.

Pinheiro, Paulo Sérgio. 1994. "The Legacy of Authoritarianism in Democratic Brazil." In *Latin American Development and Public Policy*, ed. Stuart S. Nagel. New York: St. Martin's Press.

Pinheiro, Paulo Sérgio. 1996. "O passado não está morto: Nem passado é ainda." Preface to *Democracia em Pedaços: Direitos Humanos no Brasil*, ed. Gilberto Dimensein. São Paulo: Companhia das Letras.

Rosenn, Keith S. 1990. "Brazil's New Constitution: An Exercise in Transient Constitutionalism for a Transitional Society." *The American Journal of Comparative Law* 38 (4): 773-802.

Salas, Luis, and José María Rico. 1993. *Administration of Justice in Latin America: A Primer on the Criminal Justice System*. San José, Costa Rica: Centro para la Administración de Justicia.

Santos, Wanderley Guilherme dos. 1979. *Cidadania e Justiça*. Rio de Janeiro: Campus.

Schumpeter, Joseph A. 1947. *Capitalism, Socialism, and Democracy*, 2nd ed. New York: Harper.

Seade. Various years. *Anuário Estatístico do Estado de São Paulo*. São Paulo: Fundação Seade.

Stotzky, Irwin P., ed. 1993. *Transition to Democracy in Latin America: The Role of the Judiciary*. Boulder, Colo.: Westview Press.

*Uniform Crime Report for the United States*. 1993. Washington, D.C.: U.S. Department of Justice, Federal Bureau of Investigation.

Valenzuela, J. Samuel. 1992. "Democratic Consolidation in Post-transitional Settings: Notion, Process, and Facilitating Conditions." In *Issues in Democratic Consolidation: The New South American Democracies in Comparative Perspective*, eds. Scott Mainwaring, Guillermo O'Donnell, and J. Samuel Valenzuela. Notre Dame, Ind.: University of Notre Dame Press.

# Part IV

## The Military in a New Context

# CHAPTER ELEVEN

# Civil-Military Relations in Argentina, Brazil, and Chile: Present Trends, Future Prospects

## WENDY HUNTER

Military governments have vanished from Latin America, where as recently as 1978 the armed forces ruled in more than one-half of all countries. To what extent have these regime changes shifted the balance of power between elected civilian leaders and the military? How are Latin American militaries adjusting to the dynamics of democratization in the diverse forms it has taken in the region? What perils to the stability and quality of democracy do the armed forces continue to pose? If democracy is characterized by civilian control of the government — in addition to regular competitive elections, a free press, and constitutionally guaranteed rights — then the military cannot enjoy undue influence.

Interactions between the armed forces and civilian governments in three important South American countries — Argentina, Brazil, and Chile — have revealed opportunities for rolling back military influence, as well as constraints to further subordinating the institution to civilian control, shrinking its jurisdiction, and shaping the attitudes of its members in directions more compatible with sustained democratic government.

Elected governments have reduced the influence of the armed forces in many non-military areas since the transition to civilian rule, notably in Argentina and Brazil and somewhat in Chile. Particularly in Argentina and Brazil, accommodation and normalization have replaced the overt, pronounced contentiousness that marked civil-military interactions in the early phases of civilian rule. Military forces have assumed a lower political profile, while civilian governments and senior officer corps have so far managed their conflicts without destroying or severely compromising democratic systems. In no Latin American country, with the partial exception presented by Peru under Alberto Fujimori, have the armed forces returned to power.

Less clear is whether deeper changes in civil-military relations have been effected. Do civil-military relations continue to represent a fault line of democratic governance? Will problems arise if and when civilians decide to reduce military power and privilege to a significantly lower level? Are the directions in which military missions are being redefined auspicious for democracy's future? Have underlying attitudes within the officer corps changed in ways that will help undergird democratic rule, especially under adverse economic conditions? Or, should economic crisis and political polarization revisit Latin America, will the military emerge from political dormancy and launch a new wave of interventions?

This chapter 1) examines and analyzes the overall decline of military power and the attenuation of civil-military conflict in Argentina since 1983, Brazil since 1985, and Chile since 1990; 2) raises questions about the impact of certain persistent military practices, attitudes, and institutional arrangements on the quality and stability of democracy; and 3) outlines areas for further inquiry and research. The chapter's central argument is that civilian governments and the military leadership in these countries have reached a stabilizing settlement but that this settlement has inhibited further reforms from taking place. The armed forces enjoy substantial autonomy over defense matters and their own corporate affairs in exchange for basic political subordination. Deeper or more extensive reforms have been slow in coming, if not altogether elusive. While not posing an immediate threat to the stability of democracy, remaining pockets of military autonomy, specific missions that the armed forces persist in advocating or adopting, and attitudes that officers continue to harbor inhibit civilian supremacy and impair the quality of democracy. If popular sovereignty is the cornerstone of democracy, the military — unelected and not subject to democratic accountability — cannot remain a central political player.

## NORMALIZATION IN CIVIL-MILITARY RELATIONS

Military forces in Argentina, Brazil, and Chile enjoy less political power and fewer privileges today than in the initial period following the countries' return to civilian rule. Similarly, the "military question" has ceased to loom over elected presidents as ominously as it once did. Although the armed forces are still a "factor of power" and not just another state actor, the pervasive fear they engendered and the disruptive effects they sometimes exercised on the political standing of governments have subsided, especially in Argentina and Brazil and to a lesser extent in Chile. What explains the reduction in the military's broader influence over politics, as well as the attenuation of open conflict in civil-military relations? To address this question, the interests of civilian governments and the military must first be examined.

Nearly all of Latin America's new civilian governments have sought to establish greater authority over the armed forces. They have done so in the context of judging whether to hold officers accountable for human rights violations committed in the authoritarian period; determining which of the military's institutional prerogatives (many expanded during authoritarian rule) will be allowed to persist in the new regime; and deciding what priority defense expenditures have in a national budget subject to heightened interest-group pressures and the competition for resources among vote-seeking politicians.

Various factors have motivated Latin America's civilian governments to challenge and try to rein in the military on these fronts. In countries such as Argentina and Chile where the armed forces committed severe and large-scale human rights violations, politicians have faced public demands to hold members of the officer corps accountable for their misdeeds and to weaken the military institution politically. Such demands confer on government leaders a mandate to address human rights concerns and to challenge vestiges of the authoritarian period.

Moreover, democratization, coupled with the diminution of internal security threats in the post-Cold War era, has led many elected presidents to regard the armed forces more as a competitor for power and influence than as a potential ally. Institutional prerogatives that enhance the military's political and economic influence tend to restrict the margin of latitude that politicians have to attract votes, by supporting popular political positions (which are often at odds with military preferences) and/or using state resources in electorally minded ways.[1] With respect to defense expenditures, the imperatives of electoral competition tend to motivate politicians to wrest resources away from military projects that have little electoral appeal and toward civilian projects that will gain them more votes. In some countries, such as Argentina and Brazil, neoliberal restructuring and International Monetary Fund (IMF) dictates have put further pressure on public officials to keep military budgets low as part of a broad emphasis on promoting austerity.

What factors shape military interests in the current era? Institutional preservation ranks first among the military's concerns. Senior military leaders have gone to great lengths to protect the officer corps from prosecution for human rights abuses and to resist proposals to transform the military into a qualitatively different institution, such as a regional defense force. Another core interest involves retaining autonomy over the areas senior leaders regard as within their own corporate domain — such as the education, socialization, and career advancement of officers. Also important is that virtually all militaries seek to maintain or improve their professional standing, reflected by salaries, budgets, equipment, training, and organization — factors central to modernization. Additionally, many militaries would like to retain institutional prerogatives that enhance their leverage over broader political, social, and economic matters, but the aspiration to exercise influence over wide-ranging extra-military issues is typically secondary to that of protecting basic corporate integrity.

New civilian governments and the armed forces have come into conflict along several of the lines mentioned above. However, a basic mutual interest in maintaining instead of overturning the democratic order has restrained both parties and inhibited conflict from spiraling out of control. Leaders of new civilian regimes place a high priority on preserving stability. Besides the obvious interest that these leaders have in preserving their elected positions, a wide array of groups in society — some of whom in the 1960s dismissed democracy as a "bourgeois institution" and attached greater importance to the realization of substantive goals, such as socioeconomic equality — have come to value democracy as a system of government in and of itself.

As for the military, most senior officers do not appear to want a return to authoritarian rule, which politicized and factionalized the military institution, invited corruption, and often led to a loss of combat capabilities. Furthermore, many militaries that have recently exited from political power feel compelled to repair their image. Opinion polls suggest that high levels of saber-rattling turn public opinion against the institution. Given that public opinion can well affect the policies that democratically elected politicians adopt toward the military, officers need to consider the impact of their actions on the public. Hence, today's militaries pick their political fights carefully. The pro-democracy orientation of the U.S. government since the end of the Cold War further restricts U.S. militaries as they react to efforts to reduce their power and privilege, causing them to be more circumspect and perhaps less forceful in their responses.

How then have civil-military conflicts evolved in the specific countries under study? What courses have they followed? The first *directly* elected presidents of Argentina, Brazil, and Chile — Raúl Alfonsín, Fernando Collor de Mello, and Patricio Aylwin — all tried to assert authority over the armed forces and shrink the military's sphere of influence. The three presidents and their respective Congresses tested how far they could go in reducing military prerogatives, even if it meant provoking conflict. The skirmishes taking place in their governments yielded distinctive patterns of gains and losses. With respect to specific issues, civilian governments generally found it extremely difficult to triumph over the military in disputes involving human rights. Yet, the Alfonsín, Collor, and Aylwin administrations discovered that it was possible to reduce defense expenditures and military claims to other public resources, as well as to cut certain political prerogatives.

Over time, mutual testing between the civilian governments and military forces and the gains and losses that resulted from it established precedents and expectations. Seeking to assert their own interests and authority while avoiding fueling dangerously high levels of conflict, civilian governments came to learn when they could stand firm and when they would be wise to yield. Presidents Alfonsín, Collor, Aylwin, and their successors in office confined their battles with the military increasingly to issues that experience suggested were possible to win. On issues for which the military could be expected to "go to the mat," the presidents either compromised or conceded entirely. As a result, civilian governments and the military have developed a more stable coexistence. Nevertheless, each of the countries examined here has experienced a variation of this process.

## ARGENTINA

The shift from overt civil-military conflict to accommodation took its most dramatic form in Argentina. Public repudiation of the military junta's dictatorship was strongest in Argentina, where from 1976 to 1983 the armed forces committed unspeakable human rights violations, led the economy down a ruinous course, and in 1982 suffered a disastrous defeat in the Malvinas/Falklands War. President Raúl Alfonsín (1983-1989) acted boldly to break the tradition of military impunity, weaken it operationally, and subordinate it to civilian control. The government took the unprecedented steps of prosecuting officers for human rights abuses, eliminating countless military prerogatives (economic and political), and imposing severe budgetary cuts on the institution. These policies, especially the mushrooming trials against human rights violations, provoked a series of uprisings by junior and mid-level officers (Norden 1996). In response, President Alfonsín pardoned all officers below the rank of colonel. He backtracked only slightly on decisions to curb the political and economic prerogatives of the military and to slash defense expenditures. The Alfonsín government's battle with the armed forces wound down with a fragile truce.

Alfonsín's successor, Carlos Saúl Menem (1989-present), has deftly depoliticized the armed forces. President Menem's policy has been to yield where implacable military hostility could be expected to persist and fester, allow the officer corps a high degree of autonomy over corporate and defense matters, and offer compliance-enhancing inducements. Thus, Menem has managed to keep the military's political prerogatives in check and to cut defense expenditures further.

Exemplifying the policy of conceding to the military over intractable problems, President Menem granted blanket pardons to officers imprisoned for committing human rights crimes in the 1976-1983 dictatorship (including all junta members) and for leading uprisings under the Alfonsín government.[2] With respect to allowing military autonomy to persist over explicitly military affairs, President Menem has set down general guidelines for restructuring but has left the details of demobilization to active-duty officers working in or with the civilian-led defense ministry. Similarly, he has not tried to influence junior officers directly; instead, he holds senior leaders accountable for promoting subordination among the ranks. To integrate the armed forces into the government and induce them to adhere to civilian authority, President Menem has encouraged their engagement in international peacekeeping (which provides officers with higher wages) and opportunities to train with some of the world's most advanced militaries, involving foreign experience — fostering a sense of the continuing importance of the military's role. As analysts of military affairs know, morale-boosting is critical for keeping down unrest in the barracks.

These and related policies enacted by President Menem have helped to stabilize civil-military relations, a notable accomplishment in light of the historical unwieldiness of the Argentine military, and to reduce the high levels of conflict that marked civil-military relations as recently as the Alfonsín government.

## BRAZIL

Civilian actions have reduced military clout and privileges in Brazil as well since the initial stages of the new regime, and civil-military relations are relatively calm. The equilibrium of this relationship, however, has stabilized in Brazil at a higher level of military influence than in Argentina. This is due in no small measure to greater support orchestrated by the Brazilian military regime during its rule from 1964 until 1985, placing the armed forces in a better bargaining position at the outset of the new civilian regime.

Military influence began to decline markedly only with the election of President Fernando Collor de Mello (1990-1992). The military remained a privileged and prominent political player under President José Sarney, who led Brazil in the first five years of the new civilian regime (1985-1990), due to the military government's significant control over the transition from authoritarianism, as well as to President Sarney's lack of predisposition and capacity to challenge the armed forces. Sarney, who had been a leader of the Aliança Renovadora Nacional (ARENA), the pro-government party under military rule, became president by default. Newly elected President Tancredo Neves died shortly before taking office, so as Vice President-elect, Sarney assumed the presidency, but he lacked the electoral mandate necessary to challenge established powers.

President Fernando Collor attacked several of the military's key political prerogatives. He abolished the old military-dominated intelligence service and security council, organs synonymous with the dictatorship, and replaced them with agencies directed by civilians. Likewise, he confronted the armed forces' previous monopoly over nuclear issues by signing an agreement with Argentina allowing for inspections by the International Atomic Energy Agency. Collor began to cut defense expenditures as well. Under the Collor administration, the military intervened far less extensively in extra-military affairs (Hunter 1997).

The Collor period constituted a critical turning point in the reduction of military influence. Although the military recovered some of its earlier clout under Itamar Franco (October 1992-December 1994), the politically weak president who finished out Collor's term after his impeachment, at no point did the military regain the influence it wielded under the Sarney government. The armed forces have become even less visible under Brazil's current President, Fernando Henrique Cardoso (January 1995-present), although it is still too early to tell whether Cardoso will try to reduce military prerogatives further. Thus far, President Cardoso does not appear intent on "rocking the boat," as he has not advocated additional reforms to subordinate and weaken the military.[3] In light of the lower political profile the officer corps has assumed since 1990 and its reduced interference in areas that clash with important civilian interests, military forces in Brazil constitute a less formidable obstacle to civilian politicians today than they did under Sarney. Accordingly, Cardoso may well have made a decision to "live and let live" with respect to the armed forces and to concentrate instead on addressing issues more immediately relevant to economic performance and social welfare.

## CHILE

The balance of power between the constitutionally elected government and the armed forces remains far less resolved in Chile than in Argentina or Brazil. Vestiges of the 1973-1990 authoritarian regime under General Augusto Pinochet persist in the form of substantial political and economic prerogatives for the armed forces. The Constitution promulgated in 1980 and the Leyes Orgánicas Constitucionales for the armed forces conferred substantial guarantees of autonomy on the military, including the provision for General Pinochet to remain commander-in-chief of the army until 1998 and immunity for all officers — from the commander-in-chief down — from dismissal by the president (Ensalaco 1994).

The continuing presence of General Pinochet and the solid representation of the political right in the Congress have impeded initiatives by the Concertación (the center-left coalition that has headed both post-authoritarian governments) to reduce military power and privilege. Christian Democratic President Patricio Aylwin (1990-1994) attempted to curb prerogatives that endow the military with inordinate political autonomy. He also tried to impose some accountability on the institution by creating a Truth Commission charged with conducting investigations of human rights violations without naming the perpetrators of crimes or calling for their punishment. In his efforts to assert authority over the armed forces, President Aylwin provoked conflict. Twice, the army resorted to shows of force. Toward the end of his administration, Aylwin seemed resigned to the fact that existing constraints would preclude reforms aimed at checking military power further.

For the most part, the military policies of President Eduardo Frei (1994-present) reflect a continuation of this outlook. Observing the difficulty his predecessor had in gathering congressional support for a reduction of military prerogatives, he has dedicated little energy and political capital to this cause. This has contributed to diminishing the overt hostility that existed between the army and the civilian government under President Aylwin. Frei, nevertheless, faced one particularly difficult power struggle with the armed forces. When Chile's Supreme Court upheld a lower court order convicting General Manuel Contreras and his second-in-command of ordering the 1976 assassinations of Orlando Letelier (former ambassador to the United States under President Salvador Allende) and Letelier's assistant, sectors within the army helped Contreras elude arrest. Only after five months of high drama, which included negotiations between the Frei government and the army high command, was the president able to enforce the court's sentence against the general.

Pinochet's departure from office in 1998 and the possibility of a leftward shift in the composition of the Congress in subsequent elections may provide reformists within the Concertación the opportunity to pass long-awaited military reforms. Seizing this opportunity will break apart the terms of the existing truce and will doubtless lead to renewed conflict. All the same, the difficulty the Frei government had in forcing General Contreras into prison suggests that reformist civilians will not easily prevail in future conflicts with the armed forces.

Where, then, do civil-military relations in Argentina, Brazil, and Chile stand? All three relationships have undergone a certain "normalization," arriving at a more stable equilibrium in Argentina and Brazil than in Chile. As far as the conduct of the armed forces is concerned, in no country is the preservation of democracy in immediate question. Democracy's stability is due not only to the accommodation civilians have reached with the armed forces but also to the relatively successful economic performance that current administrations in these three countries can claim. Good governance deprives the military of a traditional motivation for intervention and makes civilian support highly unlikely should the military try to take over the government. Recent high levels of unemployment notwithstanding, Argentina continues to pull out of a decades-long economic decline and to keep inflation low, accomplishments that helped Menem win a second presidential term in May 1995. Chile is demonstrating the ability of a free market economy to provide for growth as well as equity-enhancing reforms. Brazil's economic program under President Cardoso has provided considerable hope for a sustained economic turnaround for the first time since the beginning of Brazil's new democracy. In all three countries, the reduction of military power and autonomy from the early stages of civilian rule, coupled with progressive normalization, represents progress.

Yet, a normalization of civil-military relations is not equivalent to the assertion of civilian supremacy or a fundamental redefinition of the proper role of the military. The three countries' current accommodations place limits on how far elected public officials may go in challenging the officer corps over remaining enclaves of autonomy, insubordinate behavior, and undemocratic attitudes. This suggests that civilian governments have "agreed to disagree" with the military in several areas rather than attempt reform. Argentina, Brazil, and Chile have a long way to go before popular sovereignty, the cornerstone of democracy, becomes robust and assured, especially in Chile. In short, while the stability of democratic governments in the region may not be in question, the contribution of civil-military relations to the quality of the region's democracies leaves much to be desired.

# REMAINING PROBLEMS

As far as the conduct of the military is concerned, what are the fault lines, real and potential, that pose a threat to the integrity of democracy in Latin America? These can be grouped into the following categories: the presence of institutional prerogatives that provide the military with legal legitimation for meddling in extra-military matters, de facto military autonomy over corporate as well as defense and security issues, the persistence and/or emergence of military missions that draw the armed forces into domestic functions, and undemocratic attitudes among military officers as well as civilians.

## Legal Prerogatives

Scholars have paid much attention to the legal prerogatives that enhance military power and undermine the sovereignty of elected governments (see, for example, Stepan 1988 and Zaverucha 1993). Without dwelling on this issue, suffice it to mention that legal prerogatives remain most substantial in Chile and least pronounced in Argentina. In Chile, the military's most outstanding prerogatives include an oversight capacity on the National Security Council, limitations on the president's powers to appoint and dismiss military chiefs, and restrictions on the power of the government to affect the military budget. In Brazil, they include the existence of three military-dominated service ministries in place of a civilian-led ministry of defense, effective control over some aspects of internal intelligence, and the right to intervene in issues of "law and order." In Argentina, former President Alfonsín made significant progress in reducing military prerogatives. While President Menem has maintained most of the reforms enacted under Alfonsín, he has approved legislation allowing the military a slightly greater role in combating threats to internal security.

These legal prerogatives doubtless endow the militaries in the three countries with a greater degree of political power and autonomy than they would have otherwise. The prerogatives contribute to the armed forces' capacities to function as pressure groups and, hence, reduce the civilian regimes' abilities to respond effectively to their citizens' interests and demands. Alfred Stepan argues that prerogatives equal power "if the exercise of these prerogatives helps to turn potential issues on the political agenda into non-issues, if their existence facilitates the appeal to their exercise by civilians who have interests to protect and thus want the military to remain strong players in the political systems, or if the strong defense of the prerogatives prevents major political initiatives from being implemented once they have begun" (Stepan 1988, 106). In these ways, prerogatives exert a limiting effect on democracy.

More research needs to be undertaken to determine the actual effects that institutional prerogatives have had on military influence. The mere existence of prerogatives does not mean that armed forces always use them or that their members necessarily prevail when they do. In this light, the military's failure to combat government policies prejudicial to its institution in recent years (for example, widespread budget and salary cuts, reductions in force size, the elimination of sensitive high-technology weapons systems, and so on) merits explanation. Prerogatives make up only one component of influence. The military's capacity and will to exercise prerogatives hinges on a host of other factors as well. For example, concerns about negative public reactions sometimes inhibit the hierarchy from using its legal attributions to gain political leverage. Also, the exercise of prerogatives can fail to realize officers' policy preferences when these preferences clash with important civilian interests. Thus, institutional prerogatives do not automatically give the military strong influence on civil decisionmaking.

## De Facto Autonomy over Corporate and Defense Issues

Beyond legal attributions that enhance the potential political influence of the officer corps, de facto military autonomy remains pronounced over corporate matters and policies related to security and defense. Military education, training and doctrine, the system of military justice, defense organization, force levels, and the nature of weaponry rest largely within the purview of active-duty officers everywhere in Latin America. Civilian politicians, who have not targeted these issues as priorities, are as much to blame for this as the armed forces themselves. Beyond lacking the necessary knowledge and expertise to participate effectively in these areas, the vast majority of civilian politicians dedicate their attention to more electorally strategic goals. Corporate and defense issues are not high-priority concerns for most citizens. Politicians prefer to confront the armed forces over issues that carry greater resonance with the public (for example, human rights and defense expenditures) and have a greater impact on their reelection potential.[4]

Permitting the military considerable autonomy in corporate and defense matters in exchange for political quiescence is part and parcel of the accommodation described above. Yet, civilians need to make inroads into these residual spheres of military autonomy in order to extend popular sovereignty and consolidate democracy. At first glance, military dominance in corporate and defense matters may seem innocuous, perhaps even a small price to pay for their depoliticization. However, when civilians neglect issues such as the numbers and location of troops in the country and the kinds of weapons they have at their disposal, civilians give up a crucial opportunity to influence the role definition and orientation of the armed forces, for example, whether they focus on internal or external conflicts. Similarly, when civilians leave issues like military education, socialization, and doctrine in the hands of uniformed officers — who are likely to be steeped in the undemocratic traditions of the institution — they do not try to affect or reshape the attitudes of people who could exert a critical impact on the future of democracy.

## ARGENTINA

Even in Argentina, where civil-military relations are the most stable and military subordination to civilian authority is the most extensive of the three countries under study, civilians have permitted the existence of a great deal of military autonomy in certain corporate and defense issues. Critics note that de facto military autonomy continues to flourish in the defense ministry and that, in effect, men in uniform decide the country's defense policy, despite the progress that has been made in the training of civilian defense experts.[5] As a result, the three service branches have protected vested interests within their own ranks instead of adapting to recent geostrategic changes, have failed to coordinate their restructuring projects, and have not adequately shifted security programs to reflect broader government goals (Scheetz 1995, 76-93). Similarly, civilians have left education largely in the hands of the military, risking the perpetuation of military ideology and culture.

## BRAZIL

Military autonomy over corporate and defense issues is even greater in Brazil, where a unified defense ministry has yet to be formed. Although both houses of Congress have committees whose approval is necessary for certain projects, such as the development of new military weaponry, other issues, such as the location of commands and bases, remain within the military's domain. A fundamental reorientation of the country's armed services away from domestic involvement and toward external defense would demand a transfer of troops away from major urban centers on the coast (where internal security is a likely role) to Brazil's borders. The largest concentration of army troops in the country remains in the state of Rio de Janeiro. The failure of civilians to try to change this and related arrangements contributes to keeping the military immersed in activities and roles that do not bode well for democratic consolidation.

## CHILE

Chile's defense sector remains more immunized from democratic processes than the defense sectors in either Argentina or Brazil. Although Chile has a civilian-led Ministry of Defense, which has made a commitment to training greater numbers of civilian defense experts, the armed forces also possess important aspects of de jure autonomy in the area of defense. In this respect, they enjoy two important economic privileges. The first, enshrined in the Ley Orgánica de las Fuerzas Armadas of 1989, ensures that the armed forces receive allocations equivalent to at least those of 1989 military expenditures in real terms. The second is that the armed forces receive 10 percent of all profits from copper exports of the state monopoly, CODELCO. In recent years, the armed forces have extracted upwards of US$400 million per year from this extra-budgetary source (Rojas Aravena 1994, 239-277; Patillo 1992, 1-13). The resources channeled to the military through the copper fund are divided equally among the three forces and designated for the purchase of new weaponry. No other state actor enjoys this degree of economic privilege. The budget floor and copper fund symbolize the military's overall immunity and special status of being shielded from civilian decisions and popular sovereignty. From time to time, civilian politicians have proposed reallocating money from the copper fund for education, health, or other social programs, but so far no such proposal has come to fruition. A serious effort to eliminate the copper fund would surely meet with the resistance of the hierarchy.

In sum, in various ways and degrees, the armed forces of Argentina, Brazil, and Chile enjoy autonomy over corporate and defense concerns. Future research is needed to investigate further the extent of de facto military autonomy in these areas and its effect on keeping the armed forces entrenched in patterns and practices counter to democracy's consolidation. While such autonomy may contribute to ensuring that the military obey government authority, the pursuit of a more profound process of military reform would have to address more problematic consequences. Confronting the issue might well be seen by the military as a violation of the accommodation that has evolved and hence disrupt government-military relations. However, democracy does not stand on firm ground when civilians feel the need to refrain from any activities that could erode military privilege.

## Military Missions

Democratization, the end of the Cold War, the decline of the radical left, neoliberal restructuring, and the resulting reduction of military participation in the economy have called for a redefinition of military missions in Latin America. The precise missions that the armed forces develop will doubtless affect the extent to which they remain political players. To give the military a stake in the current democratic system and to break the recurring authoritarian-democratic cycle of governments, missions that are credible, honorable, and nonpolitical need to be defined. As much as possible, these missions should focus on strictly military functions and draw the military out of broader involvement.

Certain developments augur in favor of a contraction of the military's jurisdiction to external defense, strictly defined. Democratization and the wide-spread disappearance of guerrilla insurgencies and their foreign sponsors have rendered internal security missions for the armed forces less pressing. Privatization and economic restructuring have reduced military participation in strategic sectors of the economy. Will these developments reverse the trend toward the "new professionalism of internal warfare and military role expansion" that Latin American militaries underwent beginning in the 1950s (Stepan 1973, 47-65)?

Posed against these developments are factors that complicate reform and threaten to expand the definition of the military's role. Many of the most immediate threats to national security in the 1990s lie in the "gray area" between strictly defined military functions and law enforcement. Drug trafficking, immigration, ethnic (indigenous) conflicts, and environmental protection are becoming more significant national security issues in a region where traditional border conflicts have either been resolved or have diminished in importance.[6] Economic integration between Argentina and Brazil and border resolutions between Argentina and Chile have helped to transform old hypotheses of conflict and to convert former rivals into commercial partners. While positive for regional peace, economic integration and the resolution of border disputes deprive the military of credible external defense functions. Use of the military in internal conflicts and law enforcement functions is counterproductive from the standpoint of contracting its overall influence. Militaries that engage in such functions often begin to conduct intelligence, administer justice, and violate civil and human rights. The line between conducting such operations and staying out of broader social and political conflicts is a fine one. One analyst encapsulates the dilemma posed by the nature of current threats to national security: "How [Latin American] military institutions retain a legitimate institutional function in modern democracies while at the same time defining security missions that assign meaningful but politically unintrusive roles to those institutions is a tough act" (Fauriol 1995, 31). As a result of "gray area" threats to public security, members of the military may be drawn into politics, even if they do not wish to become involved. At the same time, if they are already inclined to intervene, such security threats can offer an "excuse" that may be credible.

The renewed attention of Latin American governments to social problems, coupled with the armed forces' need for organizational justification in an era when diminished external as well as internal threats exert heavy pressures to downsize, has led to the enlargement of civic action and social development roles for military personnel in many countries. As with law enforcement, civic action is not a glamorous or highly valued military mission. Yet, civic action compensates the armed forces somewhat for the severance of the traditional military-development connection incurred with the decline of Latin America's state-led development model and enhances the military's organizational justification. Civic action and development roles — the provision of food and health services and construction of infrastructure in poor and remote areas — make a useful contribution to the nation. The problem lies in the potential expansion of the military's role in development beyond that intended or desired by civilian authorities. As Felipe Agüero points out, "Whereas a larger role for the military in development will result in a more encompassing concept of security, such an expanded conception, including development-related issues, will, in turn, tolerate larger military roles" (Agüero 1994, 244).

## ARGENTINA

Of the three cases under examination, Argentina is the least problematic as far as the adoption of questionable military missions is concerned. The role of the Argentine military has the most circumscribed definition. Conventional defense is its main mission, followed by international peacekeeping as an important secondary role. Peacekeeping operations, while hardly a panacea, do offer the possibility that military missions will be defined increasingly as external to the country. Logistical support in anti-narcotics operations and aid to the community in the event of natural disasters provide subsidiary roles. Only under very exceptional circumstances are the Argentine armed forces authorized to participate in internal security.[7] The strict limits on military participation in internal matters stem from the "Dirty War," when the armed forces earned society's antipathy for the abuses they committed under the 1976-1983 military junta. Many military officers — while not wanting the organizational justification to shrink further — have voiced serious reservations about resuming involvement in internal conflicts and risking reassociation with the repression of their own citizens.[8]

# BRAZIL

The Brazilian army is engaged in a broader array of missions than its counterparts in either Argentina or Chile. It carries out internal security roles and civic action on a regular basis and engages in conventional defense and some international peacekeeping. Contributing to this diversified role definition are a tradition of domestic involvement by the military, the inclusion of internal conflicts in current definitions of threats to security, a relatively favorable public opinion of the armed forces, and the officer corps' perceived need to enhance its organizational justification. Historically, Brazil's armed forces have played a leading role in developing the vast and resource-rich country and in quelling internal conflicts, including clashes among different social sectors and regional revolts that threatened to disrupt the social and political order. The military continues to be viewed by many public officials and citizens as the appropriate institution to combat the most severe internal conflicts, including drug trafficking. In 1994 and 1995, the army made regular raids into the *favelas* of Rio de Janeiro to root out gang violence, racketeering, and the trafficking of arms and drugs. President Cardoso recently has sought to enlist military help in arresting the wave of kidnappings in Brazil's urban centers. For the most part, public opinion has been favorable toward military involvement in drug and crime control. The first manifestation of public support for internal security came in 1992, when army troops guarded Rio de Janeiro for the Earth Summit. In 1994, 82 percent of citizens polled in Rio de Janeiro expressed support for army participation in combating violence in the city.[9]

The education of army officers reflects an institution committed to more than defending national borders. The 1995 curriculum for the Army Staff and General Command School (Escola de Comando e Estado-Maior do Exército — ECEME), a training ground for all officers aspiring to the rank of general, included 219 hours of instruction devoted to internal security out of a total of 3,280 hours. As listed in the course description, this section includes treatment of the doctrine of national security and the communist movement of Brazil (Movimento Comunista do Brasil).[10]

The problems of public security related to poverty, crime, and underdevelopment in Brazil indeed demand attention; however, faced with the choice of drawing the military out of the kinds of activities that led to their deepening involvement in politics in the past, civilian authorities would be well advised to keep military personnel away from regular involvement in internal security as well as civic action roles. Instead, civilian means of addressing these problems need to be developed.

# CHILE

Chile's armed forces are deepening their involvement in developmental roles, notwithstanding their renewed attention to military aspects of national defense. The institution's tradition includes civic action but not nearly on the order practiced by militaries of the less-developed, less-integrated nations of Latin America, such as Brazil, Peru, and Ecuador. The Chilean army's developmental role has certain parallels with the activities of the U.S. Army Corps of Engineers. The development projects currently being pursued by Chile's armed forces have to do primarily with the occupation and exploitation of land and sea in the name of economic modernization and sovereignty.

The Chilean army's project is entitled Fronteras Interiores (Interior Borders). Territorial occupation, national integration, and economic modernization are the project's goals. In the army's view, having a presence in otherwise empty areas is essential not only to increasing the economic vitality of the country but also to guarding sovereignty. The areas targeted — the extreme north, south, and eastern strip of Chile adjacent to Argentina — are at the margins of the economic and social growth that the rest of the country has experienced. By helping to develop these regions, thus enhancing their economic value, the military hopes to distribute Chile's concentrated population over the national territory.[11] The army has conducted studies on the border regions and drawn up proposals on how to develop them. The plan awaits approval by civilian authorities.[12]

Similarly, the navy recently formulated a 20-year plan to project its presence into the Pacific Ocean, fortify Chile's territorial water rights, and expand scientific and oceanographic discoveries. This project, entitled Mar Presencial (Sea Presence), reflects the navy's perception of the ocean as the natural space for Chile's growth, as well as its institutional commitment to being an agent of development. Conceived in 1989, Mar Presencial envisions staking out Chile's claims beyond its exclusive economic zone to include a huge area extending westward to Easter Island and southward to the South Pole. International law (UN Convention on the Law of the Sea, 1982) recognizes this area as part of the "high sea," and as such it is open to all nations. Based on a unique interpretation of this convention, Mar Presencial contradicts U.S. policy on the Law of the Sea. The navy wants to open up this ocean space to Chilean forces, such that other countries do not benefit at Chile's expense from what the navy sees as resources that rightfully belong to Chile. While staking out claims for scientific exploration and economic exploitation of deep sea resources is undoubtedly part of the reason for Mar Presencial, projecting Chilean power and sovereignty onto the high seas undoubtedly also motivates this program. Naval power would be used to establish and defend Chile's presence in ocean territory.[13]

Are military proposals for projects such as Fronteras Interiores and Mar Presencial cause for concern? They do suggest that the long period of military rule may have led to a lasting entrenchment of the armed forces in the political, social, and economic fabric of the country.[14] This is consistent with the observation that during the 1970s and 1980s the Chilean military moved toward a "new professionalist" orientation to national problems along the lines of other hemispheric military institutions, such as Peru's Center for Higher Military Studies (Centro de Altos Estudios Militares — CAEM) and Brazil's War College (Escola Superior de Guerra — ESG) (Nunn 1995, 20). As Frederick C. Nunn notes, "Democracy and the New World Order or no, Chilean officers saw no end to the need for the armed forces' talents and expertise to be put to domestic use" (Nunn 1995, 21). Military role expansion rarely augurs well for democracy, yet such a development in Chile is likely to be less injurious than in countries with weak civil societies and frequently ineffective civilian governments. In countries such as Brazil, Peru, and Ecuador, where nation-states are less integrated and political and economic stability more precarious, military role expansion (into internal security as well as civic action) carries the risk that key sectors of society and the officer corps itself come to regard the armed forces as more competent to manage governmental affairs than civilians. The impressive performance of Chile's center-left elected governments since 1990 — in maintaining the trajectory of economic growth set in motion under the Pinochet dictatorship, in advancing equity-enhancing social reforms, and in keeping social order — leaves little room for the military to project itself or be seen as a superior governing alternative, at least for the present time.

## Military Role Beliefs and Attitudes

Above and beyond legal prerogatives, de facto autonomy, and specific missions that the armed forces adopt, military role beliefs and attitudes shape the extent to which the officer corps remains an important political actor. Three questions are central to an examination of military attitudes: Has the officer corps adopted the internal norm that subordination to civilians is not only tactically necessary but fundamentally appropriate? Do officers perceive themselves as accountable to the public or above the law? Do they legitimize a tutelary role for themselves by harboring notions about the superiority of their own norms, such as order and discipline, relative to those of civilian politicians and interest groups?

With respect to the depth of the military's commitment to the democratic order, a distinction needs to be drawn between a conditional acceptance of political noninvolvement and an independent commitment to honoring the principles of political neutrality and subordination. If democracy is to thrive, the military's acceptance of the democratic order cannot be based on such factors as the economic performance of a given government or the generosity of its policies vis-à-vis the military. Whether and to what extent the military remains obedient when political and economic performance is poor and/or defense expenditures and related resources decline constitutes the true test of the military's commitment to the rules of the democratic game. Militaries that adhere unconditionally to political neutrality and subordination do not react to national political crises by becoming politically involved themselves or by trying to extract concessions from the government. Militaries that have not internalized norms of political neutrality and subordination may well engage in role expansion and saber-rattling when government performance falters.

The quality of democracy in Latin America also hinges on officers' perceptions of whether they are accountable to society for their actions. If the equality of all citizens before the law is a guiding principle of democracy, then *uniformados* cannot remain exempt from judgment. Yet, a common dilemma of new civilian governments — how to consolidate a regime founded on the principle of equality before the law and, at the same time, obtain the acquiescence of the armed forces — frequently has inhibited civilians from prosecuting the military for human rights violations. In the absence of efforts to make the military accountable — through methods ranging from truth commissions to actual trials — deeply rooted attitudes among officers about their own immunity are unlikely to change, auguring poorly for democratic norms.

Similarly, the extent to which military officers regard themselves as "moral reservoirs" in wayward societies, "guardians of the nation," or watchdogs against corrupt, incompetent civilian politicians affects democracy's future. Such self-definitions, especially when shared by key sectors of society, have contributed to the military becoming one of the most powerful political players in twentieth-century Latin America. Have officers set aside such notions, adopting instead a narrow professional self-conception? Has society ceased to view the military as a guarantor of law and order?

Regarding role beliefs and attitudes conducive to democracy, the Argentine military reflects the most progress and the Chilean army the least. Brazil's military lies in between. The compatibility of officers' attitudes with democratic consolidation varies inversely with the success of the most recent period of authoritarian rule. In Argentina, the total delegitimation the armed forces suffered eventually led a new generation of senior leaders to engage in self-criticism and to try to reshape attitudes within the institution. By contrast, the Chilean officer corps credit themselves with creating order out of chaos and putting the economy on an upward trajectory after 1973. A high degree of support for the military in Chilean society — reflected by the 43 percent of votes that General Pinochet won in the 1988 plebiscite to decide whether he would stay in power for eight more years — reinforces this self-perception.[15] Confident and unapologetic, senior leaders regard the institution as uniquely qualified to guide Chile into the future (Nunn 1995, 23). Members of the Brazilian military, while far less discredited than their Argentine counterparts, could not claim the success of the Chilean dictatorship. While they are somewhat sobered by having seen Brazil's economic policies of 1964-1985 founder, they retain some elements of their former self-concept as prime defenders of "national values," champions of development, and keepers of social order. As became clear through the many interviews I conducted between 1988 and 1995, most Brazilian military officers do not see themselves as just one among many other important state actors.

## ARGENTINA

The Argentine military's acceptance of civilian rule appears solid. Despite severe downsizing and loss of resources, members of the Argentine officer corps are obedient to their commander-in-chief, Carlos Menem. Similarly, they have all but ceased to present themselves as morally superior to and more able than civilians to manage the affairs of government. Over time, they have come to adhere to a relatively narrow professional role definition.

Of the three cases under study, only in Argentina were large numbers of officers prosecuted for human rights violations. This event forced the military *as an institution* to recognize the costs of its actions and the risks of repeating them, in spite of the "due obedience" exemption President Alfonsín eventually granted to lower ranking officers and the pardon granted by President Menem to the remainder (Acuña and Smulovitz 1995). Due obedience is the argument that all orders must be followed simply because they come down the chain of command. Illegitimate orders are those that defy constitutional authorities. Only in Argentina has the military leadership publicly recognized the illegitimacy of state terror unleashed during the military junta's dictatorship. Its admission to this effect, in April 1995, is one sign of a gradual cultural shift within the institution promoted by General Martín Balza. Army chief since November 1991, Balza has prompted the army to reexamine its conduct in the Dirty War and the Malvinas/Falklands War and to redefine its role beliefs. He has contended consistently that under no condition should the institution ever assume power again and that military officers are responsible for their own actions and cannot seek refuge in due obedience.[16]

Does General Balza have an audience within the army for these changes? It would be an exaggeration to claim that the ranks are full of officers eager to adopt the attitudes he is trying to inculcate. Yet, by virtue of being a hierarchical organization, the army has mechanisms for bringing about a shift in attitudes. Stiff competition for promotion to the top of the shrinking institution, coupled with the loyalty to General Balza exhibited by those who are promoted, help to weed out anti-democratic elements within the institution and provide hope for the spread of democratic attitudes. So, too, does another dynamic. Low-profile political behavior and a return to more strictly professional duties have brought about higher public approval ratings for the military, a development that the officer corps understands and welcomes.[17] If "good behavior" reinforces democratic attitudes, the military's once begrudging acceptance of civilian rule might become transformed into a deeper commitment to the norms necessary to consolidate democracy.

## CHILE

Unlike the Argentine military, the army in Chile believes that its leadership is vital to "protect" Chilean democracy. The Pinochet dictatorship reversed decades of military subordination to civilian governments and inculcated in officers a belief in the appropriateness of a broader vocation, including a governing role. However, military attitudes remain ill-suited for a deepening of democracy. The Chilean army, much more than its counterparts in Argentina or Brazil, regards itself in heroic terms. According to one analyst, "Chileans who wear the army uniform still see themselves as symbolizing the finest attributes of the Fatherland, as having a historical vocation, and as playing social and developmental roles — and doing so successfully" (Nunn 1995, 20).

In contrast to Argentina, the Chilean army has taken no responsibility nor shown any sign of regret for the "disappearance" of over two thousand people under the military dictatorship. Despite the Truth Commission's revelations of massive human rights violations, at no point did General Pinochet admit that the military committed errors or excesses. Not once has he backed away from the official contention that a "state of war" (that is, a justification for repression) existed in the early years of military rule. An example of officers of the Chilean army viewing themselves as above the law was manifested most clearly in efforts to resist civilian directives and protect retired General Manuel Contreras, former head of the secret service, from going to jail. General Pinochet backed down from his position against Contreras' jail term only after President Frei made concessions, including a pay hike for soldiers and a proposed cut-off date for most remaining trials of military officials accused of human rights violations. Such behavior on the part of the army commander hardly serves as a model of military subordination to the government to cadets and junior officers.

Despite the prevalence of such attitudes, members of the officer corps have remained notably detached from daily matters of government and politics since 1990. The solid performance of Chile's two center-left governments has left the armed forces without much reason or justification for deeper political involvement. A faltering in governance, however, might test the military's restraint and commitment to the democratic order. The military forces' historic pride in their own talents, coupled with substantial societal support for the institution many citizens credit with "saving the fatherland" in 1973, could lead them back into assuming a more active political role.

## BRAZIL

Members of the Brazilian military also evince attitudes that appear to be in conflict with the accepted norms of democracy. Like the Chilean military forces, they have remained largely immune from prosecution or punishment for past crimes and have not assumed responsibility for their actions.[18] Nor have they completely internalized the norm of political subordination. The army continues to define "permanent national objectives." Some army officers also deem it appropriate to issue pronouncements on issues of broad political and social significance. These issues include the military's perceptions of the corruption since Brazil's democratic transition and the spiral of crime that afflicts Brazil's urban centers.[19] Military statements on these and related issues suggest that the army has not entirely abdicated its role as a watchdog of the government or defender of the nation.

In Brazil, the inconsistency of military obedience to civilian authority reflects a lack of fundamental adherence to the norm of subordination. When popular support for the president is weak, the military forces have proved quick to expand their visibility and make demands on the government. This dynamic was evident from mid-1993 until mid-1994, the low point of the Itamar Franco administration. Revelations of widespread corruption among Brazil's political elite, coupled with budgetary and salary restrictions on the armed forces, prompted high-ranking officers to make veiled threats and to extract salary concessions and funding for military projects from President Franco.[20]

Civilian attitudes in Brazil reinforce nondemocratic inclinations within the army. Opinion polls indicate that the public consistently ranks the military as one of the most trustworthy institutions in society. The public by and large also supports a greater role for the military in crime control and law enforcement. Data from the public opinion project, Latinobarómetro, revealed several interesting points. When asked what three groups or institutions the respondents would like to see gain more power, a higher percentage of those surveyed in Brazil answered "the military" than in Argentina or Chile. Choices besides the military included large firms, unions, small businesses, banks, political parties, multinational corporations, the government, and Congress. Whereas 32.9 percent of respondents in Brazil answered "the military," only 10.6 percent and 4.3 percent did so in Chile and Argentina, respectively. Only 19.5 percent of Brazilian respondents said they would like to see Congress have more power, compared with 50.5 percent in Argentina and 31.0 percent in Chile.[21] In two other questions, a higher percentage of Brazilian respondents (than Argentine and Chilean) listed "the maintenance of order" and "combating crime" as important policies to strive for.[22] As James Holston and

Teresa P.R. Caldeira suggest in this volume, many who embrace a "law and order" perspective are ordinary citizens who themselves might be victimized and left defenseless by the arbitrariness of authoritarian methods.

Future research needs to be conducted on the current redefinition of military missions and on the state of officers' attitudes. Given the hermetic nature of the institution, officers' attitudes are difficult to discern directly. Only one analyst, J. Samuel Fitch (1995), has conducted extensive formal surveys among officers. Important divisions within the armed forces exist with respect to both missions and attitudes. The navy and air force have tended to be more liberal and internationalist, more concerned than the army to meet narrower professional and technological needs. These and other divisions will affect the ability of civilian politicians to erode further military influence and assert control over the institution. While the majority of Argentine officers now evince a professional orientation (in the narrow sense of the term), not all do. Similarly, while segments of the officer corps in Brazil and Chile harbor antidemocratic views, other segments are interested in a contraction of the military's role definition and a refocusing on defense and war-fighting activities.

## CONCLUSION

In conclusion, civilian governments in Argentina, Brazil, and Chile have made progress in eroding military influence and in stabilizing their relations with the armed forces. In none of these countries is the stability of democracy in question in the foreseeable future. An accommodation or normalization of civil-military interactions has evolved in all cases. In Argentina, civil-military relations are the most stable, and military influence is lowest. In Chile, civil-military relations are the least resolved, and military influence is greatest. In Brazil, civil-military relations remain fluid, yet more resolved than in Chile, and military influence is greater in Brazil than in Argentina but less than in Chile.

Despite the progress that has occurred, in various ways and degrees, de jure and de facto military prerogatives, military missions, and officers' attitudes remain problematic for democracy's consolidation. Institutional prerogatives and guarantees protect the armed forces from democratic processes and help them assert themselves politically. Missions and roles that allow officers to remain involved in social, developmental, and law enforcement activities are questionable from the standpoint of a democracy that actually rests on a confined sphere of military jurisdiction. Also disconcerting are the attitudes of officers who sometimes fail to recognize their subordination to civilian authorities.

In which country, then, is democracy's consolidation in greatest jeopardy? A response to this question necessitates a consideration of the military's status as well as the broader viability of civilian governments. The latter greatly affects the extent to which the military's potential influence will become actualized. Regarding both factors, Argentina presents the least cause for concern, as not only have the military forces been tamed the most, but the economy has improved since 1991, and the political system appears to rest on fairly solid ground. While Argentina's overall economic turnaround is thought by some to be fragile,[23] a serious downturn in the economy would be unlikely to provoke an expansion of military influence, much less bring the military back into power. The fact that the armed forces so discredited themselves in the eyes of the elite and ordinary citizens over an extended period virtually precludes their return.

Analyzing the military alone might lead one to believe that democracy's integrity is most threatened in Chile. Yet, taking into account the performance of civilian governments would suggest that Chile is not likely to see an expansion of military influence any time soon. Chile's military government left behind a much stronger economy and fiscal situation than was the case in either Argentina or Brazil. Chile's and Argentina's postauthoritarian governments have been able to build on this legacy. Fiscal health and new growth, investment, and social spending characterized economic performance in the early 1990s (Mainwaring 1995, 137-140). Moderation has been the norm for the political climate. Such a situation leaves little room for a restoration of military power.

Rather, it is in Brazil where the threat to democracy — its quality as well as stability — is greatest. This has as much to do with civilian governance as with the military itself. For most of the postauthoritarian period, the economy has been characterized by high levels of indebtedness, inflation, and erratic growth (Mainwaring 1995, 133-137). Only since the implementation of the Plano Real in 1994 and the presidency of Fernando Henrique Cardoso have the prospects for the Brazilian economy begun to look brighter. One corruption scandal after the next emerged in the political system, the most prominent the one that led to the impeachment of President Collor. Crime in Brazil's urban centers has reached alarming proportions. Public security constitutes a leading concern among citizens. Coupled with these problems, society appears to retain considerable trust in the military to arrest corruption, impose order on the streets, and to "set things straight" in general. So far, Brazilian democracy has withstood these strains. The current domestic and international climate is conducive to the survival of constitutionally elected governments. Yet, as the expansion of the *uniformados'* influence under the beleaguered Itamar Franco government suggested, poor governance and a not fully reformed military constitute a potentially dangerous combination.

Thus, comparisons among Argentina, Brazil, and Chile suggest that the stability and quality of democracy in fledgling regimes rests not only on civilians reforming the military but also on civilians putting and keeping their own houses in order. Insofar as military forces continue to present obstacles to the deepening of democracy, civilians need to enact military reforms. At the same time, they need to deprive officers and citizens of reasons to endorse expanded military influence.

# Notes

1. For a fuller explanation of this point, see Wendy Hunter, 1997, *Eroding Military Influence in Brazil: Politicians against Soldiers* (Chapel Hill, N.C., and London: University of North Carolina Press), chapter one.

2. The first pardon came in October 1989. It included officers implicated in human rights violations, the Malvinas/Falklands War, the military uprisings under the Alfonsín government, and civilians condemned for terrorism. The second pardon was announced in December 1990, after the last uprising of the *carapintada* rebels. It included former junta leaders and the former head of the urban guerrilla organization, the Montoneros.

3. One sign of Cardoso's caution is the several-month lag between the announcement of his intention to substitute the three traditional service ministries with a civilian-led ministry of defense and actual steps taken toward this goal. Cardoso has even expressed a commitment to expanding defense expenditures.

4. Notably, because of the public resources involved, civilian politicians constrain the military's autonomy with respect to force levels and weapons systems more than some of the other issues noted above.

5. Confidential author interviews with high-ranking civilians in Argentina's Ministry of Defense, Buenos Aires, March 1995.

6. The most recent Conference of American Armies recognized economic inequality, terrorism, drug trafficking, and ethnic conflict as the primary threats to security within the region. Robert Olson, 1995, "Concepts for Future Defense and Military Relations with Counterparts," in *Hemispheric Security in Transition: Adjusting to the Post 1995 Environment*, ed. L. Erik Kjonnerod (Washington, D.C.: National Defense University Press), 205.

7. See "Misión principal y subsidiarias del ejército," 1993, *Verde Oliva* 8 (November), 7.

8. J. Samuel Fitch documents a rather marked change in sentiment among officers regarding the assumption of internal security roles between interviews conducted in 1985 and 1992. See J. Samuel Fitch, 1995, "Military Role Beliefs in Latin American Democracies: Context, Ideology, and Doctrine in Argentina and Ecuador," paper presented at the XIX International Congress of the Latin American Studies Association, Washington, D.C. (September 28-30).

9. "Cariocas apóiam Exército na luta contra violência," 1994, *Jornal do Brasil*, August 23.

10. Ministério do Exército. Brazil. 1995. Escola de Comando e Estado-Maior do Exército. *Curso de Comando e Estado-Maior: Currículo* (Brasília: Ministério do Exército), 10-12.

11. Ninety percent of Chile's population is concentrated between the cities of La Serena and Puerto Montt.

12. For descriptions of the program, see "Ejército plantea crear comisión sobre 'Fronteras Interiores,'" *El Mercurio*, July 19, 1994; and "Pinochet llamó a dejar de lado confrontaciones," *El Mercurio*, August 20, 1993. See also "La conquista de las fronteras interiores," *La Nación*, July 5, 1994; and "Ejército pide desarrollar nuevos polos de población," *El Mercurio*, July 11, 1994.

13. For a description of Mar Presencial, see Jorge Martínez Busch, 1991, "El Mar Presencial: Actualidad, desafíos y futuro," Part I, II, III, *El Diario*, May 28, 29, and 31.

14. In an author interview with Jorge Burgos, Under-Secretary of the Army, Burgos stated that Fronteras Interiores represents an extension of the army's drive to modernize Chile under the dictatorship, Santiago, February 7, 1995.

15. For a direct comparison of public opinion of the armed forces in Argentina and Chile, see Andrés Fontana, 1992, *Chile y Argentina: Percepciones acerca del rol de las fuerzas armadas* (Buenos Aires: Fundación Simón Rodríguez). See also "Chilenos y argentinos opinan de sus FF.AA.," *La Nación*, October 18, 1992.

16. See "Mensaje del gral. Balza a sus subordinados en el Día del Ejército: Recuerden siempre que cada nivel de comando es responsable de lo que ordene y de como se cumplen sus ordenes," *Tiempo Militar* 2, 30 (June 3, 1994).

17. See "Predominio de imagen positiva en la opinión pública sobre las Fuerzas Armadas," *Tiempo Militar* 1, 3 (April 9, 1993).

18. The 1979 amnesty has remained completely intact. The only governmental challenge to the military in this area was President Cardoso's recent signing of a proposed law recognizing the deaths of 136 political prisoners under the dictatorship and calling for the indemnification of the families of victims of the dictatorship. Cardoso was determined to veto any provisions that would investigate responsibility for these abuses.

19. See, for example, "As fardas falantes," *Veja*, December 15, 1993.

20. See "Tucano e quepes: Reforma ministerial fortalece FHC e militares," *Istoé*, March 9, 1994; "Itamar chama a guarda," *Istoé*, March 30, 1994; and "Acordo com a caserna," *Istoé*, May 26, 1993.

21. See *Latinobarómetro 1995: Datos Preliminares*, 1995, Question P61B (May-June). (Distributed by the University of Michigan, Institute for Social Research, Survey Research Center, Ann Arbor, Michigan.)

22. When asked which of the following was most important (maintaining order, citizen participation, combating inflation, or protecting free expression), 32.1 percent of Brazilian respondents chose "maintaining order" as compared to 20.7 of Chilean respondents and 31.1 percent of Argentine respondents. When asked to rank order the importance placed on a stable economy, a more humane and less impersonal society, and combating crime, 49.3 percent of Brazilian respondents listed "combating crime" first, versus 6.5 percent in Argentina and 19.0 percent in Chile. See *Latinobarómetro 1995*, Questions P68 and P69.

23. For a brief explanation of the concerns about the future consequences of Argentina's overvalued currency, trade imbalance, dependence on privatization to balance the budget, and lack of new investment, see Scott Mainwaring, 1995, "Democracy in Brazil and the Southern Cone: Achievements and Problems," *Journal of Interamerican Studies and World Affairs* 37, 1 (Spring): 113-179.

# References

Acuña, Carlos H., and Catalina Smulovitz. 1995. "How to Guard the Guardians: Feasibility, Risks and Benefits of Judicial Punishment of Past Human Rights Violations in New Democracies." Paper presented at the XIX International Congress of the Latin American Studies Association. Washington, D.C., September 28-30.

Agüero, Felipe. 1994. "The Latin American Military: Development, Reform, and 'Nation-Building.'" In *Security, Democracy, and Development in U.S.-Latin American Relations*, eds. Lars Schoultz, William C. Smith, and Augusto Varas. Coral Gables, Fla.: North-South Center at the University of Miami.

Burgos, Jorge. Interview conducted by Wendy Hunter. February 7, 1995, Santiago, Chile.

Ministério do Exército, Escola de Comando e Estado-Maior do Exército. 1995. *Curso de comando e estado-maior: Currículo*. Brasília: Ministério do Exército.

Ensalaco, Mark. 1994. "In with the New, Out with the Old? The Democratising Impact of Constitutional Reform in Chile." *Journal of Latin American Studies* 26(2): 409-429.

Fauriol, Georges. 1995. "Thinking About U.S. Defense Policy in Latin America." In *Hemispheric Security in Transition: Adjusting to the Post-1995 Environment*, ed. L. Erik Kjonnerod. Washington, D.C.: National Defense University Press.

Fitch, J. Samuel 1995. "Military Role Beliefs in Latin American Democracies: Context, Ideology, and Doctrine in Argentina and Ecuador." Paper presented at the XIX International Congress of the Latin American Studies Association. Washington, D.C., September 28-30.

Fontana, Andrés. 1992. *Chile y Argentina: Percepciones acerca del rol de las fuerzas armadas*. Buenos Aires: Fundación Simón Rodríguez.

Hunter, Wendy. 1997. *Eroding Military Influence in Brazil: Politicians against Soldiers*. Chapel Hill, N.C., and London: University of North Carolina Press.

*Istoé*. 1993. "Acordo com a caserna," May 26.

*Istoé*. 1994a. "Tucano e quepes: Reforma ministerial fortalece FHC e militares," March 9.

*Istoé*. 1994b. "Itamar chama a guarda," March 30.

*Jornal do Brasil*. 1994. "Cariocas apóiam exército na luta contra violência," August 23.

*Latinobarómetro 1995: Datos Preliminares*. 1995. Questions P61B, P68, and P69. Distributed by the University of Michigan, Institute for Social Research, Survey Research Center, Ann Arbor, Michigan.

Mainwaring, Scott. 1995. "Democracy in Brazil and the Southern Cone: Achievements and Problems." *Journal of Interamerican Studies and World Affairs* 37(1): 113-179.

Martínez Busch, Jorge. 1991. "El mar presencial: Actualidad, desafíos y futuros." *El Diario*, Part I, II, III, May 28, 29, 31.

*Mercurio, El*. 1993. "Pinochet llamó a dejar de lado confrontaciones," August 30.

*Mercurio, El*. 1994a. "Ejército plantea crear comisión sobre 'Fronteras Interiores,'" July 19.

*Mercurio, El.* 1994b. "Ejército pide desarrollar nuevos polos de población," July 11.

*Nación, La.* 1992. "Chilenos y argentinos opinan de sus FF. AA.," October 18.

*Nación, La.* 1994. "La conquista de las fronteras interiores," July 5.

Norden, Deborah. 1996. *Military Rebellion in Argentina: Between Coups and Consolidation.* Lincoln, Neb.: University of Nebraska Press.

Nunn, Frederick M. 1995. "The South American Military and (Re)Democratization: Professional Thought and Self-Perception." *Journal of Interamerican Studies and World Affairs* 37(2): 1-56.

Olson, Robert. 1995. "Concepts for Future Defense and Military Relations with Counterparts." *In Hemispheric Security in Transition: Adjusting to the Post 1995 Environment,* ed. L. Erik Kjonnerod. Washington, D.C.: National Defense University Press.

Patillo, Guillermo. 1992. "Evolución y estructura de gasto de las fuerzas armadas de Chile, 1970-1990." *Fuerzas Armadas y Sociedad* 7(2): 1-13.

Rojas Aravena, Francisco. 1994. "Chile y el gasto militar: Un criterio histórico y jurídico de asignación." In *Gasto militar en América Latina: Procesos de decisiones y actores claves,* ed. Francisco Rojas Aravena. Santiago: Centro Internacional para el Desarrollo Económico (CINDE) and Facultad Latinoamericana de Ciencias Sociales (FLACSO).

Scheetz, Thomas. 1995. "El marco teórico, político y económico para una reforma militar en la Argentina." In *Defensa no provocativa: Una propuesta de reforma militar para la Argentina,* eds. Gustavo Cáceres and Thomas Scheetz. Buenos Aires: Editorial Buenos Aires.

Stepan, Alfred. 1973. "The New Professionalism of Internal Warfare and Military Role Expansion." In *Authoritarian Brazil: Origins, Policies, Future,* ed. Alfred Stepan. New Haven, Conn., and London: Yale University Press.

Stepan, Alfred. 1988. *Rethinking Military Politics: Brazil and the Southern Cone.* Princeton, N.J.: Princeton University Press.

*Tiempo Militar.* 1993. "Predominio de imagen positiva en la opinión pública sobre las fuerzas armadas," 1(3), April 9.

*Tiempo Militar.* 1994. "Mensaje del gral. Balza a sus subordinados en el Día del Ejército: recuerden siempre que cada nivel de comando es responsable de lo que ordene y de como se complen sus ordenes," 2(30), June 3.

*Veja.* 1993. "As fardas falantes," December 15.

*Verde Oliva.* 1993. "Misión principal y subsidiarias del ejército," November 8.

Zaverucha, Jorge. 1993. "The Degree of Military Political Autonomy During the Spanish, Argentine and Brazilian Transitions." *Journal of Latin American Studies* 25(2): 283-299.

# CHAPTER TWELVE

# The Changing International Environment and Civil-Military Relations in Post-Cold War Southern Latin America

## MICHAEL C. DESCH

### INTRODUCTION

How will the end of the Cold War and the emerging international environment affect the relationship between civilian leaders and military institutions in southern Latin America (Argentina, Brazil, and Chile)? Some believe that the end of the Cold War should coincide with improved civil-military relations in this previously coup-plagued region (Lowenthal 1987, 21-22). Optimism about the future no doubt reigns because much of the literature on civil-military relations shares Harold Lasswell's assumption that periods of high international threat — such as the Cold War — increase the influence of the military and, therefore, make it harder for civilians to control it (Lasswell 1941; Snyder 1985). By that reasoning, the end of the Cold War should make it much easier for civilian leaders to control their militaries.

My argument is that this optimism needs to be substantially qualified. First, it is not clear that Lasswell was correct that a more challenging international environment leads to poor civil-military relations. In fact, I will claim just the opposite: a challenging *external* threat environment leads to relatively good civil-military relations — defined here primarily in terms of civilian control of the military — while a challenging *internal* threat environment undermines civil-military relations. Further, in the case of Latin America, I will argue that it was the real or perceived internal threat from indigenous leftist groups — not always closely aligned with the Soviet Union — that led to military interventions and other manifestations of bad civil-military relations during the Cold War.

Second, the post-Cold War international system is far more complex than is generally acknowledged. While it is certainly true that the post-Cold War international security environment has become less challenging, it is not clear that optimism about better civil-military relations in southern Latin America — or indeed in other parts of the world (Desch 1993, 1995) — is fully warranted. There have been other important changes in the international system that could also affect civil-military relations. These include a widespread crisis in the strength of the nation-state, the effects of the globalization of production and exchange in the international economy, and a growing recognition that technological progress has produced what is increasingly being recognized as a "revolution in military affairs" (RMA). The implications of these developments for civil-military relations have not been thoroughly explored, and their initial consideration generally suggests reasons for both caution and optimism.

This chapter proceeds by first considering why the less challenging international security environment of the post-Cold War period may not coincide with good civil-military relations. It then considers how other aspects of the changing international environment will affect civil-military relations. There have been three important changes in the new international environment: the end of the Cold War, the expanding reach of economic globalization, and the advent of what may be a period of revolutionary change in military technology. All of these changes are likely to have important but also unexpected or counterintuitive implications for future civilian control of the military. The effects of these changes are explored, using examples from southern Latin America and other parts of the world. The chapter concludes with an examination of the theoretical implications of these findings and some concrete policy recommendations.

## WHY THE END OF THE COLD WAR MAY NOT PROMOTE GOOD CIVIL-MILITARY RELATIONS

Despite the break-up of the Soviet Union and the end of the Cold War, there are few grounds for optimism about the prospects for maintaining firm and reliable civilian control of Latin American militaries. The conflict-ridden civil-military relations in southern Latin America of past years cannot be explained meaningfully in terms of the effects of the Cold War, and so its end will not necessarily improve relations. This section argues that the key explanation for the pattern of a state's civil-military relations is the external and internal threat environments faced by that state. States facing a challenging external threat environment will tend to have good civil-military relations, while states facing a serious internal threat environment will tend to have poor civil-military relations. Given that the post-Cold War international security environment is likely to remain quite benign and that domestic security environments could easily deteriorate again in Latin America, it is not at all certain that good civil-military relations will endure among the states of the Western Hemisphere.

This section begins with a conceptual discussion of how different combinations of internal and external threat environments affect civil-military relations. These varied effects are illustrated with a consideration of changing patterns of civil-military relations in the United States and the Southern Cone of Latin America. An assessment of the future prospects for the maintenance of civilian control in the post-Cold War Western Hemisphere concludes the section.

Most of the literature on civil-military relations almost exclusively considers domestic factors, such as the structure of the military institution or the state of civilian governmental institutions, to explain various patterns of civil-military relations.[1] Both of these factors are necessary parts of the explanation of a state's pattern of civil-military relations, but they are not sufficient because these military and civilian governmental variables are ultimately shaped by structural factors, such as the nature of the domestic and international threat environments.

Threats affect both military and civilian institutions. First, the location of the threat orients the military in either an internal or external direction. Second, the intensity of the threat affects the cohesion of both civilian and military institutions (Nordlinger 1977). Put in theoretical terms, the greater the threat, the more cohesive the institution; the lower the threat, the less cohesive the institution. To simplify the argument, there can be four different sorts of threat environments. First, a state might face a high external threat and no internal threat. This should lead to the best pattern of civil-military relations. Both civilian and military institutions will be highly cohesive, and the military will be oriented outward. Second, a state might face neither external nor internal threats. This should lead to fair civil-military relations. While the military will probably not be oriented inward, neither the military nor the civilian institutions will be very cohesive, and this could lead to low-level civil-military conflict. Third, a state might face an external and an internal threat. This sort of situation could lead to relatively incohesive military and civilian institutions and may also produce an inwardly oriented military. This could lead to difficult civil-military relations. Fourth, a state might face no external but high internal threats. This should lead to the worst pattern of civil-military relations. Civilian institutions will lack cohesion while the military institution will probably be cohesive and inwardly oriented.

A number of cases illustrate these propositions well. First, the best patterns of civil-military relations exist in states facing significant external threats and few internal threats. A clear case in point was the United States during the Second World War and the Cold War. In fact, the United States was widely regarded as a model of stable civilian control of the military (Huntington 1968, 194). Second, one might look to the post-Cold War United States as an example of a state facing neither external nor internal threats. The current low-level tensions in U.S. civil-military relations can be explained by the changed threat environment. Third, the difficult patterns of civil-military relations in states facing significant external and internal threats are evident historically in the cases of Germany during the Hindenburg-Luddendorf dictatorship during the First World War and France during the Algerian crisis (Craig 1956; Ambler 1966). Fourth, good illustrations of the pathologies in civil-military relations faced by states with no external threats but significant internal threats were the military dictatorships of southern Latin America (Rouquié 1987). In short, the structural threat environment facing a state goes some way toward explaining that state's pattern of civil-military relations. Let us consider the Western Hemisphere cases in greater detail.

The Cold War United States was a model of stable civilian control over the military. Despite incidents such as the Truman-MacArthur conflict during the Korean War, civilian leaders were generally able to prevail over the military in most major disputes. For instance, President Harry S. Truman overcame fierce military opposition to ending racial segregation in the military and integrated the military well before civilian society was integrated. Similarly, President Dwight D. Eisenhower was able to impose his strategic and fiscal programs on a reluctant U.S. military throughout the 1950s. President Lyndon B. Johnson overcame military resistance to limitations on the conduct of the ground and air wars during the Vietnam conflict. In fact, if one considers the aggregate pattern of U.S. civil-military relations during the Cold War, one is forced to agree with historian Allan Millett:

> One cannot assert that military organizational preferences or the advice of senior military officers have dominated foreign policy decisions, let alone domestic policy. . . . Despite successive buffetings administered by civilian leaders and foreign enemies, the American system of civilian control has shown a resilience and strength that few predicted thirty years ago (Millett 1979, 38).

A high external and low internal threat environment produced very good civil-military relations in the United States during the Cold War.

Unfortunately, the same is not true of the post-Cold War United States. While discussion of a "crisis" in contemporary U.S. civil-military relations is overdrawn,[2] it is nonetheless true that U.S. civil-military relations are not as stable as they once were. A few examples follow. There is widespread agreement that military resistance to intervention in the Yugoslav civil war — manifested most dramatically by the unprecedented public activities of then Chairman of the Joint Chiefs of Staff General Colin Powell[3] — forced the administrations of George Bush and Bill Clinton to retreat at first from playing a larger role in the Balkans. Similarly, the military services initially were resistant to Senator Sam Nunn's efforts to get them to rethink seriously their "roles and missions." Also, the military played a key role in getting the Clinton administration to endorse the standard of two simultaneous military regional conflicts (MRCs) as the benchmark for post-Cold War U.S. force posture. In addition, the military made only token concessions to the Clinton administration's efforts to expand the opportunities for women in combat arms and combat support positions. Military resistance also undermined President Clinton's efforts to lift the Department of Defense's exclusionary policies on homosexuals in the armed services. In the much more benign external threat environment of the post-Cold War era, the United States has experienced an increase in low-level civil-military conflict.

To be sure, the United States has not faced the sort of extreme breakdowns in civil-military relations experienced by many developing states. The reason that the United States is unlikely to experience the most extreme manifestations of bad civil-military relations — outright military insubordination or even a military coup — is that the institutions of civilian rule are still extremely robust. In addition, the U.S. military has not been asked to take on an extensive internal military role.[4] Therefore, my expectations about future U.S. civil-military relations are that they will probably not worsen beyond the low-level conflict we are seeing today. Nonetheless, U.S. post-Cold War civil-military relations are not as good as those of the Cold War period.

However, I am more pessimistic about stable civil-military relations in Latin America because of the relative weakness of civilian institutions throughout the region and the recent history of extremely poor civil-military relations in a number of Latin American states. In the past 30 years, three of the largest and most developed states of Latin America suffered from severe breakdowns in civilian control of the military and even periods of direct military rule.

In Brazil as early as the mid-1950s, the military institution began to focus upon internal "threats" such as economic underdevelopment, elite corruption, and leftist subversion. In 1964, when the military came to the conclusion that the João Goulart regime was contributing to the growth of an internal threat, they assumed a direct role in Brazilian politics. In fact, the military remained in power in Brazil until 1985, by which time pressures for a democratic transition had crested, and the military concluded that the internal threat had been eliminated. Given the remaining weakness of Brazil's civilian institutions and the dramatic increase in internal problems such as crime, who is to say that this sort of civil-military conflict could not re-emerge?

A similar pattern was evident in Argentina, especially in the mid-1970s. While the Argentine military had taken power in 1966 and relinquished it again in 1973, the period after 1976 was qualitatively different. Indeed, there was a widespread perception that the Perón regime was hopelessly weak, which, in turn, undermined the civilian institutions of the Argentine government. Further, the internal threat to Argentine society and the military from the growing urban insurgency of the Montoneros (guerrillas) seemed quite significant to many Argentine citizens. This set the stage for another military coup and a much longer and deeper period of military rule. However, once the Argentine junta had eliminated the Montoneros as a serious internal threat, the unity of the regime began to crumble. This led Gen. Leopoldo Galtieri to try to rally the Argentine military and civilians by invading the British-held Falkland/Malvinas Islands in 1982 (Eddy, Linklater, and Gillman 1982). After years of focusing on internal military operations, the Argentine military performed so badly in the war with Britain that they lost the war along with political power in Argentina. The Argentine case, therefore, not only shows how internal threats might lead to worse civil-military relations but also how deep military involvement in politics might render a military organization incapable of fighting a conventional external adversary.

The Chilean case lends further support to the argument that internal threats can undermine civil-military relations. Until the early 1970s, Chile had been a model both of civilian democracy and reliable civilian control of the military. In contrast to Brazil and Argentina, which had unfortunate histories of frequent military excursions into politics, Chile had experienced only one previous period of military usurpation of civilian authority. What changed this situation was the breakdown of one of the key civilian institutions in Chile, the Christian Democratic Party (Partido Demócrata Cristiano — PDC) (Fleet 1985), and the growth of a serious internal threat from the militant extremes of the right and the left. After the election of socialist President Salvador Allende in 1970, initially the extreme right began to use violence to try to destablize Chilean politics. However, by 1973, the extreme left also began to adopt violent means to advance its political agenda. In early 1973, in the face of growing social unrest and economic chaos, President Allende invited a number of military officers to join his government and assume control of certain ministries. This played a key role in legitimating an internal role for the military in the minds of the public and the officer corps. Allende himself turned the military inward. By September 1973, the situation had deteriorated so badly that the military overthrew Allende and seized control of the country. Once the internal threat had been eliminated, the grip of the Chilean military on power loosened, and the military establishment took a back seat in the personalistic regime of Gen. Augusto Pinochet. Once again, the weakness of internal institutions and the emergence of a serious internal threat made a crisis in Chilean civil-military relations inevitable. It is not clear that entirely stable civil-military relations have yet been reestablished in Chile.

In sum, given the weakness of the civilian institutions of the unconsolidated democracies of Latin America, the significant possibility that the internal threat environments in those states might again deteriorate, and the few counterbalancing external threats,[5] the military moment may not be over in the Western Hemisphere (Millett 1995). Even if the era of coups and direct military rule is over, it is still possible that less dramatic manifestations of civil-military conflict (for example, indirect military involvement in political affairs and resistance to civilian commands) will occur.

## THE CRISIS OF THE POST-COLD WAR STATE AND FUTURE CIVIL-MILITARY RELATIONS

This section investigates the relationship between the changing international security environment and the future of different types of states.[6] The principal argument is not that we are about to witness the end of the state or the states' system. Rather, as a result of the end of the Cold War, the state as we know it will change: Some states will disintegrate, many will cease growing in scope and may even shrink a little, and a few will remain unaffected. In addition, the accelerating process of globalization is contributing to the further weakening of the state. The implications of this crisis of the state for civil-military relations are dire because a strong set of civilian governmental institutions is critical for stable civil-military relations (Huntington 1968, 1-31).

There are essentially two groups of theories about the state that make diametrically opposed predictions about the effect of the changing international security environment on various aspects of state structure. "State persistence" theories maintain that despite the end of the Cold War and the dramatic changes in the international security environment, states will remain basically unchanged in scope and cohesion. "The nation-state," according to Michael Mann, is "not in any *general* decline, *anywhere*" (Mann 1993, 18). Some versions of this argument hold that states facilitate internal economic or other non-military tasks, such as dealing with market failures or mobilizing for collective action, that will continue to justify their existence despite international changes. Others hold that states are shaped by internal and external factors, such as ideas or transaction costs that could also continue to justify the state. Yet, others argue that the state is primarily a response to continuing external economic vulnerability.

"State deformation" theories, in contrast, maintain that the changed international security environment makes the continued broad scope and in a few cases even the viability of some states extremely doubtful.[7] The basic argument of the state deformation position is that threats are critical for bringing groups of individuals together and keeping them together. That is, *insecure* environments make for *secure* states. This argument is based on two assumptions: 1) Expansion in state scope is justified primarily by war, and 2) some states are so deeply divided that without external threats to hold them together they would collapse. In short, the state deformation theorists would predict that the changed external military threat environment brought by the end of the Cold War should have very dramatic effects on the scope and cohesion of a variety of different types of states.

If the state persistence theorists are correct, the future looks much like the past; however, if the state deformation predictions are right, then the post-Cold War period may present a host of international and domestic challenges to governments that need to be addressed to avoid future conflict and instability. I shall argue that the state persistence and the state deformation arguments both contain elements of truth. The state persistence arguments are right in that most states will not fall apart as a result of the end of the Cold War because they retain other functions besides external defense. However, the state deformation arguments contain a large element of truth, too. Specifically, war and external defense were the single most powerful engines in the growth of the scope of the state. Without these threats, the maintenance of the broad scope of the state is unlikely. Also, there are a few states that are so deeply divided internally that they are held together largely by common external threats. The less intense international security competition of the post-Cold War period should witness the demise of these threats. With respect to Argentina, Brazil, and Chile, while their scope has often been extensive, their capacity has been quite weak. The less challenging international security environment of the post-Cold War era should weaken them even further.

The general argument is that "[w]ar was a great stimulus to state building, and it continues to be, if not a great stimulus, then at least a major factor" (Rasler and Thompson 1989, 2). Historical evidence suggests that the functions of the state were overwhelmingly military rather than economic and predominantly international rather than domestic (Mann 1988). The consensus among historians and sociologists is that while war was not the only justification for the state, it was the most important one (Fried 1961; Titmuss 1959). War and external threats played a key role in increasing the scope and cohesiveness of states.[8] External military threats make states more cohesive because they reduce what Albert O. Hirschman labeled the "exit" option and tend to suppress the "voice" option, leaving only the "loyalty" option (Hirschman 1970, 1978). This argument is undergirded by the conflict/cohesion thesis, which holds that threats increase group cohesiveness or unity under specific conditions (Simmel 1955; Coser 1956). Further, the voluminous literature on war and state formation argues that various aspects of state structure are reducible to external factors in important ways (Howard 1979). Max Weber and Otto Hintze made some of the earliest arguments along these lines,[9] and this perspective on the impact of war on the modern state continues to find widespread acceptance.[10]

Historically, while wars might have strengthened the First World states of Western Europe and North America (Bayley 1993), Third World states did not experience the same challenging external threat environment (although they did often face significant internal threats), and so their state structures turned out to be quite different.[11] They evolved in far less cohesive and effective ways. Developing nations are generally characterized by weak governments, little effective control of the economy, a low level of political institutionalization, and chronic political instability. The absence of war and serious external threats at the time of their emergence as new states may explain much of this. Indeed, it was only widely held ideas about sovereignty by the great powers that account for the persistence of weak states in Africa and other areas of the Third World (Jackson and Rosberg 1982, 1-24). In contrast, those few Third World states that faced harsh external environments developed much more extensive and more cohesive states, such as Israel, Cuba, Korea, and China (Migdal 1988, 274).

Given this explanation, will the long-term reduction in the intensity of the international security competition have the opposite effect? The reason it might is that "war and peace are," as William Graham Sumner observed, "so intimately related that peace creates the problem that war is required to solve" (cited in Park 1941, 569). George Simmel noted, "A group's complete victory over its enemies is thus not always fortunate in a sociological sense. Victory lowers the energy which guarantees the unity of the group; and the dissolving forces, which are always at work, gain hold" (Simmel 1955, 98). Logically, the state deformation theory should predict that the end of the Cold War will produce a general crisis for the state. Weak states have poor civil-military relations.

Another of the key international changes of the post-Cold War era is the process known as "globalization." Like many terms in the field of international political economy, globalization is amorphous and used in a number of different senses.[12] To a large extent, globalization refers to increasing economic integration.[13] The key question is, "Why has there been an acceleration in the level of economic integration in recent years?" There are three main reasons: first, the costs of transportation of goods and services have fallen dramatically; second, the speed of communication has increased exponentially; and, third, foreign direct investment by transnational corporations has increased markedly. These factors have increased the economic integration of the global economy.

The process of increasing economic integration has produced many effects — the most important, a marked weakening of the nation-state. With the end of the Cold War, the security rationale for the state has clearly diminished. One might argue that despite the diminution of the security rationale, the state might continue to prosper for other reasons. For example, in the past, that state has performed important equity functions such as wealth transfers. In addition, nationalism has proved to be a potent ideological buttress for the state. Globalization undermines both of these non-security rationalizations for the state. The equity role of the state is threatened by the growing belief that states are economically inefficient actors (Stiglitz 1989). The state as the repository of nationalism is undermined by the fact that in a world of economic competition, economic interests tend not to be national but, rather, sectoral or even individual (Ohmae 1993). The net effect of globalization is, therefore, to further weaken the nation-state. This weakening of the nation-state is likely to make civil-military relations quite problematic. The situation in Brazil suggests how this may be the case. In particular, two manifestations of the weakening of the state are undermining civilian control. First, violent crime in Brazil has reached epidemic proportions. In the early 1980s, the Brazilian military was reluctant to get involved in combating domestic crime.[14] However, since 1994, it has done so in a very significant way.[15] At times, the army has taken control of the Federal Police force.[16] The rising level of street crime is assuming the same proportions of an internal threat that the military once attributed to leftist subversion.

Second, growing manifestations of official corruption have weakened public faith in the civilian institutions of the Brazilian government. Army High Commander Gen. Benedito Leonel warned of a "dangerous generalization of disbelief in institutions and their leaders."[17] Some feared that this weakening increased the likelihood of a coup. Their fears were fed by the statement of a spokesman for the prestigious Clube Militar, who warned, "If the military were to feel that the country was breaking up, there would be no hesitation in intervening to restore morality" (Brooke 1995). Public support for such a military intervention at times may be quite high. The weakening of the Brazilian state due to increasing crime and corruption clearly portends more difficult civil-military relations.

While the Brazilian military is not monolithic with regard to economic thought, it is fair to say that economic nationalism is a popular perspective among many Brazilian military officers. The problem is that the process of economic globalization directly conflicts with many of the tenets of this military economic nationalism (Nunn 1995). For instance, globalization has clearly contributed to the decline of the arms industry in southern Latin America (Smith and Acuña 1995). In Brazil, as in the states of the Southern Cone, the domestic arms industry was central to Brazilian military nationalist desires to obtain greater autonomy for Brazil in the international environment.

It should come as no surprise that the Brazilian military was deeply displeased by the civilian government's decisions in 1991 concerning the Brazilian defense industry: First, foreign investors were allowed to participate in EMBRAER (aircraft), AVIBRÁS (missiles), and ENGESA (tanks). Second, the Fernando Collor de Mello government also gave in to pressure from the United States to curb Brazilian arms exports.[18] Not only did this conflict with military economic nationalism; it also seemed to many Brazilian military officers to threaten the economy and social stability. Employment in each of these three important pillars of the Brazilian defense industry had dropped rapidly since the mid-1980s. For instance, the number of employees in AVIBRÁS was reduced from 6,000 in 1986 to 900 in 1990. Similarly, ENGESA dropped from 3,300 to 1,100. Only EMBRAER did not significantly downsize (Brooke 1990). In short, economic globalization threatens some of the traditional core values of the Brazilian military. To the extent that the civilian government tries to make Brazil adapt to changes in the global economy, it may come into conflict with the military.

A similar potential exists with regard to growing global concern about the effects of Brazil's development efforts in the Amazon basin — an effort enthusiastically supported by many Brazilian military officers. Many in the military fear that world efforts to protect the ecological balance of the Amazon basin will result in its being "internationalized."[19] These concerns have clearly influenced the policies of the civilian government. To the extent that globalization of ideas about protecting the Amazon basin affects the policies of the government, this issue could become a source of civil-military conflict in Brazil. Extending the argument, to the extent that globalization increases and the state further weakens, the re-emergence of civil-military conflict in Brazil is increasingly possible.

# THE REVOLUTION IN MILITARY AFFAIRS AND FUTURE CIVIL-MILITARY RELATIONS

A final change in the post-Cold War international environment is the widely heralded phenomenon, revolution in military affairs, which refers to:

> ... the application of new technologies into a significant number of military systems combine[d] with innovative operational concepts and organizational adaptation in a way that fundamentally alters the character and conduct of conflict. It does so by producing a dramatic increase — often an order of magnitude or greater — in the combat potential and military effectiveness of armed forces (Krepinevich 1994, 30).

Much discussion about the impact of the technological revolution in military affairs upon the nature and conduct of war has taken place.[20] However, its impact upon domestic politics — especially civil-military relations[21] — has been discussed infrequently. Some might conclude that a revolution in military technology might exacerbate civil-military conflict by erasing the distinction between civilian and military areas of competence. It is my hypothesis, however, that the revolution in military affairs is likely to have a positive rather than negative impact on civil-military relations. This is because, if the revolution is actually occurring, the resulting gains in combat potential will increase rather than decrease the level of international threat, which should, in turn, make civil-military relations better rather than worse. This was clearly the case in the Soviet Union during the *perestroika* period, and I also believe that it has had a similar effect in Argentina and Brazil since the Falklands/Malvinas War.

Perestroika — Soviet President Mikhail Gorbachev's radical domestic and foreign policy restructuring — could have been seen as a threat to the Soviet military's interests and, therefore, a source of serious civil-military conflict because it directly threatened the institutional interests of the Soviet military. The puzzle is why the Soviet military did not actively oppose perestroika and, in some cases, actively went along with it. The solution to this puzzle is that the interests of some in the military and those of civilian reformers overlapped to a considerable extent. In fact, there were two particular areas of convergence: Many in the military shared Gorbachev's desire to reform the stagnant Soviet civilian economy (Alexiev and Nurick 1990). In addition, large numbers of officers were sincerely interested in exploring some of the same programs that civilian reformers were advocating (Gelman 1989). The bottom line is that there was a substantial overlap between the interests of some military officers and the civilian proponents of perestroika, which meant that reform did not threaten the interests of all parts of the military equally.

An important caveat needs to be made about this convergence between the Soviet military and civilian reformers: It was animated by very different motives on each side and was thus bound to be only temporary (Azreal 1987). The motives of Gorbachev and his civilian coterie of "new thinkers" have been thoroughly analyzed elsewhere. Suffice it to say, from their point of view, perestroika represented a whole new way of doing business both internationally and domestically.[22] And to the extent that perestroika was instrumental, it was intended mostly to save money (Meyer 1988). Most military officers had substantially different motivations; reform and a relaxation of tensions were the means of obtaining "breathing space" in the ongoing military competition with the West, which they believed was moving in an entirely new direction (Gelman 1988; Herspring 1990; Alexiev and Nurick 1990).

The Soviet Union's technological revolution had important effects on civil-military relations. Initially, some analysts thought that the Soviet Union's technological backwardness would strain relations between civilian and military authorities.[23] In fact, the effects of the new technological revolution (NTR) on civil-military relations were far more positive. In the final analysis, the NTR led many Soviet officers to support reform despite its threat to their institutional interests.

Because many Soviet military officers saw the West as being well ahead of the Soviet Union in many of the most important areas of military technology, the NTR represented a fundamental change in the international distribution of military capabilities that presented a greater threat to Soviet security. The Soviet military reacted both externally and internally to this perceived shift, causing important consequences for international relations and domestic civil-military relations.[24] In fact, this change is an important reason why many Soviet officers were ambivalent about perestroika at home and abroad.

Clearly, the NTR and the West's lead in high technology threatened to tilt the international distribution of capabilities against the Soviet Union (Fitzgerald 1991). The appropriate response to this was not immediately clear, however. Some in the Soviet military advocated balancing the West's qualitative lead by a quantitative build-up. This was roughly Soviet strategy from the late 1960s until the late 1970s. But the problems with this strategy were obvious. It was extremely costly, ultimately unsuccessful, and perhaps even counterproductive. The Soviet military's next response was to try to incorporate high technology and change conventional strategy to match it. However, this new strategy also failed because the Soviet Union lacked the requisite technology to make it work. The final response, which began in the late 1980s and continued until the Soviet Union's ultimate disintegration, was for many Soviet military officers to support, albeit in many cases quite grudgingly, both domestic reform and Gorbachev's new foreign policy of accommodation with the West.[25]

A similar argument can be made about the impact of the revolution in military affairs upon civil-military relations in Argentina and Brazil. The key lesson that the Argentines learned from their total defeat in the 1982 Falklands/Malvinas War was that they lost primarily because they were at a technological disadvantage vis-à-vis the British.[26] In order to avoid such a debacle in the future, the Argentines decided that they would have to make two major changes: First, they would shift their military thinking from an emphasis on quantity to quality as the key to military victory, and, second, they would focus on increasing the level of "professionalism" of their armed forces.[27] Inextricably tied to this was the realization that a modern, professional military force was not likely to be capable of running the domestic politics of the country while simultaneously conducting an external war with a serious adversary.[28] These conclusions tended to bolster the "professionalist" faction of Argentina's armed forces, who were advocating high technology-oriented modernization.[29] This contributed to better civil-military relations in Argentina because it gave the professionalist faction of the military the edge over the faction more inclined toward domestic political involvement. There is some evidence that the Brazilian military learned similar lessons.[30] In sum, the more challenging international security environment as a result of the revolution in military affairs is likely to have the paradoxical effect of making civil-military relations better, rather than worse, in the states of southern Latin America.

## CONCLUSION

The end of the Cold War and the many other dramatic changes in the international system will have unanticipated effects on civil-military relations in the post-Cold War Western Hemisphere. The less challenging security environment, rather than making civil-military relations better, as Lasswellian optimism would expect, is likely to make them more difficult. Challenging external threat environments have coincided with the best patterns of civil-military relations. Conversely, challenging internal threat environments have coincided with the worst patterns of civil-military relations. The states of southern Latin America clearly face few external adversaries at present, and the possibility of increasing internal problems is ever present.

One of the main sources of internal problems may be that the post-Cold War state is likely to experience something of a crisis. Even during the Cold War, the states of southern Latin America were never very cohesive or effective. The accelerating process of economic globalization is likely to undermine the state further. In the less challenging threat environment of the post-Cold War era, they are likely to weaken even more. This may be evident in the increasing levels of crime and corruption in Brazil, for instance, which clearly have adversely affected Brazilian civil-military relations.

Finally, and paradoxically, one reason for optimism is that the widely recognized revolution in military affairs is likely to enhance, rather than undermine, civil-military relations. This was clearly its impact in the Soviet Union during the latter Gorbachev period. And there is some evidence from Argentina and Brazil that the technological revolution has had similarly positive effects. The revolution in military affairs is likely to encourage better civil-military relations because it tends to push militaries toward Western notions of military professionalism. Specifically, it leads to a military with an external orientation and discourages internal political intervention.

Given these findings, the main policy recommendations are twofold: First, states in the region should devote a great deal of attention to bolstering the strength of their civilian governmental institutions. Second, civilian leaders should make sure that their militaries remain focused on external missions and eschew internal roles. Obviously, with all of the domestic problems associated with the weak states of the region, this will be difficult. However, the lessons of the Falklands/Malvinas conflict and the more general recognition of the emerging revolution in military affairs should provide a set of powerful incentives for regional militaries to stay focused on external threats.

# Notes

1. The two dominant theoretical perspectives on civil-military relations that epitomize these two domestic approaches are Morris Janowitz, 1971, *The Professional Soldier: A Social and Political Portrait* (New York: The Free Press); and Samuel P. Huntington, 1957, *The Soldier and the State: The Theory and Politics of Civil-Military Relations* (Cambridge, Mass.: The Belknap Press of Harvard University Press).

2. Proponents of the "crisis" school include Richard H. Kohn, 1994, "Out of Control: The Crisis in Civil-Military Relations," *The National Interest*, No. 35 (Spring): 3-17; Edward N. Luttwak, 1994, "Washington's Biggest Scandal," *Commentary* 97, 5 (May): 29-33; and Charles Dunlap, 1994, "Welcome to the Junta: The Erosion of Civilian Control of the U.S. Military," *Wake Forest Law Review* 29, 2 (Summer): 231-92.

3. See, for example, Colin L. Powell, 1992, "Why Generals Get Nervous," *New York Times*, October 8, 21.

4. But there is definitely pressure from some Clinton appointees to do so. See the letter from Deborah R. Lee, Assistant Secretary of Defense for Reserve Affairs, 1995, "Our Civil-Military Program Is Small, But It's Paying Big Dividends," *Washington Times*, May 24, 22.

5. Obviously, there remain some potential or perceived external threats to states in the region both from each other (for example, Chile and Argentina, Argentina and Brazil, Ecuador and Peru) as well as from the United States.

6. This section draws heavily upon Desch, 1996, "War and Strong States, Peace and Weak States?" *International Organization* 50, 2 (Spring): 237-268.

7. General arguments about the uncertain future of the state can be found in Gianfranco Poggi, 1990, *The State: Its Nature, Development and Prospects* (Cambridge, U.K.: Polity Press), 190; Charles Tilly, 1992, "Prisoners of the State," *International Social Science Journal* 44, 3 (August): 329. For interesting arguments about why the American state is likely to be problematic in the near future, see James Kurth, 1992, "The Postmodern State," *National Interest*, No. 28 (Summer): 26-36; Bruce D. Porter, 1993, "Can American Democracy Survive?" *Commentary* 96, 5 (November): 37-40; and Daniel Deudney and G. John Ikenberry, 1994, "After the Long War," *Foreign Policy*, No. 94 (Spring): 21-36.

8. Morton H. Fried, 1991, "Warfare, Military Organization, and the Evolution of Society," *Anthropologia* 3, 2: 134-147; and Richard Titmuss, 1959, "War and Social Policy," in *Essays on the Welfare State* (New Haven, Conn.: Yale University Press), 75-88.

9. See Otto Hintze, 1975, "Military Organization and the Organization of the State," in *The Historical Essays of Otto Hintze*, ed. Felix Gilbert (Oxford: Oxford University Press), 178-215. For lucid summaries of their arguments, see Randall Collins, 1986, *Weberian Sociological Theory* (Cambridge: Cambridge University Press), 145; and Felix Gilbert, 1980, "From Clausewitz to Delbruck and Hintze: Achievements and Failures of Military History," *Journal of Strategic Studies* 3, 3 (December): 11-20.

10. See, for example, Robert E. Park, 1941, "The Social Function of War: Observations and Notes," *The American Journal of Sociology* XLVI, 4 (January): 551; Charles Tilly, 1975, "Reflections on the History of European State-Making," in *The Formation of National States in Western Europe*, ed. Charles Tilly (Princeton, N.J.: Princeton University Press), 51; Robert D. Carneiro, 1970, "A Theory of the Origin of the State," *Science* 169, 3847 (August 21): 734; and Paul M. Kennedy, 1993, *Preparing for the Twenty-First Century* (New York: Random House), 124.

11. For an excellent comparative treatment of the role of war or its absence in European and African state formation, see Jeffrey Herbst, 1990, "War and the State in Africa," *International Security* 14, 4 (Spring): 117-139; Alain Rouquie, 1987, *The Military and the State in Latin America,* Paul Sigmund, trans. (Berkeley, Calif.: University of California Press), 98-99; and Alexander Wendt and Michael Barnett, 1993, "Dependent State Formation and Third World Militarization," *Review of International Studies* 19, 4 (October): 321-348, who draw a similar contrast between Europe and different parts of the Third World.

12. See the discussion of the term in Hendrick Spruyt, 1995, "Globalization, Autonomy and National Identity: Does Globalization Challenge Sovereign Territoriality?" Columbia University. Unpublished manuscript, 3, fn. 4.

13. This section draws heavily upon Vincent Cable, 1995, "The Diminished Nation-State: A Study in the Loss of Sovereignty," in "What Future for the State?" *Daedalus* 124, 2 (Spring): 23-54.

14. "Military Resist Pressure to Play Anti-drugs Role," 1982, *LARR-B* RB-82-7 (July 9): 8.

15. "Military Want Anti-crime Role in Rio," 1994, *LARR-B* RB-94-08 (September 22): 4.

16. "Militarisation of Police Opens Way to Deep Reform under Armed Forces' Rule," *1993, LARR-B* RB-93-07 (August 12): 1.

17. "Scale of Corruption Scandal Provokes New Fears of Military Intervention," *1994, LARR-B* RB-94-01 (January 13): 1.

18. "Foreign Stake in Defence Companies," 1991, *LARR-B* RB-91-07 (August 15): 3.

19. "'Internationalization' of Amazon Is Rallying-point for Military Hardliners," 1992, *LARR-B* RB-92-03 (March 19): 1.

20. See, for example, A.J. Bacevich, 1994, "Preserving the Well-Bred Horse," *The National Interest*, No. 37 (Fall): 43-49; Bradley Graham, 1995, "Revolutionary Warfare," *The Washington Post National Weekly Edition*, March 6-12, 6-7; and Art Pine, 1994, "Pentagon Looks to Start High-Tech Revolution in Ways of War," *Los Angeles Times*, July 27, 7.

21. There was some limited discussion of this in David Jablonsky, 1994, "U.S. Military Doctrine and the Revolution in Military Affairs," *Parameters* 24:3 (Autumn): 18-36.

22. See, for example, Jack Snyder, 1987/1988, "The Gorbachev Revolution: A Waning of Expansionism?" *International Security* 12, 3 (Winter): 93-131; and Jack Snyder, 1988, "Limiting Offensive Conventional Forces: Soviet Proposals and Western Options," *International Security* 12, 4 (Spring): 48-77. For a Soviet source making this case, see Andrey Vladimorvich Kozyrev, 1988, "Confidence and the Balance of Interests," *Mezhdunarodnaya Zhizn* No. 10 (October) in *Foreign Broadcast Information Service* [FBIS] - *Soviet Report* (October 25): 1-7.

23. Thane Gustafson, 1990, "The Response to Technological Change," in *Soldiers and the Soviet State: Civil-Military Relations from Brezhnev to Gorbachev,* eds. Timothy Collor and Thane Gustafson (Princeton, N.J.: Princeton University Press),194.

24. This has obvious relevance to the debate concerning whether and how "peace through strength" contributed to the end of the Cold War. Participants include John Lewis Gaddis, 1989, "Hanging Tough Paid Off," *Bulletin of Atomic Scientists* 45, 1 (January): 11-14; Daniel Deudney and G. John Ikenberry, 1991/1992, "The International Sources of Soviet Change," *International Security* 16:3 (Winter): 74-118; and Thomas Riesse-Kappen, 1991, "Did 'Peace Through Strength' End the Cold War? Lessons From INF," *International Security* 16, 1 (Summer): 162-188.

25. This might be considered a shift from "balancing" to "band wagoning." For further discussion of these concepts, see Stephen Walt, 1987, *The Origins of Alliances* (Ithaca, N.Y.: Cornell University Press), 17-21.

26. "Lessons of the Falklands," 1982, *LARR-SC* RS-82-07 (September 10): 7.

27. "Military Re-think Is in Progress," 1982, *LARR-SC* RS-82-6 (July 30): 6.

28. "Malvinas Post-mortem Hits the Fan," 1983, *LARR-SC* RS-83-07 (September 9): 6.

29. "Services Ponder 'Reform' Policies," 1994, *LARR-SC* RS-84-06 (August 3): 6.

30. "Survival Depends on Exports," 1984, *LARR-B* RB-83-05 (June 3): 7; and "Electronic Warfare Centre Established," 1984, *LARR-B* RB-84-06 (August 10): 6.

# References

Acuña, Carlos H., and William C. Smith. 1995. "Arms and Democracy in the Southern Cone: Demilitarization and Regional Cooperation." *North-South Issues* 4 (1): 1-8.

Alexiev, Alexander R., and Robert C. Nurick. 1990. *The Soviet Military Under Gorbachev: Report on a RAND Workshop* [R-3907-AF]. Santa Monica: RAND Corp., xii and 62-3; F.

Ambler, John Steward. 1966. *The French Army in Politics: 1945-1962*. Columbus: Ohio State University Press.

Andersen, Martin Edwin. 1988/1989. "The Military Obstacle to Latin Democracy." *Foreign Policy* 72 (Winter): 94-113.

Azreal, Jeremey R. 1987. *The Soviet Civilian Leadership and the Military High Command, 1976- 1986* [R-3521-AF]. Santa Monica, Calif.: RAND Corp., (June): 40-1.

Bacchus, Wilford A. 1986. "Development Under Military Rule: Military Factionalism in Brazil." *Armed Forces and Society* 12 (3): 415-416.

Bacevich, A.J. 1994. "Preserving the Well-Bred Horse." *The National Interest* 37 (Fall): 43-49.

Bayley, David H. 1993. "The Police and Political Development in Europe." In *The Formation of National States in Western Europe*, ed. Charles Tilly. Princeton, N.J.: Princeton University Press.

Brooke, James. 1990. "Peace Unhealthy for Brazilian Arms Industry." *New York Times*, February 25.

Brooke, James. 1994. "Use of Army to Fight Crime in Rio Makes Many Feel Safer in Streets." *New York Times*, November 26.

Brooke, James. 1995. "A Vast New Scandal Is Shaking Brazilian's Faith in Democracy." *New York Times*, January 4.

Cable, Vincent. 1995. "The Diminished Nation-State: A Study in the Loss of Sovereignty." In "What Future for the State?" *Daedalus* 124 (2): 23-54.

Carneiro, Robert D. 1970. "A Theory of the Origin of the State." *Science* 169 (3847): 734.

Collins, Randall. 1986. *Weberian Sociological Theory*. Cambridge, Mass.: Cambridge University Press.

Coser, Lewis. 1956. *The Functions of Social Conflict*. Glencoe, Ill.: Free Press.

Craig, Gordon A. 1956. *The Politics of the Prussian Army: 1640-1945*. New York: Oxford University Press.

Desch, Michael. 1993. "Why the Soviet Military Supported Gorbachev and Why the Russian Military Might Only Support Yeltsin for a Price." *Journal of Strategic Studies* 16 (4): 455-489.

Desch, Michael. 1995. "U.S. Civil-Military Relations in a Changing International Order." In *U.S. Civil-Military Relations: In Crisis or Transition?* eds. Don M. Snider and Miranda A. Carlton-Carew. Washington, D.C.: CSIS.

Desch, Michael. 1996. "War and Strong States, Peace and Weak States?" *International Organization* 50 (2): 237-268.

Deudney, Daniel, and G. John Ikenberry. 1991/1992. "The International Sources of Soviet Change." *International Security* 16 (3): 74-118.

Deudney, Daniel, and G. John Ikenberry. 1994. "After the Long War." *Foreign Policy* 94 (Spring): 21-36.

Dunlap, Charles. 1994. "Welcome to the Junta: The Erosion of Civilian Control of the U.S. Military." *Wake Forest Law Review* 29 (2): 231-292.

Eddy, Paul, Magnus Linklater, and Peter Gillman. 1982. *The Falklands War: The Full Story.* London: Sphere Books, Ltd.

Ensalaco, Mark. 1995. "Military Prerogatives and the Stalemate of Chilean Civil-Military Relations." *Armed Forces and Society* 21 (2): 255-270.

Fitzgerald, Mary. 1991. "Soviet Military Doctrine — Implications of the Gulf War." *International Defense Review* 8: 809-810.

Fleet, Michael. 1985. *The Rise and Fall of Chilean Christian Democracy.* Princeton, N.J.: Princeton University Press.

Fried, Morton H. 1961. "Warfare, Military Organization, and the Evolution of Society." *Anthropologia* 3 (2): 134-147.

Gaddis, John Lewis. 1989. "Hanging Tough Paid Off." *Bulletin of Atomic Scientists* 45 (1): 11-14.

Gelman, Harry. 1988. *The Soviet Military Leadership and the Question of Soviet Deployment Retreats.* Santa Monica, Calif.: Rand Corporation.

Gelman, Harry. 1989. *The Soviet Turn Toward Conventional Force Reductions: The Internal Variables at Play* [R-3876-AF]. Santa Monica, Calif: RAND Corp. (December), 3.

Gilbert, Felix. 1980. "From Clausewitz to Delbruck and Hintze: Achievements and Failures of Military History." *Journal of Strategic Studies* 3 (3): 11-20.

Gottemoeller, Rose E. 1989. *Conflict and Consensus in the Soviet Armed Forces* [R-3759-AT] Santa Monica, Calif.: RAND Corp. (October): 1.

Graham, Bradley. 1995. "Revolutionary Warfare." *The Washington Post National Weekly Edition* (March 6-12): 6-7.

Gustafson, Thane. 1990. "The Response to Technological Change." In *Soldiers and the Soviet State: Civil-Military Relations from Brezhnev to Gorbachev,* eds. Timothy Collor and Thane Gustafson. Princeton, N.J.: Princeton University Press.

Herbst, Jeffrey. 1990. "War and the State in Africa." *International Security* 14 (4): 117-139.

Herspring, Dale. 1990. *The Soviet High Command 1967-1989: Personalities and Politics.* Princeton, N.J.: Princeton University Press.

Hilton, Stanley E. 1987. "The Brazilian Military: Changing Strategic Perception and the Question of Mission." *Armed Forces and Society* 13 (3): 346.

Hintze, Otto. 1975. "Military Organization and the Organization of the State." In *The Historical Essays of Otto Hintze,* ed. Felix Gilbert. Oxford: Oxford University Press.

Hirschman, Albert O. 1970. *Exit, Voice, and Loyalty: Responses to Decline in Firms, Organizations, and States.* Cambridge, Mass.: Harvard University Press.

Hirschman, Albert O. 1978. "Exit, Voice, and the State." *World Politics* 31 (1): 90-107.

Howard, Michael. 1979. "War and the Nation-state." *Daedalus* 108 (4): 101-110.

Huntington, Samuel P. 1957. *The Soldier and the State: The Theory and Politics of Civil-Military Relations.* Cambridge, Mass.: The Belknap Press of Harvard University Press.

Huntington, Samuel P. 1968. *Political Order and Changing Societies.* New Haven, Conn.: Yale University Press.

Jablonsky, David. 1994. "U.S. Military Doctrine and the Revolution in Military Affairs." *Parameters* 24 (3): 18-36.

Jackson, Robert H., and Carl G. Rosberg. 1982. "Why Africa's Weak States Persist: The Empirical and the Juridical in Statehood." *World Politics* 35 (1): 1-24.

Janowitz, Morris. 1971. *The Professional Soldier: A Social and Political Portrait.* New York: Free Press.

Kennedy, Paul M. 1993. *Preparing for the Twenty-First Century.* New York: Random House.

Kohn, Richard H. 1994. "Out of Control: The Crisis in Civil-Military Relations." *The National Interest* 35 (Spring): 3-17.

Krepinevich, Andrew F. 1994. "Cavalry to Computer: The Pattern of Military Revolutions." *The National Interest* 37 (Fall): 30.

Kurth, James. 1992. "The Postmodern State." *National Interest* 28 (Summer): 26-36.

Larabee, Stephen. 1988. "Gorbachev and the Soviet Military." *Foreign Affairs* 66 (5).

Lasswell, Harold. 1941. "The Garrison State." *The American Journal of Sociology* 46 (4): 455-469.

*Latin American Regional Reports-Brazil.* 1982. "ROTA: An Institutionalized Death Squad." RB-82-05 (May 28): 7.

*Latin American Regional Reports-Brazil.* 1982. "Military Resist Pressure to Play Anti-drugs Role." RB-82-7 (July 9): 8.

*Latin American Regional Reports-Southern Cone.* 1982. "Military Re-think Is in Progress," RS-82-6 (July 30): 6.

*Latin American Regional Reports-Southern Cone.* 1982. "Lessons of the Falklands," RS-82-07 (September 10): 7.

*Latin American Regional Reports-Brazil.* 1983. "Survival Depends on Exports." RB-83-05 (June 3): 6-7.

*Latin American Regional Reports-Southern Cone.* 1983. "Malvinas Post-mortem Hits the Fan." RS-83-07 (September 9): 6.

*Latin American Regional Reports-Brazil.* 1984. "Electronic Warfare Centre Established." RB-84-06 (August 10): 6.

*Latin American Regional Reports-Southern Cone.* 1988. "Argentina Restructures Defense Industry." RS-88-05 (June 30): 4-5.

*Latin American Regional Reports-Brazil.* 1991. "Pay Levels Only One of the Reasons for Mounting Military Dissatisfaction." RB-91-07 (August 15): 1.

*Latin American Regional Reports-Brazil.* 1991. "Foreign Stake in Defence Companies." RB-91-07 (August 15): 3.

*Latin American Regional Reports-Brazil.* 1991. "Growth of 'Urban Misery' Worries Military." RB-91-10 (October): 4-5.

*Latin American Regional Reports-Brazil.* 1992. "'Internationalization' of Amazon Is Rally-ing-point for Military Hardliners." RB-92-03 (March 19): 1.

*Latin American Regional Reports-Brazil.* 1993. "Militarisation of Police Opens Way to Deep Reform under Armed Forces' Rule." RB-93-07 (August 12): 1.

*Latin American Regional Reports-Brazil.* 1993. "Franco Responds to Military Concerns: Go-ahead for Amazon Watch System." RB-93-08 (September 16): 1

*Latin American Regional Reports-Brazil*. 1994. "Scale of Corruption Scandal Provokes New Fears of Military Intervention." RB-94-01 (January 13): 1.

*Latin American Regional Reports-Southern Cone*. 1994. "Services Ponder 'Reform' Policies." RS-84-06 (August 3): 6.

*Latin American Regional Reports-Brazil*. 1994. "Military Want Anti-crime Role in Rio." RB-94-08 (September 22): 4.

Lee, Deborah R. 1995. "Our Civil-Military Program Is Small, But It's Paying Big Dividends." *Washington Times*, May 24.

Lowenthal, Abraham F. 1987. *Partners in Conflict: The United States in Latin America*. Baltimore: The Johns Hopkins University Press.

Luttwak, Edward N. 1994. "Washington's Biggest Scandal." *Commentary* 97 (5): 29-33.

Mann, Michael. 1988. *States, War and Capitalism*. Oxford: Basil Blackwell.

Mann, Michael. 1993. "Nation-States in Europe and Other Continents: Diversifying, Developing, Not Dying." In "Reconstructing Nations and States." *Daedalus* 122 (3): 118.

Meyer, Stephen M. 1988. "Sources and Prospects of Gorbachev's New Political Thinking on Security." *International Security* 13 (2): 129.

Migdal, Joel. 1988. *Strong Societies and Weak States: State-Society Relations and Capabilities in the Third World*. Princeton, N.J.: Princeton University Press.

Millett, Allan. 1979. *The American Political System and Civilian Control of the Military: A Historical Perspective*. Columbus: The Mershon Center of the Ohio State University.

Millett, Richard L. 1995. "An End to Militarism? Democracy and the Armed Forces in Central America." *Current History* 94 (589): 71-75.

*New York Times*. 1994. "Brazil's Justice Minister Tells of '93 Coup Plot." January 7.

Nordlinger, Eric. 1977. *Soldiers in Politics: Military Coups and Governments*. Englewood Cliffs, N.J.: Prentice Hall, Inc.

Nunn, Frederick M. 1995. "The South American Military and (Re)Democratization: Professional Thought and Self-Perception." *Journal of Interamerican Studies and World Affairs* 37 (2): 27.

Ohmae, Kenichi. 1990. "Beyond Friction to Fact: The Borderless Economy." *New Perspectives Quarterly* 7 (2): 20-21.

Ohmae, Kenichi. 1993. "The Rise of the Regional State." *Foreign Affairs* 72 (2): 78-86.

Park, Robert E. 1941. "The Social Function of War: Observations and Notes." *The American Journal of Sociology* XLVI (4): 551.

Pine, Art. 1994. "Pentagon Looks to Start High-Tech Revolution in Ways of War." *Los Angeles Times*, July 27.

Poggi, Gianfranco. 1990. *The State: Its Nature, Development and Prospects*. Cambridge, U.K.: Polity Press.

Porter, Bruce D. 1993. "Can American Democracy Survive?" *Commentary* 96 (5): 37-40.

Powell, Colin L. 1992. "Why Generals Get Nervous." *New York Times*. October 8.

Rasler, Karen, and William Thompson. 1989. *War and State Making: The Shaping of Global Powers*. Boston: Unwin and Hyman.

Riesse-Kappen, Thomas. 1991. "Did 'Peace Through Strength' End the Cold War? Lessons From INF." *International Security* 16 (1): 162-188.

Rouquié, Alain. 1987. *The Military and the State in Latin America*. Paul Sigmund, trans. Berkeley, Calif.: The University of California Press.

Simmel, George. 1955. *Conflict and the Web of Group Affiliation.* Kurt H. Wolff and Rheinhard Bendix, trans. New York: The Free Press.

Smith, William C., and Carlos H. Acuña. 1995. "Arms and Democracy in the Southern Cone: Demilitarization and Regional Cooperation." *North-South Issues* 4 (1). North-South Center at the University of Miami.

Snider, Don M., and Miranda A. Carlton-Carew, eds. 1995. U.S. Civil-Military Relations in a Changing International Order." *U.S. Civil-Military Relations: In Crisis or Transition?* Washington, D.C.: CSIS.

Snyder, Jack. 1985. "Civil-Military Relations and the Cult of the Offensive, 1914 and 1984." In *Military Strategy and the Origins of the First World War,* ed. Steven E. Miller. Princeton, N.J.: Princeton University Press.

Snyder, Jack. 1987/1988. "The Gorbachev Revolution: A Waning of Expansionism?" *International Security* 12 (3): 93-131.

Snyder, Jack. 1988. "Limiting Offensive Conventional Forces: Soviet Proposals and Western Options." *International Security* 12 (4): 48-77.

*Soviet Acquisition of Militarily Significant Technology — An Update.* 1985. Washington, D.C.: U.S. Government Printing Office, September.

Spruyt, Hendrick. 1995. "Globalization, Autonomy and National Identity: Does Globalization Challenge Sovereign Territoriality?" Columbia University. Unpublished manuscript, 3, fn. 4.

Stiglitz, Joseph. 1989. "On the Economic Role of the State." In *The Economic Role of the State,* ed. Arnold Heertje. New York: Oxford University Press.

Tilly, Charles. 1992a. "Prisoners of the State." *International Social Science Journal* 44 (3): 329.

Tilly, Charles. 1992b. *Coercion, Capital, and the European State, AD 990-1992.* Cambridge, Mass.: Blackwell.

Tilly, Charles. 1995a. "Western State-Making and Theories of Political Transformation." In *The Foundation of National States in Western Europe,* ed. Charles Tilly. Princeton, N.J.: Princeton University Press.

Tilly, Charles. 1995b. "Reflections on the History of European State-Making." In *The Formation of National States in Western Europe,* ed. Charles Tilly. Princeton, N.J.: Princeton University Press.

Titmuss, Richard. 1959. "War and Social Policy." In *Essays on the Welfare State.* New Haven, Conn.: Yale University Press.

Vladimorvich Kozyrev, Andrey. 1988. "Confidence and the Balance of Interests." *Mezhdunarodnaya Zhizn* 10 (October). In *Foreign Broadcast Information Service* [FBIS] - *Soviet Report* (October 25): 1-7.

Walt, Stephen. 1987. *The Origins of Alliances.* Ithaca, N.Y.: Cornell University Press.

Wendt, Alexander, and Michael Barnett. 1993. "Dependent State Formation and Third World Militarization." *Review of International Studies* 19 (4): 321-348.

CHAPTER THIRTEEN

# Democracy, Civilizational Change, and the Latin American Military

## FERNANDO BUSTAMANTE

## INTRODUCTION

The end of the Cold War in 1989 is often seen as the starting point of a critical period of uncertainty for Latin American military establishments in relation to their tasks and missions. For some observers, the period portends a slow but sustained tendency for a "hollowing" of the regional armies' raison d'être. It is also a matter of concern for all civilians interested in military and security matters and for those having to deal with decisions affecting or involving the military.

Latin American armed forces seem to be struggling simultaneously with several problems: 1) the lack of a clearly defined ideological threat, 2) the emergence of new and unconventional challenges, 3) the problems that macroeconomic considerations pose to funding and budgets, 4) the vastly changed international context, 5) the reawakening in some places of internal challenges to the process of unified nation-building, and 6) a reappraisal of the meaning of the concepts of security and state sovereignty in an increasingly globalized world. In many cases, the armed forces also have been dealing with the troubling legacy of their past political roles and their failures in exerting domestic power.

The dissipation of the whole Cold War problematic has brought forward a complex mixture of uncertainties and a bewildering array of new potential priorities that compete for the top of the agenda. Some pertain to new internal and internationalized public order issues, some to the effects of globalization on domestic governance and social integration, and others to the proper place and role of the military in the new, democratic political systems almost universally in place throughout the region.

This chapter discusses some of these dilemmas and possible ways for them to be confronted and resolved by the existing military establishments, as well as by civilian actors involved in decisionmaking about security issues. It also examines some ways in which solutions to the foregoing problems could have an impact on the future shape of the Latin American armed services and Latin American politics.

## THE QUESTION OF THE "END OF THE COLD WAR"

When Fernando Cortés landed on Mexico's shores, he reportedly saw Indian temples as "mosques" (Parker 1993). In this way, he and his men were bringing the novelty of the American experience within the framework of their own ancestral experience. "Otherness" in the new continent was assimilated as "otherness" meant within the realm of European historical memory. As a consequence, the conquest was read as a new chapter in the struggle of militant Christianity to roll back the dark forces of heathendom and as a new stage for the confrontation with alien, threatening civilizations. The expansion of European civilization to the Americas was seen as a new crusade, a crusade featuring the Sword and the Bible in commensurate, central roles.

Throughout the history of Iberian America, the legitimacy of colonial and republican elites has been built to a large extent on the claim of being the main actors of this epochal struggle to conquer the pagan and idolatric "other" on behalf of "Christian Civilization." Different foes have been postulated as the enemy to be subdued by arms or religion, but they always have been confronted, openly or not, in relation to a civilizational mission. Therefore, Samuel Huntington's observation that after the Cold War new global conflicts would be centered around civilizational and cultural conflicts is cognizant with the deep meaning that Latin American elites traditionally have ascribed to their own historical task (Huntington 1996).

The military establishments formed at the turn of the twentieth century throughout the continent were part of the desire of ruling civilian elites to "civilize" military life, uprooting in the process the "proto-populist" warlord armies of the first decades after independence. These new professional armies were to become the leading edge of the process of subduing the forces of alien barbarism and unchristian evil. The means of the crusade had changed, but the ethos was still there, albeit often under the guise of a positivistic modernizing task. Indians in Amazonia were exterminated in the name of progress and of a certain notion of modernization, which can be seen as the thinly secularized furtherance of the Christian cosmopolis. For most military officers during the twentieth century, the railway and the public school were the modern equivalents of the mission and the colonial city, and, of course, compatible with the use of force when still necessary.

The Cold War was viewed by the Latin American military establishment through this ancestral lens. Communism was the contemporary equivalent of Cortés' mosques. In Latin military minds, the Soviet Union could easily take the place of the sultan, Islam, and heathendom. If one examines classical military readings about the bipolar conflict, it is striking that members of the military saw themselves defending "Christian civilization," and, only in second place (and not very convincingly), such values as capitalism, democracy, or freedom. The most recurring and heartfelt meanings were associated instead with the protection of a cherished civilization against a threat from a dreaded external foe. Communism was not seen as a particular Western heresy but as a reincarnation of the cultural "other," as the force of oriental darkness and despotism in the midst of history — not as the presence of a mistaken or misguided system, but as the bearer of obscure metaphysically rooted forces that could destroy the supreme common good of a universalistic

Christian civilization (Lagos and Chacón 1987). In this interpretation, Latin American cold warriors were civilizational crusaders, much before Huntington's theories were published at the end of the Cold War.

If the cultural substratum of the Cold War commitment to the "West" by Latin American military establishments lies much deeper than post-1945 alignments and if the meaning of that commitment is not crucially connected to the values of post-Enlightenment liberal democracy, then the depth of the post-Cold War "mission crisis" ought not be as huge as sometimes posited. Perhaps the retreat of the particular civilizational threat that international communism represented may not have eliminated nor made worthless the military's deeper underlying commitment to Christian civilization and its secularized progeny. What has evaporated is a particular embodiment of the metahistorical struggle against heathen otherness, but the latter could be construed as lying low somewhere else — not dead, but metamorphosed into new (or ancient but ready to reemerge) objects of fear. The missionary tasks of civilizational crusade are not exhausted by the rollback of a particular threat; the metahistorical mission can still survive any particular incarnation of evil otherness (Perelli 1990). The problem for military establishments is to define where the otherness may lurk and what new tools have to be invented or reinvented to resume the age-old task of containing or eliminating it.

In that sense, one could suggest that at a deeper level there is no mission crisis in the Latin American armed forces. The military's basic ideological and cultural frame of mind might still remain untouched; moreover, it has been validated by the verdict of history that the alignments of the past were justified and correct. The outcome of the Cold War has shown, it could be said, that the telos or ultimate ends of history coincide with the telos of the Christian West. From that perspective, the demise of the Soviet challenge can be interpreted much the same as Suleiman's failure at the gates of Vienna — a sign, a portent of the ultimate truth and godliness of Christian civilization: *In Hoc Signo Vinces* ("In this sign you shall conquer").

The problem of the "mission," therefore, may not be understood properly if one disregards this deep, underlying thread of the Latin American military ethos, which, incidentally, connects the officer corps culturally to various civilian elites in different countries of the hemisphere. This thread is common to officers of different political and religious persuasions, from the Catholic fundamentalist right to the progressive reformist left (from Jorge Videla to Juan Velasco Alvarado, for instance). The main task is still the same for all: to operate as an institutional tool for the assimilation, integration, surveillance, and deletion of the civilizational "other." This gives ample room for the accommodation of many specific threat hypotheses and opens up a discursively contested ground where ideological arguments may be advanced.

In some ways, the main problem faced by military establishments in the region is the fact that some of the most powerful external and internal actors refuse to share the above understanding of military tasks. For instance, for the United States and its European allies, the struggle is over, in the sense that the values of capitalism and democracy as understood in the post-Enlightenment tradition seem irreversibly triumphant. If the job of the armed forces were to be reduced to winning that particular conflict, of course, little else is left to be done for the Latin American armies, beyond some ancillary constabulary tasks, of which the "war against drugs" is only a small twist. However, if the mission is to be seen in the strong sense of a metahistorical drama, not exhausted by any particular foe, much is left to be done, and preparedness is not to be sacrificed but must be sustained, even though the particular characteristics of new enemies may warrant an organizational retooling.

One of the main threats confronted by the Latin American military is understanding the nature of the historical task to be met (which is quite different from the military's) held by international and national actors who want to declare the job accomplished and recommend the shelving of the most important axioms of military institution-building in Latin America. A view among some members of the military has thus turned toward a new "paranoid" way of thinking: chased from their abodes, the forces of darkness subtly penetrate new subjects and deflect their minds toward fighting the "good fighters." Moreover, since evil is infinitely resourceful and resilient, it may even infect former friends and allies by obscuring their understanding of the proper role of the military and clouding their vision — for example, the sudden lack of U.S. interest in the preservation of strong conventional armies south of the Rio Grande.

For Latin American militaries, the obvious need for strong defense forces is a constant. There are two problems to resolve: 1) how to convince civilians and the regional hegemon that the crusade is an unending battle and 2) how to detect and make a plausible account of the new incarnations of the enemy and of the specific means that have to be designed for this new phase of the struggle.

One central concept that can connect perennial discourses to post-Cold War facts of life is the question of "order." Formerly, many Latin military establishments were able to muster the discourse of "progress" to the cause of institutional self-promotion. The new civic action-minded, developmentalist officer would be the linear successor to those soldiers who opened up the wilderness for the railway and human (Westernized) habitation and exploitation in the nineteenth century or to those military modernizers who gave a boost to the task of building the organizational underpinnings of a modern bureaucratic state in the early and mid-twentieth century. Order can be connected to the tasks of civilization as a substitute for the notion of "progress," as is clearly stated in the Brazilian national motto: *Ordem e Progresso*.

Alas, this no longer seems true. Although here and there a few armies still lead a rearguard fight against neoliberalism, the bell seems to be tolling for the formerly ambitious Gerschenkronian plans of military-led technological and economic modernization, and such plans, built around state-centered development models, have become the object of derision. Since the task of bringing modernity to Latin American countries seems to have been confiscated by other actors, equipped with very different intellectual and technical tools, there is an increasing awareness among military leaders that a new sense of institutional mission ought to be searched for elsewhere, and this is where the discourse of order may provide the means for the symbolic reconversion.

In order to outline the relevance and applications of the topic of "order" to the question of mission, recall Cortés in awed and horrified contemplation of Mayan and Aztec temples. Once the relatively brief period of military conquest was over,

Iberian civilization in the New World settled into a routine in which the defense tasks were marked by alertness against two foes. The first was the "internal other," the Indian and partly Indian populations to be surveilled, educated, and kept in their place through a complex system of geographical and social internal borders (still present to a large extent), and the second was the threat of Protestant powers and their heretical and powerful wickedness. These two threats alternately have held sway over the imaginations of Creoles and their military establishments, though their relationship with the latter experienced important transformations after independence.

However, given the marginal role of Iberian-America in the confrontation of Catholic powers with Protestantism and its growing subordination to the Anglo-Saxon world after 1823, the main day-to-day military task was to secure the moral and physical safety of the missionary Christian realm against the subtle threat of forced and routine coexistence with the bearers of dissolution and disorder, as represented by the endogenous non-Western cultural worlds. As nation-building has proceeded, this has meant that the prevailing concern of military forces has been connected to the question of internal order and of state-building. In fact, it is quite interesting to realize that, for the most part, Latin armies have been political instruments of civilizational disciplining, while their value as international war-fighting machines has been very dubious.

Latin American armies' secular pragmatics are dedicated to integrating the disparate elements of nationhood and geography within a political order that has had little capacity to integrate heterogeneity through the classical means of political economy. This is seen not only in the militaries' roles as colonizers, in civic action, in social repression, and in conscription as education, but also in their still not well-understood roles as functional stabilizers of regional internal political systems (such roles as "tutelary," "moderator," or "guarantor"). The relevance of the military to these problems has not been fully resolved, as present discussions of governance, democratic stability, military autonomy, and civil-military relations bear witness.

Certainly, conventional territorial defense concerns also have been important. However, although they have been crucial in terms of self-legitimation, they obscure a still more basic cultural commitment connected to civilizational self-images. Of course, border wars have been fought, and Latin American officers are extremely aware of the conflict scenarios around them. Nevertheless, it strikes any detached observer that these armies seem much more consistent in their preparation and deployment for peacetime tasks rather than those of conventional border defense. In fact, compared to other regions' militaries, Latin American armies always have been undermanned, underequipped, underfunded, and undertrained for the classic missions of territorial defense. Also, particularly after military professionalization, Latin America has been an area of high social and internal conflict and relatively low levels of interstate violence. Wars between neighboring countries have been few, low-scale, and low-intensity for the most part. Except for the Chaco War between Bolivia and Paraguay in the 1930s, all other "major" outbursts of fighting would qualify as nothing more than mere skirmishes by global standards. Closer scrutiny shows that, in spite of geopolitical discourse and conventional conflict scenarios, Latin American armies are organized, trained, deployed, and equipped in ways that reveal a notorious lack of actual concentration on conventional warfare. Instead, most of their means and actual operations are turned toward policing, political, nation-building, and educational tasks. Real as they are, territorial defense concerns are less crucial than one may be led to believe by initial perceptions of the institutional behavior and self-image of Latin American military organizations.

Thus, although there is no denying that territorial defense and conventional deterrence are real concerns for regional militaries, they must not obscure the deeper importance of civilizational commitments, values, and pragmatics, which, in my opinion, go a long way toward accounting for Latin American military culture and priorities.

## THE MILITARY AND SYSTEM STABILIZATION

From the 1980s until today, the prevailing concern for analysts has been how to stabilize a system of civil-military relations that offers some guarantees that no new military coups or overt political influence are exerted by the military, simultaneously ensuring enhanced civilian control over the officer corps (see, for example, Varas 1988). The question of internal order, therefore, is strongly linked to the issue of the stabilization of democracy. Regarding this concern, there are several assumptions that are worth highlighting.

First, the military is seen by many analysts as a latent threat to democratic institutions. The armed forces are potential challengers to democratic governance, and the whole question of their role under democracy has taken a strongly negative and defensive tone. From this follows a certain tendency to see the question in terms of a zero-sum game. Everything that strengthens the military in organizational, political, cultural, or economic terms is suspected of increasing the probabilities that it will have the means and the will to increase its weight in the political sphere. Whatever is good for the military may be bad for democratic governance, according to this view.

This is an understandable concern, given that the past has left a legacy of deeply ingrained suspicion and resentment in many Latin American countries as well as institutional privileges and prerogatives that directly diminish the authority of civilian governments over some crucial policy areas, including military oversight and issues not directly connected to national defense (O'Donnell, Schmitter, and Whitehead 1986). There is still a series of accounts to be settled with the authoritarian past, as, for example, in the case of the so-called "authoritarian enclaves" in the Chilean political system. However, as Scott Tollefson (1995) has attempted to show for the Brazilian case, there is a long-term trend at work that seems capable of slowly reducing this legacy and gradually reasserting civilian control over the barracks.

In spite of some cases to the contrary (Peru, Venezuela), the prevailing tendency is for the military to have less weight within the state apparatus and in national politics. The military is increasingly having trouble defending its prerogatives, budgets, and influence, even in countries where it was never before challenged or curtailed. Instances of reorganization (for example, in Honduras, El Salvador, and Nicaragua), human rights cases, drastic budget cuts, and the reduction of areas of competence are sufficient proof of this.

Even in cases such as Peru's, the political influence retained or regained by the military can come at a heavy cost in terms of professional capabilities. As the dismal performance of the Peruvian forces in the 1995 Cenepa War demonstrated, political clout may be associated with a heavy price tag in terms of preparedness and operational capabilities. Thus, although the question of civilian control and reduction of undue military political influence is still open, it has ceased to have the urgency that it seemed to have 10 years ago. While much remains to be done in this area, there is a widespread sense that the military poses a much smaller threat to republican civilian government than it did in the past.

Further, it may be argued that institutionally weak military establishments are not necessarily politically quiescent or submissive to civilian authority. In fact, corrupt and badly managed, weak, or deprofessionalized militaries may be quite detrimental to enhanced and stable civilian control. The common-sense idea that weakening the military may improve the chances of democratic consolidation may be in need of revision. In fact, factors that promote military political activism often are unconnected to organizational and professional strengths and can be sought in the nature of the military's political links with the state, with other political actors, and with the institutional framework in which the armed forces perform their duties.

If this is so, the problem of civilian control should be understood in more nuanced and disaggregated ways. Arguably, strengthening access by the military to those resources and tools linked to professionalism may constitute a very real and positive contribution to more democracy-friendly roles and attitudes, while other aspects of military strength may have correlations with system stability. Therefore, it is essential to determine which dimensions of institutional military strength are conducive to a firmer commitment of the armed services to civilian rule and which dimensions undermine such a commitment.

Hence, military professionalization and formalized rules supporting professional roles should be strongly promoted, while nonprofessional roles and roles connected to corporatist political prerogatives should be discouraged and, whenever possible, reduced. We may hypothesize that certain types of strengthening help the military to fit more easily into a "normal" model of democratic civil-military relations. The problem should be seen in terms of the redeployment of organizational strengths and capabilities, not merely reducing the size of the military. This, then, leads to consideration of which organizational steps can be taken with no risk to democratic governance or even may result in positive benefits toward this goal.

The second, often unstated assumption is that any kind of civilian control over the armed forces is equivalent to a commensurate deepening of democratic governance. This facile equation has to be contemplated with a critical eye.

Civilian rule is only contingently democratic. One cannot assume that because civilians or civilian organizations control the military, citizen power over government and popular participation has gained importance in defining the goals and the activities of the military professional establishment (Varas 1988). Civilian governments may be more or less democratic, more or less open to the influence of citizens, more or less oriented toward defending and upholding constitutional values, the rule of law, and civil liberties (O'Donnell 1994). One must be aware of the wide possibilities still open for the manipulation of military force by civilian authorities, including purposes not connected to legitimate uses of power (Loveman 1993). A case in point has been the subordination of the Mexican armed forces to the semi-authoritarian Mexican civilian government. The same point could be made in relation to the support the military has given to the thinly disguised authoritarianism of the Alberto Fujimori regime in Peru.

This opens a new problem: What is to be said about the role of the military in internal politics when civilian politicians and authorities covertly or openly challenge the values and practices of democracy? Military officer corps have confronted and may continue to confront such dilemmas. In some instances, submitting to legal and formal civilian controls may undermine the substantive values of democratic governance. In such cases, the military may be involved in deep dilemmas, for which easy rules and responses may not be found. A theory of democratic civil-military relations cannot avoid the issues that emerge when the democratic nature of civilian institutions is ambiguous or altogether lacking (Stokes 1995, 59-81).

Similarly, how should Latin American armed forces react to noncatastrophic breakdowns of governance, public order, and public life without an overt dissolution of the formal aspects of electoral democracy? Answers in the past were relatively easy to produce. The implicit political rules of Latin American states gave the military some margin for maneuver in exerting their influence or stepping in as a last resort referee (Rial 1986). The military could act as "moderators" or "tutors" of a political system in disarray (O'Donnell, Schmitter, and Whitehead 1986). Nowadays, this route seems problematic or blocked. The military's classic role as ultimate defenders of state legitimacy has been decisively challenged by political processes both within and without the region. Civilian leaders in democracies ought to sort out their crises without the help or tutelage of military organizations. The problem is that civilian politicians cannot always find proper and workable solutions by themselves. As a result, military officers in many countries of the region ask what their roles should be when democratic institutions seem unable to handle adequately drawn-out crises of state legitimacy, public order, national identity, corruption, crime, and massive inefficiency of the public and private sectors.

The kinds of crises now confronting Latin American countries have largely changed. No longer is the region confronted by wrenching challenges in the political sphere, led by ideological factions or social groups willing to capture the state to reshape their nations "from above." On the contrary, the most usual crisis seems to be connected to the slow-motion disintegration of social bonds, public and private morality, and the most basic efficacy of social and political mechanisms of collective self-regulation. To these questions, standard ideas about civilian control and democratic governance are sometimes unable to provide convincing answers.

This means it is time to move to the question of how a crisis in civilian governance can be solved in ways that will not force the officer corps to confront severe dilemmas independent of their wishes. Civilian leaders may be faced not only with military institutions that have to check their allegedly inherent interventionist tendencies but also with strong pressures from without the military that ask them to "step in and do something to fix the mess," shoving aside delegitimized civilian authorities and government institutions. This is a conceivable situation in a number of countries: Ecuador, Venezuela, and perhaps even Paraguay, Colombia, and Mexico.

The question of military subordination to civilian and democratic government in contemporary Latin America cannot be separated from the resolution of the pending issues of the institutionalization of workable democratic political systems and practices and the effective rule of law. Therefore, the question of military political restraint has to be tackled simultaneously from both spheres — from the point of view of the structure, roles, and internal ethos of the armed services themselves and from the perspective of the current political practices, institutions, and conflict-resolution mechanisms prevalent in civilian politics and social life in general.

The case of Brazil during the crisis of the Fernando Collor administration provided a good example of a successful resolution of both aspects of the question of democratic stability. In that case, the military was able to stay out of the whole process because of the previous changes in the structure of military-civilian relationships, tasks, and institutional outlooks *and* because the normal mechanisms of republican democracy were successful in handling the challenges posed by massive corruption within the executive. Thus, Collor's downfall was the result of efficient crisis management by democratic institutions making use of their internal resources. The Brazilian system was quite capable of solving the crisis without resorting to military tutelage, as was often the case in the past.

## THE LATIN AMERICAN ARMED FORCES IN THE GLOBAL CONTEXT

New strategic realities have changed perceptions about the uses of military force in the hemisphere. In the Cold War years, local armies were seen by the two superpowers as important factors in their own struggles. For the United States, Latin American militaries had to be cultivated as potential or actual allies in the effort to curb communism. Their role was to secure the rearguard of the West, mainly by keeping watch, but potentially by fighting armed attempts by internal groups that could be connected to the socialist bloc. Theirs was a mixed lot of political, constabulary, and internal war-fighting tasks. Other Latin American national strategic concerns (territorial disputes) were seen as irrelevant or nuisances that could detract from efforts toward the main task or, worse, create instabilities that could provide openings for the penetration of the opposing superpower. Whatever their actual relevance in the Cold War, Latin American armies were seen as minor but useful players in the Western alliance against the socialist bloc.

In the 1990s, however, this usefulness has been curtailed drastically. There are still, of course, remnants of those former goals. The Colombian, Mexican, and Peruvian armies continue to contend with armed revolutionaries who claim to promote leftist or radical political change. However, internal guerrillas have lost much of their potency as systemic threats insofar as they cannot be linked with powerful extracontinental strategic actors. Whatever successes they may have in weakening their governments are bound to remain local events and have little hemispheric impact.

Thus, Latin American military forces may retain value as tools of internal order against ideologically motivated challenges, but this usefulness is now somewhat restricted in scope, consequences, and global import. Nevertheless, the practice of assigning them a crucial role in internal matters has taken a new twist, which is connected to a new agenda that is a matter of strong concern for the United States.

In the days of the Cold War, concern for local armies was linked to Washington's global Realpolitik and what may be termed classic strategic considerations. The cultivation of Latin armies was a part of an outward-oriented, geopolitical policy and discourse set within the framework of the worldwide superpower struggle. Today, the list of priorities that U.S. policy circles suggest to their southern counterparts is connected for the most part to North American domestic policy topics. The big threats now are seen as linked to the ways in which questions of public order in Latin America can affect social and political debates and realities within the North American political system: immigration, drugs, Cuba, and, to a certain extent, crime and the environment. Therefore, Latin American armies are being asked to become part of the efforts of U.S. administrations to handle questions that directly affect internal social and political debates within the U.S. electorate.

From this perspective, one may ask whether Latin American military establishments and their roles have been "nationalized" by U.S. governments and become increasingly separated from the usual concerns of realist geopolitics. Latin American military roles seem to be increasingly devoid of substantive, classical strategic importance, insofar as the focus has shifted toward their potential impact on a completely different set of issues. The question of the Latin American armed forces' role has become more a question to be dealt with by parochial politicians, intellectuals, and bureaucrats than a matter within the purview of global strategists and military officers.

This "destrategization" of perceptions in the United States about roles for Latin military establishments has had its counterpart in Latin America. During the Cold War, it was easy to interpret the alliance with Washington as part of the task of protecting Christian civilization from Eastern barbarism. It was an ancillary but valuable service provided to the common crusade, and it could provide the Latin armed forces with the gratifying feeling that they were part of a struggle endowed with global and historical meaning, even if providing these services to the "West" implied foregoing a professional identity grounded in conventional tasks.

Once the common threat disappeared, Latin military forces could not easily find other shared civilizational tasks. Instead, they increasingly were being asked to perform duties that could only be connected to the particular concerns of domestic U.S. politics. This role change threatened the self-perceptions of the officer corps, which had been built on the assumption that the reason for their existence was civilizational struggle. Constabulary tasks could not always be identified with such lofty principles. Their sense of mission was kept alive wherever the military met threats of "internal barbarism" (for example, in Colombia or Peru) but not in other cases.

From that point on, a communicational short-circuit started to develop. U.S. politicians and policymakers had ceased to see Latin American armies as part of a strategic, historically meaningful crusade, and, conversely, the Latin armies could not cease seeing themselves in such a light. They were motivated toward sharing the aftermath of the struggle in ways that would preserve their sense of global mission; however, they were being asked to devote their limited energies to issues that they perceived as being tied to the ignoble ups and downs of U.S. domestic political debates. This is one of the reasons why, for instance, the Argentine government insisted on being given a role in the Persian Gulf in 1991 and later stressed its military role in the Balkans. In this way, the sense of mission of the officer corps could be maintained while their internal political and conventional roles were being reduced drastically, cushioning already high levels of resentment and alienation widespread in the ranks. The Argentine case shows that it is possible to connect survival and ideological justifications in the search for a mission. The self-image of the Argentine officer corps was threatened on both accounts, and peacekeeping helped solve them simultaneously.

Yet, no matter what governments do to provide the armed forces with a vital sense of mission, and whether they succeed or not, the fact is that for most of the officer corps throughout the region, the United States already has ceased for some time to be a valid provider of answers, and it has become instead part of the problem. The crux of the matter is that the U.S. government is seen as intent on denying the military in Latin America valid grounds upon which military life, as understood in the barracks, can be anchored. Valid, uplifting missions can only be acquired despite, against, or independent of Washington's advice and wishes. The internal issues that concern the United States cannot be linked to the symbolic validation of the transcendental role of the Latin American officer corps. Worse yet for Latin military forces, they are being pressured into relinquishing all the undertakings that they saw as ultimate symbolic validators. Gone is the fight against communism; military developmentalism and civic action are under heavy attack from policymakers who support neoliberalism, which in turn is encouraged by many institutions seen as connected with the U.S. government; nation-building from the barracks is suspect; involvement in traditional border issues is frowned upon or just ignored; and no relevant task in defending Christendom has been proposed in a systematic way, although peacemaking could be a promising approach if taken seriously by both sides. The demands coming from Washington are seen as petty, threatening, irrelevant, and/or hostile — to the point that some Latin American officers feel that the United States may have an unspoken interest in eliminating their forces altogether, shrinking them into irrelevance and pushing ahead a radical agenda of demilitarization.

Another factor that irritates Latin militaries is that U.S. support of civilian elected governments appears to be less than sensitive to the fact that these governments do not always promote or operate upon the highest values of Western civilization. Many officers think that by focusing solely on protecting the rituals of electoral democracy, the United States is countenancing corruption, inefficiency, demagoguery, and gross socioeconomic unfairness. They often believe that U.S. policy is myopic and unable to perceive the full scope and meaning of civilizational processes, which may clash with the formal strictures of democracy and polyarchy.

In fact, inside Latin American military establishments, the United States always has been suspected of being too idealistically liberal and out of touch with the hard Machiavellian realities of power and nation-building. Support for civilian leaders can be seen at times as support for a debased "demagogic-plebiscitarian" form of popular government. One must remember that from the perspective of Latin American elites, including the military, "the people" does not have the ring of sanctity that it has in Anglo-Saxon or revolutionary democracies. In the Latin American tradition, the concept of "the people" among elites is still heavily embedded within civilizational "otherness" — groups that have to be tutored, surveilled, and educated by the most Westernized parts of society. The people are not seen as fully deserving to be enfranchised, given the belief in *capitis diminutio* (diminished capacity) that constituted the central axis of legitimation of social distance and deference in colonial and nineteenth-century Latin America. Support for unrestricted and untutored popular rule may easily be seen as the promotion of the rule of a partially civilized mob and not as the virtuous workings of a body of equally worthy *citizens.*

## THE QUESTION OF CIVILIZATIONAL PLURALISM

The crisis of "civilizational" models of military mission has been compounded recently by local echoes of the renewed salience that long-standing national-istic, ethnic, and religious conflicts have acquired in many "hot areas" of the world. In fact, the decade of the 1990s has witnessed the rekindling of issues that earlier nation-building ostensibly had solved in many countries of the region.

This leads directly to issues related to internal heterogeneity in Latin American countries. The last few years have seen developments that give new prominence to the fact that most Latin American states have not fully achieved the post-Enlightenment ideal of fusing society into a single citizen body under the purview of the nation-state. This question is being confronted — in some cases, tragically — in other areas of the world.

The fact is that the achievement of the nineteenth-century dream of a homogenous citizenship closely identified with the abstract nation-state, to which loyalty is granted beyond and above any other ascriptive status and identity, has not been completed. This may be due to certain features inherent in the cultural attitudes of ruling elites in the southern part of the Western Hemisphere. The cultural prestige of European ways and ideas was so overwhelmingly dominant that it almost by itself explains the subjective need of local elites to attempt to imitate and reproduce at least the outward trappings of European concepts and institutions. Being able to do so was the mark of true civilization and of success in the struggle against "otherness." By resembling on the surface the idealized image of what a modern state should be, one could perhaps become a part of the coveted Western cosmopolis.

On the other hand, the authority of elites over the internal "barbarian" required the permanent renewal of their status as paternalistic protectors of the not-so-European masses. However, the permanence of this paternalistic role demands the perpetuation of the status of the mass of people as somewhat less than fully adult. In this sense, the implicit covenant between rulers and ruled took a different form in Iberian-America than in "old" democracies. In the latter, the claim to legitimacy of social and political elites is based on the assumption that the ruled are fully able to provide consent and demand accountability. The rulers continuously have to demonstrate and prove that they are doing nothing but faithfully performing commands given by the citizens. This image of a leader is one of a delegated agent of a public interest that is primarily constructed by the autonomous will of a cohesive body politic. Notwithstanding lip service given to formal liberal ideas and discourses, the traditional pact between Latin American elites and the masses, however, has been of a quite different nature. It is not based on the idea of an autonomous citizen but on the conviction that rulers and social elites ought to take care of the people in much the same way as parents take care of their offspring. The elites ought to have as a paramount concern the best interests of the masses, but the definition of those best interests is not necessarily left to the masses themselves. The elites are assumed to know better what those best interests are and should educate the masses accordingly. Thus, ruling is not the performance of an implicit command or delegation by fully competent citizens but is the result of a trust whereby the ruled define who is going to be charged with the task of interpreting and enforcing the public interest. The ruled do not expect the rulers to be the agents of their own autonomous free will, but the providers of certain satisfactions and loosely defined forms of "protection." This is what gives the structure of governance in many countries the profile of a paternalistic relationship and why the imagery of the patriarchal family is so dominant in common-sense political discourse.

Liberal and Jacobin elites in Latin America had, therefore, an impossible task. They had to become the rulers of a "normal" post-revolutionary political order if they were to become the elites of a bona fide, modern, Eurocentric political order, but in order to maintain this role, they had to reproduce the patrimonialist compact with their own populations inside the limits of the nation-state, and that meant the preservation of a heterogeneous republic of symbolically and practically segregated orders. This particular framework, of course, has many local variants and is not the same everywhere. In some countries lacking important indigenous or non-European populations, the rationality of social paternalism has taken more subdued forms, although it can still be argued that these are very much alive, even in countries such as Argentina, Chile, Uruguay, and Costa Rica, which have more developed liberal state systems and cultural institutions. At the root of this dilemma was an ambivalent understanding of what being part of the West meant. Two conflicting meanings were adopted simultaneously. The first was connected to the question of civilization and Christianity and the other to the liberal values of democratic republicanism.

Local Latin American militaries have been wrenched by this dilemma. Yet, their predominant sense has been that their main internal task was securing the discipline and order that made this two-edged predicament stable and reproducible in time — thus, the enormous emotional importance that educational activities have for most of them. Conscription and civic action have enabled local militaries to feel that they are part of the elite task of producing and reproducing diversity while enacting the drama of its suppression: the never ending, circular tale of reproducing otherness through efforts to assimilate and tame it.

It is at this point that the question of "nationalities" becomes important for the understanding of the present predicament of military establishments in Latin American countries. During the last decade, the question of ethnicity and racial pluralism has steadily gained prominence within the region. Emerging indigenous and Afro-American political activism represents a major breakthrough in the way in which those citizens' relationships with the nation and political life have been handled previously.

The hitherto dominant view has been that indigenous ethnic groups were either to be "protected" (the conservative and populist position) or assimilated into the mainstream of national life (the liberal and leftist position). The assimilationists differed regarding methods to achieve this goal. For the liberals, indigenous people had to be incorporated as individuals, becoming property owners and market actors, thus losing the differentiating characteristics of specific civilizational groups within the countries. The only acceptable (if any) particularism to be maintained was in the realm of folklore. The indigenous condition was a form of backwardness that only full socialization into mainstream, westernized lifestyles could overcome. Indigenous culture and lifestyles were a "burden" that only hindered the personal development and freedom of individuals. The task of modernization was to erase gradually the distinctiveness of Indianness (or Africanness) in order to save the Indians and Africans from their "inherently inferior" conditions. The road to progress for these groups was via some form of color-blind "whitening" (both symbolic and socioeconomic). Left-wing, pro-indigenous ideologies equated this process with the ethnic groups acquiring a new identity as proletarians or being part of some other national-popular collective actor. In any case, ethnic identity could not become on its own the springboard of a process of empowerment and social liberation.

The new ethnic movements in Latin America have in different ways introduced the idea of "ethnic citizenship," in which indigenous people demand to be given rights and powers as members of such ethnic groups. Equal respect is being demanded for indigenous groups in their collective capacity as discrete, semi-sovereign entities. Thus, the rights and prerogatives that the new movements demand are frequently not liberal individual rights but ethnic forms of self-rule, which in some cases may even conflict with the former.

In terms of the previous discussion, the new ethnic movements are demanding nothing other than the abolition of the two founding assumptions of the Latin American political order: liberal-republican governance and the missionary-civilizational ethos. They want the whole concept of citizenship to be disengaged from presumptions about the individual being the locus of sovereignty and civil, political, and social rights; simultaneously, they demand that Creole elites forfeit their self-assigned task of acting toward the indigenous peoples in a paternalistic fashion. They are aiming toward a concept of political order in which rights are recognized for cultural and ethnic aggregates as such (as in the colonial order), while the assumption of cultural inferiority is to be dropped (contrary to the colonial order) and adjusted to some of the latent implications of a full liberal understanding of otherness. The demands voiced by these groups imply a situation in which a multinational state may emerge but without the present structures of ethnic dominance. The serious implementation of such a vision could involve some form of autonomous self-rule, special status, or, in extreme cases, direct independence from traditional nation-states. In any case, such perspectives imply some degree of undermining the classic notion of what a modern nation-state should be.

In fact, some of the demands of ethnic-based organizations point toward reestablishing the idea of *fueros,* that is, special juridical statuses for specific social and functional groups, which might or might not have a territorial basis. The old Spanish and pre-modern polities were rife with such arrangements, which gave status groups a special set of rights, duties, exemptions, and forms of authority. Special jurisdictions such as those proposed in ethnic demands would be, in fact, a sort of reestablishment of pre-republican practices.

Now, these types of demands squarely challenge the sense of political order present in contemporary military establishments. The military views political order as something founded on an essentialist definition of nationhood that has no place for the indigenous except as a symbolic ingredient that blends into the dominant myths of Creole nationhood. The possibility of a confederation of civilizations is alien to the republican credo and to the ethos of the Christian cosmopolis. This rejection is reinforced by the lessons supposedly learned from the experience of multinational empires before World War I and in the aftermath of the Cold War. Military establishments fear that multinationalism is the first stage of national disintegration, secessionism, and state decay, as many historical precedents seem to illustrate. Thus, the present ethnic movements are seen primarily as a central threat to national security.

However, the appropriate response to this perceived challenge is not as clear. There are several alternatives, from the Guatemalan "ethnic war," to the intense civic-action efforts undertaken by the Ecuadorian military, to the political co-optation strategies followed by the Bolivian government.

However, questions of multinationality and their impact on traditional concepts of state security are deserving of closer scrutiny. For instance, one can examine whether the historical record effectively supports the contention that multiethnic states are inherently less stable or weaker than one-people-one-state systems.

Such scrutiny does not seem to support the idea that multinational states in themselves are always weaker or lacking in stability and staying power. For example, the colonial system itself: Colonialism was a very durable and peaceful state of affairs that decayed only under the extreme tension of international factors and stresses produced by attempts to develop a modern, legal-rational system of government, which tended to weaken and abolish traditional *fueros* and achieved statuses. The United Kingdom is another example, and the same could be said of other solid European powers (for example, Switzerland, Belgium, and Spain), while unitarian Poland or unitarian Turkey have demonstrated that classic nation-states can be weak and unstable for long periods of time. Moreover, if one looks at the fate of exploded multiethnic empires or nations, it is apparent that the weaknesses that proved their undoing were connected to failures in dealing with the problems of "ethnic dominance" and their inability to provide different nationalities with a sense of full belonging and respect by the dominant group (for example, Germans in

Austria-Hungary, Great Russians in the former Soviet Union, Turks in the Ottoman Empire, or Serbs in Yugoslavia). These examples show that questions related to the security implications of multinationalism should be kept open and a deeper search for the mediating factors involved could be a fruitful and timely undertaking. As Juan Linz and Alfred Stepan (1996) have pointed out, political engineering, institutional crafting, and leadership may be important mediating factors in explaining why and how certain multinational or multicultural polities succeed or fail.

In any case, the Latin American militaries will become major players in the solution of the new questions of ethnic citizenship and the political status of ethnic groups and organizations, particularly as they already have a tradition in these areas, which they may take as a point of departure. In other historical contexts, armies have been institutions in which different national groups have found a common space, where differences and commonalities have been lived and expressed. Armies often have operated as crucibles for processing and negotiating ethnic and national identities, sometimes quite successfully. Concrete and specific policies regarding this issue have very different outcomes. The question is how recruitment, civic action, deployment, training, and missions might be managed so that the military can become an organizational space for promoting a new modus vivendi and addressing certain groups' feelings of marginalization and deprivation in a constructive way that gives ethnicity a recognizable and non-destabilizing place.

## INSTITUTIONAL TASKS AND MISSIONS

To recapitulate, some of the main questions that frame the discussion about future roles for the Latin American armed forces are 1) the quest for a civilizing, historic task; 2) the question of identifying roles in a globalized, cosmopolitan context; 3) the question of the military as a system-stabilizer in political systems lacking a definite source of symbolic legitimacy; and 4) questions of nationality and state sovereignty. Each one of these questions points toward a certain type of institutional task or some general criteria that may help to determine possible relevant and meaningful future missions.

First, unless and until the civilizational ethos is weakened effectively, the civilizational role could be redirected in connection with multinational and global needs of peacemaking and peace enforcement. The efforts to develop international regimes to provide cooperative security for increasing numbers of human beings can be linked to the traditions of Christian civility, entailing the "pacification" of nations and peoples and questions of a just order. Conversely, tasks should be provided for the armed forces that minimize the chances for Latin American militaries to consider themselves as warring crusaders against "other civilizations." Thus, cosmopolitan roles ought to be developed in close association with wider cooperative efforts aimed at mediating among conflicting parties or, at minimum, interposing buffers between them.

Second, due consideration should be given to remaining border defense issues, which are still part of the security problem for many Latin American countries. However, efforts should be made to modify traditional geopolitical and "realist" approaches to the question of conventional security (Child 1985), introducing new ideas about ways in which these conflicts can be managed so as to enhance chances of not having to fight wars with neighboring armies (Galtung 1982).

Third, Latin American armies still may have limited internal social, political, and cultural roles and tasks connected to nation-building and nation-maintenance. Regarding this point, the military establishments in the region may perform useful, although not central roles as organizational settings for the resolution of the emerging questions of national identity and for the reconsideration of the nature of relationships between the liberal and republican ideas on citizenship and the special status of different ethnic groups and cultures within each country.

Fourth, Latin American armed forces may retain certain political roles, conceived in terms of system stabilization. At a symbolic level, Latin American armies continue to serve as expressions of national sovereignty. However, what is needed is a new look at the question of the military's relationship with civilian powers and governance. It is necessary to go beyond the mere question of noninterference in civilian prerogatives and the (unavoidable) issue of settling accounts with the past (Zagorsky 1992). Likewise, it seems that a more nuanced consideration of the meanings of institutional strength and weakness must be developed, showing that in some capacities and areas (professionalism and modernization), the strengthening of the military should be seen as promoting the ability of republican institutions to provide for an adequate level of governance for their countries.

The fifth and final point is that governments should avoid the temptation of giving the military a crucial and routine role in issues of public security that properly belong in the sphere of competence of civilian and police organizations. As has been abundantly shown, such tasks can only erode true professionalism and distort the relationships between citizens and military personnel. Those public security tasks normally are not seen as worthy undertakings by the more professional military establishments in the region — trying to push armies into them will only be an irritant in their relationships with internal or external actors who are trying to shape a crime-fighting or a constabulary role for the armed forces.

## GOVERNANCE, MILITARY BUDGETS, ECONOMIC GROWTH, AND EXPENDITURES

Beginning in the 1980s, and especially after 1989, it frequently has been claimed in public and academic discussions that military expenditures slow economic growth (Spinetta 1995). As a consequence, reducing the funds for national defense has become a very popular and well-accepted part of adjustment programs. Even without a well-defined economic theory regarding the connection between growth and defense expenditures, the sheer lack of money in certain cases (for example, in Argentina and Brazil) has imposed sharp budget cutbacks as a matter of pure financial necessity. Likewise, with the demise of the policies of state-led growth, the rationale for many ambitious military undertakings in industry, technology, arms production, and basic infrastructure definitely has lost much of its appeal and feasibility. At the same time, of course, it is often thought that smaller and leaner armies are less threatening to democracy itself.

While after 1960 it was a commonly held belief that military forces as economic actors could provide a boost to national industrialization, economic modernization, and development, the trend in the 1990s is to deny forcefully that the armed forces perform well as economic modernizers. Many econometric studies have tried to show the full opportunity costs of military expenditures, both traditional and entrepreneurial (see Deger 1986). Yet, privatization and disinvestment largely have prevented military efforts to consolidate and expand a military-controlled sector of the economy, with only a few exceptions (Spinetta 1995).

The discussion on arms control and reduction also has been focused on growth and efficiency concerns (Deger and Smith 1983). In fact, in Latin America, unlike in Europe, arms control and expenditure reduction are predominantly part of the discourse of development and growth rather than being centrally focused around the security implications of such reductions. International organizations have nurtured and sometimes led this debate, in which the armed forces are seen as a hindrance to economic well-being.

All this is part of the unhappy legacy of "military Keynesianism," which evolved in the United States after World War II, had its heyday in the 1960s and 1970s, and had its local counterparts in different schools of "military developmentalism" in Latin America until the 1980s. According to this school of thought, military investment could provide a boost to growth and full employment as well as provide an incentive for technological advances, with beneficial spinoffs for civilian economies. Proponents of this perspective wanted to legitimize expanded military budgets in purely economic terms, showing that they could be justified regardless of their strict utility for security purposes and goals. This represented a break with an ancient tradition that held that defense was an unavoidable burden for the economy. Traditionally, military budgets had to be defended in terms of the threat that they were supposed to help defeat or prevent, but a growth-related rationale could somewhat isolate military budgets from the ups and downs of the international situation, decoupling them from actual or perceived changes in the strategic context.

To this tendency belong studies such as the famed attempt by Emile Benoit (1973) to show that military expenditure is beneficial and positively correlated to economic performance. Since 1974, however, a host of other studies have shown that such a correlation cannot be sustained, thus casting considerable doubt on the basic tenets of military Keynesianism, which has fallen in disrepute (Grobar and Porter 1989). The problem is that defenders of big military budgets became trapped in their own preferred argument. If the main rationale for big investment in the military was to be economic development, and it could be shown that no such linkage existed, then advocates of large military budgets and role expansion were deprived of one of their main lines of reasoning. Thus, they had to fall back on more traditional arguments about impending security dangers. However, in the present context in Latin America, such impending conventional dangers are hard to find or to defend. Pushed to its limit, this perspective makes it easy to see in the armed forces nothing but a bad investment that ought to be cut as much as possible or even eliminated.

However, if we accept that military investment cannot be seen as an expenditure whose economic value is subject to straightforward econometric modeling, and if we accept that the primary goods that it uses are related to state security, then the question of budgets and size can be approached again in a more conventional sense.[1] The economic debate on military budgets should focus on the intended efficacy and efficiency of those allocated funds, not to promote growth or modernization, but to provide the state with a series of goods that only democratic, open, and transparent debate can determine. The question is then, the extent to which money spent on the armed forces is providing for the fulfillment of those strategic goals that the civilian polity has defined as crucial for the well-being, stability, and survival of the political community. Defense funds should be seen as buying primarily the ability of the state to remain sovereign and fulfill goals related to the attributes of sovereignty, such as secure borders, a minimum of political autonomy within the international system, and adequate strategic deterrence or other incentives for potential foes not to engage in hostile action.

Seen in these terms, military budgets can then both be justified in terms of security considerations and be open to public and democratic scrutiny. This helps to free the whole question of defense budgets from the fetters of the discussion that simply shows that any amount spent on defense has opportunity costs associated in terms of other public goals. In its narrowest form, the outcome of that debate is fixed beforehand: expenditures should be lowered or eliminated. Yet, this latter conclusion, if taken seriously by civilian and international organizations, can only block a meaningful debate with military forces about their tasks and goals, increase mutual mistrust, and leave unanswered the question of actual and realistic missions that these forces can perform. A consideration of expenditures in terms of their internal economies and specific objectives can, instead, help introduce into democratic debate the whole question of the goals and missions of the military forces within each country, as well as legitimize a meaningful role for civilian concerns in shaping the defense agenda.

## THE MILITARY, CITIZENSHIP, AND DEMOCRATIC GOVERNANCE

Remarks that conclude this chapter concern the internal political role of the Latin American armed forces. In the past, the main concern has been to find means by which the military throughout the continent could be kept away from politics. In fact, the problem is not that simple. Keeping the military out of the wrong kind of politics really is the most crucial concern.

Modern professional military forces are not apolitical organizations. As a part of the state apparatus, they participate in certain areas of public policymaking and in statecraft, understood in the widest sense. Denying their inherently political nature in the name of apoliticism may end by bringing into existence among the officer corps the politics of anti-politics instead of the benevolent abstention many people consider as properly befitting the professional officer corps (Loveman and Davies 1989).

As the processes of democratic consolidation proceed, a "second generation" agenda of civil-military relations should be prepared for discussion. This agenda should focus on the question of military life and citizenship. It may imply some form of military repolitization, but by this we should mean something quite different from the kind of involvement witnessed in the past. In this second stage, detailed consideration should be given to appropriate ways for the military to be brought back into the mainstream of national life to become full-fledged social and civic actors.

One of the first issues that could be posed is the topic of enfranchisement and civil rights. In most Latin American countries, the officer corps and other personnel are deprived of voting rights. This exclusion was prudent decades ago, when political and electoral systems could not prevent enlisted soldiers from being used as "electoral cannon fodder" by civilian or military politicians. Likewise, this exclusion aimed at preventing officers from becoming partisans of any given faction. The assumption was that if they were not part of the electorate, candidates and parties would not become interested in wooing or cultivating them, thereby reducing the chances that officers could be subject to political recruitment or to taking sides in internal power struggles. Of course, this could not prevent officers from becoming partisans through other, nonelectoral mechanisms, but it did have the effect of making military personnel distant from the workings and rationality of civic participation. They could easily see normal politics as something in which they had no interest or involvement, and, from that stance, viewing all politics as merely debased "politicking" was the logical next step (Tulchin 1995).

As political systems throughout the region become more stable and institutionalized, there should be a gradual lessening of those conditions that increase the likelihood that military involvement in politics would lead to praetorianism and clientelism (both inside and outside the barracks). The effective consolidation of democratic governance would permit the taking-hold of rational-legal and normative mechanisms that would serve as barriers to the kind of civic culture that justified excluding soldiers from fuller involvement in political and social life. Admittedly, this point has not yet been reached, and crucial prior and enabling conditions are not yet present in many countries of the region. Before this agenda can be addressed, civilian government and civil-military relations have to achieve a certain degree of predictability, stability, reliability, and responsiveness to democratic practices, routines, and culture.

In Chile, the step of enfranchising soldiers and officers has been taken, and so far — contrary to fears voiced during the transition to elected government — there is no evidence nor public concern that this move has led to undue partisanship or politicization within the ranks. Granting the full franchise to people in uniform may be a modest but meaningful way for democratic institutions to become part of the barracks' ethos and civic culture. Enfranchisement may reduce the likelihood that members of the military will continue to feel that there is a gap between civil and military life; it might also make citizenship a part of the military lifestyle.

Should full citizenship and the weakening of the cultural isolation of the armed forces proceed even further? Making soldiers part of the wider civic culture and allowing them to become familiar with the pragmatics of liberal democracy may contribute to the erosion of the old missionary civilizational ethos and its authoritarian secondary effects. At some point, discussion should take place regarding the possibility that people in uniform also could have the right to participate in other ways, including belonging to and participating in civilian public interest organizations. In the past, there have been some attempts to bring in the military as actors within representative institutions. The argument here would be that modern liberal institutions and legal systems have built-in mechanisms that separate the official status of a person from his or her private status as a citizen.

In fact, one important issue in terms of military civic culture is the need to let soldiers have private lives and opinions, separated and relatively autonomous from their roles as public servants. Within such a private realm, they increasingly ought to be considered "normal" citizens. Such an evolution must confront squarely two antidemocratic traits of present military life: their *fuero* or special legal status (clearly a colonial and authoritarian legacy) and an all-encompassing lifestyle, both of which help to allow antidemocratic values and practices to take hold in the minds of enlisted personnel and officers. Private civic participation must be seen as a means of breaking down the monolithic, militant makeup of military social psychology, giving way to world views more compatible with the roles of professional civil servants in a modern, secularized political order of citizens.

There is nothing in democratic theory that in principle should deny soldiers the right to be elected or belong to associations other than the military. Such a move may be threatening for professionalism and institutional neutrality in politics whenever the overall system of government is weakly embedded, but not in well-consolidated democracies. In fact, the military as an organization is being represented in some crucial decision-making arenas outside its own immediate sphere of competence. In several Latin American countries, soldiers are key members of "National Security Councils" or other such organizations. In that capacity, they have a say in political matters not strictly related to their professional tasks. Bringing them into citizen arenas would transfer present forms of participation from sites where accountability, transparency, and public visibility are very low (Zagorsky 1992) to other forums where military participation would be channeled into the give-and-take of civic debate and discussion. Alfred Stepan has suggested that the military should have regular institutional outlets where they can express and share their concerns with civilian politicians and authorities outside the nondemocratic framework provided by current National Security Councils (Stepan 1988).

On the other hand, if forms of participation are chosen that stress the individual rights of military personnel, the first steps could be taken toward developing in society the modern concept that people in public life (including officers) can separate their individual personas from their official positions. These deeper forms of enfranchisement could enhance the exposure of military personnel to civic culture and a wider set of civilian concerns, lowering the "moral" barriers built around the barracks.

The question of citizenship and the military need not stop there, however. Latin American militaries are just beginning to consider the question of how the rights and duties of special groups relate to military life. One case in point is the topic of gender: Women traditionally have been accepted within the military in ancillary or support roles, but the implementation of full equality across gender lines entails, in principle and practice, the fullest incorporation of women into all kinds of military roles, including combat positions and the opening of the officer corps to women. The Chilean and Argentine militaries recently have taken a few steps in that direction by admitting women to regular officer training. As military careers become more open to traditionally excluded groups and as their concerns, interests, and perspectives are taken more fully into account, new elements of civic culture gradually may become part of the military ethos. Armies on the continent have been showing sensitivity to such issues in a few places. For instance, the Ecuadorian army has been experimenting with ethnically defined and based units, in which members of a given indigenous group identify with a certain battalion or regiment that becomes "theirs."

The classic attitude of the military toward the ethnic question has been to see the barracks as places where the "other" members of various ethnic and indigenous groups are educated into the ways of civilization and integrated into a supposedly homogeneous national culture and ethnicity. Recruitment and training practices may have to be reformulated in the future so that the demands and special needs of ethnic citizens are taken seriously, their diversity is respected, and they are provided equal opportunity, regardless of their refusal to blend completely into the dominant cultural milieu of the Creole officer corps.

Regional balances also might be the object of conscious policy. In some countries, citizens from certain regions are overrepresented or underrepresented; for example, in Ecuador and Peru, people from the highlands still are overrepresented in the officer corps, and traditionally in Venezuela and Brazil, members of the military tend to be recruited preferentially from certain specific areas. This weakens the claim of the military to be a "national" and "representative" institution. If a more universalistic profile and a closer identification with civilian society are goals, then recruitment practices must take these regional biases as something to be corrected.

Similar considerations apply to the social origins of the officer corps. Within Latin American armies, there is a tendency toward self-recruitment and for careers to be opened preferentially to the offspring of active officers. This style of social self-selection allegedly has increased the cultural and social isolation of the armed forces, among other factors, and has contributed to insensitivity toward civic opinions beyond the barracks. Ways to bring more varied social experiences and backgrounds into military life should be considered, as well as a more varied set of incentives to attract officer candidates from different walks of life. One of the main weaknesses in the social reproduction of the officer corps is that in most countries upper-class people do not consider a military career dignified or prestigious. Officers are predominantly middle or lower-middle class in their social backgrounds, which detracts from the social bearing of the career. Means ought to be discussed to enhance the social prestige of a military career so that civilian elites cease to underestimate its value and social meaning.

Finally, the question of military law and personal rights should be addressed. Personnel throughout the region are subject to a series of disciplinary constraints that restrict their enjoyment of basic civil rights. Experience shows that adequate discipline does not require a deep curtailment of the personal freedoms of officers and enlisted personnel, and, conversely, the more soldiers share the rights and duties of civilians, the more likely they will be to develop a commitment to the same political and social values promoted by a supposedly democratic, free society. The current cleavage between forms of military discipline and forms of civic discipline cannot continue indefinitely. Traditional forms of military discipline in many ways hark back to a premodern and feudal past, while forms of civil discipline have become increasingly grounded in the assumptions of the liberal ethos. The enhancement of the democratic ethos of citizenship will become increasingly hard to reconcile with the persistence of an important realm of public life that still seems to cling to the practices, routines, and assumptions of nineteenth-century, authoritarian class relations.

All of these matters have a direct bearing on the question of the gradual introduction and institutionalization of a liberal, civil ethos of citizenship within and toward military life in Latin America. Success in achieving the goals outlined in this chapter may create the basis for renewed and open discussions of the question of missions within the Latin American armed forces. Certainly, achievement of these goals would create a better climate for civilians and military officers to discuss the tasks and ultimate objectives of the defense sector within the framework of mutually compatible intellectual and emotional paradigms. Such a context would be conducive to dealing with the legacy of a military self-image still centered around the colonial images of the "civilizing mission" and of the reproduction of paternalistic social and cultural relations (Loveman 1994). If such discussions occur, there may be a reshaping of the military agenda toward the question of the military's role as providers of order against socially constructed forces of chaos and barbarism. Then, understanding of military tasks may be reshaped in terms of a secularized and instrumental mission of protecting the contractually conceived will of a fully acknowledged body of fellow citizens.

# Notes

1. On the problems of weighing the evidence for or against military investment as a hindrance on growth, see Steve Chan 1985.

# References

Benoit, Emile. 1973. *Defense and Economic Growth in Developing Countries.* Boston: Lexington Books.

Chan, Steve. 1985. "The Impact of Defense Spending on Economic Performance: A Survey of Evidence and Problems." *Orbis:* 29:2 (Summer): 424-433.

Child, Jack. 1985. *Geopolitics and Conflicts in South America, Quarrels Among Neighbors.* New York: Praeger.

Deger, Saadet. 1986. *Military Expenditure in Third World Countries: The Economic Effects.* Chicago: University of Chicago Press.

Deger, Saadet, and Ron Smith. 1983. "Military Expenditure and Growth in Less Developed Countries." *Journal of Conflict Resolution* 27: 338-349.

Department of Disarmament Affairs. 1983. *Economic and Social Consequences of the Arms Race and Military Expenditures.* New York: United Nations.

Fredrikson, Peter, and Robert Looney. 1993. "Expenditures in Pakistan: Short-Run Impacts and Long-Run Adjustments." *Journal of Peace Research,* 99-107.

Galtung, Johann. 1982. *Environment, Development and Military Activity: Towards Alternative Security Doctrines.* New York: Columbia University Press.

García Pino, Gonzalo, and Juan Esteban Montes Ibáñez. 1993. *La subordinación del poder militar al poder civil: Un aporte desde la teoría democrática.* Santiago: Centro de Estudios del Desarrollo.

Grobar, Lisa M., and Richard C. Porter. 1989. "Benoit Revisited." *Journal of Conflict Resolution* 33 (June): 318-345.

Huntington, Samuel P. 1996. *The Clash of Civilizations and the Remaking of World Order.* New York: Simon & Schuster.

Lagos, Humberto, and Arturo Chacón. 1987. *La religión en las fuerzas armadas y de orden.* 2d ed. Santiago: Presor Lar.

Linz, Juan J., and Alfred C. Stepan. 1996. *Problems of Democratic Transition and Consolidation: Southern Europe, South America, and Post-Communist Europe.* Baltimore: The Johns Hopkins University Press.

Loveman, Brian. 1993. *The Constitution of Tyranny: Regimes of Exception in Spanish America.* Pittsburgh: University of Pittsburgh Press.

Loveman, Brian. 1994. "Protected Democracies and Military Guardianship: Political Transitions in Latin America 1978-1993." *Journal of Interamerican Studies and World Affairs* 36 (Summer): 105-189.

Loveman, Brian, and Thomas Davies, Jr. 1989. *The Politics of Anti-Politics: The Military in Latin America.* 2d ed. Lincoln, Neb.: University of Nebraska Press.

O'Donnell, Guillermo. 1994. "Delegative Democracy." *Journal of Democracy* 5 (January): 55-70.

O'Donnell, Guillermo, Philippe Schmitter, and Laurence Whitehead, eds. 1986. *Transitions from Authoritarian Rule.* Baltimore: The Johns Hopkins University Press.

Parker, Cristian. 1993. *Otra lógica en América Latina: Religión popular y modernización capitalista.* Santiago: Fondo de Cultura Económica.

Perelli, Carina. 1990. "The Military's Perception of Threat in the Southern Cone of South America." In *The Military and Democracy, The Future of Civil-Military Relations in Latin America*, eds. Louis Goodman, Juan Rial, and Joanna Mendelsson. Lexington, Mass.: Lexington Books, D.C. Heath and Company.

Rial, Juan. 1986. *Las FFAA: ¿Soldados políticos garantes de la democracia?* Montevideo: Ediciones de la Benda Oriental (EBO).

Spinetta, Lawrence. 1995. "Strengthening Economic Performance & Competitiveness in an LDC: The Effects of Military Expenditure in Ecuador." Master's thesis. Boston: John F. Kennedy School of Government, Harvard University.

Stepan, Alfred. 1988. *Rethinking Military Politics: Brazil and Southern Cone.* Princeton, N.J.: Princeton University Press.

Stokes, Susan. 1995. "Democracy and the Limits to Popular Sovereignty in South America." In *The Consolidation of Democracy in Latin America*, ed. Joseph Tulchin. Boulder, Colo.: Lynne Rienner Publishers.

Tollefson, Scott. 1995. "Civil-Military Relations in Brazil: The Myth of Tutelary Democracy." Paper presented to the XIX International Conference of the Latin American Studies Association, Washington, D.C.

Tulchin, Joseph, ed. 1995. *The Consolidation of Democracy in Latin America.* Boulder, Colo.: Lynne Rienner Publishers.

Varas, Augusto. 1988. *La autonomía militar en América Latina.* 1st ed. Caracas: Nueva Sociedad.

Zagorsky, Paul W. 1992. *Democracy vs. National Security: Civil Military Relations in Latin America.* Boulder, Colo.: Lynne Rienner Publishers.

# Conclusion

## FELIPE AGÜERO AND JEFFREY STARK

This volume has been animated by a spirit of open inquiry into the new conditions affecting the functioning and reach of democratic regimes in Latin America. Consonant with that approach, our aim in this concluding chapter is not to presume to offer a definitive assessment of the fault lines of democracy analyzed and discussed in the preceding chapters. Rather, we simply hope, in a short compass, to bring some of these concerns into higher relief and to suggest areas of inquiry that are deserving of further study. One of our main goals has been the identification of new or neglected questions and issues in the study of Latin American democracies, and we hope that these topics will serve as the basis for the research of others.

We began by noting, in Felipe Agüero's chapter, that the nature and status of the region's democracies, all of which resurfaced or underwent important transformations in the course of the past two decades, have been subject to conflicting assessments. For a number of analytic and conceptual reasons, appraisals of democracy by social scientists have differed. Disparate intellectual traditions, varying angles of analysis, divergent choices in the comparisons made, and incongruities in the very nature of the concepts employed all have helped establish those differences. To those factors one might have added the practical interests of politicians, functionaries, and technocrats, sometimes recruited from the fields of the social sciences, in praising the accomplishments of the new democracies to which they attached the fate and prestige of their own leadership. Moreover, the truth is that differences also stem from the subject itself. Democracy, as a political regime embedded in the institutions and culture of society, unfolds along multiple pathways.

In some of its manifold expressions, democratization may be appraised positively, and we have acknowledged its progress. Throughout this volume, the authors' chapters have implicitly or explicitly recognized the persistence of democratic regimes, which often have traversed long stretches of difficult terrain in the post-transition era. This persistence, sometimes accompanied by the expansion of pluralist and competitive politics, has created opportunities to deepen democratization. New movements and organizations, as well as the strengthening and empowerment of previously fragile identities, became possible in the midst of the dislocations created by the destruction of the old order during the preceding military-authoritarian wave and the realities of the new political economy. In some cases, unforeseen results were realized in the invigoration of women's demands, the fuller expression of the aspirations of ethnic groups, and the growth of more autonomous working class organizations. At the same time, political elites have been able to advance in the formalization of rights aimed at imbuing political regimes with greater degrees of responsibility and accountability. In many countries, new constitutions, major constitutional reforms, and significant pieces of legislation have created opportunities for increasing guarantees for individual rights and for checking the powers of state agencies. With just a few exceptions and as a result of a complex set of factors, the military has been forced out of the realm of political intervention.

And yet, the actual realization of the new opportunities created is, at best, uncertain. The practice of electoral democracy is accompanied by a number of factors that limit its reach and erode the very principles needed for the health and sustenance of democratic regimes. As was made particularly clear by Frances Hagopian, one such factor is the decline in the political representation of societal interests as a result of the weakening of old and more or less institutionalized networks without their replacement by new forms of representation. The picture is certainly diverse throughout the region, but common trends are to be found in weakened parties, declining support for political institutions, and diminished participation. Taking another example, the politics of intermediation and participation are made problematic by the uncertain consequences of television, advances in communications technology, and the appearance of the sort of technobureaucracies discussed by Augusto Varas. Government accountability may well suffer at times as a consequence of these changes. Questions about government accountability also derive from new forms of "economic citizenship" that link states to the claims of global economic actors such as international investors, firms, and capital markets (Sassen 1996, 38).

Hugo Frühling and James Holston and Teresa Caldeira highlighted enormous deficiencies in the actual exercise and enjoyment of citizenship issuing from a fragile rule of law and weakened or distorted judicial institutions. Violence, insecurity, and an absence of legal guarantees are the lot of many individuals whose experience of citizenship is diverse and fragmented. Underlying this impoverished experience of citizenship is the reality of socioeconomic exclusion and social fragmentation so vividly described by Atilio A. Borón. Marysa Navarro and Susan C. Bourque brought to our attention that the increased activism of women in nongovernmental organizations has not yet found a corresponding echo in the more formal settings of political parties and labor organizations. Although relatively encouraged by the progress made on ethnic-cultural grievances in Peru and Bolivia, Carlos Iván Degregori reminded us that in Peru the recognition of such concerns remains largely symbolic and lacking in institutional expression. As indicated by Wendy Hunter, Michael C. Desch, and Fernando Bustamante, although the military no longer monopolizes power as it did in some countries only a few years ago, it still does not appear to be fully subjected to the control of elected authorities. In some places it maintains considerable domains of autonomy, while nearly everywhere it faces the challenges of role definition and institutional adaptation.

## Rethinking Democracy in Latin America

Clearly then, Latin American democracies, as hybrid regimes, are easily characterized in both positive and negative terms. They are regimes that feature competitive elections for the selection of leaders at regular intervals, and they maintain many of the political arrangements and constitutional provisions envisioned within democratic theory, but they are embedded in sets of political, economic, and social institutions and practices that often negate the principles of equality before the law (universal individual rights, citizenship) that are supposed to sustain democratic regimes. It is from this realization that we have criticized the uses of the notion of democratic consolidation. In their urge to ascertain the stability and endurance of democracies, scholars using the concept of democratic consolidation have often skirted the question of how incomplete, contradictory, and disjointed these regimes are.

Thus, a major implication of the chapters in this volume is the need to conceive of Latin American democracies as regimes that simultaneously display elements typical of electoral competitive regimes and elements that corrode the components of democratic citizenship. This realization carries three important consequences. One is the need to upgrade the status of theorizing about democracy for the purposes of rigorous social science studies on democratic regimes in Latin America. A first step is to rethink the decoupling between procedural and substantive versions of democracy that took place at the time of the demise of authoritarianism and the early stages of democratic transitions. In the framework of transitions, scholars needed an easily identifiable dependent variable for what was hoped would be the endpoint of transition processes, namely political democracy. Ridding the concept of democracy of "substantive" social components facilitated the task. But the decoupling that became so much a part of the consolidation paradigm has now become — to borrow Albert O. Hirschman's (1970) phrase — a "hindrance to understanding" in the new context of seemingly enduring democracies displaying the features mentioned above.

We do not mean that we ought to discard the benefits of a useful analytic distinction or that we ought to assess current regimes with excessively loaded concepts. It is simply a matter of reassessing the sufficiency of our analytic and conceptual resources to see what we might need to bring back into the analysis if we want to understand and explain Latin America's multifaceted democracies. In emphasizing the social, economic, and civil dimensions of citizenship and democracy, we are also, in a sense, calling for a considerable lessening in the treatment of Latin American democracies as a "special case" apart from other democracies. The countries of the region will always have their distinctive characteristics and historical specificities, but these need not result in the application of what amounts to variable treatment in the analysis of their democracies. Part of the overall analytic adjustment entails setting aside the view of democracy as a point of arrival and regarding it instead as an ongoing, nonlinear process of institutional and symbolic construction that encompasses contradictory elements. The chapters by Agüero, Borón, Varas, Holston and Caldeira, and Norbert Lechner provided, in their conceptual treatments of democracy, useful suggestions in this regard.

A second consequence is that the study of democracy in Latin America must become more interdisciplinary. If, as we believe to be the case, such issues as gender, ethnicity, law, and globalization are crucial to the prospects for democratization in Latin America, the contributions of specialists in women's studies, anthropology, history, sociology, legal reform, international relations, and other fields are indispensable. Many of the chapters in this volume lend support to this outlook. However, achieving a more interdisciplinary discussion will take time and effort. We note, for example, that Navarro and Bourque in their treatment of gender, Degregori in his discussion of ethnicity, and Frühling in his analysis of the judiciary all chose to broach their topics through a historical review. Clearly, there is a need for establishing certain baselines of shared information and context in order to proceed meaningfully down this road.

The third consequence is the need to advance further in the development of clear hypotheses about the changing political, social, and cultural terrains on which these democracies unfold. As we would be the first to recognize, many of the concerns and issues identified in this volume are not immediately translatable into ready-made research questions. There is considerable conceptual and methodological spadework to be done. But this is in the very nature of what is in many respects a shift toward investigating the qualitative dimensions of democracy in Latin America, and we believe the potential benefits of that endeavor far outweigh any loss of parsimony in our research agendas.

## AREAS FOR FURTHER REFLECTION AND RESEARCH

In his chapter, Lechner suggests that there has been a transformation of politics itself that affects the manner in which democratic politics operates. The changing context of politics resulting from the processes of globalization, marketization, and the generation of a new cultural climate leads to what he calls the decentering and the informalization of politics. In this context, the meaning of democracy, facing new challenges and difficulties, often becomes uncertain. New forms of politics develop outside the domains of democratic institutions, leading to an emptying of the political system. Therefore, Lechner calls for empirical research to validate claims about changes in the nature of politics and for combining this research with innovative thinking aimed at discovering and taking advantage of the possibilities offered by these new forms of politics.

With greater force and directness than any of the other chapters, Borón's essay challenges our thinking about democratization in Latin America in two fundamental ways. First, Borón reminds us that, in fact, the application of Schumpeterian, procedural notions of democracy is not limited to recent analyses of the Latin American democracies but, rather, is symptomatic of certain limitations of modern capitalist democracies and reflective of a more general straying from the richer conceptualizations characteristic of much traditional Western political theory. In this sense, our democratic theorizing may profit from recouping that which has been left behind. Second, he warns us against falling too easily into new teleological traps. Similar to various forms of neoliberalism today, Keynesianism and laissez-faire economics were, indeed, once "the only game in town." Yet, over time, they disappeared from view. This admonition prompts us to be alert for longer-term antisystemic or counterhegemonic currents running through the Latin American democracies.

Jeffrey Stark's inclusive and systematic notion of globalization, aimed at putting a degree of order in an often confusing discussion, highlights constituent elements that resonate with Lechner's references to a changing cultural climate and that find expression in Stark's own notion of new political cultures. His conceptualization of globalization allows him to capture a number of phenomena that produce dislocations affecting Latin American polities — for example, the diffusion of power away from the state toward other arenas of human activity, the ascendance of complex forms of economic life, the shifting and weakening of economic bases for political solidarities, and the intensification of socioeconomic and sociocultural disparities. Stark also emphasizes the importance of global linkages that lend support to the democratic claims of Latin American citizens (a point amply confirmed in the chapters by Navarro and Bourque, Degregori, and Frühling), and he identifies a number of democratic opportunities embedded in the norms associated with economic globalization (transparency, rule of law, and regulatory protection). This latter point, in particular, has not yet received sustained attention in the literature on Latin American democratization.

It is worth pausing here to focus more closely on the relationships among globalization, the state, and democracy. Perhaps too much attention has been given to globalization's impact on the weakening of state powers. It is true that power has been distributed among many more actors than in the past, but the state remains at the fulcrum of relations among the global, the national, and the local. As it becomes increasingly clear that Latin American democracies are moving from a phase of state downsizing to state redesign, it also becomes apparent that, in many ways, globalization is less about "breaking the state" than "making the state." Simply put, globalization entails not the superseding but the engagement of state powers, and those powers must be configured in certain ways. Hence, the key research question is: What kinds of states are being created in Latin America through globalization, and what do they mean for democratization? This represents an important research agenda that will require ongoing dialogue between Latin Americanists and those working in international relations and international political economy. Part of this research agenda, as mentioned by Stark, is a closer examination of the paradox to be found in the calls by global institutions and actors for state reforms of a scope and type whose implementation is, in fact, inhibited by the very forces unleashed by globalization.

Hagopian tackles a question pertaining to the context of politics and to the very configuration of democratic politics: political representation. Changes in the context of politics, involving mainly the retreat of the state, have, as she so nicely puts it, "stirred the political waters on which vessels of political representation in the post-war era were custom-built to navigate." Hagopian says that it is too soon to tell whether political representation is undergoing a process of secular decline or will recover and reorganize in the near future, but her thorough investigation finds political representation "disorganized to a greater extent than it has become reconfigured." Her analysis of partisan and electoral dealignment, the decline of corporatism, and new associational possibilities lead to the conclusion that the political dislocations in Latin America are greater in scope and intensity than they were in Western Europe as a result of the latter's economic adjustment and preparations for the monetary union.

Hagopian assesses with skepticism the views that see emerging voluntary associations, non-governmental organizations, and new types of associative networks as promising substitutes for the decline of older organizations for political representation. She warns that political decentralization, the prospects of which often are perceived with enthusiasm, is fraught with dangers of reinvigorated clientelism. Clearly, these are areas where those who hold conflicting views must confront each other with conceptual clarity and empirical research. Hagopian urges us to embark on such research and to contribute to frameworks that can help us understand when, how, and why the reorganization of societal interests and their reattachment to political institutions take place. She also advocates, as do several other authors in this volume, the use of surveys both to gauge changes in attitudes about political representation and to make broader assessments concerning its structure and quality.

Varas addresses the changing contexts of social differentiation, technological revolution, globalization, decreasing legitimacy of the state, social exclusion, and the emergence of what he calls new absolutist powers, such as the mass media and public and private technobureaucracies. In his view, these are challenges to democratization that may be contested through strategies of citizen empowerment, the possibilities for which may be partially found in several of the constitutional reforms that have taken place in Latin America in the past few years. However, further empowerment could result from policy research on such specific areas as citizen access to the media, standards in advertising, and public financing of political campaigns. Varas calls for research into these and other issues aimed at detecting opportunities for the expansion of citizen rights.

Navarro and Bourque, focusing on the impact of changing conditions on the promotion of equality and women's rights, note the opportunities that emerged during the struggle against authoritarianism and the establishment of democracy. Yet, the fulfillment of many of the aspirations that emerged in the course of that struggle has proved to be elusive. Thus, the meaning of democracy remains contradictory from a gender perspective as well. They assign particular importance to the role played by NGOs and international forums in the affirmation of women's rights and in fostering the possibility that these rights might find formal expression in national polities. Several conferences sponsored by the United Nations and animated by governmental as well as non-governmental organizations support the authors' view of the role of local-transnational connections in the advancement of citizen rights for women. Navarro and Bourque advocate research on the opportunities and constraints facing the expansion of the representation of women in political parties and other political institutions, with attention to the efficacy of institutional designs. A specific suggestion is a survey of the attitudes and self-conceptions held by female legislators. Navarro and Bourque call attention as well to the need to explore elements of political culture in the difficulties of promoting the expansion of equality in domains such as the family and the workplace.

Degregori adds to the discussion of participation and citizenship from the perspective of ethnicity. Through a historical contrast of the Quechua and Aymara peoples of Peru and Bolivia, Degregori examines the impact that changing forms of expression of ethnic-cultural diversity have had on national institutions and the ways they have, in Peru, intersected with class and region. By means of the critical bridge of migration, ethnic groups have influenced both their regions of origin and their urban destinations, questioning the old parameters of national integration and advocating the recognition of diversity. This sociopolitical shift presents a challenge for the state and its institutions. Will they be able to function, Degregori asks, as the "representative of unity in diversity?" The manner in which this challenge is faced, with what leadership, under what conditions, and with what impact on democratic governance and the structures of representation is a major focus of research in this area. However, Degregori also speculates that, in the future, ethnic-cultural concerns may be combined with issues of class and economic inequality, and ethnic politics may be recast within the context of broader citizen demands put forward by "more plural subjects."

Grappling with the contradictory and multifaceted unfolding of democracy requires a focused view of the problems of citizenship and their relationship to the embeddedness of democratic regimes in a fragile rule of law, marked by weaknesses and shortcomings of the judiciary. As the conference leading to this volume was being conceived, we saw it imperative to take steps to recover these concerns from the domain of narrow legal circles and to place them at the center of comparative study in the social sciences. Frühling's and Holston and Caldeira's chapters in this volume make significant contributions toward this end.

Both chapters highlight the indispensable role a judiciary must play in the protection and promotion of citizen rights and in the exercise of accountability by government agencies. If the democratic rule of law is to have any significance, a strong and effective judiciary must be in place. Frühling gives an account of the historic lack of independence of the judiciary and of the several efforts at judicial reform in the post-war era. He concludes, however, that only now are many Latin American countries experiencing relatively strong movements toward judicial reform. If successful, these movements would result in a more active and open judicial branch and real improvement in the quality of the region's democratic regimes. Factors behind this movement include the long-standing dissatisfaction in many quarters with the judiciary, the new political environment brought about by democratization, the exigencies of economic liberalization and market reform, and sustained international interest in such measures. These changes face numerous obstacles, however, with respect to the existing legal culture, the place of the judiciary in the political system, the corporate entrenchment of judicial officers, and the entanglement of the judiciary with other institutions, such as the police. Ultimately, Frühling argues, the development of a strong and independent judiciary requires a broad agreement on its proper role in democracy and, most important, the existence of active groups and organizations in civil society that are willing and prepared to use the law to defend civil rights and enforce legal claims.

Focusing on Brazil, Holston and Caldeira depict the judiciary as the branch of government most resistant to democratic transformation. Its inability to perform its role to protect and guarantee individual rights has led to judicial discredit and this, in turn, has led to the privatization of justice. In the context of the crime and violence pervading many areas of Brazil, a vicious cycle has been generated. The people's distrust of the justice system and the police has led to a culture of fear and delegitimation of the rule of law. As a striking demonstration of what Holston and Caldeira call "disjunctive democracy," Brazil appears to be relatively successful in the institutionalization of democratic politics but at the same time defective, given the delegitimation of many of its institutions of law. This situation seriously impairs the exercise of citizenship and legality. From the analysis of Brazil's "disjunctive democracy," Holston and Caldeira urge social scientists studying democratization to cease neglecting the rule of law, "the crucial question of the performance of the justice system," and the civil component of citizenship. More specifically, they urge us to study the dynamics surrounding the disjuncture between evidence of real democratic change, such as that witnessed in Brazil, and the simultaneous delegitimation of the rule of law.

The disjuncture noted by Holston and Caldeira, which has also been cited using different terminology by Guillermo O'Donnell (1996), who has written of the gap between formal and informal institutionalization, and by Juan Linz and Alfred Stepan (1996), who have written of the unequal development of democracy's arenas, should emerge as a major area of research. What accounts for the judiciaries' weakness in fulfilling their role with regard to the rule of law? How may opportunities created at the formal-legal level be translated into real advances in the universalization of rights and their effective protection? Who are the major actors and what are the main variables involved in the creation of this major fault line? Additionally, research in this area should assess the series of constitutional and legal reforms affecting the judiciary and related powers that have taken place in a number of countries, such as Colombia, Peru, Brazil, Argentina, El Salvador, Guatemala, Costa Rica, and others. Comparative studies of these reforms and their actual effects on the expansion and promotion of rights should be balanced with studies of frustrated reform attempts in other countries.

The final section of this volume highlights a lingering problem of democratization: the role and position of the military institution. Just as the study of law and the judiciary should be strongly established as part of the study of democratization, we think that the study of the military should not be dropped simply because it has retreated from the direct control of executive power. On the contrary, the new context provided by the post-transition democracies should be a fruitful time for the study of the evolving roles of military institutions. The emphasis on consolidation has tended, among some scholars, to render the military a quasi-obsolete problem of transitions. However, even if its visibility has receded relative to that of political parties or other political institutions, the military remains a central state institution and one that bears direct relevance to some of the questions of order and rule of law mentioned above. More often than would be expected in a period of democratic ascendancy, the military remains significantly involved in repression and human rights violations, operating with immunity and autonomy, in countries such as Colombia, Mexico, and Peru. The search for new roles for the military in the context of changing international politics should not be allowed to fall outside our field of vision, lest we succumb to the "liberal bias" indicated by Stepan (1988), which leads to ignoring central questions of organized force in society. Against the dangers of letting the military fall into oblivion and isolation, the social sciences should vigorously pursue the changing paths of accommodation followed by the military in these new contexts and times. At the same time, we should attend to the policies of and connections with other state institutions in matters of security, law, and order. The chapters by Hunter, Desch, and Bustamante offer us important steps in this direction.

Wendy Hunter assesses the status of civil-military relations in Argentina, Brazil, and Chile and their linkages with the process of democratization. She concludes that these relations have reached a stabilizing settlement at different levels of civil-military balance in each of the countries while pointing out that the settlements have inhibited the pursuit of further reforms. Normalization, she argues, is not equivalent to democratic civilian supremacy, which remains elusive. Hunter proposes that research should monitor the evolution of "normalization" with a focus on the consequences that actual military autonomy might entail for the affirmation of democratic regimes. Research also ought to monitor the definition of external and internal roles for the military, which come from within and without military quarters. Additionally, to monitor change and continuity, Hunter suggests that attention be directed to military role beliefs, attitudes toward democracy, and, conversely, civilian attitudes toward the military. These matters are of no small importance, as the military often surpasses all civilian institutions when evaluated for performance and prestige in public opinion surveys.

Michael C. Desch introduces an international relations perspective to address the role of the changing international environment on domestic civil-military relations. His analysis leads to caution: the end of the tensions of the Cold War, of which the Latin American militaries were a part, does not necessarily bode well for civil-military relations. The combination of a less challenging security environment with the ever-present perception of domestic threats leads to the expectation of higher levels of tension in civil-military relations. Although Desch recognizes the presence of favorable factors, such as the impact of the "revolution in military affairs" (new technology), he suggests the need for policies specifically aimed at bolstering civilian governmental institutions vis-à-vis the military and the primacy of a focus on external missions instead of internal roles.

Delving into the military's self-image in an interesting way, Fernando Bustamante warns us that, despite the many contextual changes that have taken place, the Latin American military still maintains the institutional notion of a civilizational mission against a threatening "other" that has existed since its inception. What has changed over time and what is especially acute with the end of the Cold War is the specific content of the "otherness" to be subjugated or conquered. In his view, the problem for the military today is to define where the contemporary "otherness" may lurk and what new tools have to be developed against it. Bustamante then explores ways in which the quest for a civilizing historic task gradually may be made compatible with the pluralist and liberal demands of democratization. In his search, Bustamante reflects on the potential of identifying military roles in more globalized, cosmopolitan contexts, and he explores the benefits of expanding citizenship to include explicitly the military. His analysis also deals with the critical issue of the military as a system stabilizer in political systems with weak political parties and institutions. This, too, is a topic that calls for corresponding research dealing with the civilian side of civil-military relations.

In this volume, we certainly have not exhausted all the relevant areas for research on the fault lines of democracy in post-transition Latin America. However, we have provided support for that research through studies in areas that we deem most relevant to the current dynamics of democratization in Latin America, and we have made our case for the need for new concepts or for the rethinking of old ones. We have advocated a focus on the transformations of politics, the shifting terrains underpinning democratic politics, the global influences that both threaten and nurture democracy, the potential for new democratic dispensations in relation to gender and ethnicity, and the many specific weaknesses and vulnerabilities of democratic politics as practiced in Latin America at the turn of the century.

In closing, however, we would like to offer a mild caution: Perhaps, at times, as in Shakespeare's *Hamlet*, we "doth protest too much." Are today's Latin American democracies as thoroughly riddled with fault lines as our social science searchlights make them out to be? What, exactly, are our expectations? We would like to conclude by advocating a larger historical perspective in the approach to these problems in order to discern what about them is of new or recent creation and what is more truly a legacy of the past. The source of the problems facing Latin America's democracies is often left obscure, and the literature is equivocal. Studies may find the source in the distant past (for example, a long tradition lacking in pluralism and the rule of law) or in the more recent past (the ill-fated consequences of authoritarian regimes). Alternatively, the source may be found immediately present in one of the features of the post-transition era, for instance, in the effects of globalization or the consequences of newly adopted institutional arrangements.

Hence, as a final recommendation, we believe that studies of the fault lines of democracy in post-transition Latin America should compare current situations with those of previous democratic periods. This would allow for a sharper identification of new problems as well as a more nuanced understanding of how some problems intertwine and combine with past legacies, institutions, and practices. Arriving at such clarifications and historical perspective might temper somewhat our profusion of critical judgments, while identifying useful strategies and wise policies for the strengthening of democracy.

# References

Hirschman, Albert O. 1970. "The Search for Paradigms as a Hindrance to Understanding." *World Politics* 22 (3).

Linz, Juan, and Alfred Stepan. 1996. *Problems of Democratic Transition and Consolidation: Southern Europe, South America, and Post-Communist Europe*. Baltimore and London: The Johns Hopkins University Press.

O'Donnell, Guillermo. 1996. "Illusions About Consolidation." *Journal of Democracy* 7 (2).

Sassen, Saskia. 1996. *Losing Control: Sovereignty in an Age of Globalization*. New York: Columbia University Press.

Stepan, Alfred. 1988. *Rethinking Military Politics: Brazil and the Southern Cone*. Princeton, N.J.: Princeton University Press.

# Contributors

**Felipe Agüero** is associate professor at the School of International Studies of the University of Miami and senior research associate of the North-South Center at the University of Miami. He is the author of *Soldiers, Civilians, and Democracy: Post-Franco Spain in Comparative Perspective,* and his co-edited book, *Gobernabilidad democrática: perspectivas regionales,* is forthcoming with the press of the Universidad de Chile.

**Atilio A. Borón** is executive secretary of CLACSO, the Latin American Council of Social Sciences, and professor of political theory at the University of Buenos Aires. He is author of *State, Capitalism and Democracy in Latin America* and is currently working on a book on citizenship, democracy, and neoliberal policies in recent Argentine history.

**Susan C. Bourque** is the E.B. Wiley Professor of Government at Smith College. Her most recent book is *The Politics of Women's Education: Perspectives from Asia, Africa, and Latin America,* co-edited with Jill K. Conway. Professor Bourque and Professor Marysa Navarro are currently editing a volume of essays on ethnicity, race, gender, and class in Latin America and the Caribbean.

**Fernando Bustamante**, Ecuadorian political scientist and sociologist, is currently a Visiting Fulbright Professor at the University of Ohio (Athens). He has held positions as professor and researcher at FLACSO in Quito and in Santiago and has served as chairman of the Sociology Department and associate dean at the Liberal Arts College of the Universidad San Francisco de Quito. Dr. Bustamante has written many articles and essays on democracy and governability and has advised the negotiating team working on the Ecuadorian-Peruvian border conflict.

**Teresa P.R. Caldeira** is professor of anthropology at the University of California, Irvine, and is an associate researcher at the Brazilian Center for Analysis and Planning (CEBRAP) in São Paulo. She is author of *A Política dos Outros,* and her book, *City of Walls: Crime, Segregation, and Citizenship in São Paulo,* is forthcoming with the University of California Press.

**Carlos Iván Degregori** is professor of anthropology at the Universidad Mayor de San Marcos (Lima) and is a senior researcher at the Instituto de Estudios Peruanos. He is coeditor of *The Peru Reader: History, Culture, Politics* (Duke 1995) and coauthor of *Las rondas campesinas y la derrota de Sendero Luminoso* (IEP 1996).

**Michael C. Desch** is associate professor and associate director of the Patterson School of Diplomacy and International Commerce at the University of Kentucky. He is author of *When the Third World Matters: Latin American and U.S. Grand Strategy* (Johns Hopkins 1993) and *Civilian Control of the Military: The Changing Security Environment* (Johns Hopkins, forthcoming 1999).

**Hugo Frühling** is professor of political science at the University of Chile and is senior researcher at the Center for Development Studies in Santiago. He has edited *El estado frente al terrorismo* and is currently working on a book on public policies toward crime in South America.

**Frances Hagopian** is associate professor of political science at Tufts University and is affiliated with the Weatherhead Center for International Affairs at Harvard University. She is the author of *Traditional Politics and Regime Change in Brazil* and numerous articles on Latin American politics and democratization. She is currently working on a book on economic liberalization and political representation in Latin America.

**James Holston** is professor of anthropology at the University of California, San Diego, and is affiliated with the University of São Paulo. He is author of *The Modernist City*, editor of *Cities and Citizenship*, and currently working on a book about the disjunctions of democratic citizenship in São Paulo.

**Wendy Hunter** is associate professor of political science at Vanderbilt University. She is author of *Eroding Military Influence in Brazil: Politicians against Soldiers* (University of North Carolina Press 1997). Her current research is on social policy in several Latin American countries.

**Norbert Lechner** is research professor of political science at the Facultad Latinoamericana de Ciencias Sociales (FLACSO) in Chile and Mexico and a consultant at the United Nations Development Program in Santiago. He is the author of *Los patios interiores de la democracia: subjetividad y política* (3rd ed. 1995).

**Marysa Navarro** is the Charles Collis Professor of History at Dartmouth College. Her most recent book is *The Reader's Companion to U.S. Women's History,* with Wilma Mankiller, Gwendolyn Mink, Barbara Smith, and Gloria Steinem. In collaboration with Professor Susan Bourque, she is editing a volume of essays on ethnicity, race, gender, and class in Latin America and the Caribbean.

**Jeffrey Stark** is the director of research and studies for the North-South Center at the University of Miami. He is the editor of the *North-South Agenda Papers* and *North-South Issues.* He is currently working on a study of the conflicting effects of globalization on Latin America.

**Augusto Varas**, political sociologist and former researcher and professor at the Latin American Faculty of Social Sciences (FLACSO-Chile), is the Democratic Governance Program Officer at the Andean and Southern Cone Regional Office of the Ford Foundation in Santiago. He is the editor of *Democracy Under Siege: New Military Power in Latin America* and the author of *The United States and Latin America: Beyond the Cold War.*

# Index